Criminal Justice in Canada

Fifth Edition

Colin Goff

University of Winnipeg

NELSON EDUCATION

NELSON / EDUCATION

**Criminal Justice in Canada,
Fifth Edition**

by Colin Goff

Vice-President, Editorial Director:
Evelyn Veitch

Editor-in-Chief, Higher Education:
Anne Williams

Senior Acquisitions Editor:
Lenore Taylor-Atkins

Senior Marketing Manager:
David Tonen

Developmental Editor:
Theresa Fitzgerald

Photo Researcher:
Sandra Mark

Permissions Coordinator:
Sandra Mark

Production Service:
MPS Limited, A Macmillan
Company

Copy Editor:
Wendy Yano

Proofreader:
Dianne Fowlie

Indexer:
Maura Brown

Manufacturing Manager:
Joanne McNeil

Design Director:
Ken Phipps

Managing Designer:
Franca Amore

Interior Design:
Fernanda Pisani

Cover Design:
Christa Johnston

Cover Image:
© Brand X/First Light

Compositor:
MPS Limited, A Macmillan
Company

Printer:
Edwards Brothers

**Library and Archives Canada
Cataloguing in Publication**

Goff, Colin H., 1949–

Criminal justice in Canada/
Colin Goff. – 5th ed.

Includes bibliographical references
and index.
ISBN 978-0-17-650173-0

1. Criminal justice, Administration
of–Canada–Textbooks.
I. Title.

HV9960.C2G63 2009   364.971
C2009-904511-7

ISBN-13: 978-0-17-650173-0
ISBN-10: 0-17-650173-8

CONTENTS

LIST OF EXHIBITS

PREFACE

On the first day of classes each semester, when I teach a course related to the area of the Canadian criminal justice system, I always remark to students how much our justice system has changed since the previous edition of this book was published. I also tell them they will be learning about numerous social issues that deserve our attention. Issues such as how does a certain type of behaviour become a crime? How do we decide whom to charge and whom to release without any charges at all? Who is a criminal? How should we punish criminals? How do wrongful convictions occur? Who goes to prison, and who gets probation? Do high-technology solutions, such as electronic monitoring, help control criminal behaviour? What happens to people once they get out of prison? Should there be different programs for women and men who are incarcerated?

The fifth edition of *Criminal Justice in Canada* continues with the approach used in previous editions—that is, it attempts to describe in as much detail as possible our criminal justice system. This approach involves a discussion of the major agencies and the manner in which they operate to identify, apprehend, process, and control offenders. The text is designed to cover what most people consider to be the central facets of the Canadian criminal justice system. It does not attempt to describe every aspect and nuance of each criminal justice agency, but rather to highlight the policies, legal cases, decisions, and issues that shape the operations of the various agencies in fundamental ways. Criminological research studies are also reviewed, as are government statistics.

In the fifth edition, some of the recent initiatives to control crime and criminals are included and updated: anti-terrorism legislation, gun control measures, and mandatory minimum sentences. In addition, there are discussions about critical issues facing our justice system, such as the use of Tasers by the police, wrongful convictions, and what—if any—should be the limits on police and jailhouse interrogations. Recent proposed legislation is reviewed, including Internet luring and the 2-for-1 credit for those awaiting trial while in remand. Newly instituted policies and programs are discussed, such as intelligence-led policing and specialized courts, including drug and mental health courts. Finally, some recent Supreme Court of Canada decisions that have had a significant impact upon the operation of our justice system are also examined, such as the right to silence (*R. v. Singh*).

NEW TO THE FIFTH EDITION

As the demands of and challenges to the Canadian criminal justice system are constantly evolving, the inevitable result is seen in various types of change: changes to legislation, changes to available services, changes in the types of policies used to direct criminal justice agencies, as well as changes in what types of behaviour are being criminalized. To keep this textbook at the forefront of these changes, the fifth edition includes a number of these changes that have occurred over the past few years. While perhaps the fundamental operations of our criminal justice system have not changed significantly over this time, there have still been a number of changes that have impacted almost all components of our criminal justice system. The following is a chapter-by-chapter list of some of the new content added to the fifth edition. As well, at the end of each chapter, a section entitled "Critical Issues in Canadian Criminal Justice" highlights a specific issue relevant to our criminal justice system. This section will hopefully allow students to discuss each of these issues in detail and apply the concepts they have learned in that chapter.

Chapter 1 has a new introduction that discusses the recent proposals made by the federal government in an attempt to control organized criminal activity in Canada. These new initiatives include creating new offences as well as revising existing laws. An updated section on Canada's anti-terrorism law concludes the chapter.

Chapter 2 contains a new section on HIV disclosure and the issue of criminalization. Additions have been made to the right to silence and disclosure. It also contains updates on research in the area of sexual assault and the Ontario Safe Streets Act.

Chapter 3 updates the information about sex offender registries and the DNA data bank in the area of deterrence. It also provides new discussions on the rehabilitation of sex offenders as well as the applicability of restorative justice in the area of family violence. This chapter ends with a discussion of the Peter Whitmore case, a sex offender who abducted two children in Manitoba and Saskatchewan in 2006. This case raises issues about plea bargaining and civil commitment.

Chapter 4 includes a new topic—forcible confinement—in the category of "crimes against the person." It also updates the issue of identity theft in the discussion about cybercrime. This chapter ends with a discussion about Internet luring and how the federal government has responded to individuals who engage in such activities.

Chapter 5 contains an updated introduction about CCTV (closed-circuit television). It also has updates on the First Nations Policing Policy and the expanding role of DNA data banks.

Chapter 6 contains updates about the use of Tasers as an alternative to deadly force. It also discusses the growing issues of the police and private security in Canada and the public oversight of police forces.

Chapter 7 contains new information about police interrogations and the law of electronic surveillance. In addition, there is a whole section discussing heat emissions (FLIR) and the reasonable expectation of privacy.

Chapter 8 introduces the idea of specialized courts in Canada, specifically mental health courts.

Chapter 9 has a new introduction that focuses upon the role and importance of pre-sentence reports in the sentencing process. As well, there are updates to the sections on mandatory minimum sentences for gun crimes and victim participation in sentencing. The chapter concludes by assessing whether or not mandatory minimum sentencing laws achieve their stated goals.

Chapter 10 begins with a brief overview of the federal government's recent pilot project involving electronic monitoring. There is also a discussion of the recent proposals to restrict the use of conditional sentences. As well, the section on drug treatment courts is updated. The chapter ends with an extensive review of the community justice movement.

Chapter 11 starts with a new section focusing upon the rule of law in Canada's federal correctional system. There are also updates found in the sections on prison violence and prison gangs. The chapter concludes with a discussion of the recent proposal by the federal government to end the credit given to individuals who waited for their trial in pretrial custody.

Chapter 12 updates the various conditional release programs and policies used by correctional systems across Canada to determine the risk levels of individuals who are incarcerated. It ends with a discussion of the two different approaches to the treatment of women inmates—the "what works" approach and the gender responsive approach.

ACKNOWLEDGMENTS

Writing a text for an area as diverse and challenging as the Canadian criminal justice system more than often requires the assistance of people who are willing to share their knowledge, time, and support. Two individuals deserve recognition for their assistance in seeing this project through to its completion. In particular, the comments and suggestions of Meghann McLaghlan made the finished text a much better product. Her tireless efforts, continual enthusiasm, and perceptive comments and criticisms throughout (especially in the Critical Issues sections) were always more than appreciated. Inspector Robert W. Bangs of the RCMP was more than generous in giving up his personal time to offer his expertise, and it too was always much appreciated.

Other thanks go to the librarians at the University of Winnipeg and at the University of Manitoba Law School. The training and continued support given to me by Gil Geis of the University of California, Irvine, and Francis Cullen of the University of Cincinnati, both teachers and colleagues, has contributed to this text in many intangible ways. As well, the editorial assistance of Sarah Goff continues to enhance the overall quality of the final product.

Many individuals who work at Nelson Education deserve recognition. Their enthusiasm, patience, tact, and positive support was always appreciated. Specifically, the advice and assistance of Theresa Fitzgerald was always more than welcomed. Her efforts and advice throughout made the writing of this edition more than enjoyable, so much so that it was completed on time.

Finally, the reviewers of this and past editions deserve special mention for their detailed comments. I appreciate all of their efforts, and many of their suggestions were incorporated into the final text. My thanks go to the following: Michelle Coleman, Acadia University; John Jones, Sault College; Joan Nesbitt, Kwantlen Polytechnic University; and Ken Sauter, Lethbridge College.

ABOUT THE AUTHOR

Colin Goff received his M.A. in sociology from the University of Calgary and his Ph.D. from the University of California (Irvine). Since graduating, he has taught at Simon Fraser University, the University of New Brunswick (Fredericton), and the University of Winnipeg. His areas of research include all aspects of the criminal justice system as well as corporate and white-collar crime, the history of criminology, and Aboriginal justice. In addition to *Criminal Justice in Canada*, he has published *Corporate Crime in Canada* (with C. Reasons) and *Corrections in Canada*. He has also published many articles on the work of Edwin H. Sutherland (many with Gil Geis), on the development of criminology as a discipline in the early twentieth century, and on corporate crime in Canada, particularly in the Atlantic provinces. He is currently studying life course criminology and the sentencing of white-collar criminals in Canada as well as the development of the discipline of criminology in the United States during the early twentieth century. With the assistance of Gil Geis, he has recently published manuscripts on Edwin H. Sutherland, Thorsten Sellin, and the Michael-Adler Report.

CHAPTER 1

An Overview of the Criminal Justice System in Canada

CHAPTER OBJECTIVES

✓ Identify the major agencies of the criminal justice system and discuss the role of each in processing the accused through the criminal justice system.

✓ Outline the structure of the criminal justice system.

✓ Examine the operations of each criminal justice agency within the formal structure of the criminal justice system.

✓ Discuss the importance of the "informal" criminal justice system and the ways it affects the legal rights of defendants.

✓ Contrast the crime control and due process models.

T he criminal justice system in Canada consists of three major agencies: the police, the courts, and the correctional system. Although these agencies are very different from one another, all three work together in a formal manner and follow legal procedures that have been developed to guide their actions. This formal system has an informal side as well; each agency operates in accordance with its goals and mandates, sometimes to the detriment of the other agencies and of the rights of those charged or convicted. This chapter identifies the major components of the Canadian criminal justice system and discusses the costs of operating them. It then outlines the formal and informal operations found within that system.

GUN CRIME IN CANADA AND THE CRIMINAL JUSTICE SYSTEM

On February 12, 2009, gunmen opened fire on a gang member at a shopping mall in Langley, B.C., who later died from his wounds. The next morning, at about 4 a.m., there was a shootout involving two vehicles whose occupants exchanged gunfire at a gas station. RCMP, responding to reports of gunshots, discovered a bullet-ridden pickup truck near a store, but no sign of either the occupants or the other vehicle. A gas station employee told reporters that a security video showed two vehicles speeding around the lot while the occupants shot at each other. These two incidents followed seven others, four of them fatal. Commenting on these latest incidents, a spokesperson for the Integrated Gang Task Force in the Lower Mainland of B.C. said that things could soon get worse, as criminal organizations might view the chaos as a chance to attack their enemies, leading to further gunplay. According to the spokesperson, the police "expect that people involved in the drug trade or criminal organizations may see this as an opportune time to settle their disputes" (Bailey 2009a, A5).

Less than a week later, another shooting in Vancouver left one man dead when two armed men burst into a home and confronted two brothers, one of whom wrestled and killed one of the intruders. According to family members, the intruders were looking for someone that they didn't know. This occurred just hours after the police identified the victim of an attack in Surrey, B.C., in which gunmen shot at the victim as she drove with her four-year-old son in the back seat of her vehicle. The police did not specify whether her death was gang-related. The shooting came roughly 12 hours after a very similar shooting, also in Surrey, that has been "at least peripherally linked to known gang member." In the latter incident, the occupants of a SUV pulled alongside another vehicle at a red light and opened fire on the four occupants, injuring the driver. According to RCMP investigators, the driver was an acquaintance of a known member of the area's drug and gang scene (Hammer 2009, A10). These incidents were followed by the deaths of two more people and injuries to three others in shootings across the Lower Mainland on the evening of March 3 and the morning of March 4, although the police stated that it wasn't clear that any of these shootings were linked to gang activity. When asked about the failure of the police to make arrests in cases involving in major shootings during the recent past, a Vancouver Police spokesperson replied, "these investigations are extremely complex and take a lot of time and effort and resources to have a successful conclusion" (Bailey and Stueck 2009, A4).

According to Li (2007), across Canada during 2006, approximately one of every six homicides was gang-related (about the same number as in 2005). There were 104 homicides in that year linked to organized crime groups or street gangs, of which 61 were reported by the police as "confirmed" gang-related while 43 more were reported as being "suspected" of being gang-related. The most common method used to commit a gang-related homicide was by a weapon—almost 75 percent of all homicides were committed with a firearm, most typically a handgun. In comparison, 23 percent of all non-gang-related homicides committed in 2006 were shootings. Dauvergne and Li (2006) found that gang-related homicides are difficult for the police to solve. The police were able to solve only 45 percent of such killings in 2006, compared to 80 percent of non-gang-related homicides.

In the first three months of 2009, there were more than 40 shootings and 17 gun deaths in the Lower Mainland of Vancouver (Stueck 2009). The shootings occurred at supermarkets, shopping malls, on quiet residential streets, and close to parks and golf courses. In response to these shootings, the B.C. government announced in mid-February that it would hire 168 more police officers, take control of firearms regulations within the province, and increase awards for tipsters who gave the authorities information about gang-related activities. The new police officers would be hired mainly in the Metro Vancouver area, with some placed in Prince George and Kelowna. In addition, a 10-member police task force dedicated to seizing illegal guns would be formed in Vancouver. The funding for these new positions, $69 million over three years, would be shared by Ottawa and the provincial government. The provincial government also stated that it would outlaw modified armoured vehicles and regulate the sale of body armour (Hunter 2009a). In March, the RCMP in Surrey increased the number of officers in their anti-gang unit by transferring 17 members from auto theft investigations (Bailey 2009b).

On March 5, 2009, the Federal Minister of Public Safety, Peter Van Loan, flew to Vancouver to meet the mayors, police, and crime victims, including family members of innocent bystanders killed during gang shootouts. The minister said that the police estimate that there are more than 120 criminal organizations operating in B.C. alone (there are an estimated 900 organized groups operating across Canada) and that both their numbers and degree of sophistication makes the Vancouver area the centre of organized crime in Canada (Bailey and Stueck 2009). Van Loan stated that the recent shootings pointed to the need to introduce laws that would bring about an end to gang violence. While the federal government has already introduced some changes to the Criminal Code, such as mandatory minimum sentences for offences involving guns (see Chapter 9), Van Loan also pointed out the need for other similar laws, such as mandatory sentences for drug crimes.

Almost two weeks later, the federal government announced it was going to introduce two new bills during the week: the first would amend the Criminal Code to target organized crime while the second would focus on illicit drugs. While the content of the bills were not divulged, Van Loan noted that the government's priorities include making all gang-related homicides result in first degree murder charges and imposing mandatory prison terms for some drug crimes. He stated that these new bills were designed to counteract "the wave of gang killings in British Columbia [which are] all driven by criminal organizations that all function on the drug trade and it is the drug trade that's making those communities unsafe, and that's why we need to give the police the tools they need in the form of mandatory prison sentences for drug crimes" (Chase 2009, A4).

This first bill (An Act to Amend the Criminal Code—Organized Crime and the Protection of Justice System Participants) focuses upon gang violence and other serious crimes. It is intended to provide law enforcement officials and other agencies in the criminal justice system to better deal with organized crime activities, in particular murders committed by gang members and drive-by shootings. The new bill is intended to strengthen the Criminal Code through the following:

- Making murder an automatic first degree charge when it is committed in connection with a criminal organization. First degree murder is subject to a mandatory sentence of life imprisonment without eligibility of parole for 25 years.
- Creating a new broad-based offence to target drive-by and other intentional shootings involving the reckless disregard for the lives and safety of others. This offence would include a mandatory minimum sentence of four years in prison with a maximum period of imprisonment of 14 years. The minimum sentence would increase to five years if the offence was committed for the benefit of, at the direction of, or in association with a criminal organization or with a restricted or prohibited firearm such as a handgun or automatic weapon.
- Creating two new offences for assault with a weapon or causing bodily harm and aggravated assault against a peace or public officer. This offence would be punishable by a maximum penalty of 10 and 14 years, respectively.
- Strengthening and lengthening "gang peace bonds" (i.e., preventive court orders requiring an individual to agree to specific conditions to govern their behaviour). The peace bond could be issued for up to 24 months (as opposed to the usual 12 months) against a defendant who has been previously convicted of intimidating participants in the criminal justice system or of committing an organized crime or terrorist offence. Judges would have broad discretion to impose any reasonable condition necessary to protect the public in such a case.

In the middle of March 2009, the premiers of British Columbia, Alberta, and Saskatchewan met to announce they were uniting to fight gang violence. While most of the attention on gangs has been focused on the Vancouver area, both Alberta and Saskatchewan have also experienced increased gang activity. They agreed to unite in an effort to have the federal government make amendments to the Criminal Code in order to make laws "tougher" in order to better combat gang violence. Their first proposal called for an end of the "two-for-one" provision that allows time spent in pretrial custody to be doubled and applied against an offender's sentence (see Chapter 11). Their second recommendation was to update wiretap provisions (some of which have existed in the same form for 35 years) in order that the police could use the latest technologies against gangs. And finally, the provinces agreed to ask for a reduction in paperwork that leads to lengthy delays

in trials, specifically that defence lawyers would have to justify their requests for disclosure by making sure that what they are asking for is as relevant as possible to the case at hand (Hunter 2009b).

Toward the end of April, the federal government continued on its "get tough" stance on organized crime by tabling a bill that would make "theft of a motor vehicle" and "altering, destroying or removing a vehicle's identification number" new offences under the Criminal Code. Federal Justice Minister Nicholson told reporters that the "laws are very much out of date and they're not capturing the organized crime element that is involved with auto theft" (Cohen 2009, A8). He said that one out of every five car thefts is the work of organized crime, and that many vehicles end up in chop shops to be dismantled for parts. If convicted, under the legislation, an individual could face up to 14 years in prison, four years more than the current maximum sentence for the possession of property obtained by crime. It also proposed a mandatory six-month jail sentence for a third theft of a motor vehicle, and seeks to give Canadian border guards additional powers to prevent stolen property from leaving the country.

But not everyone is supportive of these new initiatives. Some critics believe there is no need for stiffer legislation because the problem has largely been addressed by more aggressive enforcement of existing laws. For instance, gun-related crime in Toronto decreased in 2006, a drop attributed to a focus on community-based policing (Tibbetts 2007a). Other critics pointed out that increasing mandatory minimum sentences is not always helpful. They may in fact prove to be an added inflexibility on sentences, amounting to no more than a disincentive to accused persons to plead guilty. In addition, when prosecuting gang members, Crown prosecutors often need the testimony of some of its members in order to establish a gang's motives and plans and indeed its very existence. As such, without gangs members "who turn Queen's evidence, whole gangs may get off scot-free" ("The First . . ." 2009, A14).

While these changes have received support from many Canadians; however, a number of questions have been raised regarding whether they will achieve their goals. For example, some contend that the new proposals designed to "toughen up" various parts of the Criminal Code may lead to the removal of all discretion from judges at sentencing. This could result in Crown prosecutors exercising more discretion to "withdraw charges in some cases rather than subject an offender to an automatic sentence far greater than they believe he deserves" ("Sentenced . . ." 2006). Also, many accused individuals who in the past might have accepted a plea bargain may insist on a trial, in the belief that they have little to lose ("Harper's Inflexible . . ." 2006). It has also been pointed out that these changes could "lead judges to acquit more people or convict them of lesser offences rather than see them get lengthy sentences" (Curry 2006, A9). Yet another concern relates to the impact these new policies may have in terms of sending more criminal cases through the criminal justice system. Some commentators argue that unless more resources are given to assist the various criminal justice agencies, it is very likely that "the system will completely fail and charges will be stayed because of excessive delay . . . More judges, more Crown attorneys and more (very considerably more) legal aid funding will be required" (Morton 2006, A13). As one observer of attempts to introduce similar types of changes in the United States has noted, most of these types "of crime control policies and proposed alternatives are not effective" (Walker 2001, 290).

SOCIAL CONTROL, CRIME, AND CRIMINAL JUSTICE

The cultural patterns of a society are shaped by common ways of thinking, feeling, and acting. Because some individuals engage in activities that are inconsistent with the welfare of society, it is of cultural importance for a society to establish approved folkways, mores, and norms for people to follow. A society often develops a system for indicating its disapproval of those who break with approved ways of thinking and acting. In Western societies, an important function of governments has been to develop and administer systems of criminal justice. Various social control systems have emerged over time—for example, the introduction of both formal and informal sanctions to regulate behaviour.

The term "social control" is commonly used to refer to the various types of organized reaction to behaviour viewed as problematic. As societies develop, they adjust the ways in which they respond to criminal behaviour. For example, criminal behaviour has been attributed to immorality, wickedness, and poverty (among other things). At the same time, the mechanisms for maintaining social control have also changed. For example, societies have attempted to control criminals through capital punishment as well as rehabilitation. Whatever approaches are followed to understand and control criminal behaviour, the objective is always to control behaviour viewed as criminal in some way. In contemporary society, the usual approach to controlling both crime and criminals is to establish a system of criminal

justice that will enable the various institutions of social control—the police, the courts, and the correctional system—to investigate, detect, prosecute, and punish offenders. Remember, though, that these institutions do not enjoy a totally free hand—limits are always placed on them by various laws, such as the Charter of Rights and Freedoms.

How does a society define crime? And how should we deal with issues such as equality, justice, privacy, and security? There are no easy answers to these questions, as people hold different opinions on how we should define crime and achieve justice.

What Is Crime?

Criminal law is reserved for wrongful acts that seriously threaten the social values of Canadians. These wrongful acts are reflected in the various categories of crime found in the Criminal Code: weapons crime, property crime, crimes against persons, and so on. According to Bowal and Lau (2005, 10), crime "largely defines a society because it mediates the powerful forces of security, morality, and control." They also point out that criminal law is not static, because as social attitudes change, "our definitions of crime are constantly refashioned in response."

In this context, there are two commonly used definitions of crime. The first focuses on the violation of a criminal law, the second on the determination of guilt in a criminal court. According to the first definition, an act can be called a crime only when it violates the existing legal code of the jurisdiction in which it occurs. However, breaking the law is not always regarded as a crime in our society. This is because criminal responsibility requires more than a "guilty act"—it also requires a "guilty mind" (see Chapter 2). The second approach—sometimes referred to as the "black letter" approach—stipulates that no act can be considered criminal until a duly appointed representative of the criminal court (e.g., a judge or a jury) has established the guilt of an offender and attached a punishment to that determination.

These two definitions have two important consequences. First, without the criminal law there would be no crime. In other words, no behaviour can be considered criminal "unless a formal action exists to prohibit it." Second, no behaviour or individual "can be considered criminal until formally decided upon by the criminal justice system" (Muncie 2002, 10). In essence, then, a criminal act can only be established once it is determined that it violates the criminal law and/or when an accused person is found guilty in a court of criminal law.

A number of criticisms have been directed toward the use of these two definitions in determining crime. According to Muncie (2002), these criticisms include the fact that not every individual who violates the criminal law is caught and prosecuted. Another is the fact that many criminal acts are not prosecuted even after the authorities have discovered them. Muncie also raises the issue that these two definitions neglect "the basic issue of why and how some acts are legislated as criminal, while others remain subject only to informal control" (ibid., 12). He also points out that these definitions separate the criminal process from its social context—in other words, they don't consider the ways in which the law is not applied by the criminal court, but rather "is actively made and interpreted by key court personnel (for example, in plea bargaining, the quality of legal representation, and judicial discretion)" (ibid.).

According to other legal theorists, crime is better viewed as a violation of social norms (see Exhibit 1.1). This definition was first used by Edwin Sutherland, whose research into corporate crime led him to argue that crime shouldn't be defined on the basis of criminal law, but rather on the basis of two more abstract notions: "social injury" and "social harm." According to Sutherland (1949, 31), the essential characteristic of crime is that it is "behaviour which is prohibited by the State as an injury to the state." He also noted that there are two abstract criteria that are necessary elements in a definition of a crime—the "legal descriptions of an act as socially harmful and legal provision of a penalty of an act." According to him, some sort of social normative criteria must be applied before any definition of crime can be developed. In part, this means that we need to consider how crime, law, and social norms are linked. We can do this by asking, "What behaviours should be regulated?" Today, this type of approach is visible in attempts to classify behaviour as "criminal" on the basis of normative decision-making. For example, some Canadian cities now equate crime with disorderly conduct (such as panhandling), arguing that such conduct undermines public safety and security.

Crime has also been defined as a social construct. In other words, crime is a result of social interaction, the consequence of a negotiated process involving the alleged offender, the police, court personnel, and even lawmakers. According to this definition, the actions of alleged offenders are important, but so is how those actions are perceived and evaluated by those involved with the criminal justice system, including the police and Crown prosecutors, who decide whether a crime has been committed as well as how serious it is.

All of these definitions are used to analyze the nature of crime in our society. Since the three major institutions of social control in our society—the police, the courts, and the correctional system—are all involved with the control of crime and criminals, many questions can be raised about how we respond to crime and about the role of the criminal justice system. For example, is the criminal law applied equally to all, or unequally toward some? How does the use of discretion in our criminal justice system influence the processes and outcomes of that system? Can that system simultaneously promote liberty and security? Many people would agree that it is easy to declare that the planned and deliberate killing of one individual by another is a homicide and that the perpetrator of this act should be given a lengthy punishment. However, there may be other issues involved in the case that some people feel should be considered before guilt or punishment is determined. Exhibit 1.2 discusses a case in Canada that can be analyzed from the perspective of each of these differing definitions of crime.

EXHIBIT 1.1 Differing Definitions of Crime

Legal:
Crime is that behaviour prohibited by the Criminal Code.

Social:
Crime is that behaviour that violates social norms.

Social constructionist:
Crime is that behaviour so defined by the agents and activities of the powerful.

Source: Walklate, S. 2005. *Criminology: The Basics*. London, Routledge.

THE OPERATIONS AND ROLE OF CANADA'S CRIMINAL JUSTICE SYSTEM

Canada has developed a number of major agencies—the police, the courts, and the correctional system—to protect the public from individuals who violate the law. These agencies constitute a vast network of organizations and facilities charged with the investigation, detection, prosecution, and punishment of offenders. They are linked together in what is commonly called the criminal justice system. Viewing the operation of criminal justice as a system allows us to comprehend the "interdependency of the parts of the entire process" in that "many factors

EXHIBIT 1.2   Assisted Suicide in Canada

The word "euthanasia" derives from the Greek "euthanos," which refers to "good death." People often distinguish between "active" euthanasia (e.g., mercy killing) and "passive" euthanasia (e.g., turning off a life-support system). Passive euthanasia is legal in most countries while active euthanasia is a controversial topic.

Euthanasia is not a crime specifically defined in the Criminal Code. It is, however, related to other Criminal Code offences such as murder; manslaughter; assault; criminal negligence; poisoning; and helping, encouraging, or advising someone to commit suicide. The issue that helped develop the legal view of euthanasia was the Sue Rodriguez case in 1993. Ms. Rodriguez was suffering from amyotrophic lateral sclerosis and was told she had 14 months to live. She then requested assistance to commit suicide and applied for an order that would find s. 241(b) of the Criminal Code, which prohibits giving assistance to commit suicide, invalid as it violated her rights under ss. 7, 12, and 15(1) of the Charter of Rights and Freedoms. The Supreme Court ruled, in a 5–4 decision, that "a Charter violation was present but that the violation was necessary in order to protect society's weak, vulnerable and disabled" (Canadian Bar Association 2003, 28).

In 2001, in the case of Robert Latimer, who killed his severely disabled daughter "to end her suffering," the Supreme Court of Canada held that mercy killing was legally murder, whatever the motive. The Supreme Court upheld Mr. Latimer's second degree murder conviction and his sentence of life imprisonment with no chance of parole for at least ten years.

Another case in Canada occurred in 2004, when, just after 5 p.m. on September 25, 36-year-old Charles Fariala of Montreal called his mother and told her, "Today is the day." He had decided to end his life, and he was asking his mother to assist him in his suicide attempt.

At the age of 25, Charles had begun to feel the effects of multiple sclerosis. Over the following years, his condition worsened, and he was finally diagnosed in his thirties (Peritz 2006, A24). Charles had been an orderly in a Montreal chronic-care facility, helping people as their health deteriorated. In May 2005, he confided to a friend that he was dealing with the same issues of illness and control himself—that he was afflicted with multiple sclerosis and had decided "to put an end to his life." The friend said that Charles knew people at the facility where he worked who also had "multiple sclerosis, lying in stretchers and unable to move, but with all of their faculties." His friend added that Charles "had no intention of going there. Charles was in full control of his faculties. He had made a decision to end his life" (Peritz 2004, A1). As his illness developed, Charles "began to repeat incessantly to his mother, Marielle Houle, that he wanted to end it all. She tried to stall him, but to no avail" (Peritz 2006, A24).

He began to formulate a plan to take his life. He searched the Internet to learn how to combine drugs so that he could "die with dignity," and he arranged to have his bills paid. His decision to end his life also involved his mother, an auxiliary nurse at the same facility where Charles worked. She agreed to help her son because she did not want him to die alone. Arriving at his apartment at 11 P.M. that same night, Ms. Houle began to follow the instructions he had left her. When she arrived, he had already drunk his specially concocted medication. He soon went to bed, at which time she placed a plastic bag over his face and tightened it with a rubber band, then tied his hands together with leather strips (Wilton 2006, A7).

Charles had advised his mother that when she called a taxi, she was to use a nearby address so that no one would suspect her. Ms. Houle agreed to all of her son's requests except for the last one. Early on Sunday morning, September 26, she called the police from her son's apartment an hour after he died. Instead of hiding her role, she freely admitted it to the police, telling them "the whole truth" about her involvement in her son's death. According to her lawyer, she did this "as a gesture of love for her son . . . She believes she did the right thing, to alleviate him from the suffering" (ibid.).

On Monday, September 28, Ms. Houle was arrested and charged with assisting her son's suicide. She was released without bail with the consent of the Crown, having been charged under s. 241 of the Criminal Code with aiding suicide, an offence that carries a maximum sentence of 14 years but no minimum sentence. Her lawyer was "relieved at the charge because, in some similar cases, first-degree murder charges are laid. Conviction on that charge means an automatic life sentence with no chance for parole for 25 years" (Thanh Ha 2004, A5).

When her case came to trial in January 2006, Ms. Houle pleaded guilty. Her lawyer told the court that his client "was suffering from depression, diabetes, and arthritis, and was a virtual recluse in a nursing home" (Thanh Ha 2006, A5).

EXHIBIT 1.2 Assisted Suicide in Canada . . . Continued

Her lawyer argued that Canadian laws lag behind those found in other jurisdictions, most notably Belgium, the Netherlands, and the state of Oregon, all of which allow different forms of assisted suicide. He offered the opinion that justice would not be served by sending her to prison and that it would be appropriate for the court to give Ms. Houle a sentence that would allow her to remain in the community.

Four days later, the judge agreed with the defence lawyer that it would be futile to sentence his client to a period of time in a correctional facility. Instead, he sentenced her to three years' probation, which meant that she would only have to keep the peace and report her whereabouts to the authorities. The judge stated that his decision was based "only from the unusual circumstances of the case" and that he found her actions "very reprehensible and unlawful." He also noted that in those few jurisdictions that allow assisted suicide, decisions are made under very specific medical supervision. The Crown prosecutor and defence lawyer concurred with the judge's ruling, with both agreeing that it was tailored specifically to the circumstances of the case and shouldn't be interpreted as setting a precedent or as advocating leniency for individuals who assist suicide (ibid.).

At the time that Ms. Houle was charged with assisting in her son's death, it was estimated that about 60 to 65 percent of Canadians favoured a legal way to help someone to take his or her own life. Polls have shown a consistent high level of support among Canadians for allowing physicians to help terminally ill people commit suicide (as high as 75 percent in 1995). In Quebec, this support has been as high as 86

percent (Agnell 2004, A4). However, there is significant institutional opposition to this idea. It is estimated that only about 20 percent of Canadian lawyers favour doctor-assisted suicide. And many groups such as disabled people's organizations, palliative health-care professionals, and the Canadian Medical Association are strongly opposed to any such system (Thanh Ha 2004, A9).

Eckstein (2007) studied the history of euthanasia in Canada and found only 40 reported cases that relate to euthanasia and patient-assisted suicide. Of these 40 cases, 8 involved either doctors, nurses, or nurse's aides; 15 involved "mercy killings" (7 of which involved parents deciding that their children had had enough suffering and pain and were alleged to have assisted in their suicide; 5 involved an individual who alleged their spouse had experienced enough suffering; and 3 in which children felt their parent had experienced enough pain and suffering); 11 were classified as "assisted suicides"; 5 were considered to be a murder-suicide; and 1 case involved infanticide. Eckstein points out that many more cases of euthanasia are thought to have occurred in Canada. For instance, she notes a member of the Special Senate Committee on Euthanasia and Assisted Suicide stated that "there are thousands of cases in Canada in which doctors have illegally helped patients to die" (Eckstein 2007, 1).

Sources: Agnell 2004; Canadian Bar Association 2003; Eckstein 2007; Peritz 2004, 2006; Thanh Ha 2004, 2006; Wilton, 2006; R. v. Latimer (2001), Rodriquez v. British Columbia (Attorney General) (1993).

influence each decision and decision maker in the justice process" (Travis 1990, 34). Conventional wisdom holds that all the parts of the criminal justice system interact with one another in a coordinated fashion, although this image is not completely accurate. These agencies are related in the sense that they are involved in the apprehension and control of criminals, but "they have not yet become so well coordinated that they can be described as operating in unison" (Senna and Siegel 1995, 11).

Very few, if any, of the other agencies in our society provoke as much debate as our criminal justice system. Concerns about the role and operations of the

major agencies in this system arise almost daily. These agencies and the people they employ work to detect and apprehend law violators, to determine whether they have committed crime(s), and to punish those found guilty.

Our criminal justice system is a vast organization of independent government agencies organized into three general categories—the police, the courts, and corrections. As Figure 1.1 shows, this system involves different types of police organizations, levels of courts, and correctional facilities, as well as a variety of federal statutes (including the Criminal Code and the Youth Criminal Justice Act).

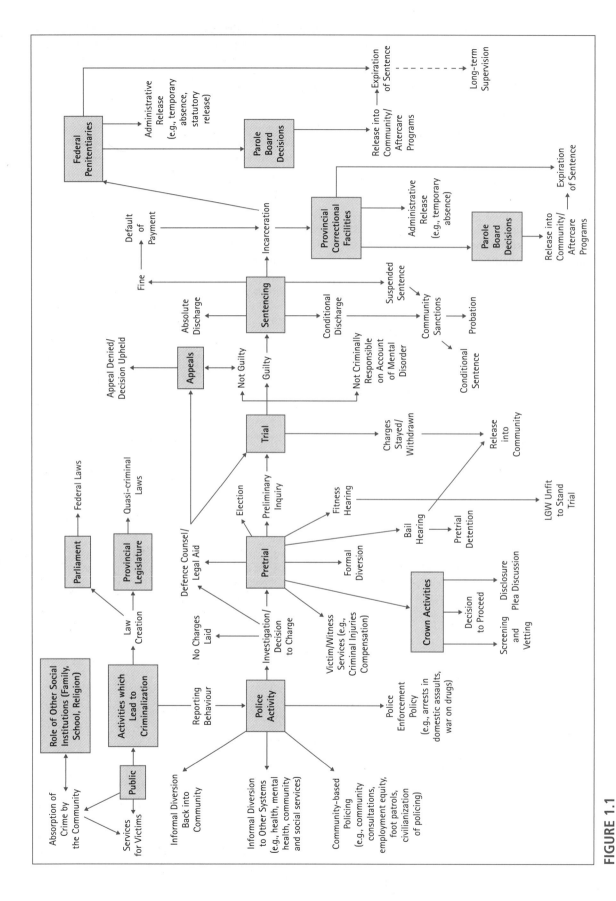

FIGURE 1.1

Overview of the Operation of the Canadian Criminal Justice System

The Purpose of the Criminal Justice System

For the purposes of study, the Canadian criminal justice system can be said to have three main aims: to control crime, to prevent crime, and to maintain justice. Controlling crime is possible in part by the arrest, prosecution, and punishment of those who commit crimes. This system also anticipates that actions related to controlling crime will achieve the second goal, the prevention of crime. This is largely accomplished by punishing offenders in the hope they will refrain from committing crime in the future (i.e., specific deterrence) and by warning others that if they commit a criminal act, they too will be punished when caught (i.e., general deterrence). The third goal is achieving justice—a difficult task, since justice is difficult to define in concrete terms and potentially involves conflicting views about what is "fair" and "just" in our society.

As we saw in the discussion about assisted suicide in Exhibit 1.2, justice can be interpreted in different ways by different groups and individuals. Achieving collective agreement on a definition of justice is not necessarily an easy task in our society. Although all members of our society share certain legal rights, these same rights may conflict with one another at certain times. Determining which rights should have precedence in any given situation can be terribly difficult. There is no doubt that our criminal justice system has assigned minimal importance to the rights of certain groups over the decades, such as the rights of minority group members who are victims of hate crimes and the rights of women who are victims of violence.

In general terms, justice means that all citizens are equal before the law and that they are to be protected from arbitrary decisions made by those working within the criminal justice system. One of the most popular views of what justice is in Western society was developed by John Rawls in *A Theory of Justice* (1971). According to Rawls, the concepts of justice and fairness are essentially the same. He holds that justice is connected to fairness since we want our laws to be written, administered, and enforced in a fair manner. People want the fairest rules possible so that no one person or group will be protected by any type of advantage. Fairness within the criminal justice system is also viewed as the balance between the state's interest in apprehending criminal suspects and the public's interest in avoiding unnecessary government interference in the lives and activities of individuals (Albanese 1999).

The three major agencies of the Canadian criminal justice system are supposed to achieve justice by making fair decisions. Sometimes their actions are interpreted by all parties as fair and just; at other times, serious questions are raised about their actions. An overview of the formal operations of each of these agencies and of how those agencies are supposed to guarantee justice to citizens will be presented later in this chapter. For now, let us explore the notion of "criminal justice."

WHAT IS CRIMINAL JUSTICE?

We have just seen that the study of our criminal justice system involves the study of the police, the courts, and the correctional system and how individuals are processed through these agencies. However, we also need to know what criminal justice is. When we start to look at our criminal justice system, it is important to ask, "What are its underlying values? What is its purpose in our society?" Some contend that the best answer is to say that our criminal justice system is designed to catch criminals, charge and prosecute them in court, and, if they are found guilty, punish them. Others may feel that it is better to view our criminal justice system in a broader social and political context.

In Canadian society today, when most people speak of justice they are referring to the fairness of our criminal law system, and their view is informed by three different assumptions. First, guilt, innocence, and the sentence should be determined fairly and in accordance with the available evidence. Second, punishment should fit the offence as well as the offender. Third, like cases should be treated alike and different cases differently (Law Reform Commission of Canada 1977).

This view of criminal justice currently guides most Canadians' thinking regarding the most appropriate form for justice to take in our society. It is most closely related to what is called the **justice model** (see Chapter 3). This approach emphasizes that justice is achieved when the various agencies of our criminal justice system follow legal rules and procedures that are publicly known, fair, and just. Key components of this approach are ideas such as the presumption of innocence, procedural fairness, and the need to follow legal rules. Discretion and unequal treatment must be reduced as much as possible. It is argued that when these rules and procedures are followed, our criminal justice system operates in an efficient, fair, and impartial manner (von Hirsch 1976).

Why should we be concerned about fairness in our criminal justice system? Probably the easiest way to answer this question is to say that the activities within our criminal justice system shouldn't lead to unfairness or to inequities, as we don't want it to operate in a way that leads to biases against individuals or groups. When we talk about bias in our criminal justice system, two words often arise: "disparity" and "discrimination."

It is important, however, to recognize that discrimination and disparities can be permitted under exceptional conditions in our criminal justice system. For example, an individual who is found not criminally responsible for committing a crime may in fact face a longer sentence than a criminally responsible offender convicted of the same offence. This is because the potential exists for the individual found not criminally responsible to receive an indeterminate sentence, whereas the criminally responsible offender receives a designated term of punishment. It has been argued (*Winko v. Forensic Psychiatric Institute* [1999]; *R. v. LePage* [1999]) that this policy discriminates against the mentally disordered. The Supreme Court of Canada upheld the relevant Criminal Code provision (s. 672.65) even though a disparity resulted. The Court held that for an individual convicted in a criminal court, a specific period of incarceration is punishment for the criminal act. A more flexible approach is warranted for offenders who are not criminally responsible, given that they are not morally responsible for their actions. In such cases, the purpose of punishment is the protection of society and the treatment of the offender (Mewett and Nakatsuru 2000).

Disparity

Disparity refers to a difference, but one that doesn't necessarily include discrimination. Concerns about disparity in our criminal justice system arise when inconsistencies appear as a result of the authorities using illegitimate factors when making their decisions. In contrast, legitimate factors include appropriate legal factors such as the seriousness of the offence and the prior record of the offender. These are considered to be legitimate reasons for differences in our treatment of alleged offenders and those convicted of a crime within our criminal justice system since they are specifically concerned with the criminal behaviour of the offender. Illegitimate factors are extralegal factors, such as race, religion, and gender, which involve decisions about the group the alleged offender belongs to and are unrelated to the criminal activity of any particular individual. For example, our criminal justice system is not supposed to operate or decide about a person's criminality on the basis of his or her social class. If it did, it is entirely possible that middle- and upper-class individuals who commit crimes would serve their sentence within the community, while members of the working class would receive a prison sentence.

Discrimination

Discrimination refers to the differential treatment of individuals based on negative judgments relating to their perceived or real membership in a group. In other words, something about an individual (e.g., religion and/or race) overrides his or her other qualities (e.g., innocence, education, and abilities). Various types of discrimination have been identified, and each has the potential to influence fairness in a variety of different ways in our criminal justice system. *Systemic discrimination* refers to discrimination (e.g., race and/or gender) existing in all aspects of the operations of our criminal justice system. This means that discrimination can consistently be found in the rates of arrest, the type of charges laid, and the decision to prosecute or stay charges, as well as in the conviction rates and types of sentences given to those convicted without any significant variation over a selected time period. Provincial inquiries into the treatment of racial minorities within the Canadian criminal justice system during the 1990s (e.g., the Manitoba Aboriginal Justice Inquiry) reported the existence of systemic discrimination.

With *institutionalized discrimination*, disparities appear in the outcomes of decisions. Such disparities are the result of established (i.e., institutionalized) policies in the criminal justice system. These policies do not directly involve extralegal factors such as an individual's employment status, race, gender, or religion. The main issue here is one of system outcomes or results rather than any intent to discriminate against a specific individual or member of a group. One example involves decisions made within the criminal justice system based on the employment status of those accused of a crime when they are applying for bail. A policy granting bail made on the basis of the employment status of the accused can be legitimized on the basis of research showing that employed persons are better risks for showing up for trial than those who are unemployed. But what if all men are employed and very few women are? Since women are disproportionately overrepresented among the unemployed, they are more likely to be denied bail. This result is referred to as a *gender effect*, which means that discrimination is the result of a policy that is not concerned with the gender of those who apply for bail. Discrimination is the result of a policy; it does not exist because of individuals who are prejudiced.

Contextual discrimination arises from organizational policies within criminal justice agencies such as the police and the courts. One example is when a police service fails to enforce the criminal harassment (or anti-stalking) provisions of the Criminal Code simply because it foresees the complainant dropping charges before the case enters the courts. Another example is when a judge sentences the members of one racial minority group more harshly when they victimize the members of another racial group, but less severely when they victimize a member of their own racial group.

Individual discrimination occurs when an individual employed within the criminal justice system acts in a way that discriminates against the members of certain groups. For example, a police officer may discriminate against members of a certain social class and/or ethnic group by arresting them in all circumstances while only giving warnings to all others.

Substantive and Procedural Justice

How does our criminal justice system operate to make sure that its decisions are fair and equal and do not discriminate? The answer to this question is found in part by looking at what our society considers the most important components of justice. The first component is *substantive justice*—specifically, the accuracy or correctness of the *outcome* of a case. If a criminal suspect is in fact guilty, a verdict of "guilty" is a just decision. However, if the suspect is in fact innocent of the charge, then the verdict of "not guilty" is just. Substantive justice is primarily concerned with the truthfulness of the allegation, the accuracy of the verdict, and the appropriateness of the sentence. The high expectations we have of our criminal justice agencies to make correct decisions are the result of our concern with substantive justice.

The second component is *procedural justice*, which relates to the fairness of the procedures used to arrive at the verdict in a case. If fair procedures aren't used, the trial cannot be just, whether or not substantive justice was attained. For example, a person who is found guilty could in fact have violated the law (substantive justice), but if unfair procedures were used at some point during the investigation and/or trial, the conviction will be considered unjust according to procedural justice. This situation is sometimes brought to our attention when a higher court in this country such as a Provincial Appeal Court or the Supreme Court of Canada rules that there was a problem with the procedural fairness in a case (e.g., the interrogation of the suspect by the police did not follow appropriate procedures). In Canada today, issues involving procedural justice are more common than those involving substantive justice.

While it is possible to analytically separate procedural from substantive justice, they are in fact closely related. Our system of criminal justice attempts to make sure that all individuals charged with and convicted of a criminal offence are treated fairly. We think of procedural justice as the best way to guarantee substantive justice. In fact, our criminal courts operate under an adversarial system, an approach that values procedural justice (e.g., a fair trial) as the best way to attain substantive justice.

The Adversarial System

An **adversarial system** of justice has a number of components. Both parties involved hope to win the case and have the right to argue about what evidence the court will consider. A feature of this system is that a prosecutor (representing the state) is concerned initially that justice be done (e.g., that charges are laid only where enough evidence exists to support them) and later on with the successful prosecution of the case. Second, the trial is heard by an impartial fact finder—the judge—who is trained in the law and who is not involved in presenting evidence or questioning witnesses. This guarantees that the defendant receives a fair trial. The judge ensures that the appropriate questions are asked and that the rules of a criminal court case are followed.

In theory, all levels of our court system operate in an adversarial manner, with the Crown prosecutor and defence lawyer opposing each other and debating the facts of the case. The purpose of the adversarial system is to search for the truth—specifically, to determine the guilt or innocence of the accused. This system has been designed to ensure that the accused's fundamental legal rights are protected, that the trial is fair, and that the final decision is impartial. Critics of this image (e.g., Ericson and Baranek 1982) argue it operates only in theory and that the legal protections given to the accused are frequently ignored or plea bargained away by the defence counsel and prosecutor. As such, "legal justice" does not exist. Instead, most defendants receive a form of "bargain justice," where the accused is encouraged to plead guilty in return for a reduced sentence or the dropping of a number of charges. These critics argue that the final result is a court system in which the vast majority of the accused plead guilty before any item of evidence is contested in open court. Guilty pleas usually involve a reduction in the number of charges or a recommendation to the judge that the sentence be reduced. Significant issues have been raised about the benefits and limitations of the adversarial system of justice. These are outlined in Exhibit 1.3.

THE STRUCTURE OF THE CRIMINAL JUSTICE SYSTEM

In order to understand the structure of the Canadian criminal justice system, we need to look at its three major agencies. As indicated by Figure 1.1 this system

EXHIBIT 1.3   Benefits and Limitations of the Adversarial System

BENEFITS OF THE ADVERSARIAL SYSTEM	LIMITATIONS OF THE ADVERSARIAL SYSTEM
• A clear division exists among the various actors and agencies. • As much evidence as possible is looked at in each case, particularly as it benefits each side, since each is committed to winning. • The legitimacy of the criminal justice system is promoted through the appearance of fairness operating throughout the criminal justice system.	• The opposing sides often cooperate in order to reach a desired result, thereby undermining procedural justice in favour of efficiency. • The length of a trial becomes a concern, since each side has to present as much information as possible in the hope that they will be able to win the case. • Relevant evidence may be excluded if the judge considers that its use will violate the Charter of Rights and Freedoms.

comprises a vast number of agencies, which are organized into three major categories: the police, the courts, and corrections.

The Police

There are three main levels of police agencies in Canada: municipal, provincial, and federal. Although police agencies vary in their organizational structures and mandates, they usually cooperate with one another should the need arise. The most common type of police agency is found at the municipal level. Some municipalities establish their own police force and hire their own police personnel; others contract with the RCMP to provide police services. In 2008, almost 62 percent of sworn police personnel in Canada were employed by municipal police services (Minister of Industry 2008). Municipal police services are found in almost every major Canadian city, including Vancouver, Calgary, Edmonton, Winnipeg, Toronto, Montreal, and Halifax. The ten regional police services in southern Ontario (including the Halton Regional Police and the Peel Regional Police) are classified as municipal police services. Some larger municipalities (including Burnaby and North Vancouver, B.C.) contract out with the RCMP, but most municipalities that do so have a population between 50,000 and 100,000. Most provinces and territories in Canada have some municipal police services; the exceptions are Newfoundland and Labrador, Yukon, the Northwest Territories, and Nunavut.

Each province is responsible for developing its own municipal and provincial policing services (ibid.). This means that a province may require all cities within its jurisdiction that reach a certain population size (e.g., any city with more than 10,000 people) to form and maintain its own municipal police service. Provincial police services enforce all relevant laws in those parts of the province that are not under the control of a municipal police service. Besides the RCMP, which operates at the provincial level in most provinces, there are currently three provincial police services: the Ontario Provincial Police, the Sûreté du Québec, and the Royal Newfoundland Constabulary.

The federal government, through the RCMP, is responsible for enforcing laws created by Parliament.

Police Chief Gorden McGregor of the Kitigan Zibi Police Service in Quebec and president of the First Nations Chiefs of Police Association of Quebec discusses with reporters drug raids conducted by the Aboriginal Combined Forces Special Enforcement Unit designed to put a significant dent into a major organized crime network of marijuana production and distribution. (CP PHOTO/Graham Hughes)

The RCMP is organized under the authority of the RCMP Act and is part of the portfolio held by the Solicitor General of Canada. The RCMP, while involved in municipal and provincial policing across Canada, is also charged with other duties such as enforcing federal statutes, carrying out executive orders of the federal government, and providing protective services for visiting dignitaries. In addition, it operates forensic facilities and an educational facility in Ottawa (the Canadian Police College), as well as the Canadian Police Information Centre (CPIC), the automated national computer system used by all Canadian police services.

In 2008, there were 65,283 sworn police officers in Canada, an increase of just under 500 from the previous year. In addition, over 25,000 civilians were employed by the various police organization, a number which accounted for 28 percent of all police personnel, or 1 civilian for every to 2.5 police officers. Ontario had the largest number of sworn police officers (24,495), followed by Quebec (15,403) and British Columbia (8,137). Most police officers work at the municipal level, including with the RCMP and OPP (67 percent), 26 percent work at the provincial level, and 7 percent at the federal level (ibid.).

The Courts

The adult criminal courts across Canada process a significant number of cases each year. During 2006–07, the adult criminal courts in nine provinces and Yukon processed nearly 372,000 cases (the same number compared to 2005–06) involving 1,079,062 charges in all (Marth 2008).

All provincial/territorial court systems in Canada with the exception of that of Nunavut have three levels, though their formal titles differ by province (Russell 1987). The **lower courts** are called the provincial courts in most jurisdictions, although in Ontario they are referred to as the Court of Justice and in Quebec as the Court of Quebec. One level higher are the **superior courts**, usually known as the Court of Queen's Bench or Supreme Court (Trial Division). In Ontario, these courts are called the Superior Court of Justice, and in Quebec, the Superior Court. The highest level of criminal court in any province or territory is the appeal court. The court with the greatest authority in any criminal matter is the Supreme Court of Canada. The Nunavut Court is unique in Canada in that it consists of a single-level trial court. Superior court judges hear all criminal, family, and civil matters. This system was introduced in order to simplify the structure of the courts, improve accessibility to the court, and reduce the travel of judges.

The provincial courts are the first courts most Canadians encounter when they are charged with a criminal offence. These courts are typically organized into specialized divisions that deal with different areas of the law. For example, a province may decide to divide its provincial court into a criminal court, a family court, a small claims court, a youth court, and a family violence court. These courts deal with the majority of criminal cases, including disorderly conduct, common assaults, property offences, traffic violations, municipal bylaws, and provincial offences, as well as violations of the Youth Criminal Justice Act.

Provincial criminal court dockets are crowded with individuals waiting to have their cases heard. The courtrooms themselves have an air of "assembly-line justice"; defendants line up to enter the courtroom, only to have their cases summarily dispatched. Defendants in these courts rarely contest their cases in front of a judge. Researchers and observers report that most defendants who enter the provincial courts plead guilty to the charges during their initial appearance or find the charges either stayed (postponed indefinitely) or withdrawn by a prosecutor (Ericson and Baranek 1982; Wheeler 1987; Ursel 1994; Desroches 1995). Desroches (1995, 252) reported that 90 percent of the 70 robbers he interviewed pleaded guilty in provincial court, quickly averting any argument over the charges in an open courtroom. Most indicated they pleaded guilty simply because they wanted to "get the thing over with." Most criminal cases in Canada end up being heard in the provincial courts, which handle routine criminal cases. This is the extent of most Canadians' involvement in the court system.

For most indictable offences, the accused has the right to be tried in either the provincial court or the superior court. However, the superior courts must hear certain indictable offences such as first and second degree murder (see Chapter 2). These courts also hear the appeals of cases decided at the provincial court level. The accused is present at trials heard in provincial and superior courts. A fundamental constitutional right in Canada guarantees those individuals charged with a criminal offence that during all stages of a trial their legal rights will be protected. These rights include the right to representation by a lawyer, the right to a speedy court trial, and the right to face and cross-examine the accuser in court, as well as the opportunity to testify on one's own behalf (see Chapter 2).

The highest level of court in a province or territory—the appeal court—hears appeals from the superior courts and occasionally from provincial courts. These courts do not try criminal court cases; rather, they deal with issues concerning sentence lengths and the possibility of procedural errors. Defendants rarely appear in cases heard in appeal courts. Instead, lawyers representing the Crown and the defendant argue the case before a panel of appeal court judges.

Corrections

An accused, having been found guilty, may be sentenced to a term in the federal or provincial/territorial correctional system. In Canada, the correctional system involves a vast array of facilities, agencies, and programs. The responsibility for adult corrections is divided between the provincial/territorial governments and the federal government. Provincial and territorial governments are responsible for any individual serving a term of incarceration under two years and all for non-custodial sentences (e.g., probation). The federal government, through the Correctional Service of Canada, is responsible for any adult sentenced to a prison term of two years or more. A person sentenced to a term of two years or more who decides to appeal the conviction or sentence will first be incarcerated in a provincial facility. Those who waive the right to an appeal are sent directly to a federal institution to start serving the sentence.

During 2005–06, 85,915 adult offenders were admitted to a federal or provincial/territorial facility. This was almost the same number compared to the previous year. There were 192 adult correctional facilities across Canada at the end of 2005–06. Of these, 76 (18 of which were designated as community correctional centres) were operated by the federal authorities. There was a capacity of 14,131 spaces in federal institutions and 516 spaces in federal community correctional centres. The other 116 facilities were operating under provincial/territorial jurisdiction and their total capacity was 23,367 spaces. Of these institutions, 90 percent were designated as secure and the remaining 10 percent as open (e.g., halfway houses). During 2005–06, 77,360 individuals served all or part of their sentence in a provincial/territorial correctional facility and 8,857 in a federal facility (Landry and Sinha 2008).

The majority of individuals in the correctional population are serving all or part of their sentence under community supervision. Community supervision includes parole, probation, conditional sentence, statutory release, and temporary absences. In 2005–06, 109,089 offenders were serving their sentence on some form of community supervision. Most of these offenders (101,885, or 74 percent) had been sentenced to a term of probation; the rest were serving a conditional sentence (18,580) or provincial parole (1,875). Another 7,654 individuals were participating in a federal conditional release program (e.g., parole, statutory release, or

temporary absence). In 2005–06, the total number of individuals admitted to a correctional facility (including those incarcerated and/or serving their sentence in the community) was 342,349 (ibid.).

When we think of an individual serving a period of time in a Canadian correctional facility, we usually think of an inmate (typically a male) serving a long period of incarceration. This image is only partly accurate. Most inmates are male. In 2005–06, adult female offenders accounted for 11 percent of those sentenced to a term of incarceration in a provincial/territorial facility; for federal facilities, the figure was only 6 percent. Custodial sentences are longer for males compared to females. According to Landry and Sinha (2008), about 60 percent of all males received a sentence of less than one month compared to 69.9 percent of all females in 2005–06. In the same year, 56.9 percent of all males were given a sentence of less than six months, compared to 85.8 percent of all females.

Those who work in the correctional system have been criticized by the public as well as by other criminal justice personnel for some of their decisions that seem to reflect a disregard of public safety (Harris 2002). Critics point to what they consider to be high recidivism rates as an indication that institutions are failing to rehabilitate offenders. They also contend that correctional officials are easily fooled by inmates, and that as a result some who should remain incarcerated are released, resulting in higher crime rates. The correctional system, however, continues to play a number of important roles in the criminal justice system. Some of these roles may seem contradictory: it is expected to deter crime, to incapacitate those convicted of numerous serious crimes, and to rehabilitate offenders. Within this system, competing beliefs about what to do with offenders must be addressed on a day-to-day basis. Notwithstanding differing opinions about how to deal with offenders, the correctional system reinforces society's disapproval of their actions.

PROCESSING CASES THROUGH THE CANADIAN CRIMINAL JUSTICE SYSTEM

The Formal Organization of the Canadian Criminal Justice System

According to the Law Reform Commission of Canada (1988), a key function of our criminal justice system is to bring offenders to justice. At the same time, our legal system has developed a number of legal rights and protections for those accused of crimes. Various fundamental principles exist that attempt to ensure that no arbitrary actions violate these principles. Our criminal justice system is based on the presumption of innocence of all defendants and is supposed to conduct itself in a manner that is fair, efficient, accountable, participatory, and protective of the legal rights of those arrested and charged with the commission of a criminal action.

An integral part of these guarantees is found in what is known as criminal procedure. Criminal procedure is concerned with how criminal justice agencies operate during the interrogation of suspects, the gathering of evidence, and the processing of the accused through the courts. Criminal procedure also ensures that the agents of the state act in a fair and impartial manner in their search for truth. Our system of criminal procedure has two major parts: pretrial procedure and trial procedure.

Pretrial Criminal Procedure

Arrest, Appearance Notice, and Summons

The main purpose of arresting someone is to ensure that the accused appears in a criminal court, in which that person's guilt or innocence will be determined. Another purpose of arrest is to prevent the commission of any further crimes. With or without a warrant, police officers can arrest a suspect for violating the law.

A warrant is issued after a crime has been committed and the police, through their subsequent investigation, have collected enough evidence that they have reasonable and probable grounds to suspect that a certain person committed the offence. Once the evidence has been collected, the police must go to a justice of the peace and lay an information against the suspect, indicating why they feel it is in the public interest to arrest the suspect. Once the arrest warrant has been signed, the police execute the order by arresting the individual named on the warrant. Most warrants are issued only for the province in which the police investigated the crime. A Canada-wide warrant is issued only after an individual fails to appear in court after being charged with a violent or serious property offence. Even without a warrant, police can arrest an individual. This generally occurs when police officers have no chance to lay an information—for example, when they discover a crime in progress.

Police officers need not arrest an individual when the offence in question is either a summary conviction offence or an indictable offence that does not allow the accused to choose a jury trial. Nor do police officers need to arrest a suspect (1) when they are certain the suspect will appear in court at the designated time and date, (2) when the prosecutor can proceed by way of a summary or indictable offence (that is, a hybrid offence), or (3) when the offence involves a charge of keeping a gaming or betting house, placing bets, or keeping a common bawdyhouse.

Police may issue an appearance notice to a suspect or request a justice of the peace to issue a summons. An appearance notice is given to the suspect by a police officer at the scene of the crime. In these cases, the police officer hands the accused a form with information pertaining to the offence as well as the time and place the accused has to appear in court to answer the charge (or charges). The police officer must lay an information with a justice of the peace as soon as possible thereafter. Another alternative to an arrest is a summons. Here the accused is ordered to appear in court by a justice of the peace. The summons must be handed to the accused by a police officer or person granted special powers by provincial authorities. It can also be left at the accused's last known address with an individual who appears to be at least 16 years old. When this document is served, the accused is compelled to appear in court at a designated time and place (Barnhorst and Barnhorst 2004).

Detention

After an individual is arrested, the police have a number of decisions to make about the suspect. For one, they have to determine whether the person arrested should be held in custody before the trial. The law in Canada states that the accused must be released unless there is good reason for keeping him or her in detention. The police cannot hold an individual for an undetermined reason; Section 9 of the Charter of Rights and Freedoms states that "everyone has the right not to be arbitrarily detained." In addition, Section 10(a) states that "everyone has the right on arrest or detention to be informed promptly of the reasons thereof." If the arresting officer decides that the accused is to be formally detained, the officer in charge at the police station to which the accused is taken has the discretion to release the suspect. The officer usually exercises that discretion unless the suspect is being charged with a criminal offence punishable by imprisonment of five years or more, the suspect is felt to pose a threat to the public, or the suspect is believed unlikely to appear in court. If the officer decides the accused is to remain in custody, the accused must be taken before a justice of the peace within 24 hours or—if this is not possible—at the earliest possible time. While the accused is in detention, the police may take fingerprints and photographs if the individual is charged with an indictable offence.

Bail or Custody

The purpose of bail is to make sure that the accused appears at the ensuing trial. In Canada today, the Criminal Code requires all individuals arrested to be brought before a justice of the peace, who decides whether the accused is to be released before trial. This hearing is formally known as the **judicial interim release hearing** but is commonly referred to as the bail hearing. The justice of the peace is expected to release the accused unless the prosecutor supplies evidence to show either that the individual should not be released or that conditions should be attached to the release. Those charged with first or second degree murder can be released on bail only by a superior court judge.

Bail is such an important part of the Canadian legal process that s. 11(e) of the Charter of Rights and Freedoms guarantees the right of the accused "not to be denied reasonable bail without just cause." According to s. 457 of the Criminal Code, bail may not be granted when it can be shown to be in the public interest or necessary for the protection or safety of the public, and/or when denial is necessary to ensure the appearance of the accused on the designated date of the trial. In certain circumstances, it is up to the accused to inform the judge why he or she should be released pending trial.

Whether the accused is granted bail or is held until the trial, almost all criminal prosecutions in Canada start with an information. According to Mewett and Nakatsuru (2000), this serves two important purposes in the Canadian legal system. First, it compels the accused to appear in court on a specific date and at a designated time. Second, it forms the written basis for the charge that the accused faces in court.

Fitness Hearings

In Canada, an accused person is presumed to be fit to stand trial—that is, able to understand the trial proceedings and to instruct defence counsel throughout the trial. If this fitness comes into doubt, there is a system in place to establish whether the accused should have a trial. If issues about the ability of the accused to stand trial are raised at the bail hearing, an assessment can be ordered "on the court's own motion, on application by the accused, or on application of the prosecutor but the latter may apply only if the accused puts it into issue or there are reasonable grounds to doubt fitness" (ibid., 192).

As a result, if there is a **preliminary inquiry**, or a trial where there is no jury, there will be some evidence concerning the fitness of the accused to stand trial. In these instances, the judge alone will make the decision after hearing all the evidence. As we have seen, however, trials involving a judge alone are not as common as trials

by judge and jury. If the trial involves a jury, and the issue arises before the trial starts (which is the usual case), a special jury is empanelled to determine whether the accused should be tried. If the jurors agree that the accused is unfit, there won't be a trial; if they agree the accused is fit, the trial will proceed. If the issue is raised during the trial itself, the same jury hearing the trial will determine whether the accused is fit to stand trial.

If it is determined that the accused is fit, there is a trial (or the trial continues). However, if the accused is determined to be unfit, special provisions exist: a judge may decide he or she has enough information to make a decision right away, or may order a review board to formally assess the accused and provide the court with the necessary information—a process that usually takes no more than 45 days. If the accused is found to be unfit to stand trial, there will be no verdict one way or other. Technically, the accused is ordered to be returned to court for trial when it is decided that he or she is fit—although based on a number of factors, such as the seriousness of the charge, the prosecution may decide not to try the accused.

Trial Procedure
The First Court Appearance

In most jurisdictions, the accused is **arraigned**—that is, hears the charges that are being brought and enters a plea in response—not at the first appearance in court but at the preliminary hearing or at trial. Young offenders, however, are often arraigned at their first appearance. During the arraignment, the accused is brought before a provincially appointed judge. All formal charges are read by the court clerk at this time and the accused (or the accused's lawyer) makes the initial plea.

Sometimes the defence counsel or prosecutor indicates to the judge that he or she is not ready to proceed. This usually happens in cases that involve complex issues, where more time is needed to prepare the defence or prosecution. In such cases, the presiding judge agrees to set aside the case until a later date. During the postponement, the conditions that governed the accused individual before the initial appearance will apply. The Charter of Rights and Freedoms guarantees the right to a trial within a reasonable period of time; for this reason, the accused may be asked to waive for the record that Charter right before the court proceeds further (see Chapter 8). Only for that particular adjournment is the right waived; it can be raised again with respect to subsequent delays.

If a plea of not guilty is entered, a trial date is specified. However, if the accused decides to enter a plea of guilty, the judge sets a sentencing date and decides whether the accused is to be held in custody until sentencing. If a plea of not guilty is entered, an information is drafted; but before the actual trial takes place, the accused may have the right to a preliminary inquiry. (It is only if the case goes to the Supreme Court is an indictment drafted.)

The Indictment and Preliminary Inquiry

When the charge involves an **election indictable offence**—that is, when the accused has the right to choose between trial by judge alone and trial by judge and jury—the next step is to hold what is referred to as the *preliminary inquiry*. Few cases in Canada involve a preliminary inquiry. In 1999–2000, for example, only 6 percent of cases involved a preliminary inquiry (Pereira and Grimes 2002, 6). And it is estimated that in each year, about 80 percent of these cases end with the accused pleading guilty on first appearance in court. However, a preliminary inquiry is a right of the accused and is supposed to be held prior to the formal trial. Preliminary inquiries are heard by a provincial court judge. Summary conviction offences proceed differently from indictable offences in our court system and don't involve a preliminary inquiry.

The purpose of a preliminary inquiry is not to determine the guilt or innocence of the individual charged with a crime but rather to determine whether there is enough evidence to send the accused to trial. During a preliminary inquiry, a prosecutor attempts to show the judge that enough evidence exists for a criminal trial. The prosecution has the power to call as few or as many witnesses as it thinks necessary to prove to the judge that a case merits a trial. Once a witness testifies for the prosecution, defence counsel has the right of cross-examination.

The defence has the right to call witnesses to support a claim of innocence. If the defence can prove to the judge that the prosecution doesn't have a good case, there won't be a trial. Thus, a good defence during the preliminary inquiry can lead to the discharge of the accused. Another reason why the defence may call witnesses is to get their testimony on record, especially if witnesses are sick or about to leave the country. The evidence provided by witnesses during the preliminary inquiry may be used during the trial. Most preliminary inquiries last less than a day, and only rarely does a preliminary inquiry end in a judicial decision to discharge the accused or withdraw the charges. An inquiry is important to defendants because it allows them to "hear the nature and judge the strength" of much of the evidence that the prosecution will use during the trial (Barnhorst and Barnhorst 2004, 21). The defendant may then decide to plead guilty. In a study by the Law

Reform Commission of Canada (1984), 71 percent of preliminary inquiries resulted in a plea of guilty once the case reached the actual court trial.

When the judge decides that enough evidence exists to proceed to a trial, the offence for which the accused is to stand trial is written in the form of an indictment. The indictment, which replaces the information, forms the basis of the prosecution. It is a formally written allegation that states that the accused has committed a particular offence.

However, even if the judge decides to discharge the accused, this does not mean that the accused is acquitted. It simply means that insufficient evidence exists at this time to proceed to trial. Mewett and Nakatsuru (2000, 88) point out that a discharge means that "the accused cannot be tried on that information and that proceedings on that information are terminated." If, at a future date, new evidence is produced and strongly indicates the accused was involved in the crime, the prosecution usually proceeds by way of a direct indictment instead of requesting another preliminary inquiry. Whichever avenue is chosen, the attorney general or a senior official in the provincial justice department is required to give personal approval of the Crown's actions.

The Trial

For most indictable offences, the accused can elect trial by judge alone or by judge and jury. Some exceptions apply— for example, with first and second degree murder charges the accused must be tried by judge and jury unless both the defendant and the attorney general of the province agree to proceed with a judge alone. Some indictable offences (e.g., gaming offences) are considered so minor that they are almost always heard by a judge alone.

In Canada, the accused has the right to change his or her mind about the type of trial chosen, although some restrictions apply. In a re-election, as this process is called, an accused who initially selected trial by a provincial court judge has 14 days to change his or her mind and request a trial by a judge and jury. An accused who originally selected trial by judge and jury has 15 days after the completion of the preliminary inquiry to change his or her mind and select a trial heard by a provincial court judge alone.

Once the indictment is read to the accused in court, that person has to plead to the charge(s) by entering a plea of either guilty or not guilty. If the accused pleads not guilty, the prosecution has to prove that the defendant is guilty of the offence beyond a reasonable doubt. In this situation, no reasonable amount of doubt concerning the guilt or innocence of the accused can be left unresolved. If reasonable doubt exists, the accused is acquitted of all charges.

The Supreme Court of Canada. It is the final and highest Court of Appeal in Canada. Each year, it receives between 550 and 650 applications for leave to appeal and hears around 80 appeals. (Philippe Landreville/Supreme Court of Canada. Copyright © Supreme Court of Canada.)

Sentencing

If the accused is found guilty, the judge has numerous sentencing options available. Commonly applied sentences in Canada include a discharge (either absolute or conditional), probation, incarceration, a suspended sentence, and a fine. A judge may decide to combine two of these sentences, such as a period of incarceration with a fine. The sentence depends in large part on the charges the individual was found guilty of and the prior record of the offender. In a few instances, a judge has no choice in setting the penalty. For example, a judge who finds an offender guilty of first or second degree murder must sentence the accused to life imprisonment.

In many instances, a judge also relies on a pre-sentence report compiled by a probation officer. This report may evaluate such things as the employment record of the offender and any family support. Other sources of information that a judge may use to determine a sentence include a victim impact statement, information given

about the accused at the sentence hearing by the Crown prosecutor or the defence lawyer, and any mitigating or aggravating circumstances surrounding the commission of the crime. These can be significant factors in the sentencing.

Incarceration

If the sentence involves a period of incarceration, the offender is sent to either a provincial jail or a federal institution. If sentenced to a federal institution, the offender can apply for day parole six months before being eligible to make an application for full parole. Full parole is possible for most offenders after one-third of the sentence or seven years, whichever period is shortest. Most offenders in Canada do not serve the full term of their sentence; if they don't receive full parole, they receive statutory release after serving two-thirds of the sentence. While incarcerated, offenders can receive some form of rehabilitation or treatment. Programs have been designed to help offenders reintegrate into society. The amount of treatment given to offenders varies, however. After their release, offenders on parole must contact their parole officer on a regular basis. They may be required to spend some time in a halfway house or under some other form of community supervision.

THE CRIMINAL JUSTICE "FUNNEL"

The Informal Operations of the Criminal Justice System

An alternative approach to explaining the processing of cases through the criminal justice system is referred to as the criminal justice "funnel." When a crime is committed and the offender is charged by the police, the case enters the top of the funnel. From there, it passes through ever-narrowing stages until it exits. Sometimes this exiting occurs at the bottom of the funnel, with the offender being sent to a correctional facility, but it can also exit higher up the funnel, such as when all charges are dropped because a witness refuses to testify or because the prosecutor feels the evidence is not sufficient. Between the top and bottom of this funnel, then, are key decision-making points; at each, the case load has the potential to be reduced.

The actors and agencies in our criminal justice system are controlled by the formal rules of law; that said, they enjoy considerable leeway in how they prioritize and carry out their activities. According to those who study the informal criminal justice system, the system as a whole is best perceived as a process. This view emphasizes the key decision points through which cases pass. Each decision point is, in effect, a screening stage that involves a series of routinized operations; its efficacy is gauged primarily in terms of its ability to move a case to its next stage and a successful conclusion. The processing of individuals through our criminal justice system has in effect become a system of human resource management. The various actors go about their daily activities without stepping on toes, all the while bending informal social and agency rules. Part of this system is dedicated to the search for simple solutions. Simple routine justice treats similarly situated defendants in the same ways. Its central elements correspond more to the personal and political needs of justice personnel than to any abstract concept of justice or the rule of law.

All of those who work in criminal justice agencies detecting, prosecuting, and sentencing offenders use their discretion in many professional matters (see Exhibit 1.4).

EXHIBIT 1.4 Discretion within the Criminal Justice System

POLICE
Enforcement of the law
Investigation of crimes
Search and seizure
Arrest suspects

PROSECUTORS
Filing charges on the basis of evidence brought to them by the police
Reducing charges
Dropping cases
Plea bargaining

JUDGES
Decide to eliminate certain pieces of evidence
Impose sentences
Correctional officials
Set a conditional release date (e.g., parole)

Figure 1.2 illustrates the crime funnel at work in Canada during 2006–07. Of the total number of offences reported to the police that year (2,564,951 incidents were reported to the police), 242,988 (or 9.5 percent) resulted in conviction in a court. Of those convicted, just over 32 percent were sentenced to custody in a provincial/territorial or federal correctional facility (2005–06 figures). In 2006–07, 97 percent of those sentenced to custody were admitted to a provincial/territorial correctional facility; the rest were admitted to a federal correctional facility.

The Courtroom Work Group

One of the most important components of the crime funnel is referred to as the courtroom work group. The existence of this group disputes the belief that the criminal courts operate as a formal, rational legal system (i.e., a bureaucracy) with all of its members following the rule of law and well-defined rules as they go about their daily business. Instead, courts consist of informal work groups whose members hold considerable discretion, largely as a result of professional bonds that have developed among the members (Eisenstein and Jacobs 1974). One important feature of this group is group cohesion—that is, everyone involved cooperates with everyone else, and the members establish shared methods and values that help the group as a whole achieve its goals. As a result, the needs of the group members take precedence over concerns about the system's fairness and equality. The

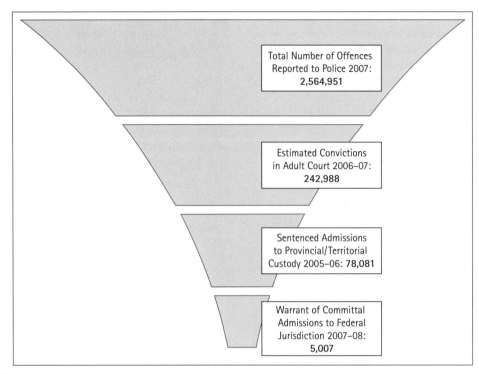

Total Number of Offences
Reported to Police 2007:
2,564,951

Estimated Convictions
in Adult Court 2006–07:
242,988

Sentenced Admissions
to Provincial/Territorial
Custody 2005–06: **78,081**

Warrant of Committal
Admissions to Federal
Jurisdiction 2007–08:
5,007

FIGURE 1.2
Relatively Few Crimes Result in Sentences to Federal Penitentiaries

Source: Corrections and Conditional Release Statistical Overview, Public Safety Canada, 2008. Reproduced
with the permission of the Minister of Public Works and Government Services Canada, 2009.

relationships among the individuals in this group have a significant impact on the day-to-day operations of the various criminal justice agencies and on the outcomes of individual cases.

There are three other characteristics of the courtroom work group, all of which essentially allow its members to accomplish their tasks: (1) There is an emphasis on speed—that is, on disposing of cases rather than dispensing justice; (2) guilt is presumed—in other words, it is generally understood that individuals charged by the police are in fact guilty; (3) secrecy is prized, because it enables all members to decide cases among themselves and to keep these negotiations private. All of these have a significant impact on the daily operations of our justice system and on the type of justice administered to and experienced by both offenders and victims.

The police, for example, have the function of collecting sufficient evidence to lay charges, thereby allowing the case to pass into the hands of a Crown prosecutor. Of course, Crown prosecutors can't try a case if the police don't collect enough evidence to lay a charge. Similarly, at the parole stage, a decision is made by parole board members about whether to release an inmate directly into society, to place him or her in a community facility, or to keep him or her institutionalized. Each decision is crucial. If an error is made, members of the public may be placed at risk or an innocent person may be incarcerated for a crime he or she didn't commit.

The criminal justice system does not inevitably secure a conviction in all cases where those who are charged with a crime appear in court. At each stage in the system, the number of accused persons is reduced, sometimes because they plead guilty, and sometimes because charges are dropped on account of insufficient evidence.

Reporting the Crime

Some people who have been victimized in a crime may not realize they have been victimized; others who have been victimized realize what has happened but don't report the crime to the police. They may decide not to report a property crime because they feel it isn't worth the effort. Police forces themselves may refuse to investigate a property crime or fraud case because they feel it is too minor or because they stand only a slight chance of discovering the perpetrator. It may not be feasible for the police to investigate the theft of a bicycle (though it is worth a few hundred dollars) or a bad cheque under $100 because of the amount of time required to investigate the crime and the low probability of solving the case. But if the police accept the complaint, an occurrence report is recorded.

Victimization studies in Canada reveal that a substantial number of victims of violent crimes do not report these crimes to the police. In the Canadian Urban Victimization Survey (Statistics Canada 1985), the four most common reasons victims gave researchers for not reporting an incident to police were, in order of priority, "too minor," "the police couldn't do anything," "inconvenience," and "nothing taken." It was discovered that victims didn't report 62 percent of the sexual assaults, 55 percent of the robberies, and 66 percent of the assaults committed against them. Questions about victimization included in the 1993 national survey (the General Social Survey) found that 90 percent of sexual assaults, 68 percent of assaults, 54 percent of vandalism, 53 percent of robberies, 48 percent of motor vehicle thefts or attempted thefts, and 32 percent of all break and enters were not reported to the police. In total, only 42 percent of the above six types of criminal incidents were reported to the police (Gartner and Doob 1994).

In the most recent General Social Survey, Gannon and Mihorean (2005) found that victims continued to report only a minority of the offences committed against them to the police. Overall, only 33 percent of all violent victimization incidents involving sexual assault, robbery, and physical assault were reported to the police. The main reasons why these crimes were not reported: the incident was not considered important enough (66 percent); the victim felt that the incident wasn't important enough (53 percent); or they didn't want the police involved (42 percent) (see Chapter 4).

Recording of the Incident as a Crime by the Police

Even if the police are contacted about a possible criminal act, they may decide after an investigation that an official report and the laying of formal criminal charges is not required. Such cases are categorized as "unfounded"—in other words, after a preliminary investigation, the police have decided that crime was neither attempted nor actually committed.

There are many reasons why the police may classify an incident as "unfounded." Ericson (1982), in his study of policing in the Toronto region, found that patrol officers used many tactics to record an incident as "unfounded." Often they did not "officially record an incident because, in

spite of their efforts, they are frustrated by the complexities and the lack of citizen assistance in sorting them out." In addition, Ericson found it rare for a minor complaint, such as a traffic accident involving damage under $200, to be recorded as a crime.

According to Ericson (ibid.), patrol officers reacted quite differently when they were contacted by victim-complainants about one or more of four types of complaints considered "major": interpersonal incidents, property disputes, automobile disputes, and "other" disputes. When one of these complaints was reported, the police officially recorded the event as a crime in 52 percent of their investigations. Official reports were more likely to be turned in incidents in situations where property damage or loss occurred. Incidents were also more likely to be recorded as crimes when no personal injury to the victim was involved. Interpersonal disputes, however, were often not officially recorded as crimes. The reason for this was that "a prior relationship between a victim and a suspect substantially decreases the probability that the suspect will be convicted if charged" and "there are usually greater problems in sustaining a charge for assault arising out of interpersonal conflicts" (ibid., 119). As a result, officers "routinely dealt with interpersonal troubles by informal means, while property-related troubles were more routinely processed as officially determined crimes."

Laying a Charge

Once a suspect has been identified and there is sufficient evidence to lay an information, the incident is considered "cleared by charge." Incidents may also be classified as "cleared otherwise"; here, the complainant has declined to proceed with the charges or the suspect has died before a charge can be laid. If a suspect is present at the scene when the police arrive, and if the officer decides the complaint has merit, one would think that a strong possibility exists that the individual will be arrested, taken to the police station, interrogated, and subsequently charged with a criminal offence.

Ericson (ibid.) found that patrol officers didn't always arrest an identifiable suspect even when they decided a crime had been committed. Ericson found that of the 392 individuals formally classified as "criminal suspects," no further formal action or report was taken against 137. Official reports were made on 40 other suspects, but again, no further action was taken against them for a variety of reasons. Thus, almost half the individuals classified as "criminal suspects" were not processed to the next stage of the criminal justice system. Only 107 (27 percent) of the criminal suspects were arrested and subsequently formally prosecuted.

Rigakos (1997) studied responses by police officers in one police organization located in the B.C. Lower Mainland. These incidents required a mandatory arrest response according to provincial and departmental policies. Yet the officers said they rarely arrested offenders even when (1) the woman complainant presented them with a signed protection order; (2) the male in violation of the court order remained at the scene; (3) the complainant requested that the police officer arrest the offender; and (4) a zero tolerance domestic violence policy was in effect for the police service.

Overall, police officers arrested the suspect in only 35 percent of cases involving criminal peace-bond breaches and only 21 percent of instances involving civil order violations.

Bail (Judicial Interim Release Hearing)

One of the most important decisions the criminal justice system makes is whether or not to grant the accused bail. Many concerns were raised during the 1960s about the relationship between the ability of an accused to raise bail and the consequent judicial determination of guilt or innocence. Studies conducted in the United States—which influenced Canadian policy on the granting of bail—found that only 18 percent of individuals jailed pending trial were acquitted, while 48 percent of those granted bail were acquitted (Vera Institute of Justice 1992). In response to concerns about the relationship between bail and trial outcomes, Canada passed the Bail Reform Act (1972), which allowed an accused to be released on his or her own recognizance; however, the accused had to promise to appear in court on the date of the trial and had to be considered a good member of the community; also, the crime being charged could not be a serious or violent one.

However, in a series of studies conducted within a decade of the enactment of the Bail Reform Act, Canadian researchers found that many accused persons who were eligible for bail still weren't receiving it and that the denial of bail significantly increased their chances of being convicted and receiving a longer sentence (Koza and Doob 1975). In addition, Hagan and Morden (1981), who studied individuals held in detention while awaiting a bail hearing, found that detention increased the likelihood that an accused would be found guilty and subsequently incarcerated.

Canadian law states that an accused person can be detained before trial only if he or she might not appear for the trial or if there is a risk that the accused might commit another offence while awaiting trial. Kellough (1996), in her study of bail hearings in Toronto during 1992, concluded that "the norm of conditional release operates differently in practice than in theory." She noted that many applicants were being denied bail not because of concern about their posing a possible threat to society or because they might fail to appear at trial when scheduled. In fact, she pointed out, many were being detained on "secondary grounds"—that is, for reasons other than community safety and to ensure appearance at the trial.

Prosecution

Research has consistently revealed that the greatest amount of attrition of major or indictable cases within our criminal justice system occurs between the time the police lay a criminal charge and the time a prosecutor decides to accept the case and take it to court. The common assumption holds that prosecutors accept any case in which the police decide there are "reasonable and probable grounds" that a crime has been committed and that the individual charged did in fact commit it. What actually happens is that before proceeding to the courtroom, prosecutors review most (if not all) of the cases involving serious crimes handed to them in order to assess the quality of the evidence. Concern about the quality of evidence collected by the police often leads prosecutors to stay charges or drop them altogether (Petersilia et al. 1990).

Factors other than evidentiary issues may be involved in a case, however. Charges involving minor offences often follow a procedure different from the one that is followed in cases involving major criminal charges. Also, issues relating to the role of witnesses and victims can have an impact on the prosecution of cases. Through their interviews with Crown prosecutors in Manitoba, for example, Gunn and Minch (1988) discovered that approximately 10 percent of cases of sexual assault were not prosecuted because the victim decided not to proceed to trial. According to the prosecutors, the victim's decision not to proceed arose from her fear of testifying in court, her fear of revenge, pressure from family and friends, her prior relationship with the offender, or sympathy for the offender.

Most people think that at the prosecution stage, the Crown prosecutor takes over the file and the police—before they appear in court—are no longer involved. In fact, cases usually remain in the hands of the police, generally until they are scheduled to be heard in provincial court. What the police tell the prosecutor about a case can therefore have a significant impact on any decision made about proceeding with the case (Wheeler 1987).

The police sometimes strike deals with offenders in order to gain information about other crimes and criminals. Here, too, the police can have considerable impact on the decision a Crown prosecutor makes about the charges or sentence in any particular case. Defence lawyers, usually without their clients, often negotiate with the police on behalf of their clients; after an agreement has been reached, the police then confirm the agreement by discussing it with the Crown prosecutor (Ericson and Baranek 1982; Klein 1976). As a result, criticism has been aimed at the control that police have over many minor court cases. This control means that prosecutions in such cases "are not as subject to checks and balances as formal legal procedures would have it. In only a tiny fraction of cases does the accused actually have a trial. In the vast majority, the 'trial' is the plea bargaining session and the accused is not allowed to attend" (Wheeler 1987).

Sentencing

As noted previously, most accused persons in Canada plead guilty on first appearance in provincial court, thus eliminating the opportunity to argue the facts of the case with the prosecution. In Desroches's (1995) study of robbers, the reasons given by accused persons for pleading guilty were numerous. Some of them simply wanted to "get the thing over with," while others had already confessed their guilt to the police. Others believed that the police had enough evidence to convict them anyway or that a trial might actually lead to a longer sentence. Still others agreed to a guilty plea prior to the court case in the hope that they would receive a lenient sentence. Whatever their hopes, most considered their sentence too harsh. As one convicted robber said, "You can molest children or kill somebody in this country and get a slap on the wrist. But don't you dare steal our money or we'll put you in prison and throw away the key" (ibid., 253).

This inmate was referring to discrimination against some offenders in the matter of sentencing. One might well expect the perpetrators of the most serious crimes to receive the harshest sentences, but this is not always the case. Extralegal factors such as race, gender, age, and social class may be significant when sentencing decisions are made by the judge. Research results vary across Canada, but generally, studies have found that race is a significant factor in sentencing. For example, Correctional Service of Canada statistics consistently reveal that an Aboriginal person is more likely to be sent to federal prison than a White person with a similar criminal record (Moyer et al. 1985). Ontario's Commission on Systemic Racism came to a similar conclusion in 1995 when it compared sentences in the Toronto criminal courts in terms of race (Roberts and Doob 1997). Studies in Manitoba (Hamilton and Sinclair 1991) and Alberta (Alberta Task Force 1991) reported that Aboriginal offenders were more commonly sentenced to a correctional facility when controlling for prior record and type of offence among all offenders. Other researchers have pointed out that the poor may not be able to afford quality legal representation and as a result receive harsher sentences (Winterdyck 2000).

VALUES AND THE CRIMINAL JUSTICE SYSTEM

If the informal processing of the accused through our criminal justice system disturbs you, then you will no doubt question the values of the system. While social scientists agree that all individuals possess values—that is, ideals, or ultimate aims and standards about what is desirable—it is also true that values are held by our criminal justice system. Packer (1968) developed two models of our criminal justice system, both of which represent very different value systems.

The Due Process and Crime Control Models of the Criminal Justice System

What do we want our criminal justice system to achieve? The answer to this question is not as straightforward as it might seem. Certainly, most if not all people want the system to be fair and just. But how can these ideals be attained? Herbert Packer, who was both legally and academically trained, attempted to answer this question by developing two ideal models of criminal justice (see Exhibit 1.5). One shows how criminal justice should work, and the other addresses its appropriate goals. He called these two models the due process model and the crime control model. The focus of the due process model is on prioritizing the rights of the suspect. According to Packer, the best mechanism for accomplishing this is an accurate, fair, and reliable system of laws and legal procedures. Central to this approach is that, every step of the way within the justice system, the rights of the suspect or accused must not be violated and that only the guilty are to be punished. In

EXHIBIT 1.5   Crime Control vs. Due Process Models

CRIME CONTROL MODEL

Goals

Deter crime
Protect citizens and the community
Punish offenders
"Assembly line" (efficient) justice

Policies

Increase the number of police officers
Increase the number of correctional facilities
Increase sentence length
Guilty until proven innocent
Give criminal justice agencies more legal powers

Purpose

Reduce the number of criminals on the street

Case Example

R. v. Hall (2002), S.C.C. 64. The Supreme Court upheld the trial judge's decision to deny bail to Hall in order to maintain public confidence in the criminal justice system. Hall had been charged with first degree murder.

DUE PROCESS MODEL

Goals

Protect individuals from the powers of the state
Enhance the legal rights of the accused
Fairness, equality, and justice

Policies

Limit and control the powers of the police
Limit discretion and control the activities of Crown prosecutors and judges so that all accused are treated fairly
Make sure that the powers of all agencies are controlled

Purpose

Ensure that the rights of the defendant are protected

Case Example

R. v. Feeney (1997), 2 S.C.R. 117. A murder suspect was arrested without a warrant, an action the Supreme Court felt was not legitimate. As a result, the Court ruled against the police, restricting their powers of search.

---

contrast, the crime control model emphasizes the control and suppression of criminal activity. This control is maintained by a criminal justice system that focuses on speed, efficiency, and incarceration for those found guilty. Because of its emphasis on repressing criminal behaviour, the crime control model cannot be effective if delays occur as a case moves through the legal system and if negotiated outcomes, such as plea bargains, come into play. On rare occasions, innocent people are found guilty; however, the model maintains that such incidents are more than countered by the deterrent impact of the justice system.

The Crime Control Model

According to Sykes and Cullen (1992), the crime control model is best characterized by such statements as "get tough on crime" and "the criminal justice system is weak on criminals." It holds that the most important goal of the criminal justice system is to reduce crime by incarcerating criminals for lengthy periods of time. This reduces lawlessness, controls crime, and protects the rights of law-abiding citizens. To achieve this goal, the criminal justice system operates like an assembly line—it moves offenders as efficiently as possible to conviction and punishment so that effective crime control is

attained. Certainty of punishment is achieved through mandatory sentences, longer prison terms, and the elimination of parole.

The crime control model rests on the presumption of guilt. That is, most individuals who are arrested are in fact guilty. Thus the model places great trust in the decisions made by criminal justice officials, who wish to protect society. The model assumes that these individuals make few if any errors, since most defendants are guilty. Each stage of the criminal justice system involves a series of uniform and routine decisions made by officials. Finality is important to officials, because it indicates that there are few problems with the system and that, as a result, there will be few challenges to the system. Support for the use of discretion throughout the system is a key feature of this model, since legal technicalities would reduce its efficiency. When the criminal justice system is allowed to operate as efficiently as possible, it is thought that a reduction in the crime rate results. It follows that concerns for legal rights should not be allowed to erode the system's ability to reduce crime. Furthermore, when issues about the administration of justice come into conflict with the goal of protecting society, the crime control model errs in favour of protecting the rights of the law-abiding citizenry.

A witness is sworn in during trial. All individuals who give evidence in court must swear or, if they object to taking an oath, make a solemn affirmation to tell the truth. (Photodisc Green/PNC/Getty Images)

The Due Process Model

In contrast to the crime control model, the due process model emphasizes the protection of the legal rights of the accused. This approach emphasizes "the need to administer justice according to legal rules and procedures which are publicly known, fair and seen to be just" (Hudson 2001, 104). The most important goal of this model is not to reduce crime but to see that justice is done—specifically, by protecting the legal rights of the accused. This ensures that innocent people are not convicted. If they are, a serious wrong has occurred somewhere in the justice system and it needs to be corrected immediately. The best way to protect the rights of the accused is to limit the powers of criminal justice officials. The criminal justice system under this model operates very differently than it would under the crime control model—it's like an obstacle course.

When people are arrested and prosecuted, every effort is made to ensure that they are treated with fairness and that justice is served. All offenders are presumed innocent, regardless of their apparent guilt. Criminal justice officials are constantly monitored to ensure that they do not abuse their power and make errors in judgment when processing and convicting individuals. The high-profile cases of Donald Marshall and Guy Paul Morin involved officials who convicted innocent people (Harris 1986; Makin 1993). As a result of these abuses, legal controls have been introduced to make sure that officials don't abuse their power.

It is difficult, if not impossible, for the criminal justice system to reduce crime, say the supporters of this model, because criminal sanctions have a limited ability to stop criminal behaviour. It follows that justice should not be sacrificed in the name of crime control. Issues that bring the administration of justice into disrepute are of great concern to the due process model. This is why, even when an accused is factually guilty, he or she is allowed to go free if a member of a criminal justice agency violated the criminal procedures that govern it.

Due Process or Crime Control?

While these models are idealized and do not exist in reality as Packer presented them, they do help clarify the expectations individuals have of the criminal justice system. For example, after the terrorist attacks in the United States on September 11, 2001, most Canadians wanted the federal government to introduce strong measures in order to counter the threat of terrorism in this country (see "Critical Issues in Canadian Criminal Justice" at the end of the chapter). Public opinion polls found that 80 percent of Canadians wanted mandatory fingerprinting and identification cards for all Canadians, while a majority of citizens were supportive of giving the police extraordinary powers even though this meant that their home telephones could be wiretapped and their mail screened. They also informed the pollsters that they wanted an end to policies that favoured immigration. By January 2002, however, this support for the crime control model to deal with terrorism had decreased, with the public now informing the pollsters that they favoured new immigration and that they were not as supportive of giving the police and security forces more legal powers to combat terrorism. In part because of changing public perceptions of terrorism, by late May 2002 the federal government had withdrawn some of the most controversial proposals dealing with terrorist activities, such as one that would have given Cabinet the power to infringe on the civil rights of individuals living in Canada without any involvement of Parliament (Fife 2002). It replaced the most onerous pieces of the proposed law with less harsh measures.

THE ANTI-TERRORISM LAW: CRIME CONTROL OR DUE PROCESS?

Laws usually evolve in a deliberate manner in our society. However, this approach changed immediately after 8:45 A.M. on the morning of September 11, 2001, when American Airlines Flight 11 was flown into the North Tower of the World Trade Center in New York City by hijackers. Many Canadians asked whether we were sufficiently prepared to handle such actions. More specifically, if laws had been in place in this country, could the 9/11 attacks have somehow been prevented? And how should we react to such actions if they ever take place in this country? Even in situations like this, with almost all Canadians demanding some form of legal response, the creation of new legal powers is not as straightforward as would seem at first glance.

THE GOVERNMENT'S RESPONSE

After 9/11, the federal government introduced two pieces of legislation to deal with terrorism in Canada. The first, introduced on October 15, 2001, was the Anti-Terrorism Act (Bill C-36), which created measures to (1) identify, prosecute, convict, and punish terrorists and terrorist organizations; and (2) give new investigative powers to law enforcement and security agencies. Some of the measures directed toward terrorist organizations would have done the following:

- Defined and designated terrorist groups to make it easier to prosecute terrorists and their supporters.
- Made it an offence to knowingly participate in, contribute to, or facilitate the activities of a terrorist group or to instruct anyone to carry out a terrorist activity or an activity on behalf of a terrorist group.
- Created tougher sentences and parole supervision for terrorist offenders.
- Cut off financial support for terrorists by making it a crime to knowingly collect or give funds to them, either directly or indirectly.

Bill C-36 also proposed to extend law enforcement and security agencies powerful new investigative tools to collect information about and prosecute terrorists and terrorists groups. These tools would have done the following:

- Made it easier to use electronic surveillance against terrorist organizations.
- Created new offences targeting unlawful disclosure of certain information of national interest.

- Amended the Canada Evidence Act to guard certain information of national interest from disclosure during courtroom or other judicial proceedings.
- Within certain defined limits, allowed the arrest of suspected terrorists and their detention for 72 hours without charge, in order to prevent terrorist acts and save lives.
- Established investigative hearings with the power to compel individuals possessing information about a terrorist organization to disclose that information to a judge even in the absence of a formal trial.

Abdul Qayyum Jamal and his lawyer Ansar Farooq talk to media outside court in Brampton, ON, west of Toronto, Tuesday, April 15, 2008. Charges have been stayed against Jamal and three other suspects in an alleged Toronto terror plot. (CP PHOTO/Toronto Star-Tony Bock)

PREVENTIVE DETENTION AND INVESTIGATION HEARINGS

In the Anti-Terrorism Act, many considered the "preventive detention" and "investigation hearings" sections to be the most controversial. Investigative hearings (s. 83.28 of the Criminal Code) are designed to allow the Crown to approve an application for an order requiring an individual who has not yet been charged with an offence to appear before the court for questioning about a terrorist offence. After an order is granted under s. 83.28, the individual in question could be arrested, compelled to give answers to questions, and charged with contempt for refusing to testify or for providing false testimony (Diab 2008, 65).

The investigative hearing provision of the Criminal Code was upheld as constitutional by the Supreme Court of Canada in 2004 after a challenge launched by the wife of Inderjit Singh Reyat, the only man convicted in the Air India bombing (*Application under the Criminal Code* 2004). The RCMP was planning on summoning 15 people to appear before a judge to answer questions about their knowledge of this unprecedented action, but the hearing never actually occurred (Bolan 2007).

The preventive arrest clause (s. 83.3 in the Criminal Code) enables the police to arrest suspects without a warrant and detain them for up to 72 hours without charge before a judge has to decide to impose a peace bond if the authorities had reason to believe a terrorist act would be committed. Once a peace bond is issued, the detention ends. Bonds can be used to impose stringent conditions on the person up to a maximum of 12 months. If the bond's conditions are violated or refused, the judge can extend it.

When the investigative hearing and preventive arrest sections were included in the Anti-Terrorism Act, there were concerns expressed that they would override civil liberties. As a result, the federal government placed a "sunset" clause on the provisions of the law enabling "preventive arrests" and "investigative hearings." Both provisions were to expire at the end of February 2007, unless the House of Commons and Senate passed a resolution to extend them. After five years, they had not been used; nevertheless, the federal government decided to attempt to renew both the investigative arrest and preventive arrest clauses of the Anti-Terrorist Act. Both the House of Commons and Senate committees reviewing these two provisions recommended that these provisions be extended subject to certain safeguards. However, the opposition parties defeated the legislation introduced in the House of Commons to extend these clauses as they were originally written.

SECURITY CERTIFICATES

Security certificates were introduced in the Immigration Act in 1988. This provision was strengthened in 2002 after the 9/11 attacks in order to give authorities a faster and more efficient way to remove non-citizen terrorist suspects from Canada without having to lay charges and then process the accused through the criminal justice system as they would a citizen of Canada. Under a security certificate, a non-resident could be classified as a national security risk and could be quickly deported. Suspects who argue that they would face torture in their homelands could spend an indefinite amount of time in jail, without criminal charges, as their cases work their way through the courts. This process was described by some as "draconian" as accused persons and their counsel are only provided with a vague summary of the allegations against them. Evidence to back up the allegations is received in secret by a judge, and neither the accused nor his or her lawyer can attend (Makin 2007).

Security certificates were challenged in the Supreme Court (*Charouki v. Canada Minister of Citizenship and Immigration* 2007). The Supreme Court, in a 9–0 ruling, invalidated provisions of the Immigration and Refuge Protection Act that denied persons named in security certificates a right to a fair hearing—the right to know and be able to rebut the information against them. In their decision, the Supreme Court wrote that "the state can detain people for significant periods of time; it must accord them a fair judicial process." They also decided that "without this information, the named person may not be in a position to contradict errors, identify omissions, challenge the credibility of the informants or refute false allegations." The court also stated that foreign nationals who do not live in Canada should be treated on par with permanent residents and given the chance to file applications for judicial review of a security certificate immediately after being detained, instead of having to wait 120 days to make any filing, as they do under the post-9/11 rules.

In their decision, the Supreme Court made several suggestions to "Charter-proof" the certificates, including allowing a security-cleared "special advocate" into a hearing to look out for the interests of the accused, a system that existed in the United Kingdom. At the same time, the court cautioned that a suspect's right to the government's case "is not absolute" and some evidence may have to remain secret to protect national security (Tibbetts 2007b).

NEW LEGISLATION

In early October 2007, the Conservative government introduced a bill (Bill C-3) to reinstate both the preventive detention and investigative

Continued on next page

hearings. The new legislation would preserve the controversial security certificate system but create "special advocates"—lawyers with security clearance who would act on behalf of the accused, with access to the secret information the government uses to detain and deport suspects.

The revisions to the Act would give foreign nationals the same 48-hour detention limit as permanent residents before a closed-door judicial review. While the new legislation would preserve the controversial security certificates, it would create the position of "special advocates," who would be appointed from a pre-approved list of security-cleared lawyers. These special advocates would have access to the government's evidence, but would not be allowed to disclose it to the accused. Special advocates would also be able to argue before federal judges that certain evidence should not be secret, and they could cross-examine government witnesses. After the new revisions gained the approval of Parliament, the federal government filed five new certificates, re-designating Mr. Charkaoui and four others as threats to national security who were to be expelled from Canada (Thanh Ha 2008).

Only a few cases have been prosecuted under Canada's Anti-Terrorism Act to date. The first successful prosecution occurred on September 26, 2008. The accused individual, who was 17 at the time he was arrested on June 3, 2006, was the first Canadian found guilty of participating in a terrorist group despite the fact there was "no evidence that he planned, or even knew about, any specific plot. However, he was found to be an 'eager acolyte' to more senior adult suspects who discussed attacking Parliament, as well as exploding truck bombs in downtown Toronto" (Freeze 2008, A4). It was in the context of this case that an issue relating to entrapment (see Chapter 2), specifically whether or not a RCMP

agent had entrapped the youth. A judge ruled that entrapment did not take place; as a result, the youth was to be sentenced at the end of May 2009 (El Akkad, 2009).

On March 29, 2004, Mohammad Khawaja, a Canadian citizen, was arrested and charged with violating the provisions of the Anti-Terrorism Act. When he was arrested, he was developing a remote detonating device. The next day, six members of a group of people that Mr. Khawaja was connected with were arrested in the United Kingdom. In October 2008, Mr. Khawaja was convicted of seven offences and became the first Canadian to be sentenced under the Anti-Terrorism Act, receiving a sentence of just over 10 years (see *R. v. Khawaja* [2008]). The Crown, arguing that Mr. Khawaja was "a grave and palpable threat to society" had argued for a sentence of two life sentences plus an additional 44 years. In April 2007, five of the members of the group arrested in the United Kingdom received sentences of life imprisonment.

Questions
1. Do you think that the provisions found in the Anti-Terrorism Act will help deter terrorist acts?
2. Do you believe that the creation of "special advocates" for the accused under the Anti-Terrorism Act is sufficient to ensure that the due process of rights of the accused are upheld?
3. In the wake of terrorist acts, how can the federal government protect the legal rights of all residents of Canada while at the same time ensuring the safety of the rest of the public?
4. In a time of crisis, should the federal government be allowed to give itself extraordinary legal powers even if they violate individual rights?

SUMMARY

Criminal justice has developed into a major field of study over the past 30 years. It combines various disciplines—including criminology, law, psychology, political science, and social welfare—in an attempt to gain a better understanding of the crime problem, of how to improve the operations of criminal justice agencies, and of how best to punish criminals. Much effort has gone into improving our knowledge of crime and determining

how our agencies should fight crime. The effort is extremely costly, and more so every year.

Criminal justice can be viewed as both a system and a "funnel." As a system, it functions in a formal and highly visible manner, with all the major agencies working together. In its actual operations, the system resembles a funnel, in the sense that many crimes are committed but relatively few individuals are convicted. The highest profile cases are representative of the formal operations of the criminal justice system, with lawyers debating the facts and an impartial judge ensuring that the rules of legal procedure are followed. Most individuals don't enjoy the luxury of a formal trial, however. Their cases are resolved during their initial appearance in court or—if a trial is conducted—in a matter of hours or days. Thus, two opposing models of the criminal justice system emerge.

According to the crime control model, criminal law establishes an important difference between the law-abiding and the lawbreakers. Those who support the crime control model say that the focus should be on the capture, processing, and control of individuals who break the law. In contrast, the due process model emphasizes the legal rights of individuals. This model's adherents view the legal system as an obstacle course; they emphasize the rights of the accused. Even when the accused is factually guilty, the prosecution must prove legal guilt before the accused can be convicted and punished. In the due process model, the operations of all agencies in the criminal justice system are open to investigation and questions about their actions.

Discussion Questions

1. Do you think the measures introduced by the federal government to combat terrorism will prevent such actions from occurring? What civil liberties are you willing to give up?

2. Discuss the relative strengths and weaknesses of the crime control model.

3. Discuss the relative strengths and weaknesses of the due process model.

4. Discuss the efforts made to reduce crime in our society. What stops us from attaining a crime-free society? Is a high crime rate the price that our society must pay to have legal rights?

5. What should be the predominant function of the police in contemporary society?

6. Should we try to control the discretion of our criminal justice agencies? If we do, and succeed, what would the impact be?

7. Why don't victims report their crimes to the police? Have you or members of your family ever witnessed or been a victim of a crime and not reported it? If so, why was the crime not reported?

Suggested Readings

Ericson, R.V., and P.M. Baranek. *The Ordering of Justice: A Study of Accused Persons as Dependants in the Criminal Justice Process.* Toronto: University of Toronto Press, 1982.

Godfrey, R. *Under The Bridge.* Toronto: HarperCollins, 2006.

Harris, M. *Con Game: The Truth about Canada's Prisons.* Toronto: McClelland and Stewart, 2002.

Hartnagel, T.F., ed. *Canadian Crime Control Policy: Selected Readings.* Toronto: Harcourt Brace Canada, 1998.

Roberts, J.V., and M.G. Grossman, eds. *Criminal Justice in Canada: A Reader,* 3rd ed. Toronto: Nelson, 2008.

References

Agnell, S. 2004. "Every Case Is Different, Euthanasia Advocates Say." *National Post*, September 28, A4.

Albanese, J. 1999. *Criminal Justice.* Boston: Allyn and Bacon.

Alberta Task Force. 1991. *Justice on Trial: Report of the Task Force on the Criminal Justice System and Its Impact on the Indian and Métis People of Alberta.* Edmonton: Attorney General and Solicitor General of Alberta.

Bailey, I. 2009a. "Gang Gunplay Rattles Metro Vancouver Communities." *The Globe and Mail*, February 12, A5.

———. 2009b. "RCMP in B.C. Defend Investigation of Gangs after Mayor's Comment." *The Globe and Mail*, March 6, A9.

Bailey, I., and W. Stueck. 2009. "Vancouver Losing Fight with Gangs, Mayor Says." *The Globe and Mail*, March 5, A4.

Barnhorst, R., and S. Barnhorst. 2004. *Criminal Law and the Canadian Criminal Code,* 4th ed. Toronto: McGraw-Hill Ryerson.

Bolan, K. 2007. "Air India Probe Faces Hindrance if Terror Laws Change." *National Post*, February 15, A5.

Bowal, P., and B. Lau. 2005. "The Contours of What Is Criminal." *LawNow* 29: 8–10.

Canadian Bar Association. 2003. "Euthanasia: The Debate Is Far from Over." *National*, August/September, 28.

Chase, S. 2009. "Conservatives to Target Gang Violence." *The Globe and Mail*, February 25, A4.

Cohen, T. 2009. "Tories' Car-Theft Bill Takes Aim at Organized Crime." *The Globe and Mail*, April 22, A8.

Curry, B. 2006. "Saskatchewan Fears More Natives Will Be Jailed." *The Globe and Mail*, May 5, A9.

Dauvergne, M., and G. Li. 2006. *Homicide in Canada, 2005*. Ottawa: Canadian Centre for Justice Statistics.

Desroches, F.J. 1995. *Force and Fear: Robbery in Canada*. Scarborough, ON: Nelson Canada.

Diab, R. 2008. *Guantanamo North: Terrorism and the Administration of Justice in Canada*. Halifax: Fernwood.

Eckstein, C. 2007. History of Euthanasia, Part 1. www.chninternational.com. Retrieved May 9, 2009.

Eisenstein, J., and H. Jacobs. 1974. *Felony Justice: An Organizational Analysis of Criminal Courts*. Boston: Little Brown.

El Akkad, O. 2009. "No Entrapment in Terror Case, Judge Rules." *The Globe and Mail*, March 25, A11.

Ericson, R. 1982. *Reproducing Order: A Study of Police Patrol Work*. Toronto: University of Toronto Press.

Ericson, R., and P.M. Baranek. 1982. *The Ordering of Justice: A Study of Accused Persons as Defendants in the Criminal Process*. Toronto: University of Toronto Press.

Fife, R. 2002. "Canadians Lose Fear of Terrorism." *National Post*, July 6, A1, A6.

Freeze, C. 2008. "Jihadist Found Guilty of Terrorist Crimes." *The Globe and Mail*, October 30, A4.

Gannon, M., and K. Mihorean. 2005. *Criminal Victimization in Canada, 2004*. Ottawa: Canadian Centre for Justice Statistics.

Gartner, R., and A.N. Doob. 1994. *Trends in Criminal Victimization, 1994*. Ottawa: Statistics Canada.

Gunn, R., and C. Minch. 1988. *Sexual Assault: The Dilemma of Disclosure and the Question of Conviction*. Winnipeg: University of Manitoba.

Hagan, J., and C. Morden. 1981. "The Police Decision to Detain: A Study of Legal Labelling and Police Deviance." In C.D. Shearing, ed., *Organizational Police Deviance: Its Structure and Control*. Toronto: Butterworths, pp. 9–28.

Hamilton, A.C., and C.M. Sinclair. 1991. *Report of the Aboriginal Justice Inquiry of Manitoba, Volume 1*. Winnipeg: Province of Manitoba.

Hammer, K. 2009. "B.C. Man's Quick Thinking Leads to Grim Discovery." *The Globe and Mail*, February 17, A1–A10.

"Harper's Inflexible Steps to Get Tough on Crime." 2006. *The Globe and Mail*, April 5, A14.

Harris, M. 2002. *Con Game: The Truth about Canada's Prisons*. Toronto: McClelland and Stewart.

———. 1986. *Justice Denied: The Law versus Donald Marshall*. Toronto: Totem Books.

Hudson, B. 2001. "Crime Control, Due Process, and Social Justice." In E. McLaughlin and J. Muncie, eds., *The Sage Dictionary of Criminology*. London: Sage, 104–5.

Hunter, J. 2009a. "Province Moves to Add Police, Prosecutors." *The Globe and Mail*, February 14, A5.

———. 2009b. "Western Premiers Unite to Combat Gang Violence." *The Globe and Mail*, March 3, A1, A4.

Kellough, G. 1996. "'Getting Bail': Ideology in Action." In T. O'Reilly-Fleming, ed., *Post Critical Criminology*. Scarborough, ON: Prentice-Hall, pp. 159–83.

Klein, J. 1976. *Let's Make a Deal: Negotiating Justice*. Toronto: D.C. Heath.

Koza, P., and A.N. Doob. 1975. "The Relationship of Pre-Trial Custody to the Outcome of a Trial." *Criminal Law Quarterly* 17: 391–400.

Landry, L., and M. Sinha. 2008. *Adult Correctional Services in Canada, 2005/06*. Ottawa: Canadian Centre for Justice Statistics.

Law Reform Commission of Canada. 1988. *Compelling Appearance, Interim Release, and the Pre-Trial Detention*. Ottawa Law Reform Commission of Canada.

———. 1984. *Questioning Suspects—Working Paper 32*. Ottawa: Minister of Supply and Services.

———. 1977. *Our Criminal Law*. Ottawa: Minister of Supply and Services Canada.

Li, G. 2007. *Homicide in Canada, 2006*. Ottawa: Canadian Centre for Justice Statistics.

Makin, K. 2007. "Top Court to Rule on Security Certificates." *The Globe and Mail*, February 20, A10.

———. 1993. *Redrum the Innocent*. Toronto: Penguin, 1993.

Marth, M. 2008. *Adult Criminal Court Statistics, 2006/07*. Ottawa: Canadian Centre for Justice Statistics.

Mewett, A.W., and S. Nakatsuru. 2000. *An Introduction to the Criminal Process in Canada*, 4th ed. Scarborough, ON: Carswell.

Minister of Industry. 2008. *Police Resources in Canada, 2008*. Ottawa: Statistics Canada.

Morton, J. 2006. "When Reforming Justice, Recall Bacon's Famous Words." *National Post*, April 21, A13.

Moyer, S., F. Kopelman, C. LaPrairie, and B. Billingsley. 1985. *Native and Non-Native Admissions to Provincial and Territorial Correctional Institutions*. Ottawa: Solicitor General of Canada.

Muncie, J. 2002. "The Construction and Deconstruction of Crime." In J. Muncie and E. McLaughlin, eds., *The Problem of Crime*, 2nd ed. London: Sage.

Packer, H.L. 1968. *The Limits of the Criminal Sanction*. Stanford, CA: Stanford University Press.

Periera, J., and C. Grimes. 2002. *Case Processing in Criminal Courts, 1999/00*. Ottawa: Canadian Centre for Justice Statistics.

Peritz, I. 2006. "Assisting in Her Son's Suicide Was Final Act of Compassion, Court Told." *The Globe and Mail*, January 24, A24.

———. 2004. "Mother's 'Pure Love' and Son's Fears Cited in Suicide." *The Globe and Mail*, September 28, A1, A6.

Petersilia, J., A. Abrahamse, and J.Q. Wilson. 1990. "The Relationship between Police Practice, Community Characteristics, and Case Attrition." *Police Studies* 1, 1: 23–38.

Rawls, J. 1971. *A Theory of Justice*. Cambridge, MA: Belknap Press of Harvard University Press.

Report of the Commission on Systemic Racism in the Ontario Criminal Justice System: A Community Summary. 1995. M. Gittens and D. Cole, co-chairs. Toronto: Queen's Printer for Ontario.

Rigakos, G. 1997. "Constructing the Symbolic Complainants: Police Subculture and the Nonenforcement of Protection Orders for Battered Women." *Violence and Victims* 10: 235–47.

Roberts, J.V., and A.N. Doob. 1997. "Canada." In M. Tonry, ed., *Ethnicity, Crime, and Immigration: Comparative and Cross-National Perspectives*. Chicago: University of Chicago Press, pp. 469–522.

Russell, P. 1987. *The Judiciary in Canada: The Third Branch of Government*. Toronto: McGraw-Hill Ryerson.

Senna, J.J., and L.J. Siegal. 1995. *Essentials of Criminal Justice*. Minneapolis, MN: West.

"Sentenced by Politics." 2006. *The Globe and Mail*, January 13, A14.

Statistics Canada. 1985. *Victims of Crime: Canadian Urban Victimization Survey*. Ottawa: Solicitor General of Canada.

Steuck, W. 2009. "Gang Wars Shooting Holes in Vancouver's Budget." *The Globe and Mail*, March 24, A5.

Sutherland, E. 1949. *White Collar Crime*. New York: Dryden.

Sykes, G.M., and F.T. Cullen. 1992. *Criminology*, 2nd ed. Fort Worth, TX: Harcourt Brace Jovanovich.

Thanh Ha, T. 2008. "Updated Security Certificates to Face Legal Challenge." *The Globe and Mail*, February 29, A8.

———. 2006. "Mother Spared Jail in Son's Assisted Suicide." *The Globe and Mail*, January 28, A5.

———. 2004. "Mother Charged in Son's Death." *The Globe and Mail*, September 28, A9.

"The First Degree Oversold." 2009. *The Globe and Mail*, February 27, A14.

Tibbetts, J. 2007a. "Tories' Gun-Crime Bill on 'Deathbed': Grits." *National Post*, February 12, A6.

———. 2007b. "Supreme Court Strikes down Security Law." *National Post*, February 24, A13.

Travis, F.T. 1990. *Introduction to Criminal Justice*. Cincinnati: Anderson.

Ursel, J. 1994. *The Winnipeg Family Violence Court*. Ottawa: Canadian Centre for Justice Statistics.

Vera Institute of Justice. 1992. *Programs in Criminal Justice Reform*. New York: Vera Institute of Justice.

von Hirsch, A. 1976. *Doing Justice: The Choice of Punishments*. New York: Hill and Wang.

Walker, S. 2001. *Sense and Nonsense about Crime and Drugs*, 5th ed. Belmont, CA: Wadsworth.

Walklate, S. 2005. *Criminology: The Basics*. London, Routledge.

Wheeler, G. 1987. "The Police, the Crowns, and the Courts: Who's Running the Show?" *Canadian Lawyer*, February.

Wilton, K. 2006. "Mother Pleads Guilty to Aiding MS Son's Suicide." *National Post*, January 24, A7.

Winterdyck, J. 2000. "Do the Rich Get Richer and the Poor Injustice? *LawNow* 24: 19–21.

Court Cases

Application under the Criminal Code (Re) (2004), S.C.C. 42.

Charkaoui v. Canada (Minister of Citizenship and Immigration) (2007), 1 S.C.R. 350.

R. v. Khawaja (2008), O.J. 4245.

R. v. Latimer (2001), 1 S.C.R. 3.

R. v. LePage (1999), 2 S.C.R. 744.

Rodriguez v. British Columbia (Attorney General) (1993), 3 S.C.R. 519.

Winko v. Forensic Psychiatric Institute (1999), 2 S.C.R. 625.

Weblinks

To read the Supreme Court of Canada decisions in *R. v. LePage* (1999) an d *Winko v. Forensic Psychiatric Institute* (1999), go to http://scc.lexum.umontreal.ca/en/index.html. Click on the year "1999," and then "Volume 1." The decisions for these cases were released on June 17, 1999. If you are interested in reading the Supreme Court of Canada decision concerning an assisted suicide case, go to the same website, then to "1993," and find the following case: *Rodriguez v. British Columbia (Attorney General)* (1993), 3 S.C.R. 519. The decision for this case was announced on September 30, 1993.

Criminal Law and Criminal Justice in Canada

CHAPTER OBJECTIVES

✓ Identify the ways in which criminal law can be established, including the common law, case law, and statute law.

✓ Understand what offences are included in the three main categories of crime.

✓ Discuss the difference between substantive and procedural laws.

✓ Recognize the basic principles used by legislatures and the courts in developing and interpreting substantive laws.

✓ Identify what protections are given to the accused by the Charter of Rights and Freedoms.

✓ Understand the different categories of legal defences and the defences found within each category.

For many people, the criminal justice system is exclusively concerned with the enforcement of the law, the processing of accused violators of the law, and the punishment of individuals convicted of violating the law. However, studying the criminal justice system also involves investigating and questioning the role of law in our society. Many aspects of the law have an impact on the processing of the accused. For example, what are the legal aspects of determining whether an individual has broken the law? What are the technical grounds for assessing such activities? How do we make laws in Canada? And what legal protections are given to those accused as they progress through the criminal justice system? To gain a complete picture of the operations of the Canadian criminal justice system, one must know something about the source, nature, purpose, and content of law in our society, as well as differences among types of laws.

There are two important terms one must be familiar with when studying the role and practice of criminal law in the criminal justice system. The first is **substantive criminal law**, which refers to the body of legislation that declares which actions will be punished by the state. In essence, substantive criminal law is what legally defines crime in our society. The main components of most criminal laws are *mens rea, actus reus,* and harm (all of which will be discussed later in this chapter). Laws provide the framework for defining criminal acts. However, they are not static entities: the various actors involved in the criminal justice system must interpret these laws. Sometimes they interpret the laws in question with no controversy; other times their decisions become major issues because someone appeals the outcome or public opinion decidedly opposes the formal decision.

The second type of criminal law is **procedural criminal law**, which tells us how the rights and duties of individuals can be enforced. It focuses on the criminal process— that is, the legal steps through which an offender passes. Examples of the procedural criminal law include the rules of evidence, the law of search and seizure, and the right to counsel. These are procedural safeguards designed to protect the accused, and they can be found in the Charter of Rights and Freedoms (which will be discussed later in this chapter) as well as in the Criminal Code and the common law. Many people use the shorthand term "due process" when referring to procedural criminal law. Whichever term is used, it is an important part of our criminal justice system because it signals "the primacy of demonstrating legal guilt rather than factual guilt and raises a number of obstacles to conviction in order to protect the rights of criminal suspects" (Hiebert 2002, 135).

Most of the procedural law is found in Sections 8 to 14 of the Charter of Rights and Freedoms. Those who drafted the Charter preferred not to use the terms "due process" and "procedural criminal law." Instead, they preferred—and this is the most common term in use today—the words "principles of fundamental justice." According to s. 7 of the Charter (see below), no individual can be deprived of life, liberty, and security of the person unless the principles of fundamental justice are followed. As a consequence, the Supreme Court rules on cases involving procedural issues that, though they are not found in ss. 8 to 14, even so involve issues of fundamental justice.

What are these principles, and where are they found? The Supreme Court has stated that they are "to be found in the basic tenets of our legal system and that it is up to the courts to develop the limits of these tenets" (Barnhorst and Barnhorst 2004, 10). In other words, the courts get to decide whether a case has followed the principles of fundamental justice or there has been a violation. Since the introduction of the Charter, the Supreme Court has been making rulings on what exactly is included as fundamental justice. The areas it has ruled on include disclosure (see below), the right to silence, the right to a fair trial, and the right not to make self-incriminating statements.

Since the Charter's introduction, the constitutionality of substantive criminal law and procedural criminal law has been ruled on in many criminal court cases. Discussed next is the development of Canada's **sexual assault** laws, during which both types of criminal law have been examined and, in some cases, redrafted after rulings by the Supreme Court of Canada.

Before 1983, offences of sexual aggression were dealt with in Sections 139 to 154 of Part VI of the Criminal Code. The offences in those sections dealt with "Offences Against the Person and Reputation." Four principal offences were recognized by the courts as relating to rape. Rape itself was one of them. The key provision of the Criminal Code dealing with rape was found in s. 143. It stated that before a person could be found guilty of rape, the following general conditions needed to be established:

1. The complainant had to be female.
2. The accused had to be male.
3. The complainant and accused were not married to each other.

4. Sexual intercourse occurred.
5. The act of intercourse occurred without the consent of the woman.

The other three principal offences in Part VI were attempted rape (s. 145), indecent assault against a female (s. 149), and indecent assault against a male (s. 156). The penalties for these four offences were life, ten years, five years, and ten years, respectively.

Many criticisms were raised against these laws over the decades. For example, some argued that they reflected "the gender dichotomy and cultural perceptions of gender relations that were functional to the male status maintenance" (Los 1994). In response, the federal government enacted new legislation (referred to as Bill C-127) on January 1, 1983. Bill C-127 brought a number of significant changes—for example, sexual assault was reclassified and placed in Part VIII of the Criminal Code ("Offences Against the Person and Reputation"), so as to emphasize that "sexual assault involves physical violence against another person." Other significant changes included the recognition that the victim could be male or female and that a spouse could be charged with sexual assault. The changes also established protections for women against cross-examination in criminal court trials regarding their past sexual history.

Also, the law covering sexual assault now included three degrees or levels of harm, in order to reflect the seriousness of the incident. Level 1 sexual assault (s. 271) refers to incidents in which the victim suffers the least physical injury; it carries a maximum punishment of ten years' imprisonment. Level 1 is the most common charge for sexual assault. Ninety-eight percent of all sexual assault charges in 2008 were Level 1.

Level 2 sexual assault (s. 272) involves the use of a weapon, threats to use a weapon, or bodily harm; it carries a maximum punishment of 14 years' imprisonment.

Level 3 sexual assault (s. 273) involves wounding, maiming, disfiguring, or endangering the life of the victim. An offender convicted of this offence can receive a maximum term of life imprisonment.

Level 1 sexual assault is a **hybrid offence**, which means that a Crown prosecutor has the power of discretion to proceed by way of indictment or summary conviction. That decision has a huge impact on the offender in terms of penalties. If the prosecutor proceeds by way of indictment, the maximum punishment is ten years' incarceration, but if the case proceeds by way of summary conviction, the maximum punishment is 18 months. Canada's sexual assault law has been the focus of much debate since its inception.

Probably the most controversial aspect of the new sexual assault law was in the provisions restricting the right of the accused to introduce evidence concerning the victim's past sexual conduct. Evidence of the victim's sexual reputation was now inadmissible (s. 277). The victim's sexual history with people other than the accused also became inadmissible unless it was required to counter the prosecution's evidence concerning past sexual conduct, to prove the identity of the perpetrator, or to establish that there had been sexual activity with others on the same occasion (s. 276). Under the pre-1983 legislation, it was an ordeal for the victim of a sexual assault to testify in court because her reputation and prior sexual history could be held against her. As a result, many sexual assaults were not reported to the police since the trial itself "could be almost as agonizing to a victim of sexual assault as the offence itself" (Bowland 1994, 245).

There have been many legal changes and challenges to the sexual assault legislation over its brief history (see Exhibit 2.1). In 1991, for example, the Supreme Court of Canada struck down s. 276 of the Criminal Code, ruling that it favoured the victim at the expense of the accused. In its decision involving the cases of *Seaboyer* and *Gayme*, for example, two men who had been accused of rape argued successfully that their right to a fair trial had been violated, since they were prevented from questioning the complainant about her prior sexual conduct. The following year, amendments were made through the introduction of Bill C-49, which outlined "the legal parameters for determining the admissibility of a victim's past sexual history as evidence in sexual assault trials" (Mohr and Roberts 1994, 10). In addition, "implied consent" was eliminated as a defence; actual consent would now be required.

Three years later, in 1994, the Supreme Court of Canada accepted the argument of "extreme drunkenness" as a defence to general-intent crimes, including the crime of sexual assault. In this case, *R. v. Daviault*, the Court overturned a Quebec Court of Appeal decision denying this defence. The Supreme Court's decision was based largely on the assumption that the defendant's intoxication was so extreme that the situation would rarely arise again. However, over the next few months, a number of men charged with sexual assault successfully defended themselves by using this defence. As a result, in 1995, the federal government passed amendments to the Criminal Code that eliminated this defence for offences requiring *general* intent, such as sexual assault and assault, but not *specific* intent, such as murder.

Later that same year, in a 5–4 decision, the Supreme Court ruled that a woman's records must be handed over to a judge if the defence can persuade the judge that the records may contain information useful to the defendant. This ruling occurred in *R. v. O'Connor*

and was based on the logic that barring such records from the proceedings would violate the defendant's right to a fair trial. After this decision, it became common practice for judges to order full disclosure of records.

As a result of *O'Connor*, in 1997, the federal government passed new legislation (Bill C-46) restricting the full disclosure of records. This bill established a two-stage process for judges to determine whether the victim's records would be disclosed to the defendant. In the first stage, the accused must convince the trial judge that the documents are likely relevant to his or her defence. In the second stage, the judge must consider whether it is "necessary in the interests of justice" to view them. In November 1999, the Supreme Court upheld Bill C-46 in *R. v. Mills*, stating that when judges decide to order the production of records concerning a complainant, they must consider "the rights and interests of all those affected by disclosure" and that the three relevant principles in this are (1) full answer and defence, (2) privacy, and (3) equality.

In 1997, in *R. v. Carosella*, the Supreme Court threw out a case involving sexual assault in which the victim's counselling records had been destroyed. This decision placed any third-party records on the same standard as police and Crown prosecutor documents. The federal government then passed amendments to Bill C-46, in an attempt to clarify when records concerning the victim should have restricted access. The amendments introduced a two-stage application process. In the first stage, trial judges have to decide whether the sought-after record is likely to be of sufficient relevance to the defence. The second stage involves balancing information contained in the document with the position forwarded by the defence on the basis of its importance to the defence, as well as with the threat its exposure might pose to the complainant's right to privacy, dignity, and security of the person.

In the fall of 2000, the Supreme Court unanimously upheld the 1992 law that restricted the freedom of defence lawyers to question sexual assault victims about their past sexual history. The Court ruled that forcing the victim to give such evidence invaded her right to privacy and would discourage the reporting of crimes of sexual violence (Anderssen 2000, A7). In this case *(R. v. Darrach)*, the defendant argued that he had been denied a fair trial because he had been unable to raise specific aspects of his prior sexual relationship with the complainant. Darrach argued that he had formed the "honest but mistaken belief" that the incident was consensual. His argument failed to influence the Court that the evidence was of significant probative value.

Critics of these rulings argued that they resulted in unfair trials for men accused of sexual assault in that they were "sometimes totally unable to raise relevant facts and arguments" ("Rape Shield . . ." 2000). Supporters of the law countered that lawmakers had created "a fair way to keep prejudicial myths about women out of the courtroom while preserving the right of the accused to a fair trial" (Chwialkowska 2000).

How have the courts reacted to these decisions by the Supreme Court? McDonald and Wobick (2004) examined 48 reported sexual assault cases between December 1, 1999, and June 30, 2003. They found that the most common reasons given by judges for ordering production of the complainant's records (as opposed to disclosure to the defence) were the potential prejudice to personal dignity and the right to privacy upon disclosure (both mentioned in 29 cases), and the defendant's right to a full answer and defence. The next two most common reasons given by judges were the reasonable expectation of privacy of the complainant (24 cases) and the probative value of the record (19 cases). The least common reasons included society's interest in reporting offences (9 cases), the influence of discriminatory beliefs or biases (8 cases), encouraging victims to seek treatment (5 cases), and the integrity of the trial process (4 cases). McDonald and Wobick (ibid., 13) found that judges in

these cases "frequently cited the defendant's right to full answer and defence and the complainant's right to privacy as competing concerns in their reasons with respect to record production; the concept of equality, however, was only mentioned in 4 cases." In the 40 cases in which there was a ruling on disclosure/production, no production was ordered in 15 cases, and partial or full disclosure to the defence in 14 cases. In the other 11 cases, after full or partial disclosure to the judge, the case ended. McDonald and Wobick (ibid., 14) concluded that since *R. v. Mills* (1999), judges have interpreted the law inconsistently when deciding whether to order production. They also found that judges varied both in their emphasis on the relevant factors found in the Criminal Code and in their emphasis on the reported decision of the Supreme Court. Overall, "privacy has been a key factor in decision-making whereas mention of equality has been quite sparse" (ibid.). Gotell (2002, 257) studied 37 trial and appellate sexual assault cases between 1999 and 2002 where there had been requests for records by the accused after the Supreme Court decision in *R. v. Mills* and concluded that complainants "remained vulnerable to disclosure post-Mills . . . ." In her most recent research study of

---

EXHIBIT 2.1   Sexual Assault Legislation in Canada

Since the enactment of sexual assault legislation in 1983, numerous changes have occurred:

1991   The Supreme Court of Canada rules that the law favours the victim at the expense of the accused (*Seaboyer v. R.* [1991] and *Gayme v. R.* [1991]). The Supreme Court strikes down s. 276 of the Criminal Code, which limits the questioning of victims in sexual assault trials by the defence.

1992   Bill C-49 is passed, allowing sexual history to be introduced in a case but only when strict guidelines are used. It also provides a legal definition of consent specific to the offence of sexual assault.

1993   The Supreme Court accepts the extreme drunkenness defence in sexual assault cases *(R. v. Daviault).*

1995   The Criminal Code is amended (Bill C-72) to disallow the extreme drunkenness defence for a number of violent offences, including sexual assault.
The Supreme Court rules that counselling records of the victim must be produced when requested by the court *(R. v. O'Connor).*

1996   An Alberta judge rules that the new law covering the disclosure of third-party

therapy or counselling records is unconstitutional, as it places too much of the burden of proof on the accused.

1997   The Supreme Court of Canada decides that when a sexual assault victim cannot produce her counselling records at the request of the court, the case must be thrown out of court *(R. v. Carosella).*
The Criminal Code is amended (Bill C-46) to introduce guidelines that instruct all parties on when the sexual assault victim's records are relevant during a trial.

1999   The Supreme Court of Canada upholds, in *R. v. Mills*, the constitutionality of the Bill C-46 provisions.
The Supreme Court of Canada, in *R. v. Ewanchuk*, rejects the defence of implied consent.

2000   The Supreme Court of Canada, in *R. v. Darrach*, upholds the provision of the sexual assault law that restricts defence lawyers in their questioning of sexual assault victims about their past sexual history.

Sources: Bowland 1994; Los 1994; Majury 1994; Roberts and Mohr 1994; Makin 1999.

---

16 sexual assault cases where there had also been requests from the defence for records about the complainants between 2002 and 2006, Gotell (2008, 153) concluded that it "was clear from a detailed reading of these recent decisions that records continue to be produced to judges and disclosed to the accused on the basis of bare assertions and discriminatory rationales."

SOURCES OF THE CRIMINAL LAW IN CANADA

Canadian criminal law is derived from British common law. Thus, the structure of our criminal law is modelled closely on the British experience. The **common law** is an important source of our criminal law and is an important component of the substantive law in Canada. It originated during the reign of Henry II (1154–1189) as a result of his desire to establish a strong central government. Part of his vision was a court system that would try cases on the basis of laws passed by the government and applicable to all citizens. To this end, he appointed judges to specific territories (or circuits) to hear cases in order to ensure that the "King's Law" was administered and enforced. Over time, judges exchanged information about their legal decisions, and this growing body of knowledge slowly began to replace laws based on local customs. In the traditional system, serious crimes such as murder, rape, and assault had been viewed as wrongs between private citizens. Judges now began to redefine these as wrongs against the state—that is, as criminal offences. A common law gradually developed, forming legal principles that were equally applicable to all citizens regardless of local customs or place of residence.

Another significant change emerged about this same time. A system gradually developed in which judges decided cases on the basis of previous judgments in similar cases. Crimes had general meanings attached to them, so that most people now knew what was meant by murder and other criminal offences. This shared knowledge resulted in a practice that continues today in our system of criminal law: deciding trials on the basis of precedents, even if such precedents are not necessarily binding. This practice evolved into a principle or rule known as *stare decisis* ("based on situations of similar facts"), which requires the judiciary to follow previous decisions in similar cases. Thus, by a process of making decisions in case after case, and guided by the rule of precedent, these early English judges created a body of law that applied to all the people of England. This law was *common* to all. Today, judges in Canada still follow precedent. This generally means that the lower courts must follow the decisions of higher courts and that courts of equal rank should try to follow one another's decisions.

The principle of *stare decisis* is still in use today. When a criminal court has to make a decision, the judge will research how other courts have reached their decisions in similar cases, and these earlier decisions will be used as guides. This principle lends itself to stability in the legal system, since it allows one to predict how a court will probably decide a case. This practice does not necessarily lead to a rigid system of criminal law, because a judge can still make rulings that deviate from existing precedent. This can happen when, for example, conditions in a society have changed so that a judge feels warranted in departing from existing precedents.

Written Sources of the Criminal Law

Originally, the common law was uncodified—in other words, it was not written down and preserved in a central location. This meant that judges had to discuss the rulings among themselves, a situation that often led to long waiting periods before a final judgment was given. This system proved to be extremely cumbersome and led to the creation of written sources of the criminal law.

Contemporary Canadian criminal law has four main sources: the Constitution, statute law, case law, and administrative law. Canadian criminal law is modelled closely on the British experience and makes use of British legal precedents and procedures. However, changes were gradually introduced when it became apparent that some legal issues facing Canadians were inapplicable to the British experience and British precedents and procedures. Clearly, some of the legal issues facing Canadians were unique and called for made-in-Canada alternatives.

The Constitution

The fundamental principles that guide the enactment of laws and the application of those laws by the courts are found in the Constitution Act. Thus, only the federal government can enact criminal laws and procedure. However, a criminal law may be found to be unconstitutional "if it infringes upon a right or a freedom protected under the Canadian Charter of Rights and Freedoms and if it cannot be justified under s. 1 of the Charter as a reasonable and demonstrably justified limit on a right" (Roach 2004, 6).

Statute Law

Another source of criminal law is **statutes**. Statutes are laws that prohibit or mandate certain acts. These laws are systematically codified and placed in a single volume, such as our Criminal Code. Most offences are updated over time in order that they can include more detailed definitions of a criminal act. In order to change the existing law, governments must either modify existing laws or introduce new ones by enacting statutes. Statute law is today considered the most important source of law in Canada. It is through the use of statutes that criminal law is created, changed, or eliminated.

The power to enact statute law in Canada is divided among the federal government (that is, Parliament), the provinces, and municipalities. However, only Parliament has the power to enact criminal law. Statute law always overrules case law, except in conflicts over the Canadian Charter of Rights and Freedoms. Under the Charter, citizens possess certain rights and freedoms "that cannot be infringed upon by the government"; in this way, the Charter "limits the legislative authority of the government" (Barnhorst and Barnhorst 2004, 8). In Canada, all statutes are consolidated about every ten years when Parliament replaces the existing statutes with revised versions.

Case Law

Case law involves the judicial application and interpretation of laws as they apply in a particular case. Every time a judge in Canada makes a decision in a court case, he or she has the discretion to interpret the relevant statutes. Statutes may need to be interpreted, because they are stated only in general terms while the court case may call for a specific meaning. For example, a judge may decide that all previous decisions are problematic because they are outdated or vague, given the facts of a case at hand. As a result, the law may be redefined to make it reflect specifics. Once a judge makes a decision that changes the traditional legal definitions, an appeal is usually made to the provincial court of appeal in that jurisdiction. The appeal court decision too will likely be appealed to the Supreme Court of Canada. If the Supreme Court refuses to hear the case, the ruling made by the provincial court of appeal stands. However, if the Supreme Court decides to hear the case, its decision becomes law.

Administrative Law

Another source of criminal law is **administrative regulations**. These regulations are considered to have the power of criminal law, since they can include criminal penalties. These laws are written by regulatory agencies that have been given the power by governments to develop and enforce rules in specific areas, such as the environment, competition policy, and protection from hazardous products. Violations of administrative laws are sometimes referred to as regulatory offences. The federal government, the provinces, and municipalities can enact them.

The Rule of Law

From the review of these various written forms of criminal law, it is easy to see their applicability to our criminal justice system. Yet questions abound regarding their use. For example, many people ask whether they can be used by powerful groups to gain personal advantages through the criminal law. It is a clear possibility, but according to the rule of law, in our system of justice there is a "sense of orderliness, of subjection to known legal rules and of executive accountability to legal authority" (*Resolution to Amend the Constitution* [1981]). In other words, society must be governed by clear legal rules rather than by arbitrary personal wishes and desires. Central to this is that no one individual or group has a privileged exemption from the law. Everyone is subject to the laws that have been introduced by the government. To protect society from the self-interest of individuals or groups, the rule of law ensures that laws are created, administered, and enforced on the basis of acceptable procedures that promote fairness and equality. The rule of law plays a central role in our society as it "forms part of the supreme law of our country, binding on all levels of government and enforceable by the courts" (Billingsley 2002, 29). Davison (2006, 11) points out that the rule of law means that "all members of society must follow and obey the law no matter what their area of activity or endeavour . . ." and that it "provides certainty and stability in our dealings with one another."

The basic elements of the rule of law include the following:

- *Scope of the law*. This means that there should be no privileged exemptions to the law. All people come under the rule of law. There are political and social aspects to this statement. Government under law is the political component. Both the government and public officials are subject to the existing law. The social aspect is equality before the law.
- *Character of the law*. This means that the law should be public, clear enough that most people can understand it, and relatively clear and determinate in its requirements.
- *Institution of the law*. In the anglo legal system, this means that there are certain rules that the institutions of the law must produce in order for the law to be fair and just. These include an independent judiciary, written laws, and the right to a fair hearing.

The Canadian Charter of Rights and Freedoms

One of the most important additions to the Canadian legal system was the Charter of Rights and Freedoms, enacted on April 17, 1982. The Charter differs from common law and statute law in that it applies mainly to the protection of the legal rights of criminal suspects and convicted persons, the powers of the various criminal justice agencies, and criminal procedure during a trial. It is a complex piece of legislation, and only parts of it deal with issues relevant to the criminal justice system. However, the sections concerned with the operation of the justice system have had a tremendous impact on criminal procedural issues in Canada, especially as they apply to the rights of the accused and the powers of criminal justice agencies involved in detecting and prosecuting criminals.

Since its introduction, the Charter has done much to establish and enforce certain fundamental principles relating to the operation of the criminal justice system—principles such as a fair trial, the protection of due process rights, and freedom from cruel and unusual punishment (see Exhibit 2.2). The Charter divides these legal principles into a number of sections. Section 7 is the most general; it guarantees that no individual will be denied his or her basic rights in Canadian society "except in accordance with the principles of fundamental justice" as specified by s. 1 of the Charter.

Sections 8, 9, and 10 of the Charter deal with the rights of individuals when they are detained and arrested by the police. Section 8 provides everyone with the right to be secure against unreasonable search or seizure. It involves the protection of citizens' property and privacy against unwarranted intrusions by state agents. This section has generated a significant amount of case law, since most criminal trial evidence is collected by the police and the propriety of how they obtained that evidence is often raised in court. This section concerns an individual's right to privacy; however, this right has to be balanced with the need for the police to be able to conduct searches and seize evidence as a part of their law enforcement activities. Section 8 is therefore referred to as a "relative" right, since an individual is protected only against unreasonable searches and seizures.

The Supreme Court set out the basic framework for police searches and seizures in one of its earliest decisions, *Hunter v. Southam, Inc.* (1984). The Court, while agreeing that individuals have a right to be secure from an unreasonable search and seizure, established that certain procedural elements must exist in order for the police to do their work. As a result, the police are now required to justify their need to search by producing sworn evidence that meets an objective standard. The Court also recognized that in some exigent circumstances (such as a "hot pursuit") the police need not have a warrant before they act. Other limitations surround a citizen's right to privacy—for example, if there is the threat or danger that evidence connected to a crime will be destroyed or removed, if a person has contacted the police because of an emergency, or if the police are involved in a reasonable search.

Section 8 is designed to protect all reasonable expectations of privacy, and it is not to be ignored even when an individual is caught committing a crime. In *R. v. Duarte* (1990), the police placed a body-pack recorder on an informer to record a conversation with a suspect. No warrant had been obtained; the police assumed that their action was legal because one of the individuals involved had given consent to being taped. The Supreme Court, however, ruled that the individual in question had the right to a reasonable expectation of privacy. Similar conclusions were reached in *R. v. Wong* (1990) and *R. v. Kokesch* (1990), where the police acted prior to obtaining a warrant. In the first case, the police made a surreptitious video surveillance tape; in the second, they conducted a search around a person's house to see whether the suspect was growing marijuana. Note that s. 8 applies to personal information (where an individual has a right to be protected from intrusive activities by the authorities) as opposed to commercial records (which are not subject to this protection).

Section 9 guarantees that everyone has the right to be free from arbitrary detention or imprisonment. This means that the police do not have complete discretion to detain citizens; rather, they have to follow an objective standard determined by the federal government. One area that was brought to the attention of the Supreme Court involved the provincial power of the police to conduct random "spot checks" in order to identify impaired drivers. In *R. v. Hufsky* (1988), the Court ruled that randomly stopping a driver was in fact an arbitrary detention under s. 9 of the Charter since it represented total discretion on the behalf of the police officer as to who would be stopped. However, the Court then stated that randomly stopping a driver thought to be impaired could be justified under s. 1 of the Charter due to the importance of highway safety and the need to protect other citizens from potential harm. However, the police should possess reasonable suspicion based on objective standards (*R. v. Duguay* [(1985]).

Before detaining and arresting someone, the police must have reasonable grounds or else their actions will be judged as arbitrary and in violation of s. 9. *R. v. Simpson* (1993) focused on the meaning of reasonable

LEGAL RIGHTS

1. The Canadian Charter of Rights and Freedoms guarantees the rights and freedoms set out in it subject only to such reasonable limits prescribed by law as can be demonstrably justified in a free and democratic society.

7. Everyone has the right to life, liberty and security of the person and the right not to be deprived thereof except in accordance with the principles of fundamental justice.

8. Everyone has the right to be secure against unreasonable search or seizure.

9. Everyone has the right not to be arbitrarily detained or imprisoned.

10. Everyone has the right on arrest or detention

    (a) to be informed promptly of the reasons therefore;

    (b) to retain and instruct counsel without delay and to be informed of that right; and

    (c) to have the validity of the detection determined by way of habeas corpus and to be released if the detention is not lawful.

11. Any person charged with an offence has the right

    (a) to be informed without unreasonable delay of the specific offence;

    (b) to be tried within a reasonable time;

    (c) not to be compelled to be a witness in proceedings against that person in respect of the offence;

    (d) to be presumed innocent until proven guilty according to law in a fair and public hearing by an independent and impartial tribunal;

    (e) not to be denied reasonable bail without just cause;

    (f) except in the case of an offence under military law tried before a military tribunal, to the benefit of trial by jury where the maximum punishment for the offence is imprisonment for five years or a more severe punishment;

    (g) not to be found guilty on account of any act or omission unless, at the time of the act or omission, it is constituted an offence under Canadian or international law or was criminal according to the general principles of law recognized by the community of nations;

    (h) if finally acquitted of the offence, not to be tried for it again and, if finally found guilty and punished for the offence, not to be tried or punished for it again; and

    (i) if found guilty of the offence and if the punishment for the offence has been varied between the time of the commission and the time of sentencing, to the benefit of the lesser punishment.

12. Everyone has the right not to be subjected to any cruel and unusual treatment or punishment.

13. A witness who testifies in any proceedings has the right not to have any incriminating evidence so given used to incriminate that witness in any other proceedings, except in a prosecution for perjury or for the giving of contradictory evidence.

14. A party or witness in any proceedings who does not understand or speak the language in which the proceedings are conducted or who is deaf has the right to the assistance of an interpreter.

EQUALITY RIGHTS

15. (1) Every individual is equal before and under the law and has the right to the equal protection and equal benefit of the law without discrimination and, in particular, without discrimination based on race, national or ethnic origin, colour, religion, sex, age or mental or physical disability.
(2) Subsection (1) does not preclude any law, program or activity that has as its object the amelioration of conditions of disadvantaged individuals or groups including those that are disadvantaged because of race, national or ethnic origin, colour, religion, sex, age or mental or physical disability.

ENFORCEMENT

24. (1) Anyone whose rights or freedoms, as guaranteed by this Charter, have been infringed or denied may apply to a court of competent jurisdiction to obtain such remedy as the court considers appropriate and just in the circumstances.
(2) Where, in proceedings under subsection (1), a court concludes that evidence was obtained in a manner that infringed or denied any rights or freedoms guaranteed by this Charter, the evidence shall be excluded if it is established that, having regard to all the circumstances, the admission of it in the proceedings would bring the administration of justice into disrepute.

grounds for an arrest. In this case, a police officer observed a man leaving a house reputed to be inhabited by persons selling drugs. While the man was driving away, the police officer pulled him over and asked to see his driver's licence and registration. The man informed the officer he was driving without a valid driver's licence. He was arrested and subsequently charged with driving while under suspension. The officer then continued her search under the assumption that he had bought drugs at the residence. She discovered several grams of crack cocaine, which led to additional charges. When the case reached court, all charges were dropped; it was ruled that the police officer had conducted an improper investigation that violated the suspect's s. 9 Charter rights. Educated "guesses" do not constitute reasonable grounds to arrest someone.

Section 10 deals with certain specific rights given to individuals when they are detained by the police. These rights are found in the three subareas of this section. Section 10(a) stipulates that everyone who is arrested has the right to be informed as soon as possible of the reasons for that arrest. Arrest and detention constitutes a significant intrusion into a private citizen's life, and it is a basic right for that person to know why he or she has been arrested and detained (*R. v. Borden* [1994]). Section 10(b) states that "everyone has the right on arrest or detention to retain and instruct counsel without delay and to be informed of that right." This section has been one of the most controversial in the Charter. Its purpose is to control police conduct after initial charges have been laid against the suspect. In *R. v. Therens* (1985), the Supreme Court ruled that evidence obtained by the police without first informing the suspect of his or her right to a lawyer cannot be used. This interpretation was expanded in *R. v. Manninen* (1987), in which the right to legal counsel was extended to all persons detained by the police. Law enforcement officers were later instructed that before conducting questioning, they had to inform all persons in their **custody** as to how they could exercise this right. In *R. v. Brydges* (1990), the Court extended the police duty to advise individuals of their right to legal counsel by giving the accused a reasonable length of time to retrain and instruct counsel. The police now have to refrain from questioning any suspect until the accused has been given a reasonable opportunity to exercise this right.

However, certain limits have been placed on the rights of the accused to obtain legal counsel. In *R. v. Tremblay* (1987) and *R. v. Ross* (1989), the Supreme Court ruled that the rights set out in this section of the Charter are not absolute and that a suspect's right to retain and instruct counsel must be exercised diligently by the suspect. This means that a suspect cannot refuse

An accused person is led into court in order to give a judge his initial plea. (© Gaetano/Corbis)

the opportunity to contact legal counsel, be questioned by the police, and then complain about having said things he or she should not have said because no lawyer was present. Furthermore, in *R. v. Thomsen* (1988), the Court ruled that owing to the need to protect the public, a motorist who has been asked to provide a breath sample is not entitled to request and then wait for legal counsel to appear before doing so.

Section 10(c) is concerned with **habeas corpus,** a common-law remedy against unlawful detention. *Habeas corpus* entitles an individual who is detained to request an assessment as to whether he or she is being unlawfully detained. The rights provided by this rule of common law are guaranteed by other Charter provisions, such as the right to be secure from arbitrary arrest and detention and the right not to be denied reasonable bail.

The Charter also addresses the activities of the courts. While s. 7 of the Charter provides the basic guarantee that everyone has the right to life, liberty, and security, s. 11 outlines the rights of individuals charged with a criminal offence as they proceed through the criminal courts. This section has nine components and deals with issues concerned with the presumption of innocence, court delays, and the right not to be denied reasonable bail. Section 11(a) states that the police must tell the accused the precise nature of the charges he or she is facing without unreasonable delay. This enables the accused to challenge the proceedings if they are unlawful or to prepare a defence if the case is proceeding to court. This section also has the effect of defining and narrowing the proceedings, "thereby limiting the scope of the prosecution and the powers of the police" (Sharpe and Roach 2005, 258).

Section 11(b) includes the right of the defendant to be tried within a reasonable time (*R. v. Askov* [1990]). However, the Supreme Court has drawn a distinction between pre-charge and post-charge delays. For example, over the past few years a number of charges have been laid against individuals years after the alleged incident. The Court has ruled that a delay in charging an individual will rarely lead to a successful challenge about an unreasonable delay (*R. v. Mills* [1986]), although unexplained or unjustified delays may lead to a successful challenge (*R. v. Kalanj* [1989]).

Section 11(c) protects the accused from having to testify during trial. Section 11(d) deals with the "presumption of innocence." Thus, an individual is innocent until proven guilty by an independent and impartial tribunal in a fair and public hearing. Concerns about the presumption of innocence led the Supreme Court of Canada, in *R. v. Oakes* (1986), to strike down a section of the Narcotic Control Act that presumed the guilt of the accused, in that it demanded that the accused prove to the court that he did not possess a narcotic for the purposes of trafficking. The other parts of Section 11 give the accused the right to reasonable bail (s. 11[e]) and the right to a jury trial for any offence for which the maximum punishment is five years or more (s. 11[f]). An individual's act or omission can be construed as an offence only if it was illegal at the time of the offence (s. 11[g]). Individuals are protected from double jeopardy (s. 11[h]). The accused, if convicted, can be punished only on the basis of the penalties that were available at the time of the offence (s. 11[i]).

Section 12 protects individuals from any form of cruel and unusual punishment. The criterion here is whether the punishment handed out is excessive—that is, violates our standards of decency. In *Smith v. R.* (1987), the Supreme Court ruled that laws mandating a minimum of seven years' punishment for importing narcotics were in violation of this section of the Charter. Its reasoning was based on the fact that this section of the relevant act included too many prohibited activities and did not distinguish between small amounts of drugs to be used for personal consumption and large amounts for trafficking. While the Court did not provide a precise definition of "cruel and unusual punishment," it regarded the minimum sentence as disproportionate to the seriousness of the offence.

Other minimum sentences have been upheld by the Court, such as the mandatory minimum punishment of seven days' suspension for driving while under suspension (*R. v. Goltz* [1991]). Indefinite sentences for those classified by the system as dangerous offenders have also been upheld by the Court (*R. v. Luxton* [1990]).

As a result of the above cases and others, guidelines have been established to prevent punishments from becoming grossly disproportionate. These guidelines indicate whether a punishment is required to achieve a valid penal purpose, whether a sentence is based on proper guidelines, and whether appropriate alternatives are available. An indeterminate sentence given to a person considered a dangerous offender is not a violation of this section, and neither is a long period of incarceration before parole after the offender is convicted of murder, since incarceration does not violate our standard of what we consider decent.

Section 13 protects witnesses from self-incrimination and from having charges laid against them as the result of their statements. The right given to witnesses in this section is restricted to not having the evidence they give in one trial used against them in a later trial in order to prove their guilt (*R. v. Mannion* [1986]) (Sharpe and Roach 2005). However, in *R. v. Kuldip* (1990), the Supreme Court decided that evidence given at a previous trial could be used to later cross-examine a witness in order to assess his or her credibility as an accused. Section 14 guarantees the accused and any witnesses the right to an interpreter; also, that interpreter must translate the key testimony in full instead of simply summarizing the accused's statements (*R. v. Tran* [1994]).

Sections 15(1) and 15(2) concern equality rights. They specify the need for the equal protection of all individuals within our system of justice as well as for equality before and under the law. Section 28 guarantees that equality rights extend to both women and men.

Section 24 deals with remedies in the criminal process in the event of any violation of the above rights. Section 24(1) allows for a stay of proceedings so that a prosecutor cannot proceed with the case. This remedy is not common, as it is considered to be an extreme measure. In addition, the Supreme Court has stated that it can only be applied in "the clearest of cases" (*R. v. O'Connor* [1995]).

The most common remedy for a violation of a Charter right in the criminal process is found in Section 24(2). This section outlines a test to determine whether the rights of the accused have been infringed on and the justice system brought into disrepute because of illegal evidence. The purpose of this section is not to control the conduct of the police but rather to uphold the integrity of the judicial system (*R. v. Collins* [1987]). In general, this section protects the accused by preventing evidence illegally collected by the police from being used during the trial. However, there are no hard rules for the police to follow. The Canadian system stands markedly in contrast to the approach developed in the United States, where a strict law known as the "exclusionary rule" makes it illegal to use evidence collected in an improper manner. The courts in Canada decide on a case-by-case basis whether or not evidence can be entered into court. A number of questions have to be asked before evidence is excluded or admitted. The first is whether the evidence in question was obtained in a manner that infringed on or denied any rights or freedoms guaranteed by the Charter. However, evidence that violates the Charter could have been discovered later. So the courts must consider a second issue: Would the admission of the evidence "bring the administration of justice into disrepute"?

The closest the Supreme Court has come to establishing a test for determining the admissibility of evidence is found in *R. v. Collins* (1987). The Court adopted the "reasonable-person test," which asks the question, "Would the admission of the evidence bring the administration of justice into disrepute in the eyes of a reasonable man, dispassionate and fully apprised of the circumstances of the case?" (Stuart 1994, 82). The Supreme Court summarized the specifics of this test the following year in *R. v. Jacoy* (1988):

> First, the Court must consider whether the admission of evidence will affect the fairness of the trial. If this inquiry is answered affirmatively, "the admission of evidence would tend to bring the administration of justice into disrepute and, subject to a consideration of other factors, the evidence generally should be excluded" . . . One of the factors relevant to this determination is the nature of the evidence; if the evidence is real evidence that existed irrespective of the Charter violation, its admission will rarely render the trial unfair.

Section 7: The Principles of Fundamental Justice

In addition to the rights guaranteed by the Charter reviewed above, s. 7 of the Charter has been applied by the Supreme Court of Canada to introduce and subsequently require certain procedural rights. These rights are not specifically guaranteed by ss. 8 to 14 of the Charter. However, the Court has determined that the principles of fundamental justice are broader than the rights provided by the Charter. The rulings made in this context have had a significant impact on the processing of defendants through the criminal justice system. Four areas have been affected: the right to silence, disclosure, the right to make full answer and defence, and the detention of those persons found not guilty by reason of insanity.

The Right to Silence

In *R. v. Hebert* (1990), an undercover police officer posing as a fellow prisoner engaged the accused in a discussion about his activities. The officer was placed in the same cell in order to initiate conversations about the alleged offence and obtain incriminating evidence after the suspect (on instructions from his legal counsel) had refused to make a statement to the police. The Supreme Court ruled that in this case the Charter protections of s. 10(b) (the right to legal counsel) and s. 11(c) (the right against self-incrimination) did not apply. The Court, however, continued on, saying that the principles of fundamental justice implicitly include a broader right to silence and that the police cannot use their "superior powers" in attempt to overstep the accused's decision to invoke his legal rights. The use of an undercover agent was ruled as "trickery," designed to deprive the accused of his choice to remain silent. The accused has a right not to be deprived of life, liberty, and security of the person except in accordance with the principles of fundamental justice, and in this case these rights were violated by the police. In this case, however, the Supreme Court was divided over the exact parameters of the right to silence.

The Supreme Court once again dealt with the issue of right to silence in *R. v. Singh* (2007). In this case, Mr. Singh was arrested three days after a murder during April 2002, in Surrey, B.C. No forensic evidence or weapon linked Mr. Singh to the murder, but a doorman identified him as the shooter in a photo line-up (Burnett 2007). He was later interviewed by the police while in custody. At the time of his arrest, Mr. Singh was given a Charter warning by the police and was permitted to talk to a lawyer. In one of his two interviews with the police, Mr. Singh repeatedly requested to the police that he no longer wanted to be interviewed and be returned to his cell. In total, Mr. Singh asserted his right to silence 18 times during the lengthy police interrogation. At each request, the police officer ignored Mr. Singh's wishes and continued with the interrogation. Mr. Singh was persuaded by the police officer to admit his presence at the location where the victim had been murdered, but he pointed out to the police that he had already left the vicinity when the victim was murdered. He was later charged and convicted of second degree murder. The British Columbia Court of Appeal upheld the trial court judge's decision, pointing out that this case had to be distinguished from *Herbert* as that case involved police trickery but Mr. Singh had been aware of the police officer's intentions. Mr. Singh appealed to the Supreme Court of Canada, challenging the admissibility of his statements made during the interrogation as they were made involuntarily and violated his Charter right to remain silent. The Supreme Court of Canada, in a 5–4 decision, ruled against Mr. Singh. According to the majority, if the police cannot use "legitimate means of persuasion" to get a suspect to talk, "then the police will lose a valuable method of fighting crime . . . One can

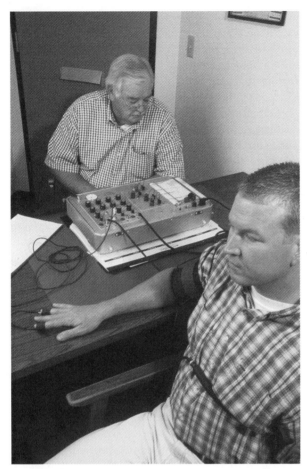

A polygraph (or lie detector) is a device which measures and records several physiological variables such as blood pressure during questioning. Are the results of polygraph tests admissible at trial in Canada?
(Robert E. Daemmrich/Getty Images)

readily appreciate that the police could hardly investigate crime without putting questions to persons from whom it is thought that useful information may be obtained" (Makin 2007, A6).

In a subsequent case, the police hired an inmate (who was then placed in the same cell) to talk to the alleged offender in order to elicit incriminating evidence (*R. v. Broyles* [1991]). The Supreme Court applied the same principle as in *Hebert*, ruling that this action violated the principles of fundamental justice.

In *R. v. Turcotte* (2005), the defendant was convicted of murder. During questioning by the police, he had refused to answer some questions. At trial, the judge suggested to the jury that it could draw an inference of guilt from Turcotte's refusal to answer, and he was convicted. On appeal, the Supreme Court ruled that Turcotte should be given a new trial. In their judgment, the Court stated that "the right to silence would be illusory if the decision not to speak to the police could be used by the Crown as evidence of guilt . . . The right to silence . . . exists at all times against the state."

The Right of Disclosure

In a number of cases, the Crown failed to give all the relevant evidence in its possession to the defence. The Supreme Court responded by ruling, in *R. v. Stinchcombe* (1991), that s. 7 imposed a duty on the prosecution to disclose all the evidence it would be using in the trial as well as any other evidence the defence might find useful. This ruling has had a tremendous impact on the activities of both prosecutors and police (see Exhibit 2.3 for a further discussion of disclosure).

The Right to Make Full Answer and Defence

One of the most significant common-law rights provided to a defendant is the right to question the complainant during a criminal trial. This became an issue in the sexual assault trials *R. v. Seaboyer* (1991) and *R. v. Gayme* (1991), mentioned earlier in this chapter. In these cases, the Criminal Code provision denying the accused's right to question the victim during the trial about her prior sexual conduct was found to be in violation of the principles of fundamental justice. The Supreme Court determined that a complete ban was excessive as it could prevent the accused from providing a legitimate defence. It ruled that this Criminal Code provision violated the principles of fundamental justice; however, it ultimately accepted strict guidelines detailing the specific circumstances in which such questions would be allowed.

The Detention of Those Found Not Guilty by Reason of Insanity

The principles of fundamental justice apply at the post-trial *and* pre-charge stages of the criminal justice system. Until recently, the law governing the detention of those found not guilty by reason of insanity stated that if an individual was found to be unfit to stand trial, he or she would be confined without a hearing and held indefinitely at "the pleasure of the Lieutenant-Governor." This meant that the accused could be held without the benefit of a trial to determine actual guilt or innocence (McKay-Panos 1998–99). This confinement amounted in most cases to an indefinite period of detention, since there was no provision for a hearing or for any procedural protections.

In *R. v. Swain* (1991), the Supreme Court ruled that this situation violated s. 7 of the Charter and instructed the provinces to change their legislation to alleviate it. The following year, the federal government mandated the creation of provincial review boards to take over the decision-making authority. One activity of these boards is to hold hearings no less often than every 12 months to review those individuals who are subject to their authority.

THE NATURE OF CRIME

Canada practises a federal system of criminal law, which means that all criminal law is passed by the federal government. Only Parliament has the authority to enact criminal laws. Different approaches—the general and the legal—are used to explain what a crime is in our society.

The general level has it that a crime can be defined as any action

1. that is harmful;
2. that is prohibited by the criminal law; and
3. that can be prosecuted by the state
4. in a formal court environment
5. for which a punishment can be imposed. (Senna and Siegel 1995)

The legal definition of crime encompasses mental and physical elements as well as "attendant circumstances"—that is, a causal link between the act and the harm that resulted. It also specifies that certain aspects of the criminal act in question must be proven in a court of law. Our criminal law is based on seven principles traditionally determined and followed by legislators and the courts. Our system of criminal law is based on the existence of these essential features in every criminal act. These principles are summarized by the term *corpus delecti,* which means literally "the body of the crime." In order to convict someone, the state must usually prove each of the following seven elements:

1. legality
2. *mens rea*
3. *actus reus*
4. concurrence of *mens rea* and *actus reus*
5. harm
6. causation
7. punishment

As Hall (1947, 17) noted, "[the] harm forbidden in penal law must be imputed to any normal adult who voluntarily commits it with criminal intent, and such a person must be subjected to the legally prescribed punishment."

Legality

Legally, a crime is defined as "an intentional act or omission in violation of the criminal law, committed without defense or justification and sanctioned by the state"

Robert Sharpe leaves court after being found guilty of possessing pornographic photographs and innocent of two pornography charges related to his writings. (CP PHOTO/Richard Lam)

(Tappan 1966, 10). This means that an act, to be considered criminal, must be "forbidden in a penal law" (Brannigan 1984, 25). The idea is that there can be no crime unless a law forbids the act in question. This is embodied in the phrase *nullum crimen sine lege,* or "no crime without a law."

Mens Rea

An assumption found in the Criminal Code is that the act of becoming involved in a criminal act results from a guilty mind. This is referred to as *mens rea,* or the mental element of a crime. *Mens rea* is commonly translated as "guilty mind," although it is often referred to as intent. It rests on the idea that a person has the capacity to control his or her behaviour and has the ability to choose among different courses of action. Many people may fantasize about committing "the perfect crime," but no crime is committed until some action is taken to realize this fantasy. In addition, a person is not culpable (i.e., blameworthy) unless he or she intends to commit an act prohibited by law or to avoid doing something that the law requires him or her to do. Police officers and judges

CHAPTER 2 Criminal Law and Criminal Justice in Canada

are often asked for forgiveness by an accused on the grounds that the accused, in committing a harmful act, "didn't mean to do it."

Intent is commonly confused with *motive*, although the two concepts are distinct. Intent refers to an individual's mental resolve to commit a criminal offence; motive refers to the reason for committing the actual illegal act. While motive is distinct from *mens rea*, Barnhorst and Barnhorst (2004, 42–43) contend that it is relevant to the criminal justice system in two ways. First, motive provides evidence of intent by establishing a reason why a person committed a crime (e.g., out of greed or jealousy). Second, motive may assist a judge in sentencing the accused in the same way—by providing a reason why the person committed the crime. According to Barnhorst and Barnhorst (ibid., 43), the accused may receive a lighter sentence if there was a good reason for committing the crime (e.g., mercy killing, as opposed to killing someone out of greed for an inheritance).

The intent to commit a crime may take either of two forms, each of which requires a different amount of proof. Some offences require only general intent, which means that *mens rea* is inferred from the action or inaction of the accused. In these crimes (e.g., homicide), there is no need for the prosecution to prove, through an

independent investigation, the state of the defendant's mind at the time of the offence. It is necessary only for the prosecution "to prove that the accused committed the prohibited act intentionally and with the necessary knowledge of the material circumstances" (Verdun-Jones 1989, 120). For example, the intent to commit a homicide is inferred from the fact that the accused pointed a weapon at the victim and discharged it. The offence of homicide is found in s. 222 of the Criminal Code:

> 222. (1) A person commits homicide when, directly or indirectly, by any means, he causes the death of a human being.
> (5) A person commits culpable homicide when he causes the death of a human being
> (a) by means of an unlawful act[.]

Therefore, the elements of culpable homicide are (1) the unlawful death (2) of a human being (3) by another human being.

Specific intent requires that the prosecution prove beyond a reasonable doubt the intent specified in the statute's definition of the elements of a crime. These offences are identified by phrases such as "with intent" or "for the purpose of" (Barnhorst and Barnhorst 2004). In these cases, the prosecution must prove "not only an

---

EXHIBIT 2.3 The Issue of Disclosure: *Stinchcombe* and *McNeil*

Disclosure is one of the most important features of our criminal justice system. The Law Reform Commission of Canada contends that disclosure of relevant information among all the parties involved in a court case is an important factor in the fairness and efficiency of the Canadian justice system. According to that commission, fairness in our criminal justice system depends largely "upon the quality of information available to litigating parties . . . Our rules of criminal procedure, however, do not provide for such disclosure, although the preliminary inquiry is commonly used by defense counsel as an opportunity to discover the strength and the scope of the Crown's case" (Law Reform Commission of Canada 1974, 1).

However, clear guidelines as to exactly how disclosure should operate were never developed. The lack of any principles governing disclosure was one of the most important legal issues that emerged from the investigation into the wrongful conviction of Donald Marshall in Nova Scotia. One of the problems with the original court case was the lack of disclosure among all the parties involved during both the pretrial actions and the subsequent trial (Brucker 1992). The investigation that followed Marshall's release found that both

the police and the prosecution had withheld information from the defence. That withholding, together with the failure of the defence counsel to seek disclosure from the Crown, was a major contributing factor in the wrongful conviction. According to the final report on Marshall's wrongful conviction, if "the police are not candid in their dealing with Crown prosecutors, the whole policy on disclosure may go for naught. It is trite to say that a dishonest cop who wishes to subvert the system may do so, and rules are not likely to completely contain such abuse" (House of Commons Debates 1986). As a result, recommendations were made in the hope that guidelines on disclosure would emerge and that the authorities would comply with them in order to achieve the "sound administration of criminal justice." One of the problems with this case was the lack of clear directives concerning the role of disclosure during the prosecution.

The guidelines for disclosure emerged from the decision reached by the Supreme Court of Canada in *R. v. Stinchcombe* (1991). This case involved an Alberta lawyer who was convicted in the Alberta Provincial Court of misappropriating funds from a client. Stinchcombe argued the client

---

had actually made him a business partner; thus he had done nothing wrong. He appealed his conviction to the Alberta Court of Appeal, but the appeal was dismissed. The Supreme Court of Canada decided to hear the case, however, perhaps because it saw the opportunity to develop clear directives concerning disclosure in criminal trials.

The key issue concerned certain information given to the police after the preliminary inquiry but before the actual trial. This information concerned a taped statement given to the RCMP by Stinchcombe's secretary. The tape supported the claim that Stinchcombe was innocent. The Crown prosecutor informed the defence of this taped statement but declined to indicate the exact nature of its contents. In addition, the secretary refused all offers to be interviewed by the defence. During the trial, defence counsel discovered that the secretary was not going to be called as a witness by the Crown. As a result, the defence requested that the judge make the Crown disclose the contents of the taped statement. The judge refused, since there was no obligation on the part of the Crown either to put the witness on the stand or to disclose her statements.

The Supreme Court of Canada overturned the decision made by the lower court. In a unanimous 7–0 vote favouring Stinchcombe, it ruled that Crown prosecutors must disclose to the defence any information in serious criminal matters that is capable of affecting the accused's ability to prepare a defence— and to do so early enough to allow the accused time to prepare that defence. However, this rule is not absolute and is subject to judicial interpretation. For example, the police are not required to give the name of any informant who supplies them with information relevant to a case. The Supreme Court decision is based on the fundamental right of the accused to give full answer and defence to the charges. However, the Court also ruled that "the defense has no obligation to assist the prosecution and is entitled to assume a purely adversarial role."

In January 2009, the Supreme Court unanimously ruled in *R. v. McNeil* that police have to hand over records of the discipline and misconduct of its officers as part of its disclosure obligation to the defence in criminal proceedings. In *McNeil*, the accused was charged with the possession of crack cocaine for the purpose of trafficking. The main witness at the trial was the arresting officer. While McNeil was awaiting sentencing after being convicted at trial, it was learned that the arresting officer in the case was standing trial for a number of criminal offences, and had no less than 71 pending Police Act offences concerning the ongoing

use, sale, and transportation of narcotics. This led to questions about the officer's credibility at McNeil's trial. The implication of this case is that if judges are satisfied that a record has relevance to the current case, the record will be produced to the defence.

Stinchcombe created guidelines about disclosure for both the police and prosecutors. But what about guidelines for the defence counsel? This issue came before the courts in the trial of Ken Murray (*R. v. Murray* [2000]). Murray was the first lawyer hired to defend Paul Bernardo, whose crimes (along with those of his wife, Karla Homolka) had made national headlines. Following a 71-day search of his residence by the police, Bernardo instructed Murray to take from the house some videotapes he had hidden. About a month later, Murray viewed the six horrific tapes and, despite their damaging content, decided they could be used to direct some of the attention from the crimes away from his client (Homolka had already struck a plea bargain with the Crown). For the next 17 months, Murray kept the videotapes in his possession, without informing the authorities about them or their contents. About a month before the trial, Bernardo suggested to his lawyer that the tapes shouldn't be used in his defence. Faced with an ethical dilemma, Murray withdrew from the case. The lawyer who took over handed them to the police through an intermediary (Blatchford 2000).

Murray was charged under s. 139(2) of the Criminal Code with attempting to willfully obstruct the course of justice in that he had failed to disclose the tapes to the police. Murray's defence rested in part on the grounds that the law society's Professional Conduct Handbook states only that a lawyer must not suppress "what ought to be disclosed." In June 2000, Murray was acquitted of the charges in the Ontario Superior Court, with the trial judge ruling that there was reasonable doubt concerning Murray's actions "after considering the accused's evidence in the context of the evidence as a whole" (ibid., 33). As a result of this trial, the Law Society of Upper Canada established a panel to deal with the ethical questions faced by lawyers when they uncover incriminating evidence (Abbate 2000). But some legal commentators felt that the practical lesson to be gleaned from this case "may simply be not to touch anything that smells of evidence" ("Smoking Guns" 2000, 409).

Sources: Law Reform Commission of Canada 1974; Tochor and Kilback 1999; Abbate 2000; Blatchford 2000; "Smoking Guns" 2000. The quoted extract is from "Discovery in Criminal Cases," Law Reform Commission of Canada, 1974, Justice Canada.

intention to commit an *actus reus* of the crime in question but also the 'intention' to produce some further consequence beyond the *actus reus*" (Verdun-Jones 1989, 121). For the offence of breaking and entering, the element of intent to commit an indictable offence typically must be established separately from the act of breaking and entering. According to s. 348(1)(a) of the Criminal Code, the prosecution must prove that an individual not only intended to commit the offence of break and enter but did so "with the specific intent to commit an indictable offence such as theft," although "it is not necessary to show that the person actually committed an indictable offence" (Barnhorst and Barnhorst 2004, 41). Section 348(1) of the Criminal Code states:

> 348. (1) Every one who
> (a) breaks and enters a place with intent to commit an indictable offence therein
> (b) breaks and enters a place and commits an indictable offence therein . . . is guilty of an indictable offence[.]

In the case of breaking and entering, therefore, the elements of the crime are (1) the breaking (2) and entry (3) of a dwelling house (4) of another (5) with the intent to commit an indictable offence therein.

In addition to the concepts of general and specific intent, there are three distinct levels or degrees of *mens rea*, ranging from the most to the least culpable states of mind: intent, knowledge, and recklessness. The highest level of culpability is purposefully or intentionally causing harm, and such offences are identified with the word "intent." These offences are indicated in the Criminal Code by words such as "intentional" and "willful" and refer to those actions that purposefully or intentionally cause harm. For example, a person commits theft when he or she takes or converts anything with the intent of depriving the owner or person who has a special interest in it. According to s. 332(1) of the Criminal Code:

> 322. (1) Every one commits theft who fraudulently . . . converts to his use or to the use of another person, anything whether animate or inanimate, with intent[.]

"Knowledge" is used to indicate that the accused possessed an awareness of a particular circumstance. For example, if someone utters a threat to another individual, the question is whether the accused knowingly stated the threat. According to s. 264.1 of the Criminal Code:

> 264.1 (1) Every one commits an offence who, in any manner, knowingly utters, conveys or causes any person to receive a threat
> (a) to cause death or serious bodily harm to any person
> (b) to burn, destroy or damage real or personal property, or

> (c) to kill, poison or injure an animal or bird that is the property of any person[.]

"Recklessness" refers to a situation in which an individual violates a law simply by lacking the appropriate care about and attention to something he or she is doing. For example, a man who decides to practise shooting a weapon in a crowded schoolyard during a break, and who kills a child, may argue that he did not have the intention to harm anyone. Yet he would probably be charged with the criminal offence of manslaughter because he was acting with reckless disregard for the safety of those nearby. Recklessness is a requirement for the offence of criminal negligence; according to s. 219(1) of the Criminal Code:

> 219. (1) Every one is criminally negligent who
> (a) in doing anything, or
> (b) in omitting to do anything that it is his duty to do, shows wanton or reckless disregard for the lives or safety of other persons.

Some defences in court can be made on the basis that the *mens rea* element does not apply. The issue here is the notion of criminal responsibility, and Canadian law allows certain individuals to be unable to form the mental state necessary to commit a crime. This means that a person might be excused for committing an action that would normally be classed as criminal. For example, children under 12 cannot be charged with a criminal offence in Canada. *Mens rea* is also lacking when people commit a crime in self-defence or while under duress.

Actus Reus

Another criterion that has to be met before a criminal charge can be laid against a suspect is known as **actus reus**. This is the physical or action element of a crime, and it is generally referred to as the "guilty act" or "evil act." In the Criminal Code, *actus reus* usually refers to the physical act performed by the accused—a punch, shove, or similar type of action directed against another individual. The actor, and the actor alone, is responsible for his or her actions. In other words, a person cannot blame someone else for the criminal act he or she has carried out. However, efforts are being made to modify this idea. Some legislators and crime control officials are now arguing that parents who are in control of their children should be subject to criminal prosecution for the illegal acts committed by the children over whom they have control.

Actus reus usually involves the commission of an illegal act; however, it refers also to the failure to do something—in other words, an omission of an act when the Criminal Code specifies that there is a duty to act.

Sections 219 and 220 of the Criminal Code, for example, refer to the offences of criminal negligence and criminal negligence causing death:

219. (1) Every one is criminally negligent who
(a) in doing anything, or
(b) in omitting to anything that it is his duty to do, shows wanton or reckless disregard for the lives or safety of other persons.
(2) For the purposes of this section, "duty" means a duty imposed by law.
220. Every one who by criminal negligence causes the death of another person is guilty of an indictable offence and is liable to imprisonment for life.

For some criminal offences a person doesn't have to become physically involved in an action. The Criminal Code specifies that in certain circumstances the mere act of talking (or speech) can be interpreted as a physical act. In fact, a crime can be committed by speech (as opposed to thought) in our legal system. Section 465 of the Criminal Code specifies that it is illegal for two or more persons to agree to commit a crime. If both individuals are in agreement about the plan, the act of criminal conspiracy has transpired. In addition, s. 131 of the Criminal Code specifies that an individual is guilty of a criminal offence when he or she commits perjury, and s. 225 states that any individual who causes the death of another individual through threats, fear of violence, or deception is guilty of a crime.

Concurrence between *Mens Rea* and *Actus Reus*

While not an "official" element of a crime, **concurrence** requires that "intent both precede and be related to the specific prohibited action or inaction that was or was not taken" (Brown et al. 1991, 68). Concurrence is usually not considered a controversial issue, since in most instances the connection between act and intent is obvious.

Harm

An important element in our legal system is that conduct is criminal only if it is harmful. This idea is "reflected in the notion of due process, which holds that a criminal statute is unconstitutional if it bears no reasonable relationship to the matter of injury to the public" (Territo et al. 1995, 33–34). This means there has to be a victim for the action to be harmful. Others argue that if the offence is a "victimless" crime—for example, gambling, abortion, prostitution—it is "not the law's business" (Geis 1974). The basis for this view is

that **victimless crimes** violate morality, not the law, and that making them illegal doesn't contribute to the good of society.

Criminal harm may result in physical injury, but such harm is by no means restricted to physical injury. For example, physical injury is not inflicted when perjury is committed, yet perjury is still considered harmful. This is because the criminal law has to deal with intangibles, such as harm to public institutions and the harm that results from fear for one's own well-being. An example is Canada's anti-stalking law, the purpose of which is to protect citizens from criminal harassment (see Chapter 3). In addition, Canada has developed "hate laws." These are usually attached as a sentence enhancement to acts of violence or crimes against property if such crimes are committed because of the victim's race, gender, or sexual preference (see Chapter 9).

Causation

Causation refers to the requirement that the conduct of the accused produce a specific result (i.e., a crime). In other words, when the act (or omission) of the accused started a series of events that led to harm, there is causation. Important concerns have been raised about causation when a long time has passed between the *mens rea* and the *actus reus*. Sometimes it is easy to see the harm that has resulted from an act, but it is not so easy to establish the *mens rea* element. This is particularly true for actions generally referred to as corporate crime.

Take, for example, an employee of a corporation who is told that because the spraying of a particular chemical mixture is "safe," she need not wear safety equipment. If she dies immediately after applying the chemical, concurrence can easily be determined. But what if that worker suffers no ill health for 15 years and then suddenly dies from a blood disease that is associated with exposure to the chemical? The lack of concurrence will make it difficult to prove that a crime was committed. This situation can be further complicated if many other workers applied the spray at the same time without contracting a terminal disease, or if some suffered from seemingly unrelated illnesses.

Punishment

The law must state the sanctions for every crime so that everyone is aware of the possible consequences of certain actions. The Criminal Code therefore specifies the sanctions for every crime. In Canada, there are sanctions for two types of offences: indictable and summary conviction offences. These are discussed in detail later in this chapter.

LEGAL DEFENCES AND THE LAW

Legal defences fall into two categories, *excuse* defences and *justification* defences. The difference between these "is that where conduct is justified, it is not wrong in the context in which it occurs" whereas conduct that is excused is wrong "but because certain circumstances exist, the actor is excused from criminal liability" (Barnhorst and Barnhorst 2004, 65).

Excuse Defences

With excuse defences, the defendant admits to committing a criminal act but contends that he or she cannot be held criminally responsible for it because there was no criminal intent. In these cases, then, the disposition of the accused is an important consideration. Examples of excuse defences are age, mental disorder, and mistake of fact.

Age

In Canada, there are three distinct stages of criminal responsibility. The law considers people (i.e., children) under the age of 12 to lack criminal responsibility. Thereafter, until their eighteenth birthday, they are classified as youths and have limited criminal accountability (or "diminished responsibility") under the Youth Criminal Justice Act. Adulthood starts when a person turns 18, at which point people face full legal accountability; however, they also possess full legal rights. These distinctions of legal accountability based on age are part of the very foundations of our criminal law. The fundamental criminal law concept "of moral accountability and the policy objective of social protection through deterrence of crime and rehabilitation apply differently to children and youth than to adults, because youths are different than adults" (Bala 1997, 2).

Mental Disorder

An accused with a mental disorder lacks the *mens rea* to commit the offence. Section 16(1) of the Criminal Code sets out the defence:

> 16. (1) No person is criminally responsible for an act committed or an omission made while suffering from a mental disorder that rendered the person incapable of appreciating the nature and quality of the act or omission or of knowing that it was wrong.

Section 16 of the Criminal Code also states that everyone is presumed not to be suffering from a mental disorder unless that issue is raised. If the issue is raised, the burden of proof rests with the party that raises the issue. In *R. v. Chaulk* (1994), the Supreme Court ruled that while the presumption of sanity violates the constitutional right to be presumed innocent, that violation is justified in a free and democratic society as it would be an "onerous burden" for the Crown to disprove insanity in every case.

Mental disorder is defined as a disease of the mind. Whether a specific condition is a disease of the mind is a question of law, and two important aspects of a judge's determination are expert medical evidence and public safety (Barnhorst and Barnhorst 2004). Examples of mental disorder include schizophrenia, paranoia, and melancholia. Self-induced states caused by alcohol or drugs are excluded, as are temporary conditions such as hysteria. "Appreciating the nature and quality of the act" refers to the defendant's capacity to perceive the consequences, impact, and results of the physical act. If it is determined that the accused was incapable of knowing the act was wrong, this defence may succeed.

When someone is found not guilty in a criminal court, he or she is usually acquitted. However, if the defence of mental disorder is successful, that person is not acquitted until a hearing is held to determine whether he or she is a danger to the public.

Automatism

Automatism (or dissociative amnesia) refers to unconscious or involuntary behaviour. People who are in a dissociative state are not in conscious control of their bodily movements, and thus they act abnormally. This defence is rarely used because there must be strong evidence from expert witnesses affirming the condition. The accused's behaviour is considered "automatic" because he or she did not have the *actus reus* of the crime (Barnhorst and Barnhorst 2004). The Supreme Court of Canada has defined automatism as "unconscious, involuntary behaviour, the state of a person who, though capable of action, is not conscious of what they are doing. It means an unconscious, involuntary act, where the mind does not go with what is being done" (*R. v. Rabey* [1977]). When this defence is used, it cannot be based on a mental disorder or voluntary intoxication by alcohol or drugs. If this defence succeeds, the accused is immediately released from custody. In *R. v. Stone* (1999), the Supreme Court ruled that a defence of automatism doesn't necessarily mean that the accused has to be unconscious; it does, however, mean that the consciousness must be so impaired that the accused lacks voluntary control. Examples of automatism include someone who commits a crime while sleepwalking (*R. v. Parks* [1992]), while in a dazed condition following a concussion (*R. v. Bleta* [1965]), or who has taken a drug without knowing its effects

(*R. v. King* [1962]). In *R. v. Graveline* (2006), the Supreme Court upheld a 2001 jury verdict that acquitted a defendant charged with second degree murder for shooting her sleeping husband after suffering from years of mental and physical abuse. Automatism is sometimes confused with self-defence (see below). The fundamental premise of automatism is that the behaviour is involuntary; in contrast, self-defence implies deliberate conduct (Tibbetts 2006, A6).

Mistake of Fact

Someone who commits an illegal act while believing that certain circumstances exist may use the defence of mistake of fact. This defence focuses on the *mens rea* of the offence. It will be a defence to a criminal charge if (1) the mistake was an honest one, and (2) no offence would have been committed if the circumstances had been as the accused believed them to be.

The Criminal Code limits the use of this defence. For example, an accused person cannot use this defence when charged with touching a young person under the age of 14 for a sexual purpose unless the accused took all reasonable steps to determine the age of the youth. In addition, there are special rules for using this defence when the charge is sexual assault (see s. 150.1[4]). The mistake-of-fact defence has been very controversial in Canada in sexual assault cases (*R. v. Pappajohn* [1980]) and in drug offence cases (*R. v. Burgess* [1970]; *R. v. Kundeus* [1975]).

Mistake of Law

The general rule that "ignorance of the law is no excuse" is found in s. 19 of the Criminal Code. That is, everyone is presumed to know the criminal law. If a mistake-of-law defence is used, it concerns an error regarding the legal status of a circumstance or fact. The Supreme Court of Canada has stated that the mistake-of-law defence is no excuse by noting that "it is a principle of our criminal law that an honest but mistaken belief in respect of the legal consequences of one's deliberate actions does not furnish a defence to a criminal charge, even when the mistake cannot be attributed to the negligence of the accused" (*R. v. Forster* [1992]). Individuals "rely on their own knowledge of the law, or even a lawyer's advice, at their peril," even when they have "made genuine and reasonable attempts to ascertain what the law is and to comply with it" (Roach 2004, 82).

Justification Defences

Justification defences involve a defendant admitting that while he or she did commit the criminal act in question,

that act was justified in the circumstances. There are five justification defences: duress, necessity, self-defence, provocation, and entrapment. These defences (except provocation and entrapment) are known as "complete defences" because if they are accepted by the court, they result in acquittal. The Supreme Court of Canada has ruled that a defendant who is acquitted after arguing justification will not be punished because "the values of society, indeed of criminal law itself, are better promoted by disobeying a given statute than by observing it" (*R. v. Perka* [1984]). The exceptions here are the defences of provocation and entrapment. Provocation is a partial defence in the sense that it only applies to a charge of murder, and if successful reduces that charge to manslaughter. Entrapment results in a permanent stay of proceedings rather than acquittal.

Justification defences "to some extent require a person to have acted reasonably in response to external pressures" (Roach 2004, 278). The Supreme Court of Canada in *R. v. Hibbert* (1995) ruled that three of these defences—self-defence, necessity, and duress—"all arise under circumstances where a person is subjected to an external danger that otherwise would be criminal as a way of avoiding the harm the danger presents." In all of the justification defences, the burden of proof is on the Crown to prove guilt beyond a reasonable doubt. For example, in *R. v. Hibbert* (1995), a new trial was ordered by the Supreme Court of Canada because the trial judge did not explain to the jury that the accused didn't have to prove the defence of provocation. However, a judge does not have to instruct a jury about every defence in every case. The accused has to reach a threshold evidential burden in every case (Roach 2004, 284). In *R. v. Cinous* (2002), the Supreme Court stated that an "air of reality" test should apply to all defences. This test requires sufficient evidence to exist on each necessary element of the defence and that the evidence permit a properly instructed jury the possibility of acquitting the accused.

Duress

Duress exists when the wrongful threat of one person makes another person commit a crime he or she would not otherwise have committed, when there was an imminent threat of death or bodily harm (*R. v. Ruzic* [2001]), and when there was no realistic alternative course of action (*R. v. Hibbert* [1995]). In these situations, duress is seen as negating the *mens rea* necessary to commit a crime.

There are two defences of duress: compulsion, which is found in the Criminal Code; and the common-law defence of duress. An accused who uses the defence of compulsion (found in s. 17 of the Criminal Code) must establish the following:

- The accused committed an offence not found in s. 17 (e.g., murder, attempted murder, sexual assault, forcible abduction).
- The accused committed the offence because he or she believed that the threats of immediate death or immediate grievous bodily harm would be carried out.
- The threats were delivered by a person who was present at the time the accused committed an offence.
- The accused was not a member of the group planning to commit the offence.

In 1993, the Quebec Court of Appeal (*R. v. Langlois* [1993]) ruled that s. 17 violated s. 7 of the Charter of Rights and Freedoms because it allows an individual who is innocent to be convicted of an offence. Its decision was based on the following:

- The defence is not available for all offences.
- The accused must have faced threats of immediate death or bodily harm by a person who was present when the crime was committed.
- The defence does not apply when the threats are made against a member of the accused's family.

In 2001, in *R. v. Ruzic*, the Supreme Court struck down a requirement that the individual who threatened the accused had to be present at the time *and* the place when the offence was committed. Once again, it was decided that this requirement violated s. 7 of the Charter of Rights and Freedoms.

The common-law defence of duress can be used in those situations not covered by s. 17. The common law does not exclude any defences and does not require the threat of immediate death or bodily harm (as in a threat made concerning the future). Moreover, the person threatening the accused does not have to be present when the crime is committed. However, the common law cannot be used if the accused had an opportunity to escape the situation in safety.

Necessity

Necessity is actually related to the defence of duress because duress is actually a type of necessity. In *R. v. Hibbert* (1995), the Supreme Court of Canada stated that in cases of duress, the danger is caused by intentional threats of bodily harm, while in cases involving necessity, the danger is caused by forces of nature or human conduct other than the intentional threats of bodily harm.

The defence of necessity is rarely used (Barnhorst and Barnhorst 2004, 80). The Supreme Court decided

in *R. v. Perka* (1984) that the defence of necessity applies in those cases where:

- there was imminent peril or danger;
- the accused had no reasonable legal alternative to the course of action he or she took; and
- there was proportionality between the harm inflicted and the harm avoided.

One of the most controversial Canadian cases involving the defence of necessity occurred in November 1993, when Robert Latimer was charged with first degree murder for the death of his 12-year-old daughter, Tracy. She was suffering from a severe form of cerebral palsy that had left her physically and developmentally disabled and in extreme pain, a condition that could not be helped by medication. During the first trial, Latimer's lawyer offered the defence of necessity, arguing that his client was attempting to prevent a tragedy greater than that of his daughter's death. The Supreme Court, however, ruled that the accused had not met the air-of-reality test. It decided that there had been no imminent threat to Tracy's life because her pain was ongoing—that is, it was not an emergency. It also ruled that there were reasonable legal alternatives for Tracy. Finally, it considered that the harm avoided was "completely disproportionate to the harm caused" (Sneiderman 2000, 513–14). In the second trial, the judge decided there wasn't an air of reality that would justify placing the defence of necessity to the jury.

Self-Defence

Self-defence (which involves defending oneself as well as others and property) justifies the use of force against another person. The general rule, found in s. 26 of the Criminal Code, is that only as much force as necessary can be used in the circumstances. If excessive force is used, the individual can be charged with a criminal offence (e.g., an assault) or be subject to a lawsuit in a civil action. Section 27 of the Criminal Code states that anyone can use as much force as is reasonably necessary to prevent the commission of certain offences that are likely to cause severe harm to a person or to property (Barnhorst and Barnhorst 2004, 82). Other sections of the Criminal Code also deal with self-defence. For an example, force can be used to protect oneself against assault, be it provoked or not, or to prevent an assault from occurring. Also, individuals can use force to defend movable property in their possession as well as a dwelling house or real property.

Section 34(2) is one of the more controversial sections relating to self-defence because it deals with situations where the accused intends to cause bodily harm or death but at the same time claims justification in using force. In this section of the Criminal Code, an individual who causes grievous bodily harm or who kills another in self-defence must meet all three of the following requirements:

- There must be an unlawful assault.
- The accused must have been under a reasonable fear of death or serious bodily harm.
- The accused must have believed on reasonable grounds that there was no other way to survive.

The case of *R. v. Lavallee* (1990) is a well-known Canadian example of a woman using force to protect herself. The accused was unable to leave her husband despite being constantly abused by him over the previous four years. On the day of the killing, he found her hiding in a closet. He then gave her a gun and dared her to shoot him, saying that if she didn't shoot him, he would kill her later. When he started to leave the room, she shot him in the head. During the trial, experts testified that the accused felt "trapped, vulnerable [and] worthless." The Supreme Court of Canada accepted the evidence of "battered woman syndrome" and upheld her acquittal. It ruled that battered woman syndrome can be resorted to when there is a well-founded anticipation of peril—in other words, the accused does not have to prove imminent peril.

Provocation

Provocation, as defined in s. 232 of the Criminal Code, involves a wrongful act or insult that deprives an ordinary person of the power of self-control. This defence can only be used for the offence of murder. If it succeeds, the accused will be found guilty of the less serious offence of manslaughter.

According to s. 232 of the Criminal Code, provocation consists of the following elements:

- a wrongful act or insult . . .
- sufficient to deprive an ordinary person of the power of self-control . . .
- that actually provoked the offender, who acted in response to it . . .
- on the sudden, before there was time for his or her passion to cool.

These four elements are used to form two tests—(1) "a wrongful act or insult" and (2) "upon the sudden"—both of which must be satisfied if the defence of provocation is to be used successfully.

Entrapment

Entrapment is a justification defence. It arises when a police officer or government agent deceives a defendant into committing a wrongful act. The police can use legitimate means to gain information to arrest a suspect, but only up to a point. Entrapment occurs when an agent of the state (such as a police officer) offers an individual an opportunity to commit a crime without reasonable grounds to suspect that the individual in question was involved in a criminal activity. Entrapment also occurs when the state actually induces the individual to commit a crime. In *R. v. Mack* (1988), for example, the Supreme Court of Canada held that this defence exists as part of the doctrine of abuse of process.

The entrapment defence may be available when someone has been "set up" to commit a crime by the police or police informants. The defendant must prove that he or she was entrapped on a balance of probabilities. The finding that entrapment occurred is always reached by a judge, and only after the guilt of the accused has been determined. A finding of entrapment results in a permanent stay of proceedings rather than an acquittal of the accused.

THE CLASSIFICATION OF CRIMINAL OFFENCES

In Canada, decisions on how to classify crimes are made by the federal government. An important factor when crimes are being classified is the penalty attached to a given offence. Two major crime classification systems are used in Canada. *Legal* classifications include indictable offences, summary conviction offences, and hybrid offences; *general* classifications are employed by police and other criminal justice agencies to classify criminal offences, and include violent crimes and property crimes.

Summary Conviction, Indictable, and Hybrid Offences

Summary conviction offences are generally punishable by a period of incarceration not exceeding six months and a maximum fine of $2,000, although for some offences (such as sexual assault level 1) the Supreme Court of Canada has increased the maximum punishment to 18 months. Summary conviction trials are always heard by a provincial court judge. In addition, charges for summary conviction offences must be laid within six months of the commission of the offence. If a period of imprisonment is part of the sentence, the offender serves the sentence in a provincial facility.

In contrast, there are three methods of trial for **indictable offences**. The less serious indictable offences (e.g., theft under $5,000) are also known as **absolute jurisdiction indictable offences**. The accused has to be

The North Vancouver RCMP Youth Intervention Unit, concerned about an apparent increase among youths participating in the sex trade, many of whom are advertising on Craigslist, announced that there appears to be a small group of individuals within the community who are pressuring women as young as 16 to prostitute themselves online. (Les Bazso / The Province)

tried by a provincial court judge. The most serious crimes (e.g., first and second degree murder) are referred to as **Supreme Court exclusive indictable offences**. These crimes must be tried by a federally appointed judge and a jury in a provincial superior court. The accused may sometimes request that the case be heard by judge alone, but this request has to be permitted by the provincial attorney general or the justice minister. For all other indictable offences, the accused can choose to have the trial by a provincially appointed judge without a jury, or by a federally appointed judge with or without a jury. These offences, which make up the majority of indictable offences in Canada, are known as *election indictable offences*. If convicted of an indictable offence, the accused may receive a variety of sentences. Some offences (e.g., homicide) bring life sentences; for others (e.g., sexual assault), the punishment depends on the degree of harm inflicted on the victim. Few minimum punishments are stipulated by the Criminal Code, so it is up to the judge to select the appropriate sentence up to the most severe provided for by law.

Hybrid offences give prosecutors the discretion to decide whether they wish to proceed with a case as a summary conviction offence or an indictable offence. The prosecutor's decision is formally based on such factors as the previous record of the offender and any mitigating factors (e.g., the social status of the offender) or aggravating factors (e.g., crimes involving violence) associated with the crime. In reality, prosecutors' decisions are often influenced by police officers. Ericson studied Peel Regional detectives and found that they were able to "fundamentally affect the outcome of a case both in terms of what the accused is convicted of and in terms of

sentencing" (Ericson, in Wheeler 1987, 27). However the final decision is reached, it will have a significant impact on most of the procedures that apply to the accused. For example, the decision determines possible appeals, the maximum length of sentence, whether a fine is imposed in addition to imprisonment, and whether an offender can serve the sentence in the community.

THE SERIOUSNESS OF CRIME

Criminal statutes prescribe punishments that reflect the seriousness of the crime committed. Some offences in the Criminal Code recognize different levels of violence, along with differences in the maximum amount of punishment applicable to each. Examples of single offences with gradations of seriousness are homicide and sexual assault.

Sexual assault actually consists of three offences, the least serious of which is found in s. 271 of the Criminal Code. This is a hybrid offence, so if the Crown prosecutor elects to proceed by way of an indictable offence, the maximum length of punishment is ten years. However, the Crown prosecutor has the discretion to proceed by way of summary conviction, in which case the accused, if convicted, faces a maximum punishment of 18 months. For a person convicted of sexual assault of the next highest level of seriousness—s. 272 of the Criminal Code, which addresses sexual assault with a weapon, threatening bodily harm, or causing bodily harm—the maximum prison term is 14 years. The most serious form of sexual assault, dealt with in s. 273 of the Criminal Code, is aggravated sexual assault. An individual convicted of this offence can receive life imprisonment (Roberts and Mohr 1994).

Homicide has four categories in the Criminal Code. A person who commits homicide, according to s. 222, "directly or indirectly, by any means, causes the death of a human being." This section specifies that only culpable homicide is punishable. Once the police have determined that a homicide is culpable, they can lay one of the following charges: first degree murder, second degree murder, manslaughter, or infanticide.

First degree murder is planned and deliberate. However, an individual can be charged with first degree murder even if the act wasn't planned and deliberate if the victim is a police officer, a prison guard, an individual working in a prison setting, or "is another similar person acting in the course of duty." In addition, a charge of first degree murder can be laid if anyone dies during the commission of one the following crimes: s. 76(1)—hijacking an aircraft; s. 271—sexual assault; s. 272—sexual assault with a weapon; s. 273—aggravated sexual assault; s. 279—kidnapping and forcible confinement; and s. 279.1—hostage taking. All murder that is not first degree murder is **second degree murder** (Silverman and Kennedy 1993).

The charge of **manslaughter** can be laid if the Crown prosecutor is unable to establish all the elements of murder. Usually a charge of manslaughter is laid when the death in question (an accidental death) is caused either by an unlawful act, such as assault, or by criminal negligence. Manslaughter is an indictable offence for which the maximum punishment is life imprisonment.

Infanticide is one of the rare sections of the Canadian Criminal Code that specifies the gender of the alleged perpetrator of the crime. This charge can be laid only against a "female person" when she "causes the death of her newly born child." An infant, in the eyes of the law, is a person under one year of age. The maximum punishment for the offence of infanticide is five years in prison. This law is based on the reasoning that a woman may be "mentally disturbed of giving birth . . . and thus less responsible for her actions. In this situation the law mitigates the severity of punishment for what would otherwise be murder or manslaughter" (Barnhorst and Barnhorst 2004, 230).

The punishment for both first and second degree murder is life imprisonment. There is an important difference between the two, however, and that is the possibility of release on parole. At the sentencing of a person convicted of second degree murder, the judge can state that the accused is eligible for parole after serving a designated amount of the sentence. At the present time, a judge has the right to grant an offender eligibility for full parole after ten years have been served. An individual convicted of first degree murder must serve life imprisonment. That person must serve at least 25 years of the sentence before applying for full parole.

In theory, any individual convicted of first or second degree murder will be spending the rest of his or her life in prison; such people have no guarantee of ever leaving a federal correctional institution. However, since 1991, most individuals convicted of first and second degree murder and still serving their sentence after 15 years can apply for a judicial review of their parole ineligibility under s. 745.6 of the Criminal Code for the purpose of receiving parole. This is often referred to as the "faint hope" clause. A jury decides whether to allow the application for reducing the number of years before the person receives parole. If this is allowed, the National Parole Board reviews the case and agrees or refuses to grant parole. Since the first application in 1987, there have been 169 court decisions. Of these cases, 141 have resulted in a reduction of the time period that must be served before parole eligibility. Of the

125 offenders who have been released to date, 15 have been returned to custody, 11 offenders are deceased, 1 is unlawfully at large, and 3 have been deported (Public Safety Canada 2008).

CRIMINAL LAW REFORM

During the past few decades, the federal government has introduced and revised various substantive laws and ruled on countless procedural issues in an attempt to deal with contemporary issues. As Davison (2005, 18) has pointed out, the trend of these new laws has been toward increasing the crime control powers of the state. Rarely do these changes "involve decriminalizing prohibited conduct or enhancing and protecting the rights of those accused of crime." Instead, most of the recent changes reflect stricter laws and "a clear willingness on the part of government to listen to and accommodate the results or demands of law enforcement, victims groups, and similar bodies and interests within society."

At the same time, new concerns have been raised about the protection of the legal rights of the accused in Canada. For example, is it possible to create laws to control the activities of gangs and of those who want to join gangs? And can activities such as panhandling in public areas be prohibited in order to reduce perceived disorder on the streets? If the answer to both questions is yes, how can we develop meaningful punishments for panhandlers and for those who become affiliated with criminal gangs?

Anti-Gang (Criminal Conspiracy) Legislation

In an attempt to combat criminal gangs and appease the public and the law enforcement agencies, in 1997, the federal government developed anti-gang legislation (Bill C-95). This law applied to "any or all of the members of a gang which engage in or have, within the preceding 5 years, engaged in the commission of a series of such offences." An accused found guilty of participating in a criminal organization could receive up to 14 years in prison. The new anti-gang measures expanded the powers of police officers. Some highlights of these measures:

- *Participation in a criminal organization.* Anyone guilty of a criminal act performed for the benefit of or in association with a criminal organization was now subject to tougher penalties referred to as "sentence enhancements." For example, a known gang member convicted of a violent crime was now subject to a much longer sentence than a person acting alone. A *criminal organization* had been redefined as any group, association, or other body consisting of five or more individuals who had as a primary activity the commission of a series of indictable offences punishable by a sentence of five years or more. This offence was now punishable by up to 14 years in prison.

- *Explosives offences.* An individual was now guilty of an offence who possessed explosives for the benefit of, or at the direction of, a criminal organization. Anyone using explosives to commit murder was now guilty of first degree murder. This offence was now punishable by up to 14 years in prison (more than the maximum for possession of explosives). Also, this sentence was to be served consecutively—that is, added to any other offence.

- *Peace bonds.* On application of an attorney general, a judge could now issue a restraining order placing strict conditions on a gang leader so as to bar the leader from associating with other known gang members and from visiting known gang hangouts. If this order were breached, the gang leader could now be sentenced to a jail term. No longer did the suspect have to commit an offence to be subject to the gang peace bond.

- *Electronic surveillance.* The police now enjoyed greater access to electronic means of surveillance in order to observe the movements and actions of gang members. Previously, the police had had to convince a judge that they needed electronic surveillance as a "last resort." The limits on wiretap authorizations had been extended from 60 days to one year.

- *Proceeds of crime.* This change allowed for the seizure and forfeiture of the proceeds from all criminal organization activities on conviction. Property such as weapons and vehicles used in the commission of a crime could also be seized, as well as property such as a gang clubhouse built or modified for the purpose of facilitating the commission of criminal organization activities. Also, police could now obtain a court order to access the income tax information of those being investigated for participating in a criminal organization.

- *Bail.* Anyone charged with a criminal organization offence was now subject to pretrial detention unless he or she could prove that it was not justified. Previously, the onus had been on the Crown to show why the person should be detained.

- *Sentencing.* Any evidence of an offence committed for the benefit of, at the direction of, or in association with a criminal organization could now be considered by a judge at sentencing as an "aggravating" factor that could lead to a longer sentence. Also, judges were now able to delay parole eligibility for anyone convicted of a criminal organization offence.

- *National and regional coordinating committees.* Six national coordinating committees on organized crime were formed across Canada (Newfoundland, the Maritimes, Quebec, Ontario, the Prairies, and British Columbia/Yukon) to share information and assist in enforcement efforts against gangs.

The first application of Canada's anti-gang legislation occurred in Manitoba, where 35 men, alleged members of the Manitoba Warriors street gang, were arrested after a year-long police operation involving 120 officers. These gang members were charged with drug and weapons offences, as well as with offences under the federal anti-gang legislation targeting participation in a criminal organization. All of those charged were denied bail, except for the last individual to have a trial (this person received bail after all of the others pleaded guilty). Two of the accused had their charges stayed in exchange for their testimony. Thirty-two of the remaining 33 were convicted on drug charges and received sentences ranging from time served to nine years. Only 2 of the 33 pleaded guilty to participating in a criminal organization, and both had extra time added to their sentence (McIntyre 2000).

Even though at least 14 individuals have since been convicted across Canada under the anti-gang provisions, some believed that the law needed to be amended to make it a much stronger legal tool for controlling criminal organizations. Others objected to this law, arguing that the legislation was "bad law" and that it was unlikely to "solve the problem of biker or other gangs committed to rebelliousness and lawlessness" (Stuart 1997, 216). These critics contended that Canada already had strong laws, which rendered the various provisions of the law unnecessary.

Most critics, however, argued a different point— that Canada's anti-gang legislation was so difficult to apply that it needed to be amended in order to make it more effective. These people argued strongly that the new laws were inadequate for effectively controlling such activities. For example, the president of the Canadian Police Association declared, "We're not winning the war. Things are going out of control and it's time to do something about it." Some parliamentarians felt that the police were being "handcuffed by ineffective laws and ineffective programs"; an organized crime expert stated that Canada had become a centre of global crime activity "in part because of federal regulations and laws" (Humphreys 2001, A4).

On January 31, 2001, the anti-gang law "survived a critical test" when a Quebec judge ruled that the law did not infringe on individual liberties or violate the Charter of Rights and Freedoms (Panetta 2001, A7).

Despite this success, prosecutors argued that the law placed "an unduly heavy burden" on them; some contended that the law "requires proof the accused is aware that others in the gang committed a series of major crimes" (Thanh Ha 2001, A3).

Three months later, in April 2001, a new anti-gang bill (Bill C-24) was brought before the House of Commons. This bill addressed some of the issues raised concerning the first law; it also provided "sweeping" new powers for law enforcement agencies and the courts. Its highlights are listed below:

- *Definition of a criminal organization.* Prosecutors had faced a difficult task when trying to convict someone based on the original definition. The proposed amendment defined a criminal organization more loosely, as a group of three or more people who had committed a crime for financial gain.
- *The criminalization of participation in a criminal organization.* This proposed change would expand the definition of participation in a criminal organization. It would no longer be necessary for an individual to break the law. The point here was to make it easier for prosecutors to charge non-criminals such as accountants who knowingly work for criminal organizations. The maximum sentence for participation would be five years.
- *The criminalization of benefiting from a criminal organization.* Anyone who committed a crime for the benefit of a criminal organization and who was found guilty would face a maximum sentence of 14 years.
- *The criminalization of directing others to commit crimes.* Gang leaders would now face a maximum sentence of life imprisonment for directing others to commit crimes, whether or not their instructions were followed.

Many groups are well organized and have come under increasing criminal justice scrutiny through new legislation passed to combat organized-crime groups. (CP PHOTO/Le Journal de Montreal)

In addition, the amendments included proposals to extend the police new wiretapping powers and to grant undercover investigators immunity for actions carried out in the course their investigations (and not just for those associated with criminal gangs). However, police would not have the right to intentionally or recklessly cause death or bodily harm, obstruct justice, or commit sexual offences. The police were also to be given the power to authorize their own activities (instead of waiting for a judge's authorization) because their work would now require them to make split-second decisions.

Bill C-24 received Royal Assent in December 2001 and became law in 2002. Critics argue that this new law has expanded the powers of the state's agents. According to Don Stuart, a law professor at Queen's University, one of the biggest problems with it is that the police can now break the law: "Police authorizing police to break the law is a perversion of the rule of law" (Chwialkowska 2001). Others have pointed out that this legislation, which is similar to the anti-terrorist legislation (see Chapter 1), will not be more effective in controlling gang activities but will erode the civil rights of Canadians (Daniels et al. 2001).

Crime control officials are pleased with the amendments, and have stated that they will enable investigators to be more proactive in combating criminal organizations. Also, prosecutions will now be easier and sentences will be much harsher.

In December 2004, the law suffered a major setback when the B.C. Supreme Court ruled a section of it unconstitutional. The section in question was the one stating that any member of a criminal organization who knowingly instructs another person directly or indirectly to commit an offence is subject to life in prison. The court ruled that this was too vague as it did not specify who was a member of a criminal organization and who was not.

The first significant conviction under the anti-gang legislation was in Ontario in 2005. Here, the judge found that two men had committed extortion against an Ontario businessman and that they had done so "in association with" an identifiable criminal group, the Hells Angels Motorcycle Club. In this case, the police had tape-recorded one of the accused warning the victim that he would be dealt with violently if he failed to pay the $75,000 debt. Since the two men wore Hells Angels insignia when they confronted the victim, the judge ruled that "they used the Angels' reputation for violence and intimidation as a tool in the abortive shakedown" (Appleby 2005, A5). The two members of the Hells Angels Motorcycle Club appealed this decision and at the same time challenged Ottawa's anti-gang law. At the end of June 2009, the Ontario Court of Appeal upheld both their conviction and the constitutionality of stiffer sentences for individuals who are members of a gang (Humphreys 2009).

On February 26, 2009, the federal government introduced amendments to the Criminal Code in an attempt to control violence related to street gangs and other forms of organized criminal organizations (see Chapter 1). In addition, in May 2009, it was announced that the House of Commons Justice Committee was considering whether or not the government should create a list of banned criminal organizations, similar to the list of terrorist organizations (created in 2001) that are "officially blacklisted" (Tibbetts 2009). The idea was proposed by the Bloc Québécois, who believe that criminal trials in Quebec are moving too slow because the Crown must prove in each case that a suspect group meets the criteria set out in Canada's definition of "criminal organization." A member of the Bloc Québécois informed the members of the justice committee that under current legislation each trial has to start "at square one" and that it would be better to have criminal organizations declared illegal (ibid.).

The Safe Streets Act

Concerns about the relationship between disorder and crime have grown over the past 20 years, ever since the publication of the "broken windows" theory in 1982 (see Chapter 5). This theory has led the Province of Ontario to enact legislation and cities to pass bylaws that prohibit activities believed to contribute to disorder. In an attempt to eliminate disorderly behaviour that some felt was threatening the safety of citizens, Vancouver and Winnipeg passed bylaws (in 1998 and 1995, respectively) focusing on controlling "aggressive" panhandling in certain locations at certain times. In 1999, Ontario passed the Safe Streets Act in an attempt to control similar behaviour as well as any type of solicitation involving a "captive audience." All three pieces of legislation have generated controversy and led to court challenges based on questions about their constitutionality.

The Safe Streets Act defines "aggressive" soliciting as soliciting in a manner likely to cause a "reasonable person" to be concerned about his or her personal safety. It also identifies numerous activities, all of which are automatically considered to involve aggressive soliciting. Examples:

- Threatening the person with physical harm.
- Obstructing the path of the person who is being solicited.
- Using abusive language during or after solicitation.
- Continuing to solicit a person in a persistent manner after the person has said that he or she doesn't want to give any money.

An RCMP officer stands over a large quantity of heroin in September 2000. The seizure totalled 156 kilograms, making it one of the largest busts in Canadian history. Since many of the groups involved with the transportation of heroin are transnational organized criminal groups, do you think that Canada's anti-gang legislation is a sufficient deterrent to such activities? (CP PHOTO/Tannis Toohey)

The act also identifies specific places where an individual cannot solicit a "captive audience." Examples include the following:

- Near a pay telephone or in a public washroom facility.
- Near an automated teller machine.
- On a public transit vehicle.
- In a parking lot.

The punishments vary according to jurisdiction, but all include a fine or a short period of confinement. In Vancouver, the maximum fine is not to exceed $2,000, while in Ottawa the maximum fine is $5,000. In Winnipeg, the fine is not to exceed $1,000 or a jail term of up to six months. In Ontario, the Safe Streets Act specifies that the first conviction is to be a fine not exceeding $500; subsequent convictions involve fines of up to $1,000 and a jail term of no more than six months.

This legislation has inspired controversy. Constitutional challenges to city bylaws have been launched in Vancouver and Winnipeg. Critics of these bylaws and the Safe Streets Act argue that these laws discriminate against the poor and are essentially a continuation of laws that over the centuries have attempted to outlaw similar types of activities by applying various terms such as "vagrancy," "tramps," "hoboes," and the "homeless." In addition, they argue that these laws are vague, in that they do not define in any specific way exactly what types of activities are outlawed in any detailed way (Hermer and Mosher 2002). Others (e.g., Ruddick 2002) contend that this legislation—in particular, the Safe Streets Act—lists so many prohibitions that it in effect controls the places where homeless people can pursue their activities. Such laws, they point out, focus on those least able to defend themselves or pay fines (thereby raising the possibility of a jail sentence). These critics also approach the problems addressed by this legislation in a broader context; the real problem, they say, is that welfare programs are being eliminated and that adequate housing is in short supply.

Supporters of this legislation argue that many citizens want these types of laws as they fear disorder and its effects. In addition, they believe that street crime increases as the result of disorder. In their view, to control activities in certain places and times is not a blanket prohibition; it only controls certain undesirable actions in very specific locations.

Eighteen months after the Safe Streets Act was introduced in Ontario, more than 100 individuals who were panhandling or squeegeeing had been charged with an offence. In August 2001, 80 of the individuals charged

decided to challenge the constitutionality of the act. The facts surrounding the activities of 13 of these individuals were agreed upon by defence counsel and the Crown (the other 67 individuals had their charges withdrawn). In this challenge (R. v. Banks [2005]), nine of the individuals were charged with "soliciting on the roadway," three were charged under the provincial Highway Traffic Act, and one was charged with soliciting "in a persistent manner." Defence lawyers challenged the act on the constitutional grounds that it denied freedom of expression, violated equality rights, and denied life, liberty, and security of the person. A provincial court judge ruled in August 2001 that the Safe Streets Act was constitutional. He agreed that it limited people's freedom of expression, but he also stated that such infringement was justified in terms of public safety. In addition, he wrote that poverty "is itself not an analogous ground of discrimination under s. 15," that the defendants "failed to establish that the Act discriminates against the extremely poor," and that the Act "does not apply only to the poor." In 2007, the Ontario Court of Appeal unanimously agreed that concerns about public safety and the flow of traffic overrides violations of freedom of expression (R. v. Banks [2007]). The police in Toronto continue to enforce the Safe Streets Act: during the first seven months of 2007, the police laid more than 1,400 charges against aggressive panhandlers, a figure higher than the total number of charges laid in 2006 (Canadian Broadcasting Corporation 2007).

CRITICAL ISSUES IN CANADIAN CRIMINAL JUSTICE

HIV DISCLOSURE AND CRIMINALIZATION

Governments often examine their substantive laws. Since the law reflects, in part, public opinion and morality regarding various forms of behaviour, what was considered to be criminal many—or even a few—years ago may not be considered so today. When a government decides to remove a crime from the Criminal Code to civil law, it is referred to as decriminalization. In the following paragraphs, it is evident that the courts have decided to make HIV-nondisclosure a criminal offence. Others, who argue that given our greater understanding of how to treat HIV-infected individuals, suggest that it is better to approach this issue from outside the criminal law.

On April 4, 2009, a Toronto jury of nine men and three women, after deliberating for two and one-half days, found 52-year-old Johnson Aziga

guilty of two counts of first degree murder, ten counts of aggravated assault, and one count of attempted aggravated assault. Mr. Aziga's crime was spreading the HIV/AIDS virus—not only did he become the first Canadian to be found guilty of murder for spreading the virus that causes HIV/AIDS, but legal observers thought his conviction to be the first-ever conviction for the reckless transmission of HIV/AIDS (Prokaska 2009, A10). One of the women he infected died of AIDS-related cancer three weeks after the police videotaped an interview with her on November 19, 2002 about her relationship with Mr. Aziga. Prosecutors alleged that Mr. Aziga "failed to inform his partners about his HIV-positive status, although he had been aware of it since 1996 and was under public-health orders to do so" (Perkel 2009, A11).

Continued on next page

In recent years, a number of other Canadian men have received harsh sentences for similar repetitive duplicity resulting in HIV-infected women (Kay, 2009). In April 2008, Carlos Leone pleaded guilty to 15 counts of aggravated sexual assault after failing to inform his sexual partners of his HIV status. The Crown attempted to seek a life sentence and dangerous offender status against Mr. Leone, but the judge dismissed the Crown's application for a dangerous offender status or as a long-term offender. Instead, he sentenced the accused to 15 consecutive terms ranging from two to five years each and totalling 49 years. The judge then stated that the justice system "required that he not impose an unduly harsh sentence that violates the 'totality principal' and then adjusted the prison term downward to 18 years" ("Leone Jailed . . ." 2008). In 2006, in a British Columbia case, Adrien Nduwayo received a 15-year sentence for similar crimes.

HIV/AIDS infection cases have increasingly involved more serious charges over the years. Grant (2008), in her study of the criminalization of the nondisclosure of HIV between 1989 and 2007, found 43 cases where this condition was a vital element in the definition of the offence itself across Canada. Between 1989 and 1998, the charges for these cases varied, ranging from common nuisance to criminal negligence causing bodily harm, sexual assault, and aggravated assault. She also found the sentences varied, from one-year imprisonment and probation in the first case (*R. v. Sumner* [1989]) to 11 years in *R. v. Mercer* (1993), which was the first case in Canada to impose consecutive sentences for more than one complainant. Grant points out that in most of the cases before 1998 assault-based charges were unsuccessful due to the apparent consent given by the complainant to engage in sexual activity.

In 1998, the Supreme Court decided to hear its first HIV-related case when an individual failed to disclose his condition to his sexual partners (*R. v. Cuerrier*). In this case, the accused had been charged with two counts of aggravated assault on the basis that his nondisclosure of his HIV-positive status constituted fraud under s. 265(3) of the Criminal Code. Mr. Cuerrier had been informed by public health officials in 1992 that he had tested positive for HIV and told to use a condom whenever he engaged in sexual intercourse and to inform any potential partners that he was HIV-positive. However, Mr. Currier refused the advice and had unprotected sexual intercourse. Two complainants testified in court that they wouldn't have engaged in unprotected sex with Mr. Currier if they had realized that he was HIV-positive. Mr. Currier was acquitted by both the trial judge and the British Columbia Court of Appeal. The Supreme Court unanimously held that any individual who conceals or fails to disclose that he or she is HIV-positive has committed a type of fraud that vitiates any apparent consent on the part of the victim to engage in sexual activity. According to the Supreme Court, persons who know that they are HIV-positive and fail to inform their sexual partners may be found to fulfill the traditional requirements for fraud, namely dishonesty and deprivation. Until this case, s. 265(3) stated that no consent was obtained when a complainant submits or does not resist as a result of the actual use of force or fear of the use of force, either to them or someone else. This section also stated that an alleged consent obtained by fraud or by the use of authority is not real consent. The Supreme Court sent the case back to British Columbia on the charge of aggravated sexual assault, but the Crown decided not to retry the case.

After 1998, Grant found 31 completed cases during the next nine years (1999 to 2007) where the accused were charged with either aggravated assault or aggravated sexual assault, with some of the cases involving other charges such as nuisance and criminal negligence causing bodily harm. Of these 31 cases, convictions were obtained in 26 (more than 50 percent of these cases involved guilty pleas), 4 ended in acquittals, and in the remaining case the accused was found guilty of sexual assault causing bodily harm against the five-year-old daughter of the original adult victim. The HIV virus was transmitted in 15 of the 31 cases to at least one complainant, sometimes more.

Since *Currier,* the Supreme Court of Canada has considered the willful transmission of HIV in two other cases (*R. v. Thornton* [1993]; *R. v. Williams* [2003]). In both of these cases, the Supreme Court upheld the convictions. In *R. v. Mercer* (1993), it denied leave to appeal in which the Newfoundland Court of Appeal had raised a sentence from 30 months to 11 years. According to Grant (2008, 14), the decisions made by the Supreme Court indicates "we have a clear indication from the Court, without a single dissenting voice, that criminal law is an appropriate tool to use in the most serious cases involving an accused who knows he is HIV-positive but fails to inform that status to sexual partners. The majority of the Supreme Court has given short shrift to the various arguments against criminalization . . ."

A number of arguments have been made in favour of removing HIV-nondisclosure from the Criminal Code. Those who support the idea of noncriminalization point out that recent research indicates that "the possibility of transmitting HIV is dramatically reduced when treatments are used," the need to update criminal justice system in order "to reflect the idea that HIV is no longer the immediate death sentence it was when the legal obligation to disclose HIV was set" as well as what the implications of criminalization "will be on public health strategies for HIV prevention" (Mykhalovskiy 2009, A12). Grant (2008) adds that issues such as the stigmatization of the offender needs to be considered as well as the difficulties in prosecuting these cases need to be considered. Those who support the criminalization of HIV-nondisclosure argue that there is a

need to isolate the accused, to deter others, as well as retribution (ibid.).

Questions

1. Do you agree that individuals who know they are HIV-positive but fail to inform their sexual partners after they have been told to by the authorities should be dealt with in the criminal courts?
2. The Crown prosecutor wanted to apply the dangerous offender to Mr. Leone. Do you believe that people with HIV and who fail to disclose that fact to their partners despite being warned to do so by the authorities should be given a dangerous offender status?
3. As medical treatment for those with HIV advances do you think the criminalization of those who engage in sex without disclosure will end?
4. Do you believe that by implementing the nondisclosure law that individuals with HIV who practise safety in their relations with others will be stigmatized?

SUMMARY

The basis of our criminal justice system is protection of law-abiding citizens through the operation of the law. The criminal justice system develops, administers, and enforces the criminal law. The federal government defines crime, but the actual administration of justice is in the hands of provincial governments; thus, one can find variations in the operation of our legal system across Canada. Crimes are categorized as indictable or summary conviction offences, depending on their seriousness.

Our understanding of what constitutes criminal conduct changes over time. Today the Criminal Code is a complex document, because our knowledge of criminal behaviour has increased dramatically over the past

decade. In recent years, Canada has passed laws designed to combat panhandlers as well as organized criminal groups such as gangs. These changes in the law have been both procedural and substantive in nature.

In our system of law, all individuals are considered innocent until proven guilty. To establish guilt, the court must find that the accused possessed *mens rea* and that he or she committed the act in question. The prosecution must prove these facts in court beyond a reasonable doubt. Whatever the standards our criminal justice system employs in the courtroom, the public's perception of our legal system is different from that of our legal professionals. In general, the public considers violent actions to be more serious offences than property crimes.

Discussion Questions

1. Define the word "law."
2. What are the goals of the criminal law?
3. What is a crime? When are individuals criminally liable for their actions?
4. Discuss the kinds of crime classifications that we use in Canada. Should we use other classifications, such as an offence index or a white-collar-crime index?
5. Can you think of any laws that should be revised and made stronger? How would this help control the behaviour you have in mind?
6. Do you think Crown prosecutors should have the power to determine whether a hybrid offence will proceed as an indictable offence or a summary conviction offence?
7. Do you think public opinion should be considered by legal officials as an important component in the development of or change in crime and legal policies?
8. Why do you think some people don't consider most white-collar crimes to be serious offences? Can you think of any recent examples that show that white-collar crimes have serious results?
9. Do you think the punishments for summary conviction offences should be made harsher?

Suggested Readings

Barnhorst, R., and S. Barnhorst. *Criminal Law and the Canadian Criminal Code,* 4th ed. Toronto: McGraw-Hill Ryerson, 2004.

Boyd, N. *Criminal Law: An Introduction,* 2nd ed. Toronto: Harcourt Brace Canada, 1998.

Hiebert, J.L. *Charter Conflicts: What Is Parliament's Role?* Montreal: McGill-Queen's University Press, 2002.

Mewett, A.W., and S. Nakatsuru. *An Introduction to the Criminal Process in Canada,* 4th ed. Scarborough, ON: Carswell, 2000.

Roach, K. *Essentials of Criminal Law,* 3rd ed. Concord, ON: Irwin Law, 2004.

Roberts, J.V., and R.M. Mohr, eds. *Confronting Sexual Abuse: A Decade of Legal and Social Change.* Toronto: University of Toronto Press, 1994.

Verdun-Jones, S. *Canadian Criminal Cases: Selected Highlights.* Toronto: Harcourt Brace Canada, 1999.

References

Abbate, G. 2000. "Lawyers to Get Code of Conduct on Evidence." *The Globe and Mail,* November 30, A8.

Anderssen, E. 2000. "Supreme Court Upholds Rape-Shield Law." *The Globe and Mail,* October 13, A7.

Appleby, T. 2005. "Bikers Convicted in Extortion Case." *The Globe and Mail,* July 1, A5.

Bala, N. 1997. *Young Offenders and the Law.* Concord, ON: Irwin Law.

Barnhorst, R., and S. Barnhorst. 2004. *Criminal Law and the Canadian Criminal Code,* 4th ed. Toronto: McGraw-Hill Ryerson.

Billingsley, B. 2002. "The Rule of Law: What Is It? Why Should We Care?" *LawNow,* 26, no. 5: 27–30.

Blatchford, C. 2000. "Ken Murray's Not-So-Excellent Adventure." *Canadian Lawyer* 24, no. 10: 28–33.

Bowland, A.L. 1994. "Sexual Assault Trials and Protection of 'Bad Girls': The Battle Between the Courts and Parliament." In J.V. Roberts and R.M. Mohr, eds., *Confronting Sexual Assault: A Decade of Legal and Social Change.* Toronto: University of Toronto Press, pp. 241–67.

Brannigan, A. 1984. *Crimes, Courts, and Corrections: An Introduction to Crime and Social Control in Canada.* Toronto: Holt, Rinehart, and Winston.

Brown, S., F.A. Esbensen, and G. Geis. 1991. *Criminology: Explaining Crime and Its Content.* Cincinnati: C J Anderson.

Brucker, T.M. 1992. "Disclosure and the Role of the Police in the Criminal Justice System." *Criminal Law Quarterly* 35: 57–76.

Burnett, H. 2007. "Decision Creates Concern." www.lawtimesnews.ca. Retrieved November 18, 2007.

Canadian Broadcasting Corporation. 2007. "Panhandling Charges Soar in 2007: Toronto Police." www.cbc.ca. Retrieved April 16, 2009.

Chwialkowska, L. 2001. "Judge's OK Not Needed for Officers to Break Law." *National Post,* December 22, B4.

———. 2000. "Rape-Shield Law Upheld by High Court." *National Post,* October 13, A14.

Daniels, R.J., P. Macklem, and K. Roach, eds. 2001. *The Security of Freedom: Essays on Canada's Anti-Terrorism Bill.* Toronto: University of Toronto Press.

Davison, C. 2006. "The Rule of Law Is Our Legal Bedrock." *LawNow* 31: 8–11.

———. 2005. "Developments in Criminal Law." *LawNow* 29: 18–20.

Gazette. 2006. "Behind the Antigang Law." Ottawa: RCMP.

Geis, G. 1974. *Not the Law's Business.* New York: Schocken.

Gotell, L. 2008. "Tacking Decisions on Access to Sexual Assault Complainants' Confidential Records: The Continued Permeability of Subsections 278.1–278.9 of the Criminal Code." *Canadian Journal of Women and the Law,* 20: 111–54.

———. 2002. "The Ideal Victim, The Hysterical Complainant, and the Disclosure of Confidential Records: The Implications of the Charter for Sexual Assault Law." *Osgoode Hall Law Journal,* 3 & 4: 251–95.

Grant, I. 2008. "The Boundaries of the Criminal Law: The Criminalization of the Non-disclosure of HIV. *Dalhousie Law Journal* 31, Spring. www.lexisnexis.com. Retrieved April 5, 2009.

Hall, J. 1947. *Theft, Law and Society,* 2nd ed. Indianapolis: Bobbs-Merrill.

Hermer, J., and J. Mosher. 2002. *Disorderly People: Law and the Politics of Exclusion in Ontario.* Halifax: Fernwood.

Hiebert, J.L. 2002. *Charter Conflicts: What Is Parliament's Role?* Montreal: McGill-Queen's University Press.

House of Common Debates. 1986. 26 May. Hansard VI: 62.

Humphreys, A. 2009. "Appeals Court Quashes Hells Angels' Anti-gang Law Challenge." *National Post,* June 29. www.nationalpost.com. Retrieved June 30, 2009.

———. 2001. "Anti-Gang Law to Get Tougher." *National Post,* April 5, A4.

Kay, B. 2009. "A Fraudster, Not a Murderer." *National Post*, April 8. www
.nationalpost.com. Retrieved May 1, 2009.

Law Reform Commission of Canada. 1974. *Discovery in Criminal Cases*. Ottawa:
Justice Canada.

"Leone Jailed 18 Years for HIV Sex Crimes." 2008. *National Post*, April 4.
www.nationalpost.com. Retrieved May 1, 2009.

Los, M. 1994. "The Struggle to Redefine Rape in the Early 1980s." In J.V. Roberts
and R.M. Mohr, eds., *Confronting Sexual Assault: A Decade of Legal and Social
Change*. Toronto: University of Toronto Press, pp. 20–56.

———. 1999. "Top Court Bows to Will of Parliament." *The Globe and Mail*,
November 26, A1, A7.

Majury, D. 1994. "Seaboyer and Gayme: A Study Inequality." In J.V. Roberts and
R.M. Mohr, eds., *Confronting Sexual Assault: A Decade of Legal and Social Change*.
Toronto: University of Toronto Press, pp. 268–92.

Makin, K. 2007. "Top Court Ruling Criticized as Attack on Right to Silence."
The Globe and Mail, November 2, A6.

McDonald, S., and A. Wobick 2004. "Bill C-46 Case Law Review." *JustResearch*
11: 14–19.

McIntyre, M. 2000. "Warriors Case Ends with a Whimper." *Winnipeg Free Press*,
July 6, A1, A4.

McKay-Panos, L. 1998–99. "Indefinite Sentence/No Criminal Conviction."
LawNow, 23: 24–31.

Mohr, R.M., and J.V. Roberts. 1994. "Sexual Assault in Canada: Recent
Developments." In J.V. Roberts and R.M. Mohr, eds., *Confronting Sexual
Assault: A Decade of Legal and Social Change*. Toronto: University of Toronto
Press, pp. 3–19.

Mykhalovskiy, E. 2009. "HIV Legal Policy Needs Debate." *The Globe and Mail*,
April 9, A12.

Panetta, A. 2001. "Judge Rules against Bikers, Upholds Law against Group." *The
Globe and Mail*, January 31, A7.

Perkel, D. 2009. "AIDS-trial Jury Asks to Review Deathbed Interview." *The Globe
and Mail*, April 3, A11.

Prokaska, L. 2009. "HIV Murder Conviction the Right Thing to Do." *Winnipeg
Free Press*, April 9, A10.

Public Safety Canada. 2008. *Corrections and Conditional Release Statistical Overview*.
www.publicsafety.gc.ca. Retrieved April 24, 2009.

"Rape Shield for All." 2000. *National Post*, March 6, A19.

Roach, K. 2004. *Criminal Law*, 3rd ed. Concord, ON: Irwin Law.

Roberts, J.V., and R.M. Mohr, eds. 1994. *Confronting Sexual Assault: A Decade of
Legal and Social Change*. Toronto: University of Toronto Press.

Ruddick, S. 2002. "Metamorphosis Revisited: Restricting Discourses of Citizenship."
In J. Hermer and J. Mosher, eds., *Disorderly People: Law and the Politics of
Exclusion in Ontario*. Halifax: Fernwood, pp. 55–64.

Senna, J.J., and L.J. Siegel. 1995. *Essentials of Criminal Justice*. Minneapolis, MN: West.

Sharpe, R.J., and K. Roach. 2005. *The Charter of Rights and Freedoms*, 3rd ed.
Toronto: Irwin Law.

Silverman, R., and L.W. Kennedy. 1993. *Deadly Deeds: Murder in Canada*. Scarborough,
ON: Nelson Canada.

Skolnick, J. 1966. *Justice without Trial.* New York: Wiley.

"Smoking Guns: Beyond the Murray Case." 2000. *Criminal Law Quarterly* 43, 409–10.

Sneiderman, B. 2000. "Latimer in the Supreme Court: Necessity, Compassionate Harm and Mandatory Sentencing." *Saskatchewan Law Review* 64: 511–44.

Stuart, D. 1997. "Politically Expedient but Potentially Unjust Legislation against Gangs." *Canadian Criminal Law Review* 2: 207–16.

———. 1994. "Policing under the Charter." In R.C. MacLeod and D. Schneider, eds., *Police Powers in Canada: The Evolution and Practice of Authority.* Toronto: University of Toronto Press, pp. 75–99.

Tappan, P. 1966. "Who Is the Criminal?" *American Sociological Review* 12: 96–102.

Territo, L., J.B. Halsted, and M.L. Bromley. 1995. *Crime and Justice in America,* 4th ed. Minneapolis, MN: West.

Thanh Ha, T. 2001. "Biker Case Puts Quebec Antigang Law on Trial." *The Globe and Mail,* January 16, A3.

Tibbetts, J. 2009. "Ottawa Mulls Gang Blacklist." *National Post,* May 11. www .nationalpost.com. Retrieved May 11, 2009.

———. 2006. "Top Court Clears Wife Who Killed in a Trance." *National Post,* April 28, A6.

Tochor, M.D., and K.D. Kilback. 1999. "Defence Disclosure: Is It Written in Stone?" *Criminal Law Quarterly* 43: 393–408.

Verdun-Jones, S. 1989. *Criminal Law in Canada: Cases, Questions, and the Code.* Toronto: Harcourt Brace Jovanovich.

Wheeler, G. 1987. "The Police, the Crowns, and the Courts: Who's Running the Show?" *Canadian Lawyer.* February.

Court Cases

Gayme v. R. (1991), 6 C.C.C. (3d) 321 (S.C.C.)

Hunter v. Southam Inc. (1984), 2 S.C.R. 145, 11 D.L.R. (4th) 641

R. v. Askov (1990), 59 C.C.C. (3d) 449, 59 C.C.C. (3d) 449

R. v. Banks (2005), O. J. 98

R. v. Banks (2007), ONCA 19

R. v. Bleta (1964), S.C.R. 561

R. v. Borden (1994), 3 S.C.R. 145

R. v. Broyles (1991), 3 S.C.R. 595, 68 C.C.C. (3e) 308

R. v. Brydges (1990), 1 S.C.R. 190, 53 C.C.C. (3d) 330

R. v. Burgess (1970), 3 C.C.C.268 (Ont. C.A.)

R v. Carosella (1997), 112 C.C.C. (3d) 289 (S.C.C.)

R. v. Chaulk (1994), 91 C.C.C. (3d)

R. v. Cinous (2002), 2 S.C.R. 3

R. v. Collins (1987), 1 S.C.R. 265, 33 C.C.C. (3d) 1

R. v. Cuerrier (1998), 2 S.C.R. 371

R. v. Darrach (2000), 2 S.C.R. 443

R. v. Daviault (1994), 33 C.R. (4th) 165

R. v. Duarte (1990), 1 S.C.R. 30

R. v. Duguay (1985), 46 C.C.C. (3) 1 (S.C.C.)

R. v. Ewanchuk (1999), 131 C.C.C. (3d) 481

R. v. Forster (1997), 70 C.C.C. (3d)

R. v. Gayme (1991), 2 S.C.R. 577, 7 C.R. (4th) 117

R. v. Goltz (1991), 3 S.C.R. 485, 67 C.C.C. (3d) 481

R. v. Graveline (2006), S.C.C. 16

R. v. Hebert (1990), 2 S.C.R. 151, 57 C.C.C. (3d) 1

R. v. Hibbert (1995), 2 S.C.R. 973

R. v. Hufsky (1988), 40 C.C.C. (3d) 398 (S.C.C.)

R. v. Jacoy (1988), 45 C.C.C. (3d) 46

R. v. Kalanj (1989), 1 S.C.R. 1594, 48 C.C.C. (3d) 459

R. v. King (1962), 133 C.C.C. 1

R. v. Kokesch (1990), 3 S.C.R. 3, 61 C.C.C. (3d) 207

R. v. Kuldip (1990), 3 S.C.R. 618, 61 C.C.C.(3d) 385

R. v. Kundeus (1971), 24 C.C.C. (2d) 276

R. v. Langlois (1993), 19 C.R. (4th) 87 (Que. C.A.)

R. v. Lavallee (1990), 55 C.C.C. (3d)

R. v. Luxton (1990), 2 S.C.R. 711, 58 C.C.C. (3d) 449

R. v. Mack (1988), 44 C.C.C. (3d)

R. v. Manninen (1987), 34 C.C.C. (3d) 385

R. v. Mannion (1986), 2 S.C.R. 272, 28 C.C.C. (3d) 353

R. v. Marshall (1971), 1 C.C.C. (2d) 505

R. v. McNeil (2009), S.C.C. 3

R. v. Mercer (1993), 84 C.C.C. (3d) 41

R. v. Mills (1986), 1 S.C.R. 863, 29 D.L.R. (4th) 161

R. v. Mills (1999), 3 S.C.R. 668

R. v. Murray (2000), 186 D.L.R. (4th) 125

R. v. Oakes (1986), 24 C.C.C. (3d) 321

R. v. O'Connor (1995), 123 C.C.C. (3d) 487 (B.C.C.A.)

R. v. Pappajohn (1980), 52 C.C.C. (2d) 483

R. v. Parks (1992), 75 C.C.C. (3d) 287

R. v. Perka (1984), 2 S.C.R. 232

R. v. Rabey (1977), 37 C.C.C. (2d) 463

R. v. Rodgers (2006), S.C.C. 15

R. v. Ross (1989), 49 C.C.C. (3d) 475

R. v. Ruzic (2001), 1 S.C.R. 687

R. v. Seaboyer (1991), 66 C.C.C. (3d) 321 (S.C.C.)

R. v. Simpson (1993), 79 C.C.C. (3d) 482 (Ont. C.A.)

R. v. Singh (2007), S.C.C. 48

R. v. Stinchcombe (1991), 3 S.C.R. 326, 68 C.C.C. (3d) 1

R. v. Stone (1999), 134 C.C.C. (3d) 353

R. v. Sumner (1989), 98 A.R. 191

R. v. Swain (1991), 1 S.C.R. 933

R. v. Therens (1985), 18 C.C.C. (3d) 481

R. v. Thomsen (1988), 40 C.C.C. (3d) 411(S.C.C.)

R. v. Thornton (1993), 2 S.C.R. 445

R. v. Tran (1994), 2 S.C.R. 951, 117 D.L.R. (4th) 7

R. v. Tremblay (1987), 37 C.C.C. (3d) 565 (S.C.C.)

R. v. Turcotte (2005), 2 S.C.R. 519

R. v. Williams (2003), 2 S.C.R. 134

R. v. Wong (1990), 3 S.C.R. 36, 60 C.C.C. (3d) 460

Resolution to Amend the Constitution, Re, (1981), 1 S.C.R. 753, 125 D.L.R. (3d) 1

Seaboyer v. R. (1991), 6 C.C.C. (3d) 321 (S.C.C.)

Smith v. R. (1987), 34 C.C.C. (3d) 97 (S.C.C.)

Weblinks

This chapter mentions some of the most influential decisions made by the Supreme Court of Canada during the 1990s. For three of its decisions regarding sexual assault in Canada, go to http://scc.lexum.umontreal.ca/en/index.html and read the following cases by clicking on the year that the decision was announced and then locating the relevant volume number for the case:

R. v. Seaboyer (1991) and *R. v. Gayme* (1991) Vol. 2, August 22, 1991.

R. v. Carosella (1997) Vol. 1, February 1997.

R. v. Ewanchuk (1999) Vol. 1, February 25, 1999.

Control Philosophy and Criminal Justice Policy

CHAPTER OBJECTIVES

✓ Understand the differences and similarities among the four different punitive models of criminal justice in terms of criminal sanctions and the operations of the major components of the criminal justice system.

✓ Understand the differences between the two different non-punitive models in terms of criminal sanctions and the operations of the major components of the criminal justice system.

✓ Identify the differences between the punitive and non-punitive approaches to crime control in society.

✓ Recognize the basic elements of an Aboriginal justice system and how they differ from those in all other approaches.

✓ Recognize how each of these models approaches the general category of "sex offenders."

U nderlying our criminal justice system are four distinct philosophies. Two of these—**deterrence** and **rehabilitation**—have traditionally guided criminal justice. Deterrence emerged in the eighteenth century, while rehabilitation gained prominence in our criminal justice system in the early twentieth century. Over the past 35 years, these two philosophies have been joined by two others: selective incapacitation and the justice model. The **selective incapacitation model** focuses primarily on those individuals labelled "dangerous"; the **justice model** is probably the dominant criminal justice policy today, as it forms the basis of the Canadian Charter of Rights and Freedoms. More recently, restorative justice and Aboriginal justice systems have been introduced as alternatives to the crime control approaches long used in Canadian society. Restorative justice has been embraced by the federal and provincial governments; the acceptance of Aboriginal justice systems—particularly those separate from the Canadian justice system—has been much slower. This chapter summarizes how each of these major crime control philosophies would operate in Canada today if it operated as a "stand-alone" system. The discussion of each of these crime control philosophies also features an example: how it would deal with sexual offenders.

Concerns about how our criminal justice system should respond to sexual offenders and sexual offending have become a major issue in Canada in the past decade or so. Sexual offences do not account for a large number of the crimes reported each year in this country—24,233 incidents involving sexual offences were reported to the police in Canada during 2007, accounting for 1 percent of total Criminal Code incidents. Due to the violent nature of such offences and high profile nature of some of the cases reported by the media, members of the public are constantly demanding that the criminal justice system do a better job of controlling those who are convicted of committing these offences. Consequently, new laws and programs have been introduced (some of which are discussed in this chapter) in the past decade or so, and other approaches have been revised to allow the authorities more control over sexual offenders once they have been released back into society.

Some sexual offences involve violent behaviour—in 2008, for example, sexual offences accounted for 5 percent of all incidents reported to the police in the category "Violent Crime." The majority of these offences were sexual assaults. Sexual assault (level 1) accounted for 86 percent of all reported sexual offences; the category "other sexual offences" accounted for 12 percent; sexual assault (levels 2 and 3) accounted for the remaining 2 percent (Dauvergne 2008).

Sexual offenders are often charged with committing more criminal offences than are other types of offenders. For example, Kong and colleagues (2003) report that during 2001–02, adult sexual offenders—in particular those charged with offences in the category of "other sexual offences"—appeared in criminal court with a higher percentage of multiple charges per case, "indicating a higher tendency toward repeat offending prior to being reported to the police." They also found that in those same years 33 percent of all individuals appearing in adult criminal courts across Canada charged with a sexual offence as the most serious charge faced three or more charges—a figure higher than for those individuals convicted for either violent or property offences.

A number of offenders convicted of sexual offences are sentenced to long terms of incarceration, with many serving their time in a federal correctional facility (i.e., serving a sentence of two years or more). In May 2003, for example, there were 2,859 sexual offenders serving a sentence of two or more years in Canada. Of this total, 19 were women. Approximately 70 percent of these offenders were incarcerated; the remaining individuals were under some form of community supervision. Sexual offenders accounted for approximately 16 percent of the total number of individuals incarcerated in the federal correctional system in 2003, a slight decrease from 18 percent in 2001.

One of the biggest questions facing policymakers is how best to control criminal behaviour. In attempting to exert this control, policymakers must consider an array of choices. For example, should they try to rehabilitate offenders? Or should they try to develop prevention programs in an effort to stop criminal activities before they start? Sometimes it might be better to sentence offenders to very long periods of incarceration since this would protect society over the long term. Other times, however, depending on the type of offence and the background of the offender, it may be better to consider alternative approaches, such as restorative justice. Whichever approach is chosen, the legal rights of the offender must always be considered.

This chapter presents different ways of understanding how each of the crime control philosophies has the potential to influence the criminal justice system.

First, the four major contemporary criminal justice policies—the justice model, deterrence, selective incapacitation, and rehabilitation—are presented in as pure a form as possible. This discussion is followed by a review of the two most recent models to emerge—restorative justice and Aboriginal justice. Then each of these crime control philosophies is considered in the context of a single issue: What is the best way to deal with sexual offenders?

CRIME CONTROL IN CANADA

One of the most common complaints made against the criminal justice system is that it is too soft on criminals. Critics readily point to a series of shortcomings—criminals are granted parole and then commit more crimes, plea bargaining is rife, judges' sentences are too lenient, and police officers warn too many offenders instead of arresting them. When left unchecked, critics argue, these approaches contribute to rising crime rates. Others argue, in contrast, that parole boards make informed decisions concerning prisoners, that plea bargaining is a useful and valid practice, and that judicial discretion in sentencing is a positive thing. These people insist that social problems are the greatest contributors to increasing crime rates and that such problems cannot be addressed by a hardening of the criminal justice system.

These opinions spill over into significant public-policy debates. Should there be mandatory sentences for all convicted criminals? Should convicted violent offenders never be allowed out of prison? Should plea bargaining be banned? Should police budgets be increased dramatically so that more officers can be hired? Finally, should judicial discretion be banned outright or at least closely controlled?

Many observers say that because of the complexity of the criminal justice system today, it would be extremely difficult to introduce clear policy directives capable of influencing that system's operations. The informal operations of the system, and the self-interests of the various groups that work within it, would make improvement difficult. All of these "real world" points are valid; even so, in the following sections the major crime control models will be discussed as ideals.

CRIME CONTROL PHILOSOPHY AND CRIMINAL JUSTICE POLICY

Four main philosophies guide our criminal justice system: the justice model, deterrence, selective incapacitation, and rehabilitation. Because these philosophies are constantly being revised and updated, many people speak of "neo-deterrence" and "neo-rehabilitation" systems. While legislators and other policymakers use these models to guide their policies, none of the philosophies exclusively guides our criminal justice system. Usually, two or more are combined. For example, when the Young Offenders Act was enacted in 1984, it was grounded almost exclusively in the strategies of the deterrence and justice philosophies—in fact, the rehabilitation of young offenders was rarely mentioned. In 2003, when the Youth Criminal Justice Act was introduced, replacing the Young Offenders Act, deterrence, rehabilitation, and the justice model were combined to form the Act's Declaration of Principles (s. 3[1]). In addition, s. 4 of the new Act added restorative justice principles to the Declaration of Principles. Combining models leads to confusion about which strategy is most important in a given situation; it also raises questions about what leads to the success or failure of any particular crime control initiative.

These philosophies address different issues, although some share certain features. For example, only rehabilitation focuses on the criminal actor, so it emphasizes treating most convicted criminals. The other three philosophies focus on the criminal act, albeit in different ways. For example, the justice model focuses exclusively on the criminal act committed by the alleged perpetrator, with punishment based on the seriousness of the offence. The deterrence and selective incapacitation philosophies, like the justice model, focus on the act, but for the purpose of preventing future crimes. In contrast to the justice model, however, the issue of the current criminal offence is of secondary importance.

Though some overlap exists among some of these philosophies, they are better understood in terms of their differences. Price and Stitt (1986) developed a framework for comparing the philosophies and policies, showing how each strategy approaches crime control through criminal sanctions and showing the policy implications of each. The following description of the four philosophies follows the Price and Stitt outline.

THE JUSTICE MODEL

History

The justice model, though a recent creation, has had a strong impact on the criminal justice system. The first important document to offer support for the justice model appeared in *Struggle for Justice* (1971), written by the American Friends Service Committee. This committee, developed as a response to an analysis of a prison riot near New York City, recommended that the criminal justice

system be guided by the ideals of justice, fairness, and the need to protect human rights and dignity. It also recommended the elimination of the discretionary powers held by prosecutors, the judiciary, and parole boards.

One of its most important findings was that a sentence needed to fit the offence, not the offender. All individuals convicted of a certain offence must receive the same sentence; however, repeat offenders ought to be given longer sentences than first-time offenders for the same crime. This message was repeated by Marvin Frankel, a U.S. federal judge, whose book *Criminal Sentences: Law without Order* (1972) recommended that the justice system be based on the principles of objectivity, fairness, and consistency. He also argued that criminal offences should be ranked according to their severity and that punishments should reflect the severity of the crimes.

Perhaps the most influential argument for a justice model–based criminal justice system came from the Committee for the Study of Incarceration. It published a book, *Doing Justice* (1975) which proposed the creation of sentencing guidelines based on the seriousness of the crime and the prior record of the offender. It also proposed shorter punishments for most crimes as well as the expansion of alternative sanctions.

The first criminal justice systems based on the justice model emerged in the United States during the 1970s and early 1980s. Maine enacted its new legislation in 1975, followed by California (1976), Minnesota (1981), Pennsylvania (1982), and Washington (1984). While these states varied in the particulars, their systems shared a number of features—namely, the elimination or control of prosecutorial discretion, the abolition of individualized sentencing practices, limited treatment programs for prisoners, and the termination of early-release programs such as parole (Griset 1991). During the late 1980s in Canada, the Canadian Sentencing Commission (1987) proposed a similar approach, but it was never introduced into public policy.

The Criminal Sanction

According to the justice model, the essential factor "is to punish offenders—fairly and with justice—through lengths of confinement proportionate to the gravity of their crimes" (Logan 1993). The punishment must be proportionate to the crime—specifically, the most serious crimes deserve the most severe punishments, in accordance with the doctrine of proportionality. In addition, the rights of the accused must be guaranteed through due process protections, from arrest to incarceration (Hudson 1987).

The justice model assumes that a direct relationship exists between the seriousness of the offence and the severity of the punishment. Ideally, any personal circumstances of those involved in the crime are ignored. The only information the justice model needs to know about an offender is that person's prior record. This "ensures the individual is not made to suffer disproportionately for the sake of social gain" and that "disproportionate leniency" as well as "disproportionate severity" are not allowed (Hudson 1987; von Hirsch 1976). An example of a violation of the principle of proportionality would be a mandatory five-year prison term for parking violators; here, the punishment would far outweigh the seriousness of the offence, since we can assume that parking violators could be dissuaded by other, lighter sanctions, such as towing or fines.

In Canada, the federal government determines the proportionality of sentences that link a criminal offence to its punishment. While it is easy to conclude that a violent criminal should receive a more severe punishment than an individual convicted of a lesser offence, such as an act of vandalism, the development of a comprehensive scale of proportional punishments is a difficult task, given the wide variety of crimes found in our Criminal Code. Should a person who sexually assaults a child receive a longer sentence than a person who robs a bank at gunpoint? If we are to create a workable system of punishment based on proportionality, much discussion will be required, since the seriousness of crimes and the unpleasantness of crimes are not objective facts.

One major contribution of the justice model to the area of punishment is that it supports the creation and proliferation of alternative sanctions, such as when a convicted person is allowed to serve part or all of the punishment in the community. The justice model prefers alternative sanctions for minor offences. Thus, any individual who is convicted of an offence in those categories designated as minor usually receives an alternative sentence allowing him or her to serve the sentence in the community. Community service orders and probation orders are favoured for many first- and second-time property offenders. This means that many offenders don't serve time in a prison facility, unless of course the number of their prior convictions grows beyond a certain point. Dangerous violent offenders, however, will always be incarcerated for the longest periods of time, even if they have no prior convictions.

One significant aspect of the justice model is that it guarantees due process rights for all individuals accused of committing a crime (see Exhibit 3.1). Pretrial, trial, and post-trial procedural rights are guaranteed, so that every suspect receives protections to ensure that criminal justice officials do not overextend their powers. In addition, anyone under investigation or charged with an offence is presumed to be factually innocent before proven legally guilty. Thus, although someone may admit to police investigators that he or she committed the crime (i.e., factual guilt), that person's guilt nonetheless has to be established (i.e., legal guilt) in a court of law. Due process ensures that only the facts of the case are at issue, that evidence is collected according to the rules established by the courts, that formal hearings with impartial arbitrators are held, and that procedural regularity is maintained. Extralegal issues are considered to be inconsistent with fundamental justice.

The Operations of a Justice Model-Based Criminal Justice System

The main concern of the justice model is to eliminate or control discretion within the criminal justice system, particularly as exercised by prosecutors, the judiciary, and parole boards. Supporters of the justice model argue that the main barrier to the attainment of justice is the discretion held by the key agencies in the criminal justice system. Concerns about discretion lead to concerns about the protection of rights for all accused. The solution is to operate the justice system in a fair and equitable manner. The main recommendations of the justice model are (1) to eliminate or control discretion; and (2) to enhance due process protections for all who enter the criminal justice system.

The role of the police is pivotal here, because their decisions affect all other groups involved in the later stages of the crime control process. The police will allocate most of their resources to investigating crimes classified as the most serious. Justice model considerations also will direct the way the police react to a crime, with minor offenders being recommended for diversion or other similar types of alternative sanction programs. Arrest and prosecution is more likely if the individual commits a serious crime and has an extensive criminal record.

Prosecutors would then have to prosecute the accused on the basis of all charges laid. This means that plea bargaining would be eliminated or strictly controlled by guidelines enacted by the legislative authorities. In reality, however, plea bargaining has proved to be difficult to ban. The State of Alaska banned all forms of plea bargaining in 1975, but the policy lasted only a few years, because, among other problems, the ban had no influence on the disposition of cases involving serious crimes. In addition, other criminal justice agencies (notably the police) increased their discretion prior to laying any charges (Rubenstein et al. 1980). The most popular policy has been to permit some plea bargaining

EXHIBIT 3.1   Have the Legal Rights of Sex Offenders Gone Too Far?

There will always be a debate between those who advocate for the accused's legal rights and those who argue that crime control should take precedence in judicial decisions. But can one side be taken too far? Many Canadians feel that the courts have gone too far in protecting the accused, much to the detriment of the law-abiding. In particular, some of the recent decisions made by the Supreme Court of Canada have been criticized for expanding the rights of the accused too far. This has led supporters of crime control to argue that Canada's top court is focusing too much on the principles of justice in its decisions while ignoring the reality of horrific crimes committed by sex offenders. Some of the most controversial decisions made by the Supreme Court in this area follow.

R. V. BORDEN

This case had a strong impact on the legal system because it created a law according to which bodily substances can be legally taken by the police for DNA analysis (see Chapter 6). Police in Nova Scotia were investigating two sexual assaults that occurred within a few months of each other. The police arrested a suspect for the second sexual assault, and they were certain that the same individual had committed the first, which involved a 69-year-old woman who had just returned from a prayer meeting. They requested a blood sample from the accused, but informed Borden that they only wanted it for the second investigation. The police didn't inform him that they really wanted to use the DNA analysis in connection with the sexual assault on the senior citizen. DNA linked this individual to both sexual offences. Borden was convicted and sentenced to six years' imprisonment, based on the results of the DNA test. The Appeal Division of the Supreme Court of Nova Scotia overturned Borden's conviction on the grounds that his legal rights had been violated under s. 8 of the Charter of Rights and Freedoms, which controls unlawful searches and seizures. The Crown appealed this verdict, but the Supreme Court of Canada agreed in a 7–0 ruling that the DNA evidence could not be admitted as evidence because the police did not tell Borden that the blood sample and the subsequent DNA analysis could be used against him. Although the suspect had voluntarily signed a consent form for the police, the Supreme Court ruled that the proper test was not consent but rather whether or not the suspect had enough information to give up the right to be secure from unreasonable seizure. It was up to the police to inform the suspect that they were going to

use his consent for a DNA test for both offences, not just the second one.

R. V. SWIETLINSKI

Swietlinski was convicted of the first degree murder of Mary Francis McKenna in 1976. He had stabbed her 132 times with five different knives. Although sentenced to a minimum of 25 years in a federal correctional facility, he applied for early parole under s. 745 of the Criminal Code. That section sets out a process for those convicted of first degree murder to apply for parole eligibility after 15 years (see Chapter 12). Swietlinski was granted the hearing, but during the proceedings the jurors were subject to "appeals" directed at their "passions" by the Crown prosecutor. The prosecutor told the jury, among other things, not to forget the victim in their decision, saying that "she doesn't have a chance to come before a group of people to ask for a second chance." Furthermore, the minimum security prison where Swietlinski was incarcerated was described as "too comfortable," and "his residency there was reward enough for good conduct in jail." Surprisingly, the lawyer representing Swietlinski took no exception to these and other similar comments made by the prosecutor. Ultimately, the jury refused the accused's request for the possibility of early parole, instead setting November 6, 2001, as the date on which he could again apply for parole (a date that corresponded to the end of the first 25 years of his sentence).

Swietlinski appealed the decision, arguing that in questioning certain witnesses and in his address to the jury, the Crown prosecutor had made "inflammatory" and "highly prejudicial remarks." The Supreme Court, in a 5–4 ruling, agreed with Swietlinski that he had been denied his right to a fair hearing and therefore deserved another jury review. The majority ruling was based on the opinion that the Crown prosecutor's role at a review hearing is much the same as it is at criminal trials—to assist the judge and jury in making decisions that lead to "the fullest possible justice" while avoiding "any appeal to passion." The minority ruling was based in large part on the silence of Swietlinski's lawyer, a silence that the jury interpreted as agreeing that the prosecutor's comments were not unfair.

R. V. SHARPE

In 1995, Sharpe was found possessing child pornography. He was charged with violating Canada's child pornography laws after police seized books, manuscripts, a computer disk, and photographs (Persky and Dixon 2001). At his trial in November 1998, Sharpe argued that two sections of Canada's child pornography law violated the Charter's freedom of expression guarantees. Mr. Justice Shaw of the B.C. Supreme Court agreed with Sharpe's defence and ruled that the child pornography section of the Criminal Code (which makes simple possession of such items a crime) was illegal since it violated s. 2 of the Charter. The provincial government appealed the ruling, but on June 30, 1999, the B.C. Court of Appeal (by a 2 to 1 vote) ruled in favour of Sharpe. The case was appealed to the Supreme Court of Canada, which in January 2001 overturned the B.C.

ruling and unanimously upheld the child pornography law. However, it also specified that certain exceptions existed: works of artistic merit and works of the imagination by a private individual as well as photographic depictions of oneself. The case was returned to British Columbia to be retried, and on March 26, 2002, Sharpe was convicted of two charges of possession of child pornography but acquitted of the two charges of possessing written child pornography. On May 2, 2002, Sharpe was sentenced to four months' home confinement.

Sources: Fine 1994a, 1994b, 1994c, 1997.

but to control it by developing strict guidelines to govern its use as it allows prosecutors to bargain with the accused about their knowledge of other, more serious, crimes or to gain evidence about other criminals who would otherwise not be charged.

Supporters of the justice model argue that the problem with traditional sentencing approaches is the great amount of discretion held by judges. This discretion has led to concerns about discrimination in sentencing, as some defendants receive more severe punishments apparently on the basis of their group characteristics—such as race or gender—instead of their crimes. To eliminate this problem, the justice model favours a determinate sentencing approach, in which all judges are required to follow sentencing guidelines. When deciding how much punishment a convicted offender receives, judges are to be influenced by the crime committed and the offender's prior record. Once the seriousness of the crime and prior record is established, the judge refers to the sentencing guidelines to determine the actual sentence. The research evaluating whether or not judges follow sentencing guidelines has found that they do (Kramer and Ulmer 1996; Marvell and Moody 1996).

The seriousness of the crime and the blameworthiness of the offender are the most significant criteria for determining the type of correctional facility or diversion program to which an offender is sent. Canadian correctional facilities are classified by security risk: maximum, medium, and minimum, with the most serious of all offenders being sent to a Special Handling Unit located in Quebec (see Chapter 12). Since most sentences in Canada only specify the maximum amount of time an individual is to serve before being released, the decision about the exact length of an inmate's period of incarceration is actually made by the parole board rather than a judge. The discretionary powers held by parole boards are

of concern to justice model advocates, since those boards can decide to release inmates before they have served the full length of their sentence. The justice model's solution is either to eliminate the parole board altogether (by eliminating parole) or to remove it from the decision to release an inmate. In the latter case, the parole board would be responsible only for parole supervision. It is conceivable, however, that the elimination of parole could lead to prison overcrowding, since no prisoners would be released early. To prevent overcrowding, convicted criminals would serve all their sentences, but sentence lengths would be shortened. When the justice model was instituted in Minnesota, almost all sentence lengths were reduced. The exception was for first degree murder, which remained punishable by a mandatory life sentence. The only exceptions to these policies would be the reduction of a sentence by 15 percent in exchange for an inmate's good behaviour during incarceration. Finally, while treatment programs would be offered to inmates, such programs would be limited in scope and voluntary in nature.

DETERRENCE

History

Deterrence is the oldest of the four major criminal justice philosophies. Its roots are in eighteenth-century Europe, where two reformers, one Italian (Cesare Beccaria) and the other English (Jeremy Bentham), proposed significant reforms to the criminal justice system. Both argued that the goal of the criminal justice system should be to prevent future crimes by individuals who had already been caught (i.e., **specific deterrence**) and by members of the broader society who might contemplate committing a crime (i.e., **general deterrence**).

Faced with a biased and barbaric system, Beccaria wrote *On Crimes and Punishment* (1764) in the hope of achieving equitable reforms that would eliminate favouritism. Note that Beccaria's recommendations became the source of modern criminal justice systems, including those in Canada and the United States. His book was the first widely read text to demand that due process rights be placed throughout the criminal justice system, that sentences reflect the harm done to the state and the victim, and that punishments be quick, certain, and contain a degree of deterrence. His key points (Beirne and Messerschmidt 1991, 290) were as follows:

- The right of governments to punish offenders derives from a contractual obligation among the citizenry not to pursue self-interest at the expense of others.
- Punishment must be constituted by uniform and enlightened legislation.
- Imprisonment must replace torture and capital punishment as the standard form of punishment.
- The punishment must fit the crime. It must be prompt and certain, and its duration must reflect only the gravity of the offence and the social harm caused.

Bentham argued that legislators must calculate the amount of punishment required to prevent crimes and punish criminals. This system, which he referred to as a calculus, could include both positive sanctions (rewards) and negative sanctions (punishment). In addition, he argued that the criminal justice system should operate in a manner that allows it to catch suspects with certainty, process criminal cases in a speedy yet efficient manner, and punish those convicted of a crime with an appropriate (not excessive) amount of punishment.

An important basis of this approach was the reformers' strong belief that all people are rational—that is, possess free will. Criminals differ from law-abiding individuals only because they choose to engage in criminal as opposed to non-criminal activities. Over time, however, legislators have recognized a number of limitations to these arguments. Today most Western legal codes recognize limits to criminal responsibility, including such factors as age, duress, and mental disorder.

Today, the **deterrence model** assumes that people participate in an action only after carefully considering the risks (or costs) and the benefits (or rewards). Punishment is supposed to induce compliance with the law, since people fear punishment and do not want to jeopardize their stake in conformity. According to the deterrence model, then, the point of punishment is to affect future behaviour rather than to inflict any pain that offenders might deserve as a result of their prior actions.

In reality, however, not all criminal actions are governed by careful consideration of the costs and benefits—some of them are unplanned and habitual. Some individuals choose not to engage in illegal behaviour because they lack the skills or opportunities to commit an act. At the same time, rational choice is involved in some criminal activity. Some offenders try to minimize the risks by planning their crimes, and select their targets on the basis of what they are to gain. However, many of these individuals make poor selections because they lack good information or overestimate what they will gain. On the other hand, they may underestimate the risk of punishment. In addition, many offenders have been found to act on impulse.

The Criminal Sanction

It is possible that a criminal penalty can act as a negative inducement, by discouraging people from engaging in behaviour that violates the law. According to Grasmick and Green (1980), deterrence is actually the threat of legal punishment, or fear of physical and material *deprivation* through legally imposed sanctions. Deterrence is an objective phenomenon, as it implies a behavioural result—specifically, the potential offender acts (or chooses not to act) because of fear that the illegal act could lead to capture and punishment. Supporters of the deterrence doctrine hope that any individual contemplating a crime will be deterred because of the certainty, or risk, that he or she will be caught and punished. Deterrence is also a perceptual phenomenon in the sense that potential criminals decide not to commit crimes on the basis of their perception that they may be caught and punished. Gibbs (1975, 2), a strong advocate of this model, defines deterrence as "the omission of an act as a response to the perceived risk and fear of punishment for contrary behavior."

The deterrence approach assumes a direct relationship between the certainty of punishment and the severity and swiftness of punishment. The severity is set at a level that maximizes its deterrent effect—that is, where "the pain of punishment would exceed the pleasure of the offense for a majority of potential offenders" (Price and Stitt 1986, 26). The deterrence philosophy places great emphasis on the efficient operation of the criminal justice system—specifically, on a reduction in court delays and in the time between arrest and trial (Feeley and Simon 1992). Yet researchers report that individuals have imperfect knowledge of the maximum penalties for various crimes. Behaviour choices are based on perceptions about the severity of sanctions, the certainty that the punishments will be applied, and the swiftness of the punishment (Apospori and Alpert 1993; Decker, Wright, and Logie 1993; Sherman and Berk 1984).

According to Chambliss (1969), some crimes are more easily deterred than others. Instrumental or goal-oriented behaviour, such as robbing a bank, is more easily deterred than expressive behaviour that results from the inner needs of the offender, such as a violent outburst. This distinction between instrumental and expressive acts is not easy to make: a person might commit a robbery to gain a sense of superiority over others (an expressive act) rather than to gain any material item (an instrumental act). Chambliss also states that the success or failure of deterrence is linked to the offender's commitment to crime. Offenders who are highly committed to a criminal lifestyle are more difficult to deter than those offenders who do not see crime as a way of life.

The Operations of a Deterrence-Based Criminal Justice System

Any deterrence-based criminal justice system would introduce policies to achieve the greatest certainty of capture, swiftness of prosecution, and—in cases of conviction for a crime—severity of punishment. The goal of this system is to prevent future crime. More emphasis is placed on protecting society and the law-abiding public than on protecting the individual rights of defendants. To ensure that the justice system and its agencies work to their maximum efficiency, more money would have to be spent on all criminal justice agencies. More police officers, prosecutors, judges, and correctional personnel would be hired, and more facilities such as jails, courts, and prisons would be built. Furthermore, the government would have to revise existing statute laws and pass new ones that would grant more powers to the police in the areas of investigation and apprehension, for the sole purpose of increasing the likelihood that suspected criminals are caught (see Exhibit 3.2). Essentially, the criminal justice system would operate like an assembly line, pushing offenders as efficiently as possible from arrest through conviction to punishment.

The number of police officers and resources involved in crime detection within a deterrence-based criminal justice system would increase, since police are the frontline agency in the "war on crime." Police patrol tactics would change to ensure that the maximum deterrent effect would be achieved by highly visible patrol vehicles. Police officers would be better educated and better trained, and receive the latest technology in order to increase the certainty of capture of criminals. But not all the new resources given to the police would be involved in actual crime fighting. Procedural laws that inhibit the police during their search for and arrest of criminals would be reduced. Emphasis would be placed on crime control and factual guilt. If, for example, a police officer accidentally violated the rights of an alleged offender during an investigation, this violation would probably be overlooked, assuming that the individual in question is guilty of the offence.

Not all of this increase in police resources would go to hiring more police for street-level patrols. The deterrence doctrine also supports the prevention of crime. As a result, more money would be given to proactive policing activities such as Neighbourhood Watch, Operation Identification, and Crime Stoppers programs. These programs, because they involve members of the community in the fight against crime, enable police to spend more time pursuing criminals, thereby increasing the probability of capture and subsequent punishment.

Deterrence advocates the control of all forms of plea bargaining. Price and Stitt (1986, 27) point out that controlling plea bargaining "could be the greatest single step to increase both certainty and severity of punishment." In addition, suspects awaiting trial would find it more difficult to receive bail, since they are presumed guilty. This means that most of the individuals arrested are guilty, particularly as they move past arrest and into the court system (Packer 1968). As was the case in the justice model, prosecutors would pursue all charges laid against the defendant by the police.

Judicial discretion would be eliminated. Governments would provide judges with a system of mandatory determinate sentences. This would lead not only to the uniformity of punishment but also to the certainty that an individual would receive a designated punishment. However, in contrast to the justice model, most sentences under a deterrence approach would become longer, in order to impress on individuals contemplating a crime that, if caught and convicted, they will be punished severely.

Parole would be abolished. More prisons would be built to house those guilty of an offence and to discourage potential criminals from committing a criminal offence by making them fearful of being caught and incarcerated. Risk assessments of offenders would become normal practice. Offenders would be placed into groups based on their predicted future behaviour. All sanctions would therefore be viewed in terms of their effectiveness at reducing the risk of further offences. At one extreme would be secure incarceration; at the other would be probation, with levels of intermediate punishments between (Morris and Tonry 1990).

EXHIBIT 3.2   Sex Offender Registry/DNA Data Bank

Two significant additions to the Criminal Code over the past decade have established a national DNA data bank (which contains the profiles of individuals convicted of the most serious crimes in Canada) and a national Sex Offender Registry (which contains the pertinent personal information of individuals convicted of committing a sexual offence). The purpose of the DNA bank is to help the police:

- solve crimes by linking crimes together when there are no suspects;
- identify suspects;
- eliminate suspects (i.e., when there is no match between crime scene DNA and a DNA profile in the National DNA Data Bank); and
- determine whether a serial offender is involved.

Before the DNA Identification Act was introduced, DNA samples could only be taken from declared dangerous offenders and those convicted of murder, attempted murder, sexual assault, robbery, assault, and break and enter with intent to commit an offence. Since this Act and the one establishing the Sex Offender Registry are both federal, both the bank and the registry are maintained by the RCMP.

The DNA Identification Act, enacted on June 30, 2000, requires convicted persons to provide blood or other bodily samples, which are then placed in the data bank. In other words, persons convicted of the most serious criminal offences in Canada (referred to as primary offences) are required to provide samples for the data bank. Primary offences include threatening violence, hijacking, sexual interference, murder, aggravated assault, and sexual assault. In addition, a judge can order an individual convicted of a less serious offence (i.e., a secondary offence) to provide a DNA sample as long as the facts of the case warrant it. Secondary offences include possession of child pornography, indecent acts, criminal negligence causing death, assaulting a peace officer, and robbery. The information in the data bank can then be used to ascertain whether someone previously convicted of an offence is involved in a current case.

The DNA bank consists of two distinct indexes. The Convicted Offender Index has been developed from the DNA profiles collected from offenders convicted of designated primary and secondary offences. The Crime Scene Index consists of DNA profiles collected through investigations of criminal acts mentioned in the DNA Act. As of May 1, 2006,

the DNA Data Bank had given the police 5,142 crime scene to offender "hits" and 751 crime scene to crime scene "hits." Over the same period, 94,299 DNA profiles have been entered into the Convicted Offender Index and another 28,457 DNA profiles into the Crime Scene Index.

DNA has greatly assisted the police in their criminal investigations. In addition, it has exonerated over 200 wrongfully convicted persons in North America. (Copyright © 2009 HER MAJESTY THE QUEEN IN RIGHT OF CANADA as represented by the Royal Canadian Mounted Police (RCMP). Reproduced with the permission of the RCMP.)

Bill C-13 (passed by Parliament in May 2005) expanded the criteria regarding who could be included in the DNA bank. DNA samples can now be gathered from all persons convicted before June 30, 2000, of murder, manslaughter, or a sexual offence who are still under sentence. After one year , approximately 2,000 individuals were compelled to give DNA samples retroactively. This policy was upheld by the Supreme Court of Canada in April 2006 in *R. v. Rodgers* (2006). In *Rodgers,* a repeat sex offender challenged the constitutionality of the provisions requiring him to hand over a DNA sample although he had been convicted before Parliament passed the new law. In a written opinion, one Supreme Court justice stated that the DNA database does in fact create a "proper balance" between the principles of privacy, individual security, and procedural fairness guaranteed by the Charter of Rights and Freedoms, as a sample can be obtained only through a judge's order and for those convicted of certain crimes. In addition, individuals convicted of serious offences have a reduced expectation of privacy and can't expect their identity to remain secret from the police.

Bill C-13 also brought a number of new sexual offences, such as indecent assault and

EXHIBIT 3.2   Sex Offender Registry/DNA Data Bank . . . Continued

gross indecency, within the purview of the DNA bank. It was estimated that these changes would add just under 5,000 additional offenders to the database. In addition, Bill C-13 compels an offender to give a blood sample when a judge orders it. Previously, offenders had been able to avoid giving a sample because they had already been released from custody on a conditional sentence (see Chapter 10) or because they had served all of their punishment. Now an arrest warrant can be issued for an individual who does not give a sample.

The first sex offender registry in Canada was established in Ontario in 2001. The Ontario Sex Offender Registry (also known as "Christopher's Law") was introduced after the brutal slaying of 11-year-old Christopher Stephenson in 1988. During the 1993 inquest into the slaying, the coroner's jury recommended the creation of a national registry for convicted sex offenders. The Ontario registry compiled the names of those individuals convicted of sexual assault, child molestation, and other sex offences. These registries were established owing largely to public concern about the exploitation, assault, and murder of children by sex offenders. The Ontario registry requires all those convicted of a sex offence to register with the local police within 15 days of moving into a community; this enables the police to access the names and addresses of convicted sex offenders released into the community. Failure to register can result in fines of up to $25,000 and/or a jail term for a first offence (Mackie 1999). In its first 12 months, the Ontario registry placed more than 5,000 names on its list; by January 2007, there were 7,400 registered offenders. In 2008, the Ontario Court of Appeal upheld the constitutionality of the Ontario sex offender registration legislation (*R. v. Dyck* [2008]). One shortcoming of Ontario's approach is that an offender who leaves the province need not register the new address.

The federal government has passed two laws to help the police monitor convicted sex offenders who had been released into the community. In 1994, the National Screening System was introduced; this allows volunteer and other community organizations to access the criminal records of applicants for positions of trust with children and vulnerable adults. The second piece of legislation, Bill C-7, established a special flagging system within the Canadian Police Information Centre for those offenders who had been pardoned of offences against children and vulnerable adults. Both these laws have been strongly criticized. According to an OPP spokesperson, both lack a search capability: "Without a name of the offender you can't do anything" (Elliott 2001). Another criticism was that the system did not force offenders to report a change of address. Not until February 2002 did the federal Solicitor General announce—after two years of intense pressure from federal opposition parties, provincial governments, and public organizations—that his department would be introducing a national registry system. The proposed new national system would require all convicted sex offenders to register their new addresses with local law enforcement officials when they move, along with other information such as a name change. This system would also allow police investigators to search by geographical area, such as postal code, so that when a sex crime was committed they would be able to determine quickly whether anyone who had been convicted of a similar offence was living in that area (Clark 2002).

The national Sex Offender Information Registration Act (Bill C-16) added sections 490.011 through 490.32 to the Criminal Code and came into force on December 15, 2004. The legislation states that any individual convicted of a designated sexual offence may be ordered by the court to register with the registry within 15 days of conviction and/or after release from prison. Pertinent information such as address and telephone number, past offences, alias(es), and identifying marks are to be included in the national database. In addition, persons convicted of any designated sex offence are required to re-register or notify the provincial or territorial registration centre any time they change their address or their name. Persons convicted of a sexual offence are required to remain registered for periods of 10 years, 20 years, or life depending on the maximum length of the sentence for their crime. The National Sex Offender Registry is retrospective—that is, it includes the names of offenders convicted of sex offences who were incarcerated, on parole, on probation, or under another form of sentence when the law came into force. As of January 2007, there were 9,408 offenders registered federally.

SELECTIVE INCAPACITATION

History

Selective incapacitation policies attempt to separate high-risk offenders from low-risk ones and to incarcerate for a long time those who are most likely to be dangerous once released. This approach is very recent in criminal justice; it emerged as a major force only in the 1970s. James Q. Wilson, a prominent criminologist, gave this model strong support in *Thinking about Crime* (1975). He wrote that serious crimes could be reduced by about one-third if each individual convicted of a violent crime received a sentence of three years and was not paroled. Then a study conducted by the Rand Corporation and authored by Peter Greenwood, titled *Selective Incapacitation,* appeared in 1982. This study became famous because on the basis of their investigations the researchers devised a system that they felt would successfully separate those offenders who should be "incapacitated" because they posed a long-term threat to society from those who should serve shorter sentences because they could be successfully reintegrated back into society once released.

In this study, Greenwood studied 2,190 prison and jail inmates in California, Texas, and Michigan. He found that the offenders who had committed the most crimes had the following characteristics:

1. An earlier conviction for the same offence.
2. Imprisonment for more than one-half of the two years prior to the current arrest.
3. A conviction before the age of 16.
4. Previous commitment to a juvenile institution.
5. Use of heroin or barbiturates during the previous two years.
6. Use of heroin and barbiturates as a juvenile.
7. Unemployment for half or more of the preceding two years.

He contended that a sentencing approach based on the Rand findings could reduce robberies by 15 percent and prison populations by 5 percent. The imprisonment of more chronic offenders would be more than offset by the elimination of low-risk offenders from prisons. This report received strong attention, since it suggested that more effective crime control could be achieved at less cost. Another study by E.D. Zedlewski, *Making Confinement Decisions* (1987), concluded that, assuming the average chronic offender committed 187 crimes a year, a saving of $430 million could be made annually if these individuals were sentenced to lengthy periods of incarceration (Walker 1994).

Despite these claims, critics argued that many errors would be made since prediction can never be precise. In other words, there would always be some "high-risk" individuals who would never commit another crime, and some "low-risk" individuals who would do so soon after being returned to the community. Zimring and Hawkins (1988) have argued that the reduction in crime promised by supporters of selective incapacitation has not materialized. They contend that the figures used by this theory's proponents are based on estimates of the number of crimes a chronic offender remembered committing each year. Many of the critics' harshest criticisms are based on their contention that attempts at reducing crime may be limited by a number of factors. These include problems in the identification of high-risk offenders and the possibility that one offender, if arrested, will simply be replaced by another. Also, if the offender who is incarcerated is a gang member, the gang may continue to commit the same amount of crime. Selective incapacitation no doubt has some limited influence on the crime rate, but its success depends on the ability of the criminal justice system to identify chronic offenders in the early stages of their career (Visher 1995).

The Criminal Sanction

The selective incapacitation approach focuses on those few individuals who commit the greatest number of crimes, be they property crimes or violent crimes. Most of the attention to date has been on individuals classified as chronic, career, or repeat offenders.

According to the criminal sanction approach, the crime rate is a function of the total number of offenders less those imprisoned (i.e., incapacitated), multiplied by an average number of crimes per offender. It follows that if chronic criminals are incarcerated for long periods of time, the crime rate will go down. Research has shown that a relative handful of offenders are responsible for the vast majority of violent offences. An example of that research is a book by Wolfgang, Figlio, and Sellin titled *Delinquency in a Birth Cohort* (1972), which has been lauded as "the single most important piece of criminal justice research in the last 25 years" (Walker 1993, 55). Focusing on 10,000 juvenile males born in Philadelphia in 1945 and living in that city between the ages of 10 and 18, the researchers measured crime as the number of times the police took a juvenile into custody. They discovered that nearly 35 percent of all males had a record of an offence. At least 627 of them had committed at least five offences. Even more important was their finding that only 6 percent of the males in the study accounted for more than half of all offences committed by the entire group and that 6 percent accounted for well over half of all violent crimes. Other studies (Hamparian et al. 1978; Shannon 1988; Tracy, Wolfgang, and Figlio

Selective incapacitation advocates support much longer prison terms for criminals who have committed serious crimes. Inmates will serve their sentences in prison cells like the one pictured above. (© Don Hammond/Design Pics/Corbis)

1990) turned up similar findings for both juveniles and adults. These studies identified small groups of high-rate offenders who were responsible for most criminal offences as well as most violent crimes.

The selective incapacitation philosophy does not apply to all offenders; it focuses only on those who are deemed the most dangerous to society. A key feature of this approach is that individuals are considered dangerous not only because of their deeds in the past but also because of the crimes they are likely to commit in the future. Future crimes are determined either by the number of prior convictions or by the number of crimes that similar offenders committed once they were released from prison.

In 1990, the Solicitor General of Canada recommended the elimination of parole for those convicted of dealing drugs. This policy was to be instituted if members of the National Parole Board suspected convicted drug dealers would be at risk to sell drugs after they were released. Such individuals were to be denied parole—they were to be punished, in essence, for crimes they had not yet committed. An example of this type of philosophy is found in the State of Washington's "sexual predator" law, which allows the state to "indefinitely lock up anyone who has committed at least one violent sex crime—after he has served his time" (Richards 1992, A1). Legislation has now been introduced in this country in an attempt to incarcerate and/or carefully control in the community those who are considered to be potential high-risk offenders (see Exhibit 3.3).

While there is undoubtedly support for such policies, there are potential pitfalls to such laws as well as problems associated with implementing them. The most serious criticism of the selective incapacitation of violent offenders is that the criminal justice system lacks the capacity to accurately predict future violent behaviour. This criticism directly challenges the legitimacy of selective incapacitation as a legal sanction.

The judicial maxim that "it is better to let ten guilty people go free than to let one innocent person suffer" embodies the value that our society places on individual liberty. The criminal sanction approach would extend judges the power "to prevent violent offenders . . . and drug offenders from obtaining parole until they have served half of their sentences." Those identified as dangerous would be incarcerated longer than those who are not. For Price and Stitt (1986, 28), this would mean that "two offenders could commit the same act but receive different sentences because one is thought to be more likely to commit that or a related act in the future."

The Operations of a Selective Incapacitation-Based Criminal Justice System

According to Price and Stitt (1986), the selective incapacitation approach is based on the idea that the best predictor of future behaviour is past behaviour. For the vast majority of offenders, the criminal justice system would operate on the basis of the deterrence doctrine. However, once an individual entered the system and was considered dangerous, the system would assign special resources and individuals to process the case as quickly as possible. Thus only some of the resources of the criminal justice system would be dedicated to the selective incapacitation approach.

Furthermore, because it contained such a narrow interest, this approach could easily be attached to any of the other three models. Such is the case in Washington, which employs the justice model for most offenders but also has a sexual predator law to ensure that certain sex offenders are not released for a long time. This is the most specific of all the models in the sense that it looks only at a narrow group of criminals.

The role of the police would be to arrest suspected offenders, conduct careful background checks, and then place offenders in a pretrial detention centre if they are considered to be chronic offenders. Plea bargaining would be eliminated, enabling prosecutors to process all such cases as quickly as possible in order to ensure that offenders aren't released back into the general population. Judges would have little discretion in these cases. Once an offender was perceived as a chronic offender, he or she would be sentenced to a lengthy determinate prison term. Parole would be abolished and the correctional system would become little more than a holding facility for such offenders. Policies such as "three strikes and you're out" are consistent with the selective incapacitation approach.

THE REHABILITATION APPROACH

History

Supporters of this model assume that crime is a result of factors outside the control of the individual. They argue that since criminals don't freely choose their behaviour, punishment is the wrong policy. Instead, they recommend the individualized treatment of offenders in the hope that the causes of their criminal behaviour can be discovered and eliminated. As Allen (1981, 2) points out, a central purpose of the rehabilitative approach "is to effect in the characters, attitudes, and behavior of convicted offenders, so as to strengthen the social defense against unwanted behavior [as well as] to contribute to the welfare and satisfaction of the offenders."

Under the **rehabilitation model**, more attention is placed on the offender than on the criminal act itself. Criminal sanctions are intended to meet the needs of the offender instead of being "based on considerations of social harm and deterrence" (Cullen and Gilbert 1982, 34). To

facilitate this approach, indeterminate sentences are essential—specifically, offenders must remain in prison for as long as it takes to find the appropriate "cure."

In the late nineteenth and early twentieth centuries, to facilitate an individual-based justice system, probation and parole were introduced as well as indeterminate sentences. The idea behind these policies was that the type of punishment (probation or incarceration) would be based on an offender's need for treatment. If the individual needed treatment, the duration of that person's punishment "would be determined by his or her behavior after sentencing as much as by the crime itself" (Clear 1995, 460). Inmates who showed improvement would be released earlier than those who resisted treatment or who failed to respond to it. Treatment at the turn of the century involved "programs of work, moral instruction, discipline, and order," all designed "to develop those personal habits that were prerequisites to a useful law-abiding life" (Carrigan 1991, 356).

Probably the test most often used to evaluate the success of rehabilitation programs is whether the offender recidivates—that is, is convicted of another offence after the sentence is completed. Indicative of the results is the

---

EXHIBIT 3.3 Dangerous Offender Designations and Long-Term Supervision Orders in Canada

In Canada, the sentencing of an individual most commonly involves a judge evaluating the past behaviour of an individual convicted of a crime and then determining the appropriate punishment (this assumes that a convicted person can be held responsible for his or her actions). However, there are currently two sentencing options in Canada that treat the risk of re-offending as the principal factor. One relates to dangerous offenders, the other to long-term-supervision offenders. This focus on the risk of future criminal behaviour is sometimes referred to as "actuarial justice," an approach that places people in categories and then estimates the risk these groups present.

In the case of dangerous offenders, over the past 60 years Canada has used various laws to allow the indeterminate confinement of those considered to be a danger to the public. In 1947, the term "habitual offender" was introduced to the Criminal Code; a year later, "criminal sexual psychopath" provisions were introduced into the Criminal Code. In 1962, a new definition, "dangerous sexual offender," replaced "criminal sexual psychopath." Then in 1977, new amendments to the Criminal Code replaced the designations of "habitual offender" and "dangerous sexual offender." This new designation, "dangerous

offender," focused on those individuals considered "dangerous" because they had committed a "serious personal injury offence"—a category that included a number of violent offences as well as several sexual offences stipulating a maximum punishment of at least 10 years. This legislation, which was in force between 1977 and 1997, meant that when an offender was declared a dangerous offender, a judge could sentence him or her to either a determinate or indeterminate sentence. The dangerous offender classification was upheld by the Supreme Court of Canada in *R. v. Lyons* (1987), in which the plaintiff argued that these provisions violated ss. 7, 9, and 12 of the Charter of Rights and Freedoms.

The current legislation on dangerous offenders, introduced in 1997, retains many of the provisions passed in 1977. One of the most important changes is that once an individual is classified as a dangerous offender, an indeterminate sentence is automatic. Another important change is that when a finding of dangerous offender is not warranted, a court may declare an individual a long-term offender, which means that the offender receives a determinate sentence of at least two years as well as a lengthy supervision order (up to 10 years) after release. This new provision allows court officials to evaluate patterns of offending over time.

If the Crown wants someone classified as a dangerous offender, it must apply for a dangerous offender hearing after the offender has been convicted of a "serious personal injury offence." Before the dangerous offender hearing, the individual in question is remanded for up to 60 days so that court-appointed experts can conduct a behavioural assessment. It is possible for an offender to become classified as a dangerous offender after committing one offence; however, most such individuals have long criminal histories. There are four possible criteria for a finding of dangerous offender. They are found in s. 753(1)(a) of the Criminal Code:

(1) (a) that the offence for which the offender has been convicted is a serious personal injury offence described in paragraph (a) of the definition of that expression in s. 752 and the offender constitutes a threat to the life, safety or physical or mental well-being of other persons on the basis of establishing

(i) a pattern of repetitive behaviour by the offender, of which the offence for which he or she has been convicted forms a part, showing a failure to restrain his or her behaviour and a likelihood of causing death or injury to other persons, or inflicting severe psychological damage on other persons, through failure in the future to restrain his or her behaviour,

(ii) a pattern of persistent aggressive behaviour by the offender, of which the offence for which he or she has been convicted forms a part, showing a substantial degree of indifference on the part of the offender respecting the reasonably foreseeable consequences to other persons of his or her behaviour, or,

(iii) any behaviour by the offender, associated with the offence for which he or she has been convicted, that is of such a brutal nature as to compel the conclusion that the offender's behaviour in the future is unlikely to be inhibited by normal standards of behavioural restraint; or

(b) that at the offence for which the offender is convicted is a serious personal injury offence described in paragraph (b) of the definition of that expression in s. 752 and the offender, by his or her conduct in any sexual matter including that involved in the commission of the offence for which he or she has been convicted, has shown a failure to control his or her sexual impulses and a likelihood of causing injury, pain or other evil to other persons through failure in the future to control his or her sexual impulses.

A long-term-supervision order application may be made if an offender has been convicted of an offence listed in s. 753.1(2)(a) of the Criminal Code: sexual interference (s. 151), invitation to sexual touching (s. 152), sexual exploitation (s. 153), exposure (s. 173[2]), sexual assault (s. 271), sexual assault with a weapon (s. 272), and aggravated sexual assault (s. 273). The offender may also have "engaged in serious conduct of a sexual nature in the commission of another offence of which the offender has been convicted" (s. 753.12[a]).

Long-term offender legislation is also found in s. 753.1:

(1) The court may, on application made under this Part following the filing of an assessment report . . . find an offender to be a long-term offender if it is satisfied:

(a) it would be appropriate to impose a sentence of imprisonment of two years or more for the offence for which the offender has been convicted;

(b) there is substantial risk that the offender will re-offend; and

(c) there is a reasonable possibility of eventual control of the risk in the community . . . . If the court finds an offender to be a long-term offender, it shall: impose a sentence for the offence for which the offender has been convicted, which sentence must be a minimum punishment of imprisonment for a term of two years; and order the offender to be supervised in the community, for a period not exceeding ten years . . .

As of April 2008, 394 Canadians were classified as dangerous offenders, with 388 serving an indeterminate sentence. In comparison, in April 2008, there were 489 offenders under a long-term-supervision order. Most long-term-supervision orders have been against sex offenders who do not meet the dangerous offender criteria (Trevethan et al., 2002). Of the 489 long-term-supervision offenders, 362 (74 percent) had at least one current conviction for a sexual offence. Ninety-three of them were being supervised in the community on their long-term-supervision order.

success rate of federal parolees who completed their first year while on parole. In 2007–08, the success rate for 3,009 individuals released from a federal correctional facility was 83.5 percent. Of those who had their parole revoked, 13 percent (391 individuals) was for breach of conditions, 3.2 percent (96 individuals) was for committing a non-violent offence, while 0.4 percent (11 individuals) was for a violent offence (Public Safety Canada 2008). The debate over the effectiveness of rehabilitation continues to this day between advocates of rehabilitation and those of the other three models.

The Criminal Sanction

Supporters of rehabilitation see this approach as necessary if we are to understand why people commit crimes. Once we understand what causes criminal behaviour, society will be able to apply appropriate sanctions. To this end, punishment needs to be flexible as well as based on the needs of the individual. This means that two individuals could commit the identical crime but end up with completely different punishments—perhaps because one individual requires a lengthy treatment program while the other needs some other treatment. A rehabilitation ("rehab") system is best described as discretionary, with all court and correctional agencies having the power to determine the type and length of sentence to individualize the punishment.

After long being criticized, rehabilitation seems to be gaining support. A national survey in the United States found that prison wardens—though they felt that the maintenance of custody and institutional order was their top priority—felt that rehab was a more significant goal than punishment and retribution (Cullen et al. 1993).

The Operations of a Rehabilitation-Based Criminal Justice System

Rehabilitation sets out to enhance the discretionary powers of the principal agencies of the criminal justice system. Since the focus of this model is on the needs of the offender, each agency must make decisions to enhance the chances that the individual will return to society as a better person.

As Price and Stitt (1986) point out, a system based on rehab would require the criminal justice system to focus on the criminal more than on the act committed. Agencies would intervene in the offender's life in order to change the offender, the hope being that the pressures that forced the individual to commit crime would be reduced and finally eliminated. Much of this model's emphasis would thus be on the sentencing and correctional stages of the criminal justice system.

The role of the police would not change dramatically. Police would continue to arrest criminals and lay charges. Prosecutors would be allowed to plea bargain as much as they wish and would encounter few if any restrictions in this regard. A case could easily be terminated or the total number of charges reduced if the prosecutor felt that it would be in the best interests of the offender. Prosecutors would rely on the pre-sentence report and make recommendations on the type of treatment needed. Both the prosecutor and judge would make use of this report during the sentencing of the offender.

Judicial discretion is an essential component of the rehabilitation approach. Prior to handing out a sentence, the judge would receive a pre-sentence report from a probation officer. Any recommendations made in this report would be carefully considered by the judge in the sentencing decision, as would any statements made by the defence lawyer and the Crown prosecutor. The sentence would reflect the "best interests" of the offender and would involve an indeterminate sentence that best fits the needs of the offender. As such, offenders would have to serve only the minimum length of their sentence. Under a rehabilitation approach, the correctional system and its related services would probably become the most important agencies of the criminal justice system. Parole services would be expanded, since they would be required in order to individualize the treatment program for each offender. This individualization would add discretion to the system, since offenders could be released at any time by the parole board after serving the minimum sentence.

Correctional services within the prison would become more treatment oriented. The correctional system would discover the needs of offenders before proceeding with a course of treatment (see Exhibit 3.4). Since treatment would be personalized, it could take a long time before that treatment succeeded for any individual. Thus, the treatment services might vary for each offender and the length of treatment as well.

ABORIGINAL JUSTICE AND RESTORATIVE JUSTICE SYSTEMS: AN INTRODUCTION

Aboriginal and restorative justice systems represent a significant shift from the above-mentioned crime control philosophies. They share several principles, including the belief that governments need to give up their monopoly

A common topic of debate over the past few decades has been the best way to control criminals convicted of sexual offences. Is it better to selectively incapacitate offenders or to rehabilitate them? Some researchers argue that psychological assessments reduce the recidivism risk of sexual offenders (e.g., Hanson et al. 2002), while others believe the current research evidence does not support such a position (Rice and Harris 2003). As a result, many believe that sex offenders should be punished for extensive periods of time. They view punishment as the only approach that "works" in the sense of keeping sex offenders from recidivating. However, they sometimes ignore the fact that almost all sex offenders will be released once they have completed their sentence. The feeling is that if they are not treated, many will re-offend.

Other correctional experts are now questioning the success of deterrence-based punishment systems, arguing that they have only a marginal positive effect and do not save any money in either the short or long term (e.g., Cullen and Applegate 1997). Problems have been discovered in deterrence-based punishments, most notably the failure to properly implement programs. Some (e.g., Andrews and Bonta 1998) argue that deterrence-based punishments fail to significantly reduce recidivism rates because they do not focus on any of the known predictors of recidivism, such as anti-social values and the influence of negative peer groups. Others believe that "the deterrence approach ignores the criminological evidence showing that the roots of crime among serious offenders typically extend to childhood or early-adolescent activities, where youths develop propensities and associations that stabilize their involvement in crime" (Cullen and Applegate 1997, xxi). This debate over the appropriate approach to reducing recidivism rates has been going on for more than 25 years in the field of corrections, ever since the publication of Robert Martinson's research (1974), which questioned the success of rehabilitation programs (see Chapter 12).

Extensive empirical data now exist indicating that rehabilitation programs can and do work—if they are well designed and effectively implemented. Paul Gendreau, a professor of psychology at the University of New Brunswick, found that "appropriate" treatment programs can reduce recidivism rates by 53 percent within six months to two years. Gendreau, along with Don Andrews of Carleton University (in Freiberg 1990), found

that the most successful programs employ behavioural modification techniques that reward prosocial behaviour and that "target those anti-social attitudes and values that fuel criminal behaviour." Gendreau noted that these techniques vary - in some correctional settings, prisoners are given more privileges or money for prosocial behaviour. Often, role-playing exercises are conducted to influence an offender's thinking and values.

Gendreau and Goggin (1996) found that rehabilitation-based programs attain better results when programs operate with optimal theoretical integrity. In other words, programs need to be properly constructed, operated by qualified and well-trained staff who provide intensive treatments, and evaluated by experts in behavioural intervention. In their analyses of rehabilitation-based programs, Gendreau and Goggin reported that those programs with therapeutic integrity are much more successful than programs that ignore or contain only partial program integrity. Programs with proper therapeutic integrity reduce recidivism by 20 to 35 percent compared to between 5 and 15 percent for those without program integrity.

But if successful sex offender treatment programs can be implemented, will the recidivism rates of sex offenders be reduced? In Canada, sex offenders incarcerated in federal correctional facilities who want to apply for conditional release (e.g., parole) are expected to attend relevant institutional programs. Their progress in these programs helps correctional and parole officials determine whether a sex offender should be released on a conditional program.

Seto (2003) reported on sex offenders released from the Warkworth Sexual Behaviour Clinic, a treatment program offered by a Canadian federal correctional facility. The main treatment approaches involved in that program included acceptance of responsibility for offences, victim empathy, understanding one's own offence cycle, and the development of an individual relapse prevention program. The performances of those who attended were evaluated at 32 and 62 months. It was found that treatment performance was not related to either general or serious recidivism—specifically, sex offenders who scored high in psychopathy were roughly twice as likely to seriously re-offend as those who scored lower in psychopathy.

(Continued)

Some studies report lower recidivism rates for sex offenders released into the community on a conditional release program. A study of a treatment program for high-risk sex offenders (recidivist rapists and pedophiles serving a federal sentence) conducted at CSC's maximum-security Regional Psychiatric Centre (Prairies) compared one treatment group to another group of federal offenders released from federal correctional facilities. Over three years, the treatment group had a 59 percent lower rate of sexual recidivism than the comparison group, even though they were followed up for more than two years longer. At the same time, however, no differences were reported in a comparison of a similar program comparing sexual and non-sexual offenders sentenced to provincial facilities (Nicholaichuk 1995).

over our society's response to crime and must stop being the sole regulator of those who are most directly affected by the crime—the victim and the offender. Another principle involves gathering people in a circle to eliminate the hierarchical relationships that exist in today's legal system (Roach 1999). Yet another principle is that the relationship between victims and offenders must be restored in a process that allows both to participate (Van Ness and Heetderks Strong 1997; Zehr 1990). The importance of these principles was formally recognized in 1996, when they were incorporated into the sentencing principles of the Criminal Code, in particular into s. 718(e) (the provision of reparations for harm done to victims or to the community) and s. 718(f) (the promotion of responsibility in offenders, and acknowledgment of the harm done to victims and the community).

Programs based on restorative justice are guided by a number of factors, including the following:

- Victims and offenders must give and also be able to withdraw their free, voluntary, and informed consent to participate in the restorative justice process; they must be fully informed about the process and its consequences.
- Offenders must admit responsibility for the offence, and both the victim and offender must agree on the essential facts of the case.
- Offenders and victims can have legal advice at any time and can withdraw if they so wish.
- Admissions of guilt cannot be used as evidence in any later legal proceedings.
- Failure to reach an agreement should not be used in any subsequent legal proceedings to justify a harsher sentence than would otherwise be given.
- The consequences of failing to honour an agreement should be clearly stated.

Aboriginal justice systems differ from restorative justice systems in that they involve the idea that crime devastates a community's quality of life. Also, such systems are more informal. Instead of focusing on the punishment of offenders, they support a healing process involving victims, offenders, and the community. Another fundamental belief of Aboriginal justice systems is that local communities should be able to determine what happens to offenders who commit crimes within their boundaries.

ABORIGINAL JUSTICE SYSTEMS

Many Aboriginal communities have traditionally emphasized elements of restorative justice. The Supreme Court of Canada, in *R. v. Gladue* (1999) (see Chapter 10), commented that in general terms, restorative justice can be described as an approach to remedying crime in which it is understood that all things are interrelated and that crime disrupts the harmony that existed prior to its occurrence, or at least that should have existed. The appropriateness of a particular sanction is determined largely by the needs of the victims and the community as well as those of the offender. The focus is on the human beings closely affected by the crime.

In the past decade there has been much discussion about the development of formal Aboriginal justice systems throughout Canada. These systems—specifically those administered by Aboriginal courts—have become a major area of interest, as they would honour traditional methods for resolving conflicts. Many officials have accepted the idea of Aboriginal justice systems, but there has been much controversy over the form such systems should take. In December 1991, for example, the Law Reform Commission of Canada published a report that supported the concept of Aboriginal justice, but it did not indicate which *type* of system it supported. The commission did, however, discuss the reasons why such a justice system was needed in Canada: "From the Aboriginal perspective, the criminal justice system is an alien one, imposed by

Inmates at the Aboriginal Healing Range home at the Stony Mountain Institution participate in a drum circle on May 19, 2006, in Stony Mountain, Manitoba. The inmates have committed to a lifestyle behind bars that follows traditional teachings, while also participating in mainstream correctional programs. Visits with elders, cultural and spiritual ceremonies, sharing circles, stints in a sweat lodge, drumming, and arts and crafts are all part of the path to healing. (CP PHOTO/Winnipeg Free Press - Ken Gigliotti)

the dominant white society . . . Not surprisingly, they regard the system as deeply insensitive to their traditions and values: many view it as unremittingly racist" (Law Reform Commission of Canada 1991, 5).

A few months after the Law Reform Commission released its report, federal Justice Minister Kim Campbell rejected the possibility of a separate system of Aboriginal justice in Canada, saying that such a system would be a "copout." She favoured a system that integrated aspects of the traditional Aboriginal value system into the broader Western legal system. In March 1996, the federal government decided to adopt Campbell's position. It continued to reject the idea of Aboriginal peoples establishing their own justice system and creating their own criminal law by stating unequivocally that the Charter of Rights and Freedoms applies to Aboriginal peoples as much as to all other Canadians. It did, however, recommend that they be given a greater role in sentencing Aboriginal offenders and in helping develop alternatives to prison.

Some provincial governments have also rejected the idea of separate legal systems. To date, most Aboriginal systems in Canada have worked together

with the existing criminal justice system with regard to accommodating Aboriginal approaches to justice. In Manitoba, for example, the Aboriginal Justice Inquiry recommended sweeping changes in the criminal justice system; these changes failed to materialize, however. The provincial government turned down a proposal for an Aboriginal court in January 1993, proposing instead a three-year pilot project that would combine Aboriginal approaches to resolving conflict with principles found in the Western legal system. This system was to focus upon cases involving summary convictions for adults as well as nonserious youth justice cases. In 1999, a new provincial government announced that it would be exploring this idea, but it ultimately decided against a separate justice system. This led one of the original authors of the Aboriginal Justice Inquiry to speculate that such a system would never be introduced (Hamilton 2001).

An Aboriginal justice system inevitably involves more than having justice programs in Aboriginal communities delivered by Aboriginal organizations. As Rudin (2005, 109) points out, in order for justice programs "to be successful, Aboriginal people must control the alternative justice processes." This involves governments and justice system providers allowing Aboriginal communities themselves "the time, opportunity and funding to determine how they wish to approach justice issues." Also, Aboriginal justice programs need to "be developed and controlled by Aboriginal organizations and communities" (ibid., 111).

Models of Aboriginal Justice Systems

How would an Aboriginal justice system operate? What shape would it take? There are many views regarding what would constitute an effective Aboriginal justice system, but "fundamental is the belief that the system must be faithful to aboriginal traditions and cultural values, while adapting them to modern society" (Law Reform Commission of Canada 1991, 7). Other essential components of an Aboriginal justice system include care for the interests of the collectivity, the reintegration of the offender into the community, mediation and conciliation within the community, and the importance of the role of community Elders and leaders (ibid.) (see Table 3.1).

According to Meyer (1998, 44), Aboriginal communities might develop and practise their own unique justice systems, but all would "focus on reparations and

making the parties 'whole' after the injury." And all would avoid, as a basic principle, blaming the offender for the harm he or she has done. Instead, efforts would be made to repair the injury and make the community whole again. Such approaches would address the need to emphasize persuasion over coercion, with the goal of restoring the parties involved. They would also recognize the need for respected community members to serve as decision-makers.

Manitoba's Aboriginal Justice Inquiry found that the meaning of justice in an Aboriginal society differs greatly from that of the broader society. European adversarial systems attempt to "prevent or punish harmful or deviant behaviour"; in contrast, Aboriginal systems attempt "to restore the peace and equilibrium within the community, and to reconcile the accused with his or her own conscience and with the individual or family who has been wronged." Thus, the underlying notion of Aboriginal justice systems when dealing with crime is "the resolution of disputes, the healing of wounds and the restoration of social harmony" (Hamilton and Sinclair 1991).

Other provinces besides Manitoba have explored the possibility of a separate Aboriginal justice system. Alberta examined the issue through its Task Force on the Criminal Justice System and Its Impact on the Indian and

TABLE 3.1 Differences in Justice Paradigm

ABORIGINAL JUSTICE APPROACH	AMERICAN JUSTICE PARADIGM
Communication is fluid. Native language is used. Oral customary law learned as a way of life, by example.	The paradigm is vertical. Communication is rehearsed. English or French language is used.
Law and justice are part of the whole.	Written statutory law is derived from rules and procedure.
The spiritual realm is invoked in ceremonies and prayer. Trusting relationships are built to promote resolution and healing. Talk and discussion is necessary.	The paradigm features separation of power. The process is adversarial, conflict-oriented, argumentative. Isolated behaviour is considered—freeze-frame acts.
Problems are reviewed in their entirety; contributing factors are examined.	A fragmented approach is taken to process and solutions.
Comprehensive problem-solving is undertaken. No time limits are put on the process; it includes all individuals affected.	The process is time-oriented. Limits are imposed on the number of participants in the process and solutions.
All extended-family members are represented. The focus is on victim and communal rights. The process is corrective; offenders are accountable and responsible for change.	Representation is by strangers. The focus is on individual rights. The paradigm is punitive and removes the offender.
Customary sanctions are used to restore the victim–offender relationship.	Penalties are prescribed by and for the state.
Offender is given reparative obligations to victims and community.	Rights of the accused are defended, especially against self-incrimination. Society is vindicated.

Source: Melton, A.P. 1998. *Indigenous Justice Systems and Tribal Society.* Washington, DC: National Institute of Justice.

Métis People of Alberta. The final Alberta report, *Justice on Trial* (the Cawsey Report), recognized that important differences exist between European and Aboriginal approaches to justice. It noted (Bryant 1999, 20–21) that the Aboriginal model incorporates different goals:

1. It focuses on problem solving and the restoration of harmony.
2. It uses restitution and reconciliation as means of restoration.
3. The community acts as a facilitator in the restorative process.
4. The impact of the actions in question is impressed on the offender.
5. The holistic context of an offence—its moral, social, economic, political, and religious and cosmic considerations—is carefully considered.
6. The stigma of the offence is removed through conformity.
7. It is important for the offender to express remorse, repentance, and forgiveness and for the community to recognize it.
8. The offender must play an active role in the restorative process.

Ross (1994, 262) has identified two essential features of Aboriginal justice systems:

1. A dispersal of decision-making among many people, as suggested by a repeated emphasis on consensus decision-making and a regular denunciation of such hierarchical decision-making structures as those created by the Indian Act.
2. A belief that people can neither be understood nor assisted so long as they are seen as isolated individuals. People must be seen as participants in a broad web of relationships.

A number of key components of Aboriginal justice systems have been identified. One is healing, which allows the spiritual needs of the individual to be addressed. Another is what has been referred to as cultural imperatives. According to Clare Brant, a Mohawk psychiatrist, these consist of four major rules in the area of conflict suppression that maintain harmony in the group. Together, they form the very basis of Aboriginal community life. The four rules (Hamilton and Sinclair 1991) are these:

1. The ethic of non-interference—that is, the promotion of "positive interpersonal relationships by discouraging coercion of any kind, be it physical, verbal, or psychological."
2. The rule of non-competitiveness, which acts to eliminate internal group conflict by "averting intragroup rivalry."

3. Emotional restraint, which controls those emotional responses that may disrupt the group.
4. Sharing, which means that those who are rich give away much of their wealth to ensure the survival of the group.

Much diversity underlies these general characteristics. Green (1998), who studied Aboriginal communities throughout Saskatchewan and Manitoba, found four approaches in use, all of which involved community participation. These included sentencing circles, an Elders' or community sentencing panel, a sentence advisory committee, and a community mediation committee. Both the circle and mediation are important elements in these practices, as they represent a more egalitarian approach, one that reflects the communal nature of the group. A variety of offences were heard by these groups. Some heard cases for which the period of incarceration is less than two years; others dealt with more serious offences, such as sexual assault. All of these different approaches incorporated certain features of Aboriginal practices, including spirituality, grassroots consultations, community consensus, and sharing (ibid., 134).

Ross (1994), discussing the operation of different Aboriginal justice systems, found they utilized various approaches when dealing with offenders. The Hollow Water First Nation (see Exhibit 3.5), located in eastern Manitoba, developed its justice system by requesting that some of the practices of the Western legal system be "modified to accommodate . . . what they wanted to continue doing on their own" (ibid., 248). In comparison, the Sandy Bay and Attawapiskat communities (both in Manitoba) requested that they be "granted roles within the Western legal system" in order to cooperate with selected functionaries of the Western legal system.

The Sandy Bay and Attawapiskat justice systems focus on integrating traditional Aboriginal values into the Western legal system by placing Aboriginal people in selected advisory roles. At Sandy Bay, the emphasis is on involvement not in the trial process but rather at the time of sentencing. A panel of Elders acts together with a provincial court judge or justice of the peace to deliver the sentence. Recommended sentences usually involve some interaction with the community, such as restitution and community service. An offender who does not fulfill his obligation is "banished" to the Western legal system, where he is subject to incarceration.

At Attawapiskat, Ross found the Elders playing a different role during the sentencing of offenders. They hear most of the cases by themselves within a community court, complete with its own summonses and subpoenas. Charges are laid in provincial court, but are stayed; they can be reactivated within a year if the offender fails to follow the sentence of the Elders' court.

CHAPTER 3 Control Philosophy and Criminal Justice Policy

The cases the Elders' court tries would not normally involve a period of incarceration. As in Sandy Bay, most of the sentences involve some form of community work.

The first Aboriginal court system in Canada opened in October 2000 on the Tsuu T'ina Nation, near Calgary. Referred to as "the first comprehensive justice system in Canada, it encompasses the desire of the Tsuu T'ina people to address the glaring problems affecting First Nations people within Canadian criminal justice" (Bryant 2002, 16). Known as the Peacemaker Court, it consists of a First Nations judge and a Peacemaker program and controls its own administration. The court blends Tsuu T'ina cultural traditions with various components of the provincial court system (Mildon 2001). Since then, other Aboriginal courts have been created in Canada—The Cree-Speaking Court and Dene-speaking Court in northern Saskatchewan; The Gladue (Aboriginal Persons) Court in Toronto, Ontario; and the First Nations Court, in New Westminster, British Columbia.

The Tsuu T'ina court works in much the same way as the Alberta provincial court system. It has jurisdiction over summary conviction offences and over hybrid offences elected to be tried as summary conviction offences. Before any trial, however, all sessions begin with a Peacemaker (who has reviewed each case and whose role is in ways similar to that of the Crown prosecutor). The Peacemaker reviews cases and requests that suitable ones be transferred to the Peacemaker program. If the Crown prosecutor feels that the case should be held in a regular court, the outcome is decided by the First Nations judge. The court is set up in a circular arrangement, and its protocols reflect Tsuu T'ina traditions. Peacemaking is an integral component of the court process (Mandamin, Starlight, and One-spot, 2003). The mandate of the Peacemaker program, which is modelled on the Navajo Peacemakers approach, is "to resolve problems, investigate and discover the root causes of the behaviour which has translated into criminal activity or disharmony in the community or among families" (Bryant 2002, 17). The Peacemaking process focuses on community harmony and restorative justice. If this approach is successful, the Crown prosecutor withdraws the charges laid against the accused.

RESTORATIVE JUSTICE

Restorative justice is a significant new development in the philosophy of crime control. This approach posits that an offender's conscience (i.e., internalized norms) and significant others (friends, family, and so on) can be incorporated into deterrence and serve as potential sources of punishment. Supporters of this approach believe that criminal behaviour can be reduced by decreasing the expected utility of criminal activity. They argue that deterrence doesn't need to be restricted to legal sanctions; it can also come about when people refrain from acting on the basis of fear or of negative consequences such as shame (Grasmick and Bursik 1990).

History

In his theory of restorative justice, Braithwaite (1989) develops what he calls *reintegrative shaming*, a system of justice that is based on the idea that it is better to try to shame some offenders than to try to punish them within the formal criminal justice system. The criminal justice system stigmatizes people and turns offenders into outcasts; in this way it severs their ties to society and actually increases criminal behaviour. The offender is labelled as evil, and in this way *criminal* becomes the individual's master status trait. In contrast, shaming is "disapproval dispensed within an ongoing relationship with the offender based on respect" (Braithwaite 1993, 1). This process involves victims and significant others confronting the offender in an attempt to moralize the individual and explain the harm the behaviour in question has caused. Disapproval of the offender's actions is counteracted by the community's efforts to build a moral conscience and strengthen social bonds (Makkai and Braithwaite 1994).

The key to reintegrative shaming, then, is to change perceptions of the offender. Instead of seeing the offender as someone to be punished (e.g., through incarceration), an attempt is made to reintegrate offenders by holding a "shaming" ceremony in which offenders realize the pain they have brought to the victim, the community, and society. Shaming is more likely to be reintegrative and successful when a high degree of interdependence exists between victim and offender, such as within a family, a group of relatives, or the community of which the offender is a member.

Restorative justice is a new approach to justice in North America. Its history is found in other nations, particularly Japan. Since the early 1950s, Western social scientists have been fascinated by the high level of social order—defined as the extent of citizens' compliance to important social norms—found in Japan. This compliance translates into a higher degree of social order and lower crime rates. Some (e.g., Befu 1990; Smith 1983) argue that the phenomenon is due to the religious ideals associated with Confucianism, an idea traditionally accepted by most Western social scientists. However, other Confucian nations have high levels of social disorder. Why, then, is Japan different?

The Hollow Water First Nation operates a program dealing with sexual abuse in the four communities surrounding Hollow Water, Manitoba. It is formally known as the Community Holistic Circle Healing Program (CHCH) and combines fundamental principles of Anishnawbe spirituality with a program designed to heal those individuals involved in the cycle of abuse and conflict. This system developed from the need to find a concrete solution to the community problem of sexual abuse. Studies in these four communities revealed that a significant number of people living in them had been sexually abused as children and were now themselves sexually abusing children (Royal Commission on Aboriginal Peoples, 1996). In the past, when sexual abuse was detected, the police were called to arrest the individual, with the case heard in a court located outside of the community. Offenders who were found guilty were incarcerated in the provincial or federal correctional system. However, when they had completed their sentence, many of the offenders returned to Hollow Water and the surrounding communities and continued to engage in sexual abuse. As a result, a number of community members met during the mid-1980s and decided to set up a program to heal sexual abusers in a way that would keep both the offenders and their victims within the local communities.

According to the protocol of this justice system, disclosure about sexual abuse is first made to a community team rather than to the police. This community team consists of volunteers, mostly women, including a child protection worker, a community health representative, the nurse-in-charge, and representatives from the local school division and community churches, as well as the local detachment of the RCMP. Criminal charges are laid as quickly as possible after the act is disclosed. The alleged offender is then given a choice: proceed through the outside criminal justice system or proceed with the healing support of the team. Either way, the offender is ultimately sentenced in a court of law. Sentencing is delayed, however, if the individual decides to take part in the healing process.

There are four components to the CHCH. First, it brings together all of the resources in the community. It is available to any community member who is prepared to take full responsibility for his or her actions in the sexual victimization of another person. All members of the community participate in the healing process. Second, the CHCH is holistic—that is, it attempts to deal with all parties involved, including the victim, the victimizer, the families, and the community, as well as all aspects of the imbalance (physical, emotional, and spiritual). Third, the CHCH is a circle. This is the strength of tradition. In the circle everyone is equal and all similarities and differences are accepted. Within the circle, the power of one becomes the power of all. Finally, the CHCH is spontaneity from within, and all members follow their hearts. The CHCH uses principles that the Elders say would have been used in the past to deal with such issues. The traditional way was for the community to bring the issue out into the open; to protect the victim in such a way as to minimally disrupt the family and community functioning; to hold the person accountable for his or her behaviour; and to provide an opportunity for balance to be restored to all parties (Community Holistic Circle Healing 1997).

To be accepted into the healing program, an alleged abuser must accept full responsibility for his or her actions and enter a guilty plea as soon as possible. The abuser then enters a program that involves 13 different steps "from the initial disclosure to the creation of a healing contract." An individual who passes them then proceeds to the cleansing ceremony (Ross 1994, 244). This process entails a painful stripping away of all the defences of the abuser over a long period of time; the rebuilding of the individual can then begin. Each case is seen as unique and is handled accordingly. Incarceration (as long as it includes input from the community) can be used as a part of this process, but only in those cases where the prognosis for healing is not good.

When the accused appears in court for sentencing, the team presents a report to the judge about the abuser's sincerity of effort and how much work, if any, still needs to be done. A Western court would sentence the offender; in sharp contrast, the healing circle fiercely rejects any recommendation of incarceration. Between 1986 and 1995, only five offenders selected to be tried by the Western courts; 48 others chose to enter the CHCH program (Moon 1995). An evaluation released in 2001 reported that since the beginning of the program, only 2 of the 107 participating offenders had recidivated (Couture et al. 2001).

In 2003, NHL player Dany Heatley was charged with first degree vehicular homicide (which could have carried a prison sentence of 2 to 15 years if convicted) for a speeding accident that led to the death of his friend and teammate, Dan Snyder. Mr. Heatley did not go to jail as Dan Snyder's family chose to forgive him. Mr. Snyder's family and other people involved in restorative justice were able to persuade the judge not to send Mr. Heatley to jail as they favoured more constructive options. (CP Photo/AP Photo/John Bazemore)

Braithwaite (1989) points out that when someone is shamed in Japan, that shame is shared by the collectivity (e.g., family, friends, school, and the workplace) to which the individual belongs. In addition, the criminal justice authorities in Japan, notably the police, work with the offender and the victim to develop alternatives to formal punishment. According to Braithwaite, one of the powerful aspects of shaming is that social control is diverted back to the family, the community, and the social environment of the offender.

Hechter and Kanazawa (1993) believe that the answer lies in Japan's high rate of social conformity—higher than that found in either Canada or the United States. They explain this high rate of conformity on the basis of three principles of social control. The first principle is that of dependence, defined as the extent to which a group is the most important source of reward. Individuals conform more to group norms the more they are dependent on the group. The second factor involves visibility—the idea that behaviour that is easily observed and monitored by the group is more likely to conform to group norms. The final factor involves how strongly norms are upheld by the group. According to Hechter and Kanazawa, the greater that strength, the greater the social order and the lower the crime rate.

Restorative Justice Sanctions

Restorative justice sanctions are developed to represent the interests of the victim, the public, and the community. These sanctions are essentially alternatives to incarceration

and generally involve sanctions served in the community or conveying to the community the decision of the court. The purpose of these sanctions is to make the offender aware of the moral wrong he or she has committed and to indicate that no more such actions are expected. According to Karp (1998), three types of shaming sanctions are currently practised in North America. The first type (and the most common) is referred to as public exposure sanctions. The purpose of such sanctions is to bring the attention of the community and other parties to the offence, the offender, and the victim. The objective is to belittle the crime and therefore shame the offender.

Another shaming sanction involves debasement penalties. These typically involve shaming through embarrassment or humiliation. Usually the offender agrees to accept a penalty that compels reflection on the feelings that the victim may have experienced as a result of the offence. The third type of reintegrative shaming sanctions, apology penalties, typically has the offender writing an apology or making a public statement about the offence and how wrong it was to commit it. To date, the few evaluation studies have found that most of these agreements have been successfully completed.

The Operations of a Restorative Justice-Based Criminal Justice System

The focus of restorative justice is not on determining guilt and punishment but rather on addressing a harm. This approach provides an alternative to the traditional adversarial system. Only certain criminal acts are to be considered for processing in a shaming context, most commonly non-serious property crimes and minor forms of violent crime. Certain criminal justice personnel, such as a police officer or a court worker, recommend that a conference take place and start the process of diverting the case to a trained facilitator. The facilitator then arranges a conference that involves the offender and the victim. A key component of the conference is the voluntary involvement of both the victim and the offender. Most restorative justice approaches take the form of a diversion program that occurs prior to any criminal charge being laid against the alleged offender. If an agreement cannot be reached within a specified time, a criminal charge may be laid and the case heard in a criminal court. Certain restorative justice programs operate a bit differently, in that they start after a criminal charge is laid but before the case is heard in criminal court. Some restorative justice programs may not start until a finding of guilt is made; others don't start until a judge sends an offender to a program as part of his or her sentence.

Latimer, Dowden, and Muisse (2001) have summarized the four entry points to restorative justice programs within our criminal justice system:

- Police (pre-charge)
- Crown (post-charge and pre-conviction)
- Courts (post-conviction and pre-sentence)
- Corrections (post-sentence and pre-reintegration)

Offenders can be referred to a restorative justice program at any one of these entry points. Unlike Aboriginal justice systems, restorative justice programs are not an alternative to the current criminal justice system; rather, these programs are integrated into the current system. According to Latimer and Kleinknecht (2000, 7), the "more serious the case, the more likely the case will be referred to a restorative justice program later in the process."

To participate in a restorative justice program, offenders have to accept responsibility for their actions. An important part of the shaming process involves the recognition of the community, so supporters of both the victim and the offender are invited to take part in the shaming process as well as serve as a social support mechanism. Professionals and law enforcement officials who have been involved or have assisted either party may also be invited. While 10 to 12 participants is the norm, 40 or more individuals may attend a conference. This group is expected to arrive at a consensus on the outcome of the case. In theory, there can be several benefits to using restorative justice programs in our criminal justice system. Victims receive the chance to participate in the system; normally they would not be allowed to take an active role. Offenders can find these programs "therapeutic" as they take responsibility for their actions and repair the harm their actions have caused. For members of the community, restorative justice programs can humanize the criminal justice system by giving them a voice in it. According to Latimer and Kleinknecht (ibid., 6), restorative justice can be "an empowering experience" for all participants (see Exhibit 3.6).

Goals of restorative justice conferences include accountability, prevention, and healing. The benefits of this approach are that it recognizes a larger group of people as victims, involves a wider group of participants than is normally the case, and acknowledges the importance of the family in the offender's life (Umbreit and Stacey 1996). At the end of the meeting a consensus is reached on the best way to deal with the harm, and a resolution document is signed by all participants.

EXHIBIT 3.6 Restorative Justice and Family Violence

Some researchers have explored the possibility of using restorative justice to reduce the incidence of family violence. At present there is more support for using restorative justice in the area of minor property crimes, not violent crime. Daly and Stubbs (2007, 160) point out although there is considerable debate on whether restorative justice should be used for partner, sexual or family violence, the empirical evidence is sparse." However, Daly (2006) in her study of about 400 sexual violence cases finalized in court, by conference or caution, concludes that restorative justice conferences are a better option for victims as there is an admission to the offence and a penalty of some sort. Recent studies of a restorative justice approach to family violence in Newfoundland reported a significant reduction in child abuse and neglect as well as in the abuse of mothers and wives (Burford and Pennell 1998; Pennell and Burford 1995, 2000). The goal of this study was to test within different cultural contexts the ability of restorative justice programs to eliminate or reduce violence against child and adult family members as well as to promote their well-being.

Thirty-two families participated in this program, and a total of 472 individuals (384 family members and 88 service providers). The program involved the following five stages:

1. The project coordinators received referrals from mandated individuals.
2. Conferences were organized by the project coordinators after consulting with family group members and involved service providers.
3. Conferences were then convened with the members of the family group as well as the service providers.
4. The referring agency personnel approved plans in terms of whether or not they met all of the areas of concern.
5. The program was then implemented. The programs typically involved services such as counselling, addiction treatment, in-home support, and child care.

The researchers, after evaluating the program and comparing the 32 families who participated with families who did not, reported that

(Continued)

EXHIBIT 3.6   Restorative Justice and Family Violence . . . Continued

the restorative justice program protected children and adult family members while at the same time unifying family group members. There was a 50 percent reduction in all types of abuse and neglect for the 32 families involved in the study compared to the year before. In addition, the incidents among families involved in a comparison group that did not receive restorative justice programs increased markedly. The lowest success rates were found in those cases where young people were abusing their mothers.

The researchers, in an earlier study, reported that victims of family violence who participated in a restorative justice–based program had high levels of satisfaction. Ninety-four percent of

family members were satisfied with the techniques used in the program; 92 percent said they were "able to say what was important"; and 92 percent said they agreed with the intervention plan that was offered to them. On the basis of all their studies, the researchers were able to conclude that their program led to a sense of shame throughout the extended families since they had not acted to protect their relations. This research suggests the power of restorative justice programs in the area of violent crime.

Sources: Sherman and Berk 1984; Pennell and Burford 1996; Burford and Pennell 1998; Pennell and Burford 2000; Daly 2006; Daly and Stubbs 2007.

CRITICAL ISSUES IN CANADIAN CRIMINAL JUSTICE

THE PETER WHITMORE CASE

On July 22, 2006, Peter Whitmore vanished with a 14-year-old teenager, the stepson of a man who he had met while working at a construction site in Winnipeg, Manitoba. The next day, Whitmore met a 10-year-old boy in Whitewood, Saskatchewan, when he went to the boy's family's farm to sell a DVD player in the hope of getting some money for gas. The boys played together for several hours, but later "the teen allegedly lured the boy out of his farmhouse on the premise of going for a bike ride" (McIntyre 2007, A4). Whitmore, who was allegedly waiting in his van, then grabbed both of the boys. When their bicycles were found discarded some hours later, a search was immediately started.

A Canada-wide warrant was issued for Whitmore, charging him with abduction. The next day, a vehicle matching the description of Whitmore's was seen at an abandoned farmhouse near Kipling, Saskatchewan, by a local resident. When the RCMP arrived, the 10-year-old boy was able to run to safety. A 10-hour standoff ensued, during which time Whitmore attempted to kill himself. He eventually surrendered and both boys were returned to their families. Shortly after Whitmore's arrest, Crown prosecutor Anthony Guerin informed reporters that he anticipated proceeding with a dangerous offender application and, given Whitmore's prior record, foresaw "no reason to compromise" since he had a solid case.

After his arrest, it was reported that Whitmore had a record of sex offences against

children dating back some 15 years. In 1993, he had been convicted of abduction and five sexual offences involving four young boys in Toronto. He was sentenced to 16 months in custody. In 1995, Whitmore was sentenced to a five-year sentence after he was found guilty for numerous sexual offences, including the abduction and confinement of an 8-year-old girl from Guelph, Ontario, and for sexual interference with a 9-year-old boy from outside Toronto. His sentence also included a ban that forbade him from being close to children under the age of 14 for the remainder of his life.

Less than a month after his release from these charges, Whitmore was found in a downtown Toronto motel with a 13-year-old boy. He was sentenced to one year in jail for breaching a court order. In 2002, a Toronto judge gave Whitmore a three-year sentence for parole violations as he had gone to British Columbia after he was found with a 5-year-old boy. In March 2004, a National Parole Board report stated that clinicians who assessed Whitmore were of the opinion that he had a 100 percent probability of recidivating.

On June 16, 2005, Whitmore was released after serving his full three-year sentence and he moved to Chilliwack, British Columbia. For the next year, he lived under s. 810 of the Criminal Code, which places restrictions on released offenders who have served their full sentence for violent attacks or sexual offences against children. On June 2, 2006, he received permission from local police to visit family members in Alberta for a few days. In early June, a probation officer with B.C. Corrections recommended that the Crown obtain a new Section 810 order for another 12 months. On June 15, Whitmore contacted the police in Alberta who told him to set up a court date to renew the Section 810 order, but he failed to appear and efforts to locate him were unsuccessful. On July 14, a Canada-wide warrant was issued for Whitmore not appearing at the June 29 hearing. Four days later, using a different last name, Whitmore was hired at a construction site in Winnipeg, where he befriended a co-worker, the stepfather of the 14-year-old boy (Walton 2006).

After Whitmore's capture, the Crown indicated it has a strong case to have Whitmore designated as a dangerous offender. A year after his arrest in Saskatchewan, however, it was reported that, in return for a guilty plea to 12 charges (which ranged from unlawful confinement to making child pornography available to both boys) during a court appearance, he would be given a life sentence without the possibility of parole for seven years. The agreement also included the Crown agreeing not to make any effort to apply to have Whitmore designated a dangerous offender, which, if successful, would have seen him kept in prison indefinitely.

Peter Whitmore was given a life sentence without the possibility of parole for seven years in return for his plea of guilty to 12 charges. (CP Photo/Troy Fleece)

This plea bargain quickly became a topic of debate. The Director of Saskatchewan's public prosecutions defended the move by stating that a life sentence was "functionally the same" as designating Whitmore a dangerous offender. He also pointed out that the agreement was made to spare both of the victims having to testify and be cross-examined during the trial. In addition, individuals given a life sentence as well as dangerous offenders are eligible for a parole hearing after seven years, and, if unsuccessful, their cases are automatically reviewed every two years afterward. Critics, however, stated that almost all dangerous offenders are denied parole, so that by giving Whitmore a life sentence, he has a better chance of being released on parole (Pruden and Hall 2007). It was noted that although individuals who received life sentences and those designated as dangerous offenders are technically judged by the same rules when they apply for parole, the National Parole Board grants 33 percent of lifers' applications for parole compared to just 1.4 percent of full parole requests from dangerous offenders ("The Importance . . . " 2007). The trial judge agreed with plea bargain, sentencing Whitmore to life (Harding 2007a, 2007b).

In October 2007, the federal government re-introduced a bill (Omnibus Bill C-2, An Act to Amend the Criminal Code – The protection of children and other vulnerable persons). This bill included five criminal justice bills that were before the House of Commons when Parliament was prorogued in September 2007. This Omnibus bill included a number of provisions regarding dangerous and violent offenders, including provisions that would make it easier for Crown prosecutors to obtain dangerous offender designations and allow judges to hand out new sentences intended to prevent dangerous and high-risk offenders from re-offending. On July 2, 2008, these new provisions came into effect.

Critics of the new bill felt that the new provisions did not go far enough. They argued that Canada should think about introducing laws currently being used in the United States that would transfer criminals such as Whitmore to secure centres where they would be held indefinitely as "patients" under civil commitment measures. A number of provincial justice ministers have indicated that they think this issue has merit and should be discussed (Freeze 2007).

In the United States, involuntary civil commitment statutes (sometimes referred to as "sexual predator statutes")—usually applied to offenders who victimize strangers, have multiple victims, and commit certain violent offences—have been in place for almost 20 years. The first such statue was introduced by Washington State when it passed its Community Protection Act in 1990.

Continued on next page

These statutes presume that such individuals have a mental abnormality or disability and that are unable to control their sexual deviancy. If prosecutors believe that a sexual offender about to be released from prison is likely to re-offend, they start an involuntary civil commitment hearing in order to assess whether or not the offender is too dangerous to be released. If prosecutors are successful, the sex offender will then be committed to a secure facility. The commitment will be for an indefinite period of time until the offender no longer poses a threat to the community.

A number of constitutional challenges to these laws have been heard by the United States Supreme Court. These cases have questioned these statutes on the basis of the U.S. Constitution's due process clause. Substantive due process prohibits states from limiting an individual's fundamental rights unless the state has a compelling interest and that the statute be specifically focused on that interest. The U.S. Supreme Court upheld the constitutionality of the State of Kansas's Sexually Violent Predator Act in two separate cases. In *Kansas v. Hendricks* (1997), a divided Supreme Court ruled that because the statute is "civil" and not part of the criminal law, the statute cannot violate the Constitution's double jeopardy clause. And five

years later, in *Kansas v. Crane* (2002), the Supreme Court clarified the definition of a sexual predator, holding that the involuntary civil commitment of a sexual predator is permissible if a sex offender is known to lack control over his or her behaviour. While it is not necessary for an offender to lack "total" control in order to be involuntary committed, the state cannot commit a person without showing that the offender suffers from a volitional impairment (such as pedophilia) and has serious difficulty in terms of controlling his or her behaviour. Mr. Crane was released after doctors concluded that his mental condition had changed and that he was no longer a threat.

Questions

1. Do you think that striking a plea bargain was the appropriate decision in this case?
2. What do you think about Canada's current long-term offender and dangerous offender legislation? Do you think they should be changed? If so, how?
3. Do you think the dangerous offender designation should have been applied to Peter Whitmore?
4. Do you think Canada should implement a system of involuntary civil commitment as practised by many jurisdictions in the United States?

SUMMARY

The different approaches and models of justice discussed in this chapter all focus on reducing crime in our society. One model may appear superior to the others in its ability to achieve that goal; in fact, it is likely that one philosophy alone can never achieve the goal, given the realities of contemporary society.

It is probably wiser to seek an integrated philosophical approach to the problem of crime. The treatment of offenders and the protection of the legal rights of alleged perpetrators are important, but so are the rights of victims and the desire of citizens to live in a crime-free society. How, then, are these issues to be reconciled? Still, it is important to remember that not all offenders can be treated (e.g., some dangerous offenders cannot be). So some offenders can and should be incapacitated for long terms of imprisonment, if not for life.

Overall, however, it seems that though most people want punishment for offenders, they also want justice done and want to see the protection of due

process rights granted them by the Charter of Rights and Freedoms. Thus, Canadians should expect to see combinations of the various crime control strategies described in the chapter, with the resulting tensions, conflicts, and problems that such approaches bring.

The different models that form the basis of our criminal justice system can be categorized according to whether they focus on the act or on the actor. Three of the philosophies emphasize the criminal act and include demands that discretion within the system be removed. These models argue that the discretion of both prosecutors and sentencing judges must be controlled by guidelines and that any deviations from these standards must be written down and forwarded to a review agency that assesses their validity. In addition, because prosecutors and judges have the power to shorten sentence lengths, advocates of the justice model support the elimination of parole.

The justice model, which is generally the basis of our criminal justice system today, posits that the accused should be punished only after being found guilty in a court of law, regardless of factual guilt. This philosophy's advocates also believe in the control of discretion and the elimination of parole. Here, they differ from advocates of the deterrence and selective incapacitation models, in that they believe that most prison terms should be short. Advocates of this position believe in alternatives to imprisonment, especially for first-time offenders. The deterrence philosophy, too, supports limitations to discretion throughout the criminal justice process, but it favours much longer periods of incarceration. Violent offenders are the focus of the selective incapacitation approach, which argues that the incarceration of these offenders reduces rates of violent crime.

The only philosophy of punishment to focus on the actor is the rehabilitation model. Since offenders differ from one another, this approach favours discretion within the criminal justice system so that the "punishment fits the criminal." The goal of this model is to reintegrate offenders back into society, so it calls for a wide variety of programs to be made available for offenders both inside and outside correctional facilities.

The philosophy of restorative justice differs from the other mechanisms of social control, largely in its emphasis on involving both the victim and the community. Aboriginal justice systems, which are based mainly on the principles of restorative justice, are now operating in various locations across Canada. The communities using these Aboriginal tenets of justice are working to integrate their concerns with those of the Western legal system in order to assist in the social control of as many Aboriginal offenders as possible. These systems comprise a large number of groups and individuals, including Elders, community members, the offender, the victim, and police officers.

Discussion Questions

1. Which philosophy of criminal justice do you think is most effective in controlling crime in our society?

2. What improvements would you make to our criminal justice system to reduce crime?

3. Why do you think the majority of the models of criminal justice want to control or eliminate the discretionary powers of criminal justice agents? How would such control reduce the crime rate?

4. Do you think that increasing the number of police on the street, as advocated by the deterrence model, would effectively control crime?

5. Do you think Aboriginal communities should operate their own justice systems?

6. What Aboriginal principles of justice do you think are superior to those held by Western legal systems?

7. Why do you think Aboriginal justice systems are so successful, compared to the Western legal system, in processing and treating Aboriginal offenders?

8. Do you think restorative justice programs should deal with violent offenders on a regular basis?

Suggested Readings

Cullen, F.T., and K. Gilbert. *Reaffirming Rehabilitation*. Cincinnati: CJ Anderson, 1982.

Elliott, E., and R.M. Gordon, eds. *New Directions in Restorative Justice: Issues, Practice, Evaluation*. Devon, U.K.: Willan, 2005.

Green, R. *Justice in Aboriginal Communities: Sentencing Alternatives*. Saskatoon: Purich, 1998.

Hudson, B. *Justice through Punishment: A Critique of the "Justice" Model of Corrections*. London: Macmillan, 1987.

Ross, R. *Returning to the Teachings: Exploring Aboriginal Justice*. Toronto: Penguin, 1996.

Whyte, J.D., ed. *Moving Toward Justice: Legal Traditions and Aboriginal Justice*. Saskatoon, SK.: Purich/Saskatchewan Institute of Public Policy, 2008.

References

Allen, F. 1981. *The Decline of the Rehabilitative Ideal: Penal Purpose and Social Purpose*. New Haven: Yale University Press.

American Friends Service Committee. 1971. *Struggle for Justice*. New York: Hill and Wang.

Andrews, D., and J. Bonta. 1998. *The Psychology of Criminal Conduct*, 2nd ed. Cincinnati: Anderson.

Apospori, E., and G. Allpert. 1993. "Research Note: The Role of Differential Experience with the Criminal Justice System in Changes in Perceptions of Severity of Sanctions Over Time." *Crime and Delinquency* 39: 184–94.

Beccaria, C. 1764. *On Crimes and Punishment*. Indianapolis: Bobbs-Merrill, 1978.

Befu, H. 1990. "Four Models of Japanese Society and Their Relevance to Conflict." In S.N. Eisenstadt and E. Ben-Ari, eds., *Japanese Models of Conflict Resolution*. London: Kegan Paul.

Beirne, P., and J. Messerschmidt. 1991. *Criminology*. San Diego, CA: Harcourt Brace Jovanovich.

Braithwaite, J. 1993. "Shame and Modernity." *British Journal of Criminology* 33: 1–18.

———. 1989. *Crime, Shame, and Reintegration*. New York: Cambridge University Press.

Bryant, M.E. 2002. "Tsuu T'ina First Nations Peacemaker Justice System." *LawNow* 26, no. 4: 16–17.

———. 1999. "Sentencing Aboriginal Offenders." *LawNow* 24: 20–22.

Burford, G., and J. Pennell. 1998. *Family Group Decision Making Project: Outcome Report*, vol. 1. St. John's: Memorial University.

Canadian Sentencing Commission. 1987. *Sentencing Reform: A Canadian Approach*. Ottawa: Ministry of Supply and Services Canada.

Carrigan, D.O. 1991. *Crime and Punishment in Canada: A History*. Toronto: McClelland and Stewart.

Chambliss, W.J., ed. 1969. *Crime and the Legal Process*. New York: McGraw-Hill.

Clark, C. 2002. "Ottawa to Create National Sex-Offender Registry." *The Globe and Mail*, February 14, A1, A8.

Clear, T. 1995. "Correction beyond Prison Walls." In J.F. Sheley, ed., *Criminology*, 2nd ed. Belmont, CA: Wadsworth.

Committee for the Study of Incarceration. 1975. *Doing Justice*. New York: Hill and Wang.

Community Holistic Circle Healing. 1997. *History*. Wampigoux, MA.

Couture, J., T. Parker, R. Couture, P. Laboucane, and Native Counselling Services of Alberta. 2001. *A Cost-Benefit Analysis of Hollow Water's Community Holistic Circle Healing Process*. Ottawa: Ministry of the Solicitor General.

Cullen, F.T., and B.K. Applegate. 1997. *Offender Rehabilitation*. Aldershot: Ashgate.

Cullen, F.T., and K. Gilbert. 1982. *Reaffirming Rehabilitation*. Cincinnati, OH: Anderson.

Cullen, F.T., E.J. Latessa, V.S. Burton, and L.X. Lombardo. 1993. "The Correctional Orientation of Prison Wardens: Is the Rehabilitative Ideal Supported?" *Criminology* 31, no. 1: 69–92.

Daly, K. 2006. "Restorative Justice and Sexual Assault: An Archival Study of Court and Conference Cases." *British Journal of Criminology*, 46: 334–56.

Daly, K., and J. Stubbs. 2007. "Feminist Theory, Feminist and Anti-Racist Politics, and Restorative Justice." In G. Johnstone and D.W. Van Ness, eds., *Handbook of Restorative Justice*. Cullumpton, Devon: Willan.

Dauvergne, M. 2008. *Crime Statistics in Canada, 2007*. Ottawa: Canadian Centre for Justice Statistics.

Decker, S.H., R. Wright, and R. Logie. 1993. "Perceptual Deterrence among Active Residential Burglars: A Research Note." *Criminology* 31, no. 1: 135–47.

Elliott, L. 2001. "Ontario Willing to Foot Bill for National Offender Registry." *Winnipeg Free Press*, September 7, B4.

Feeley, M., and J. Simon. 1992. "The New Penology: Notes on the Emerging Strategy of Corrections and Its Implications." *Criminology* 30: 449–75.

Fine, S. 1997. "Top Court Extends Rights of the Accused." *The Globe and Mail*, August 9, A1, A6.

———. 1994a. "Has the High Court Lost Touch with Reality?" *The Globe and Mail*, October 8, D2.

———. 1994b. "Murderer Denied Fair Hearing, Court Says." *The Globe and Mail*, October 1, A4.

———. 1994c. "Failure to Inform Suspect Invalidates DNA Evidence, Top Court Rules." *The Globe and Mail*, October 1, A8.

Frankel, M.F. 1972. *Criminal Sentences: Law without Order*. New York: Hill and Wang.

Freeze, C. 2007. "Should Canada Hold Sex Offenders Indefinitely?" *The Globe and Mail*, March 8, A5.

Freiberg, P. 1990. "Rehabilitation Is Effective if Done Well, Studies Say." *American Psychological Association Monitor*. September.

Gendreau, P., and C. Goggin. 1996. "Principles of Effective Correctional Programming." *Forum on Corrections Research* 8: 38–41.

Gibbs, J. 1975. *Crime, Punishment, and Deterrence*. New York: Elsevier.

Grasmick, H., and R. Bursik. 1990. "Conscience, Significant Others, and Rational Choice: Extending the Reference Model." *Law and Society Review* 24: 837–61.

Grasmick, H., and D.E. Green. 1980. "Legal Punishment, Social Disapproval and Internalization as Inhibitors of Illegal Behavior." *Journal of Criminal Law and Criminology* 71: 325–35.

Green, R.G. 1998. *Justice in Aboriginal Communities: Sentencing Alternatives*. Saskatoon: Purich.

Greenwood, P. 1982. *Selective Incapacitation*. Santa Monica, CA: Rand.

Griset, P.L. 1991. *Determinate Sentencing: The Promise and the Reality of Retributive Justice*. Albany: State University of New York Press.

Hamilton, A.C. 2001. *A Feather Not a Gavel: Working Towards Aboriginal Justice*. Winnipeg: Great Plains Publishing.

Hamilton, A.C., and C.M. Sinclair. 1991. *The Justice System and Aboriginal People: Report of the Aboriginal Justice Inquiry*, vol. 1. Winnipeg: Queen's Printer.

Hamparian, D.M., R.S. Schuster, S. Dinitz, and J.P. Conrad. 1978. *The Violent Few: A Study of Dangerous Juvenile Offenders*. Lexington, MA: Lexington Books.

Hanson, R.K., A. Gordon, A.J.R. Harris, W. Murphy, V.L. Quinsey, and M.C. Seto. 2002. "First Report of the Collaborative Outcome Data Project on the Effectiveness of Psychological Treatment of Sex Offenders." *Sexual Abuse: A Journal of Research and Treatment*, 14: 169–94.

Harding, K. 2007a. "Whitmore's Sordid Crimes Revealed." *The Globe and Mail*, July 24, A1, A4.

———. 2007b. "Notorious Pedophile Offered Plea Bargain." *The Globe and Mail*, July 19, A10.

Hechter, M., and S. Kanazawa. 1993. "Group Politics and Social Order in Japan." *Journal of Theoretical Politics* 5: 455–93.

Hudson, B. 1987. *Justice through Punishment: A Critique of the "Justice" Model of Corrections*. London: Macmillan.

Jerusalem, M.P. 1995. "A Framework for Post-Sentence Sex Offender Legislation." *Vanderbilt Law Review* 48: 219–55.

Karp, D.R. 1998. "The Judicial and Judicious Use of Shame Penalties." *Crime and Delinquency* 37: 449–64.

Kong, R., H. Johnson, S. Beattie, and A. Cardillo. 2003. *Sexual Offenders in Canada*. Ottawa: Canadian Centre for Justice Statistics.

Kramer, J.H., and J.T. Ulmer. 1996. "Sentencing Disparity and Departures from Guidelines." *Justice Quarterly* 13: 81–106.

Latimer, J., C. Dowden, and D. Muisse. 2001. *The Effectiveness of Restorative Justice Practices: A Meta-Analysis*. Ottawa: Department of Justice.

Latimer, J., and S. Kleinknecht. 2000. *The Effects of Restorative Justice Programming: A Review of the Empirical*. Ottawa: Department of Justice.

Law Reform Commission of Canada. 1991. *Aboriginal Peoples and Criminal Justice*. Ottawa: Law Reform Commission of Canada.

Logan, C. 1993. *Criminal Justice Performance: Measures for Prison*. Washington, DC: Bureau of Justice Statistics.

Mackie, R. 1999. "Ontario Plans Registry of Rapists and Pedophiles." *The Globe and Mail*, April 17, A5.

Makkai, T., and J. Braithwaite. 1994. "Reintegrative Shaming and Compliance with Regulatory Standards." *Criminology* 20: 361–413.

Mandamin, Judge T.L.S., E. Starlight, and M. One-spot. 2003. "Peacemaking and the Tsuu Tina Court." *Justice as Healing* 8.

Martinson, R. 1979. "Symposium on Sentencing: Part II." *Hofstra Law Review* 7: 243–58.

———. 1974. "What Works? Questions and Answers about Prison Reform." *Public Interest* 35: 22–54.

Marvell, T.B., and C.E. Moody. 1996. "Determinate Sentencing and Abolishing Parole: The Long-Term Impacts on Prisons and Crime." *Criminology* 34: 107–28.

McIntyre, M. 2007. "Teen Used to Lure Boy, Crown to Allege." *Winnipeg Free Press*, July 19, A4.

Melton, A.P. 1998. *Indigenous Justice Systems and Tribal Society*. Washington, DC: National Institute of Justice.

Meyer, J.A.F. 1998. "History Repeats Itself: Restorative Justice in Native American Communities." *Journal of Contemporary Criminal Justice* 14: 42–57.

Mildon, M. 2001. "First Native Court Set Up in Alberta." *LawNow*, 25, no. 5: 6.

Moon, P. 1995. "Natives Find Renewal in Manitoba Prison." *The Globe and Mail*, July 20, A1, A4.

Morris, N., and M. Tonry. 1990. *Between Prison and Probation: Intermediate Punishments in a Rational Sentencing System*. New York: Oxford University Press.

Nicholaichuk, T.P. 1995. "Sex Offender Treatment Priority: An Illustration of the Risk/Need Principle." *Forum on Corrections Research* 8: 30–32.

Packer, H.L. 1968. *The Limits of the Criminal Sanction*. Stanford, CA: Stanford University Press.

Pennell, J., and G. Buford. 2000. "Family Group Decision Making: Protecting Children and Women." *Child Welfare* 79: 131–58.

———. 1995. *Family Group Decision Making: New Roles For "Old" Partners in Resolving Family Violence*. St. John's: Memorial University, School of Social Work.

Persky, S., and J. Dixon. 2001. *On Kiddie Porn: Sexual Representation, Free Speech, and the Robin Sharpe Case*. Vancouver: New Star Books.

Price, A.C., and B.G. Stitt. 1986. "Consistent Crime Control Philosophy and Policy: A Theoretical Analysis." *Criminal Justice Review* 11, no. 2: 23–30.

Pruden, J., and A. Hall, 2007. "Whitmore Jail Deal Defended." *The National Post*, July 19, p.A8.

Public Safety Canada. 2008. *Corrections and Conditional Release Statistical Review*. Ottawa.

Rice, M.E., and G.T. Harris. 2003. "The Size and Sign of Treatment Effects in Sex Offender Therapy." *Annals of the New York Academy of Sciences*, 989: 428–40.

Richards, B. 1992. "Burden of Proof." *The Wall Street Journal*, December 8, pp. A1, A8.

Roach, K. 1999. "Four Models of the Criminal Process." *Journal of Criminal Law and Criminology* 89, no. 2: 671–716.

Ross, R. 1994. "Duelling Paradigms? Western Criminal Justice versus Aboriginal Community Healing." In R. Gosse, Y. Youngblood Henderson, and R. Carter, eds., *Continuing Poundmaker and Riel's Request*. Saskatoon: Purich, pp. 241–68.

Royal Commission on Aboriginal Peoples. 1996. *Bridging the Cultural Divide*. Ottawa: Minister of Supply and Services.

Rubenstein, M.L., S.H. Clarke, and T.J. White. 1980. *Alaska Bans Plea Bargaining*. Washington, DC: Government Printing Office.

Rudin, J. 2005. "Aboriginal Justice and Restorative Justice." In E. Elliott and R.M. Gordon, eds., *New Directions in Restorative Justice: Issues, Practice, Evaluation*. Devon, U.K.: Willan.

Seto, M.C. 2003. "Interpreting the Treatment Performance of Sex Offenders." In A. Matravers, ed., *Sex Offenders in the Community*. Devon, U.K.: Willan.

Shannon, L. 1988. *Criminal Career Continuity: Its Social Context*. New York: Human Sciences Press.

Sherman, L.W., and R. Berk. 1984. "The Specific Deterrent Effects of Arrest for Domestic Assault." *American Sociological Review* 49: 261–72.

Smith, R.J. 1983. *Japanese Society: Individual, Self and the Social Order*. Cambridge: Cambridge University Press.

"The Importance of a Dangerous Label." 2007. *The Globe and Mail*. July 20, A12.

Tracy, P., M.E. Wolfgang, and R.M. Figlio. 1990. *Delinquency in Two Birth Cohorts*. New York: Plenum.

Trevethan, S., N. Crutchon, and J.-P. Moore. 2002. *A Profile of Federal Offenders Designated as Dangerous Offenders or Serving Long-Term Supervision Orders*. Ottawa: Correctional Service Canada.

Umbreit, M., and S. Stacey. 1996. "Family Group Conferencing Comes to the U.S." *Juvenile and Family Court Journal* 47: 29–38.

Van Ness, D., and K. Heetderks Strong. 1997. *Restoring Justice*. Cincinnati, OH: CJ Anderson.

Visher, C. 1995. "Career Offenders and Crime Control." In J.F. Sheley, ed., *Criminology*, 2nd ed. Belmont, CA: Wadsworth.

von Hirsch, A. 1976. *Doing Justice*. New York: Hill and Wang.

Walker, S. 1994. *Sense and Nonsense about Crime*, 3rd ed. Belmont, CA: Wadsworth.

———. 1993. *Taming the System*. New York: Oxford University Press.

Walton, D. 2006. "Old Charge Builds New Whitmore Mystery." *The Globe and Mail*, August 5, A7.

Wilson, J.Q. 1975. *Thinking about Crime*. New York: Basic Books.

Wolfgang, M.E., R.M. Figlio, and T. Sellin. 1972. *Delinquency in a Birth Cohort.* Chicago: University of Chicago Press.

Zehr, H. 1990. *Changing Lenses: A New Focus for Criminal Justice.* Scottsdale, PA: Herald Press.

Zimring, F.E., and G. Hawkins. 1988. "The New Mathematics of Imprisonment." *Crime and Delinquency* 34: 425–36.

Court Cases

Kansas v. Crane (2002), 534 U.S. 407

Kansas v. Hendricks (1997), 521 U.S. 346

R. v. Borden (1994), 3 S.C.R. 145

R. v. Dyck (2008), ONCA 309

R. v. Gladue (1999), 1 S.C.R. 688

R. v. Lyons (1987), 2 S.C.R. 309

R. v. Rodgers (2006), S.C.C. 15

R. v. Sharpe (2001), 1 S.C.R. 45

R. v. Swietlinski (1995), 92 C.C.C. (3d) 449 (S.C.C.)

Weblinks

This chapter includes three of the most significant and controversial decisions made by the Supreme Court of Canada over the past decade. They are located at the following website: http://scc.lexum.umontreal.ca/en/index.html. To read *R. v. Gladue,* click on 1999, then Volume 1. The decision was announced on April 23. To read *R. v. Sharpe,* click on 2001, then Volume 1. It was announced on January 26. To read *R. v. Rodgers,* click on 2006, then Volume 1. It was announced on April 27.

Crime Rates, Crime Trends, and Perceptions of Crime in Canada

CHAPTER OBJECTIVES

✓ Understand the Uniform Crime Reporting system in Canada.

✓ Understand how violent and property crimes are differentiated.

✓ Follow the general trends of criminal victimization in Canada.

✓ Know the shortcomings of using crime statistics collected by official agencies.

✓ Understand the importance of public perceptions toward crime and the criminal justice system.

I f the criminal justice system is to control and reduce crime, we need current and accurate information on the nature and extent of crimes in particular locations as well as across Canada. In order to understand the dimensions of any type of crime, we need to be able to measure crime in an accurate way. A number of different measures have been developed to help officials and policymakers collect and interpret crime statistics. Official crime statistics are collected by the police and other justice officials from crimes reported to them or through interviews with individual citizens about instances in which they were victimized. Many individuals look at crime or victimization rates for a single year; others study crime trends and how particular types of crime change over time.

The crime rate is declining in Canada, but is fear of crime? There is not always a direct correspondence between the two. In the 2004 General Social Survey (GSS), Canadians were asked about their perceptions concerning the level of crime and crime trends in their neighbourhood. The GSS found that Canadians believe that crime is lower in their neighbourhood than elsewhere in Canada. Fifty-nine percent of Canadians held this opinion, while another 29 percent thought that the crime rate in their neighbourhood was about the same as in other neighbourhoods. Only a small proportion of Canadians felt that their neighbourhood experienced higher rates of crime.

Fear of crime can be measured in two ways: (1) by feelings of satisfaction with personal safety from crime, and (2) by an individual's anticipated fear or worry about becoming a victim. The 2004 GSS asked respondents about their overall satisfaction with their own personal safety from crime as well as their level of fear of crime in three situations that focused on general feelings of security (as opposed to fear of certain types of crime): (1) being home alone at night, (2) taking public transportation at night, and (3) walking alone after dark. Ninety percent of the respondents stated that they felt safe walking alone in their neighbourhood at night, a slight increase from the 88 percent reported in 1999. Eighty percent of those who stayed at home alone in the evening indicated that they were not worried about crime—the same proportion as in 1999. Waiting for and using public transportation alone after dark was the most fear-inducing activity of the three situations presented to the respondents. Only 57 percent of the respondents indicated that they weren't worried about becoming a victim of a crime when using public transportation alone at night.

Feelings of safety were slightly lower among women (93 percent) than among men (95 percent). In 2000, women's feelings of safety increased slightly more (15 percent) than those of men (12 percent). A narrowing of gender differences occurred in 2004;

however, differences did appear when specific activities at night were examined. Twice as many women as men were worried when relying on public transportation alone at night (58 percent versus 29 percent); women also had higher rates of fear than men when home alone at night (27 percent versus 12 percent) and when walking alone after dark (16 percent versus 6 percent). For all three of these situations, women's fear of crime had dropped slightly since 1999, while men's fear of crime remained stable. Fear of crime is greater for women than for men across all age groups, with this exception: women's concerns about being the victim of a crime generally decrease with age while men's concerns remain about the same.

Canadians who walked alone every night had lower rates of fear than those who walked alone less than once a month. And among those who felt that the level of crime in their neighbourhood was higher than in other parts of Canada, 18 percent indicated that they were dissatisfied with their safety. In addition, those respondents who believed that crime in their neighbourhood had increased were more likely to be fearful.

Every five years in Canada, statistics about the fear of crime and perceptions of the criminal justice system are published. But perhaps the most anticipated crime statistics are the national crime statistics, which are usually released to the public in the early summer. Criminologists are interested in the following: how much crime occurs; whether overall crime rates are increasing or decreasing; the rate of violent crime; which crimes are committed most often; how many crimes are "cleared" (i.e., solved) by the police; and which city can claim the title "murder capital of Canada." But what is meant by these national crime statistics? What problems and limitations are associated with them? Can the figures be manipulated? This chapter discusses the official crime reporting system in Canada. Official crime figures include police-generated crime data and data collected from victimization surveys. Unofficial methods of collecting crime data are also discussed.

2008 CRIME RATES

In 2008, about 2.2 million Criminal Code incidents were reported to the police (excluding traffic incidents and those involving other federal statutes such as drug offences). Overall, the volume of crime reported to and by the police decreased by 5 percent compared to 2007, reaching its lowest level in 30 years (see Figure 4.1). Twenty percent of offences were classified as violent crimes, and the remaining 80 percent were classified as non-violent Criminal Code offences. Together, seven offences accounted for approximately 80 percent of all reported crime in Canada during 2008: theft under $5,000

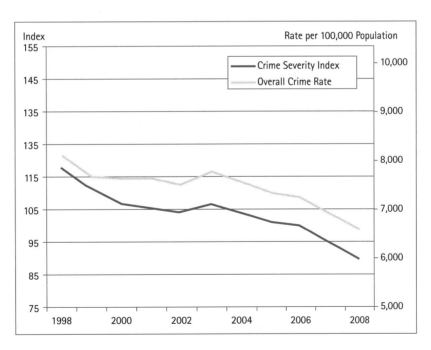

FIGURE 4.1

Police-Reported Crime Rate and Crime Severity Index, Canada, 1998 to 2008

Source: Marnie Wallace, "Police-reported crime statistics in Canada, 2008", *Juristat*, Vol. 29, no. 3, p. 13. Statistics Canada catalogue no. 85-002-X.

(25 percent), mischief (17 percent), break and enter (10 percent), common assault (8 percent), administration of justice offences (8 percent), motor vehicle theft (6 percent) and disturbing the peace (5 percent) (Wallace 2009).

In 2008, a Crime Severity Index was included for the first time to the annual crime statistics. Changes in the more serious crimes are assigned higher weights and, as a result, have a greater impact on the police-reported Crime Severity Index than on the crime rate. Approximately 50 percent of the decrease in the severity of police-reported crime in Canada in 2008 was the result of a 10 percent decline in the rate of break and enters (see Exhibit 4.1).

Violent Crime

There were almost 442,000 violent Criminal Code violations reported in 2008, a decrease of 3,500 reported violent crimes from 2007 (see Figure 4.2). Both the volume and severity of police-reported violent crime decreased during 2008. The Violent Crime Severity Index decreased by 3 percent, the result of a 7 percent decline in robberies and a 10 percent decrease in attempted murders (Wallace 2009). This decline can be explained largely by the fact that the rate of common assault, the most frequently reported violent crime,

decreased by 2 percent. Other violent crimes that experienced significant declines in 2008 compared to 2007 included attempted murder and sexual assault (level 2) (both −10 percent); firearms − use of, discharge, pointing (−9 percent); and robbery and threatening or harassing phone calls (both −7 percent). The rate of all violent crimes with the exception of homicide (+2 percent), assault (level 3) (+1 percent), other assaults (+1 percent), and criminal harassment (which remained the same compared to 2007) experienced a decline in 2008 compared to 2007.

The homicide rate (which includes first and second degree murder, manslaughter, and infanticide) increased by 2 percent in 2008. There were 611 homicides reported, 17 more than in 2007. The number of attempted murders decreased to 723 in 2008, a decrease of 70 from the previous year. The number of robberies also decreased in 2008, from 34,182 to 32,281 (Wallace 2009).

The jurisdictions that experienced increases in their violent crime rate in 2008 included New Brunswick (+7 percent), Nunavut (+6 percent), Newfoundland and Labrador (+2 percent), and Alberta (+1 percent). Prince Edward Island and Manitoba had the same violent crime rate in 2008 as in 2007. The largest decline in the violent crime rate was experienced in British Columbia (−5 percent), followed by Ontario,

---

EXHIBIT 4.1 The Police-Reported Crime Rate Crime Severity Index

The new police-reported Crime Severity Index (PRCSI) adds to existing measures of crime—namely the traditional police-reported crime rate (PRCR) and victimization data from the General Social Survey. The index was developed in response to a request by the police community to create a measure of crime that reflects the relative seriousness of different offences and addresses limitations of the current PRCR.

The police-reported crime rate, which measures changes in the volume of crime, counts each criminal incident equally. As a result, the rate is dominated by high-volume, less-serious offences.

The police-reported Crime Severity Index measures changes in the severity of crime from year to year. Each type of offence is assigned a weight derived from actual sentences handed down by courts in all provinces and territories. Weights are calculated using the five most recent years of available sentencing data.

More serious crimes are assigned higher weights; less serious offences lower weights.

As a result, when all crimes are included, more serious offences have a greater impact on changes in the Index.

Separate police-reported crime rates have traditionally been calculated for overall crime, violent crimes, property-related crimes, and all other offences. Separate severity indexes have also been created: one for overall police-reported crime, one for violent crime including only crimes against person, and one for non-violent crime such as property and drug offences. Drug offences are excluded from the traditional crime rate, along with Federal Statutes and Criminal Code traffic offences. They are, however, included in the PRCSI.

In contrast to the PRCR, which is a rate of 100,000 population, the PRCSI is an index where the base year in 2006 is equal to 100. Data for the index are available back to 1998 only.

Source: Marnie Wallace, "Police-reported crime statistics in Canada, 2008", *Juristat*, Vol. 29, no. 3, p. 7. Statistics Canada catalogue no. 85-002-X.

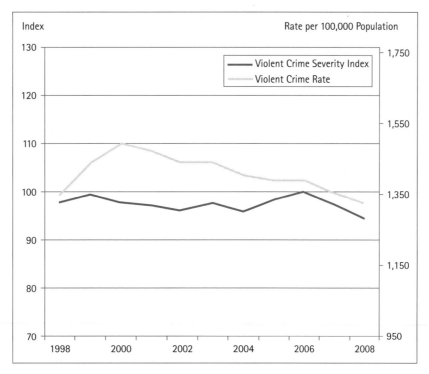

FIGURE 4.2

Police-Reported Violent Crime Rate and Crime Severity Index Values, Canada, 1998 to 2008

Note: The violent crime rate has been expanded to include a number of offences not previously included in the violent crime rate. As a result, comparable data is only available starting in 1998.
Source: Marnie Wallace, "Police-reported crime statistics in Canada, 2008", *Juristat*, Vol. 29, no. 3, p. 13. Statistics Canada catalogue no. 85-002-X.

the Northwest Territories, and Yukon (all of which declined by 4 percent). In terms of the Crime Severity Index, all provinces recorded declines in 2008 compared to 2007 with the exception of Prince Edward Island (+8 percent), Newfoundland and Labrador (+5 percent), Alberta (+3 percent) and New Brunswick (+2 percent) (see Table 4.1).

Property Crime

Property crimes are committed with the intent to acquire property without violence or the threat of violence. The most common property crimes were theft under $5,000 (non-motor vehicle), break and enter, and motor vehicle theft.

All offences in the property crime category declined in 2008 from 2007, with the exception of fraud, which experienced a rate increase of 1 percent. The largest rate decreases were found in theft of a motor vehicle (−15 percent), breaking and entering

(−10 percent), possession of stolen property (−8 percent), and theft under $5,000 (non-motor vehicle) (−6 percent). The rates of robbery decreased in every province with the exception of Prince Edward Island (+42 percent) and Nunavut (+22 percent). The largest decreases in robbery were recorded in Manitoba (−22 percent) and Saskatchewan (−18 percent). The rates of break and enter also declined in all provinces except for Prince Edward Island (12 percent) and Nunavut (9 percent). Motor vehicles theft also declined in all provinces except for Yukon (+24 percent) and the Northwest Territories (+6 percent).

Other Criminal Code

The rate of most "other" Criminal Code offences declined in 2008 from 2007. While declines were recorded for almost every offence, the most notable decline was for prostitution (−18 percent). The largest increase was found in counterfeiting (+40 percent).

TABLE 4.1 Police-Reported Crime Rate and Crime Severity Index Values, Canada and the Provinces and Territories, 2008

Province and territory	Total				Violent crime			
	Crime Severity Index	Percent change in Index 2007 to 2008	crime rate[1]	Percent change in 2007 to 2008	Violent Crime Severity Index	Percent change in Index 2007 to 2008	Violent Crime rare[2]	Percent change in rate 2007 to 2008
Newfoundland and Labrador	71.2	-6	6,321	-1	66.1	5	1,519	2
Prince Edward Island	68.2	7	6,208	2	43.2	8	1,126	0
Nova Scotia	83.6	-9	6,956	-7	87.6	-5	1,689	-1
New Brunswick	71.3	1	5,664	1	67.1	2	1,482	7
Quebec	82.5	-3	5,064	-1	82.4	-2	1,084	0
Ontario	70.6	-5	4,877	-4	81.5	-5	1,043	-4
Manitoba	128.7	-14	9,911	-9	158.2	-9	2,013	0
Saskatchewan	156.1	-5	12,892	-4	155.6	-9	2,551	-3
Alberta	110.1	-4	8,808	-4	110.9	3	1,517	1
British Columbia	120.9	-8	9,580	-8	115.0	-2	1,686	-5
Yukon	181.5	-2	21,805	5	195.2	-2	3,832	-4
Northwest Territories	337.7	1	43,509	1	339.9	-2	8,872	-4
Nunavut	324.2	2	34,867	15	466.8	-9	9,606	6
Canada	**90.0**	**-5**	**6,558**	**-5**	**94.6**	**-3**	**1,326**	**-2**

[1]The crime rate consists of all *Criminal Code* offences excluding traffic. It also excludes drug offences and all federal statutes. All offences are included in the Crime Severity Index.

[2]The violent crime rate has been expanded to include a number of offences not previously included in the violent crime rate, Incuding uttering threats, criminal harassment and forcible confinement. Data using this definition of violent crime are available back to 1998.

Source: Marnie Wallace, "Police-reported crime statistics in Canada, 2008", *Juristat*, Vol. 29, no. 3, p. 26. Statistics Canada catalogue no. 85-002-X.

TRENDS IN CANADIAN CRIME RATES

The crime statistics discussed above were those recorded by the police. However, the police are often reactive when it comes to recording crime—that is, in many instances they only realize that a crime has been committed after they have been told about it by a member the public (see Chapter 5). A number of factors besides the raw level of crime can affect police crime statistics. Behavioural patterns, such as variations in the number of individuals committing offences, as well as society's responses to criminal behaviour, can influence the crime rate. Moreover, crime rates can be influenced by the age structure of the society and the unemployment rate. This is why researchers look for correlates of criminal behaviour; they want to understand why crime rates fluctuate over time.

Crime rates in Canada between 1962 and 2003 have tended to follow shifts in the population, although there is a bit of "lag effect." For example, Pottie Bunge et al. (2005) concluded that the overall crime rate was influenced by the age cohort referred to as the "baby-boomers." After all ages in this cohort reached 15 years of age (between 1960 and 1980), the violent and property crime rates also increased almost every year. Then the overall crime rate for property and violent crimes began to change, each following its own separate path over the next decade. Property crime rates stabilized during the 1980s as the proportion of 15- to 24-year-olds began to decline, then increased for a few years during the early 1990s, then declined again. Violent crime rates, however, increased steadily until 1993, several years following the decrease in the proportion of individuals aged 15 to 24 and 25 to 34 in Canadian society.

Pottie Bunge and colleagues (ibid.) also discovered links between certain social factors and types of crime. They reported that trends in financially motivated criminal offences, such as robbery and break and enter, were positively correlated with changes in Canada's inflation rate. This could be explained by the reduction in purchasing power for goods and services, uncertainty about the economy's future, and the resulting attractiveness of illegal criminal activity to obtain desired material goods.

And while many might think that the age structure of society would have a strong impact on financially motivated crimes, this was not the case in Canada between 1962 and 2003. In fact, the researchers found that only one financially motivated crime—break and enter—was heavily influenced by the number of individuals between 15 and 24, the most criminally active age group.

The number of 15- to 24-year-olds in the population was also found to have an impact on violent crime, notably the homicide rate. The same researchers also noted two other studies that found a similar relationship between age and homicide in Canada. Leenaars and Lester (2004) noted that the proportion of the Canadian population between 15 and 24 years of age was the most significant predictor of homicide rates in Canada. And Sprott and Cesaroni (2002) estimated that 14 percent of the reduction in Canadian homicide rates between 1974 and 1999 could be explained by changes in the age composition in the population.

Decreases in the public's tolerance for certain offences—such as domestic violence, child abuse, and other offences committed within the family—can lead to an increase in the number of cases reported to the police. In addition, victims' expectations of how the police will handle a complaint can increase or decrease the likelihood that they will report a crime to the police. Other factors that can influence crime rates include new laws—for example, the sexual assault laws introduced in 1983 (see Chapter 2)—or modifications to existing laws that make it easier to file a complaint and/or for the police and Crown to enforce the law; the latter can increase the number of criminal incidents reported. Changes in enforcement tactics as well as targeted operations can also have a significant impact on crime rates. Examples of offences that reflect the level of police enforcement activities as opposed to any increase or decrease in criminal activity include drug offences and prostitution (e.g., Duchesne 1997).

CRIME STATISTICS

One of the most basic questions asked about crime in Canada—but one of the hardest to answer—is whether the crime rate is decreasing or increasing. The question is difficult to answer because it depends on the type of crime data we are using. If those data come from the police, they represent only those crimes reported to the police or those crimes the police discover themselves. If we use an alternative source of data, such as self-reports or victimization reports, are we any closer to establishing the actual number of criminal incidents? None of these three sources of crime data is accurate; even so, they have all been studied over the years to see how well they capture the true extent of criminal incidents.

What the Police Say: The Uniform Crime Reporting System

The **Uniform Crime Reporting (UCR) system** was launched in Canada in 1961 and continues, with some modifications, to this day. The UCR is designed to generate reliable crime statistics for use in all aspects of law enforcement. In order to ensure reliability in the reporting of crime data, it applies standard definitions to all offences. This approach eliminates regional and local variations in the definitions of offences. All police agencies are required to submit their crime statistics in accordance with the UCR definitions. Since some offences are "hybrid" (see Chapter 2), the UCR does not distinguish between indictable and summary conviction offences. UCR statistics indicate that the overall police-reported crime rate declined between 1991 and 1999, before increasing by 1 percent in the years 2000 and 2001. This increase was largely the result of a 4 percent rise in the number of offences reported in the category of "other" Criminal Code offences (Savoie 2002).

In order to classify crimes, the police use a guidebook, the *Uniform Crime Reporting Manual*, which contains definitions of crime as determined by Statistics Canada and the Canadian Association of Chiefs of Police (Silverman et al. 1991). Between 1961 and 1988, all police departments in Canada summarized their crime data on standardized forms on a monthly basis and forwarded those forms to Statistics Canada. Since 1982, the responsibility for collecting and reporting these data has fallen to an affiliated agency, the Canadian Centre for Justice Statistics. This organization produces the annual crime statistics as well as a bulletin known as *Juristat*. This publication, which comes out several times a year, provides reports that offer insight into specialized areas of Canadian crime statistics as well as the operations of various aspects of the criminal justice system, such as corrections.

For its first 27 years, the UCR reported crime on the basis of aggregated statistics. This survey, known as the Aggregate UCR Survey, is still used today alongside the revised system. It records the number of incidents reported to the police and includes the number of reported offences, the number of actual offences (i.e., excluding those that are unfounded), the number of offences cleared by charge, the number of adults charged, the number of youths charged, and the gender of those charged. It doesn't include victim characteristics. This approach to collecting statistics has been criticized for being "less useful for analytic purposes than information based on characteristics of individual crimes" (ibid., 62).

A new system for collecting and reporting crime statistics was introduced in 1988 but wasn't fully operational until 1992. The new system—referred to as the Incident-Based UCR Survey, or UCR2—incorporated a key change: it collected incident-based data rather than summary data and thus allowed for better analyses of crime trends. This **revised UCR system** also added the following:

1. Information on victims: age, sex, victim–accused relationship, level of injury, type of weapon causing injury, and drug and/or alcohol use.
2. Information on the accused: age, sex, type of charges laid or recommended, and drug and/or alcohol use.
3. Information on the circumstances of the incident: type of violation (or crime), target of violation, types of property stolen, dollar value of property affected, dollar value of drugs confiscated, type of weapon present, date, time, and type of location of the incident (ibid., 62–63).

Another difference between the aggregate survey and UCR2 relates to the number of police departments included. For example, while the aggregate survey reflects virtually 100 percent of the total caseload of every police service, the latter has historically consisted of only a number of police services. For example, in 2005, a sample of 127 police departments in nine provinces was used in the UCR2. That year, the UCR2 included crime data representing 62.1 percent of the national volume of substantiated Criminal Code offences. Also, the police services included in the UCR2 were non-representative, in that 41 percent are located in Ontario, 29 percent in Quebec, 11 percent in Alberta, 6 percent in British Columbia, 5 percent in Manitoba, 4 percent in Saskatchewan, and 2 percent or less in all other provinces and territories. And except with regard to the police forces selected from Ontario and Quebec, the data used in the UCR2 were collected mainly from urban police services. This difference between the two surveys gradually disappeared—in 2006, 90 percent of all police services were included in the UCR2.

A crime typically becomes known to the police when a victim or sometimes a witness reports it. At best, the police discover only a minimal number of crimes by themselves, since many victims do not report the crimes committed against them. When the police do receive a report of a criminal incident, they have to decide whether to record it as such. Sometimes they may not believe the report; and even if they do believe it, they may not feel that the incident really involved any criminal activity. And even if the police do believe that a crime occurred, they may be too busy to investigate it thoroughly or to complete all the necessary paperwork,

especially if the incident is not that serious. If the police do not record it as a crime, it will not be included on the official UCR system. One study (Silverman 1980) found that about 6 percent of all information informally processed by the Edmonton police was lost somewhere on its journey to the records section; the corresponding figure for the Calgary police was closer to 20 percent. Differences in the crime rates between cities can be attributed to the structure, organization, and operations of the information system that each police service maintains.

And even when the police do record the crime, a case successfully solved by a charge is the exception rather than the rule. Unless the victim or witness can positively identify a suspect, or unless the police are able to catch the alleged offender shortly after the offence was committed, it is unlikely they will catch the offender. Unless the crime is a serious one, the police don't have the time to investigate each criminal incident thoroughly and interview many witnesses or suspects. Generally, the proportion of thoroughly investigated crimes to the total number of crimes is small. In 2003, for example, Canadian police services solved 69.8 percent of all violent crimes but only 20.0 percent of all property crimes and 38.3 percent of "other" Criminal Code violations.

The UCR's accuracy is often questioned. How well does it measure Canada's crime rate? For the UCR to be accurate, citizens must report criminal activity to the police, and then the police must pass this information on to Ottawa. Criminologists have long been aware that this is a highly discretionary area. Citizens may not report a crime—perhaps they are afraid to do so—and because of their discretionary powers, the police themselves may not report every crime that comes to their attention. One consequence is that many criticisms have been levelled against police-generated crime statistics. The most common of these criticisms are as follows:

1. An unknown (and no doubt large) amount of crime is not reported to the police and, as a result, is not recorded in the UCR. This problem can be alleviated through the use of victimization surveys.
2. For each single series of criminal actions reported to the police, only the most serious crime is included in the UCR. The most serious offence is usually the one that carries the longest maximum sentence under the Criminal Code. For example, if a male breaks and enters a house, sexually assaults a woman (level 1), and then kills her (homicide), only the murder is recorded. Although break and enter and homicide both have a maximum penalty of life imprisonment, violent offences take precedence in the record

over non-violent offences. One exception to this approach is criminal harassment (stalking): all instances of this offence are recorded, whether or not it was the most serious violation in a series (Hendrick 1995).

3. The overall crime totals misrepresent the crime rate in any given year. When we talk of an increase or a decrease in any given year, we are comparing the totals of all crimes included in the crime statistics to totals from previous years. But what if an increase in break and enter corresponds with a decrease in level 1 sexual assault? It has been argued that since one offence is classified as a violent crime and the other as a property crime, these two offences shouldn't have the same weight.

4. There are problems with the way the UCR records criminal incidents for some crimes. For non-violent crimes, one incident is counted for every distinct or separate incident. But the UCR records violent incidents differently from other incidents. For violent crime, a separate incident is recorded for each victim, so if one person attacks and assaults five individuals, five incidents are recorded. But if five people attack and assault one person, only one incident is recorded. Robbery is an exception to this approach. One robbery equals one incident, regardless of the number of victims. This is because a single robbery can involve many victims, so to record the robbery by the number of persons it victimizes would overstate the occurrence of robbery (Martin and Ogrodnik 1996).

Crime rates are a more reliable way to measure crime than total numbers of crimes. This is because rates are not influenced by changes in the population, which can have a significant impact on the degree of risk faced by an individual. If, for example, you live in a town of 1,000 residents in which there were 200 break and enters, your chances of being a victim are 1 in 5. But if you live in a community of 10,000 with 200 break and enters, the risk is reduced to 1 in 50, even though the number of break and enters is the same. Since the term "crime rate" is used so often, it is important to know exactly what it means. Crime rates are usually based on 100,000 population. This allows researchers to standardize and compare crime rates across Canada in any given year as well as across a number of years. For example, in 2008 there were 611 homicides in Canada, and the homicide rate was 2.00 per 100,000 population. The 2008 rate continues a decline in the rate of homicide starting in 1975, when the rate was 3.03 per 100,000.

What Victims Say: Victimization Data

One of the problems with using the UCR as the only basis for crime statistics in Canada is that not all victims report crimes to the police. For example, in 2004, there were 2,863,255 crimes recorded by the police in all of the provinces and territories across Canada; in comparison, there were almost 6.0 million criminal victimization incidents involving only eight criminal offences in the ten provinces alone (Gannon and Mihorean 2005). The exact number of unreported crimes is unknown, but these unreported crimes probably fluctuate in number and type from year to year. For example, the number of crimes that went unreported to the police in 2004 was estimated to be 88 percent for all types of sexual assaults, 69 percent for all household thefts, and 67 percent for personal property thefts (ibid.). The official crime rate generated by the UCR is only as accurate as the number of incidents reported to the police and the data the police decide to process. Asking members of the public about the crimes they do not report to the police contributes significantly to our understanding of the amount of crime. Victimization surveys (1) help estimate unrecorded crime; (2) help explain why victims do not report crimes to the police; (3) provide information about the impact of crime on victims; and (4) identify populations at risk (Hood and Sparks 1970, 5).

Victimization studies also have a number of limitations, including the following:

1. *Underreporting to interviewers.* Victimization surveys always reveal more crime than the UCR does, yet they too underreport the crime rate. This is because many crimes are forgotten by victims or seem so insignificant to them that they do not report them (Sparks 1981).

2. *Response bias.* Critics of victimization surveys argue that the rate of underreporting is distributed unevenly in society. For example, White people are more likely than Black people to report having been victimized. Also, university graduates are more likely to report their victimization than those with less education (Beirne and Messerschmidt 1991).

Victimization surveys were first used in Canada during the late 1970s and early 1980s in an attempt to gain more information about the volume, types, and rates of crime. The first national study was the Canadian Urban Victimization Survey (CUVS), conducted by the federal government in the late 1970s in various urban centres across Canada. It found that huge numbers of Canadians living in these areas were not reporting crimes—including large numbers of violent crimes—to the police. For example, it found that victims had not reported 11,000 sexual assaults, 27,000 robberies, and 185,000 assaults to the police. Since 1988, a victimization survey of a national sample has been included as part of the GSS.

The GSS is based on a representative sample of about 24,000 Canadians aged 15 or older, from the non-institutionalized population in the ten provinces. Respondents are selected by computer-assisted random dialling. Interviewers ask the respondents about their experience with crime and the criminal justice system during the previous 12 months. There are a number of differences in how the UCR and the GSS collect data about crimes (see Table 4.2). One difference relates to the ability of the GSS (as compared to the UCR) to discover information about crimes not reported by victims to the police. The GSS collects data about personal and household risks. It also examines the prevalence and social and demographic distribution for eight types of criminal victimization: sexual assault, robbery, physical assault (all of which are categorized as "violent victimizations"), theft of personal property, and the following crimes classified as "household victimizations": break and enter and

attempted break and enter, motor vehicle/parts theft, theft of household property, and vandalism. Information is also collected for other facets of criminal victimization as well, including fear and perceptions of crime and perceptions about the criminal justice system.

The GSS was not intended to replace the UCR but to complement it. Comparisons between the UCR and the GSS are of dubious value, because the ideas behind each system are different. Crime rates in the UCR emerge from reports of crime incidents by the public to the police; those in the GSS emerge from reports of victimizations to survey interviewers. In other words, GSS data originate from individuals who are actually victimized, whereas UCR data are based on criminal acts reported to the police. Because their sources of data differ, the GSS and UCR give us different information about crime in Canada.

Victimization surveys are able to focus on specific types of crimes. In 1993, for example, the federal government conducted a national victimization survey, the Violence Against Women Survey (VAWS), which focused on the amount of violence committed against women in Canada.

TABLE 4.2 Comparison of the GSS and UCR

UCR	GSS
Data Collection Methods	
Administrative police records	Personal reports from individual citizens
Census	Sample survey
100% coverage of all police agencies	Sample of approximately 10,000 persons using random digit dialling
Data submitted on paper or in machine-readable format	Computer-assisted telephone interviewing (CATT); excludes households without telephones
National in scope	Excludes Yukon, Nunavut, and the Northwest Territories
Continuous historical file: 1962 onward	Periodic survey: 1988, 1993, 1999
All recorded criminal incidents regardless of victim's age	Target population: persons aged 15 and over, excluding full-time residents of institutions
Counts only those incidents reported to and recorded by police	Collects crimes reported and not reported to police
Scope and Definitions	
Primary unit of count is the criminal incident	Primary unit of count is criminal victimization (at personal and household levels)
Nearly 100 crime categories	Eight crime categories
"Most Serious Offence" rule results in an undercount of less serious crimes. Includes attempts.	Statistics are usually reported on a "most serious offence" basis, but counts for every crime type are possible, depending on statistical reliability. Includes attempts.
Sources of Error	
Reporting by public	Sampling error
Processing error, edit non-responding police department, police discretion, changes in policy and procedures Legislative change	Non-sampling error related to the following: coverage, respondent error (e.g., recall), non-response, coding, edit and imputation, estimation.

Source: Reproduced from Statistics Canada, *An Overview of the Differences between Police-Reported and Victim-Reported Crime,* Catalogue 85–542, 1997.

CRIMINAL VICTIMIZATION IN CANADA, 1988–2004

General Trends and Patterns

According to Gannon and Mihorean (2005), 28 percent of Canadians in 2004 were victimized by at least one crime during the previous 12 months, a slightly higher percentage than was reported in 1999. These researchers found that the rate of victimization increased for Canadians 15 years and over in 2004 for the crimes of theft of personal property, theft of household property, and vandalism. There were no significant changes in the rates of sexual assault, robbery, physical assault, and motor vehicle theft. There was a decrease in the rate of break and enter (see Figures 4.3 and 4.4). The level of multiple victimizations recorded in 2004 indicated that about four in ten victims were victimized multiple times. More specifically, 19 percent of all victims experienced two criminal incidents over the year, while 20 percent were victimized three or more times.

The rate for those offences categorized as violent victimizations in 2004 was 106 per 1,000 Canadians 15 years or older. In this category, the rates of theft and physical assault were the highest (75 per 1,000), followed by sexual assault and robbery (21 and 11

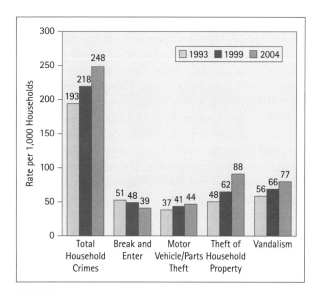

FIGURE 4.4

Rates of Household Property Theft and Vandalism Continues to Increase

Source: "Criminal Victimization in Canada, 2004", *Juristat*, Vol. 25, no. 7, p. 5. Statistics Canada catalogue 85-002. Released November 24, 2005.

incidents per 1,000, respectively). The overall rate for household victimization was higher than for personal victimization: 248 incidents per 1,000 households. Theft of household property and vandalism had the highest rates (88 and 77 incidents per 1,000), while break and enter and motor vehicle/parts theft had the lowest (39 and 44 incidents per 1,000 households, respectively).

Victimization rates for some jurisdictions and groups are much higher than for others. For example, Albertans and Nova Scotians faced the highest rates of violent victimization (160 and 157 incidents per 1,000, respectively). Quebecers reported the lowest rates of violent victimization (58 incidents per 1,000). The likelihood of being a victim of a household victimization was highest in the Western provinces. In 2004, Saskatchewan and Manitoba had the greatest number of household victimization incidents per 1,000 households (406 and 403 incidents per 1,000, respectively). The lowest rates of household victimization were in Newfoundland and Labrador (127 per 1,000) and Quebec (147 per 1,000). The only province to record a decrease between 1999 and 2004 in the rate of household victimization was Quebec (−28 percent). The rates of household victimization in all of the other provinces in 2004 were generally higher than in 1999. This increase reflected mainly increases in vandalism and the theft of household property.

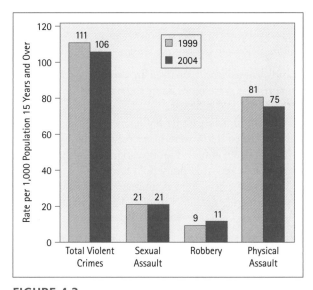

FIGURE 4.3

Rates of Violent Victimization Remain Unchanged

Note: Includes incidents of spousal sexual and physical assault.
Source: "Criminal Victimization in Canada, 2004", *Juristat*, Vol. 25, no. 7, p. 4. Statistics Canada catalogue 85-002. Released November 24, 2005.

Young people were particularly vulnerable to violent crime in 2004. That year, the rate for Canadians aged 15 to 24 was 1.5 to 19 times greater than the rates recorded for other age groups. The rate of violent victimization declined with age. For example, Canadians between 25 and 34 had a rate of violent victimization of 157 per 1,000; for those between 35 and 44, the rate was only 115 per 1,000. In addition, those individuals who indicated that they had participated in 30 or more evening activities in any given month reported the highest rates of violent victimization (174 per 1,000). This rate was four times higher than for those who stated that they had been involved in fewer than 10 evening activities during a month (44 incidents per 1,000). Also, people who were single faced a greater likelihood of being the victim of a crime (203 incidents per 1,000) relative to those who were married (52 incidents), living common law (131 incidents), or separated or divorced (159 incidents).

Personal and Household Victimization

Some of the principal findings of the 2004 GSS are noted below (Gannon and Mihorean 2005):
Risk of violent victimization

- Women and men face similar overall risks.
- Violent victimization rates are highest for young people (ages 15 to 24).
- Violent victimization rates are highest for single and separated/divorced people.
- Students face higher rates of violent victimization.
- Urban rates of violent victimization are higher than rural rates.
- Violent victimization rates are higher among those with a low household income (less than $15,000 per household).
- Gays and lesbians face higher rates of violent victimization.
  Risk of household victimization
- People living in urban areas face a higher risk of victimization than people in rural areas.
- Higher household income is associated with higher rates of household victimization.
- Rates are higher in those households with more people living in them.
- Semi-detached, row, and duplex homes face the highest risk of victimization.
- Renters face higher risks than home owners.

The GSS also provides data for three violent offences—sexual assault, robbery, and assault—by providing information about the presence of a weapon and injury to the victim. Below are some of the findings from the 2004 GSS:

- No weapons were used or present during the majority (75 percent) of violent crime incidents. Weapons were most commonly used (45 percent of the time) during robberies.
- In the majority of sexual assaults (91 percent), a weapon was not involved.
- Friends, acquaintances, or someone else known to the victim were the perpetrators in 51 percent of violent incidents involving a lone accused.
- Violent victimizations most often involved a male acting alone (76 percent).
- Nearly one in five victims of a violent crime suffered a physical injury. In 2004, the victim suffered an injury in 24 percent of these three violent crimes—an increase from 18 percent in 1999.
- Drug and/or alcohol abuse was a factor in 52 percent of violent crime incidents—an increase from 43 percent in 1999. Alcohol or drug use by the perpetrator did not vary considerably among the three types of violent victimization offences; it ranged from 48 percent (for sexual assault incidents) to 55 percent (for physical assault incidents).
- Violence was often highly disruptive to the victim's main activity. Thirty-seven percent of victims of a violent crime said that the crime interrupted their main activity for one day; 39 percent said it affected them for two to seven days; 16 percent said their main activities were disrupted for more than 14 days.

The GSS also provides a profile of household victimizations for four offences: break and enter, motor vehicle/parts theft, theft of household property, and vandalism. Below are some of the findings from the 2004 GSS:

- Individuals who had lived in their home for only a short time were more likely to be the victim of one of the household offences.
- Most victims lost under $500.
- Most stolen items were never recovered.
- The police conducted an investigation in three out of every four reported household crimes.
- Victims of a household victimization were more likely to want to participate in victim–offender mediation programs.

Victimizations Not Reported to the Police

In 2004, only 33 percent of the victims of the three violent crimes reported the crime to the police. Among the violent incidents, robberies and physical assaults were most likely to be reported to the police (46 and 39 percent, respectively). In contrast, only 8 percent of sexual assaults were reported to the police. The most common reason given by the victim of a violent crime for reporting it to the police was, quite simply, that it was their duty (83 percent said so). Almost as many said they reported the crime from a desire to see the offender arrested or punished (74 percent), or to stop the violence or gain protection from the offender (70 percent).

In 2004, 37 percent of all household victimizations were reported to the police. According to Gannon and Mihorean (2005), this low rate of reporting can be explained in part by the fact that no items were stolen in 21 percent of theft-related household crimes. When there was a significant loss of property, victims were more likely to report the crime. In 2004, eight out of ten victims of household victimization reported their loss to the police when there was a loss of $1,000 or more. Break and enter and motor vehicle/parts theft incidents had higher reporting rates as the value of the stolen property increased. About half of these crimes were reported to the police, but when the loss was more than $1,000, the rate of reporting increased to 89 percent for theft of a motor vehicle or parts and 84 percent for break and enters.

Of great interest to many who study crime are the reasons why victims do not report crimes to the police. Sixty-six percent of violent incidents during 2004 were not reported to the police. Sixty percent of the victims who did not report a crime to the police indicated that they did not do so because they dealt with it another way. Other reasons why victims did not report their violent victimization to the police: they felt that the incident wasn't important enough (53 percent); they didn't want the police involved (42 percent); or they didn't think the police could do anything (29 percent). The most common reason for not reporting a household victimization to the police was the perception that the incident was not important enough (65 percent). This was followed closely by the belief that the police wouldn't be able to do anything (60 percent). In 30 percent of all household offences, the victim stated that he or she dealt with the incident in another way (see Figure 4.5).

Self-Report Surveys

Self-report surveys are a third source of data used by criminologists for studying crimes not necessarily reported to the police. Such surveys are based on similar principles as victimization surveys, in that people are asked directly about any criminal activities they may have been involved with over a certain period, usually the previous year. Self-report surveys also include questions about subjects' attitudes, values, personal characteristics, and behaviours. The information obtained in this way is used for various purposes such as to measure

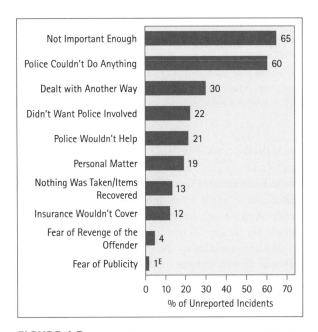

FIGURE 4.5

Most Common Reason for Not Reporting Household Victimization Was "Incident Was Not Important Enough," 2004

Note: Figures may not add to 100% due to multiple responses. ^Euse with caution.
Source: "Criminal Victimization in Canada, 2004", *Juristat*, Vol. 25, no. 7, p. 4. Statistics Canada catalogue 85-002. Released November 24, 2005.

attitudes toward criminal offences and to examine the relationship between crime and certain social variables such as family relations, income, and educational achievement.

This approach can be used to investigate the prevalence of offending among those who indicate that they have committed a criminal offence during the period under study. Most self-report surveys focus on youths and drug offenders. Youths are usually questioned about issues besides their offending, such as how their friends, schools, and families influence their lawbreaking and/or law-abiding behaviours. Drug offenders are surveyed because many of them have committed numerous crimes in order to pay for the drugs they use.

Self-report surveys help some researchers focus on specific criminological subjects. Some have used them to study the age (referred to as "age of onset") at which youths first start offending. Frechette and LeBlanc (1987) studied male youths in Montreal and discovered that the annual rate of self-reported offending was approximately twice as high for those who started their involvement with youth crime compared to those who started later. In the late 1980s, using the self-reporting approach, Hagan and McCarthy (1992) studied the criminal activities of 309 homeless youths in Toronto; they found that youths who had been homeless for one year or more were more likely to be involved in criminal activities.

CRIMES AGAINST THE PERSON

The violent crimes of homicide, attempted murder, assault, sexual assault, other sexual offences, abduction, and robbery make up the category of "violent crimes" or "crimes against the person." While they made up only 20 percent of all crimes reported to the police in 2008, they are the offences that lead to the greatest physical harm and are typically the ones feared most by the public. In 2008, the overall rate of violent crime was 3 percent lower than in 2007. Just under 442,000 violent crime incidents were reported to the police in 2008, a decrease of approximately 3,500 from the previous year. This decline was largely due to a 7 percent drop in the rate of robbery, as well as a 10 percent decrease in attempted murder (Wallace 2009).

Homicide

Homicide occurs when a person directly or indirectly, by any means, causes the death of a human being. Homicide is either culpable (murder, manslaughter, or infanticide) or non-culpable (not an offence and therefore not included in the homicide statistics). Examples

According to police officials, Robert Picton is the focus of the largest serial killer investigation in Canadian history. By the end of October 2002, he had been charged with the deaths of 15 women. (CP PICTURE ARCHIVE/HO/BCTV-Vancouver)

of non-culpable homicide include suicide, deaths caused by criminal negligence, and accidental or justifiable homicide (e.g., self-defence). A murder has been committed when a person intentionally, by a willful act or omission, causes the death of another human being, or means to cause bodily harm that the person knows is likely to cause death. Four Criminal Code offences are associated with homicide: first degree murder, second degree murder, manslaughter, and infanticide.

> First degree murder occurs when the act is planned and deliberate; or
> the victim is a person employed at and acting in the course of his or her work for the preservation of and maintenance of the public peace (e.g., a police officer or correctional worker); or
> the death is caused by a person committing or attempting to commit certain serious offences (e.g., treason, kidnapping, hijacking, sexual assault, robbery, and arson).
> Second degree murder is all murder that is not first degree murder.
> Manslaughter is culpable homicide that is not murder or infanticide. It is generally considered to be a homicide committed in the heat of passion caused by sudden provocation.
> Infanticide occurs when a female willfully causes the death of her newborn child (under twelve months of age), if her mind is considered disturbed from the effects of giving birth or from lactation.

Homicide is a unique crime for several reasons. First, it is widely perceived as the most serious of all criminal acts. Second, it is more likely than any other crime to be discovered by the police and to be the subject of a police investigation. Third, unlike other crimes, the definition of homicide tends to be fairly consistent across nations. As a result, homicide is important to examine, "not only because of its severity, but because it is a fairly reliable barometer of violence in society" (Dauvergne 2005, 2). The incidence of homicide decreased gradually in Canada between 1975 and 2001, with some yearly fluctuations; by 2003, the homicide rate was only 1.73 per 100,000 but increased slightly in 2007 to 1.80 and to 2.0 per 100,000 in 2008 (see Figure 4.6).

In 2006, 35 percent of all homicides involved a stabbing; 32 percent, firearms; 20 percent, a beating; 8 percent, strangulation or suffocation; and 2 percent, fire (by smoke inhalation or burns). Poisoning, a motor vehicle, or shaking (Shaken Baby syndrome) accounted for another 2 percent. The most common firearm used was a handgun—in 2004, these accounted for almost two-thirds (65 percent) of all firearm-related homicides; shotguns or rifles accounted for 22 percent. According to Li (2007), 83 percent of all solved homicides were committed by an acquaintance or family

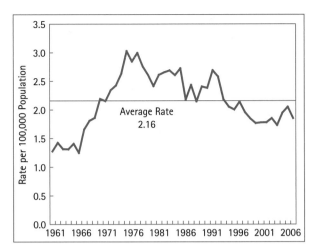

FIGURE 4.6

Homicide and Attempted Murder, Police-Reported Rate, Canada, 1978 to 2006

Source: "Homicide in Canada, 2004", *Juristat*, Vol. 25, no. 6, p. 7. Statistics Canada catalogue 85-002. Released October 6, 2005.

member; the remaining 16 percent were committed by a stranger. In 2004, 37 children (under the age of 12) were murdered. Twenty-seven of them were killed by a parent, five by a family friend, and three by another family member; no children were killed by a stranger. Fourteen of these children were less than one year old. As has been the case since 1974, infants were at the highest risk for homicide among all child victims—approximately four out of every 100,000 infants (Dauvergne 2005).

Eighty-four youths (aged 12 to 17) were accused of homicide in 2006, 12 more than the previous year. The rate of youth accused was at its highest point since 1961. Among the 84 accused youth, 72 were males and 12 were females. The number of accused males was 10 more than the previous year and 28 more than the preceding ten-year average. The number of females accused in 2006 was two more than in 2005. Youth are more likely to kill strangers. In 2006, 30 percent of all homicides with a youth accused were against a stranger compared to 16 percent of those where an adult was the accused. Youths are also more likely to kill other youth and young adults (58 percent of all incidents with a youth accused) than are adults who commit homicide (22 percent) (Li 2007).

It is well known that alcohol, drugs, and other intoxicants are involved in many crimes, and homicide is no different. In 2004, among the homicide cases where it was known whether alcohol or drugs were a factor, 73 percent of the accused and 55 percent of the victims had consumed an intoxicant at the time of the homicide. Dauvergne (2005) also points out that 49 percent of the homicide incidents in 2004 (for which data were available) occurred during the course of another offence. Of these 232 incidents, most (180) were committed during another violent offence: 106 during an assault, 45 during a robbery, eight during a sexual assault, five as the result of stalking, three during a kidnapping or abduction, and 13 during some other violent offence. Six homicides resulted from arson, 14 from property offences, and 32 from other types of criminal offences.

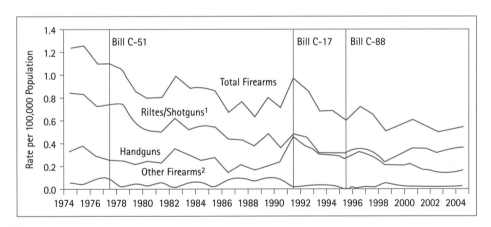

FIGURE 4.7

Rate of Firearm Homicides, Canada, 1974–2004

Note: The information is not intended to imply a causal relationship between gun-control legislation and homicide rates. See Exhibit 4.2 for details of Bills.

[1]Includes sawed-off rifles/shotguns.

[2]Includes firearm-like weapons (e.g. nail gun, pellet gun) and unknown type of firearm.

Source: Marnie Wallace, "Police-reported crime statistics in Canada, 2008", *Juristat*, Vol. 29, no. 3, p. 17. Statistics Canada catalogue no. 85-002-X.

EXHIBIT 4.2   Changes to Canadian Firearm Legislation 1969–2003

Important changes have been made to Canadian firearms laws in an effort to reduce the number of firearms-related injuries and deaths. To this end, the Criminal Code was amended in 1969, 1977, 1991, 1995, 1998 and 2003. These pieces of legislation are summarized below:

1969: Parliament enacted Bill C-150, which for the first time made it illegal to provide firearms to persons of "unsound mind" or to convicted criminals under a prohibition order. Also, the definition of a "firearm" was revised so that it now included non-restricted, restricted, and prohibited weapons.

1977: Amendments to Bill C-150 were introduced (Bill C-51) so that a firearms acquisition certificate (FAC) would now be required prior to obtaining a firearm. This legislation also introduced a variety of other provisions, including regulations on safe storage and display of firearms for businesses and bona fide gun collectors, and mandatory minimum sentences to deter the criminal use of firearms.

1991: With Bill C-17, Parliament strengthened the FAC screening provisions (Bill C-17) so

that applicants now had to provide references, a personal and criminal history, and a photograph. Also, a mandatory 28-day waiting period was established.

1995: The Firearms Act (Bill C-68) was passed, establishing a licensing system for people wishing to possess firearms. Those who met the criteria could be licensed to possess firearms that were neither prohibited nor restricted. The Firearms Act also established a system for registering all firearms.

1998: Part III of the Criminal Code was amended to create a variety of offences relating to the unauthorized possession, transfer, importing, or exporting of firearms and the use of firearms in the commission of offences.

2003: In January, all firearms owners and users were required to obtain a firearms licence and all firearms had to be registered (including non-registered rifles and shotguns).

Source: Pottie Bunge, V., H. Johnson, and T.A. Balde. 2005. *Exploring Crime Patterns in Canada*. Ottawa: Ministry of Industry.

Methods Used to Commit Homicide

Canadians are greatly concerned about the use of firearms in homicides. Since 1969, the Canadian government has introduced numerous pieces of legislation to restrict and regulate firearms (see Exhibit 4.2 and Figure 4.7). The use of firearms in homicides has declined since 1974. Homicides caused by firearms account for a relatively small percentage of all fatalities involving firearms. In 2006, there were 168 homicide incidents involving firearms, accounting for 190 victims. In the same year, there were 210 homicides committed by stabbings, 13 more than in 2005 (Dauvergne and De Socio 2008).

Over the past three decades there has been a change in the types of firearms used in homicides. Before 1990, rifles and shotguns were used more often than handguns; in the early 1990s, this began to change. In 2006, handguns accounted for 57 percent of all firearm-related homicides, rifles and shotguns for 19 percent. Thirteen percent of homicides were committed with a sawed-off rifle or shotgun. Between 1997 and 2004, when more detailed information about the firearm used in a homicide was provided to researchers, 84 percent were not registered and 79 percent of accused

persons did not possess a valid firearm licence. In 2006, among the 61 firearms used to commit homicide that were recovered by the police, 18 were reported as having been registered with the Canadian Firearms Firearm Registry, of which 12 were rifles/shotguns. Of the remaining recovered weapons, 12 were rifles/shotguns, four were handguns, and two were sawed-off rifles/shotguns. For the 45 of 61 incidents where the firearm was revered and ownership determined, 26 were owned by the accused, two by the victim, and 17 by another person.

Sexual Assault

This crime has been committed when an individual is sexually assaulted or molested or when an attempt is made to sexually assault or molest an individual. In 2008, 21,483 sexual assault incidents were recorded by the police; this was less than 5 percent of all violent crimes. Of the sexual assaults reported to the police, 98 percent were classified as level 1. The rate of sexual assault level 1 decreased by 1 percent compared to 2007, the rate of sexual assault level 2 decreased by 10 percent, while the rate of sexual assault level 3 declined by 3 percent.

The same year, the largest decreases in the rate of sexual assault were largest in Yukon (−17 percent), the Northwest Territories (−17 percent), and British Columbia (−12 percent). The jurisdictions with the highest recorded increases in their rates of sexual assault were Alberta, Manitoba, and Prince Edward Island, all of which had a 3 percent increase from the previous year.

Assault

Assault is the most frequently occurring crime in the violent crime category. In 2005, 236,934 incidents of assault were reported to the police. Between 2001 and 2007, the total number of violent crimes averaged some 305,000 offences per year. During this same period, assault offences averaged 236,000 incidents per year, or about 77 percent of all violent offences. The most common assault reported to the police between 2001 and 2007 was common assault—assault level 1—which accounted for 78 percent of all assault offences. The next most frequent category was assault causing bodily harm, or assault level 2, which accounted for 21 percent of all assault offences, followed by aggravated assault, or assault level 3 (1 percent of all assault offences).

Data from the UCRs during these years indicate that males and females are equally likely to be the victim of an assault. Females are most likely to be the victim of assault level 1 (52 percent); males are 67 percent of the victims in both level 2 and level 3 assault. Women are more likely to be assaulted by a spouse or ex-spouse (42 percent), by a casual acquaintance (18 percent), or by a close friend (12 percent). The assailants of men are most commonly strangers (37 percent) or casual acquaintances (33 percent).

Robbery

In 2007, robbery accounted for slightly less than 8 percent of all violent crimes reported in the UCR statistics. The robbery rate declined by 7 percent in 2008 over 2007, but the robbery rate has generally been declining—it is about 15 percent lower than it was a decade ago and 25 percent lower than 1991. Robbery is classified as a violent crime because it involves either real violence or the threat of violence. However, in approximately 75 percent of robberies, the victim suffers no physical injury, which implies that violence was threatened. Of the remaining victims, 22 percent receive minor physical injuries. The remaining incidents involve the victim(s) experiencing serious physical injuries (i.e., injuries requiring professional medical attention either on the scene or at a medical facility).

The highest robbery rates are in the Western provinces. Manitoba had the highest rate of robbery (158) among the ten provinces, followed by Saskatchewan (128), British Columbia (123), and Alberta (106).

Criminal Harassment (Stalking)

On August 1, 1993, amendments to s. 264(1) of the Criminal Code were introduced to protect individuals from harassment. "Criminal harassment" occurs when someone repeatedly follows or communicates with another person, repeatedly watches that person's house or workplace, or directly threatens that person or any member of that person's family, causing the person being targeted to fear for his or her own safety or the safety of someone he or she knows (see Chapter 2). That stalking is a serious matter is reflected in the fact that between 1997 and 1999 nine women were killed by a man when the precipitating crime was criminal harassment (Hackett 2000).

Before 1993, persons engaging in stalking activities were generally charged with one or more of the following offences: intimidation (s. 423 of the Criminal Code), uttering threats (s. 264.1), mischief (s. 430), indecent or harassing phone calls (s. 372), trespassing at night (s. 177), and breach of recognizance (s. 811). This section has been amended twice since August 1993. Effective May 26, 1997, murder committed during the course of criminally harassing the victim was classified as first degree murder, whether or not it was planned and deliberate, and the commission of an offence of criminal harassment when there was a protective court order became an aggravating factor when the offender was being sentenced. And effective July 23, 2002, the maximum sentence for stalking was increased from five to ten years.

In 1994, 3,200 incidents of criminal harassment were reported to Canadian police. By 1999, the number of criminal harassment incidents reported on the UCR2 had increased to 5,382. In 2002, 9,080 criminal harassments were reported. In 2002, criminal harassment incidents accounted for slightly more than 4 percent of all violent incidents reported to the police. Of these incidents, 45 percent were cleared by charge; in another 16 percent, the complainant declined to lay charges. Seventy-six percent of the victims were female. Female victims tended to be younger than male victims—42 percent of the female victims were under 30, compared to 27 percent of male victims. Of the accused, 84 percent were male. Thirty-one percent of the female victims were criminally harassed by a current or former intimate partner, while 23 percent were harassed by an acquaintance or friend. Male victims of criminal harassment were most often (39 percent) stalked by a casual acquaintance; 13 percent were stalked by a current or former intimate partner. Emotional injury was reported in all criminal harassment cases, physical injury in fewer than 2 percent (Federal/Provincial/Territorial Working Group on Criminal Harassment 2004). In 2006–07, 2,859 criminal harassment cases were heard in adult criminal courts across Canada. This represents a 3 percent increase since 2002–03 (Marth 2008). In 2008, criminal harassment accounted for 4 percent of all violent crimes; the rate of this offence was the same in 2008 as it was in 2007.

Forcible Confinement

Forcible confinement is one of the few violent crimes that has been increasing in Canada over the past three decades. In Canada, it is a criminal offence to unjustly hold an individual against his or her will by the use of threats, duress, force, or the exhibition of force. This offence, "forcible confinement," is defined by the Criminal Code (s. 279) as depriving an individual of the liberty to move from one point to another by unlawfully confining, imprisoning, or forcible seizing that person. According to Dauvergne (2009), the offence of forcible confinement is similar to kidnapping in that a person who is kidnapped is held against his or her will, but kidnapping also involves the act of transporting the victim from one location to another. Police reports do not distinguish these two offences; however, information about these two offences from the Adult Criminal Courts Survey data shows that the majority of these two offences are forcible confinement (94 percent).

One of the unique aspects of forcible confinement is that it usually involves other offences. For example, in 2007, 78 percent of all forcible confinement charges also involved offences such as assault, uttering threats, sexual assault, and robbery. In comparison, only about 25 percent of all other violent crimes occurred in conjunction with other offences. There are three primary situations in which forcible confinement occurs. The most common involves individuals being held against their will by a spouse or intimate partner (48 percent). Most of these incidents happened in conjunction with another violent offence, such as an assault (70 percent) or uttering threats (28 percent). Seventy-one percent of all victims were in a current relationship with the perpetrator. The second forcible confinement situation occurs during disputes between friend and acquaintances (20 percent of all forcible confinement charges), while the third type of situation is associated with robberies and break and enters. When these types of incidents occur in a private residence they are sometimes classified as "home invasions" (see Exhibit 4.3). In 2007, 46 percent of all robberies involving forcible

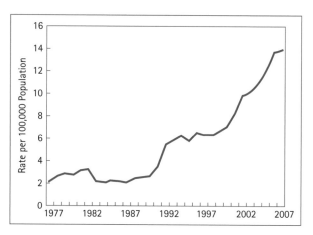

FIGURE 4.8

Forcible Confinement in Canada, 1977 to 2007

Source: Mia Dauvergne, "Forcible Confinement in Canada", *Juristat*, Vol. 29, no. 1, 2009, p. 7. Statistics Canada catalogue 85-002-X.

confinement and 96 percent of all break and enters involving forcible confinement occurred in a private residence. There were nearly 4,600 incidents of forcible confinement reported in 2007. The rate in 2007 was twice what it was a decade ago and seven times higher than 20 years ago (see Figure 4.8).

CRIMES AGAINST PROPERTY

Property crimes account for the majority of all serious crimes. Property incidents involve unlawful actions with the intent to gain property, but do not involve the use or threat of violence. Six crimes comprise the category of property crime: theft $5,000 or under, theft over $5,000, fraud, breaking and entering, motor vehicle theft, and possession of stolen goods. Theft under $5,000 is the most common property crime. In 2008, 1,022 million property crime incidents were reported to the police. These accounted for almost 47 percent of all Criminal Code incidents, reflecting a general decline in property crimes since 1984. Rates for all types of property crime decreased in 2008. The lowest decrease was for theft over $5,000 (non-motor vehicle) (−5 percent). Property crimes heard in adult court tend to receive more prison sentences than offences in the category of crimes against persons; in 2006–07, 41 percent of individuals found guilty of a property crime were sentenced to prison, compared to 31 percent of those found guilty of a violent crime (Marth 2008). Fedorowycz (2004, 8) states that this difference can be explained in large part by the fact that adults charged with a property offence tend to have long criminal records.

EXHIBIT 4.3 Home Invasions

In recent years, Canada has been experiencing a new criminal phenomenon: the home invasion. While no official definition of this crime exists, it is normally characterized by the forced entry into a private residence while the occupants are home and involves violence against the occupants. Broadly defined, home invasion encompasses both robberies that occur at a place of residence and residential break and enters involving any other type of violent offence. It is generally thought to be different from break and enter in that there is premeditated confrontation with the intent to rob and/or inflict violence on the occupants of the household. In this context, a home invasion is actually more like a robbery than a break and enter. In any case, few robberies or break and enters are characterized as home invasions.

Regardless, this type of crime is particularly frightening to the victim, as it involves an attack within the sanctity of one's home. Some police services do record the number of home invasions in their jurisdiction, although the definitions they use may vary across police agencies. Researchers have tried to use GSS data to study this type of crime, but the number of such incidents reported by victims has been too small to allow for any analysis.

Many of the police data on this type of crime are readily available from the UCR2; one need only look at residential robberies and break and enters that involve violence. A sample of police forces reported 2,470 such incidents in 1996. Almost half of these involved robbery of the occupants. These data suggest that the number of home invasions rose slightly from 1993 to 1994 (an increase of 1 percent) but then decreased to 2,504 in 1995 and to 2,480 in 1999.

It is difficult to determine the exact number of home invasions across Canada in part because there is no single definition of this offence. In Vancouver, for example, the police started to collect data on this type of crime in 1997. They recorded 17 such incidents in 1997, 61 in 1998, 30 in 1999, 35 in 2000, 38 in 2001, and 49 in 2002. The Vancouver police define a home invasion as an incident "where the suspect(s) choose a residential premise in which they know a person or persons are present with the pre-formulated plan of confronting the occupant(s), attacking them, holding them or binding them, thereby committing assault and unlawful confinement, then a theft is attempted or completed, thereby committing robbery" (Fedorowycz 2004, 7). The Toronto police use a different definition of home invasion, defining it as "a robbery committed in the living quarters of a residence" (ibid.). The Toronto police report that the number of such incidents decreased from 401 in 1994 to 175 in 1999, then to 127 in 2000, before increasing to 178 in 2001 and 173 in 2002.

An analysis of the 1999 UCR2 data found that more than half of residential robberies (58 percent) involved a weapon, most often a firearm (22 percent) or a knife or another cutting instrument (21 percent). And when the relationship between the victim and offender was known, more than half (58 percent) of the accused were strangers; another 24 percent were casual acquaintances of the victim. In addition, the elderly (i.e., individuals over 60) were the most typical victims: 18 percent of these incidents involved elderly victims, compared to 3 percent of all other violent crimes. A number of provinces have recognized the seriousness of home invasions, and individuals convicted of such offences are being given longer sentences. In Alberta, for example, the Court of Appeal has established a minimum of eight years for this offence. On June 10, 2002, the Criminal Code was amended so that it now specifically identifies home invasion as an aggravating circumstance for judges to consider at the time of sentencing.

Sources: Kong 1998, 6; Kowalski 2000, 4–5; Fedorowycz 2004, 7.

Breaking and Entering

Breaking and entering occurs when a dwelling or other premise is illegally entered by a person who intends to commit an indictable offence. Break and enter is considered the most serious of all property crimes. This is reflected in the severity of the sentencing provisions in the Criminal Code. The maximum penalty for an offender convicted of breaking and entering into a dwelling is life imprisonment. In comparison, the maximum punishment for breaking and entering into a business or any other premise is 14 years. In the UCR, breaking and entering is divided into three classifications: business, residential, and "other." A recent concern has been the incidence of home invasions, which involve criminals breaking in when the residents are at home and physically attacking them (see Exhibit 4.3). In June 2002, in an attempt to more effectively deal with this crime, the federal government passed legislation that made home invasion an aggravating circumstance to be considered by judges at the time of sentencing.

Breaking and entering is the fourth largest offence category in the UCR (after theft under $5,000 [non-motor vehicle], mischief, and assaults). It accounts for approximately one in ten Criminal Code incidents and one in five property crimes. In 2008, there were 209,755 incidents, the lowest number in four decades and a 10 percent decrease from 2007 (see Figure 4.9). In 2007, nearly 60 percent of all break-ins occurred in residences; 32 percent occurred in businesses; and the remaining 9 percent occurred in other locations such as schools, sheds, and detached garages. In 2007, the rate for break-ins decreased in all types of locations, declining by 9.0 percent for residences, 9.1 percent for businesses, and 7.8 percent for all other locations (Dauvergne 2008a). In 2002, it was reported that the most frequently stolen items from residences were audiovisual equipment (22 percent), jewellery (12 percent), and money, cheques, or bonds (12 percent). A break and enter at a business most commonly resulted in the theft of money, cheques, or bonds (22 percent), office equipment (15 percent), or consumable goods such as cigarettes and liquor (10 percent) (Fedorowycz 2004).

THEFT

Theft comprises two separate offences—"theft over $5,000" (non-motor vehicle) and "theft under $5,000" (non-motor vehicle). In 1995, the cutoff point between the two offences was raised to $5,000. Incidents of theft under $5,000 accounted for 53 percent of all property crimes in 2007. This percentage has been relatively stable since 1998. Since 1998, the rate of theft has decreased for both offences—the rate of theft over $5,000 has fallen by 32.7 percent, while the rate of theft under $5,000 has fallen by 25.8 percent. The decrease in reported incidents of theft under $5,000 has strongly influenced the decrease in both the property crime rate and the overall crime rate, as the number of "thefts under" is so large (Tremblay 1999).

Motor Vehicle Theft

Motor vehicle theft involves taking, or attempting to take, a vehicle without the permission of the owner. In 2008, there were 125,271 incidents of motor vehicle theft reported to the police, 15 percent fewer than in 2007 (see Figure 4.9). The decrease in the rate of motor vehicle theft in 2008 was the largest in 30 years. Lower rates of motor vehicle thefts were reported by every province, ranging from 39 percent in Manitoba to 1 percent in

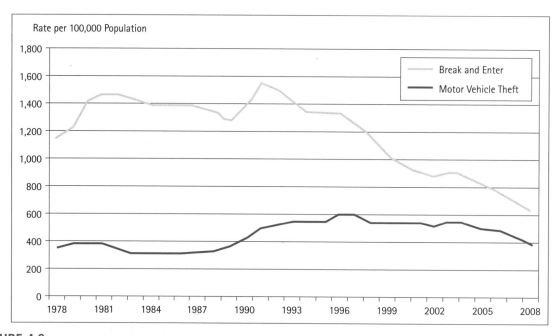

FIGURE 4.9

Break and Enter and Motor Vehicle Theft, Police-Reported Rates, Canada, 1978 to 2008

Source: Marnie Wallace, "Police-reported crime statistics in Canada, 2008", *Juristat*, Vol. 29, no. 3, p. 20. Statistics Canada catalogue no. 85-002-X.

An RCMP officer speaks at a crime scene. Do you think the police should release all the information they collect about a crime, or withhold the information until they arrest a suspect? (CP PHOTO/New Brunswick Telegraph-Journal/Noel Chenier)

Saskatchewan (Wallace 2009). Theft from a motor vehicle involves the theft of automobile accessories as well as personal property found inside the vehicle. Motor vehicle theft is an expensive crime. In 2007, the Insurance Bureau of Canada estimated that the direct and indirect financial costs of motor vehicle theft to consumers, police, insurance companies and governments to exceed $1 billion annually (Dauvergne 2008b).

OTHER CRIMINAL CODE INCIDENTS

"Other" Criminal Code offences include arson, bail violations, disturbing the peace, mischief, weapons offences, and prostitution. Almost 33 percent of all Criminal Code incidents recorded in 2008 included one of these. Offences in this category were almost the same in 2008 compared to the previous year. A large increase in counterfeiting currency (+40 percent) was offset by decreases in prostitution (?18 percent). There was also a decrease of almost 2 percent in mischief, the most common offence in this category (accounting for 54 percent of all offences during 2008).

OTHER TYPES OF CRIME

So far we have been looking only at the most serious violent and property crimes. For obvious reasons, these receive the greatest amount of attention from the public, the police, and politicians. However, other types of crimes are emerging and are posing significant threats. They can be assigned to three categories: white-collar (or economic) crime, computer crime, and organized crime.

White-Collar (or Economic) Crime

White-collar crime is a generic term that encompasses a variety of activities. Generally speaking, the term is used within the criminal justice system to describe crimes of fraud that are carried out during the course of a (seemingly) legitimate occupation. White-collar criminals exercise deceit (as opposed to force or stealth) in an effort to trick their unsuspecting victims. White-collar crimes

Bernie Madoff was sentenced to a 150-year prison term for his $65 million (U.S.) Ponzi scheme that the sentencing judge termed "extraordinarily evil." (AP Images/Jason Decrow)

EXHIBIT 4.4 Cybercrime: Identity Theft and Online Pornography

Cybercrimes are those that take place on the Internet. The "location" of these crimes—cyberspace—is raising many new issues for the criminal justice system: How can laws against it be written? And how can offenders be prosecuted? (Huey 2002) The problem is that cyberspace enables individuals to communicate, provide and receive information, and sometimes commit crimes while anonymous. There are many different types of cybercrime, including **cyberstalking,** cyber-consumer fraud, and hacking. Another form of cybercrime is identity theft, which has been referred to as the "crime of the new millennium" and "a major scourge of the information age" (Marron 2002).

In Canada, there is still no single definition of cybercrime. However, the following working definition has been accepted by many Canadian law enforcement agencies: "a criminal offence involving a computer as the object of the crime, or the tool used to commit a material component of the offence" (Kowalski 2002). Two broad categories have emerged under this definition. With the first, a computer is the tool used to commit the crime. This category includes crimes that law enforcement has long been fighting in the physical world but now is seeing more often on the Internet. Examples of these crimes include identity theft, child pornography, criminal harassment, fraud, intellectual property violations, and the sale of illegal goods and substances. With the second, the computer is the object of the crime. Here, cybercrime involves specific crimes against computers and networks and is specifically related to computer technology and the Internet. Examples include hacking—that is, the unauthorized use of computer systems—as well as the creation and malicious dissemination of computer viruses (ibid., 6).

IDENTITY THEFT

Identity theft occurs when an individual steals a form of identification, such as a name, date of birth, or social insurance number, and uses that information to access the victim's financial resources. This type of activity went on before the Internet came into common use. In its earliest forms, thieves would watch people at public telephones in order to "steal" their calling card numbers, or they would get their hands on bank credit card receipts. In either case, the object was to quickly use the information before the victim was aware of being victimized.

How easy is it to steal someone's identity? Many birth or death announcements in newspapers include the maiden name of a mother, which is the most common password used in the Canadian banking system. From this piece of information alone, the thief can start to construct a victim's identity by finding other bits of information, such as a telephone number, an address, and a place of work. Having done that, the thief can easily obtain a photo identification (perhaps from a library) and get government offices to issue a social insurance number, a birth certificate, and a driver's licence (Clark 2002).

The Internet has turned identity theft into the fastest growing financial crime in Canada and the United States. The Internet enables criminals to use stolen credit cards to purchase goods online, with near total impunity. Identity theft is widespread in Canada. The main source of information about identity theft in Canada comes from PhoneBusters, a national anti-fraud call centre jointly operated by the Ontario Provincial Police, the Royal Canadian Mounted Police, and the Competition Bureau of Canada. Between January 1, 2008 and December 31, 2008, over 11,000 complaints were received by this organization, involving more than $9 million in losses. The potential for identity theft is large: in 2001 it was estimated that there were about 1.4 million more social insurance numbers in circulation than there were people in Canada (ibid.). In comparison, there are a reported 700,000 to 750,000 victims each year (Marron 2002). It is also estimated that victims in the United States spend an average of 175 hours of personal time and over $800 to clear their name and restore their credit rating. One of fastest growing forms of identity theft is known as "fictitious identity theft." In these cases, criminals use a real piece of identification in order to create a fake person. They then use this identification to apply for the types of credit cards and loans that real people do. Once they are successful in obtaining credit of loans, the individuals who created the fictitious individual disappears. It is estimated that the average loss of these types of identify theft is $250,000 (El Akkad 2009).

Current laws for protecting individuals from theft are difficult to apply in cyberspace. As a result, new laws have had to be passed to address these issues. One such law was introduced by the Ontario government in 2001. This law increased the fine for impersonating to $50,000 (from $1,000) and tightened government control over official identity documents such as birth certificates. One police official in Canada contends that a different way must be found for individuals to establish their identity. Currently, Canadians establish their identity by obtaining various pieces of identification. This fragmented approach may have to be replaced by a national identity card (Clark 2002).

Online Pornography

The Internet has also become the site of massive amounts of pornography. The adult porn industry has made huge profits from the Internet: it is esti-mated that the online sex industry generates more than $100 million annually in Canada and more than $1 billion annually in the United States ("Everything Has a Price" 2000). The problem of online pornography is basically twofold. First, it allows surfers access to illegal sexual images or invitations; second, it facilitates the trafficking in pornographic photographs and videos. There are a number of reasons why the Internet has led to a surge in pornography, in particular, child pornography:

- *Speed*. The Internet is the quickest means of sending visual materials over long distances. Online pornographers can deliver their

products faster and more securely than by surface mail.
- *Security*. Any illegal materials placed in the hands of a mail carrier could be discovered. This risk is significantly lower when the Internet is used. For example, passwords can be used to protect an Internet site, thereby keeping non-customers from accessing the pornography site.
- *Anonymity*. Anonymity is the most important protection offered by the Internet to those in the online pornography industry and their customers (Graham 2000).

For the above reasons, lawmakers and the courts are having a difficult time controlling the online pornography industry. A survey conducted by the Crimes against Children Research Center at the University of New Hampshire found that one in every five children between 10 and 17 had been subjected to a sexual solicitation over the Internet in the previous year. The study concluded that girls were targeted at almost twice the rate of boys, and that less than 10 percent of the incidents were reported to the authorities (Foss 2002).

Senior Constable Don De Gray of Cornwall, Ontario, and a boater recover cigarettes dumped into the St. Lawrence River by thwarted smugglers. (Courtesy of Jeff Sallot)

receiving significant attention today include telemarketing fraud, consumer and business fraud, theft of telecommu-nication services, and the manufacture and use of counter-feit currency and payment cards (see Exhibit 4.4).

The federal government estimates that in 1998, economic crimes such as securities and telemarketing fraud cost Canadians $5 billion. Also, credit card fraud increased over 40 percent between 1996 and 1997, from

$88 million to $127 million (LeMay 1998). Furthermore, the smuggling of tobacco, alcohol, and jewellery results in a loss of about $1.5 billion in government tax revenues per year.

Organized Crime

Organized crime involves a number of different criminal activities, all of which revolve around the provision of illegal goods or services as well as the infiltration of legit-imate businesses. Most organized crime has emerged from the public's demand for illicit services and goods. The crime of conspiracy characterizes nearly all organ-ized criminal activities. Laws dealing with conspiracy make it possible for enforcement agencies to arrest and prosecute individuals who plan criminal activities.

In Canada, various laws have been introduced to govern such activities—for example, the Proceeds of Crime Act. In the United States, law enforcement agen-cies operate under more sweeping laws, such as the Racketeer Influenced and Corrupt Organization (or RICO) provisions of the Organized Crime Control Act, which make it illegal for people to engage in racket-eering activities. These laws are meant to make it diffi-cult for people to organize to violate the law.

In 1998, Canada's justice department estimated that the illicit drug market in this country generates between $7 and $10 billion per year. And each year between $5 and $17 billion is laundered (i.e., disguised to look like it has legitimate origins).

PUBLIC PERCEPTIONS OF THE CRIMINAL JUSTICE SYSTEM

Canada has developed an elaborate system for ensuring a safe and just society. On any given day in 2003–04, an average of 101,000 adults were under the supervision of correctional officials in the community. Another 12,600 were being held in a federal correctional facility, 9,800 in a provincial/territorial correctional facility, 9,200 in remand, and 360 in temporary detention. And every day, more than 6,800 Criminal Code incidents were reported to the police.

Mainly because of the high visibility of the decisions made by the various agencies of our justice system, most Canadians have an opinion about its effectiveness. Through their taxes, Canadians pay for this system's operations. As consumers, they expect quick and just responses to their needs. As victims, they may suffer from the system's inadequacies. Members of the public can be expected to ask whether current practices and policies are meeting their expectations. Policymakers are increasingly influenced by the public's perceptions of the criminal justice system and by the need to maintain its confidence in that system.

What perceptions of the criminal justice system do Canadians report? Researchers have consistently found that when all the major agencies are compared, the public usually holds the police in highest regard. The 2004 GSS examined public attitudes toward the police, the courts, and the prison and parole systems and reported findings consistent with past surveys. In 2004, most Canadians felt that the police were doing a good job at being approachable (65 percent), making sure citizens were safe (61 percent), treating people fairly (60 percent), enforcing the laws (59 percent), responding to calls (52 percent), and providing information about how to reduce crime (50 percent) (Gannon 2005). Overall, the level of satisfaction with the police was similar to findings made in the 1988, 1993, and 1998 GSSs.

When asked how they felt about the courts, most Canadians saw this agency as doing a poorer job than the police. In 2004, 44 percent perceived the courts as making sure that the accused were receiving a fair trial—a 3 percent increase from 1999. Twenty-seven percent indicated that they felt the courts were doing a good job of determining innocence or guilt—an increase from 21 percent in 1999. Overall, the courts were not perceived as doing enough to assist victims (only 20 percent thought they were doing so) and to provide justice quickly (15 percent) (ibid.).

Canadians are asked questions about two roles of the prison system: supervision and rehabilitation. For both, the respondents were most likely to say that the prison system was doing an adequate job. In 2004, 31 percent of Canadian respondents rated the prison system as doing a good job at supervising and controlling inmates; 18 percent considered the prison system to be doing a good job in terms of helping inmates become law-abiding citizens. However, 23 percent considered the prison system to be doing a poor job of assisting inmates in this same area (ibid.). In the 2004 GSS, Canadians ranked the parole system lowest among all the major criminal justice agencies in terms of doing a good job. Seventeen percent of respondents felt that the parole system was doing a good job of releasing inmates who were not likely to reoffend, while 15 percent considered it was doing a good job supervising inmates on conditional release programs such as parole. Both these percentages reflected small increases (both 12 percent) from the 1999 GSS (ibid.).

Canadians differ in their perceptions as to whether specific criminal justice agencies are doing a good job. Gannon (ibid.) found that women and men had approximately the same feelings about the police and the quality of their efforts. Except for the question about whether the police were doing a good job at providing information (more women [53 percent] than men [48 percent] said that they were), women and men had very similar responses to the questions about police performance. People over 65 were most likely to give a positive rating to the courts, the prisons, and the parole system. Respondents in the 15 to 24 age group gave the police the lowest rating of any age group. This age group, however, did rate the police positively in four of the six questions asked about them. It is interesting that in terms of all other areas of the criminal justice system—the courts, the prison system, and parole—younger Canadians gave the highest levels of satisfaction. In general, in terms of perceptions of the courts, the prison system, and the parole system, the older Canadians were, the more they perceived those agencies as not doing as a good a job as the police (see Table 4.3).

	Age of population (years)				
	Total	15–24	25–44	45–64	65+
			%		
Local police are doing a *good* job . . .					
Enforcing the laws	59	54	56	62	66
Responding promptly to calls	52	48	48	54	59
Being approachable	65	56	63	70	70
Supplying information on reducing crime	50	41	47	56	59
Ensuring the safety of citizens	61	61	57	63	66
Treating people fairly	59	51	57	62	66
Criminal courts are doing a *good* job . . .					
Providing justice quickly	15	24	14	12	13
Helping the victim	20	34	19	15	18
Determining whether or not the accused is guilty	27	36	26	25	21
Ensuring a fair trial for the accused	44	48	44	45	38
The prison system is doing a *good* job . . .					
Supervising/controlling prisoners	31	44	32	28	21
Helping prisoners become law abiding	18	28	16	18	17
The parole system is doing a *good* job . . .					
Releasing offenders who are not likely to re-offend	17	27	16	14	12
Supervising offenders on parole	15	30	13	10	10

[1]Only the percentage who perceive justice agencies as doing a good job is shown.

Source: "Perception of the Criminal Justice System Doing a Good Job, by Age, 2004", from the Statistics Canada publication "General Social Survey on Victimization, Cycle 18: An Overview of Findings", 2004, Catalogue 85-565, page 27, Released July 7, 2005.

For example, in terms of support for the courts, Canadians aged 15 to 24 believed that the courts were providing justice quickly (24 percent), compared to respondents who were over 65 (13 percent). Canadians between 15 and 24 were more likely than those over 65 to say that the prison system was doing a good job.

Despite their concerns about the criminal justice system, most Canadians don't perceive crime and justice issues to be of major importance relative to other social issues. A number of surveys have asked Canadians to identify the importance of various issues. These surveys have found consistently that crime and criminal justice issues are not a major concern for most Canadians. For example, on average between 1990 and 2001, 5 percent of Canadians identified crime and justice as the issue that Canada's leaders should be most concerned about; compare this to the 24 percent who identified the economy and the

27 percent who identified unemployment as the most important national concern. In 2000, only 2 percent of the public identified crime as the top priority for the government, after health care (33 percent), education and the economy (both at 9 percent), unemployment (8 percent), and taxes (7 percent). Other studies have reported similar results. It is estimated that fewer than one-third of Canadians are "very concerned" about crime, compared to those who are "very concerned" about the health care system (68 percent) and child poverty (58 percent). This finding was reported by Environics Canada (1998), which found that over the previous 15 years the percentage of Canadians identifying crime as the most important problem had never been higher than 5 percent. It is illuminating that in the summer of 2002, this issue was left off a survey developed by the Liberal Party's own polling firm studying Canadians' level of

CHAPTER 4 Crime Rates, Crime Trends, and Perceptions of Crime in Canada

INTERNET LURING

In 2002, the federal government introduced legislation (Bill C-15A); its purpose was to protect children from sexual predators in cyberspace. This bill addressed three issues: sexual exploitation, Internet luring, and child pornography. When Bill C-15A was proclaimed, the Canadian Criminal Code was amended to include the following:

- A new offence that targets individuals who use the Internet to lure and exploit children for sexual purposes.
- A new offence that makes it a crime to transmit, make available, export, or intentionally access child pornography on the Internet.
- Allows judges to order the forfeiture of any materials or equipment used in the commission of a child pornography offence.
- Enhances the ability of judges to keep known sex offenders away from children by making prohibition orders, long-term offender designations, and one-year peace bonds available for offences relating to child pornography and the Internet.
- Amends the child sex tourism law enacted in 1997 to simplify the process for prosecuting Canadians who sexually assault children in other countries (Kowalski 2002).

The new laws were created in order to assist justice officials in their efforts to crackdown on child and youths under the age of 18 being exploited via the Internet. These new amendments also made it illegal to communicate with children over the Internet for the purpose of committing a sexual offence. Under s. 172.1 of the Criminal Code (Luring of Children on the Internet), the age (real or believed) of the intended victim varies from 14 to 17, depending on the offence. It wasn't long before the first individuals were charged in the new offence of Internet luring. One such case occurred in Winnipeg where police charged a 22-year-old male after he contacted a 13-year-old girl in an Internet chat room and persuaded her to meet him. He then took the victim to his home where they engaged in sexual activity. But before they could charge the adult male with Internet luring, the police had to gain the approval of the Massachusetts' Attorney General to access the texts of the conservations between the victim and the perpetrator, since the chat room where those texts had been recorded was hosted by an ISP in the Boston area (Foss 2002). A number of other charges were also laid in this case,

including sexual assault and sexual interference. The accused later pleaded guilty to a charge of sexual assault and received a one-year conditional sentence (McIntyre 2004, B1).

Researchers have found that many Canadian youths are engaging in online activities that may increase the risk of online sexual exploitation, including Internet luring. Wittreich et al. (2008) report that many youths are sharing personal information over the Internet, e-mailing or posting photos online, chatting online with strangers, and visiting adult-only content websites and chat rooms. In the United States, the Youth Internet Safety Survey found in a 2005 national survey that 1 in 3 Internet users aged 10 to 17 was exposed to unwanted sexual materials; 1 in 7 had received unwanted sexual solicitations and 1 in 11 had been the recipient of threats or offensive behaviour during the previous 12 months (Wolak et al. 2006). Further, Wolak and her colleagues found that less than 10 percent of American children and youths sexually solicited over the Internet in 2005 reported the incident to law enforcement officials, Internet service providers, or some other authority.

In Canada, during 2006–07, a total of 464 incidents of child luring were reported by the police in Canada. During these two years, about 75 percent of all police-reported incidents involved luring as the only violation. The remainder of the child luring in incidents involved one or more additional criminal activities such as the production or distribution of child pornography, sexual assault (level 1), indecent acts, and/or sex crimes categorized as "other sexual offences" (Loughlin and Taylor-Butts 2009).

From 2003 through 2005, statistics collected by the police indicate that the number of reported offences of child luring remained consistent. However, these incidents increased by 1.5 percent in 2006 and rose another 31 percent during 2007. The increases in incidents reported to the police during 2006 and 2007 are attributed to efforts to raise awareness of child luring. In 2004, the National Strategy to Protect Children from Sexual Exploitation on the Internet was created in 2004 in order to increase resources to better deal with online child sexual exploitation. The following year, Canada's national tipline, Cypertip.ca, was created. It is dedicated to the online protection of children as well as educating the public.

According to police statistics, from 2003 to 2007, only a minority of child luring offences have been cleared by the police laying a charge or by some other means. Between 2003 and 2005, the clearance rate was about 5 in 10 incidents; during 2006 and 2007, the clearance rate was approximately 4 in 10 incidents (ibid). During 2006 and 2007, individuals were identified in approximately 33 percent of all child luring offences. This compares to an accused being identified in about 50 percent of all child pornography incidents and more than 75 percent of "other sexual offences" during the same time period. Almost 60 percent of the 158 persons accused of luring a child during 2006 and 2007 were younger adult males aged between 18 and 34. Males in the same age bracket made up just more than 3 in 10 of the accused in child pornography cases and just under 3 in 10 cases involving crimes categorized as "other sexual offences."

Between 2003–04 and 2006–07, the adult and youth criminal courts processed 122 cases where at least one of the charges included a child luring offence. Adults were accused in 113 of these cases, while the other 9 cases were heard in youth court. During these four years, 89 of the 122 cases (73 percent) resulted in a finding of guilt in criminal court. Approximately 75 percent of the cases were guilt was determined by the court included at least one guilty charge specifically related to child luring.

Both the adult and youth criminal courts imposed serious sanctions upon the individuals convicted in cases where there was at least one charge of child luring. Custody was imposed as the most serious sentence in 46 percent of all of the guilty cases, and the custodial sentences averaged just over one year (374 days) in length. Those individuals found guilty in cases that involved a charge of child luring only most often received a community-based sanction. Forty-two percent of these individuals received a conditional sentence, while another 25 percent were placed on probation. Custody was imposed in 28 percent of these cases and the average length of these sentences was 272 days. For cases involving multiple convictions, a period of incarceration was much more likely. Custody was imposed in 63 percent of the guilty cases when the accused was convicted on two or more charges. The average length of custody for these cases was 465 days (ibid.).

Questions

1. Do you believe that Canada's child luring laws are strong enough? If not, how do you think they can be improved?
2. Do you think that individuals convicted of Internet luring should be able to receive a long-term offender designation after they have finished serving their sentence?
3. How can the computer industry improve their product in order to better control Internet luring?
4. Do you think the Canadian government is doing enough in terms of funding enforcement efforts to detect and control Internet luring?

confidence in the government's handling of key social issues.

At times, though, Canadians indicate that they are very concerned about crime and criminal justice issues. Just days after the 9/11 attacks in the United States, 80 percent of Canadians said they were concerned about how our criminal justice system would deal with acts of terrorism and wanted the Canadian government to introduce strong new laws to deal with this threat. Yet eight months after the attacks, Canadians priorities had changed back to what they had been: health care, high taxes, and government spending. In fact, some of the changes in the proposed anti-terrorism law were made because public sentiment had shifted and the federal government decided they would be too intrusive.

Summary

Since the 1960s, the traditional mechanism for collecting information about crime in Canada has been the Uniform Crime Reports (UCRs). This information is based on crimes reported to police forces across Canada and then tabulated and summarized by the federal government. During the late 1980s, this reporting system was revised to include incident-based data, such as information on the victims, the accused, and the circumstances of the incident.

Critics have pointed out a number of limitations in the UCRs. Among them: many victims don't report crimes to the police, and the police include only the most serious offence in a criminal incident involving numerous criminal actions. Questions have also been raised about the accuracy of police recording practices and how police "clear," or solve, many crimes. As a result of these criticisms, the federal government started to collect crime data from victims. Over the past 15 years, the federal government has discovered that many violent crimes are not reported to the police by the victims. Yet the police are more likely to solve violent crimes than they are property crimes. The police are also much more likely to solve a murder or a sexual assault than they are to solve a motor vehicle theft.

Public perceptions of crime have become an increasingly important component of responses to crime. The 1999 GSS reported that most Canadians felt that the police were doing a good job in combating crime; however, Canadians were not as positive about the courts and the correctional system. Overall, though, most Canadians do not consider crime to be a pressing issue, and so crime is left off many public opinion polls.

Discussion Questions

1. Why did government officials revise the UCRs?
2. What are the three categories into which all crimes in Canada are placed? Do you think the government should develop new categories, such as a sexual offence category or a white-collar crime category? Why or why not?
3. Why is the clearance rate for aggravated assault lower than the clearance rate for first degree murder?
4. Why is sexual assault level 1 of the most underreported violent crimes?
5. What are the four categories of murder?
6. Why would a police force try to manipulate the number of crimes reported to the various categories?
7. Discuss the differences between the UCRs and victimization surveys.
8. What are the most common criticisms of UCRs?
9. Why is it important to study the fear of crime? Should statistics on the fear of crime be incorporated into official year-end measures of crime, as are the statistics in the UCRs?
10. What is the importance of understanding how the public perceives the operations of the Canadian criminal justice system?
11. Why don't Canadians consider crime to be a major social issue?

Suggested Readings

Beare, M. *Criminal Conspiracies: Organized Crime in Canada.* Scarborough, ON: Nelson Canada, 1996.

Gartner R., and A.N. Doob. *Trends in Criminal Victimization: 1988–1993.* Ottawa: Canadian Centre for Justice Statistics, 1994.

Sacco, V.F. *Fear and Personal Safety.* Ottawa: Canadian Centre for Justice Statistics, 1995.

Silverman, R.A., J.J. Teevan, and V.F. Sacco, eds. *Crime in Canadian Society,* 6th ed. Toronto: Harcourt Brace, 2000.

Snider, L. *Bad Business: Corporate Crime in Canada*. Scarborough, ON: Nelson Canada, 1993.

Tremblay, S. *Crime Statistics in Canada, 1998*. Ottawa: Canadian Centre for Justice Statistics, 1999.

References

Beirne, P., and J. Messerschmidt. 1991. *Criminology*. San Diego, CA: Harcourt Brace Jovanovich.

Clark, T. 2002. "Ontario Laws Toughened to Combat Identity Theft." *The Globe and Mail*, February 9, A8.

Dauvergne, M. 2009. *Forcible Confinement in Canada, 2007*. Ottawa: Canadian Centre for Justice Statistics.

———. 2008a. *Crime Statistics in Canada, 2007*. Ottawa: Canadian Centre for Justice Statistics.

———. 2008b. Motor Vehicle Theft in Canada, 2007. Ottawa: Minister of Industry.

———. 2005. *Homicide in Canada, 2004*. Ottawa: Canadian Centre for Justice Statistics.

Dauvergne, M., and L. De Socio. 2008. *Firearms and Violent Crime*. Ottawa: Canadian Centre for Justice Statistics.

Duchesne, D. 1997. *Street Prostitution in Canada*. Ottawa: Canadian Centre for Justice Statistics.

El Akkad, O. 2009. "Identity Theft among Canada's Fastest-Growing Crimes." *The Globe and Mail*, June 29, A5.

Environics Research Group. 1998. *Environics: Focus Canada Report 1998-1*. Toronto: Environics.

"Everything Has a Price . . ." 2000. *Business Weekly*, July 10, p. 10.

Federal/Provincial/Territorial Working Group on Criminal Harassment. 2004. *A Handbook for Police and Crown Prosecutors on Criminal Harassment*. Ottawa: Department of Justice Canada.

Fedorowycz, O. 2004. *Breaking and Entering in Canada–2002*. Ottawa: Canadian Centre for Justice Statistics.

Foss, K. 2002. "Winnipeg Man among First Charged with Internet Luring." *The Globe and Mail*, September 14, A9.

Frechette, S., and M. LeBlanc. 1987. *Delinquances et Delinquants*. Chicoutimi: Gaetan Morin.

Gannon, M. 2005. *General Social Survey on Victimization, Cycle 18: An Overview of Findings*. Ottawa: Minister of Industry.

Gannon, M., and K. Mihorean. 2005. *Criminal Victimization in Canada, 2004*. Ottawa: Canadian Centre for Justice Statistics.

Graham, W.R. 2000. "Uncovering and Eliminating Child Pornography on the Internet." *Law Review of Michigan State University Detroit College of Law*. Summer.

Hackett, K. 2000. *Criminal Harassment*. Ottawa: Canadian Centre for Justice Statistics.

Hagan, J., and B. McCarthy. 1992. "Streetlife and Delinquency." *British Journal of Sociology* 43, no. 4: 533–61.

Hendrick, D. 1995. Canadian Crime Statistics, 1994. Ottawa: Canadian Centre for Justice Statistics.

Hood, R., and R. Sparks. 1970. *Key Issues in Criminology.* London: Weidenfeld and Nicholson.

Huey, L.J. 2002. "Policing the Abstract: Some Observations on Policing Cyberspace." *Canadian Journal of Criminology* 44: 243–54.

Kong, R. 1998. *Breaking and Entering in Canada, 1996.* Ottawa: Canadian Centre for Justice Statistics.

Kowalski, M. 2002. *Cyber-Crime: Issues, Data Sources, and Feasibility of Collecting Police-Reported Statistics.* Ottawa: Canadian Centre for Justice Statistics.

———. 2000. *Break and Enter, 1999.* Ottawa: Canadian Centre for Justice Statistics.

Leenaars, A., and D. Lester. 2004. "Understanding the Declining Canadian Homicide Rate: A Test of Hollinger's Relative Cohort Size Hypothesis." *Death Studies* 28: 263–65.

LeMay, T. 1998. "Credit-Card Fraud Epidemic Worsens." *National Post,* December 18, D1, D4.

Li, G. 2007. *Homicide in Canada, 2006.* Ottawa: Canadian Centre for Justice Statistics.

Loughlin, J., and A. Taylor-Butts. 2009. *Child Luring Through the Internet.* Ottawa: Minster of Industry.

Marron, K. 2002. "Identity Thieves Plunder the Net." *The Globe and Mail,* June 28, E1, E2.

Marth, M. 2008. *Adult Criminal Court Statistics, 2006/2007.* Ottawa: Canadian Centre for Justice Statistics.

Martin, M., and L. Ogrodnik. 1996. "Canadian Crime Trends." In L.W. Kennedy and V.F. Sacco, eds., *Crime Counts: A Criminal Event Analysis.* Scarborough, ON: Nelson Canada, pp. 43–58.

McIntyre, M. 2004. "Net Luring Charge Cut." *Winnipeg Free Press,* May 5, B1.

Pottie Bunge, V., H. Johnson, and T.A. Balde. 2005. *Exploring Crime Patterns in Canada.* Ottawa: Ministry of Industry.

Savoie, J. 2002. *Crime Statistics in Canada, 2001.* Ottawa: Canadian Centre for Justice Statistics.

Silverman, R. 1980. "Measuring Crime: A Tale of Two Cities." In R.A. Silverman and J.J. Teevan, eds., *Crime in Canadian Society,* 2nd ed. Toronto: Butterworths, pp. 78–90.

Silverman, R., J.J. Teevan, and V.F. Sacco, eds. 1991. *Crime in Canadian Society,* 4th ed. Toronto: Butterworths.

Sparks, R. 1981. "Surveys of Victimization—An Optimistic Assessment." In M. Tonry, ed., *Crime and Justice—An Annual Review of Research.* Chicago: University of Chicago Press, pp. 1–60.

Sprott, J., and C. Cesaroni. 2002. "Similarities in Homicide Trends in the United States and Canada: Guns, Crack or Simple Demographics." *Homicide Studies* 6: 348–59.

Tremblay, S. 1999. *Crime Statistics in Canada, 1998.* Ottawa: Canadian Centre for Justice Statistics.

Wallace, M. 2009. *Police-Reported Crime Statistics in Canada, 2008.* Ottawa: Canadian Centre for Justice Statistics.

Wittreich, A., M. Grewal and R. Sinclair. 2008. *Technology: Shaping Young People's Global World.* Ottawa: The National Child Exploitation Centre.

Wolak, J., K. Mitchell, and D. Finklehor. 2006. *Online Victimization of Youth: Five Years Later.* University of New Hampshire: National Center for Missing & Exploited Children.

CHAPTER 5

Police Operations

CHAPTER OBJECTIVES

✓ Describe the three types of police agencies.

✓ Understand the two measures used to estimate the appropriate size of police forces.

✓ Understand the traditional organizational structure of the police force.

✓ Describe the preventive model of police patrol and new types of police patrols.

✓ Compare and contrast problem-oriented policing, community policing, zero tolerance policing, and intelligence-led policing.

✓ Understand DNA legislation and its due process limitations.

T he police are an important component of the criminal justice system. They play a crucial role, as was noted by the Royal Commission on the Donald Marshall, Jr., Prosecution: "The police are, in effect, the first and main keepers of the integrity and fairness of the criminal justice system" (Hickman et al. 1989, 249).

This chapter begins with a history of the police followed by a description of the types of police agencies in Canada: municipal, provincial, and federal. This description is followed by an overview of the professional model of policing, which was the dominant model of policing from the 1930s to the 1970s. The central types of police operations—patrols and criminal investigation—are then reviewed. Later in this chapter, emerging trends in policing are discussed—problem-oriented policing, community policing, zero tolerance policing, intelligence-led policing, and Aboriginal police services. One of the most significant developments in policing in the recent past has been the use of technology to help the police investigate crimes. One such technological innovation is the use of DNA to analyze evidence in order to determine whether an individual should be prosecuted. In addition, DNA evidence has been used to obtain acquittals of individuals charged with or convicted of a criminal offence.

Another type of technological device is closed-circuit television (CCTV). CCTV consists of a video camera monitor and a recording device. Multicamera systems allow images to be viewed sequentially, simultaneously, or on several monitors at once. CCTV systems can record images in black and white as well as in colour, and camera positions can be either fixed or varied by remote control to focus on activities in different locations. CCTV systems also allow cameras to zoom onto a selected target or to give a broad view of activity in a designated area. Recent developments in technology now allow CCTV cameras to be smaller (and therefore less intrusive), to use night vision, and to transmit images over the Internet. In addition, computer technology now gives CCTV systems the ability to match recorded faces against a computer database of photos—a system referred to as facial recognition.

CCTV is a type of situational crime prevention, an approach that promotes the idea that we can reduce crime through the creation of a strategy or overall plan to reduce specific types of crimes and the development of specific tactics to achieve the stated goals (Clarke 1992). One of the elements of situational crime prevention is to increase the risk of committing a crime. This would lead to, for example, increasing the risk of committing a crime by improving the surveillance of a specific location through better lighting, introducing a neighbourhood program (e.g., Neighbourhood Watch), and by increasing police and private security patrols. Some research studies have discovered that the police can reduce crime through aggressive patrol techniques as well as promotion of community safety by introducing better lighting (Braga et al. 1999).

Some jurisdictions have increased surveillance by installing CCTV in areas that are at high risk of criminal activity. For example, CCTV systems have been in use in England for a number of years. And in the United States, CCTV has been commonly used for monitoring inmates as well as for taping traffic stops (i.e., with cameras mounted in police vehicles). But do they deter criminal activity? In their study of 41 studies of CCTV used around the world, Welsh and Farrington (2008) reported that CCTV interventions (1) have a small but significant positive effect on crime reduction; (2) are most effective in reducing crime in parking lots; (3) are most effective in terms of reducing vehicle crimes, and (4) are most effective in reducing crime in England, where there is significant public support for the use of CCTV cameras in public places.

In this chapter, you will be introduced to the traditional and contemporary forms of policing. Many questions surround the issue of how to police today's society. For example, to what extent can technology be used to detect criminals? And do the laws covering new technologies such as CCTV and DNA testing balance the rights of the accused with the safety of the public, or do they infringe on individuals' reasonable expectations of privacy?

THE HISTORY OF THE POLICE

The origins of Canadian police agencies, like our criminal law, can be traced back to early English society. Prior to the Norman Conquest of England in the eleventh century, there was no regular police force. Justice was largely left in the hands of concerned citizens. Victims of a crime had to deal with the perpetrators without any assistance from the state, as there was no court system. The closest thing to a police agency was the pledge system, in which every person was responsible for assisting neighbours and protecting the village from thieves and other criminals. Gradually, however, a system of group protection emerged. Groups of ten families (known as "tithings," or the frankpledge system) were set up in villages in order to police their own minor problems. Ten tithings were then grouped in a larger area to a form a "hundred," whose affairs were looked after by a constable appointed by the local nobles. The constable,

considered by many to be the first "real" police officer, dealt with the most serious law violations. The hundreds were then amalgamated into shires (the equivalent of modern-day counties), and the top law enforcement officials became known as shire-reeves, a position that (as the phonetics suggest) developed into the position of sheriff. This individual was appointed by the Crown or local landowner to supervise a specific area to maintain law and order and apprehend law violators.

In the thirteenth century, the constable-watch system of protection was formalized by the Statute of Westminster (1285). This system was created in order to protect the property of people in larger English towns and cities. In the largest English cities, watchmen were organized within church parishes; usually they were residents of the parishes they were hired to protect. The statute allowed one man from each parish to be selected as a constable. The statute enabled constables to appoint citizens as watchmen, whose duties largely consisted of watching or guarding the local town or city. Watchmen patrolled predominantly at night and were responsible for protecting citizens from robbers, ensuring that citizens were safe, and detecting fires. Watchmen reported to the area constable, who ultimately became the primary law enforcement officer. They were not paid, and as a result many did not perform their duties as instructed. The statute also required all males between 15 and 60 to possess weapons and to be ready to participate in the "hue and cry," that is, to come to the assistance of a watchman when their assistance was needed. If they did not, criminal punishments could be handed out to the neglectful citizens on the reasoning that their inaction aided the offender. This system lasted until the eighteenth century.

In 1326, shire-reeves were replaced by justices of the peace, a position created to control an entire county. Over time, justices of the peace were assigned judicial functions. From this came the position of parish constable, who was expected to oversee criminal justice for his parishioners. Parish constables were agents of the justice of the peace; they supervised night watchmen, investigated offences, served summonses, executed warrants, and ensured the security of those charged with crimes before their trial. This system has been credited with starting the separation of the police from the judiciary, a system that has continued in our legal system for almost 700 years.

The Development of Modern Policing

As of the mid-1700s, the City of London still did not have an organized law enforcement system. Crime was commonplace, and when crime grew so common as to become unbearable, the only recourse open to city officials was to call in the military. This approach became unpopular among the local populace, however, as the soldiers used their powers in most cases to maintain a system of harsh control over those living in crime-prone areas, and they occasionally used their weapons to exert control in disorderly situations. So the military were placed under the direct control of city officials. It is a matter of historical record that these officials often abused the power of the military to their own purposes. As a result, many citizens in London were suspicious of any formal efforts to control their activities.

An alternative to calling in the military was introduced by Henry Fielding, Chief Magistrate of Bow Street, in 1748. Fielding decided to turn a group of men into professional law enforcement agents; their duties would be to catch criminals and recover stolen property. These individuals became known as the Bow Street Runners (also referred to as the "Thief Takers"), and they were volunteers. The Runners soon became so successful that they were being hired out to control crime in various other parts of England. Their efforts were largely unsuccessful; even so, the idea of a group of individuals tasked with apprehending criminals and with returning stolen property to its rightful owners helped develop the concept of a professional police force.

The Industrial Revolution dramatically increased the size of urban populations. As a result, social problems such as poverty, crime, and disorder began to increase. Concerns over the rise of the "dangerous class" drew the British Parliament into a debate about the best way to deal with criminal activity. But it wasn't until Sir Robert Peel was appointed to the position of Home Secretary that a formal plan was approved. In 1829, Peel succeeded in having the London Metropolitan Police Act passed by Parliament. This led to the creation of a 3,200-member police force with professional standards to replace the various law enforcement systems that existed in London at the time. Members were easily recognized by their uniforms (which included blue coats and top hats). The new police force had a military structure, including ranks. Two magistrates (later known as "commissioners") were appointed to oversee the force. Peel's legislation included four operational philosophies for the police (who were called "bobbies" after their creator):

- They were to reduce tension and conflict between law enforcement officers and the public.
- They were to use non-violent means in keeping the peace, with violence to be used only as a last resort.
- They were to relieve the military from certain duties, such as controlling crime.
- They were to be judged on the absence of crime rather than by high-visibility police actions (Manning 1977).

According to Peel's vision of a professional police force, the main goal was to prevent crime through the use of preventive patrols. Peel's ideas continue to have an impact on policing, and many of his goals are still being espoused by police agencies. This approach to policing became so popular that in 1835 it began to expand to towns outside London, where "new" police organizations started to replace constables and the watch in incorporated districts. In 1856, police forces became compulsory in all counties. This approach to policing quickly spread into Canada, the United States, and Australia.

The Early Canadian Police Experience

In colonial Canada, various law enforcement agencies were established. Before Canada joined the British Empire, settlers in New France created a system of policing that replicated the one in France. The first individuals involved in policing appeared in the settlement of Quebec in 1651. Twenty years later, that settlement developed police regulations (Kelly and Kelly 1976). The first permanent constables under the control of their respective town councils appeared in Quebec and Montreal in 1833.

Settlers in Ontario municipalities followed the law enforcement system being practised in England. In 1835, the City of Toronto hired six men to be its first constables; their task was to police the municipality at night. Other Canadian cities gradually formed their own municipal police forces, including Halifax (1841), Hamilton (1847), Saint John (1849), Victoria (1862), Winnipeg (1874), Calgary (1885), and Vancouver (1886). In the North-West Territories, there was no organized municipal policing. Most rural communities developed policing systems based largely on what the populace had experienced in their homelands. The Hudson's Bay Company formed its own policing system, approved by the federal government, in the areas surrounding its trading posts. In order to gain control over its Western lands, Canada established the North-West Mounted Police (NWMP) in 1873. The NWMP was organized in a different way from the municipal police forces, as it founders applied a paramilitary structure based on that of the Royal Irish Constabulary. This system was gradually adopted by all municipal forces across Canada (Guth 1994). The purpose of the NWMP (renamed the RCMP in 1920) was to police and control the lands purchased from the Hudson's Bay Company by the federal government in 1869 (Browne and Browne 1973; Kelly and Kelly 1976).

The Rise of Municipal Policing

The early municipal police departments had three main functions: to maintain public order, to prevent and control crime, and to provide services to the community (Marquis 1994).

Perhaps the most significant developments in this type of policing over the decades occurred in the area of communications. In their early stages of development, municipal police officers had to personally meet or write notes delivered by police runners in order to communicate with one another. The introduction of call boxes in the 1870s revolutionized policing. At first, patrol officers were only able to signal their location to police headquarters. Later, the call boxes were equipped with a bell system, which allowed patrol officers to send different signals to headquarters—for example, to call for back-up or an ambulance. Finally, in the 1880s, telephones were placed in the call boxes, establishing a direct link between officers on the street and those at headquarters. Over the coming decades, the police introduced more technology into their operations as it became available. Patrol vehicles, two-way communication systems, fingerprinting, a criminal record system, and toxicological analyses were all introduced during and after the 1920s. One of the most significant changes, however, was that police officers were separated from the community—a situation that was to last until the introduction of community policing in the late 1980s.

This separation of the police from the community was the result of a number of problems that plagued the police in the early twentieth century, particularly in the United States. Many of these problems were ultimately traced to the lack of training for and qualifications among police officers. Around this time, then, a number of individuals set out to reform policing. These reformers believed they could improve the police by raising the educational requirements for police officers and improving the training they received. This led to the introduction of a "new" way of policing that many today see as being the "normal" policing role and function in our society. This approach, which was slowly and carefully developed over three decades (1920 to 1950), revolutionized how policing was practised. The components of this approach to policing (most commonly known as the "professional" or "reform" model of policing) included the following:

- Reducing the police function from **social service** and the maintenance of order to crime fighting exclusively.
- Developing specialized, centrally based crime-fighting units, such as homicide and robbery.
- Shifting from foot patrols to motorized patrols.

- Creating patrol systems based on criteria such as crime rates, calls for service, and response times.
- Recruiting new police officers through psychological testing and civil service testing.

THE DISTRIBUTION OF THE POLICE IN CANADA

In 2008, 90,909 individuals were employed by police forces across Canada. Of this total, 65,283 were sworn police personnel and 25,626 were civilian employees. The number of sworn police officers had increased by 1 percent over the previous year. Since 2000, the number of civilian employees employed by police organizations in Canada increased by 23 percent.

There are three different jurisdictional levels of policing in Canada: municipal, provincial, and federal. In 2008, 42,668 (or 67 percent) of all police officers in Canada were involved with municipal police agencies. This total included more than 350 "independent" municipal police forces (i.e., non-RCMP), employing 38,217 officers—89.5 percent of all municipal police officers in Canada. There were also just over 200 RCMP municipal contract forces employing 4,451 officers.

Provincial police agencies employed 9,692 police officers, or 15 percent of all police personnel in Canada. Provincial police forces enforce the Criminal Code and provincial statutes within areas of a province not served by a municipal police force. The three provincial police forces are in Ontario (the Ontario Provincial Police [OPP]), Quebec (the Sûreté du Québec [SQ]), and Newfoundland (where the Royal Newfoundland Constabulary provides policing services to the three largest municipalities). For the other seven provinces and three territories, provincial policing is provided by the RCMP under contract.

The RCMP has complete responsibility in all provinces and territories for enforcing federal statutes, carrying out executive orders, and providing security for dignitaries. In 2008, 4,249 RCMP officers (6.5 percent of all police officers in Canada) were involved in federal policing. Other responsibilities of the RCMP include forensic laboratory services, the operation of CPIC (an automated national computer system available to all police forces), and telecommunications services for data and radio transmissions to ensure that all detachments receive current information. The RCMP also maintains the National DNA Data Bank and the Sex Offender Registry. There were 1,776 RCMP officers stationed at RCMP Headquarters and at the force's own training facility as well as in departmental and divisional administration in 2008 (Statistics Canada 2008).

The police agency with the greatest number of sworn police officers in Canada is the Toronto Police Service, with 9,585 officers. Montreal has the next largest police service, with 6,997 officers. The other police organizations with more than 1,000 sworn personnel in 2008 were Vancouver (3,410), Calgary (1,711), Edmonton (1,667), Winnipeg (1,364), Ottawa (1,350), Hamilton (1,081), and Quebec City (1,019).

There is no single model for determining the appropriate size of a police force or its workload. One problem is determining the size of the population base. Census figures are commonly used, but every large city in Canada experiences a heavy influx of workers on most days as people who live outside the city limits drive in for work or pleasure. Police agencies vary significantly in size across Canada, both in terms of personnel and in terms of the number of officers per person served. For example, in 2008, Thunder Bay had the highest number of police officers for every 100,000 population (217); Saint John, came next (205). Abbotsford, Kingston, and Saguenay had the lowest numbers of police officers for every 100,000 population (Abbotsford and Kingston both had 143, while Saguenay had 124).

Two measures are generally used to establish the appropriate size of a police force. These measures, however, are used mainly to analyze and identify trends in the population. The most common measure used is the population-to-police-officer ratio, which is used to compare changes in the number of police officers with changes in the Canadian population. In Canada in 2008, the number of police officers per capita increased by 0.7 percent from the previous year, to 196 per 100,000. The highest rate ever was 206 officers per 100,000, in 1975. By province/territory, the lowest number of police officers per 100,000 population in 2008 was in Alberta with 163 per 100,000. The highest rate among the provinces was for the Northwest Territories (419 per 100,000), followed by the Nunavut and Yukon (with 382 and 371 per 100,000, respectively).

The second technique for evaluating the appropriate police force size is to compare the number of Criminal Code incidents (excluding traffic incidents) reported to the police with the number of police officers in the force that handle those incidents. This ratio is used to indicate police workloads (Young 1995). The number of Criminal Code incidents per police officer increased from 20 in 1962 to a high of 51.1 in 1991. It has since declined almost every year since, to 35.9 in 2007.

THE ORGANIZATION OF THE POLICE

Police forces are bureaucracies, and in order to provide policing services as efficiently as possible, an ideal model, known as the "professional model of policing," emerged in the 1930s and remained dominant in policing for the next four decades. This model was characterized by four organizational characteristics:

- A hierarchical differentiation of the rank structure, with the police chief holding the highest rank and probationary constables the lowest.
- Functional differentiation, with job specializations, such as patrol, homicide investigation, traffic, and robbery, developed to better deal with crime problems.
- The routinization of procedures and practices, which were formalized and included in policy manuals that dealt with all aspects of the organization.
- The centralization of command, in which "ultimate authority rests at the top of the police hierarchy, and decision making within the hierarchy is accountable up the chain of command, while being protected from outside influences" (Reiss 1992, 68–72).

These four characteristics remain in place today, although most police forces have attempted to shift their focus toward a community policing perspective—an approach that (in theory) attempts to limit the top-down approach by eliminating many middle managers and

According to the 2009 United Nations World Drug Report, since 2003–04 Canada has emerged as the primary source of ecstasy-group substances for North American markets and increasingly for other regions. (CP PHOTO/Peterborough Examiner-Clifford Skarstedt)

giving patrol officers more discretion. However, since police forces operate on a paramilitary basis, it is difficult to eliminate the top-down approach.

Of particular importance to the professional model are specialist job roles. These roles allow the police to operate in a more efficient and effective manner. Large police departments are divided into various operational areas, including field operations, administration, and crime and support services. Each of these components is in turn divided into different specialties. For example, crime and support services can be broken into dozens of different units, including homicide, robbery, crime prevention, gang, and stolen-automobile units. This type of job specialization continues in the first decade of the twenty-first century, with many large police forces creating specialized operations such as gang units and hate crime units.

In recent years, however, complaints have been directed toward this type of organization—specifically, the contention is that it does not meet the social needs of contemporary society. For example, the number and complexity of police divisions and the lack of a clear relationship among them can lead to internal problems. One division may inadvertently implement a program that overlaps with the activities of another. This overlap illustrates the problem with a traditional top-down approach to organizational structure, in which administrators tell supervisors what to do, then supervisors tell divisional commanders what to do, divisional commanders tell subordinate police officers what to do, and then these officers talk to citizens. For the organization, the problem with this approach is that there isn't enough information flowing from the bottom to the top, especially when it comes to the sentiments of the public. Another problem with this approach is that it fails to promote personal ingenuity and that it reduces contact among the members of the police organization (Kelling and Moore 1988).

POLICE EFFICIENCY

Organizations typically measure their efficiency using statistical methods, and the police are no different in this regard. For police organizations, the traditional measures of efficiency are (1) response times, and (2) arrest rates. Response time is the time elapsed between a citizen's call to police and the arrival of the police at the scene of the incident. The speed with which the police respond to calls for service is a traditional statistical measure of efficiency because it is seen as an effective response to crime control and prevention. The belief is that if the police can respond quickly, they will catch perpetrators at the scene of the offence.

The problem with this measure is that citizens often wait several minutes before calling the police for assistance. So by the time the police arrive, the perpetrator has already fled the scene. It has been found that citizens often take between five and ten minutes to call the police from the moment the crime is committed. As a result, rapid response does not have the anticipated effect on either crime rates or police efficiency.

Management of Demand (Differential Response)

Police agencies came to realize that response times as a statistical measure were not as important as response times for emergency calls requiring immediate assistance. So these agencies began to develop systems that could distinguish between emergency and non-emergency calls. These systems utilize **management of demand** or "differential response." Management of demand for services requires the police to categorize citizen demands for services and then match these with differential police responses. This means that the police, after receiving a call for service involving an emergency, respond to it faster than for a non-emergency call. The police have developed a variety of differential responses. For non-emergency calls, for example, they may take the report over the telephone, request that the citizen go and file a report at a community police office, or ask the citizen to make an appointment when the level of calls for service is usually lower. This means the police are able to adjust workloads and thereby make better use of their resources.

Management of demand/differential response programs are now standard policy across Canada. For example, the Edmonton Police Service analyzed its calls for service and discovered "consistently, month after month . . . only about five percent of all incoming phone calls are high priority in nature" (Braiden 1993, 219). A similar study of the Halifax Police Service found that only 17 percent of incoming calls required an immediate police response, and many of these were false alarms (Clairmont 1990). If the police could identify the most serious criminal incidents, a rapid response might be the most efficient approach to apprehending offenders. In addition, by analyzing calls for service police, administrators can restructure their patrol activities without diminishing public satisfaction with the police. This can improve police efficiency without adversely affecting the crime rate. This approach has also gained support because it allows some patrol officers to become active in other areas of police operations, such as criminal investigation and crime prevention, when demand for immediate response is low.

Arrest Rates and Efficiency

The second traditional measure of police efficiency is arrest rates. Following the logic of the deterrence approach discussed in Chapter 3, it is assumed that if the police arrest most offenders, this will prevent crime and the crime rate will go down. This approach, which was accepted for decades by police administrators, is flawed because—as self-report and victim surveys reveal (see Chapter 4)—a significant amount of crime is not brought to the attention of the police. Another problem with using arrest rates as a measure of efficiency is that many people are arrested but not all are prosecuted.

Some police administrators favour clearance rates as a better indicator of police performance. The clearance rate, or the percentage of crimes solved over a specific period, allows the police to separate out and analyze various categories of crime, such as violent and property crimes. The clearance rate for violent crimes is usually the highest, since many of these offences are committed by persons known by the victim. Conversely, property crimes are committed by strangers and are typically lower in their clearance rates. For example, the clearance rate for homicides in 2003 was 65.4 percent, while the clearance rate for break and enters in the same year was only 12.8 percent. High clearance rates tell people that the police response to that crime is good, while low clearance rates typically tell the police that more resources could be applied to this area.

Yet another measure of police performance is the number of arrests that lead to prosecutions. In Chapter 1, we saw that few offences cleared by charge result in a conviction. Also, a crime may be cleared by the police but not processed, as a result of decisions made by Crown prosecutors that have nothing to do with the police. Certain events and circumstances are beyond the control of the police—for example, witnesses and/or victims may be reluctant to testify, so that prosecutors decide to stay the charges. But the fact that most arrests lead to a conviction overshadows some of the limitations found in other indicators used to evaluate police performance.

A more recent measure for evaluating police performance is *fear reduction*, which most advocates of community policing consider the most important indicator of all. When fear of crime is reduced in the community, the police gain the trust of community members. In turn, this trust provides the police with much-needed community support when it comes to reducing criminal activity or behaviours that can lead to criminal incidents.

Following are some successful approaches the police can take to reduce fear:

1. A community-organizing response team designed to build a community organization where none existed.
2. A program in which the police contact victims of crime to inform them of the progress of the case and to offer them advice about victim services.
3. A police community service centre staffed by police officers and local community volunteers.
4. Neighbourhood activity programs for youths and young adults sponsored and operated by police officers and volunteers.

THE POLICE ROLE

The police play an important role in our society, since they are the criminal justice agency that people most often see and with whom they come into contact. A "role" encompasses the rights and responsibilities associated with a particular position in society. A concept related to "role" is "role expectations"—that is, the behaviours and actions that people expect from a person in a particular role. Most people accept the police role in our society and how the police perform their various roles; however, some individuals and groups criticize the police for their performance. This can lead officers to experience "role conflict"—that is, psychological stress arising from their efforts to perform two or more seemingly incompatible responsibilities in society. For example, many people expect the police to simultaneously involve themselves with two roles that essentially conflict with each other. These roles are "social agent" and "crime fighter." The former involves the police assisting members of the public, while the latter focuses on arresting and charging lawbreakers.

Operational Style

The police role is changing in our society, from one that mainly involves investigating criminal incidents to one that involves non-crime activities. The police are becoming more active in crime prevention activities and in addressing social problems. Police work can take many different forms—peacekeeping, law enforcement, emergency medical treatment, and so on. Police work is so complex that it cannot be limited to any one form. Part of the socialization of police officers involves the development of a working attitude, or style.

Many researchers have attempted to identify the various roles in the daily activities of police officers. Muir (1977), for example, studied how police officers use their power and authority in their street activities and identified two essential criteria in terms of how the police use them. One he called "passion," the other "perspective." Passion is the recognition that force can be used to control a situation and is a legitimate means for resolving conflict. In contrast, perspective refers to the ability of the police to empathize with human suffering and to use their force both ethically and morally. Muir also recognized four different styles of policing:

- *Professionals.* These officers have both the passion and the perspective to be valuable members of the police organization.
- *Enforcers.* These officers have passion for their occupation, including enforcing the law and making decisive actions. Their values allow them to be comfortable using force to deal with situations.
- *Reciprocators.* These officers lack the passion to do their tasks. They have a difficult time deciding when to make use of their authority in any given situation, when to arrest someone, and when to enforce the law. Their values make it difficult for them to use force to solve problems.
- *Avoiders.* These officers possess neither passion nor perspective. As a result, they ignore or do not recognize the problems facing citizens and take no action to assist them.

Probably the most successful classification of these styles was developed by Wilson (1968). He studied eight police departments and he identified four policing styles: the social agent, the watchman, the law enforcer, and the crime fighter.

- *The social agent.* This style sees the need for police officers to be involved in a range of activities that are not necessarily attached to law enforcement. Instead, officers see themselves as problem solvers who work with community members. Generally, citizens expect officers working in this style to provide protection from outsiders and to respond to their concerns, whether they involve criminal violations or not. Police are also expected to direct their law enforcement actions toward strangers while giving local residents great latitude.
- *The watchman.* The **watchman** style of policing emphasizes public order. This style is tolerant of private matters between citizens as well as minor criminal offences. Much is left up to the citizenry. If the police respond for a second time to an altercation at an address, they may separate the parties involved but are unlikely to make an arrest unless a major incident occurs. This style of policing involves the restoration of "disruptive situations to normalcy without arresting the citizens involved" and "the management of situational tensions." Thus, for example, the police "move along" drunks to hostels instead of arresting them, and

they escort mentally ill patients to their facilities when they wander away from them.

- *The law enforcer.* With this **legalistic** style, the police enforce all laws to the limit of their authority. All crime-related incidents and suspects are treated in accordance with the formal dictates of the law. This means that all suspects are arrested and charged if enough evidence is found, all traffic violators are issued tickets, and discretion is minimal. This approach involves investigating all criminal incidents, apprehending, interrogating, and charging suspects, and protecting the constitutional rights of suspects as well, because the law states that this is what police officers are supposed to do.
- *The crime fighter.* Here, the most important part of policing is the detection and apprehension of criminals. The focus is entirely on serious criminals, in the belief that without the "thin blue line," society would descend into chaos. Police who adopt this approach are opposed to any sort of social service function for the police, as this would diminish their effectiveness.

In reality, police officers employ a number of policing styles in their day-to-day activities as opposed to following just one type of style. Hochstedler (1981) studied more than 1,000 Dallas, Texas, police officers and was unable to place individual officers into a single style of policing. The officers she studied thought and reacted in terms of the situation at hand.

THE PATROL FUNCTION

Patrol is considered the backbone of policing. All new officers are expected to spend their early years on patrol. Police patrols were introduced by Sir Robert Peel in London, England, in 1829. Peel believed that the presence of the police would prevent crime, and this idea became a basic assumption concerning the role and function of patrol officers. The basic purposes of police patrol have hardly changed since 1829. These purposes include the following:

- The deterrence of crime by maintaining a visible presence.
- The maintenance of public order and a sense of security in the community.
- The 24-hour provision of services that are not crime-related (Walker 1992).

The first two of these purposes—deterrence and the maintenance of public order—are almost universally agreed upon as legitimate for the police. The third purpose has been much more controversial, especially in community policing (see below).

The importance of police patrol cannot be underestimated. It continues to be the essential component of police agencies, since it is the patrol officers who are most visible to the public. The police patrol is designed to achieve a number of goals, notably the maintenance of a police presence in the community, a quick response to emergencies, and the detection of crime (Langworthy and Travis 1994). Patrol officers play an important public role because they are so visible in the community. Also, because they are mobile and located throughout a community, they are usually able to respond quickly to emergencies. Finally, officers on patrol are expected to observe what is going on in the community and stop crimes from happening.

The activities of patrol officers today are many and varied, but they can be divided into a few key areas:

1. Deter crime by maintaining a visible police presence.
2. Maintain public order within the patrol area.
3. Enable the police department to respond quickly to law violations or other emergencies.
4. Identify and apprehend law violators.
5. Aid individuals and care for those who cannot help themselves.
6. Facilitate the movement of traffic and people.
7. Create a feeling of security in the community.
8. Obtain statements from crime victims and witnesses.
9. Arrest suspects and transport them to a police facility for investigation (American Bar Association 1974; Cordner and Hale 1992).

Patrol officers are the most visible component of the entire criminal justice system. When a criminal incident occurs, they are usually the first to arrive and deal with the incident. They are typically seen in marked patrol vehicles, but they may also patrol on foot, on bicycle, or on horseback. They carry out their duties within a designated area, or beat, and rarely leave it unless in pursuit of a suspect or to back up other patrol officers. Police beats are patrolled 24 hours a day, by different shifts of officers. The activities of patrol officers are hard to enumerate, because their role is, in many ways, generalist—that is, a patrol officer plays a multitude of roles while on the job.

Sometimes patrol officers receive a detailed assignment, such as traffic patrol or security checks at business establishments. Their typical role, however, is "routine observation"; that is, they drive around a particular beat and respond to citizens' calls for service. Most of the

Toronto police officer Nicole Campbell surveys the city from her "eye in the sky" position aboard one of the force's new helicopters in August 2000. (CP PHOTO/Toronto Star/ Sean White)

activities of patrol officers are unrelated to crime. It has been estimated that at least 80 percent of all calls for police assistance involve non-crime incidents. This means that officers on patrol commonly deal with issues such as neighbourhood disputes, animal control, noise complaints, and locating lost children.

Incident-Driven Patrol

Two developments revolutionized police departments in the 1930s: the police patrol vehicle, and two-way communications. New communications technology enabled the police patrols to be in constant contact with headquarters, and the motor vehicle allowed them to respond to criminal incidents almost immediately. This led to a type of policing known as *incident-driven policing*, where the primary role of the police is to respond to citizens' calls for help. Since incident-driven policing was viewed as the most efficient way to organize patrols, police administrators moved all patrol officers into motor vehicles. In addition, it was assumed that the best way to deter crime was to conduct random patrols while ensuring a rapid response to criminal incidents.

Incident-driven policing is also referred to as *reactive policing*. When the police receive an emergency call, a patrol officer is immediately dispatched to the scene. Patrol officers are also involved in proactive policing. In other words, they initiate their own crime control activities. Examples of this kind of work include requesting information from citizens and stopping possible suspects to question them. When police departments crack down on the street drug trade or street prostitution, or set up fencing "stings," they are engaged in proactive policing.

Proactive and reactive policing styles are thought to be separate functions of the police, but they can also be used in conjunction with each other. For example, a city may be experiencing an increasing number of break and enters. When a citizen calls the police after realizing that his or her residence has been broken into, the police respond by investigating the incident. At the same time, the police can respond proactively by analyzing all such recent incidents in the hope that a pattern emerges. If a pattern is detected, the police may be able to identify potential break and enter locations and keep them under surveillance.

Deterrence through Patrol Officer Arrests

A significant measure of the deterrent effect of the police is whether the arrest of an alleged offender reduces crime. Some critics have argued that any formal action by the police can have only a limited deterrent effect on criminal activity (Ross 1982; Sherman 1990; Walker 1985). However, researchers have found that arrests made by police may in fact deter future criminal activity. Shapiro and Votey (1984), for example, discovered that an arrest for drunk driving increases the belief by the offender that he or she will be rearrested if he or she drinks and drives again. Other researchers have found support for the deterrent effect of arrest (Chamlin 1988). However, researchers have also found that despite directives from their superior officers, patrol officers may resist demands that they arrest more individuals whom they know or suspect have committed crimes (Ferraro 1989).

Jaffe and colleagues (1991) found that police officers in London, Ontario, responded favourably to a change in arrest policy for domestic violence incidents. These researchers reported that in the year prior to the introduction of the mandatory arrest policy, charges were laid in only 2.7 percent of occurrences involving wife assault. During the first year of the new policy (1983), this figure increased to 67.3 percent, and by 1990, it had reached 89 percent. In addition, over the course of the study, police officers were found to be less inclined to wait for the victims to file charges, deciding to take the initiative themselves. Choi (1994) found that Toronto police officers and OPP officers were more likely to arrest the suspect when (1) the victim accused the suspect of an assault; (2) the victim requested that charges be laid; (3) the suspect used a weapon during the assault; and (4) the suspect was hostile to the attending officers. His study suggests that if police arrests are to have a deterrent effect on domestic violence, the victims must start the legal process by laying a formal complaint.

Methods of Police Patrol

As we have seen, police officers on patrol engage in many activities, such as controlling traffic, investigating complaints, and making arrests. Police have been carrying out these activities for decades. In recent years, patrols have been organized in a variety of ways.

Directed Patrol

With **directed patrols**, officers are given orders about how to use their time on patrol. For example, they are told to spend a certain amount of their patrol time in certain locations and to watch for specific crimes. This type of patrol is usually based on crime analyses. Results of directed patrols indicate that the police can reduce the target crime, although it is not known whether directed patrols actually reduce crime or merely force it into other areas. Studies have shown that this type of patrol activity can reduce certain types of crimes, such as thefts from automobiles as well as robberies (Cordner 1992).

One form of directed patrol is referred to as **"hot spots"** patrol. This requires an analysis of all incoming calls based on their geographical origin. The Neighbourhood Foot Patrol Program (NFPP), formed in Edmonton in 1987, was based largely on an analysis of calls for service. The Edmonton police analyzed 153,000 calls for service made in 1986 and in this way located the 21 hottest areas of the city. This analysis indicated that over 80 percent of the calls from these areas came from repeat addresses. Twenty-one foot patrol officers were then permanently assigned to a beat that encompassed a hot spot. The foot patrol officers were supplemented by 80 vehicle patrol officers. One year after the NFPP was established, the department counted the number of calls coming from those addresses that accounted for at least two calls the year before. A slight reduction in the number of calls to repeat addresses (from 4,014 to 3,918) was noted, so was a reduction in the total number of calls (from 21,001 to 19,612) (Hornick et al. 1993; Koller 1990). One recent type of direct patrol focuses upon "hot spots" of criminal activity—that is, those locations that are the source of a high volume of calls for police service.

Recent technological innovations have encouraged the increased use of directed patrols. One such innovation has been crime-mapping systems such as geographic information systems (GISs). This technology identifies crime patterns in specific geographic areas, such as neighbourhoods or larger districts of a city. The police can then develop and maintain an ongoing computer analysis of both crime and criminals and use this analysis to generate crime maps. The most common type of computer mapping is referred to as "resource allocation" mapping, which involves analyzing crime patterns and then sending police officers to designated geographical locations to keep watch on the preferred targets of criminal(s). It is thought that this system gives the police a better chance of arresting the individual(s) committing the crimes.

Foot Patrol

Foot patrol was the mainstay of police forces in the late nineteenth and early twentieth centuries, but all but disappeared when motor vehicle patrols were introduced in the 1930s. However, foot patrols began to reappear in the late 1970s in response to citizens' complaints about the lack of contact with patrol officers in motor vehicles. A common feature of foot patrols today is that they emphasize greater interaction with the community and the solving of underlying community problems that may lead to crime and disorder. Most municipal police forces in Canada today have foot patrols, although many forces maintain such patrols only in the downtown core or other densely populated areas.

An experiment involving foot patrol officers in Flint, Michigan, generated a lot of interest across North America (Trojanowicz et al. 2001). An evaluation of the Flint Neighborhood Foot Patrol Program revealed that while foot patrol may reduce crime only slightly, it leads to a significant reduction in citizens' fear of crime and has a positive effect on police–citizen relationships. For example, it was found that foot patrol lowered crime rates by about 9 percent in all categories of crime except burglary and robbery, both of which increased by about 10 percent. Calls for service decreased by over 40 percent, and public support for the police increased. After four years, 64 percent of the citizens surveyed indicated they were satisfied with the police, and 68 percent felt safer in their neighbourhood.

Another early study on the effects of foot patrol was conducted in Newark, New Jersey (Police Foundation 1981). This one found that foot patrol had little or no impact on crime levels. However, a number of positive effects were identified:

- Residents noticed when the foot patrol officers were in the immediate vicinity.
- Residents were more satisfied with the service they received from the police when foot patrol officers were involved.
- Residents who were in the area frequented by foot patrol officers were less afraid than citizens who received their police service from motorized patrol officers.

Police forces in Canada have implemented a variety of foot patrols. In Toronto, 31 Division police commanders instituted foot patrols in the Jane-Finch area in 1977 to "defuse escalating tensions between the police and, in particular, members of the ethnic community" (Asbury 1989, 165). This area was selected for its long history of tensions between police and community, its high population density, and its high rate of serious crime. Foot patrol officers designed and became involved in various "community-building" activities in an attempt to help residents increase community cohesion and gain control of their community. Some residents reported "a 1000-percent" improvement in the community after the introduction of foot patrols and felt much safer.

Another major foot patrol initiative was Edmonton's NFPP (see above). Twenty-one foot patrol areas were selected on the basis of calls for service. The results of this program have been mostly positive; however, an evaluation of the program found that it worked best in stable middle-class neighbourhoods and not as well in the inner city (Bayley 1993). A survey of users of police services in these 21 beats revealed that foot patrol was favoured over motor vehicle patrol. In addition, foot patrol officers had a higher degree of satisfaction with their job than did motor vehicle patrol officers.

The evidence to date indicates that if foot patrol is to succeed, it must operate in locations where the possibility exists for frequent interaction with large numbers of community members, such as at shopping centres, in high-density neighbourhoods, and in the downtown core. The size of the foot patrol beat should be small, in some instances covering no more than a few blocks; this enables the police to walk their beat area at least once a day (Trojanowicz et al. 2001).

Does Preventive Patrol Deter Crime?

A central purpose of police patrol is to prevent crime. It is assumed that the presence of officers on general patrol in marked vehicles prevents criminal activity and reduces the crime rate. This is a core assumption of the professional model of policing, and police organizations have for decades been using marked patrol vehicles as their principal tool for deterring crime. However, during the late 1960s and early 1970s, critics began to argue that this mainstay of policing operations was not in fact reducing crime rates The assumption was not empirically evaluated until 1972 and 1973, when the Kansas City Police Department conducted perhaps the most famous of all police patrol studies, the Kansas City Preventive Patrol Experiment (Kelling et al. 1974). The results of this study forever changed how patrol officers in marked vehicles were used in both Canada and the United States.

During the one-year evaluation, the police studied the effects of preventive patrols by applying different patrol strategies in different areas. Three types of patrol were instituted: reactive, proactive, and control (i.e., preventive patrol). The reactive beats involved no preventive patrol activity whatsoever. Patrol officers who worked reactive patrol beats entered their beat only to respond to calls for assistance. When not responding to calls, the patrol officers patrolled neighbouring proactive police beats. Proactive beats were assigned two to three times the number of police patrol units through the addition of patrol vehicles from the reactive beats. Proactive patrols were highly visible, and the officers patrolled in an aggressive style, meaning they stopped vehicles and citizens if they felt there was reason to do so. The control beats maintained the normal level of patrols that were operational at that time—one car per beat.

Before this study started, most observers felt that proactive patrols would be the most successful in reducing crime and improving citizens' feelings of safety, because of the greater number of patrol vehicles and the more aggressive patrol approach. But the results, after one year of this experiment, did not support this. In fact, the results revealed that the different types of patrol did not affect (1) crime rates (as measured by the number of burglaries, motor vehicle thefts, thefts including motor vehicle accessories, robberies, and vandalism, all considered to be easy crimes to deter), (2) citizens' attitudes toward police services, (3) citizens' fear of crime, or (4) rates of reported crimes. These findings were both revealing and controversial.

They were revealing because police departments had always considered routine preventive patrol to be the most effective approach to patrolling. Yet this study concluded that preventive patrol is no more effective than reactive patrol and that adding more patrol units does not automatically lead to a reduction in crime rates or in citizens' fear of crime. According to Klockars and Mastrofski (1991, 131), this experiment led to the conclusion that it "makes about as much sense to have police patrol routinely in cars to fight crime as it does to have firemen patrol routinely in fire trucks to fight fire." The findings were controversial because they questioned traditional assumptions about preventive patrol. While it is necessary to have police patrols, the presence of more patrol officers doesn't lower crime rates. This finding led to the "mayonnaise" theory of police patrol, which states that the quantity of police patrols is similar to the amount of mayonnaise required to make a sandwich. If an area has no patrol, starting one there will reduce the crime rate, but adding more patrols to an area that already has some appears to have little if any impact on crime. This study gave police managers a reason to maintain a constant level of vehicles on patrol, but at the same time it allowed administrators to experiment with alternative tactics and strategies.

According to Walker (1994), there are several reasons why increasing police patrols has a limited impact on crime. First, patrol officers are spread so thinly across a beat that a patrol vehicle may be seen only on chance encounters rather than as a daily occurrence. Second, many crimes cannot be deterred by police patrols. Crimes that occur in residences, such as murders, sexual assaults, and child abuse, are not going to stop because more police are patrolling the streets. Finally, some people are not deterred by increasing numbers of police. Robbers, for example, will change their approach to committing an offence rather than stop their criminal behaviour altogether (Desroches 1995).

CRIMINAL INVESTIGATIONS

Criminal investigation is the second main function of the police. According to Berg and Horgan (1998), criminal investigation involves searching for people and things in order to recreate the circumstances of a criminal act in the hope that this will identify the perpetrators and ultimately determine whether or not they were involved, as well as finding and maintaining evidence that will assist in a court case to determine their guilt. Criminal investigations typically have two components: (1) a preliminary investigation, which is conducted by patrol officers; and (2) a follow-up investigation, which is conducted by detectives if the patrol officers are not able to apprehend the alleged perpetrator. The patrol officers hand over to the detectives the information they have gathered; the detectives then follow up these "leads."

The preliminary investigation usually has five steps: (1) identifying and arresting any suspects; (2) providing assistance to any victims in need of medical attention; (3) securing the crime scene to prevent the loss of any evidence; (4) collecting any physical evidence; and (5) preparing a preliminary report (Eck 1983). It has been estimated that about 80 percent of all arrests of suspects are made by patrol officers rather than detectives. This is because when the patrol officers arrive, the suspect is often still at the crime scene or is readily identified by witnesses. If the patrol officers can't make the arrest, it can mean that very little is immediately known about the suspects and, as a result, it may be difficult to make an arrest.

A case can be handed over to detectives for follow-up investigation after an arrest has been made or if further investigation is needed in order to identify the suspect(s). Follow-up investigations can be routine, secondary, and tertiary (ibid.). Routine activities include interviewing victims and witnesses and examining the crime scene. Secondary activities include looking for people who may have witnessed the crime but who left the scene before the police arrived. Tertiary activities include discussing the case with patrol officers, interviewing suspects, checking police records and those of other agencies, interviewing informants, and staking out addresses or individuals.

In most mid- to large-size police services today, 15 to 20 percent of the personnel are detectives. They have not been studied as closely as patrol officers, because the bulk of their work involves law enforcement and very little of their time goes into service and order maintenance activities. Detectives are usually organized in a different division of a police agency than patrol officers. They are often assigned to sections specializing in a particular type of criminal activity, such as vice, homicide, robbery, or prostitution; or they support services such as polygraph operations. While most of their investigative work is reactive, detectives are also involved in proactive activities. For example, a vice squad detective may pose as a prostitute in order to arrest customers; or in a sting operation, detectives may set up an operation that buys stolen goods and videotapes everyone who brings in those goods. No matter how they investigate crimes, all detectives carry out a number of critical functions. These include collecting and preserving evidence, interviewing witnesses, questioning suspects, writing reports, preparing cases for the Crown prosecutor, and testifying in court.

Advances in technology, such as DNA analysis, have allowed detectives to maintain high clearance rates for certain criminal activities such as murder (see Exhibit 5.1). Over 65 percent of all murders in Canada are solved by the police in the year they were committed. In contrast, in the United States the clearance rate for murder dropped from 86 percent in 1968 to 62 percent in 2001. The drop is thought to have resulted from the fact that strangers are responsible for more murders than they were three decades ago; thus, they are harder to identify (Parker and Fields 2000).

The Detective Function

The "ideal" criminal case is one where the offender is arrested at the scene by a patrol officer, there are many witnesses, and the suspect quickly confesses. Such cases are, of course, rare; much more often, detectives must solve crimes by interviewing the victim and witnesses, doing background checks on potential suspects, and waiting for an analysis of any forensic evidence that was available at the crime scene. According to Eck (1983), detectives categorize cases into three types:

- *Unsolvable.* These cases are considered "weak" in the sense that they cannot be solved regardless of the amount of effort put into the investigation.
- *Solvable.* These cases can be solved with a moderate to considerable amount of investigation effort.
- *Already solved.* These cases have strong evidence and so can be solved with a minimum of investigation.

Studies have found that cases with moderate levels of evidence can be solved successfully. For example, Brandl and Frank (1994) examined a number of robbery and burglary cases and found that detectives were able to solve most of those that had a moderate level of evidence.

If patrol officers are unable to solve a serious crime at the scene, detectives assume control over the case. The first step in the detection process is the preliminary investigation. If the case was launched some time previously, detectives will receive a file from the patrol division. But if the crime has just occurred, detectives will arrive to secure the crime scene, which may contain potential evidence, such as weapons, as well as fingerprints, bloodstains, clothing fibres, and hair samples, which can be sent to forensics for analysis. Also, statements are taken from any witnesses, and photographs are taken of any relevant information. Any

EXHIBIT 5.1 DNA and Criminal Justice

As pointed out earlier, forensics (i.e., the application of science to criminal investigations) plays a key role in the detection of criminals. In fact, it has become a standard part of many police investigations, and many different techniques are now available to investigators. These include lighting a crime scene with ultraviolet light to detect fingerprints and footprints as well as bloodstains so small they cannot be seen by the naked eye. DNA analysis has led to the release of a number of Canadians who were serving time for crimes for which they had been wrongfully convicted. Notable examples include Guy Paul Morin, David Milgaard, and Thomas Sophonow. In the United States, as of early 2003, DNA had been used in at least numerous cases to establish that an innocent person had been wrongfully convicted.

What is DNA? Its full name is deoxyribonucleic acid, and it is the genetic material that carries the code for all living cells. DNA is useful to criminal investigators because every person's DNA is absolutely unique (except in the case of identical twins). Thus, forensic scientists are able to test DNA samples gathered at crime scenes to ascertain whether they match the DNA profile of a known or suspected offender.

A unique genetic profile can be obtained from hair, blood, or other bodily substances discovered at the scene of a crime or on a victim. These substances can then be matched to DNA samples from a suspect. This gives the police a very high probability of identifying the perpetrators. DNA profiling has three uses. First, it can link or eliminate those suspects who have been identified as the most likely to have committed the crime in question. Second, it leads to "cold hits"—that is, when a sample from a crime scene is matched against the contents of a DNA database and a positive match is made. Third, the DNA found at the crime scene can be placed in a DNA database when no one can be found who may have committed the crime; this DNA will be stored until the individual commits another crime and has his or her DNA collected, and that DNA is found to match the DNA profile gathered from the earlier crime.

DNA was first used to secure a criminal conviction in England in 1986, when it identified Colin Pitchfork as the murderer of two schoolgirls (Wambaugh 1989). Two years later, the FBI in the United States was using it to establish guilt. Soon after, Canadian judges began to allow DNA evidence in criminal cases. This, however, led to questions about whether the police could gather

a bodily sample without the suspect's consent. Specifically, was such a practice an unreasonable seizure under s. 8 of the Charter of Rights and Freedoms? If this manner of collecting DNA was illegal, there was a chance that such evidence could be excluded on the basis of s. 24(2) of the Charter if its introduction would bring the administration of justice into disrepute. However, when confronted with this issue, the courts ruled that it would not do so; that is, an unfair trial would not result from the introduction of the DNA evidence. The first Canadian case in which the DNA results were openly debated in court did not arise until 1994, when Allan Legere was convicted of four murders on the basis of DNA profiling (*R. v. Legere* [1994]).

Today in Canada, law enforcement agencies are allowed to collect DNA samples from offenders who have been convicted of specific crimes and store the resulting profiles in a national database. Two pieces of legislation relevant to DNA have been passed by Parliament. The first (1995) established a statutory basis for securing DNA evidence; the second (1998) established the National DNA Data Bank.

DNA has transformed—some say revolutionized—many aspects of policing. One commentator has referred to it as "a scientific miracle for human justice" that "shines the light of irrefutable truth into our courtrooms and juries." By May 2005, there were about 77,000 DNA profiles in Canada's Crime Scene Index; 3,270 matches had been made between crime scene DNA profiles and convicted offender DNA profiles, and 408 "forensic matches" (i.e., crime scene to crime scene). However, to date, no study has yet looked at the proportion of cases solved through the use of DNA evidence, and the impact of DNA on police investigations has yet to be evaluated. However, it is known that in the United States, by April 2007, DNA evidence had freed 200 inmates from prison. These individuals had served an average of 12 years before they were exonerated. One hundred and seventy-six had been convicted of a sexual assault, 56 had been convicted of murder, and 14 had been on death row.

One of the main issues surrounding DNA is whether individuals arrested for committing a crime should be required to give a DNA sample prior to being convicted. Taking DNA samples from all those charged with a crime was suggested by Ontario government officials in 1990. They based their argument on the fact that

(Continued)

EXHIBIT 5.1   DNA and Criminal Justice . . . Continued

accused persons are denied liberty in other areas before being convicted—for example, the police have the right to take their fingerprints. They also wanted to have DNA samples taken from every person already incarcerated. However, federal legislation specifies that only those individuals convicted of specific crimes have to give a DNA sample.

Other critics have argued that DNA sampling would violate the legal rights of their clients. Concerns in this area focus on how the police have obtained the suspect's consent and on whether they have used an illegal seizure to obtain the sample. This issue was addressed in *R. v. Borden* (1994), where the Supreme Court of Canada ruled that the police had not given the suspect sufficient information about the charges. In order to rectify this situation, Parliament introduced legislation (Bill C-104) authorizing the police to use a warrant to collect a bodily substance that could be used as DNA evidence.

Sources: Wambaugh 1989; Blackwell 2000; Scheck, Neufeld, and Dwyer 2000; Wickham 2000; Romano 2003; Royal Canadian Mounted Police 2001; Hiebert 2002.

evidence collected is placed into evidence bags. In addition, investigators will often conduct a walkthrough of the crime scene, trying to re-create the crime as it might have happened. This enables them to determine the location of the victim as well as the offender at the time of the incident, the place of entry and exit, whether there are signs of forced entry, and so on. All relevant information must be documented by written notes. If a suspect is arrested at the scene, detectives have to interrogate that person.

The purpose of all this detective work is to provide prosecutors with evidence strong enough to result in a conviction. If the case remains unsolved, detectives and their superiors have to determine whether they will

Firefighters and volunteers use poles and scuba gear to search a farm pond. A four-year-old boy who disappeared from the backyard of his family's home was discovered drowned in a nearby pond, provincial police said. When the police arrived, they secured the site. (CP PHOTO/London Free Press/Mike Hensen)

pursue the investigation any further. This decision is based on "solvability factors," such as the existence of any witnesses or forensic evidence.

Aggressive Detective Investigation Tactics

Detectives have a number of options open to them in the course of their work. In contrast to the mostly reactive actions of patrol officers, these actions are proactive in nature. If the case involves a significant piece of property, such as jewellery or an expensive motor vehicle, detectives may choose to set up a "sting" operation, in which the offender thinks the undercover officers (called "fences") are purchasing stolen property. The "buy" will be videotaped in order to make a strong case for prosecutors and to establish that the detectives conducted themselves within the law.

Police may also decide to "go undercover" in order to obtain information concerning the crime. This is standard practice for certain crimes today, such as drug trafficking. Or they may try to "turn" a member of a gang or criminal organization—that is, persuade that individual to become an informant. In recent years, the police have often succeeded at this; this has led to the arrest of a number of crime bosses. Without informants, police would find it terribly difficult to infiltrate criminal groups. However, the use of informants has been carefully scrutinized in recent years by the Supreme Court of Canada, since the police have been known to use "dirty tricks" to obtain confessions or other evidence.

POLICING MODERN SOCIETY

Because of concerns about the proper role of the police in contemporary society, police administrators and analysts began to study what was wrong with traditional styles of policing and to develop and experiment with new ones. By the mid-1980s, two decades of research had revealed the limits of traditional styles of policing: police patrols didn't reduce the crime rate; detectives didn't solve a lot of crimes; and arrests didn't necessarily deter would-be criminals. Most police work remained reactive, but that approach didn't seem to be working well. Victim surveys found that citizens weren't reporting crimes to the police and that victims had lost faith in the police to respond quickly and effectively. When the police did respond, many citizens remained uninformed about the case until they were notified to appear at a preliminary hearing or court trial. Furthermore, officers had become removed from neighbourhoods' concerns, and therefore seemed unreliable, with the result that citizens weren't calling the

police to report crimes and were living with significant fear of crime (Sherman 1986).

Meanwhile, some communities took to hiring private security companies to protect them from criminals because they lacked faith in the ability of the police to do so (Shearing 1992). As a result, some police administrators felt there was a need for fundamental change. What emerged was community policing, which attempts to close the gap between the police and the community. There are many types of community policing; almost all police forces in Canada are involved in some aspects of it. In fact, it is seen by many as the future style of policing. How did this new type of policing develop in such a short time?

The Broken Windows Model

The start of the community policing era can be traced to a 1982 article written by two police scholars, Kelling and Wilson, for a popular American magazine, *The Atlantic Monthly*. This article, titled "Broken Windows: The Police and Neighborhood Safety," argued that the police cannot combat crime successfully all by themselves. They need the assistance and support of the community; even more important, they need to change their basic approach by allowing for community involvement in policing. Kelling and Wilson also pointed out that much of traditional policing focuses on the end result of policing activity—that is, clearance rates. They contended it would be an improvement for the police to get involved at the beginning of the process of neighbourhood deterioration—that is, at the first signs of neglect and disorder. This article introduced the concept of disorder to policing by making the point that disorder, if left unchallenged, signals that no one cares about a neighbourhood. When that is the perception, disorder

Many communities have created programs to clean up signs of disorder in the hope that criminal activity will be reduced. Are these programs successful in reaching this goal? (© iStockphoto/Frank vandenBergh)

increases and so does crime (including violent crime). The police had traditionally ignored this element of community life, since it was not part of the professional model of policing.

The **broken windows model** posits that social incivilities (such as loitering and public drinking) and physical incivilities (such as vacant lots and abandoned buildings) cause residents and workers in a neighbourhood to be fearful of crime. This fear causes some residents to move out and others to live in fear and isolate themselves. The model has three components:

1. *Neighbourhood disorder creates fear.* Those areas in a city that are filled with criminals such as drug dealers are the areas that are most likely to have high crime rates.
2. *Neighbourhoods give out crime-promoting signals.* In other words, the appearance of a community can attract criminals. Deteriorated housing, disorderly behaviour, and unrepaired broken windows send the message that no one in the area cares about the quality of life. That message attracts criminals, who feel they can go about their business without interference from the local residents.
3. *Police need citizens' cooperation.* If the police are to reduce fear of crime and the crime rate, their policies must include the involvement and cooperation of local citizens.

This approach proposes that there is a significant correlation between disorder and perceived crime problems in a neighbourhood. This type of reasoning constitutes the basis of Ontario's Safe Streets Act (see Chapter 2), which targets panhandlers, homeless people, and squeegee kids as significant sources of disorder. Supporters of these laws point to the research on community policing; these studies have found that both serious crimes and fear of crime can be alleviated by reducing disorder (Pate et al. 1986; Skogan 1990). The broken windows model recommends that police administrators change some of their policies to include local residents in decisions about policing priorities in their neighbourhoods. This model also suggests that other areas of policing that had been largely ignored over the past four decades need to be reviewed in order to reduce fear of crime, increase levels of safety, and develop order maintenance policies. These should become the main focus of the police—and of patrol officers in particular.

Problem-Oriented Policing

In 1979, Herman Goldstein published an article in which he laid out a new style of policing that he called **problem-oriented policing**. This style, according to Goldstein, represented a fundamental change in the way

the police operate. Instead of spending most of their time responding to citizens' calls about criminal incidents, the police would direct their energies at the causes of crimes and complaints in an attempt to modify these sources. This would involve a fundamental shift in the way the police operated. They would have to begin studying the underlying causes of crime, for unless those causes were modified or eliminated the problems would persist, leading to more criminal incidents and to greater fear of crime.

What is a problem? Although it is easy to point to criminal acts as problems, problem-oriented policing focuses strongly on those situations that are perceived as leading to criminal activity. Five principles of problem-oriented policing have been identified, all of which are meant to turn the police away from an incident-based focus toward one that emphasizes the potential sources of criminal activity:

- A problem is something that concerns the community and its citizens, not just police officers.
- A problem is a group or pattern of incidents and therefore demands a different set of responses than does a single incident.
- A problem must be understood in terms of the competing interests at stake.
- Responding to a problem involves more than a "quick fix," such as an arrest. Problem solving is a long-term strategy.
- Problem solving requires a heightened level of creativity and initiative on the part of the patrol officer (Bureau of Justice Assistance 1993).

As problem-oriented policing began to come into practice, four stages in the problem-solving process were developed. The first is referred to as *scanning*; here, a police officer identifies an issue and assesses whether it really is a problem. In the second stage, *analysis,* the officer collects as much information as possible about the problem. In the third stage, *response,* all relevant information is collected and solutions are developed and implemented. In the final stage, *assessment,* officers collect information about the effectiveness of their approach, changing any particular tactics if doing so is considered necessary, or even developing an entirely new approach. This same approach is also found in the RCMP's CAPRA model. Many policing initiatives have used the problem-oriented approach, often with some success. Exhibit 5.2 outlines two such projects.

Community Policing

One flaw of the problem-oriented approach is that the police don't always include the community when studying a crime problem. As Moore and Trojanowicz

EXHIBIT 5.2 Problem-Oriented Policing Programs Designed to Prevent Crime

Evaluations of problem-oriented policing programs have found that some are successful in terms of preventing firearm-related crimes. It is now clear that if these programs can accurately identify and minimize the causes of a specific type of offence, the crime rate for that offence will decline. Problem-oriented policing programs for reducing firearm-related crime generally focus on reducing the possession, carrying, and use of firearms in gun violence "hot spots" and among violent gun offenders. Two recent and relatively successful problem-oriented policing programs are discussed below. The first targeted a small number of chronic offenders in an attempt to reduce and control gun violence; the second focused on reducing the use of firearms in a hot spot.

POLICING DRUG HOT SPOTS

In 1995, David Weisburd and Lorraine Green attempted to discover if the police could reduce the selling of drugs in a location responsible for a large amount of drug sales in Jersey City, New Jersey. They evaluated an experiment that attempted to reduce the drug sales at locations (i.e., "hot spots") responsible for a substantial amount of calls for service. These locations accounted for only 4.4 percent of all streets and intersections but 46 percent of all drug sale arrests and emergency calls for narcotics. Prior to the experiment, the Jersey City police relied on techniques such as narcotics squads who had relied on unsystematic techniques such as surveillance, arrests, search warrants, and field interrogations of suspected dealers on the street. While these enforcement efforts increased over time, they didn't have any impact on the drug problem.

The experiment was designed to get local business owners and residents involved; crack down on drug hot spots, and create a maintenance program to patrol the hot spots after police crackdowns. Comparing the seven months before and after the experiment, Weisburd and Green (1995) found the following:

- Significant reductions in emergency calls to the police.
- Little displacement of crime to the areas near the experimental hot spots.
- Reduced crime in areas around the experimental hot spots.

According to Weisburd and Green (ibid., 721), the reduction in emergency calls is important since "recent studies suggest emergency calls are a more reliable measure of crime and crime-related activity than are other official indicators."

THE KANSAS CITY GUN PROJECT

The Kansas City Gun Project was developed in an attempt to reduce the carrying of firearms in high-risk locations at high-risk times. It tested the hypothesis that greater enforcement of gun-carrying laws in gun crime hot spots could reduce gun crimes overall in two Kansas City Police Department beats that had identical rates of drive-by shootings. The Kansas City Police Department directed extra patrol officers on "hot spot" crime areas identified by a computer analysis of all firearm offences. Officers were specially trained in the detection of individuals carrying concealed weapons. The police focused on seizing illegally carried firearms. Over a 29-week period in 1992–93, targeted police patrols were conducted in a 10-by-8-block area that had a homicide rate 20 times the national average. During this time, police officers made more than 600 arrests. Using frisks and searches, they seized 29 more firearms than normal. A similar area in a different part of the city showed no change in firearms offences or firearms seized.

Sherman and Rogan (1995, 681) reported that some of the activities by the police in the gun crime hot spots areas involved the following:

- *Safety frisk during traffic stops.* When a police officer asked a driver for his licence, the officer noticed a bulge in the driver's jacket when the driver leaned over to retrieve his registration from the glove compartment. The officer then grabbed the bulge, felt a hard shape and reached into the jacket, pulling out a hand gun.
- *Plain view.* When an officer approached a vehicle he had pulled over for speeding, he shined his flashlight onto the floor in front of the rear seat and saw a shotgun. Ordering the driver and passenger out of the vehicle, he discovered that the shotgun was loaded.
- *Search incident to arrest on other charges.* After stopping a vehicle for running a red light, the officer asked the driver for his licence. A computer check revealed that the driver was wanted for failure to appear on domestic assault charges. The driver was arrested and when searched, the officer discovered a handgun hidden beneath the driver's shirt.

(Continued)

During the 29 weeks prior to the start of the experiment, the designated area recorded 169 firearm offences; while the experiment was being conducted, it recorded only 86—a decrease of 49 percent. Drive-by shootings and homicides also dropped significantly, without any displacement of these crimes to other areas of the city. According to the researchers, it is possible that the firearms seized were taken from high-rate offenders who were likely to commit firearm-related offences, resulting in the overall rate

reduction. It was also suggested that the police tactics resulted in some of the criminals using firearms being taken off the streets. And as it became public knowledge what the police were doing, there may have been a general deterrent effect—that is, people contemplating using a firearm to commit a crime may have decided that the apprehension risks were unacceptably high.

Sources: Sherman, Shaw, and Rogan 1994; Sherman and Rogan 1995.

(1988) point out, community policing involves community groups, such as businesspeople, residents, and school teachers, as "key partners . . . in the creation of safe, secure communities. The success of the police depends not only on the development of their own skills and capabilities, but also on the creation of competent communities."

The goal of this style of policing is not to fight crime but to encourage public safety and confidence, reduce citizens' fear of crime, and encourage citizen involvement. Community policing is a broad-based approach that can encompass many different policies and programs. One possible approach involves establishing decentralized, neighbourhood-based mini-stations or storefronts. Since community policing was introduced about 20 years ago, a consensus has been reached regarding its basic elements and how it differs from past policing strategies. Key here is the change that community policing has brought to the role of policing in society. This new role embraces such issues as disorder, neighbourhood decay, the fear of crime, and order maintenance. This shift has been justified in two ways. The first is rooted in the belief that disorder leads to serious crime, as discussed earlier (the "broken windows" thesis). The second is that order maintenance contributes to the growth of civil society by promoting an environment in which citizens can, without fear, go about their lives (Greene and Mastrofski 1988).

Community policing has three basic aims: (1) the formation of community partnerships, (2) organizational change, and (3) problem solving. Supporters of community policing view it as the most effective way to reduce disorder in communities; they contend that it does so by developing partnerships between the police and the community. The desired result is for the police and the community to become "co-producers of crime control." According to Bayley (1994), two elements are necessary in order to introduce community partnerships:

consultation and mobilization. Consultation involves community meetings between the police and the community, while mobilization involves the introduction of community crime prevention programs that can increase neighbourhood cohesion.

Community policing also requires organizational change. Eck and Maguire (2000) contend that there are two reasons why such change is necessary: (1) to encourage officers to become active in community policing programs; and (2) to ensure that the organization is more flexible and open to developing community partnerships and creative problem solving strategies. In their opinion, before police agencies can successfully implement community policing, they will have to change (1) their structure, (2) their culture, and (3) their management approach. Regarding the first, police agencies must abandon their traditional, strongly centralized structures. Regarding the second, those agencies must abandon their focus on crime fighting and begin to emphasize problem solving and community interaction. Regarding the third, management must reduce its emphasis on departmental rules and regulations and begin working more closely with community-based police officers as they develop programs and problem-solving initiatives.

The third aim, problem solving, refers to the police and the community participating in cooperative efforts to solve neighbourhood problems. Specifically, the problem-solving process involves police and community residents addressing chronic problems in the neighbourhood. Many of these programs focus on particular small-scale issues. Such programs identify the causes of problems instead of simply reacting to those problems.

Community policing also involves an important new role for the police, a role that focuses on reducing fear of crime in the community. There are three types of fear of crime. The first is the intense fear suffered by the victims of crime and by their family, friends, and neighbours. This fear comes from physical injury, property loss, economic costs (such as hospital bills and loss of wages at work), and psychological trauma (such as depression and anxiety). Some victims also suffer from *double victimization*—that is, when they report the crime they are treated as second-class citizens by agencies in the criminal justice system.

The second type is often referred to as the "concrete" fear of crime. Here, the fear is of specific crimes, especially violent ones. Various studies have found that women, the young, racial minorities, and metropolitan dwellers are most susceptible to this type of fear. Members of these groups fear being sexually assaulted, physically assaulted, robbed, and murdered. The third type—formless fear—is the general feeling that one is unsafe. Research has found that the elderly, the marginally employed, and those with low incomes experience the highest levels of formless fear. Studies that focus on the fear of crime note that while people are afraid of serious crime, they are just as concerned—if not more so—about petty crimes and social disorder. In the past, the police failed to understand that when people say they are afraid of crime, they are talking about all types of crime and disorder, not just serious, violent crimes (Trojanowicz et al. 2001).

For community police officers, reducing the fear of crime is a core task. It's also a way to increase citizen–police cooperation. A variety of techniques can be employed to reduce the fear of crime in a community, including a police–community newsletter, a police–community contact centre staffed by patrol officers and civilians, and a variety of programs in which police officers contact victims of crime to inform them of police action on the case. Whatever programs are developed, the most successful seem to be those that allow officers the time to identify key issues with local residents and to use both personal initiative and community input to solve problems. While not all programs succeed, the evidence shows that foot patrol officers are actually able to reduce the level of fear in the community.

Criticisms of Community Policing

Community policing has been in existence for a number of decades, and many evaluations have been made of it. While most observers recognize that the benefits of community-based policing far outweigh its shortcomings, a number of criticisms have been levelled at it. These criticisms are evidence that community policing is not necessarily the crime control panacea its advocates say it is.

The basic question is whether community policing is rhetoric or reality (Greene and Mastrofski 1988). That is, does community policing represent a new strategy, or is

it simply new rhetoric for describing traditional policing approaches? Bayley (1998) contends that it is difficult to evaluate "community policing" because the concept is too difficult to describe. In his view, the programs the police and the community have started are so diverse that it is difficult to judge how widespread the changes have been and how successful the programs have been.

Another criticism is that community policing lacks a clear definition and seems to include almost any type of proactive activity by the police. The fact that it is an "approach" and not a concise set of operational procedures is damaging to its overall integrity, since this has led to a dilution of what community policing really is.

A third criticism focuses on the amount of community policing that actually becomes part of the everyday operations of the police. Community policing has become a buzzword, and its critics point out that it may be more rhetoric than an emerging new philosophy among police agencies. They point out that the two most common programs implemented by the police identified as community policing are drug prevention programs and foot patrols, both of which existed long before community policing emerged.

Other criticisms of community policing are encountered in studies that have found police officers spending more time on paperwork and other administrative duties than they do talking to members of the community or developing programs specific to the community needs (Parks et al. 1999). The issue of the police's proper role has also been raised. Should officers be working on community projects such as cleaning up vacant lots, or should they be spending their time investigating serious criminal activity? Others point out that community policing will never be accepted because it advocates a change in the command structure, thereby reducing the number of higher-level positions (Lewis et al. 1999). There are also problems associated with the police being unable to define exactly what a community really is; in these situations, the roles of community police officers remain poorly integrated with the rest of the police organization (Halsted et al. 2000).

Zero Tolerance: Aggressive Policing

In recent years, another type of policing has emerged: zero tolerance policing. This type is actually a variant of problem-oriented policing, but instead of combating a problem by analyzing various features about it within the community, the police basically eliminate most of the analysis stage and simply apply traditional law enforcement methods. The focus of this style is order maintenance on the streets, and it narrows police attention to suppressing those individuals who are seen as the main sources of disorder in public places.

As shown in Figure 5.1, zero tolerance policing differs from other forms of policing in a number of important ways. While problem-oriented and community policing emphasize crime prevention, zero tolerance policing embraces what has been termed the "crime–attack" model. In other words, it is based on suppression, which is closer to the traditional approach to policing in many Western countries. A second difference is that zero tolerance policing operates on the premise that not all communities may be able to provide support for crime prevention activities; thus, the police must take primary responsibility for crime control. A third difference is that zero tolerance policing focuses on specific types of behaviour instead of analyzing crimes to unearth their causes. Zero tolerance policing also concentrates more on place-specific interventions—that is, it maps crime and determines its hot spots. Another difference is that zero tolerance policing favours a more traditional organizational response to crime, one that favours an organizational structure that is both centralized and internally focused (Cordner 1998; Green 2000).

To eliminate disorder, then, the police pursue an aggressive policy throughout certain designated neighbourhoods that are facing disorder problems. This leads to a confrontational style of policing, as the police target those individuals they feel are responsible for disorder and incivility in the community.

Zero tolerance policing gained the attention of police services across Canada and the United States after the results of this approach were published by the New York Police Department (NYPD). This style of policing started shortly after Rudolph Giuliani became mayor in 1993. He had promised the voters that he would make New York City a safe place to live. So he hired a new police commissioner, William Bratton, who had been the police chief in Boston. Bratton radically altered the way the NYPD approached crime by employing COMPSTAT (the acronym for "computer comparison statistics"), which places current crime data in the hands of precinct commanders. Commanders were held accountable if crime rates in their precincts did not decline within a certain time, and they were replaced if their actions were not deemed adequate. Bratton also increased the powers of police officers to stop, search, and question individuals who had violated the law, even if the infraction was minor. The belief was that by stopping and questioning suspects, the police might discover a weapon or information that could assist in solving a crime or in preventing a crime from occurring. To accomplish these goals, a large number of police officers were hired—the NYPD grew in size by 39.5 percent.

The results of this approach to controlling crime and disorder gained international headlines within a few years. Official police statistics indicated that there had been a dramatic reduction in the crime rate of 37.4 percent between 1990 and in 1995. Large reductions were recorded in homicides, robberies, and burglaries.

So zero tolerance policing succeeded—but at a price. Minority neighbourhoods were most often the target of this style of policing, and as a result, the number of civil rights complaints against the NYPD had increased by 75 percent by the end of 1997. In the same time period, citizens' complaints filed with New York's Civilian Complaint Review Board rose by 60 percent. Complaints against the police in cases where no arrests were made had doubled by the end of the first year of the program. Amnesty International contended that this new policing approach had increased police brutality and the use of unjustifiable force.

Despite these accusations, there was considerable interest in the NYPD's tactics because the crime rate had in fact decreased. Other cities rushed to introduce zero tolerance programs based on the fact that the zero tolerance approach apparently reduced crime in New York. Yet, it was also noted that remarkable reductions in crime rates were being recorded in cities *that had not introduced zero tolerance policing*. Critics of the NYPD approach pointed to the experience of the San Diego Police Department (SDPD). The SDPD had taken a more community-oriented approach to policing crime and disorder by trying to work closely with the community and to develop solutions acceptable to both groups. The results of its program were interesting: between 1990 and 1995, both the crime rate and the number of complaints filed by citizens in San Diego had dropped 36.8 percent, and over the same years, the size of the SDPD had increased by only 6.8 percent. Central to the SDPD's success was that it had relied strongly on community participation when planning crime prevention efforts. In contrast, the approach taken by New York City alienated the residents of many communities (Greene 1999).

Intelligence-Led Policing

In fact, zero tolerance policing was only the most heavily trumpeted of a number of changes that were introduced by the NYPD at around the same time. Another component introduced by that department was *intelligence-led policing*, an approach that assigns reactive-style policing a secondary role in a system that emphasizes computer-assisted programs for identifying high-crime places (i.e., "hot spots") as well as certain people (i.e., repeat offenders) who are at risk of offending.

Social Interaction or Structural Dimension	Traditional Policing	Community Policing	Problem-Oriented Policing	Zero Tolerance Policing
Focus of Policing	Law enforcement	Community-building through crime prevention	Law, order, and fear problems	Order problems
Forms of Intervention	Reactive, based on criminal law	Proactive, on criminal, civil, and administrative law	Mixed, on criminal, civil, and administrative law	Proactive, uses criminal, civil, and administrative law
Range of Police Activity	Narrow, crime focused	Broad crime, order, fear, and quality-of-life focused	Narrow to broad—problem focused	Narrow—location and behaviour focused
Level of Discretion at Line Level	High and unaccountable	High and accountable to the community and local commanders	High and primarily accountable to the police administration	Low, but primarily accountable to the police administration
Focus of Police Culture	Inward, rejecting community	Outward, building partnerships	Mixed, depending on problem, but analysis focused	Inward, focused on attacking the target problem
Locus of Decision-Making	Police directed; minimizes the involvement of others	Community–police coproduction; joint responsibility and assessment	Varied, police identify problems but with community involvement/action	Police directed, some linkage to other agencies where necessary
Communication Flow	Downward from police to community	Horizontal between police and community	Horizontal between police and community	Downward from police to community
Range of Community Involvement	Low and passive	High and active	Mixed, depending on problem set	Low and passive
Linkage with Other Agencies	Poor and intermittent	Participative and integrative in the overarching process	Participative and integrative depending on the problem set	Moderate and intermittent
Type of Organization and Command Focus	Centralized command and control	Decentralized with community linkage	Decentralized with local command accountability to central admission	Centralized or decentralized but internal focus
Implications for Organizational Change/ Development	Few; static organization fending off the environment	Many; dynamic organization focused on the environment and environmental interactions	Varied; focused on problem resolution but with import for organization, intelligence, and structure	Few; limited interventions focused on target problems, using many traditional methods
Measurement of Success	Arrest and crime rates, particularly serious Part 1 crimes	Varied; crime calls for service, fear reduction, use of public places, community linkages and contacts, safer neighbourhoods	Varied; problems solved, minimized, displaced	Arrests, field stops, activity, location-specific reductions in targeted activity

FIGURE 5.1

A Comparison of Problem-Oriented Policing, Community Policing, and Zero Tolerance Policing

Source: Greene, J. 2000. "Community Policing in America: Changing the Nature, Structure and Foundation of the Police." In J. Horney, ed., *Policies, Processes and Decisions of the Criminal Justice System*. Washington, DC: National Institute of Justice.

Intelligence-led policing attempts to increase the effectiveness of the police by more strongly emphasizing (1) the collection and analysis of intelligence; and (2) the development of targeted responses to the analysis. In the Information Age, police departments have emerged as key agencies for managing information about public safety. In the new "risk society," it is the police who are in the best position to gather and store knowledge about crime and security, to assess that information, and to recommend how risks should be managed and controlled (Ericson and Haggerty 1997; Maguire 2000).

This model of policing first appeared in the early 1990s in Great Britain, when rising crime rates led to demands for the police to develop more effective and more cost-efficient policies. The sources of this change were both external and internal. The external sources included the recognition that the traditional models of policing were failing to cope with the rapid changes being brought by globalization. In particular, transnational organized crime and new technologies were causing the old, national policing boundaries to vanish. The internal sources included the recognition that changes were occurring rapidly in public policing; in particular, private policing was growing in ways that were somehow compromising public safety.

In 1993 in Britain, the Audit Commission (the equivalent of Canada's Auditor General) produced a report on police effectiveness, titled *Helping with Enquiries: Tackling Crime Effectively*. This report identified three reasons why the police were finding it difficult to be effective: (1) their various roles lacked integration, and their level of accountability was unclear; (2) they were failing to make the best use of their resources; and (3) they were emphasizing crimes rather than criminals. The report also noted that while the police were doing well at preventing certain crimes such as vehicle crime, break and enters, and drug offences, they were failing to anticipate and/or identify emergent changes in the criminal environment. Why? Because the police were basing their activities largely on performance indicators, and thus were focusing on areas in which they were already doing well. As a consequence, new areas of criminal activity were emerging unnoticed (Heaton 2000).

The report recommended that the police focus on two things: proactive policing, and repeat offenders. It argued that the police should use their data storage and collation facilities to gather, collect, and analyze key information. The results could then be disseminated to the appropriate authorities and policing and non-policing agencies. This approach was viewed as superior in terms of targeting specific types of criminal behaviour, increasing community safety, reducing crime and disorder, and controlling criminality. To work effectively, such a system would have to be in close and constant communication with police decision-makers.

Intelligence-led policing applies recent developments such as video technology and communication devices. It includes these goals: (1) targeting repeat offenders, using both overt and covert means; (2) managing crime and disorder hot spots; (3) investigating the links among crimes and incidents; and (4) developing and implementing preventive measures, especially through multiagency partnerships.

Critics (e.g., Innes 2000; Maguire 2000) of intelligence-led policing have raised a number of concerns about this approach. For example, they argue that the overreliance on informants to gather intelligence can lead to serious problems, since many informants may be motivated by factors other than the protection of society—factors such as revenge, financial gain, or the possibility of a favourable plea bargain. In addition, critics point out that many police informants continue to engage in criminal activities while supplying the police with information (Maguire 2000). Concerns have also been raised about the effectiveness, accountability, and fairness of the methods used in this type of policing. Still another issue is that this type of policing is growing more quickly than the statutory and procedural rules designed to control such activities.

Intelligence-led policing relies on computer-based methods, and in this sense shares certain features with problem-oriented policing and COMPSTAT. Problem-oriented policing has the ability to define problems as well as analyze trends. In addition, COMPSTAT is able to map crime as well as collect and manage data.

ABORIGINAL (FIRST NATIONS) POLICE FORCES

During the late 1980s and throughout the early to mid-1990s, a series of provincial and federal government commissions and reports considered the issue of First Nations policing. All of these reports concluded that policing in First Nations communities was inadequate and often culturally insensitive, that the justice system often discriminated against First Nations peoples, and that these communities were sorely lacking in crime prevention programs. These reports did not, however, agree on solutions. Some (e.g., Head 1989) felt that the best way was to make changes to the existing system, while others (e.g., Hamilton and Sinclair 1991) recommended a separate and First Nations–controlled policing service.

Aboriginal policing services, however, predate these inquiries. One of the earliest such services was founded in Quebec in 1978, when 25 reserves in that province began to receive policing services from a force known as the Amerindian Police. This force was established because it had been surmised that the dependency of Native communities on outside police forces "increases the likelihood of police interventions and 'criminalizes' behaviors that would not necessarily be considered criminal if other agencies were involved" (Hyde 1992, 370). Aboriginal police forces were founded to allow more sensitivity to Aboriginal communities.

Officers of the Amerindian Police were most often asked to perform service functions in the community. About 6,000 of the total of 17,000 requests for police assistance recorded between 1978 and 1983 were for noncriminal incidents. Almost 45 percent of these calls resulted in referrals to other agencies, such as social and health services, probation officers, and psychiatric specialists. According to Hyde (ibid.), "peace keeping, crime prevention, and crisis-intervention functions of the police are, in part, the raison d'être for the establishment of the force."

The crimes committed involved the least serious Criminal Code and provincial offences. These included public order offences, interpersonal altercations, liquor and drug offences, and break and enters. The most typical police response to an incident was "no charge," meaning the police took no action; the next most common response was "suspect detained," meaning the individual was detained by the police overnight (Depew 1992). Clearly, the Amerindian Police played an important role in crisis intervention and in providing social services. LaPrairie and Diamond (1992) found that many criminal cases were dealt with outside the measures available through the formal criminal justice system. They also found that only about 33 percent of reported criminal or potential criminal offences were officially recorded and that only 12 percent of those officially recorded made it to court.

Recognizing the importance of Aboriginal police officers on reserves, the federal government created the First Nations Policing Policy in June 1991 to allow Aboriginal communities more control over policing on reserves. The purpose of this policy was to improve the administration of justice and the maintenance of social order, public security, and personal safety on Aboriginal reserves. Specifically, the policy would:

1. help improve social order, public security, and personal safety in First Nations communities, especially for women, children, and other vulnerable groups;

2. provide a practical way to improve the administration of justice for First Nations by establishing First Nations police services that were professional,

effective, and responsive to the particular community's needs;

3. ensure that First Nations peoples enjoyed their right to personal security and public safety. This would be achieved through access to policing services that were responsive to their needs and that met acceptable standards with respect to the quality and level of service;

4. support First Nations in acquiring the tools to become self-sufficient and self-governing by establishing structures for the management, administration, and accountability of First Nations police services; and

5. implement and administer the First Nations Policy in a manner promoting partnerships with First Nations based on trust, mutual respect, and participation in decision-making (Solicitor General of Canada 1999).

By 1995, 41 agreements had been signed with 180 First Nations communities. Ten years later, in 2005, 319 Aboriginal communities with a total population of approximately 244,000 had signed agreements. Close to 1,000 police officers, most of them of Aboriginal descent, are employed under this program. Agreements exist both with single communities and with groups of communities; in one case, 44 communities joined together to establish one police service. Under the policy, a number of options are available to First Nations communities (see Exhibit 5.3). One of the most common is the self-administered police service (also referred to as stand-alone police service), which allows a community or number of communities to have their own separate police force that is not affiliated with any other police force, be it federal, provincial, or municipal. In these arrangements, the First Nations community manages its own police service under provincial legislation. Independent police commissions oversee these self-administered police services. Another option is an agreement signed with an existing federal, provincial, or municipal police force. Agreements are signed between the federal government, the province or territory in which the First Nations community is located, and the governing body of the First Nations community, represented by the Band Council. These are known as Community Tripartite Agreements, and they usually involve the RCMP providing the policing services.

The most common of these arrangements is the self-administered agreement. Of the 356 First Nations communities that had signed an agreement by 2007, 154 (43 percent) were using a self-administered approach to policing. Additionally, there were 142 communities being policed by the Aboriginal Community Constable Program (78 communities) and band constables (59 communities)

(Rastin 2007). This approach involves fully trained officers of Aboriginal ancestry providing policing services to a community or communities. Agreements under the FNPP provide for appropriate mechanisms to ensure that requirements are met to protect independent policing services from inappropriate political or partisan influence, as well as to allow for appropriate police accountability. This has led to the creation of First Nations Police Boards and Commissions that administer services in accordance with established policing standards.

Depew (1992) and Metha (1993) point out the relevance of a community policing approach to Aboriginal communities. This involves a commitment to community planning that takes into account "community-level political and economic development to ensure stability and coherence in local social organization and an appropriate legislative framework to sustain intergovernmental cooperation, coordination, and support for new native policing arrangements." However, they add that the task may be difficult, given community erosion and potentially limited community resources. A major issue is the extent to which a different style of policing—one informed by Native cultural traditions and "communitarianism" (LaPrairie 1992)—can be developed and autonomously practised in Aboriginal communities.

First Nations communities with high crime rates not only want their Aboriginal police officers to practise community policing but also want them to be skilled and effective at solving major crimes. Aboriginal law enforcement officers as well see the need to acquire conventional policing skills in order to perform their jobs. A survey of Aboriginal police officers conducted by Murphy and Clairmont (1996) rated conventional police skills as very important; these officers said they required greater skills training in both general and specialized law enforcement techniques. Some researchers (Hyde 1992; Landau 1996) have questioned the extensive funding that has gone into policing services, a policy they say leads to overpolicing. They believe that some of these funds might be better spent on other social policies within the communities.

EXHIBIT 5.3 Policing Services and the First Nations Policing Policy

The First Nations Policing Policy (FNPP) provides for several forms of policing services:

SELF-ADMINISTERED AGREEMENT
Self-Administered Agreements (SA) involve an arrangement between the federal government and a respective province as well as a First Nations community. This form of policing agreement allows for First Nations communities to directly manage and administer their police service under a respective province's Police Act. SAs are cost shared between the federal government and the province at a rate of 52–48 percent.

COMMUNITY TRIPARTITE AGREEMENT
Community Tripartite Agreements (CTA) involve an arrangement between the federal government, respective province, and a First Nations community. However, the key difference between a CTA and a SA is that instead of the First Nation administering its own policing service, under a CTA agreement, the RCMP provides policing services to the First Nations community. CTAs are cost shared between the federal government and the province at a rate of 52–48 percent.

BAND CONSTABLE PROGRAM
The Band Constable Programs (BCP) is an historical program pre-dating the inception of the FNPP and is primarily administered in Manitoba. A band constable is an unarmed officer who supplements and assists existing policing services. A band constable is not meant to replace a police officer. Under the BCP, the federal government assumes 100 percent of the costs associated with this form of policing.

FIRST NATIONS COMMUNITY POLICING SERVICE FRAMEWORK
First Nations Community Service Framework Agreements (FNCPS) are bilateral agreements between the federal government and a province or territory that allow for the future signing of individual CTA that will provide for policing services within the province or territory.

NUNAVUT COMMUNITY CONSTABLE PROGRAM AND INUIT POLICING PROGRAM (IPP)
The Nunavut Community Constable Program (NCCP) and Inuit Policing Program (IPP) are developmental initiatives. The IPP was formed in 1999 and the officers are part of the RCMP and provide culturally enhanced policing for Inuit communities in Nunavut. These programs are cost-shared 50–50 percent between the respective province/territory and the federal government.

ABORIGINAL COMMUNITY CONSTABLE PROGRAM
The Aboriginal Community Constable Program (ACCP) is similar to the BCP and is cost-shared between the federal government and the province/territory at a rate of 46–54 percent.

Source: Aboriginal Policing Update 2007, Vol. 1, No. 2, Special Edition Policy and Program Overview, pg. 3-4 (Christopher J. Rastin; Public Safety Canada). Reproduced with the permission of the Minister of Public Works and Government Services, 2009.

EXPANDING THE ROLE OF DNA DATA BANKS

One of the key issues regarding DNA data banks is determining who should be included. Another, more recent, issue is determining on what grounds, if any, they can be maintained on a data bank if they have not been convicted of a crime. When data banks were first developed, only those individuals who were convicted of certain criminal offences were included. In Canada, this remains the case today. DNA profiles and samples are included in the National DNA Data Bank's Convicted Offenders Index when individuals are convicted of a designated offence or when they become included under retroactive legislation. Under current Canadian legislation, DNA profiles and samples can be removed from this index when the conviction or DNA order is quashed on appeal, the criminal record retention period has expired in the case of a young person, one year after an individual receives an absolute discharge, or three years after a conditional discharge unless there is on the criminal record a DNA sample collection order for another designated offence (Royal Canadian Mounted Police 2008). However, information supplied to an Ontario youth court indicated that the DNA of Canadian youths "convicted of crimes as minor as petty theft have been improperly retained by the federal DNA data bank . . . (violating) youths' constitutional rights to privacy . . . In her ruling, Judge Cohen said . . . a senior data bank official stated that only 535 of 21,169 DNA samples seized from youths have been destroyed because their retention period has ended—a suspiciously small number." The judge also noted that when the data bank destroys DNA profiles taken from youths, it continues to hold a portion of the original biological material that was seized (Makin 2009).

Some countries, however, have expanded who is included in their DNA data banks. This is largely due to the fact that when DNA data banks were first established, the police found the information included in the data banks to be of limited assistance in their investigations. This was due to the fact that there was a lack of having "an optimum size of sample and a means of storage" as well as the fact that the police also lacked the power "to compel suspects to give a suitable sample that could then be matched with samples found at the scene of a crime or on a victim" (Dovaston and Burton 1996).

In Britain, these problems were removed by the government in 1994 when it introduced the Criminal Justice and Public Order Act. Part IV of this legislation made amendments to the Police and Criminal Evidence Act (1984), granting the police the right to take samples from suspects for DNA analysis during investigations. If no criminal proceeding occurred, any samples taken were to be destroyed. The following year, another amendment gave the police the power to take a DNA sample from offenders who had been convicted of a "recordable offence" (i.e., an offence punishable with imprisonment or as otherwise specified in law) starting in April 1995. Two years later, in 1997, more legislation was passed allowing the taking of DNA samples from sex offenders currently in custody. In early 1997, the National DNA database contained more than 112,000 samples; two years later, this number had risen to over 600,000. By June 2003, the number of samples had reached two million. By 2009, that number had more than doubled to 4.5 million DNA samples. The taking of DNA samples in other circumstances was voluntary, such as when individuals allowed the police to take a sample of their DNA in order to assist the police in their investigation of a local sexual offence. In addition, as of March 2008, 857,000 people were on the database who had committed no crime (Moore 2009, 19). In December 2008, the European Court of Human Rights ruled that Britain's practice of collecting DNA profiles from innocent people, including children as young as 10, violated international privacy protections.

This issue of retaining DNA samples in Britain came into dispute in 1998 when an individual was charged with committing a burglary based on a DNA sample he had voluntarily given to the police sometime before. This earlier sample was not destroyed but maintained in the DNA data bank and used by the police to match him to an earlier sexual offence. Although he was prosecuted, the case was thrown out of court because a judge ruled that it was based on an illegally held DNA sample (*R. v. B. Attorney General's Reference* No. 3 of 1999).

As a result, concerns were raised about the retention of DNA samples collected during police investigations from volunteers and those samples held although the individuals in question had been acquitted of all charges. An investigation reported that "many thousands of samples,

Continued on next page

perhaps as many as 50,000, were being held on the database when they should have been taken off" (Thomas 2005, 78). The government responded by passing the Criminal Justice and Police Act of 2001, which legalized such activities as long as the retention of the samples was specifically for the purposes of the prevention or detection of crime. In addition, samples gathered to eliminate suspects of sex offences in a local area were also allowed to be retained if the person had given their written consent.

In 2003, the Police and Criminal Evidence Act was further amended in order to allow the police to take DNA (as well as fingerprints) without consent from anyone arrested for a recordable offence and detained in a police station. This led to a match at a crime scene in over 3,000 offences, including 37 murders, 16 attempted murders, and 90 rapes (British Home Office 2006).

In the United States, the FBI announced in April 2009 that it was going to expand their collection of DNA samples from an exclusive focus upon those convicted of certain crimes "to include millions more people who have been arrested or detained but not yet convicted" (Moore 2009, 1). This move aligns the FBI collecting activities with a number of states that collect DNA samples from those awaiting trial. California is one such state, and in 2009, it started to collect DNA from individuals upon arrest. State officials predicted the DNA database will increase to 390,000 by the end of the year, from 200,000 the year before.

The new FBI database will also include immigrants who have been detained. It is predicted that this new policy will increase the FBI DNA database from its current 6.7 million profiles to an estimated 12 million by 2012, based on an increase of 80,000 new entries each month. Sixteen states currently collect DNA samples from those who have been found guilty of misdemeanors while in 35 other states minors are required to provide samples upon conviction, and in some states upon arrest.

While the courts in the United States have generally upheld laws authorizing the compulsory collection of DNA from convicts and ex-convicts under supervised release on the basis that criminal acts diminish privacy rights, critics of taking DNA samples from those not yet convicted of a serious crime argue that privacy is being undermined. They believe that the U.S. is becoming "a genetic surveillance society." They believe that the original intention of DNA data banks was to deal with those convicted of "violent sexual crimes and

homicides—a very limited number of crimes" and that now, with lesser and suspected crimes becoming included in the data banks, the "government's power is becoming too broadly applied." Over time, however, "more and more crimes of decreasing severity have been added to the database." Some believe that the police and prosecutors like it "because it gives everybody more information and creates a new suspect pool" (ibid., 19).

Other critics are concerned about the fact that expanding DNA sampling could exacerbate racial disparities in the criminal justice system. It has been estimated that African Americans, who make up about 12 percent of the population in the United States, currently make up 40 percent of the DNA profiles in the federal database, which is reflective of their percent in the adult prison population. In addition, there are concerns that Latinos, who make up roughly 13 percent of the U.S. population and who committed 40 percent of all federal offences in 2008 (of which almost half were immigration-related offences, including illegal entry) would dominate DNA databases.

Proponents of expanding who is placed onto a DNA database argue that if an innocent person's DNA was included in a data bank, it would not be used unless there is a crime scene sample to match it. Extracting DNA upon arrest, in their opinion, is no different than fingerprinting during after an arrest and that jurisdictions regularly take off any names of individuals cleared of suspicion. On the issue of race, they point out that the British National DNA database collects the "ethnic identification" of all those placed into their system. As of March 31, 2007, 78 percent of all females and 75 percent of all males on the British National DNA database were placed in the category of "White Skinned European."

Questions

1. Do you think Canada should expand the use of its DNA database so that it would follow exactly the way in which the U.S. and England operate their DNA databases?
2. Do you believe that DNA data banks violate people's reasonable expectation to privacy as guaranteed by s. 8 of the Charter of Rights and Freedoms?
3. Do you think there should be a third-party oversight agency implemented in order to monitor the activities of DNA data banks?
4. What do you predict for the future of DNA databases with technology constantly evolving?

SUMMARY

Police forces have traditionally been organized in a militaristic way. Many questions have been raised about the effectiveness of policing, especially patrol work. Police officials have spent the past two decades experimenting with different patrol styles, some of which seem to be effective in catching criminals and deterring further criminal actions.

To improve their effectiveness, many police forces have introduced community-based policing. Although the nature of this type of policing varies from location to location, most of the time it involves elements of community involvement and problem solving. These new approaches have led many police forces into a new era of policing. They are using their resources differently in an attempt to achieve better results for their efforts. These new models have established themselves as the future of policing in our society; even so, many issues have yet to be resolved. Police forces are reluctant to change their organizational structure, particularly in any way that would decentralize their decision-making authority and split that authority with the community. There is also the issue of change occurring among the police; more research is needed to understand the nature and extent of this change in all aspects of policing.

Aboriginal police forces have emerged in recent decades as part of efforts to deal more effectively with the issues facing Aboriginal communities. In many ways, the members of those forces are peacekeepers, in that they serve as police officers, social workers, and community activists. The origins of Aboriginal policing are found in the community policing model.

Discussion Questions

1. What should be the primary function of the police in our society?

2. What should be the primary role of the police in our society?

3. Should the police become more proactive? If so, how could this be accomplished, and what would the impact be?

4. What problems and benefits are associated with a highly structured model of police organization?

5. Would there be benefits to a decentralized model of police organization? Why do you think many officers resist attempts to move police departments toward a community-policing model?

6. Can the efficiency of detectives be increased? How?

7. Discuss the positive aspects of community policing for the police and the public. Can the police and community ever form a unified front to fight crime?

8. Discuss how problem-oriented policing led some police forces to practise zero tolerance policing, although their mandate was to introduce community policing.

9. Do the benefits of zero tolerance policing outweigh its associated problems?

10. What do you think the benefits of intelligence-led policing on policing within Canada will be?

11. Discuss the impact of Aboriginal police forces. What are the benefits of Aboriginal police forces? Should each province have a unified Aboriginal police force for all Aboriginal communities?

Suggested Readings

Forcese, P. *Policing Canadian Society.* Scarborough, ON: Prentice-Hall, 1992.

Stansfield, R.T. *Issues in Policing: A Canadian Perspective.* Toronto: Thompson Educational Publishing, 1996.

Trojanowicz, R.C., V. Kappeler, and L. Gaines. *Community Policing: A Contemporary Perspective,* 3rd ed. Cincinnati, OH: Anderson, 2001.

Weisburd, D., and T. McEwen. *Crime Mapping and Crime Prevention.* Monsey, NY: Criminal Justice Press, 1998.

Whitelaw, B., and R.B. Parent. 2010. *Community-Based Strategic Policing in Canada.* Toronto: Nelson.

References

American Bar Association. 1974. *Standards Relating to Urban Police Function.* New York: Institute of Judicial Administration.

Asbury, K.E. 1989. "Innovative Policing: Foot Patrol in 31 Division, Metropolitan Toronto." *Canadian Police College Journal* 13: 165–81.

Audit Commission. 1993. *Getting Things Right: Quality of Service Committee Report.* London: Audit Commission

Bayley, D.H. 1998. *Policing in America: Assessment and Prospectus.* Washington, DC: Police Foundation.

———. 1994. *Police for the Future.* Oxford: Oxford University Press.

———. 1993. "Strategy." In J. Chacko and S.E. Nancoo, eds., *Community Policing in Canada.* Toronto: Canadian Scholars' Press, pp. 39–46.

Berg, B.L., and J.J. Horgan. 1998. *Criminal Investigation,* 3rd ed. Westerville: Glencoe/McGraw-Hill.

Blackwell, T. 2000. "Collect DNA from All Charged with a Crime, Ontario Urges." *National Post,* September 9, A4.

Braga, A., D. Weisburd, E. Waring, L. Green Mazerolle, W. Spelman, and F. Grajewski. 1999. "Problem-Oriented Policing in Violent Crime Places: A Randomized Controlled Experiment." *Criminology* 37, 541–80.

Braiden, C. 1993. "Community-Based Policing: A Process for Change." In J. Chacko and S.E. Nancoo, eds., *Community Policing in Canada.* Toronto: Canadian Scholars' Press, pp. 211–32.

Brandl, S., and J. Frank. 1994. "The Relationship between Evidence, Detective Work, and the Dispositions of Burglary and Robbery Investigations." *American Journal of Police* 13, no. 3: 149–68.

British Home Office. 2006. *National Policing Improvement Agency: The National DNA Database Annual Report for 2006-07.* www.npia.police.uk. Retrieved April 23, 2009.

Browne, L., and C. Browne. 1973. *An Unauthorized History of the RCMP.* Toronto: James Lewis and Samuel.

Bureau of Justice Assistance. 1993. *Problem-Oriented Drug Enforcement: A Community-Based Approach for Effective Policing.* Washington, DC: Office of Justice Programs.

Chamlin, M. 1988. "Crime and Arrests: An Autoregressive Integrated Moving Average (CARIMA) Approach." *Journal of Quantitative Criminology* 4: 245–55.

Choi, A. 1994. *An Examination of Police Intervention in Domestic Disturbances in a Canadian Context.* Lampeter, Wales: Edwin Mellen Press.

Clairmont, D. 1990. *To the Forefront: Community-Based Zone Policing in Halifax.* Ottawa: Canadian Police College.

Clarke, R. 1992. *Situational Crime Prevention: Successful Case Studies.* Albany, N.Y.: Harrow and Heston.

Conway, C. 2007. "The DNA 200." *The New York Times,* May 20, A14.

Cordner, G.W. 1998. "Problem-Oriented Policing vs. Zero Tolerance." In T. O'Connor Shelly and A. Grant, eds., *Problem Oriented Policing.* Washington, DC: Police Executive Research Forum.

———. 1992. "Patrol." In G. Cordner and D. Hale, eds., *What Works in Policing? Operations and Administration Examined.* Cincinnati, OH: Anderson.

Cordner, G.W., and D.C. Hale. 1992. *What Works in Policing? Operations and Administration Examined.* Cincinnati, OH: Anderson.

Depew, R. 1992. "Policing Native Communities: Some Principles and Issues in Organizational Theory." *Canadian Journal of Criminology* 34, nos. 3–4: 461–78.

Desroches, F.J. 1995. *Force and Fear: Robbery in Canada.* Scarborough, ON: Nelson Canada.

Dovaston, D., and C. Burton. 1996. "Vital New Ingredient." *Policing Today,* 44–48.

Eck, J.E. 1983. *Solving Crimes: The Investigation of Burglary and Robbery.* Washington, DC: Police Executive Research Forum.

Eck, J.E., and E. Maguire. 2000. "Have Changes in Policing Reduced Violent Crime?" In A. Blumstein and J. Wallman, eds., *The Crime Drop in America*. Cambridge, MA: Cambridge University Press.

Ericson, R., and K. Haggerty. 1997. *Policing the Risk Society*. Toronto: University of Toronto Press.

Ferraro, K. 1989. "Policing Woman Battering." *Social Problems* 36: 61–74.

Goldstein, H. 1979. "Improving Policing: A Problem-Oriented Approach." *Crime and Delinquency* 25: 236–58.

Green, J. 2000. "Community Policing in America: Changing the Nature, Structure and Foundation of the Police." In J. Horney, ed., *Policies, Processes and Decisions of the Criminal Justice System*. Washington, DC: National Institute of Justice.

———. 1999. "Zero Tolerance: A Case Study of Police Policies and Practices in New York City." *Crime and Delinquency* 45: 171–88.

Greene, J., and S. Mastrofski. 1988. *Community Policing: Rhetoric or Reality?* New York: Praeger.

Guth, D.J. 1994. "The Traditional Common-Law Constable 1235–1829: From Bracton to the Fieldings of Canada." In R.C. Macleod and D. Schneiderman, eds., *Police Powers in Canada: The Evolution and Practice of Authority*. Toronto: University of Toronto Press.

Halsted, A., M. Bromley, and J. Cochran. 2000. "The Effects of Work Orientations and Job Satisfaction Among Sheriffs' Deputies." *Policing* 23: 82–104.

Hamilton, A.C., and C.M. Sinclair. 1991. *The Justice System and Aboriginal People: Report of the Aboriginal Justice Inquiry of Manitoba*, vol. 1. Winnipeg: Queen's Printer.

Head, R. 1989. *Policy for Aboriginal Canadians: The RCMP Role*. Ottawa: RCMP.

Heaton, R. 2000. "The Prospect for Intelligence-Led Policing: Some Historical and Quantitative Considerations." *Policing and Society* 9: 337–55.

Hickman, Chief Justice T.A., Associate Chief Justice L.A. Poitras, and the Honourable G.T. Evans, QC. 1989. *Royal Commission on the Donald Marshall, Jr. Prosecution*, vol. 1. Ottawa: Ministry of Supply and Services.

Hiebert, J.L. 2002. *Charter Conflicts: What Is Parliament's Role?* Montreal: McGill-Queen's University Press.

Hochstedler, E. 1981. "Testing Types: A Revision and Test of Police Types." *Journal of Criminal Justice* 9: 451–66.

Hornick, J.P., B.A. Burrows, D.M. Phillips, and B. Leighton. 1993. "An Impact Evaluation of the Edmonton Neighbourhood Foot-Patrol Program." In J. Chacko and S.E. Nancoo, eds., *Community Policing in Canada*. Toronto: Canadian Scholars' Press, pp. 311–32.

Hyde, M. 1992. "Servicing Indian Reserves: The Amerindian Police." *Canadian Journal of Criminology* 34, nos. 3–4: 369–86.

Innes, M. 2000. "Professionalizing the Role of the Police Informant: The British Experience." *Policing and Society* 9: 357–84.

Jaffe, P., D. Reitzel, E. Hastings, and G. Austin. 1991. *Wife Assault as a Crime: The Perspectives of Victims and Police Officers on a Changing Policy in London, Ontario from 1989–1990*. London, ON: London Family Court.

Kelling, G.L., and M.H. Moore. 1988. *Perspectives on Policing*. Washington, DC: National Institute of Justice.

Kelling, G.L., T. Pate, D. Dieckman, and C. Brown. 1974. *The Kansas City Preventive Patrol Experiment: A Summary Report*. Washington, DC: Police Foundation Report.

Kelling, G.L., and J.Q. Wilson. 1982. "Broken Windows: The Police and Neighborhood Safety." *The Atlantic Monthly* 249.

Kelly, W., and N. Kelly. 1976. *Policing in Canada*. Toronto: Macmillan.

Klockars, C., and S. Mastrofski. 1991. "The Police and Serious Crime." In C. Klockars and S. Mastrofski, eds., *Thinking About Crime*. New York: McGraw-Hill.

Koller, K. 1990. *Working the Beat: The Edmonton Neighbourhood Foot Patrol*. Edmonton: Edmonton Police Service.

Landau, T. 1996. "Policing and Security in Four Remote Aboriginal Communities: A Challenge to Coercive Models of Police Work." *Canadian Journal of Criminology* 38: 1–36.

Langworthy, R.H., and L.F. Travis. 1994. *Policing in America: A Balance of Forces*. Don Mills, ON: Macmillan.

LaPrairie, C. 1992. *Justice for the Cree: Communities, Crime and Order*. Nemaska, QC: Cree Regional Authority.

LaPrairie, C., and E. Diamond. 1992. "Who Owns the Problem? Crime and Disorder in James Bay Cree Communities." *Canadian Journal of Criminology* 34, nos. 3–4: 417–34.

Lewis, S., H. Rosenberg, and R. Sigler. 1999. "Acceptance of Community Policing among Patrol Officers and Police Administrators." *Policing* 22: 567–88.

Maguire, M. 2000. "Policing by Risks and Targets: Some Dimensions and Implications of Intelligence-Led Social Control." *Policing and Society* 9: 315–37.

Makin, K. 2009. "Court Raises the Bar in Seizing DNA from Juveniles." *The Globe and Mail* April 8, A7.

Manning, P. 1977. *Police Work*. Cambridge, MA: MIT Press.

Marquis, G. 1994. "Power from the Street: The Canadian Municipal Police." In R.C. Macleod and D. Sneiderman, eds., *Police Powers in Canada: The Evolution and Practice of Authority*. Toronto: University of Toronto Press.

Metha, V. 1993. *Policing Services for Aboriginal Peoples*. Ottawa: Ministry of the Solicitor General Research Division.

Moore, M., and R.C. Trojanowicz. 1988. *Corporate Strategies for Policing*. Washington, DC: National Institute of Justice.

Moore, S. 2009. "F.B.I. and States Vastly Expanding Databases of DNA." *New York Times*, April 19, 1, 19.

Muir, W. 1977. *Police: Streetcorner Politicians*. Chicago: University of Chicago Press.

Murphy, C., and D. Clairmont. 1996. *First Nations Police Officers Survey*. Ottawa: Solicitor General of Canada.

Parker, L., and G. Fields. 2000. "Unsolved Killings on the Rise." *USA Today*, February 23, 1A.

Parks, R., S. Mastrofski, C. DeJong, and M.K. Gray. 1999. "How Officers Spend Their Time with the Community." *Justice Quarterly* 16: 483–519.

Pate, A., M.A. Wycoff, W.G. Skogan, and L. Sherman. 1986. *Reducing Fear of Crime in Houston and Newark*. Washington, DC: Police Foundation.

Police Foundation. 1981. *The Newark Foot Patrol Experiment*. Washington, DC: Police Foundation.

Rastin, C.J. 2007. "Policy and Program Overview 2007." *Aboriginal Policing Update* 1, 2–9.

Reiss, A. 1992. "Police Organization in the Twentieth Century." In M. Tonry and N. Morris, eds., *Crime and Justice: A Review of Research*, vol. 15. Chicago: University of Chicago Press, pp. 51–98.

Romano, L. 2003. "When DNA Meets Death Row, It's the System That's Tested." *Washington Post*, December 12, A1.

Ross, H. Laurence. 1982. *Deterring the Drinking Driver: Legal Policy and Social Control*. Lexington, MA: D.C. Heath.

Royal Canadian Mounted Police. 2008. *The National DNA Data Bank of Canada Annual Report 2007–2008*. Ottawa: RCMP.

———. 2001. *The National DNA Bank of Canada: Annual Report 2000/2001*. Ottawa: Royal Canadian Mounted Police.

Scheck, B., P. Neufeld, and J. Dwyer. 2000. *Actual Innocence: Five Days to Executing and Other Dispatches from the Wrongfully Convicted*. New York: Doubleday.

Shapiro, P., and H. Votey. 1984. "Deterrence and Subjective Probabilities of Arrest: Modelling Individual Decisions to Drink and Drive in Sweden." *Law and Society Review* 18: 111–49.

Shearing, C.D. 1992. "The Relation between Public and Private Policing." In M. Tonry and N. Morris, eds., *Crime and Justice: A Review of Research*, 15. Chicago: University of Chicago Press, pp. 399–434.

Sherman, L.J. 1990. "Police Crackdowns: Initial and Residual Deterrence." In M. Tonry and N. Morris, eds., *Crime and Justice*, vol. 12. Chicago: University of Chicago Press, pp. 1–48.

———. 1986. "Policing Communities: What Works?" In A.J. Reiss and M. Tonry, eds., *Crime and Justice: A Review of Research*, vol. 8, pp. 343–86.

Sherman, L.J., and D. Rogan. 1995. "Effects of Gun Seizures on Gun Violence: 'Hot Spots' Patrol in Kansas City." *Justice Quarterly* 12: 673–94.

Sherman, L.J., J. Shaw, and D. Rogan. 1994. *The Kansas City Gun Experiment*. Washington, D.C.: National Institute of Justice.

Skogan, W. 1990. *Disorder and Decline: Crime and the Spiral Decay in America's Neighborhoods*. New York: Free Press.

Solicitor General of Canada. 1999. *The First Nations Policing Policy*. Ottawa: Solicitor General of Canada.

Statistics Canada. 2008. *Police Resources in Canada, 2008*. Ottawa: Minister of Industry.

Thomas, T. 2005. *Sex Crime: Sex Offending and Society*, 2nd ed. Cullompton, Devon: Willan.

Trojanowicz, R., V.E. Kappeler, and L.K. Gaines. 2001. *Community Policing: A Contemporary Perspective*, 3rd ed. Cincinnati, OH: Anderson.

Walker, S. 1994. *Sense and Nonsense about Crime*, 3rd ed. Belmont, CA: Wadsworth.

———. 1992. *The Police in America: An Introduction*, 2nd ed. New York: McGraw-Hill.

———. 1985. "Setting the Standards: The Efforts and Impact of Blue-Ribbon Commissions on the Police." In W.A. Geller, ed., *Police Leadership in America: Crisis and Opportunity*. New York: Praeger.

Wambaugh, J. 1989. *The Blooding*. New York: William Morrow.

Weisburd, D., and L. Green. 1995. "Policing Drug Hot Spots: The Jersey City Drug Market Analysis Experiment." *Justice Quarterly* 12, 711–37.

Welsh, B.C., and D.P. Farrington. 2008. *Making Public Places Safer: Surveillance and Crime Prevention.* New York: Oxford University Press.

Wickham, W. 2000. "Don't Use DNA Test to Excuse Bad Idea." *USA Today,* January 2, 5A.

Wilson, J.Q. 1968. *Varieties of Criminal Behavior.* Cambridge, MA: Harvard University Press.

Young, G. 1995, *Police Personnel and Expenditures in Canada—1993.* Ottawa: Juristat.

Court Cases

R. v. Borden (1994), 3 S.C.R. 145

R. v. Legere (1994), 95 C.C.C. (3d) 139 (N.B.C.A.)

R. v. B. Attorney General's Reference No. 3 of 1999

Weblinks

To read the Supreme Court of Canada's decision in *R. v. Borden,* go to http://scc.lexum.umontreal.ca/en/index.html, click on 1994, and go to volume 3. The decision for this case was announced on September 30, 1994. The New Brunswick Court of Appeal's decision in *R. v. Legere* (1994) is available at http://quartet.cs.unb.ca/8080/dspace/handle/1882/209.

CHAPTER 6

Issues in Canadian Policing

CHAPTER OBJECTIVES

✓ Discuss the practice of police discretion.

✓ Examine the changing social composition of the police.

✓ Discuss the use of deadly force by and against police officers in Canada.

✓ Examine the amount and types of police misconduct and attempts to control these actions by outside agencies.

✓ Identify differences between private security agencies and the public police.

T his chapter considers a number of topics in contemporary policing. First, it discusses police activities that are of concern to due process advocates—in particular, the use of **discretion**, the use of force (including **deadly force**), and police misconduct. The reasons why due process violations occur is also discussed during a review of the "police subculture."

The second major topic discussed is the composition of police agencies. Who should be recruited as police officers? Are women and minority groups being treated fairly by the police agencies they work for? What experiences have they encountered as police officers? And what is the relevance of a college or university education for the police?

This chapter begins with the issue of police discretion, particularly as it concerns the fairness of police decisions to arrest and charge. This discussion reviews the three main factors thought to influence the use of discretion. The chapter then discusses the police subculture and its impact on police officers and how they react to the various situations they face. After this, the chapter examines deadly force and police misconduct, and discusses efforts to control the latter. In addition, women and visible-minority police officers are discussed, along with issues related to the recruitment of these groups to police forces. The current status of female and minority officers in Canadian law enforcement agencies is reviewed. Concerns about the performance of women police officers are considered, as are gender conflicts at work.

In recent years, the issue of racial profiling by the police has made headlines and has been an issue in a number of court cases across Canada. Racial profiling occurs when a police action is initiated by a statistical profile of race, ethnicity, or national origin of a suspect, rather than by any evidence or information that the suspect had broken the law. According to Callahan and Anderson (2001), racial profiling involves the police moving from their standard practice of "case probability" to "class probability." Case probability is defined as those situations where some factors relevant to a particular event are comprehended, while class probability describes those situations where enough is known about a class of events to describe it using statistics, but nothing about a particular event other than the fact that it belongs to the class in question. That is, before the police have evidence of a crime, they start to "investigate a high proportion of people of some particular race, ethnic group, age group and so on. Their only justification is that by doing so, they increase their chances of discovering some crime" (ibid., 40). Once class probability, or racial profiling occurs, "there is a strong claim that certain groups of people are being denied equal protection under the law."

Individuals protest against the alleged racial profiling by members of the police. Much of the controversy arises from what young persons say is racial profiling by police officers who are attempting to crack down on street gang activity. (CP Photo/Graham Hughes)

It is argued that racial profiling has been used by the police in many Western countries for a lengthy period of time. Supporters of racial profiling favour the crime control model discussed in Chapter 1, defending the practice by saying it is a good and efficient approach to catching criminals since the police use the laws of probability to make the best use of their resources. Others supportive of this position point out recent research that found although race does have a significant impact in some traffic stops, age and gender have a greater influence upon police decision-making (Schafer et al., 2004) and that there is no pattern of discriminatory actions directed toward members of minority groups during traffic stops, although there was some evidence of unequal treatment after the traffic stop (Alpert et al., 2007). Critics of racial profiling follow the logic of the due process model, and argue that racial profiling involves discriminatory police actions against minority group members. This is revealed, they argue, by empirical research finding that minority group members more likely to be arrested for assaults (Eitle et al., 2005) and

more likely to be illegally searched by the police (Gould and Mastrofski 2004). Some (e.g., Skolnick 1994) argue that law enforcement involves stereotyping, a practice that they feel is integral to the world of policing.

Concerns about the constitutional aspects of racial profiling in Canada were raised over the introduction of Canada's Anti-Terrorism Bill when it was introduced in late 2001 (Choudhrey 2001). In an early Canadian court case, the issue of racial profiling was raised by the defence. This case involved an African American member of the Toronto Raptors basketball team who was stopped for going slightly over the speed limit on a Toronto expressway on November 1, 1999. During the trial, his lawyer argued that his client was the victim of racial stereotyping and had been stopped arbitrarily by the police because "black men in big cars must be criminals" (Mitchell 2002, 8). The trial judge dismissed the argument of racial profiling, stating that such allegations were "distasteful" and "really quite nasty, malicious accusations based on, it seems to me, nothing" (ibid.). The trial court judge convicted the defendant. The case was appealed to the Ontario Superior Court and there it was determined that race was a factor in the actions of the police officers and as a result the conviction was overturned. In a 3–0 ruling, the Ontario Court of Appeal stated that the police engaged in racial profiling. The court concluded that the trial court judge "had sufficient evidence to find that racial profiling was at play . . . but he found the idea too distasteful to consider" (Makin 2003, A1). In another Ontario court case during 2004, an Ontario Superior Court judge dismissed drug trafficking charges against a Black real estate developer "because she says Toronto police engaged in racial profiling" (Kari 2004, A4). In an effort to combat racial profiling, the federal government has invested $2.2 million until 2010 to promote "bias-free policing" (Thompson 2005).

Another issue for the police today is their search for non-lethal weapons. In their search for non-lethal alternatives to firearms, more than 7,000 police forces worldwide have selected Tasers (sometimes referred to as "stun guns") as an alternative to firearms in life-threatening situations. In Canada, the main user of Tasers is the RCMP, but many other Canadian police services have purchased them, as have a number of provincial correctional services and the federal Court Services Branch.

"Taser" is an acronym for "Thomas A. Swift Electric Rifle," based on the Tom Swift science fiction novels written for children early in the twentieth century. They are manufactured by Taser International of Scottsdale, Arizona. When a Taser is used, the chances of an innocent bystander being hurt or killed are minimal at best.

Tasers are hand-held weapons that deliver a jolt of electricity from up to six metres away. Two small metal probes, attached to wires, are fired into an individual. If both probes make contact (the probes can penetrate up to five centimetres of clothing), the circuit is completed and the individual's muscles are immobilized by 50,000 volts of electricity. The electrical charge is intermittent and continues for five seconds, giving the police time to subdue the individual.

Two types of Tasers are currently used by police forces. The first model, the M26, is the one carried by most police officers. In 2004, the company began selling the X26, a smaller but less powerful model. It puts out a charge that is only 25 percent of the M26 model; however, company officials have stated that the new model allows the electrical charge to enter a person's body much more efficiently.

Tasers are often introduced after a heavily publicized incident in which the police have used deadly force. The early results suggest strongly that Tasers are highly effective. American police forces have reported that where Tasers have been introduced, the incidence of deadly force confrontations has fallen dramatically. For example, in 2003, the Miami, Florida, police had no fatal shootings for the first time in 14 years. And the same year, police in Phoenix, Arizona, reported that deadly police shootings had fallen to the lowest rate in 14 years. No records are kept on the use of Tasers, but it has been estimated that they have saved more than 4,000 citizens' lives in North America alone (Kershaw 2004).

Concerns about Tasers has generally centred on their safety. By the middle of 2004, more than 50 deaths had been associated with the use of Tasers in the United States. By February 2006, 13 deaths of Canadians had been associated with the police use of Tasers. However, Taser company officials are quick to point out that investigations into the deaths of individuals as a result of the police use of their products have failed to conclude that the use of a Taser has been the direct cause of an individual's death. They point out that officials have determined that the deaths are the result of health problems, such as a heart condition, or a drug overdose.

Critics argue that Tasers have never been adequately tested to ensure their safety. To date, there have been no independent, controlled studies of the effects of Tasers. They point out that while the company that produces the Tasers says they are safe, they have rarely been tested independently. The most comprehensive report, produced by the British govenment in 2002, concluded that Tasers are "not safe," and for that reason they have not been approved for general police use. In 1999, the U.S. Department of Justice reported that a much less powerful electrical weapon than a Taser could cause cardiac arrest in a person with a heart condition (Berenson 2004).

A Taser being used by a police officer. These types of devices are playing a more important role in policing than ever before. In the near future, law enforcement agencies will likely need independent means to establish appropriate guidelines for their use. (Copyright © 2009 HER MAJESTY THE QUEEN IN RIGHT OF CANADA as represented by the Royal Canadian Mounted Police (RCMP). Reproduced with the permission of the RCMP.)

POLICE DISCRETION

Discretion involves police officers using their judgment in deciding when to intervene in a situation and when to ignore it. Discretion is a crucial part of policing because it is difficult to develop a system of laws and rules that will divide appropriate from inappropriate behaviour in every context. For example, the police always use discretion when deciding whether to engage in a high-speed pursuit, as well as when to end it once started.

The discretionary powers of the police have been subject to appeals in court cases since the Charter of Rights and Freedoms was proclaimed in 1982. In fact, some cases involving questions about police discretion have been heard by the Supreme Court of Canada. The most significant case involving this issue to date involved a decision by the Saskatchewan Court of Appeal, which ruled that the police enjoyed too much discretionary power. The appeal court ruled that the power for this discretion is granted by the Criminal Code, but it also ruled that the police were using too much discretionary power in their daily decisions. This was particularly the case with decisions about reasonable grounds for believing the accused had committed an indictable offence (*Beare v. R.* [1988]).

On appeal, the Supreme Court of Canada disagreed with the Saskatchewan court. It ruled that "discretion is an essential part of the criminal justice system . . . The Criminal Code provides no guidelines for the exercise of discretion in any of these areas. The day-to-day operation of law enforcement and the criminal justice system nonetheless depends upon the exercise of that discretion" (ibid.). In other words, police officers are in a unique position to use discretion in their decisions about enforcing the law.

The Supreme Court also said that discretion can be contested in court by an individual who feels that the police used their discretionary powers in a wrongful manner. Section 24 of the Charter is a remedy for cases involving the use of discretion in an "improper or arbitrary" manner. And while it was not developed to deal specifically with police discretion, s. 15(1) of the Charter stipulates that numerous extralegal factors are not to be considered within the law or the application of the law. Legal questions surrounding the discretionary powers of a police officer can be stayed on the basis of an abuse of process or as an infringement of equality as specified by equality provision (s. 15[1]) of the Charter: "Every individual is equal before and under the law and has the right to the equal protection and equal benefit of the law without discrimination and, in particular, without discrimination based on race, national or ethnic origin, colour, religion, sex, age, or mental or physical orientation."

The discretion of police officers is rarely questioned during a case. This is because the Supreme Court requires that a judicial stay be allowed only in cases where "compelling the accused to stand trial would violate those fundamental principles of justice which underlie the community's sense of fair play and decency" (*R. v. Mack* [1988]). If an appeal is made under s. 15(1), there must be clear evidence of discrimination (*R. v. Andrews* [1989]; *R. v. Turpin* [1989]).

Studies of Police Discretion

When deciding to invoke their powers (which may include discretion), the police typically consider three factors. The most important is the type of crime committed: the more serious a crime, the more likely the officer will use his or her legal powers to enforce the law. The second factor is the attitude of the citizen involved in the offence. If a suspect acts in a highly disrespectful manner to the officer, chances are that officer will detain the individual and lay some charge. Third and finally, departmental policies can limit the amount of discretion a police officer will use in a given situation. During the past two decades, for example, zero tolerance policies have attempted to limit the amount of discretion used by officers when they respond to a domestic violence complaint (see Chapter 5). However, police officers still use considerable amounts of discretion, even when organizational policies say otherwise (see Chapter 1). As McKenna (2002, 120) points out, it "may be put forward as a general principle that it is virtually impossible to provide rules and regulations for police officer activity in the field that would eliminate the need for officers to use their discretion."

Goldstein (1960), in one of the first analyses of police discretion, noted that a decision by a police officer to arrest a suspect "largely determines the outer limits of police enforcement." This statement reveals the power inherent within police discretion and that police do not have to arrest everyone they find breaking the law. Discretion is the choice or decision—the judgment call—made by a police officer to make an arrest or not. In reality, it is difficult for the police to arrest and charge everyone they catch breaking the law because they lack the resources to do so. So a police officer may decide to give a warning or reprimand instead. Many citizens fully expect to be "let off" with a warning.

Police discretion becomes a factor when officers must use their powers of arrest or investigate an alleged criminal offence when available evidence indicates they should not. According to Roberg and Kuykendall (1993), police discretion involves three elements:

- Deciding whether to get involved in an incident in the first place, although no choice may be open if the officer is responding to a citizen complaint.

- Determining how to behave in any particular incident, or how to interact with the victim, witnesses, or the public.
- Selecting one of many alternatives in dealing with the problem.

In any given situation, a police officer may decide to do nothing, even though he or she observes the commission of a criminal offence or lets one person off with a warning while arresting another for the same offence.

Goldstein (1960) developed two categories of police discretion based on the type of approach used to enforce the criminal law: (1) invocation discretion, and (2) non-invocation discretion. Invocation discretion refers to situations in which a police officer decides to arrest an individual. Non-invocation discretion refers to situations in which a police officer can arrest someone but chooses not to do so. Goldstein was most concerned about non-invocation discretion, because such decisions have "low visibility" and are not reviewed by superiors. The low visibility of police discretion means that unlike other criminal justice agencies, the police can "hide" or "obscure" their discretionary decisions. Thus, discretion "may sometimes deteriorate into discrimination, violence, and other abusive practices" (Senna and Siegel 1995, 233).

Police discretionary power has been one of the most visible issues in policing for more than 40 years. Researchers have studied police discretion and its relationship to the unequal enforcement of the law, specifically as it relates to possible discrimination against certain groups in our society. If in fact discretion is found, then it creates unfairness within the criminal justice system, violating the various due process protections designed to protect all citizens (see Chapter 2).

Factors Affecting Police Officers' Decision to Arrest

Most studies on police use of discretion focus on the specific factors that led to an officer's decision to make an arrest. As Stansfield (1996, 142) states, the focus should not be on whether or not the police decide to use discretion but "which criteria police use when enforcing the law." The factors most often influencing a police officer's discretion are situational variables, as well as a suspect's social class, age, sex, and race; the relationship between victim and complainant; the amount of respect or deference given to the police officer; the nature of the offence or problem; and the amount and quality of the evidence.

Situational Variables

The dynamics vary between any two situations, so police officers differ in the ways they respond to incidents. The dynamic derives in part from the location of the incident (see Exhibit 6.1). Police are more likely to arrest suspects in public settings than in private ones. Still, a number of different agents can influence police use of discretion in these situations, such as the need to be in control of the situation, especially if members of the public are watching. The presence of other police officers is another influence on police discretion—if a police officer thinks other officers expect a punitive response, that officer will probably comply. Indeed, police officers working alone behave very differently than if they are working with a partner—they usually make more arrests, since they are concerned about gaining control of a situation as quickly as possible. Chappell et al., (2006) examined data from a nationally representative sample of 182 American municipal police agencies serving populations of at least 100,000 and concluded that when making arrests, police officers "appear to be more driven by the situational exigencies that vary from community to community."

Both legal and extralegal factors can be involved in a police decision to arrest someone. The first two of the situational factors identified below are legal in nature; the rest are extralegal.

- *Seriousness of the crime.* The more serious the crime, the more likely a police officer is to make an arrest. Black (1980) reported that the police officers he was studying arrested 58 percent of suspects involved in serious crimes but only 44 percent of those involved in less serious offences.
- *Strength of the evidence.* The police are more likely to arrest a suspect when the evidence in a case is strong. If there is a witness to a crime, it is more likely that an officer will arrest someone. When there are no witnesses, an arrest is much less likely.
- *Preference of the victim.* An arrest is more likely when a victim or the complainant requests that the officer make an arrest. On the other hand, police officers may decide not to arrest someone if the victim or complainant indicates that he or she does not want someone to be arrested.
- *Relationship between the victim and the suspect.* A police officer is more likely to arrest someone when the victim and offender are strangers, and are least likely to do so if they are family members.
- *Demeanour of the suspect.* A number of researchers have found that the demeanour of the suspect can precipitate an arrest. In most cases, the argument goes that if a suspect is disrespectful toward the officer, it is more likely that he or she will be arrested. However, Klinger (1994) challenges this view, arguing that in many cases disrespect toward a police officer occurs only after a suspect is arrested and is therefore a consequence, rather than a cause, of the arrest.

- *Characteristics of the neighbourhood.* Smith and colleagues (1984) found that police officers were more likely to arrest someone in low-income neighbourhoods compared to higher income neighbourhoods. The result: a greater likelihood of poor people being arrested and processed through the courts.

Community Variables

An important factor in police decision-making is the racial and social-class composition of a community. Research conducted in Canada and the United States has found that police officers make more arrests in minority and working-class communities. The police view these communities as locations where violent crimes are more likely to occur and where residents are more likely to challenge their authority. Police, as a result, are more suspicious and concerned for their safety when in these areas. These feelings revolve around the idea of a symbolic assailant—an individual who, the police believe, tends to be potentially dangerous or troublesome (McGahan 1984; Skolnick 1966).

Some communities have higher rates of reported crime, and these higher rates can influence an officer's perception of danger. The greater the danger police officers perceive, the more likely they will respond with an arrest. But at the same time, police officers tend to ignore certain types of criminal activity in these areas, perhaps because of the greater amount of police work they entail or because they are more tolerant of minor violations. In addition, the attitudes of citizens in a particular community can influence police behaviour, since most police–citizen encounters result from a citizen's call to police. McGahan (1984) found that police form a "model" of troubled areas, which they then use to predict the types of calls and the most appropriate responses; this allows them "to cope with a threatening and troublesome segment of their environment."

Officer discretion can be influenced by the local legal culture. This refers to the fact that different communities request that their police officers enforce certain criminal offences more than others. For example, one community might want them to enforce panhandling laws much more strictly than the next community. The local legal culture does not necessarily involve a written formal policy specifying what a neighbourhood wants enforced and what it wants underenforced—most times it exists in an informal relationship between local officials and the police department.

Extralegal Factors

Perhaps the most controversial issue connected to police use of discretion is whether the police take into account the race, class, and gender of a suspect when deciding to make an arrest—that is, whether police discretion favours the members of a certain social class or racial group. The issue of race and police discretion in Canada has interested researchers for more than 30 years. In one of the earliest studies conducted in this country, Bienvenue and Latif (1974) studied 1969 arrest data for the City of Winnipeg in order to determine whether differences existed in the arrest and charge rates between Aboriginal people and non-Aboriginal people. They found that Aboriginal women and men were overrepresented for all offences except drug and traffic violations. However, when the distribution of offences within each group was compared, it was found that Aboriginal people were arrested more often for minor offences and that White people were arrested more often for the most serious, indictable offences. While these arrest patterns perhaps reflected variations in socioeconomic status, Bienvenue and Latif suggested that they were the result of police discretion. This was evident when they looked at police decisions to charge; they discovered that Aboriginal people were overrepresented for every type of charge at the time of sentencing. Numerous studies (e.g., Forcese 1999; Hamilton and Sinclair 1991; Havemann et al. 1985; Mosher 1998; Ontario Commission on Systemic Racism 1995) published since the work of Bienvenue and Latif have found that race is a determining factor in the police use of discretion.

Police discretion has also been found when extralegal variables other than race are studied. For example, Gunn and Minch (1988) found extensive use of police discretion in sexual assault cases in Winnipeg. Of the 211 charges laid against offenders, 122 (or 58 percent) were terminated, either because the police officer decided that no sexual assault had occurred or because the officer foresaw difficulties for the complainant. Because police were using discretionary power to choose not to arrest or charge alleged offenders, mandatory arrest and charge policies in sexual assault cases is now policy in all Canadian police forces. In 1992, the Metropolitan Toronto Police Force required all its officers to lay charges when the evidence supported such an action; if officers did not lay a charge, they had to file a report indicating the reason for inaction.

In the area of sexual orientation, Fleming (1981) discovered evidence of police discretion in his study of police decisions concerning whether to proceed with an investigation after the victim of a violent crime was determined to be gay. Abell and Sheehy (1993, 225) note that when police investigate these crimes, the "violence and homophobia and lesbophobia underlying [them] are often downplayed or excused." Assailants receive more lenient treatment simply because "their crimes are crimes against gay men or lesbians."

Other studies have found that the race and social class of the victim rather than the criminal is the basis for police decisions to use discretion. For example, Ericson (1982) found that when a crime involved property damage or theft, the police proceeded by way of arrest when the suspects were poor and members of minority groups.

These studies have led some observers and researchers to say that police discretion works against males, the poor, and members of minority groups while protecting those who are members of the privileged groups in our society. Yet, other studies (e.g., De Lisi and Regoli 1999) have concluded that the police do not discriminate when they use their discretionary powers to arrest and charge members of certain groups. Instead, they argue that legal variables (such as the seriousness of the crime and the prior record of the suspect) determine whether the police will arrest and charge a suspect.

These conflicting positions may be the result of differences in the techniques used by researchers to study this issue. A meta-analysis of these various studies has drawn the following conclusions as to why discretion is found in some situations and not others:

1. Most of these studies examine only a few factors that may influence police decision-making; they do not attempt to explain it comprehensively.
2. Most do not cover a wide enough range of offences to account adequately for discretion in serious and non-serious cases.
3. Studies reporting on factors influencing police decisions in one city may not hold true for police decisions in other cities.
4. Many studies rely on responses to hypothetical scenarios rather than on actual observations of police work.
5. Even factors that are found to be important in police discretion cannot be used to make accurate predictions more than 25 percent of the time (Albanese 1999, 187).

EXHIBIT 6.1 Discretion and High-Speed Pursuits

The police have long enjoyed considerable discretion when deciding whether to start a high-speed pursuit. This discretion has come under scrutiny in recent years because of the many serious accidents resulting from such pursuits. Between 1991 and 1995 in Canada, 19 deaths were attributed to 4,200 pursuits. One-third of these chases resulted in collisions, 14 percent in injuries (Bell 1999). Between 1991 and 1997, 33 people (26 suspects, 1 police officer, and 6 bystanders) died in police chases in Ontario. In British Columbia, the RCMP and 12 municipal police forces were involved in 4,468 high-speed pursuits between 1990 and 1997, and 21 people were killed and 748 injured as a result (Appleby et al., 1999). In 1999, eight people died during police chases (Alberts 2000). And in the United States, the National Highway Safety Administration estimates that more than 250 people are killed each year (about one-third of whom are bystanders) and more than 20,000 injured as a result of high-speed pursuits by police officers (Mitchell 1990).

Most police departments in Canada and the United States now have written policies governing high-speed pursuits. In Canada, these policies vary among jurisdictions, but they are similar in such key areas as public safety and the discharging of weapons. The safety of the public is supposed to be the most important consideration in any police decision to begin, continue, or end a pursuit. According to OPP policy, a police chase "shall be the choice of last resort and will be considered only when other alternatives are unavailable or unsatisfactory." The RCMP's policy on pursuits informs its officers to consider the seriousness of the offence before starting a pursuit, but "it is silent on what constitutes a serious offence" (Bell 1999). In addition, most jurisdictions prohibit police officers from discharging their weapons at or from a moving vehicle in an attempt to stop a fleeing vehicle.

An RCMP cadet learns how to drive in a high-speed pursuit of a vehicle. (Copyright © 2009 HER MAJESTY THE QUEEN IN RIGHT OF CANADA as represented by the Royal Canadian Mounted Police (RCMP). Reproduced with the permission of the RCMP.)

EXHIBIT 6.1   Discretion and High-Speed Pursuits . . . Continued

In 2000, most if not all police departments in the United States had written policies. These policies can be placed into three different categories. Sixty percent of police forces had restrictive policies governing pursuits—that is, their policies limited the discretion of officers by specifying the conditions under which pursuits could be initiated. Seven percent of police forces had discouraging policies—that is, policies advising officers against pursuits in certain situations. However, these policies were not as limiting as restrictive ones. And 23 percent of police forces followed a discretionary or judgmental policy—that is, their policies gave officers broad discretion regarding whether they should engage in a pursuit (Bureau of Justice Statistics 2000).

Canadian police forces require their officers to have reason to believe that a criminal offence has been, or is about to be, committed before starting a chase; they also require that the immediate apprehension of the vehicle and its driver outweigh the danger created by the chase. When a non-criminal offence is involved, most police forces allow an officer to give chase but only for the purpose of identifying the vehicle; once this is accomplished, the officer must stop the pursuit. The RCMP relies instead on different classifications of pursuits. In a "hazardous" pursuit, a motorist has been signalled to stop by the police and has deliberately chosen to flee to avoid being stopped. Police officers then give chase using emergency equipment such as sirens and flashing lights to alert members of the public to potential danger. In a "routine" pursuit, the police often exceed the speed limit and violate other traffic regulations without using their sirens or lights, in order to gauge the speed or to intercept a fast-moving vehicle. The rationale for not using sirens or flashing lights during a routine pursuit is the concern that the suspect(s) will attempt to outrun the police. Although these pursuits are referred to as "routine," they are sometimes considered more hazardous to the public than hazardous pursuits.

Many jurisdictions don't allow more than two police vehicles to engage in a pursuit at any given time. Restrictions also govern when a police officer can ram a patrol car into the fleeing vehicle (only in an extreme emergency or when a major crime is committed). Other jurisdictions require their police officers to have both their lights and sirens on during a chase. In British Columbia, if lights and sirens aren't on, officers must stop at all red lights and stop signs and observe the speed limit in school zones (Appleby et al. 1999).

Various alternatives have been tried to reduce the number of high-speed pursuits. Some jurisdictions have increased the number of hours of training that police officers receive. Such initiatives, however, have been criticized for not reflecting real-life situations, in which officers must decide quickly whether to continue or end the pursuit. Other alternatives have been proposed for heavily populated areas. In Calgary, for example, the purchase of a helicopter by the Calgary Police Service in 1995 has assisted in pursuits. Every pursuit it has been involved in has ended in an arrest, and no accidents have occurred. Legal issues are also important in the determination of pursuit policies.

Ontario and the federal government have introduced new offences in an attempt to stop motorists from fleeing police officers. The first jurisdiction to introduce such legislation was Ontario in 1999; that province allows judges to suspend a driver's licence for 10 years to life in cases where the fleeing motorist caused death or injury. The federal government added a new offence to the Criminal Code in 2000 that provides for specific penalties against motorists who refuse to stop after being requested to do so by the police. This offence gives judges the power to impose penalties to a maximum of life imprisonment for motorists whose flight from police results in death. An incident causing injury has a maximum sentence of 14 years, while a conviction for evading the police could lead to a maximum sentence of five years (Alberts 2000; Laghi 2000).

A number of studies have explored police officers' attitudes toward pursuits. The police officers that Falcone (1994) studied in Illinois indicated that the seriousness of the offence was strongly associated with the decision to engage in a high-speed pursuit. Most officers answered that the most important reasons for stopping a pursuit were (in descending order) traffic conditions, certain speed zones, seriousness of the offence, and weather conditions. Alpert and Madden (1994) studied police supervisors in Florida, South Carolina, Nebraska, and Arizona and found that they regarded the need to apprehend a suspect immediately as more important than the risks posed to either police officers or the public. Finally, Britz and Payne (1994, 130–31) found that supervisors and patrol officers differed significantly in their "perceptions of policy, supervisory support, the adequacy of training, liability issues and discretionary issues regarding police pursuit." They also found that 38 percent of the police officers reported that the pursuit policy was difficult to understand and implement; 80 percent of the supervisors stated that they had given no pursuit training whatsoever to their officers; and 35 percent of the officers who had been in pursuits had not reported them.

THE POLICE CULTURE

All professions possess unique characteristics that distinguish them from other occupations and professions. Policing is no different. Police veterans and policing experts have long talked about certain factors, such as the nature of the job itself, that make police officers form tight bonds, or an occupational culture. Occupational cultures consist of "accepted practices, rules and principles of conduct that are situationally applied, and generalized rationales and beliefs" (Manning 1995). Occupational cultures in general, and police culture in particular, have been heavily researched. The police culture is considered to be an important concept in terms of understanding a large number of issues surrounding policing, including how new members of the police organization "learn the ropes" of policing, the success or failure of attempts to reform the police, and how the police function on a day-to-day basis.

Members of the police culture share certain common values. These values, it is argued, arise from the hazards of police work and the ways in which officers attempt to minimize those hazards and protect the members of the subculture (Brown 1988). A number of these basic values have been identified:

1. *Police are the only real crime fighters.* The public wants the police officer to fight crime; other agencies, both public and private, only play at crime fighting.
2. *No one else understands the real nature of police work.* Lawyers, academics, politicians, and the public in general have little concept of what it means to be a police officer.
3. *Loyalty to colleagues counts above everything else.* Police officers have to stick together because everyone is out to get the police and make the job more difficult.
4. *It is impossible to win the war against crime without bending the rules.* Courts have awarded criminal defendants too many civil rights.
5. *Members of the public are basically unsupportive and unreasonably demanding.* People are quick to criticize the police unless they themselves need police help.
6. *Patrol work is the pits.* Detective work is glamorous and exciting (Sparrow et al., 1990, 51).

The importance of studying the police subculture is found in the significance it has for the everyday activities of police officers. Researchers who have investigated the police subculture have noted that it has both positive and negative aspects. Most, however, have discussed the negatives. For example, some have argued that the subculture is a major reason why the police resist new or innovative ideas such as **community policing** (e.g., Skogan and Harnett 1997), while others have pointed out that it is used to support violations of the legal rights of citizens as well as the misuse of police authority (e.g., Skolnick and Fyfe 1993). Others have commented that this subculture is a major factor in police officers' resistance to police accountability. This has led to the "blue curtain" (also known as the "blue wall of silence"), a term referring to the value placed on secrecy and the general mistrust of the outside world shared by many police officers. The "blue curtain" is regarded as a major reason why the police are so deeply separated from the very citizens they are supposed to protect (Walker 2001). Other researchers have pointed out that the police subculture has positive aspects. It creates a sense of "collectiveness" that helps officers deal with their unique stresses (e.g., Waddington 1999), and it can be a mechanism for regulating and preventing inappropriate police activities (e.g., Crank 1997). Another positive aspect of the police culture is based on research that has found it enables new members of the police to learn the "craft" of policing (e.g., Manning 1995; Van Maanen 1974).

Most of the research on the police culture has focused on its use as a coping mechanism enabling the police to insulate themselves from the stresses and hazards of policing activities. In particular, two environments have been studied: the relationship of police officers to the citizens they meet in the course of their duties; and the relationship between police officers and their supervisors. The most commonly studied aspects of the police culture in terms of police–citizen relationships are the presence of or potential for danger (e.g., Skolnick 1994) and the coercive powers and authority that police officers possess over citizens (Bittner 1974). Skolnick (1994, 42) points out that the police perceive their working environment as dangerous or as having a high level of risk or as having the potential to escalate to high levels of dangerousness almost instantaneously. He states that the element of danger is so integral to the work of officers that explicit recognition of such situations can create an emotional barrier for some to the occupation of policing. In addition, the police are a unique institution in our society in that they have been given the power to use force legitimately—that is, they possess "a license to threaten drastic harm to others" (Muir 1977, 37). This, in turn, reinforces the perception of police work as dangerous (Skolnick 1994).

The second component of the police environment is the organizational context in which officers work. Two major issues have been identified: the unpredictable and punitive nature of the relationship between police officers and their supervisors, and the ambiguity of the police role. Researchers have described the police-supervisor relationship as characterized by feelings of uncertainty. Police officers fully expect to deal with issues on the street in an efficient and timely manner, only to have their decisions and actions criticized later by a supervisor (Ericson 1982; Skolnick 1994). This can lead to organizational uncertainty, in that it appears to police officers that only their mistakes are noted by their superiors, and that their accomplishments go unrecognized. Another aspect of the organizational environment is the ambiguous role identification experienced by officers. This refers to the fact that officers use a number of policing styles (see Chapter 5) to accomplish their goals, but only the law enforcement–style functions are reinforced and recognized. The ambiguity exists because supervisors want the officers under their control to handle all their activities and roles on the street equally (Bittner 1974).

How do police officers—and their culture—cope with the stresses and hazards of their work? The police use two coping mechanisms in particular when dealing with citizens. Researchers refer to these as "suspiciousness" and "maintaining the edge." According to Skolnick (1994, 46), in their attempts to reduce or control the uncertainty related to their work, the police have developed a conception of order that emphasizes "regularity and predictability. It is therefore, a conception shaped by persistent suspicion." Maintaining the edge refers to the tendency of police to use their authority when interacting with citizens. The police are able to deal with situations by being in control—that is, by using enough of their authority that they can assert themselves to deal with the situation at hand. They achieve this by reading the people and the situations they come into contact with and always being "one up" on citizens (Muir 1977; Van Maanen 1974). Another coping mechanism, this one directed at avoiding the police supervisor's attention, is referred to as the "lay-low" attitude. Basically, this means that police officers learn when not to do something since it might draw undue attention to themselves (Brown 1988).

Many components of the police culture are transmitted through a socialization process that starts when an officer graduates from the training academy and that continues throughout his or her career. According to Van Maanen (1974, 86), the socialization process gives new police officers "a set of rules, perspectives, techniques, and/or tools" that allow them to participate in the police organization. The socialization process starts in the training academies, where it is presented in a formal manner. Once the new recruits start their careers

as probationary patrol officers, their field training officers offer them informal socialization—that is, "what to do and expect" versus "this is the way we really do it." Coping mechanisms within the police culture generally start during the first few months, while a new recruit is learning how to patrol, but it never really ends (Brown 1988).

THE POLICE PERSONALITY

Many researchers, and citizens generally, feel that police officers have formed a unique set of personality traits to help them in their work. They have often been criticized for the following traits, which are almost universally viewed as negative: cynicism, hostility, dogmatism, and conservatism. These attitudes are thought to influence police decisions to arrest, and ultimately they contribute to poor relationships with the community and lead to police deviance as well as to greater use of deadly force. In particular, police cynicism is characterized by a rejection of the ideals of justice and truth—the very values that a police officer is sworn to uphold and protect. Officers who become cynical lose respect for the law and replace it with other "legal" rules formed in and promoted by the police subculture. These values become more acceptable to some police officers because they think they offer a better representation of today's social realities. Police cynicism has been found at every level of policing, including among police chiefs, and throughout all stages of a police career (Regoli et al. 1990). Where police cynicism becomes entrenched, the result can be increased police misconduct, corruption, and brutality (Regoli 1977).

The existence of the police culture has led researchers to ask how it starts in the first place, prompting a study of the "police personality." This, in turn, has led to questions such as these: Do police officers and the general public have different attitudes? How did officers come by their attitude? Do the personality characteristics of officers influence their discretion and performance on the job? And do they acquire those characteristics from other officers while on the job?

The term "police personality" refers to a value orientation that is unique to police—or at least to some police. Some believe that the police are cynical—that is, motivated entirely by self-interest—and that they are pessimistic about human behaviour. But how do police officers become cynical? Is it because they already hold a different attitude by the time they become members of a police force, or is it because they become that way once they have held the job and are exposed to negative public feelings and the police culture?

The earliest studies explored the possibility that police officers are exposed to negative social events and public responses and then learn from other police officers how to best deal with them, notably by becoming part of the police culture. The first major study of police cynicism was conducted by Arthur Niederhoffer (1967), who at the time was an NYPD officer. He believed there were two types of police cynicism: (1) general cynicism, or cynicism directed against people in general; and (2) system cynicism, or cynicism aimed at the police organization itself. According to Niederhoffer, police officers embark on a policing career with a professional and committed attitude but experience frustrations on the job. This leads to disenchantment, which leads most officers to develop a cynical attitude. For a minority, however, it leads to a renewed commitment to the high standards with which they started. An officer's degree of cynicism, in Niederhoffer's view, is determined by age and experience.

He found that new officers were less cynical even than those officers who had hardly more experience. He found that almost 80 percent of new recruits questioned on their first day on the job responded that the police department was "an efficient, smoothly running organization"; less than two months later, however, fewer than one-third held this view. Niederhoffer also found that cynicism increased steadily during the first seven to ten years of a police officer's career; then, as years of experience increased beyond this time, cynicism decreased but never returned to the low levels found among the recruits. In addition, he reported that college-educated patrol officers were more cynical than non-college-educated patrol officers and that cynicism decreased as police officers became closer to retirement, and that police administrators had the lowest levels of cynicism. Based on his results, Niederhoffer concluded that police officers either left policing or were able to come to terms with the problems found within policing. Other researchers (e.g., Langworthy 1987; Regoli, Poole, and Hewitt 1979) tested Niederhoffer's ideas on other police departments but were not able to replicate his findings regarding the length of service of police officers and cynicism. However, differences were found between recruits at the beginning of their training compared to those who had just completed their training as well as those who had completed their first few months of regular policing duties (e.g., Rafky, et al. 1976).

The development of police cynicism may have a damaging impact on the job performance of a police officer. Feelings of cynicism appear to intensify the need to maintain respect and exert authority over others (Regoli and Poole 1979). And as this cynicism escalates, there can be a corresponding increase in citizens' distrust and fear of the police. This can ultimately result in the feeling that every contact with the public involves potential danger, a state of mind termed "police paranoia." All of these factors contribute to make the police conservative and resistant to change (ibid.).

The Working Personality of the Police Officer

Probably the most important result of Niederhoffer's study is that it led some researchers to investigate whether those who choose to become police officers possess personality characteristics that make them susceptible to cynicism. The classic work on the police personality was conducted by Jerome Skolnick (1966). Like Niederhoffer, Skolnick believed that the police personality emerges from certain aspects of police work, such as danger and isolation, rather than from pre-existing personality traits. Skolnick contended that the constant danger of the job leads police officers to be extremely suspicious of people, which has the effect of isolating them from the public. The fact that citizens constantly challenge their authority further isolates them. As a consequence, officers react to "vague indications of danger suggested by appearance," a feeling that is constantly reinforced by the police culture. Police officers also feel strongly that the public doesn't support them; this also leads to feelings of isolation, which in turn make police officers turn to one another for support (Skolnick 1994).

The works of Niederhoffer and Skolnick support the view that the police personality emerges as a product of the strains and pressures they encounter in their work. This view has become known as the socialization model. An alternative approach, referred to as the predispositional model, argues that the police personality is the product of the pre-existing personality traits of police officers.

One of the first tests of this model was conducted by Bennett and Greenstein (1975), who asked three groups of students at an American university—police officers (working toward a B.A. degree), police science majors, and non-police science majors—to assign priorities to the values that serve as guiding principles in their lives. These values included equality, happiness, freedom, a sense of accomplishment, a comfortable life, and so on. The researchers hypothesized that the police officers and police science majors would possess like-value orientations. However, the opposite was true, which led to a rejection of this model. The researchers found that the police science majors were most like the

TABLE 6.1 Highest Level of Education for Police Officers, Canada, 2001

	Male	Female	Total
	(%)	(%)	(%)
Less than high-school diploma	4	3	4
High-school diploma	9	6	9
Some trade and non-university	11	9	11
Trade and non-university with certificate/diploma	37	33	36
Some university	22	22	22
University with bachelor's degree or higher	17	27	19
Total	100	100	100

Source: Andrea Taylor-Butts, "Private Security and Public Policing in Canada, 2001", *Juristat*, Vol. 24, no. 7, 2004, p. 13. Statistics Canada catalogue 85-002. Released August 10,2004.

non-police science majors and that the values of both these groups were "markedly divergent from the value systems of experienced police officers." Other studies (e.g., Cochrane and Butler 1980) yielded similar results.

The significance of these studies is that any attempt to reduce value differences between the police and the community should be in the context of new training procedures rather than recruitment on the basis of personality characteristics alone. Furthermore, the training of new recruits should emphasize the social and legal aspects of policing (such as awareness of different cultures as well as the use of discretion) instead of focusing on changing personal values. Despite the evidence that police attitudes are learned on the job, most police forces today continue to rely on personality screening tests and similar interview questions when screening potential candidates for police academies (Ash, et al. 1990; Sanders, et al. 1995).

HIGHER EDUCATION AND POLICING

With the demise of the predispositional model, researchers turned their attention to the effects of higher education on police officers. A common strategy among police forces today is to use educational attainment as a measure for screening out undesirables who want to become police officers (Rodriquez 1995). This has led to research on the impact of higher education on police attitudes.

One of the earliest studies took the form of a questionnaire mailed to 100 members of the RCMP (Smith, et al. 1969). These officers were divided into four comparable groups on the basis of age, education, and experience. Each of the officers was given a per-

sonality test and was also measured on two attitude scales: one for authoritarianism, the other for liberal–conservative leanings. The point of all this was to measure the rigidity/flexibility of the officers. The results indicated that significant differences existed among officers on the basis of education level. Senior officers who had not graduated from a university or college possessed authoritarian, conservative, and rigid attitudes, while those who had attained a degree did not. Other studies yielded similar results. Roberg (1978), Murrell (1982), Meagher (1983), and Carter, et al. (1988) have reported that higher education benefits law enforcement officers by instilling a more professional demeanour and performance and by enabling them to cope better with stress. Police administrators have noted that police officers with higher education show more initiative and professionalism when performing their tasks and receive fewer public complaints (Krimmel 1996).

Table 6.1 indicates that in 2001 the percentage was 22 percent while 36 percent had a trade and non-university certificate' or diploma. of police with "university with bachelor's degree or higher" was 19 percent. The number of police officers with "some university" was 22 percent, while 36 percent had a trade or non-university certificate or diploma. The remaining three categories "high-school diploma" (9 percent) and less than a high-school diploma (3 percent). Forty-nine percent of female police officers in 2001 had some university training or had received a bachelor's degree or better compared to 39 percent of all male officers (Taylor-Butts 2004).

POLICE USE OF DEADLY FORCE

If the police subculture is largely an outgrowth of the occupational hazards of policing, then police behaviour can be measured in terms of the police use of authority.

This authority, when misused as it sometimes is, can lead to the use of deadly force.

Deadly force is defined as force that is used with the intent to cause bodily injury or death. Police use of deadly force refers to those situations where the police use firearms in encounters with citizens. But citizens may be injured or killed as the result of other types of force used by the police. For example, choke holds, which can cause death, ought to be included in any definition of deadly force (Fyfe 1988). High-speed chases ending in death can also be seen as a type of deadly force; however, such cases are not included here because the deaths that occur are unintentional and often accidental.

Until 1995, the Criminal Code permitted the shooting of a "fleeing felon" without any consideration as to whether the suspect presented a danger to a police officer or other citizens (Roach 1999). This was challenged in the trial of a Toronto police officer who shot and wounded a Black male suspected of purse snatching. In this case (*R. v. Lines* [1993]), the prosecutor successfully argued that the shooting was inconsistent with the victim's rights to life and security as provided by the Charter of Rights and Freedoms—specifically, that it deprived both victims and potential victims of police shootings of life and security of the person in that the Criminal Code "authorized lethal force regardless of the seriousness of the offence or the threat posed by the suspect" (ibid., 232).

As a result of *Lines*, Parliament introduced a new defence (found in s. 25[4] of the Criminal Code) authorizing police officers to use deadly force in order to prevent a suspect from fleeing if the officer "believes on reasonable grounds that the force is necessary for the purpose of protecting the police officer . . . or any other person from imminent or future death or grave bodily harm."

Section 25 of the Criminal Code authorizes Canadian police to use force, including lethal force, to deal with various situations they encounter in the course of their work:

25. (1) Every one who is required or authorized by law to do anything in the administration or enforcement of the law

   (a) as a private person,
   (b) as a peace officer or public officer,
   (c) in aid of a peace officer or public officer, or
   (d) by virtue of his office, is, if he acts on reasonable grounds, justified in doing what he is required or authorized to do and in using as much force as is necessary for that purpose . . .

(3) Subject to subsection (4), a person is not justified for the purposes of subsection (1) in using force that is intended or is likely to cause death or grievous bodily harm unless he believes on reasonable grounds that it is necessary for the purpose of preserving himself or any one under his protection from death or grievous bodily harm.

(4) A peace officer who is proceeding lawfully to arrest, with or without warrant, any person for an offence for which that person may be arrested without warrant, and everyone lawfully assisting the police officer, is justified, if the person to be arrested takes flight to avoid arrest, in using as much force as is necessary to prevent the escape by flight, unless the escape can be prevented by reasonable means in a less violent manner.

Subsection (1) of s. 25 of the Criminal Code states that any individual, including a peace (police) officer, can use "as much force as necessary" in the "administration of the law" if he or she "acts on reasonable grounds." Furthermore, a police officer, in order to be justified in using deadly force, must believe on "reasonable grounds" that force is necessary in order to protect himself or herself or an individual in his or her care from "death or grievous bodily harm."

Stansfield (1996; 2000) points out that this approach to deadly force raises a number of problems. First, the phrase "as much force as necessary" suggests that police can use as much force as they feel is necessary to resolve any particular incident. Second, it does not state exactly how much force should be used. In the first case where a police officer was convicted of manslaughter under this section of the Criminal Code, the officer received a conditional sentence (see Chapter 10) and 180 hours of community service. This sentence was reached on the basis of the defendant's previous record as a police officer and because he was given false information that the Aboriginal protestors at Ipperwash, Ontario, were in possession of weapons (*R. v. Deane* [1997]).

A number of mechanisms have been implemented to control the use of deadly force by police. While the Criminal Code clearly states that a police officer does not have to be physically attacked before using potentially deadly force, it does say that police officers have to follow a reasonable standard for the use of force. In brief, force is to be considered excessive when, after the officer has evaluated all the circumstances at the time of the incident, the force is unreasonable. However, even when police investigators and Crown prosecutors determine that excessive force was used, it is difficult to gain a conviction. Police officers who are witnesses to potential criminal offences committed by their colleagues have always been reluctant to assist Crown prosecutors. This problem has led to a revision of the Ontario Police Act, which now states that officers must cooperate with any investigation.

Information on the use of deadly force by police in Canada is limited to estimates about the number of people killed by police. Three categories need to be examined if the issue is to be assessed thoroughly:

1. *Death*—police use a deadly weapon, and as a result the individual dies.
2. *Injury*—the police use a deadly weapon, and the individual is wounded but does not die.
3. *Non-injury*—the police use a deadly weapon, and the individual against whom it is directed is not injured.

Roberg and Kuykendall (1993) contend that a fourth category should be added—the total number of times a police officer fires a weapon. An individual who is shot at and killed or wounded may have been shot at many times, not just once. Geller and Scott (1991) found that police officers miss their target 60 to 85 percent of the time. An officer who shoots six bullets at a suspect may miss the suspect altogether or hit the person once, injuring or killing him or her.

Data on the first category of deadly force is hard to find in Canada, since such records are not kept for public review. Case studies from newspapers cannot be analyzed for the purpose of studying anything beyond the dynamics of the situation, such as police regulations and the final results of any investigation (Forcese 1992). In contrast, figures can be obtained in the United States, as a "cause of homicide" category has been published annually by the National Center for Health Statistics since 1949 in the subcategory of "police or legal" intervention. Between 1949 and 1990, police in the United States killed approximately 13,000 people. However, Sherman and Langworthy (1979) contend that these statistics underestimate such incidents by 25 to 50 percent and that the real number is closer to 30,000 or 40,000.

Variations among Provinces and Cities

The frequency with which police use category 1, deadly force, varies among the provinces and territories. Between 1970 and 1981, the use of deadly force by police resulted in 119 deaths. Quebec accounted for the greatest number of deadly force incidents during this period (37 percent), followed by Ontario (27.7 percent) and British Columbia (11.8 percent). However, when the number of deaths caused by police use of deadly force was measured by 100,000 population, the Northwest Territories had the highest rate (2.43 per 100,000 population), followed by Manitoba (1.18 per 100,000) and Quebec (0.70 per 100,000).

The size of a police force is thought to influence the police use of deadly force, which is said to increase as the size of the police force increases. This idea is based on the argument that larger centres have more criminals, more crime, and more weapons, and that the police are more likely to intervene in situations where they think deadly force is the appropriate response. Chappell and Graham (1985) found that between 1970 and 1981 there was no discernible evidence that such a relationship existed in Canada. Although they did not analyze their data in this matter, American researchers (Kania and Mackey 1977; Sherman and Langworthy 1979) have found a relationship between lack of social cohesion in a community (e.g., high poverty and divorce rates) and police involvement in potentially dangerous situations.

Another important factor is the police organization itself—the organizational values, policies, and practices of police administrators. For example, the imposition of restrictive shooting policies will no doubt lead to a significant decrease in the use of deadly force. Also, police training and the police response to dangerous incidents may have an impact on the use of deadly force. For example, some police departments may tell their officers how to deal with certain incidents, such as whether to wait for back-up or to act in an aggressive manner (Fyfe 1988). Police forces do not always follow government recommendations to change their practices. In Ontario, the Task Force on Race Relations and Policing (Lewis 1989) recommended alternative types of interventions involving such procedures as better community relations, employment equity, and culturally sensitive training.

Police Use of Deadly Force

The following discussion of police use of deadly force in Canada is limited to those few studies that have empirically analyzed this issue. Abraham and colleagues (1981) focused on the Metropolitan Toronto Police, Chappell and Graham (1985) looked at both national and British Columbia data, Stansfield (1996) looked at Toronto, while Parent and Verdun-Jones (1998) studied police shootings in British Columbia.

Abraham and colleagues (1981) studied the use of deadly force by Toronto police officers and described seven incidents as "confrontation situations." All of the victims were armed at the time of the shooting: one had a shotgun, another an inoperative shotgun; there were also two toy weapons, two kitchen knives, a gardening tool, and a police officer's nightstick. The key problem in all seven incidents was that the police involved themselves in a way that led to a confrontation, reflecting "fundamental training defects in the Metro police" (ibid., 234).

In their study of police use of deadly force in British Columbia between 1970 and 1982, Chappell and Graham (1985, 110–11) reported that all 13 victims were males aged 17 to 52. One victim was Black, another Asian, and the rest White. Seven of the victims were armed at the time of the shooting, and two were not in possession of a weapon when confronted by the police (though they were in possession of a weapon at the time of their offence). Three individuals were not armed, while in the remaining case no weapon was discovered on the victim's body in the field, though an unloaded weapon was discovered tucked into his belt at the autopsy.

As Stansfield (2000) points out, two studies found that many of these incidents involved the use of deadly force by the police in fleeing-felon situations. Chappell and Graham (1985) reported that almost 40 percent of the fatal shootings they analyzed involved situations where the victim was fleeing the police. Stansfield (1993) found that 8 of the 14 shootings in Toronto between 1988 and 1991 involved the victim being shot while fleeing the police.

In contrast, Abraham and colleagues (1981) reported that all of the victims in their study were shot and killed while confronting the police. Also, Parent and Verdun-Jones (1998), who analyzed 58 fatal police shootings in British Columbia between 1980 and 1994, found that almost half the deaths were the result of the victim provoking an officer to use deadly force, intentionally or not. And in "the majority of these cases, the individual's statements and actions clearly reflect their intention to commit suicide" (ibid., 438).

With regard to police shootings in Canada, the issue of the victim's race has been raised many times. For example, the Ontario Commission on Systemic Racism (1995, 377) stated that "the number and circumstances of police shootings in Ontario have convinced many residents that they are disproportionately vulnerable to police violence." Between 1978 and 1995, 16 Black men were shot by the police in Ontario, 10 of them fatally. Nine of these shootings led to a criminal prosecution; all of these prosecutions ended with the officers charged being acquitted (ibid.). A number of cases involving the police use of deadly force and members of racial minority groups have received national attention; they include the cases of JJ Harper in Winnipeg (Hamilton and Sinclair 1991) and Richard Barnabe in Montreal (Peritz 2000).

Deadly Force Used Against Police Officers

Police officers can of course be the *recipients* of deadly force. The danger of their daily work was underscored in 2005 when four RCMP officers were shot and killed while conducting an investigation near Mayerthorpe, Alberta. The death of a police officer on duty is a rare event in Canada; on average, two or three officers are killed each year. In comparison, approximately 70 police officers a year are shot and killed each year in the United States.

Since 1961, a total of 128 police officers have been killed in the line of duty (Li, 2007). The decade in which the highest number of police officers were killed was the 1980s: between 1980 and 1989, 63 officers were killed. Fifty-seven police officers died between 1960 and 1969, and 61 between 1970 and 1979 (Picard 1997). The Canadian Centre for Justice Statistics (1982) investigated the deaths of Canadian police officers for the years 1960 to 1979. During this period, 118 Canadian police officers were murdered. Most of these homicides were committed by firearms—handguns, rifles, shotguns, and sawed-off rifles. Between 1960 and 1991, 11 percent of all police officers killed were shot with their own or a fellow officer's firearm (Stansfield 2000).

POLICE MISCONDUCT

Police misconduct, or police deviance as it is sometimes referred to, is a term used in its broadest sense throughout the criminal justice literature (Martin 1993). It can be defined as "a generic description of police officer activities which are inconsistent with the officer's legal authority, organizational authority, and standards of ethical conduct" (Barker and Carter 1986, 1–7). Police misconduct can be subdivided into two categories: occupational deviancy and abuse of authority. Occupational deviancy is defined as "criminal and noncriminal [behaviour] committed during the course of normal work activities or committed under the guise of the police officer's authority" (ibid., 4). Examples of police occupational deviancy include misconduct such as sleeping on duty, insubordination, and misuse of firearms.

Police misconduct has been investigated and reported by social scientists and social historians.

Examples of police misconduct in recent years are not difficult to find. For example, in Quebec, charges in a drug case were thrown out after the judge found out that the documents linking the shipment to the accused had been planted by Sûreté du Québec officers. Another incident involved a jury finding two SQ officers guilty of falsifying evidence in an attempt to prevent the daughter of one of them from being charged with drunk driving causing bodily harm (Tranh Ha 1999).

Police abuse of authority (often referred to as the use of excessive force) involves the application of various types of coercion when the police are interacting with citizens. According to Roberg and Kuykendall (1993, 200), the police use four types of coercion:

1. *Verbal*—the use of deceit, promises, threats, and derogatory language.
2. *Physical*—the use of the officer's physical strength and body.
3. *Non-lethal*—the use of a weapon instead of or in addition to the officer's body.
4. *Lethal*—the use of a deadly weapon in such a manner that a person is likely to be seriously injured or killed.

How common is the police use of excessive force? Claims have been made throughout the twentieth century that Canadian police have used excessive force. Jamieson (1973) and Brown and Brown (1978) found that various police forces across Canada have harassed and intimidated striking workers. As recently as 1982, some Regina police officers patrolled with unleashed police dogs; during 1981–82, 52 Aboriginal persons and 33 non-Aboriginal persons were bitten by those dogs (Forcese 1992).

Incidents of police use of excessive force are reported almost every week in the Canadian media. But what form does this force take? Reiss (1974), in an American study, used university students to observe police–citizen interactions in high-crime areas in Washington, D.C., Chicago, and Boston. The students reported that verbal abuse was common but that the excessive use of force was relatively rare, occurring in 44 cases out of the 5,360 observed. There was little difference between the way police treated Black people and White people, and when force was used it was typically used selectively—against those who were disrespectful of the police or who disregarded police authority after being arrested. Sherman and Cohen (1986) reported that police use of any form of violence was rare, while Bayley and Garofalo (1989) found that when police use force, it usually involves grabbing and restraining and rarely if ever involves the use of weapons.

Despite these findings, widely publicized incidents of the police use of excessive force have continued to haunt police departments in Canada (Forcese 1992, 172–76). The police are often accused of relying on excessive physical force to obtain confessions from suspects (Hagan 1977), and some say they "push the law to its limits, slip through the loopholes and employ technicalities" and that they cannot be trusted "to obey the rules society imposes on the way they question suspects" (Woods, in Martin 1993, 161). This led Brannigan (1984, 57) to conclude that "the police appear to routinely trample over the rights of accused people." In 1976, as a result of allegations of excessive police force in the Metropolitan Toronto Police, a Royal Commission was called to investigate the charges. Its chairman, Mr. Justice Donald Morand, concluded that 6 of the 17 incidents he studied involved the use of excessive force. And the Quebec Court of Appeal posthumously overturned the manslaughter conviction of Michel Jaffe, who spent five years in prison for killing a suspected drug trafficker. The court overturned Jaffe's conviction after it heard that his confession followed four hours of beatings (with telephone books) by SQ officers (Tranh Ha 1999).

A third type of police misconduct involves the selective enforcement of laws—an approach to enforcement encountered by certain populations in Canada. These "routine incidents of misconduct reflect and reinforce race, class and gender bias in a myriad of ways" (Martin 1993, 149). The selective enforcement of the law as it applies to marginalized women, such as prostitutes, became an issue in Vancouver about 10 years ago: the disappearance of more than 50 women led to accusations that the police were indifferent to their fate.

"Problem" Police Officers: Early Warning Systems

Some people believe that all police officers are involved in the illegitimate use of force, while others argue that only a small proportion of officers engage in such actions. The empirical reality, however, is that in many police services a small group of police officers account for a large number of citizen complaints. In fact, it has become a truism among police administrators that 10 percent of police officers generate 90 percent of all the problems faced by police services. Lersch and Mieczkowski (1996) in the United States found that 7 percent of all police officers were "chronic" offenders who generated a disproportionate number (33 percent) of complaints from the public. These "high-volume" officers were younger and less experienced and were accused of using force after a proactive encounter they had personally initiated. Yet these officers were actually praised by police administrators as more productive and as performing their duties to the best of their abilities. In other words, citizen complaints were often interpreted as indicators of productivity rather than a problem.

Some researchers (Sherman 1977) argue that "problem" police officers are indicative of problems that exist within entire police departments. They contend that police departments can be categorized according to the level and type of misconduct found within them. Three categories have been developed:

- *Rotten apples.* This term refers to police departments that have a few problem police officers (that is, "rotten apples"), who use their position for illegal personal gain, or who resort to the force that society has authorized to engage in questionable behaviour with suspects and/or members of marginalized groups. Sometimes a number of "rotten apples" work together; if they do, they are sometimes referred to as "rotten pockets."
- *Pervasive but unorganized misconduct.* Here, a majority of police personnel are engaged in questionable activities but cooperate little with one another, if at all.
- *Pervasive and organized misconduct.* Here, almost all of the members of a police department are involved in systemic and organized misconduct.

The phenomenon of the "problem police officer" was first identified by Goldstein during the 1970s. He wrote that problem police officers "are well known to their supervisors, to the top administrators, to their peers, and to the residents of the areas in which they work" but that "little is done to alter their conduct" (1977, 171). The Christopher Commission's investigation of the Los Angeles Police Department identified 44 problem police officers, with each averaging 7.6 complaints for excessive force or for improper tactics, compared to only 0.6 for all other officers. In 1981, the U.S. Commission on Civil Rights recommended that all police departments create an "early warning system" to identify problem police officers, "who are frequently the subject of complaints or who demonstrate identifiable patterns of inappropriate behavior" (U.S. Commission on Civil Rights 1981, 81). By 1999, almost 40 percent of all police forces in the United States that were responsible for populations greater than 50,000 either had an early warning system in place or were planning to implement one.

An "early warning system" is a data-based police management tool for identifying officers whose actions are problematic. It enables a police service to intervene before an officer creates a situation that requires formal disciplinary action. The system alerts administrators to problem officers; those administrators can then warn the officers in question and provide appropriate counselling and/or training to help them change their problematic behaviour.

According to Walker (2001), early warning systems have several capabilities, including these:

- *Individual officers.* They can improve the performance of officers who are having problems in their interactions with citizens.
- *Supervisors.* They can improve the supervision efforts of sergeants by placing systematic data in their hands relating to the performance of the officers under their command. These data let them focus on particular police officers and on particular performance issues such as the use of force.
- *The police department as a whole.* They can improve the police department as a whole by identifying unacceptable performance with the goal of reducing or eliminating it.
- *Police–community relations.* They can improve police–community relations by reducing specific problems such as the use of excessive force; at the same time, they can communicate to the public the message that the police department is addressing community concerns in a substantive manner.

Early warning systems have three basic components: selection, intervention, and post-intervention monitoring. In the selection phase, various criteria are applied in order to identify officers who should be placed in the system. These criteria include citizen complaints, the use of firearms, the use of force, civil litigation, incidents involving resisting arrest, and high-speed pursuits and vehicular damage. The primary goal of an early warning system is to change the behaviour of police officers who have been identified as problems. Intervention strategies are based on a combination of deterrence and education. Deterrence (see Chapter 3) assumes that police officers who go through the intervention process will change their behaviour in response to the perceived threat of punishment. It is assumed, as well, that this system will have a general deterrent effect, in the sense that police officers not involved with the system will change their behaviour in order to avoid being caught up in it. Early warning systems also work on the assumption that retraining the officers in question will help those officers improve their performance. About 50 percent of the police departments using early warning systems monitor an officer's performance for 36 months after the initial intervention. The other police services do not specify a time period for the follow-up, but the officers in question are constantly monitored.

Police forces have found that early warning systems can improve the actions of their officers while at the same time reducing the number of complaints received by the police directly or by a police oversight committee (see below). In Minneapolis, one year after an early warning system was introduced, the average number of citizen complaints against officers involved in the early intervention system fell by 67 percent. In New Orleans, the figure fell by 62 percent. In Miami-Dade County in Florida, use-of-force reports by officers involved in the system decreased dramatically—after intervention, 50 percent of the officers in question had no use-of-force reports.

Police Accountability: The Role of Citizen Oversight

A police department may provide excellent training, practise culturally sensitive policing, and develop excellent rapport with local residents; even so, problems such as police misconduct and the use of excessive force will no doubt surface. The question then becomes, who shall police the police? The police in a democracy are accountable to both the public and the law. This means that besides conforming to the appropriate legal standards of due process, the police have to be responsive to the citizens they serve. One important issue concerning police accountability, as Walker (2001) points out, is that these two aspects of accountability can conflict with each other. The public wants effective crime control, but some of the means used by the police to accomplish this goal may conflict with legal principles. How is a balance to be struck between these two types of accountability?

A Royal Commission or an inquiry can be struck to investigate a specific incident; this is rare, however, and usually happens only long after the fact. A Royal Commission was appointed to investigate the wrongful conviction of Donald Marshall, Jr., a Mi'kmaq man who served almost 12 years for a murder he did not commit. And the Aboriginal Justice Inquiry in Manitoba focused on the deaths of two Aboriginal people in that province, Helen Betty Osborne and JJ Harper. The ensuing reports were critical of some policing practices.

Much more common approaches to ensuring police accountability are internal investigations, citizen oversight, and civil liability. With internal investigations, the police themselves investigate allegations of wrongdoing by police officers. Many observers are critical of this approach, arguing that it is inherently biased in favour of the police and that when an officer is found guilty of wrongdoing, the resulting penalties are too lenient. A. Alan Borovoy, then-general counsel

of the Canadian Civil Liberties Union, argues that this approach is flawed because it "will scare off many potential complainants" and because "investigating officers will have a conflict of interest" (2000, A3). To illustrate his concerns, he points to the evidence collected by the Donald Marshall inquiry. That inquiry found that an RCMP officer appointed to evaluate the prosecution of Marshall soon after Marshall started to serve his sentence found no wrongdoing by investigators in Sydney, Nova Scotia, where the crime occurred. When this issue was raised at the hearings years later, another member of the RCMP stated that "police officers are like a fraternity. You feel a certain loyalty to one another." Similar scenarios have been found across Canada. In Winnipeg, the conclusions reached by an internal police review board established to look into the wrongful death of an Aboriginal man, JJ Harper, at the hands of a Winnipeg police officer were criticized by an external inquiry. They found that the police paid "much more attention to protecting the officer than . . . to uncovering the facts." And in Toronto, a police officer whose testimony helped incarcerate another police officer who had assaulted a prisoner was reportedly ostracized by other officers, with the result that he left the police.

A second approach—and the most common one today—to controlling police misconduct is to establish a separate civilian review agency to investigate allegations of police misbehaviour (Walker 2001, 5) (see also Exhibit 6.3). This opens the complaints process to individuals who are not police officers. In this way, the police are made accountable to the public (Finn 2000).

Demands for some sort of citizen oversight of the police have existed for more than 40 years in North America. In the 1960s, the idea of oversight was viewed as radical by almost everyone except civil liberties groups. Slowly the idea of citizen oversight of the police became accepted in Western countries, and today such bodies are found in the United Kingdom, the United States, Australia, and New Zealand (see Exhibit 6.2 for some of the reasons given by people who support and who criticize civilian oversight committees). In Canada, the first civilian oversight agencies were established in the 1980s in Toronto, in the provinces of Manitoba, British Columbia, and Quebec, and (federally) for the RCMP.

The first citizen review board in Canada was formed in Toronto in 1981. It enabled members of the public to direct their complaints to a non-police organization. This board was created after an investigation into the Metropolitan Toronto Police Force (as it was then known) by Judge D. R. Morand of the Ontario Supreme Court recommended that a citizen review

EXHIBIT 6.2 The Pros and Cons of Citizen Oversight

Those who favour citizen oversight committees make a number of arguments in favour of them, including these:

- Police misconduct is a serious problem, and internal police complaint systems have failed to address the real issues leading to these problems.
- Citizen oversight committees are more thorough and fair than the police's own internal reviews.
- Citizen oversight committees find in favour of more complaints.
- Such committees lead to more disciplinary actions against police officers.
- Such committees do more to deter the types of police behaviour that lead to complaints.
- Such committees are viewed as independent by citizens and therefore provide greater satisfaction among complainants.
- Such committees lead to greater professionalization within police organizations; they also improve the quality of policing.

    Critics of civilian oversight point out that this approach achieves few of its stated goals and can actually make matters worse. They identify the following problems with it (among others):

- Police misconduct is not as serious a problem as it is made out to be.
- Police officers and organizations are capable of and do conduct thorough and fair investigations.
- Internal police investigations into police wrongdoing actually find in favour of complainants more often than do citizen oversight committees.
- Police departments hand out harsher disciplinary sanctions to those officers who have been found to be involved in wrongful conduct than citizen oversight committees.
- Internal police disciplinary approaches deter more police officers from engaging in misconduct.
- Internal police investigations are actually more satisfying to complainants.
- Citizen oversight committees actually do more harm than good in that they limit the crime control initiatives of police officers and undermine the authority of police executives.

Source: Walker, S. 2001. *Police Accountability: The Role of Citizen Oversight.* Belmont, CA: Wadsworth.

board be formed. In his investigation, Morand uncovered evidence of false arrests, cover-ups, and false charges, as well as a conspiracy among police officers to protect one another from legal action. This led to the passing of the Police Force Complaints Act, which makes it possible to investigate allegations of police brutality. This legislation established a commission for investigating complaints in which both the police and civilian authorities have input.

The Public Complaints Commissioner has considerable powers of search and seizure as well as the right to subpoena witnesses and order hearings before a board of inquiry with direct disciplinary powers. One-third of the board members are lawyers, one-third are individuals jointly recommended by the Board of Police Commissioners and the Metropolitan Toronto Police Association, and one-third are appointed by the city (McMahon 1988). Although these hearings are not criminal in nature, misconduct must be established beyond a reasonable doubt, a standard usually applied to criminal matters. Between 1988 and 1990, almost 98 percent of the cases in which civilians filed a complaint against police stemmed from an incident in which those civilians themselves were charged (Ellis and DeKeseredy 1996).

The annual reports of the Public Complaints Commissioner for 1988 to 1991 have been summarized by Ellis and DeKeseredy (1996). Non-physical and physical assaults by police accounted for about half of all complaints, with the most common complaint (43 percent) being "failure to act according to police procedure," such as neglect of duty. Landau's (1994) study of the nature of allegations revealed that "improper police behavior" accounted for 49 percent of complaints, followed by physical abuse (34 percent), verbal abuse (32 percent), unprofessional conduct (29 percent), and neglect of duty (25 percent). The largest percentage of decisions by both the police chief and the Public Complaints Commissioner for a 15-month period in 1992 and early 1993 resulted in "no action taken" because of insufficient evidence—these decisions accounted for 52 percent of all "resolved" complaints. Two other categories—"no further action—evidence supports officer" and "no further action—complaint lodged in bad faith"—accounted for 16 and 23 percent of all complaints, respectively. Thus, no further action was taken in 70 (or 91 percent) of 77 decisions.

Ellis and DeKeseredy found that of the 1,915 incidents investigated, most arose from police–citizen contacts on the street (48 percent). "Residence," "police building," and "public place" accounted for another 46 percent. Similar results were obtained by Landau, who found that just over 78 percent of all complaints arose from incidents "on the street or in public" (54 percent) and the complainant's residence (24 percent). Thirty percent of the complainants were Black, 8 percent were Asian, and 4 percent were Hispanic. These rates are considered to be an "unreliable indicator of the current state of relations between police and visible minority, particularly black members of the community" (Landau 1994). Ellis and DeKeseredy (1996, 119) point out that these rates "greatly underestimate the actual number of occasions in which blacks and other visible minority community members experienced racially or ethnically biased police conduct."

But are complainants more satisfied with this type of system? Landau (1996) interviewed 104 individuals who had made formal complaints about the actions of Toronto police officers to assess whether or not they were satisfied with this system for investigating the police. She discovered that only 14 percent of the 58 complainants whose complaints had been resolved at the time of the study felt that the system was fair. In comparison, 35 percent of this same group said they considered the police investigation to be biased. Overall, Landau found that almost 60 percent of those complainants whose complaints had been resolved felt that Toronto did not have a fair system for investigating citizen complaints. And more than two-thirds of this same group of complainants indicated that they were unsatisfied or very unsatisfied with the complaint process and that they would not use the system again, preferring instead to use an alternative system such as hiring a lawyer. In addition, the role of the Office of the Public Complaints Commissioner in terms of investigating complaints made by citizens was misunderstood by many of the complainants; this led Landau (ibid., 310) to comment that this organization cannot "achieve any of the goals of accountability or control of the police or improve police-community relations from the perspective of those who use the system."

In 1990, a new Ontario Police Services Act received Royal Assent. It expanded the powers of the Police Complaints Commissioner to the entire province. This new legislation also created the Special Investigations Unit (SIU), a civilian oversight agency, as a response to concerns expressed during the hearings of the Task Force on Race Relations in 1988. During these hearings, some presenters had expressed concern about the manner in which the police conducted their investigations involving officers of other police services, a process that was criticized for its potential lack of objectivity and conflict of interest.

The SIU is intended to be an independent agency of the provincial government and is composed of civilian investigators. The SIU's jurisdiction is limited to the criminal investigation of police actions that result in serious injuries, including sexual assaults and deaths. Complaints involving police activities that do not involve a serious injury or death are handled by other agencies. Ontario is the only Canadian province with an independent civilian agency that possesses the power and authority to investigate complaints and, when the evidence permits, to charge police officers with a criminal offence.

In 1992, the SIU's jurisdiction was expanded to cover municipal, regional, and provincial police officers across the entire province of Ontario (Wells 2000). The duties of the SIU include these:

- To review and, if necessary, reinvestigate complaints made by individuals dissatisfied with decisions made by the police.
- To monitor initial police complaints, investigations, and decisions made by police chiefs and the Ontario police commissioner, as well as decisions reached in internal disciplinary hearings.
- To receive and record complaints from the public.
- To refer cases to a civilian board of inquiry, if necessary, after reviews.
- To conduct initial investigations into "two-force" complaints—allegations against officers from more than one force.
- To make recommendations to the police to improve police practices in order to avoid reoccurrences of certain types of complaints.

In 1997, allegations were made concerning the lack of cooperation between the police and SIU investigators. In addition, the media made accusations that some of the investigations were either biased and/or incompetent. In response, the Ontario government appointed a retired judge to look at the operations of the SIU in relation to the police as well as broader communities. Almost a year later, in May 1998, the judge presented the final report, which pointed out that much of the problem was the result of an ambiguous subsection relating to the duty of police officers to cooperate with SIU investigators. This led to a new regulation, which came into effect in 1999.

Between 2001 and 2005, 10,002 occurrences across Ontario were investigated by the SIU. The most common occurrences investigated fell under the categories of "custody injuries" (489), vehicle injuries (185), and custody deaths (117). The SIU also investigated 52 vehicle deaths, 43 firearm injuries, and 28 firearm deaths. During this same time period, 21 charges were laid as a result of SIU investigations. Eleven charges were laid involving "custody incidents," six involving sexual assaults, and three involving "vehicular incidents."

The third mechanism for controlling police misconduct is civil liability. In this approach, individual police officers can be held liable for their misconduct and sentenced to a period of incarceration (although this rarely occurs), or the police service itself can be sued. In 1998, for example, a rape victim successfully sued the Toronto Police Service for failing to warn her that a serial rapist was attacking women in her neighbourhood. An Ontario court awarded her $220,000 (Gatehouse and Eby 2000). In another case, a British Columbia woman attempted to sue the RCMP for allegedly failing to protect her from a "shooting rampage" by her former husband that left her best friend dead and her daughter wounded. Even though an internal RCMP investigation found the officer in question did not conduct a thorough investigation, the B.C. Supreme Court dismissed her case (Sokoloff 2001, A9).

EXHIBIT 6.3   The Commission for Public Complaints against the RCMP

What happens when a member of the public wants to make a complaint against the RCMP in the belief that one of its officers engaged in misconduct? Some people think that complainants must file with a provincial organization where the incident took place. This is not so: complaints against RCMP officers can be filed directly with the RCMP, or with the Commission for Public Complaints against the RCMP (CPC), or with a provincial body. In all cases, however, the complaint is ultimately sent to the CPC for review. The CPC is a civilian board that investigates the actions of RCMP members. The CPC can also initiate a complaint, as it did when, on October 23, 2003, an investigation was initiated to review the role of the RCMP in the case of Maher Arar. Arar, a Canadian citizen, was arrested in the United States in 2002 and then deported to Syria by American authorities. He alleged that he was tortured during his year in Syrian custody. An independent public inquiry into this matter was announced in January 2004. In September 2006, the Commission of Inquiry released its report, finding that Mr. Arar was "an innocent victim of inaccurate RCMP intelligence reports and deliberate smears by Canadian officials" (Sallot 2006, A1).

The CPC can also decide to hold a public interest investigation or conduct a hearing. The CPC uses public interest hearings to raise public awareness about important policing issues as well as to provide a complaint process that is both transparent and accessible. It can decide to pursue a public interest investigation into any complaint when the chair considers it in the public interest. In these cases, the RCMP does not have to conduct an investigation.

The CPC was established by Parliament in 1988 and is an independent group, separate from the RCMP. The CPC's mandate:

- To receive complaints from the public about the conduct of members of the RCMP.

- To conduct reviews when complainants are not satisfied with the handling of their cases by the RCMP.
- To hold public hearings and investigations.
- To report findings and make recommendations.

During 2007, the CPC received a total of 1,440 formal complaints requesting a review. When the CPC receives a complaint concerning the possibility of misconduct by an RCMP member, it contacts the complainant to describe the process. In addition, it helps the complainant to decide whether he or she wishes to make a formal complaint or proceed informally. If the complainant decides to proceed formally, the CPC helps that individual fill out the required forms. The complaint is then sent to the RCMP for a statutory investigation. The rules established for the CPC require the RCMP to conduct the first investigation into a complaint; however, it is possible that the CPC will conduct an investigation itself. During its investigation, the RCMP can decide whether a Criminal Code investigation should be conducted.

A number of options are available to the RCMP. For example, it may be able to handle the complaint informally. If the complainant agrees to this (and many of the complaints made against RCMP members are handled in this way), the investigation is then closed and the formal complaint process ends. If the complainant prefers to pursue a formal complaint, the RCMP will contact that individual after it has completed its investigation. The complainant will be informed by letter whether the RCMP has taken any steps to address the complaint. If the complainant is satisfied with the RCMP's response, this is the end of the process. However, if the complainant is not satisfied, the CPC will review the complaint. Once the CPC receives all the relevant information, it begins its review. If it rules that the RCMP acted appropriately, the complaint is closed. If it rules that the

RCMP did not act appropriately, a copy of the file is sent to the RCMP Commissioner as well as to the Ministry of Public Safety and Emergency Preparedness. The RCMP Commissioner then responds to the complainant. If the issue still cannot be resolved, the CPC may investigate the complaint itself, return it to the RCMP for further investigation, or hold a public hearing.

Public hearings are held in those cases where the CPC determines that the complaint involves issues that are of interest to the public and that are best dealt with in a public forum.

One of the unique aspects of the CPC process is that alternative dispute resolution (ADR) is available. When this process is followed, the complainant can decide to meet informally with the RCMP about the issue. One advantage of this system is the speed at which these meetings can take place; usually, the files can be dealt with within days, compared to the 6 to 12 months it takes for the formal complaint process. In the ADR process, a CPC analyst acts as a facilitator between the RCMP and the complainant. The citizen and the RCMP voluntarily agree upon a decision. If there are still outstanding issues, the complainant can still decide to file a formal complaint. During 2007, ADR was used in 438 cases.

THE CHANGING COMPOSITION OF THE POLICE

Over the past 25 years, Canadian police forces have been hiring more women, people from visible minorities, and Aboriginal people. It is widely believed that it is essential for a police force to reflect its community in terms of race, sex, and ethnicity. When it does, the result is "a psychologically positive attitude on the part of visible minorities who have felt left out and alienated from the mainstream of society" (Jayewardene and Talbot 1990; Normandeau 1990). A police force that reflects the demographics of its community can do much "[to gain] the public's confidence by helping to dispel the view that police departments are generally bigoted or biased organizations" (Senna and Siegel 1995, 239).

In Canada, not until the 1970s did pressure begin to grow for police forces to hire more female and minority officers. This was more than ten years later than in the United States. According to Forcese (1992), this pressure was the result of increasing numbers of visible-minority immigrants to Canada. Questions about the appropriate composition of the police were being raised: Were the police isolated from the community by their White male profile? How important was it to have visible-minority and female representation in police departments? What types of individuals should be recruited as police officers? While the responses to these questions varied, some police officials began to actively recruit people from visible minorities and women for their departments. In addition, the Royal Commission on the Status of Women recommended in 1971 that all police forces train and hire women. Its recommendations became the basis of the RCMP's decision to train and hire its first female members in 1974. However, the integration of women and other minorities into policing has been a slow process.

Women and Policing

The number of female police officers in Canada has always been small, at least until recently. Throughout the 1960s, the percentage of female police officers was below 1 percent, rising to 2 percent only in 1980. This figure increased to 3.6 percent in 1985, 6.4 percent in 1990, 10.9 percent in 1994, 13.7 percent in 2000, and 18.5 percent in 2003 (Sauve and Reitano 2005; Li 2008). While the number of sworn police officers has gradually increased over the past few years (see Chapter 5), the number of women police officers has increased by several thousand. In 2007, there were 11,853 women police officers, compared to 7,650 in 2000.

Female police officers are now entering the upper echelons of police administration. In 1996, for example, 1.7 percent of all senior officers in Canada were women; by 2001, this figure had more than doubled to 3.5 percent. By 2008, the number of women in senior positions in police forces across Canada had reached 7.7 percent. Women in non-commissioned ranks had increased their presence from 3.0 percent in 1996 to 6.3 percent in 2001 and to 13.3 percent in 2008. In 1996, women made up 13.5 percent of all constables; by 2001, that figure had increased to 17.8 percent; by 2008, to 21.2 percent. In terms of rank, the number of female officers occurred at the senior level increased from 3.1 percent in 2000 to 7.7 percent in 2008 (Minister of Industry 2008). In a comparison of female police officers in 26 other countries in 2002, Canada ranked seventh with a percentage of 15.3 percent. The countries with the highest percentage of

In 2006, Bev Busson was appointed interim commissioner of the RCMP, the first woman to hold that position. (CP PHOTO/Fred Chartrand)

involving social service issues, most commonly in the areas of juvenile and family violence. Female officers were seen as adding to specialized police activities and units rather than as contributors to general law enforcement duties. It was commonly believed at the time that men were more effective administrators and "were less likely to become irritable and over-critical under emotional stress" (Wilson and McLaren 1977).

Although these stereotypes of women and men in police work would ultimately be challenged, the initial breakthrough for equal treatment of women was the elimination of exclusionary physical requirements. For example, until 1979 the OPP and the Ottawa police were turning down female applicants unless they were at least 5'1" tall and at least 160 pounds. Complaints to the Ontario government resulted in changes to these standards to accommodate the recruitment of more women (Forcese 1992). Police agencies started to advertise for more women interested in policing as a career. In 1987, the Toronto police, which employed more than 5,000 officers, had only 226 female sworn officers—about 4 percent of the total. In 1988, the percentage of women in the RCMP, which didn't hire its first female officers until 1974, was 7 percent. Fourteen percent (or 2,045) of all RCMP officers were women in 1999. In 2009, there were almost 4,000 female RCMP officers, or approximately 22 percent of all regular members in the force.

Probably the most significant breakthrough for female police officers was the policy of **employment equity**. According to the federal government, employment equity involves the purposeful identification of any significant differences between the participation levels and the population figures of four targeted minority groups—people from visible minorities, women, people with disabilities, and Aboriginal people. Employment equity aims to identify any employment policies and/or practices that disadvantage these groups. The legal foundation of employment equity is the Canadian Human Rights Act (1977). Section 16(1) of this act states that it is not discriminatory to start a program designed to prevent, eliminate, or reduce disadvantages experienced by individuals because of their race, national or ethnic origin, religion, age, sex, family status, marital status, or disability.

In this matter, some observers have noted that the biggest problem facing police departments is not recruiting women but rather keeping them. This is because "many police departments are locked in a 'timewarp' that perpetuates the myth that only men can do patrol" (Hale and Wyland 1993, 4). The presence of women in a traditionally male domain is threatening to many male officers, regardless of rank, and they are treated as outsiders; this effectively prevents them from learning tasks that would help them gain promotion later (Hunt 1990; Padavic and

female police officers were Norway (30.7 percent) and Australia (29.9 percent), followed by the Netherlands (19.2 percent). In the United Kingdom, 17.8 percent of all police officers were women; the United States ranked 18th with 7.2 percent, slightly more than Japan (7.1 percent) and Greece (7.0 percent). The lowest percentage was in Mexico (2.1 percent). The first female chief of police in Canada was appointed in Guelph, Ontario, in the fall of 1994. Calgary became, in the summer of 1995, the first Canadian city with a population more than 100,000 to appoint a female police chief. Since then, women have been appointed commissioner of the OPP and chief constable of British Columbia. In the RCMP, the first female detachment commander was appointed in 1990, the first female commissioned officer in 1992, and the first female commanding officer of a division in 1998. In 2006, Bev Busson, a member of the first female recruit class trained by the the RCMP in 1974, was appointed interim RCMP Commissioner.

Unequal Treatment

Before the increase in the number of female police officers in Canada during the mid-1980s, the role of women in policing was generally restricted to assignments

Reskin 1990). Crawford and Stark-Adamec (1994) studied why both female and male officers left four major Canadian police forces. The reasons women gave for doing so were to raise a family (56 percent), to move to another city (17 percent), to join a different police force (11 percent), or because of burnout/negative views on life (6 percent), feelings of inadequacy as a police officer (6 percent), or dissatisfaction with shift work (6 percent). Male officers, in contrast, left primarily due to a change in occupation (41 percent), disillusionment with policing or the criminal justice system (32 percent), burnout/negative views on life (23 percent), dissatisfaction with shift work (18 percent), family-related issues (9 percent), and the dangers inherent in the job (5 percent).

The Performance of Female Police Officers

When questioned about their experience on the job, most female police officers say they have to work harder than men to receive credit for their work. Most say that their competence is repeatedly questioned, that they are judged by different standards, and that any mistakes they make are attributed to their being women. This type of experience is found in many Western countries, not just Canada. Brown (1994) reports that this is also the case in the United States. Holdaway and Parker (1998) have found the same in England.

Some contend that female police officers are more compassionate, less aggressive, and less competitive than their male counterparts. They see their job from a different perspective and thus develop policing styles that are different from those of men. Citizens seem to prefer having a female officer respond to their complaints, especially those involving domestic issues. In addition, female officers are more likely to possess the skills to "dial down" potentially violent situations. Also, in the United States, financial payouts in civil lawsuits for cases involving police brutality and misconduct involving male officers exceed those involving female officers by a ratio of 43 to 1 (Spillar 2000).

Female Police Officers: Gender Conflicts at Work

Despite evidence that female and male police officers perform equally, policewomen have sometimes experienced difficulty being fully accepted by their male colleagues. According to Balkin (1988, 33), male officers perceive policewomen as lacking both the physical and emotional strength to perform well in violent confrontations. Overall, male police officers hold "almost uniformly negative . . . attitudes toward policewomen."

Petersen (1982) and Martin (1991) have pointed out that since male police officers associate masculinity with the use of physical force, and view the use of physical force as the defining feature of police work, they are concerned about and threatened by women's successful integration into police work. However, Hunt (1990) reports that male and female police officers develop similar attitudes toward their occupational duties and job satisfaction.

This is not to say that female officers no longer experience gender conflicts at work. In her national assessment of female police officers in the United States in the 1980s, Martin (1991) found that a high percentage of female officers encountered some form of bias and that 75 percent of both new and experienced police officers reported being victims of sexual harassment. In fact, a higher proportion (35 percent) of rookie female officers than rookie male officers (8 percent) reported that their biggest problem as new patrol officers was harassment by other police officers. This harassment included displays of pornography, jokes or comments based on sexual stereotypes of women, and remarks on women's sexuality. Crawford and Stark-Adamec (1994) came to a similar conclusion in their study of 50 female and 68 male police officers and ex–police officers in four major Canadian police departments. Eighteen percent of the women in this study referred to sexually related problems on the job, including sexual harassment and sex discrimination. The performance of female police officers is often based on gender stereotypes, and as a result, they are snared by the perception that they are physically weak and a risk in physical confrontations; yet if they are strong and aggressive, they are perceived as an affront to the maleness of policemen (Charles 1982).

Aboriginal and Other Visible-Minority Police Officers

Visible minorities "are those persons (other than Aboriginal persons) who are non-Caucasian in race or non-white in colour" (Statistics Canada 1997, 5). Aboriginal persons are those "who reported identifying with at least one Aboriginal group, i.e., North American Indian, Métis or Inuit (Eskimo) and/or those who reported being a Treaty Indian or a Registered Indian as defined by the Indian Act of Canada and/or who were members of an Indian Band or First Nation" (ibid.). Little has been written about visible-minority and Aboriginal police officers in Canada, in part because so few have become police officers.

For example, in 1986, 645 sworn police officers in Canada were members of visible-minority or Aboriginal groups. That was 1.1 percent of all sworn officers in this country. At the time, most of them were in Ontario, where 395 officers—1.9 percent of all sworn police officers—belonged to a visible minority. There were no visible-minority officers in either Newfoundland or Prince Edward Island. By 1996, the number of visible-minority officers had grown to 1,725 (3 percent of all police officers in Canada). Of this total, 1,430 were males and 295 were females. At the same time, there were 1,785 Aboriginal police officers (3 percent of all sworn officers), of whom 1,430 were males and 355 were females. In 1989, the police force with the largest number of visible-minority officers was the Metropolitan Toronto Police Force, where 242 (or 4.2 percent) of all officers belonged to a visible minority. At that time, the population of the jurisdiction policed by the Toronto force was more than one million. In Toronto, the largest number of visible-minority officers were constables (195, or 4.7 percent of all constables), followed by sergeants (18, or 2.0 percent), staff sergeants (8, or 2.7 percent), inspectors (2, or 4.4 percent), and staff inspectors (1, or 3.0 percent) (Suriya 1993). In 1988, in the Sûreté du Québec there were no officers who represented "minority communities." In 1997, in the Montreal Community Police Department, 2 percent of police officers belonged to a visible minority (other than Aboriginal), 7.4 percent belonged to an ethnocultural group, and 0.2 percent were Aboriginal (Jaccoud and Felice 1999).

By 2001, the number of visible-minority police officers had risen to 2,775—a 38 percent increase over 1996, or 4 percent of all police officers. Of this total, 2,395 were males and 385 were females, representing increases of 40 and 24 percent, respectively. The number of Aboriginal police officers had also increased by 2001 over 1996. In 2001, there were 485 female Aboriginal police officers (a 27 percent increase from 1996) and 1,955 male Aboriginal police officers (a 9 percent increase) (Taylor-Butts 2004). By 2006, the number of minority police officers had risen to 6 percent of all police officers in Canada (Li, 2008).

The small number of visible minorities in Canadian police forces has been attributed to their restricted access to the law enforcement profession. Studies have found that unrelated job requirements have discouraged large numbers of visible minorities from applying to police forces across Canada (Jayewardene and Talbot 1990). For example, the debate over whether Sikh RCMP officers should be permitted to wear the turban as part of their uniform focused on the RCMP's traditions rather than on whether wearing a turban would interfere with the performance of duty. Hiring policies that create such obstacles for police officers are often viewed as a form of systemic discrimination,

since these policies place an arbitrary barrier between people's abilities and their employment opportunities (Abella 1984).

According to the Canadian Employment Equity Act, the goal of selecting the appropriate individual "has to be so structured as to increase the reliability of its objectivity" (Suriya 1993, 47). In his investigation of recruitment processes among Canadian police forces, Jain (1994) recommended that proactive recruitment methods be followed, such as community outreach programs. These programs would involve strategies such as providing visible-minority role models, training recruiters to seek out members of visible minorities, giving high-school presentations with visible-minority role models, and asking high-school teachers and others to identify potential visible-minority candidates. Jain also suggested that mental ability tests be reassessed, since these might be biased against women as well as those not raised in Canada (or North America). He also noted that interviews may be a questionable component of hiring processes, since they have relatively low reliability (different interviewers reach different conclusions) as well as low validity (interview ratings and job performance scores are not closely related); for these reasons, such assessments are "susceptible to the covert prejudices of individual interviewers" (ibid., 105). Interviews have also been criticized for being "not conducive to objective results" (Jayewardene and Talbot 1990, 6).

The Advisory Committee on Multicultural Police Recruitment and Selection of the Ottawa Police Force found that psychological tests, unless carefully reviewed, can easily result in "many areas where sexual, religious, and cultural assumptions . . . lead to misinterpretations of the responses." This committee also emphasized the importance of including an individual "with multicultural experience or training at the final interview as well as throughout [the] entire selection process." Wood (1989) reported that the Ontario Task Force on Race Relations and Policing found that members of visible minorities consider policing a dead-end job with few opportunities for promotion. This task force found that the "effective ceiling" for visible-minority promotions is the rank of staff sergeant. It also found that many visible-minority police officers had served for many years in the hope of attaining promotions "which have not been forthcoming."

Few researchers have studied racial-minority communities in Canada to ascertain what residents expect from the local police forces in terms of racial composition. One such study was Manitoba's Aboriginal Justice Inquiry; the authors of its report wrote that Aboriginal people "consider the police to be a foreign presence and do not feel understood by it. They certainly do not feel that the police operate on their behalf, or that the police are in any significant manner subject to a corresponding Aboriginal influence in their communities" (Hamilton and Sinclair 1991, 597). Because of these concerns, they recommended that police services in Aboriginal communities be delivered by professional regional Aboriginal police services that report to and service Aboriginal communities.

Many benefits have been associated with increasing the number of Aboriginal and other visible-minority officers serving with Canadian police services. These benefits extend to the police organization itself—the presence of such officers increases police effectiveness, prevents crime, and changes the image of the police among community members, especially young people (Jaccoud and Felices 1999).

THE POLICE AND PRIVATE SECURITY

One of the most interesting developments in policing over the past few decades has been the growth of the private-security sector (Cunningham and Taylor 1985; Shearing 1992; Shearing and Stenning 1981). The private-security sector was larger than the public-police sector throughout the 1990s. For example, in 2006 there were 62,400 police officers across Canada compared to 91,325 private security personnel and 10,200 private investigators. This reflected a 3 percent increase in the total number of police officers between 2001 and 2006 but a 15 percent increase in the private-security sector during those same years (Li 2008).

There are a number of differences between the public police and private security personnel. First, more women are employed in the private sector. In 2006, women comprised 1 in 4 of all private security guards, but only 1 in every 5 of all police officers. Second, a considerable age difference exists among individuals employed in the various sectors. A much higher percentage of private security personnel are under 25 or over 54 than in the police. Eighty-six percent of all police officers were between 25 and 55 in 2006, compared to 53 percent of security guards. Third, police officers are better educated than their private-sector counterparts. In 2006, 75 percent of police officers had at least some college certification, compared to 55 percent of private investigators and 37 percent of security guards. Fourth, more private-sector security guards are members of visible minorities. In 2006, 12 percent of private investigators and 21 percent of security guards belonged to a visible minority group, compared to 6 percent of all police officers. Finally, police earn

significantly higher incomes than private security personnel. In 2006, the average salary of police officers across Canada was $73,582, more than twice what security guards made and about 33 percent more than what private investigators made (Li 2008).

One of the major differences between the police and both private investigators and private security guards relates to how they are regulated. The police are accountable to the state, with the provincial and/or federal governments determining the appropriate standards, including training and employment requirements. Also, police are held accountable for their actions through various laws, such as the Charter of Rights and Freedoms, as well as through police commissions, external review boards, internal affairs divisions, and criminal and civil litigation. The governance of private security is very different throughout Canada. While every jurisdiction in the country (except the Northwest Territories and Nunavut) has its own legislation relating to private security, the standards vary between each jurisdiction. For example, only three provinces (British Columbia, Saskatchewan, and Newfoundland and Labrador) require applicants to meet minimum training requirements (Taylor-Butts 2004).

Private police forces are found in a number of places, including shopping centres, industrial facilities, banks, and a variety of corporations. Most of this work is visible: personnel wear distinctive uniforms, and they either are posted at a conspicuous location in a building or walk around a specific perimeter. Other security personnel work undercover. Some organizations hire them to work alongside regular employees in an attempt to uncover criminal activity. In addition, they monitor hidden surveillance cameras placed in employee work and rest areas in an attempt to detect employee wrongdoing.

How did private policing and security forces become such a major force? As early as 1972, governments in North America were interested in the growth of private security. That year, the first study of this sector commissioned by a federal government was released. The U.S. Department of Justice had commissioned the Rand Corporation to investigate private policing (Kakalik and Wildhorn 1972). The report identified private security as an "industry" that provides a "service" to the public. It referred to private policing as an "asset" that was "making a significant contribution to the American economy" and relieving taxpayers of some of the substantial costs involved in public policing.

More than ten years later, another significant research project investigated the growth of private security forces. This one, funded by the American government and conducted by the Hallcrest Corporation, examined the growth of and issues raised by the private police forces that had emerged since the Rand study. The report's authors stated that by 1985, "Americans will easily spend $20 billion per year for products and services to protect themselves—more than they'll spend to support all enforcement agencies (federal, state, local) in the United States" (Cunningham and Taylor 1985, 163).

In discussing why private police forces had grown so dramatically, the report's authors made three key points. First, there had been a profound structural change in contemporary society relating to the expansion of enclosed, private industries and developments. These places required security, and security was increasingly being provided by private police forces (while public places continued to be patrolled by public police forces). Second, much of the resistance to private policing stemmed from concerns expressed by the public police, largely to do with the loss of personnel. Third and finally, private security agencies "police" areas and conduct themselves in ways that are outside the realm of public police forces (Shearing 1992). In Canada, a report for the Solicitor General of Canada by Normandeau and Leighton (1990) recommended that Canadian policing policy include "new strategic partnerships" to integrate all types of policing in order to better preserve the peace in communities.

Some argue that private security is growing and public policing is declining largely because citizens have doubts about the ability of public forces to protect them and their property. These doubts have generated a number of related issues. For example, Reiss (1988) and Moore (1992) argue that growth in private policing can lead to (1) a distribution of security based on who can afford it, (2) less respect for the rights of those detained, and (3) lower levels of professional competence.

Another concern is that many criminal offences uncovered by the private police are not being referred to the public system. Many are dealt with privately, outside the protections guaranteed to citizens by the Charter of Rights and Freedoms. This public–private split has led to concerns that two criminal justice systems may soon be operating at the same time, one public and the other private. Will the private system be as concerned about the rights and protections of the public as the public system is? (Cunningham et al. 1990)

CRITICAL ISSUES IN CANADIAN CRIMINAL JUSTICE

ARE TASERS LETHAL OR NON-LETHAL USES OF FORCE?

On October 14, 2007, four RCMP officers in Richmond, B.C., responded to a dispatcher's call about a man said to be intoxicated and throwing objects and breaking glass at the Vancouver International Airport. Police arrived on the scene at 1:28 a.m., and two minutes later it was reported that a male "had been Tasered" (Hume and Dhillon 2007, A1). The male in question was Robert Dziekanski, 40, who had just spent more than 14 hours travelling to Canada to begin a new life with his mother, who lives in Kamloops. He had waited ten hours for his mother at the airport, but they never met. After being Tasered, he died of cardiac arrest.

When the police arrived at the airport, Mr. Dziekanski had a stapler in his hand and was in a "combative posture." No officer asked him to put down the stapler. One officer was armed with a Taser, and he used the device on the orders of the senior officer present. Mr. Dziekanski was subjected to five Taser blasts, tackled, and handcuffed. Three of the Tasers were fired by the RCMP officer in a "probe-mode" fashion where wires projected from the weapon apply electrical current, and twice in a "push stun mode" where the device causes localized pain. The Taser was used for a total of 31 seconds (Bailey and Alphonso, 2008, A6). The cause of his death was listed as "sudden death following restraint." On December 12, 2008, the British Columbia Criminal Justice Branch announced the results of its investigation, stating that there would be no charges laid against any of the four RCMP officers.

One of the key factors in the investigation was whether or not Mr. Dziekanski was experiencing "excited delirium." Medical examiners investigating Taser-related deaths have attributed some of these deaths to excited delirium, which they term a supposed overdose of adrenaline that can occur in heated confrontations with the police. Not everyone agrees that excited delirium is an actual medical condition, but it has been listed as the cause of death in some situations, particularly when the suspect was determined to be under the influence of stimulants (DiMaio and DiMaio 2005).

This issue of excited delirium was raised both prior to and after the inquiry into Mr. Dziekanski's death. An expert investigating his death prior to the inquiry concluded that the victim was in a state of delirium cased by "possible alcohol withdrawal, dehydration and a lack of sleep"

(Bailey 2009, A6). During the inquiry, another expert witness, a psychiatrist and expert in delirium hired by homicide investigators looking into the death of Mr. Dziekanski, testified that the victim was in a state of "agitated delirium" just before he was shot with the Taser. In his report, he stated that while he couldn't determine the cause of the delirium, Mr. Dziekanski's behaviour could have been the result of "alcohol and nicotine withdrawal, dehydration and exhaustion from lack of sleep . . . " (Mertl 2009, A14). This assessment was countered by the testimony of a forensic psychiatrist, who stated that the victim was "a very angry, overly stressed-out traveler." He found Mr. Dziekanski to be "responsive to his environment" and acted "in way that in my mind rules out delirium but certainly indicates he was in a highly stressed and agitated state" (ibid.).

According to the police, medical evidence shows that, without Tasers, "prolonged and dangerous struggles occur with people from what they term 'excited delirium'" (Leeder and Alphonso 2007, A1). However, the medical pathologist who conducted the autopsy ruled delirium out as the cause of death. In Mr. Dziekanski's case, various factors could have contributed to the heart attack that killed the 40-year-old immigrant. These factors included "heart disease associated with chronic alcohol abuse, an agitated state of delirium and an inability to breathe while being restrained" (Bailey and Alphonso 2008, A6).

According to an Amnesty International report, the number of Taser-related deaths is over 150 in the U.S. Other estimates put the number of deaths at over 290 since 2001 (Hume and Bailey 2008). It is estimated that the number of Taser-related deaths in Canada exceed 20. In its defence, Taser International states that its weapon has not caused any deaths. Some individuals have disputed Amnesty's findings, arguing that other factors besides just Tasers were responsible for suspect deaths in these cases, but this has not stopped police agencies, medical examiners, and researchers from calling for guidelines on the use of Tasers. According to Julian Fantino, the Commissioner of the Ontario Provincial Police, there are 150 studies worldwide showing "there is no direct link in any case where a Taser has been deployed . . . to the demise of any individual" ("Tasers Are . . . " 2009, A6).

The Chairman of Commission for Public Complaints Against the RCMP, Paul Kennedy,

released a report in 2007 reviewing the use of Tasers by the RCMP. He wrote that there had been "usage creep" of the multiple shots from these weapons by members over the years since they introduced in 2001, when they were approved for use against individuals who resisted arrest, were combative, or suicidal. Over time, Mr. Kennedy noted, Tasers were deployed "outside stated objectives . . . where individuals have exhibited behaviours that were clearly non-combative or where there was no active resistance" (Bailey 2007, A8). Just three months before Mr. Dziekanski was Tasered, the RCMP changed a protocol that allowed its officers to fire multiple shocks to control people under certain circumstances. In addition, the percentage of cases in which RCMP officers fired their Tasers more than once rose from 31 percent in 2002 to over 45 percent in 2007. Mr. Kennedy also stated that officers should have clearer directions on how and when Tasers should be used (Bailey and Bronskill 2008).

On February 13, 2009, the Commissioner of the RCMP, William Elliott, announced a new RCMP policy on the use of Tasers. "We've now made it very clear that the only time the use of a Taser can be justified is where there is a threat, either to our officers or to members of the public" (LeBlanc 2009, A4). Mr. Elliott acknowledged that in circumstances involving agitated individuals, the risks associated with Tasers can increase dramatically.

In order for police officers to better use Tasers, the Police Executive Research Forum in the United States has developed a number of recommendations for the appropriate use of Tasers and related CEDs, including the following:

- CEDs should only be used against persons who are actively resisting or exhibiting active aggression, or to prevent individuals from harming themselves or others. CEDs should not be used against a passive suspect.
- No more than one officer at a time should activate a CED against a person.
- When activating a CED, a law enforcement officer should use it for one standard cycle and stop to evaluate the situation (a standard cycle is five seconds). If subsequent cycles are necessary, agency policy should restrict the number and duration of those cycles to the minimum activations necessary to place the subject in custody.
- Training protocols should emphasize the multiple activations and continuous cycling of

Continued on next page

- a CED appear to increase the risk of death or serious injury and should be avoided when practical.
- Training should include recognizing the limitations of CED activation and being prepared to transition to other force options as needed (Cronin and Ederheimer 2006).

Questions

1. Do you agree with the RCMP's course of action in their dealing with Robert Dziekanski? Why or why not? Are there any other ways in which this situation could have been handled?
2. Tasers have proven to de-escalate many situations that may have led to a public or police officer fatality. Should the safety of the public and the police be prioritized over that of a suspect?
3. The Police Executive Research Forum in the United States has developed new policies

regarding the use of Tasers by the police. Some police services in that country have adopted some or all of these recommendations. Should Canada adopt similar policies? Why or why not?

4. Should there be stronger restrictions placed on police officers surrounding their use of Tasers? What restrictions do you believe should be implemented, if any?
5. Many potential offenders that the police come into contact with suffer from behavioural and/or mental health issues (e.g., addictions). These can increase their likelihood of suffering from "excited delirium" by making them appear to be non-compliant, thereby increasing the likelihood that the police use a Taser. In these situations, what could be done to lessen the use of Tasers in these cases by the police?

SUMMARY

Police forces and their officers today are facing many important issues as they develop policies, enforce the law, and interact with the public. One central issue involves finding effective ways to measure the overall effectiveness of the police. Some people contend that the police should arrest an individual whenever there is enough evidence, regardless of the infraction. This move toward a policy of zero tolerance has led to a debate over police discretion. Studies of the arrest practices of the police in Canada indicate that the police do not "over-arrest" members of any particular group, and also that situational and community factors play a key role in the decisions made by the police. Social issues also affect police operations.

Women and minority group members are entering police ranks in increasing numbers, and research indicates that their performance is as good as or even better

than that of other police officers. However, the percentages of women and minority group members on police forces still fall short of their percentages of the population as a whole. As their numbers increase, another important issue is sure to emerge—the number of women and people from minorities in the higher echelons of police departments.

Other critical issues are police use of deadly force and police deviance. While studies of deadly force are few, it is known that Canadian police rarely kill citizens. More information is available on police deviance. Recent initiatives by the Province of Ontario indicate that many citizens have concerns about the police overextending their powers in their contacts with citizens. Questions about the role of private security agencies have become more frequent as these agencies become more visible and as their activities appear—at least according to some Canadians—to overlap more and more with those of the public police.

Discussion Questions

1. What are some possible negative and positive consequences of the police use of discretion?
2. Why is it difficult to formulate a clear policy to guide decision-making by police officers?
3. Why were women and minority group members prevented from joining police forces throughout most of the twentieth century in Canada? Compare the Canadian experience to that of the United States. Are there any differences?
4. How do police officers' attitudes affect their performance?
5. Are women as effective as men in all types of police work? Why or why not?
6. Discuss why the police in Canada use deadly force less often than their counterparts in the United States.
7. Do you think that police deviance is as serious a problem as it was ten or more years ago?
8. What measure is the best indicator of police performance in crime control?
9. What should be the role of the private police in Canada?
10. Should the private police have the same form of governance as the public police in Canada?

Suggested Readings

Forcese, Dennis P. *Policing Canadian Society*. Scarborough, ON: Prentice-Hall, 1992.

Landau, Tammy. *Public Complaints against the Police: A View from Complainants*. Toronto: Centre of Criminology, University of Toronto, 1994.

MacLeod, R.C., and D. Schneiderman, eds. *Police Powers in Canada: The Evolution and Practice of Authority*. Toronto: University of Toronto Press, 1994.

Marquis, G. *Policing Canada's First Century: A History of the Canadian Association of Chiefs of Police*. Toronto: Osgoode Hall Law Society, 1993.

Northup, D.A. *Public Perceptions of Police Treatment of Minority Groups and the Disadvantaged in Metropolitan Toronto*. North York, ON: Institute for Social Research, York University, 1996.

References

Abell, J., and E. Sheehy, eds. 1993. *Criminal Law and Procedure: Cases, Context, Critique*. North York, ON: Captus Press.

Abella, R.S. 1984. *Report of the Commission on Equality in Employment*. Ottawa: Supply and Services Canada.

Abraham, J.D., J.C. Feld, R.W. Harding, and S. Skura. 1981. "Police Use of Lethal Force: A Toronto Perspective." *Osgoode Hall Law Journal* 19: 199–236.

Albanese, J. 1999. *Criminal Justice*. Boston: Allyn and Bacon.

Alberts, S. 2000. "Motorists Face Stiff Penalties for Fleeing Police." *National Post*, February 8, A6.

Alpert, G.P., R.G. Dunham and M.R. Smith. 2007. "Investigating Racial Profiling by the Miami-Dade Police Department: A Multimethod Approach." *Criminology and Public Policy* 6: 671–78.

Alpert, G.P., and T. Madden. 1994. "Police Pursuit Driving: An Empirical Analysis of Critical Decisions." *American Journal of Police* 13: 23–45.

Appleby, T., T.T. Ha, and R. Thomas. 1999. "Police-Chase Deaths Prompt Calls for Action." *The Globe and Mail*, March 24, A3.

Ash, P., K.P. Slora, and C.F. Britton. 1990. "Police Agency Selection Practices." *Journal of Police Science and Administration* 17: 258–69.

Bailey, I. 2009. "Mounties Regarded Stapler as a Weapon." *The Globe and Mail*, February 25, A6.

———. 2007. "Tasers Have Role in Policing, RCMP Watchdog Says." *The Globe and Mail*, December 13, A8.

Bailey, I., and C. Alphonso. 2008. "Airport Death Not Caused by Tasers, B.C. Says." *The Globe and Mail*, December 13, A6.

Bailey, S., and J. Bronskill. 2008. "RCMP Plans to Curb Taser Use in Face of Pressure." *The Globe and Mail*, June 19, A3.

Balkin, J. 1988. "Why Policemen Don't Like Policewomen." *Journal of Police Science and Administration* 16: 29–38.

Barker, T., and D.L. Carter. 1986. *Police Deviance*. Cincinnati, OH: Anderson.

Bayley, D.H., and J. Garofalo. 1989. "The Management of Violence by Police Patrol Officers." *Criminology* 27: 1–21.

Bell, S. 1999. "RCMP Watchdog Wants Police Chases Only in Serious Cases." *National Post*, December 14, A4.

Bennett, R.S., and T. Greenstein. 1975. "The Police Personality: A Test of the Predispositional Model." *Journal of Police Science and Administration* 3: 439–45.

Berenson, A. 2004. "As Police Use of Tasers Rises, Questions over Safety Increase." *New York Times*, July 18, 1, 22.

Bienvenue, R., and A.H. Latif. 1974. "Arrests, Dispositions, and Recidivism: A Comparison of Indians and Whites." *Canadian Journal of Criminology and Corrections* 16: 105–16.

Bittner, E. 1974. "Florence Nightingale in Pursuit of Willie Sutton: A Theory of the Police." In H. Jacobs, ed., *Potential of Reforming Criminal Justice*. Beverley Hills, CA: Sage, pp. 233–61.

Black, D. 1980. "The Social Organization of Arrest." In D. Black, *The Manners and Customs of the Police*. New York: Academic Press.

Borovoy, A. Alan. 2000. "Who Will Police the Police?" *National Post*, June 6, A9.

Brannigan, A. 1984. *Crimes, Courts, and Corrections: An Introduction to Crime and Social Control in Canada*. Toronto: Holt, Rinehart and Winston.

Britz, M., and D. Payne. 1994. "Policy Implications for Law Enforcement Pursuit Driving." *American Journal of Police* 13: 13–42.

Brown, J. 1994. "The Plight of Female Police: A Survey of North West Patrolmen." *Police Chief*, September: 50–53.

Brown, L., and C. Brown. 1978. *An Unauthorized History of the RCMP*, 2nd ed. Toronto: Lewis and Samuel.

Brown, M.K. 1988. *Working the Street: Police Discretion and the Dilemma of Reform* (2nd ed.) New York: Russell Sage Foundation.

Bureau of Justice Statistics. 2000. *Local Police Departments*. Washington, DC.

Callahan, C., and W. Anderson. 2001. "The Roots of Racial Profiling." *Reason* 33, no. 4: 36–43.

Canadian Centre for Justice Statistics. 1982. *Homicides of Police Officers in Canada.* Ottawa: Statistics Canada.

Carter, D.L., A.D. Sapp, and D.W. Stephens. 1988. "Higher Education as a Bona Fide Occupational Qualification (BFOQ) for Police: A Blueprint." *Policing: An International Journal of Police Strategies and Management* 7, no. 2: 1–27.

Chappell, A., J.M. MacDonald, and P.W. Manz. 2006. "The Organizational Characteristics of Police Arrest Decisions." Crime *and Delinquency* 52: 287–306.

Chappell, D., and L. Graham. 1985. *Police Use of Deadly Force: Canadian Perspectives.* Toronto: Centre of Criminology.

Charles, M. 1982. "Women in Policing: The Physical Aspects." *Journal of Police Science and Administration* 10: 194–205.

Choudhry, S. 2001. "Protecting Equality in the Face of Terror: Ethnic and Racial Profiling and s. 15 of the *Charter*." In R.J. Daniels, P. Macklem, and K. Roach, eds., *The Security of Freedom: Essays on Canada's Anti-Terrorism Bill.* Toronto: University of Toronto Press, pp. 367–81.

Cochrane, R., and A.J.P. Butler. 1980. "The Values of Police Officers, Recruits, and Civilians in England." *Journal of Police Science and Administration* 8: 205–11.

Crank, J. 1997. *Understanding Police Culture.* Cincinnati, OH: Anderson.

Crawford, B., and C. Stark-Adamec. 1994. "Women in Canadian Urban Policing: Why Are They Leaving?" In N. Larsen, ed., *The Canadian Criminal Justice System: An Issues Approach to the Administration of Justice.* Toronto: Canadian Scholars' Press.

Cronin, J.M., and J.A. Ederheimer. 2006. *Conducted Energy Devices: Development of Standards for Consistency and Guidance.* Washington, D.C.: Police Executive Research Forum.

Cunningham, W.C., J.J. Strauchs, and C.W. Van Meter. 1990. *Private Security Trends 1970 to the Year 2000: The Hallcrest Report II.* Boston: Butterworth Heinemann.

Cunningham, W.C., and T.H. Taylor. 1985. *The Hallcrest Report: Private Security and Police in America.* Portland, OR: Chancellor.

De Lisi, M., and B. Regoli. 1999. "Race, Conventional Crime and Criminal Justice: The Declining Importance of Skin Color." *Journal of Criminal Justice* 27: 549–57.

DiMaio, T.G., and V.J.M. DiMaio. 2005. *Excited Delirium Syndrome: Cause of Death and Prevention,* Boca Raton, FL: CRC Press.

Eitle, D., L. Stolzenberg, and S.J. D'Alessio. 2005. "Police Organizational Factors, the Racial Composition of the Police, and the Probability of Arrest." *Justice Quarterly* 22: 30–57.

Ellis, D., and W. DeKeseredy. 1996. *The Wrong Stuff: An Introduction to the Sociological Study of Deviance,* 2nd ed. Scarborough, ON: Allyn and Bacon.

Ericson, R.V. 1982. *Reproducing Order: A Study of Police Patrol Work.* Toronto: University of Toronto Press.

Falcone, D. 1994. "Police Officers and Officer Attitudes: Myths and Realities." *American Journal of Police* 13: 143–55.

Finn, P. 2000. *Citizen Review of Police: Approach and Implementation.* Washington, DC: Government Printing Office.

Fleming, T. 1981. "The Bawdy House 'Boys': Some Notes on Media, Sporadic Moral Crusades, and Selective Law Enforcement." *Canadian Criminology Forum:* 101–15.

Forcese, D. 1999. *Policing Canadian Society,* 2nd ed. Scarborough, ON: Prentice-Hall Allyn and Bacon Canada.

————. 1992. *Policing Canadian Society*. Scarborough, ON: Prentice-Hall.

Fyfe, J.J. 1988. "Police Use of Deadly Force: Research and Reform." *Justice Quarterly* 5: 165–205.

Gatehouse, J., and C. Eby. 2000. "Rape Victim and Family Sue Toronto Police Force for $4.5 Million." *National Post*, October 12, A9.

Geller, W.A., and M.S. Scott. 1991. "Deadly Force: What We Know." In C.B. Klockars and S.D. Mastrofski, eds., *Thinking About Police*. New York: McGraw-Hill, pp. 446–76.

Goldstein, H. 1977. *Policing a Free Society*. Cambridge, MA: Ballinger.

Goldstein, J. 1960. "Police Discretion Not to Invoke the Criminal Justice Process: Low Visibility Decisions in the Administration of Justice." *Yale Law Journal* 69: 543–94.

Gould, J., and S. Mastrofski. 2004. "Suspect Searches: Assessing Police Behavior under the U.S. Constitution." *Criminology and Public Policy* 3: 315–62.

Gunn, R., and C. Minch. 1988. *Sexual Assault: The Dilemma of Disclosure and the Question of Conviction*. Winnipeg: University of Manitoba.

Hagan, J. 1977. *The Disreputable Pleasures*. Toronto: McGraw-Hill Ryerson.

Hale, D.C., and S.M. Wyland. 1993. "Dragons and Dinosaurs: The Plight of Patrol Women." *Police Forum* 3: 1–6.

Hamilton, A.C., and C.M. Sinclair. 1991. *The Justice System and Aboriginal People: Report of the Aboriginal Justice Inquiry of Manitoba, Volume 1*. Winnipeg: Queen's Printer.

Havemann, P., K. Couse, L. Foster, and R. Mantonovitch. 1985. *Law and Order for Canada's Indigenous People*. Regina: Prairie Justice Research, University of Regina, School of Human Justice.

Holdaway, S., and S.K. Parker. 1998. "Policing Women Police: Uniform Patrol, Promotion and Representation in the CID." *British Journal of Criminology* 38: 40–48.

Hume, M., and I. Bailey. 2008. "Police across Country Checking Tasers' Safety." *The Globe and Mail*, December 10, A4.

Hume, M., and S. Dhillon. 2007. "He Spent 10 Hours Frustrated by Airport Bureaucracy. Just 24 Seconds Later, Police Shot Him with Tasers." *The Globe and Mail*, October 26, 2007, A1, A15.

Hunt, J.C. 1990. "The Logic of Sexism among the Police." *Women and Criminal Justice* 1: 3–30.

Jaccoud, M., and M. Felice. 1999. "Ethnicization of the Police in Canada." *Canadian Journal of Law and Society* 14, no. 1 (Spring): 83–100.

Jain, H.C. 1994. "An Assessment of Strategies of Recruiting Visible-Minority Police Officers in Canada: 1985–1990." In R.C. Macleod and D. Schneiderman, eds., *Police Powers in Canada: The Evolution and Practice of Authority*, pp. 138–64.

Jamieson, S. 1973. *Industrial Relations*, 2nd ed. Toronto: Macmillan.

Jayewardene, C.H.S., and C.K. Talbot. 1990. *Police Recruitment of Ethnic Minorities*. Canadian Police College.

Kakalik, J.S., and S. Wildhorn. 1972. *Private Security in the United States*. Washington, DC: U.S. Department of Justice, National Institute of Law Enforcement and Criminal Justice, Law Enforcement Assistance Administration.

Kania, R.R.E., and W.C. Mackey. 1977. "Police Violence as a Function of Community Characteristics." *Criminology* 15: 27–48.

Kari, S. 2004. "Police Used Profiling, Judge Says." *National Post*, September 17, A4.

Kershaw, S. 2004. "As Shocks Replace Police Bullets, Deaths Fall but Questions Grow." *New York Times*, March 7, 1, 14.

Klinger, D.A. 1994. "Demeanor of Crime: Why 'Hostile' Citizens are More Likely to Be Arrested." *Criminology* 32: 475–93.

Krimmel, J. 1996. "The Performance of College-Educated Police: A Study of Self-Rated Police Performance Measures." *American Journal of Police* 15: 85–95.

Laghi, B. 2000. "Bill Gets Tough with Those Who Flee Police." *The Globe and Mail*, February 8, A9.

Landau, T. 1996. "When Police Investigate Police: A View from the Complainants." *Canadian Journal of Criminology:* 291–315.

———. 1994. *Public Complaints against the Police: A View from Complainants.* Toronto: Centre of Criminology, University of Toronto.

Langworthy, R.H. 1987. "Police Cynicism: What We Know from the Niederhoffer Scale." *Journal of Police Science and Administration* 11: 457–62.

Leblanc, D. 2009. "Acknowledging High Risk of Death, RCMP Revamps Rules for Taser Use." *The Globe and Mail*, February 13, A4.

Leeder, J., and C. Alphonoso. 2007. "RCMP Revised Taser Policy to Allow Multiple Jolts." *The Globe and Mail*, November 24, 2007, A1, A9.

Lersch, K., and S.T. Mieczkowski. 1996. "Who Are the Problem Prone Police?" An Analysis of Citizen Complaints." *American Journal of Police* 15: 23–42.

Lewis, C. (chair). 1989. *The Report of the Race Relations and Policing Task Force.* Toronto: Solicitor General.

Li, G. 2008. *Private Security and Public Policing.* Ottawa: Canadian Centre for Justice Statistics.

———. 2007. *Homicide in Canada, 2006.* Ottawa: Canadian Centre for Justice Statistics.

Makin, K. 2003. "Police Use Racial Profiling, Appeal Court Concludes." *The Globe and Mail*, April 17, A1, A6.

Manning, P. 1995. "The Police Organizational Culture in Anglo-American Societies." In W. Bailey, ed., *Encyclopedia of Police Science.* New York: Garland.

Martin, D. 1993. "Organizing for Change: A Community Law Response to Police Misconduct." *Hastings Women's Law Journal* 4: 131–74.

Martin, S.E. 1991. "The Effectiveness of Affirmative Action: The Case of Women in Policing." *Justice Quarterly* 8: 489–504.

McGahan, P. 1984. *Police Images of a City.* New York: Peter Lang.

McKenna, P.F. 2002. *Police Powers I.* Toronto: Pearson Education Canada.

McMahon, M. 1988. "Police Accountability: The Situation of Complaints in Toronto." *Contemporary Crises* 12: 301–27.

Meagher, M.S. 1983. *Perception of the Police Patrol Function: Does Officer Education Make a Difference?* Paper presented at the annual meeting of the Academy of Criminal Justice Sciences, San Antonio, TX.

Mertl, S. 2009. "Dziekanski Was Angry, Not Delirious." *The Globe and Mail*, May 22, A14.

Minister of Industry. 2008. *Police Resources in Canada, 2007.* Ottawa: Minister of Industry.

Mitchell, L.P. 1990. "High Speed Pursuits." *Criminal Justice: The Americas*, vol. 2. January.

Mitchell, T. 2002. "One Judge: Two Cases about Bias." *LawNow* 26, 5: 8.

Moore, L. 2000. "Police Who Beat Man into Coma Should Keep Jobs, Judge Says." *National Post*, March 8, A5.

Moore, M.H. 1992. "Problem-Solving and Community Policing." In M. Tonry and N. Morris, eds., *Modern Policing*. Chicago: University of Chicago Press, pp. 90–158.

Mosher, C. 1998. *Discrimination and Denial: Systematic Racism in Ontario's Legal and Criminal Justice System, 1891–1961*. Toronto: University of Toronto Press.

Muir, W.K. 1977. *Police: Streetcorner Politicians*. Chicago: University of Chicago Press.

Murrell, D.B. 1982. "The Influence of Education on Police Work Performance." Unpublished doctoral dissertation, Florida State University, Tallahassee.

Niederhoffer, A. 1967. *Behind the Shield: The Police in Urban Society*. Garden City, NY: Anchor Books.

Normandeau, A. 1990. "The Police and Ethnic Minorities." *Canadian Police College Journal* 14: 215–29.

Normandeau, A., and B. Leighton. 1990. *A Vision of the Future of Policing in Canada: Police Challenge 2000*. Ottawa: Solicitor General of Canada.

Ontario Commission on Systemic Racism in the Ontario Criminal Justice System. 1995. *Report of the Commission on Systemic Racism in the Ontario Criminal Justice System*. Toronto: Queen's Printer.

Padavic, I., and B.F. Reskin. 1990. "Men's Behaviour and Women's Interest in Blue-Collar Jobs." *Social Problems* 37: 613–27.

Parent, R.B., and S. Verdun-Jones. 1998. "Victim-Precipitated Homicide: Police Use of Deadly Force in British Columbia." *Policing: An International Journal of Police Strategies & Management* 21: 432–48.

Peritz, I. 2000. "Montrealers Aghast at Barnabe Ruling." *The Globe and Mail*, March 9, A3.

Petersen, C. 1982. "Doing Time with the Boys: An Analysis of Women Correctional Officers in All-Male Facilities." In B.R. Price and N.J. Sokoloff, eds., *The Criminal Justice System and Women*. New York: Clark Boardman.

Picard, A. 1997. "A Community Makes Up for Lost Time." *The Globe and Mail*, November 4, A2.

Rafky, D.M., T. Lawley, and R. Ingram. 1976. "Are Police Recruits Cynical?" *Journal of Police Science and Administration* 4: 352–60.

Regoli, R.M. 1977. *Police in America*. Washington, DC: R.F. Publishing.

Regoli, R.M., R. Culbertson, J. Crank, and J. Powell. 1990. "Career Stage and Cynicism among Police Chiefs." *Justice Quarterly* 7: 592–614.

Regoli, R.M., and E.D. Poole. 1979. "Measurement of Police Cynicism: A Factor Scaling Approach." *Journal of Criminal Justice* 7: 37–52.

Regoli, R.M., E.D. Poole, and J.D. Hewitt. 1979. "Refining Police Cynicism Theory: An Empirical Assessment, Evaluation, and Implications." In D.M. Peterson, ed., *Police Work: Strategies and Outcomes in Law Enforcement*. Beverly Hills, CA: Sage, pp. 59–68.

Reiss, A.J. 1988. *Private Employment of Public Police*. Washington, D.C.: U.S. Department of Justice, National Institute of Justice.

———. 1974. "Discretionary Justice." In D. Glaser, ed., *Handbook of Criminology*. Chicago: Rand McNally.

Roach, K. 1999. *Due Process and Victims' Rights: The New Law and Politics of Criminal Justice*. Toronto: University of Toronto Press.

Roberg, R.R. 1978. "An Analysis of the Relationship among Higher Education, Belief Systems, and Job Performance of Police Officers." *Journal of Police Science and Administration*, 6–44.

Roberg, R.R., and J. Kuykendall. 1993. *Police and Society*. Belmont, CA: Wadsworth.

Rodriquez, M.L. 1995. "Increasing Importance of Higher Education in Police Human Resource Development Programs." *Criminal Justice: The Americas*, vol. 8 (April–May): 1–9.

Sallot, J. 2006. "How Canada Failed Citizen Maher Arar." *The Globe and Mail*, September 19, A1, A10.

Sanders, B., T. Hughes, and R.H. Langworthy. 1995. "Police Officer Recruitment and Selection: A Survey of Major Police Departments in the U.S." *Police Forum* 5: 1–4.

Sauve, J. and J. Reitano. 2005. *Police Resources in Canada, 2005*. Ottawa: Ministry of Industry.

Schafer, J., D. Carter, and A. Katz-Bannister. 2004. "Studying Traffic Stop Encounters." *Journal of Criminal Justice* 32, 159-170.

Senna, J.J., and L.J. Siegel. 1995. *Essentials of Criminal Justice*. Minneapolis: West.

Shearing, C. 1992. "The Relations between Public and Private Policing." In M. Tonry and N. Morris, eds., *Modern Policing*. Chicago: University of Chicago Press, pp. 399–434.

Shearing, C., and P. Stenning. 1981. "Modern Private Policing." In M. Tonry and N. Morris, eds., *Crime and Justice: An Annual Review of Research*, vol. 3. Chicago: University of Chicago Press, pp. 193–245.

Sherman, L.W. 1977. *Police Corruption: A Sociological Perspective*. Garden City, NY: Doubleday.

Sherman, L.W., and E.G. Cohen. 1986. *Citizens Killed by Big-City Police: 1974–1984*. Washington, DC: Crime Control Institute.

Sherman, L.W., and R.H. Langworthy. 1979. "Measuring Homicide by Police Officers." *Journal of Criminal Law and Criminology* 70: 546–60.

Skogan , W., and S.M. Hartnett. 1997. *Community Policing: Chicago Style*. New York: Oxford University Press.

Skolnick, J. 1994. *Justice without Trial*, 3rd ed. New York: Macmillan.

———. 1966. *Justice without Trial*. New York: Wiley.

Skolnick, J., and J. Fyfe. 1993. *Above the Law: Police and the Excessive Use of Force*. New York: Free Press.

Smith, A.B., B. Locke, and A. Fenster. 1969. "Authoritarianism in Police College Students and Non-Police." *Journal of Criminal Law, Criminology, and Police Science* 58: 440–43.

Smith, D.A., C.A. Visher, and L.A. Davidson. 1984. "Equity and Discretionary Justice: The Influence of Race on Police Arrest Decisions." *Journal of Criminal Law and Criminology* 75: 234–49.

Sokoloff, H. 2001. "Domestic Violence Victim Loses Suit against the RCMP." *National Post*, June 6, A9.

Sparrow, M., M. Moore, and D. Kennedy. 1990. *Beyond 911: A New Era for Policing*. New York: Basic Books.

Spillar, K. 2000. *Gender Differences and the Cost of Police Brutality and Misconduct*. Los Angeles: National Center for Women and Policing.

Stansfield, R.T. 2000. "Use of Force By and Against Canadian Police." In J.V. Roberts, ed., *Criminal Justice in Canada: A Reader*. Toronto: Harcourt Brace and Company Canada, pp. 70–76.

———. 1996. *Issues in Policing: A Canadian Perspective*. Toronto: Thompson Educational Publishing.

Statistics Canada. 1997. *1996 Census Dictionary.* Ottawa: Industry Canada.

Suriya, S.K. 1993. "The Representation of Visible Minorities in Canadian Police: Employment Equity beyond Rhetoric." *Police Studies* 16: 44–62.

"Tasers Are an Essential Tool that Saves Lives, Police Say." *The Globe and Mail,* February 25, 2009, A6.

Taylor-Butts, A. 2004. *Private Security and Public Policing in Canada, 2001.* Ottawa: Canadian Centre for Justice Statistics.

Thompson, E. 2005. "Police Outfight Racial Profiling in their Ranks." *National Post,* March 25, A5.

Tranh Ha, T. 1999. "Quebec Police Officers Guilty of Falsifying Evidence." *The Globe and Mail,* December 23, A3.

U.S. Commission on Civil Rights. 1981. *Who Is Guarding the Guardians?* Washington, DC: U.S. Commission on Civil Rights.

Van Maanen, J. 1974. "Working the Streets: A Developmental View of Police Behavior." In H. Jacobs, ed., *Potential for Reforming Criminal Justice.* Beverly Hills, CA: pp. 83–130.

Waddington. P.A.J. 1999. "Police (Canteen) Sub-Culture: An Appreciation." *British Journal of Criminology* 39: 287–309.

Walker, S. 2001. *Police Accountability: The Role of Citizen Oversight.* Belmont, CA: Wadsworth.

Wells, J. 2000. "The Watchdogs." *Toronto Life* 34, no. 16: 114–22.

Wilson, O.W., and R.C. McLaren. 1977. *Police Administration.* New York: McGraw-Hill.

Wood, C. 1989. "Police: A Call for Racial Balance." *Toronto Star,* April 12, A22.

Court Cases

Beare v. R. (1988), 1 S.C.R. 525, 68 C.R. (3d) 193

R. v. Andrews (1989), 56 D.L.R. (4th) 1

R. v. Deane (1997), O.J. No. 3057 (Prov. Ct.) (Q.L.)

R. v. Lines (1993), O.J. No. 3248 (Gen. Div.)

R. v. Mack (1988), 44 C.C.C. (3d) 513

R. v. Turpin (1989), 48 C.C.C. (3d) 8

Weblinks

To read the decisions made by the Supreme Court of Canada in *R. v. Beare* and *R. v. Mack,* go to http://scc.lexum.umontreal.ca/en/index.html. Click on "1988" and then on Volume 2. Both decisions can be found in the same volume number for that year. Beare was announced on December 1, *Mack* on December 15. The Supreme Court decision for *R. v. Turpin* can be found on the same website as above, in Volume 1. It was announced on May 4 of that year.

CHAPTER 7

Pretrial Criminal Procedures

CHAPTER OBJECTIVES

✓ Explain the key components of pretrial procedures.

✓ Consider the importance of the defendant's right to legal counsel.

✓ Discuss the rules governing search and seizure in Canada.

✓ Discuss the limitations and expectations placed on the police use of warrants.

✓ Discuss the issues surrounding false confessions as they relate to the rights of defendants.

✓ Understand the laws governing police use of electronic surveillance.

✓ Recognize the problems with using evidence from jailhouse informants.

✓ Examine the laws controlling the police interrogation while the suspect is in custody.

✓ Discuss the need for electronic surveillance and whether it violates the privacy of Canadians.

B etween arrest and trial, a series of events take place that are essential to the processing of suspects in our criminal justice system. Pretrial criminal procedures are important because most criminal cases are never formally heard in the courts; rather, they are resolved informally. Although most Canadians have seen television courtroom dramas with juries, and with defence lawyers and prosecutors arguing over details in front of a judge in a courtroom filled with spectators, these are infrequent events. So it is important to study pretrial procedures in order to understand what most individuals experience when they enter the criminal justice system.

This chapter focuses on pretrial criminal procedures that involve the actions of the police from the time a suspect is detained up until the case enters a criminal courtroom for a trial. As you will see, many procedures must be followed during this process, and many of the issues that process raises have ultimately been heard by the Supreme Court of Canada. One of the most important questions at this stage of our criminal justice system concerns the reasonable expectation of privacy. That is, what protections do Canadians have against unreasonable police intrusion into their lives? This question has been raised in a number of significant cases in recent years, and the Supreme Court has agreed to hear some of these in an attempt to resolve the issues for both suspects and the police. Part of the controversy surrounding the question arises from the fact that "privacy" is not mentioned in the Charter of Rights and Freedoms, and as a result the courts have had to interpret—and balance—this area of law between the rights of society to have effective police protection and the rights of suspects to their privacy. In *Hunter v. Southam* (1984), for example, the Supreme Court held that a reasonable expectation of privacy existed in s. 8 of the Charter and, for that reason, searches and seizures must be authorized by either statute or the common law in order to be constitutional. Since s. 8 of the Charter governs searches conducted by the police, questions can be raised as to whether or not the evidence collected by the police can be excluded from the trial if it was gathered in such a way that it violates a legal right of an individual protected by the Charter.

Privacy was a key issue in *R. v. Feeney* (1997), and the Supreme Court's ruling in that case led one legal observer to comment that the Court's decision was unprecedented (Coughlan 1998). In *Feeney*, a murder suspect was arrested without a **warrant** and evidence was seized from the location where the suspect was arrested. The decision of the Supreme Court, which favoured the defendant, was based on due process violations committed by the police, and its decision led to a restriction of police search powers. As a consequence, Parliament had to pass new legislation on warrants. In fact, the decision in this case reversed a rule previously established by the Supreme Court—that police could enter a residence to make an arrest without a warrant.

At 8:20 a.m. on June 8, 1991, the body of 86-year-old Frank Boyle was found in his mobile home in the B.C. Interior. He had been murdered. The police officer who arrived at the scene concluded from the amount of blood that Boyle's death had been extremely violent. A neighbour told the investigating officer that she had observed Michael Feeney, who lived nearby, walking away from Boyle's truck after it had been driven into a ditch earlier that morning. Another neighbour told the officer he had seen Feeney enter a storage trailer at about 7 a.m. The officer knocked on the door of the trailer and yelled out "Police!" The officer heard nothing in response, entered without a warrant, and woke up Feeney by touching him on the leg. Feeney's shirt and shoes were covered with blood, and money stolen from the deceased was found under the suspect's mattress. Feeney was later charged and convicted of second degree murder.

However, on May 22, 1997, the Supreme Court of Canada, in a 5–4 ruling, ruled that the search had been unlawful because the police had violated ss. 8 and 10(b) of the Charter. It ordered a new trial. The majority of the Court, following the due process model, decided that the police officer had acted on a hunch, since he admitted that he did not have reasonable grounds for arresting Feeney and should have obtained a **search warrant** while waiting outside the storage facility. The Court's ruling was based on the arresting officer's statement that at the time he entered the suspect's trailer, he had reason to believe that the suspect was involved in the murder but did not have sufficient reason to make an arrest (he had reason only after he saw the bloodied clothing) (Hiebert 2002). The majority ruled that although the officer was correct in his "hunch" about the accused, this did not legitimize his actions. Since Feeney was asleep when the officer arrived, he did not pose a threat of flight and exigent circumstances (such as the need to prevent the destruction of evidence prior to the arrival of a warrant) were low. In addition, the police had

not properly followed the Supreme Court's decision in *R. v. Brydges* (1990) that required them to inform the suspect of his right to free legal counsel. During the time they spent with Feeney before counsel arrived, the police asked him a number of questions, and some of his answers were incriminating. Only after they took Feeney to the police detachment did the police ask for and receive a search warrant for the trailer.

The majority of the Supreme Court justices ruled that Feeney's fingerprints and incriminating statements would have to be excluded since they involved procedural violations on the part of the police. Mr. Justice Sopinka wrote in his decision that "in general, the privacy interest outweighs the interest of the police and warrantless arrests in dwelling houses are prohibited" (*R. v. Feeney* [1997], at 154). In addition, Mr. Justice Sopinka noted that Feeney had not spoken to a lawyer for two days following his arrest and detention; the fact that the police "did not cease in their efforts to gather information, indicates a lack of respect for the appellant's rights displayed by the police" (ibid., at 15–17). Another issue of concern to the majority of Supreme Court justices was the police's delay in reading Feeney his rights. They ruled that it had taken too long for the officer to do so. They also ruled that as soon as the officer touched Feeney's leg to awaken him, Feeney had been "detained," and the law requires that the rights of a detained person be read immediately. Finally, the Supreme Court held that the police must receive prior authorization before entering the dwelling of an individual to gather evidence.

The minority of Supreme Court justices, supporting the crime control model, interpreted the actions of the officer quite differently while placing it in the context of a concern for the victim. In their opinion, the police officer had acted properly by ensuring that a suspect accused of murder was not at large in the community. Madame Justice L'Heureux-Dubé stated that the majority had seen the actions of the police officers involved "as [those of] lawless vigilantes, flagrantly and deliberately violating the Charter at every turn" (ibid., at 204). Her concern extended beyond the police to the "helpless victim," whom she viewed as having suffered a "random" and "savage beating" (ibid., at 205).

The Supreme Court ordered a new trial but ruled the bloody shirt and shoes and the money inadmissible as evidence, because its continued use by the prosecution would bring the criminal justice system into disrepute. Up until this case, the common law had permitted a police officer, in certain circumstances, to enter a private dwelling to arrest a suspect without a warrant. But now the majority of justices were ruling that the arresting officer had been incorrect to believe there were reasonable grounds to enter the dwelling and arrest the suspect.

The police officer had been within the laws concerning the arrest and detention of a suspect as they had existed up until this case; with *Feeney*, the majority of the justices were overturning those rules. Based on the Supreme Court's decision in *Feeney*, the police would now be required to gain prior authorization to enter the private dwelling of an individual in order to search for and collect evidence.

The impact of this decision on police forces was potentially so devastating that the Supreme Court allowed the previous rules governing warrants to continue for six months. Parliament responded to this by passing Bill C-16, which allows a police officer to enter a residence or other dwelling to make an arrest without a warrant if exigent circumstances exist, such as the need to prevent the loss or destruction of evidence, and/or a belief that their warnings will lead to personal harm when they enter a dwelling, and/or an urgent call for assistance having been made, especially in the context of domestic violence.

This latter exception was affirmed in *R. v. Godoy* (1997), a case that involved the police entering an apartment without a warrant after receiving a 911 call. A "nervous-looking man answered the door and suggested nothing was going on of interest to them," but "the police pushed past him" (Makin 1998). They discovered the woman who had made the call. She was sobbing and had a badly bruised eye. She told the police that the man who had tried to stop them at the door was responsible for her injury. The accused was acquitted by the lower court but on appeal was convicted by the appeal court. The accused argued that when the police entered his apartment they were infringing his constitutional right to be free of unreasonable search and seizure. The Supreme Court disagreed with the accused, and threw out his appeal.

Another exception to the decision made in *Feeney* involves the actions of police officers searching a motor vehicle without a warrant in certain circumstances. A **warrantless search** can often result in evidence being ruled inadmissible. One such case arose in October 1997 when a RCMP police officer on patrol arrested a man after he stepped out of a field of tall grass just outside Gimli, Manitoba. When questioned about his activities, the individual told the officer that he had gone into the field to relieve himself. After a quick search of the area, the officer discovered a bag containing 4 kilograms of marijuana and arrested him for marijuana trafficking. The officer then took the suspect to the police lockup in Gimli. The vehicle of the arrested individual was then towed to an impound lot; there, six hours after the arrest, the RCMP discovered cocaine and a large amount of cash during a routine inventory check of the arrested

individual's vehicle. The cocaine and money were seized by the RCMP. Defence counsel later argued that since the RCMP did not have a search warrant, the cocaine and money should be returned.

Was the RCMP search of the suspect's vehicle lawful? Should the cocaine and money found in the vehicle have been returned? And could it be used as evidence for another criminal charge? Once again, these questions involve the conflict between an individual's right to privacy and the need for the police to have some leeway in the gathering of evidence. The answers to these questions are found in the interpretations of the Canadian Charter of Rights of Freedoms. This chapter reviews the principles of the Charter as they apply to pretrial criminal procedures (especially as they apply to police actions) that affect the freedom and privacy of Canadians.

In the case just outlined, *Caslake v. R.* (1998), the Supreme Court of Canada ruled that the seizure of the cocaine and money was unjust because the search was not connected to the arrest itself. However, the court also ruled that the evidence should not be excluded. Not only did the police act in good faith, but the evidence caused no harm to the administration of justice. The court felt that "excluding the evidence would have a more serious impact on the repute of the administration of justice than admitting it, for the prosecution had no case without the evidence."

ARREST OR DETENTION

Section 10 of the Charter of Rights and Freedoms enacts the following:

> Everyone has the right on arrest or detention:
> (a) to be informed promptly of the reasons therefor;
> (b) to retain and instruct counsel without delay and to be informed of that right; and
> (c) to have the validity of the detention determined by way of habeas corpus and to be released if the detention is not lawful.

These rights only come up when an individual is arrested or detained. The fact that the Charter identifies both indicates there is a difference between the two. When is someone "detained" and when is someone "arrested"?

INVESTIGATIVE DETENTION

Many people think that an arrest is the first step in criminal pretrial procedure, but often it is not. This is because

Canadian courts have recognized that the police can detain, interrogate, and search an individual even "where there is less than reasonable grounds to believe that an offence has been committed" (Bilodeau 2001–02, 42). Today in Canada, the police can hold a person for questioning even when they do not have grounds for an arrest. However, the legality of detaining a person in this way depends on the importance of the matter being investigated and on the amount of intrusion that is necessary.

An investigative detention is currently defined as "a reactive power dependent upon a reasonable belief that the detained person is implicated in a prior criminal act" (*Brown v. Durham Regional Police Force* [1998]). The Charter is concerned about police officers misusing their powers, so s. 9 states that "everyone has the right not to be arbitrarily detained or imprisoned." According to Bilodeau (2001–02, 42–43), the police are allowed to detain an individual due to safety concerns. If, for example, a suspect runs away from the police after leaving a crack house and being told to stop, the police are allowed to protect themselves by conducting a non-intrusive search for weapons. And if during this search illegal drugs are discovered, the police officer can legally arrest the person without fear of having the case thrown out of court on a Charter challenge to have the evidence excluded. Police officers risk having the evidence thrown out if they decide they are at risk when in fact they aren't (e.g., when the individual in question doesn't run away from the police after being told to stop). Another limit on police powers in this area is when the police decide to conduct an intrusive search, such as a strip search (see Exhibit 7.4), which is more difficult to justify to the court. One example of an illegal police investigative detention is when a police officer observes an individual running from the scene of a break and enter with a sack. The police stop the individual and discover expensive machinery parts. In a short while, they are told that the parts have been stolen, and they subsequently arrest the individual. Assuming that no threats to the police were made (i.e., their safety was not at issue), the search for the stolen property is illegal. While an officer is allowed to detain an individual to determine whether he or she has been involved in a crime, this does mean the right to make an intrusive search that does not involve issues of safety.

But what happens if the police "ask" an individual to accompany them to the police station? Has this person been arrested or detained? In either case, the s. 10 Charter rights of the individual in question must be observed. When dealing with this question, the Ontario Court of Appeal in *R. v. Moran* (1987) listed several questions that should be considered, including these: What, precisely, was the language used by the police?

Was the accused given a choice by the police? Did the individual go to the police station of his or her own free will? Was that individual free to leave at any time? And at what stage of the police investigation did this occur—that is, was it still a general investigation or did the police have reasonable grounds to believe that this individual was the actual offender? (Mewett and Nakatsuru 2000).

So, why do the police resort to investigative detentions? As Nicol (2002, 234) points out, "the opportunity to stop and confront suspects is an invaluable tool." Such detentions offer several benefits to the police. For example, they allow investigators the time and opportunity to use other search powers where the circumstances permit. If during their search of the individual, they legally obtain evidence about a crime, they may then use a number of legal warrantless search and seizure powers they possess, such as the plain view doctrine (see below), certain exigent circumstances (see below), and powers relating to weapons and drugs. And if the police, during an investigative detention, find enough evidence to formally arrest an individual, then s. 495 of the Criminal Code permits them to conduct a search incident to an arrest (ibid.). However, other Charter rights may come into play for suspects or arrestees, such as found in ss. 10(a) and 10(b) (the right to be informed promptly of the reasons thereof, and the right to retain and instruct counsel without delay and to be informed of that right, respectively).

ARREST

Once it is determined that an individual should be charged with an offence, an appropriate way must be chosen to ensure that person will appear at the trial. The police have several options at this point. They can seize the person and force him or her to appear, by way of an arrest and detention. Or they can arrest the individual but then release that person with an order to appear if they are fairly certain that he or she will appear in court at the date and time given. Or they may decide not to arrest the individual, but require that he or she appear at a certain date and time in order to be tried. The Criminal Code tries "to ensure that the least unfair method is tried first before resorting to the most unfair, but at the same time [the] most certain method of arrest and pre-trial detention" (Mewett and Nakatsuru 2000, 56).

An **arrest** involves the police power to restrain an individual—in effect, to deprive an individual of liberty. Exactly how the police arrest someone depends on the facts of the case. When a crime has occurred, they may have to investigate to determine who committed it. This may involve the police, in the course of their investigation, stopping and questioning a large number of people to gain information. After collecting enough information to identify the alleged perpetrator, they go to a justice of the peace and **lay an information** against the person they have identified. The justice of the peace determines whether the case has been properly made out and, if it has been, either issues an arrest warrant authorizing the police to make an arrest or issues a **summons**—that is, an order directed to the accused requiring him or her to appear in court on a certain date. In both situations, the laying of the information occurs before the police have any procedural contact with the accused.

Sometimes, however, the police actually discover a person in the act of committing a criminal offence, or who has just committed an offence. In these cases, it is not possible for the police to go to a justice of the peace before they lay an information. So instead, they arrest the individual and *then* go to a justice of the peace to lay an information. In these situations, an information is laid only after the police have had procedural contact with the accused.

The police must believe that they have reasonable grounds to make an arrest, and these grounds have to be justifiable from an objective point of view. For the police, however, the threshold to justify an arrest is relatively low; for example, they are not required to consider whether the person they are arresting will be convicted of a criminal offence. In *R. v. Golub* (1997), the Ontario Court of Appeal stated:

> [O]ften, the officer's decision to arrest must be made quickly in volatile and rapidly changing circumstances. Judicial reflection is not a luxury the officer can afford. The officer must make his or her decision based on available information which is often less than exact or complete. The law does not expect the same kind of inquiry of a police officer deciding whether to make an arrest that it demands of a justice faced with an application for a search warrant.

The Laying of the Information First

If an information is laid first, the justice of the peace has to be satisfied that a case has been made out against the accused. If it has not been, the police will have to go back to collect more evidence. What usually happens, however, is that the justice of the peace is satisfied with the information and issues an arrest warrant or summons. A summons must be issued as opposed to an arrest warrant unless what the justice of the peace hears provides reasonable grounds to believe that it is in the public interest to issue the latter (s. 507 of the Criminal Code). If a summons is issued, it is "served" on the accused so that he or she will know what is required. If an arrest warrant is issued, it will be "executed" by the police actually arresting the named person.

Arrest without a Warrant

According to s. (1) of the Criminal Code, it is possible for a police officer to arrest someone without a warrant. A person may be arrested in this way:

- who is found committing any criminal offence (indictable, summary conviction, or federal statute);
- who is about to commit an indictable offence, on the basis of reasonable and probable grounds;
- who the police officer, on reasonable and probable grounds, believes has an outstanding warrant within the territorial jurisdiction in which the person is located; and/or
- who the police officer knows has committed an indictable offence.

A police officer's power to arrest without a warrant is restricted by s. 495(2) of the Criminal Code, which states that no arrest shall occur where the public interest is satisfied and no reasonable grounds exist to believe the accused will fail to appear in court. This means that a police officer shall not arrest an individual without a warrant (1) for a summary conviction offence; (2) for an indictable offence within the absolute jurisdiction of a provincial court judge, as listed in s. 553 of the Criminal Code (see Chapter 8); or (3) if the offence is defined as a hybrid offence. Section 495(2) states:

> 495. (2) A peace officer shall not arrest a person without warrant for
> (a) an indictable offence mentioned in Section 553,
> (b) an offence for which the person may be prosecuted by indictment or for which he is punishable on summary conviction, or
> (c) an offence punishable on summary conviction, in any case where
> (d) he believes on reasonable grounds that the public interest, having regard to all the circumstances including the need to
> (i) establish the identity of the person,
> (ii) secure or preserve the identity of the person,
> (iii) prevent the continuation or repetition of the offence or the commission of another offence, may be satisfied without so arresting the person, and
> (e) he has no reasonable grounds to believe that, if he does not so arrest the person, the person will fail to attend court in order to be dealt with according to law.

Police officers then proceed to use one of three alternatives available to them. They can issue the suspect with an **appearance notice;** or they can release the suspect with the intention of applying for a summons from a justice of the peace; or they can release the suspect unconditionally. This last one means that the police officer, after determining the identity of the suspect, releases the suspect and at a later date either issues an appearance notice or arranges for a justice of the peace to issue a summons.

The Laying of the Information Second

The police have the power to arrest without a warrant

- anyone they find committing any criminal offence (be it indictable or summary conviction);
- anyone who has committed an indictable offence;
- anyone who they believe, on reasonable grounds, has committed or is about to commit an indictable offence; and
- anyone they believe has an outstanding arrest warrant that is in force in that jurisdiction.

The Criminal Code (s. 495[2]) states that police officers will not arrest someone, although they have the power to do so,

- where the offence being committed is a summary conviction offence;
- where the offence being committed is listed as a "hybrid" offence;
- where the police determine that the public interest will be served without an arrest being made of that person; and
- where an indictable offence is within the absolute jurisdiction of a provincial court judge.

In these cases, instead of arresting the individual, the police may decide to issue an appearance notice. This notice contains the name of the accused, the substance of the offence alleged to have been committed, and the time and place where the accused must appear in court. The appearance notice also contains information pertaining to the fact that it is an offence not to appear, as well as a description of what will happen if the person fails to appear.

Part of the tradition of our legal system is that the criminal process cannot begin until someone with the power of a judicial officer—in this case, a justice of the peace—is satisfied that a case exists against the accused. But in the above-mentioned situations, it is the police who actually are commencing the proceedings that require the

accused to appear in court. So the Criminal Code (s. 505) requires any police officer who issues an appearance notice to lay an information as soon as it is practicable, but in all cases prior to the time indicated in the appearance notice for the accused's first court appearance.

Notwithstanding the powers of arrest that a police officer has, the only individuals who can actually be arrested are those

- who have committed a serious indictable offence;
- who have committed a lesser offence, but who the police have reason to believe will not appear for trial unless arrested; and
- whose arrest will serve the public interest.

Arrest with a Warrant

For the police to arrest someone with a warrant, they must suspect on the basis of reasonable grounds that the individual in question committed a crime and that the suspect's appearance cannot be compelled by a summons (see above, and Chapter 1). To obtain a warrant, the police must ordinarily go before a justice of the peace and lay an information alleging that a criminal offence has been committed. Having succeeded in obtaining an arrest warrant, the officer who executes that warrant should have it in his or her possession in case the suspect asks to see it. In some situations, the police may be granted an arrest warrant that authorizes them to enter a private residence to arrest an individual (s. 529.1 of the Criminal Code). Police officers are permitted to enter a private residence without a search warrant in certain situations—for example, if they are in "hot pursuit" of a suspect (s. 529.3 of the Criminal Code). Obviously, an arrest can be made without a warrant if the police observe a crime being committed. But if the police decide they are going to detain the individual for a period of time, the suspect must be brought before a justice of the peace as soon as possible.

Section 503.1 of the Criminal Code states that when a justice is available within 24 hours of an arrest, the accused must be taken before him within this period of time—or, if a justice is not available, within a reasonable period. If the accused does not appear before a justice within a certain amount of time, the case may be terminated on the grounds of "unreasonable delay." The Supreme Court of Canada dealt with the meaning of "unreasonable delay" in *R. v. Storey* (1990), where it ruled that the police could delay this process for 18 hours so that a line-up could be put together. However, when an accused was detained for 36 hours (*R. v. Charles* [1987]), the Supreme Court ruled that it was a violation of s. 9 of the Charter.

In order to arrest someone legally, the police officer has to verbally inform the suspect that he or she is under arrest. An arrest also involves the taking of physical control or custody of an individual with the intent to detain that individual. This action will require the use of force if the individual being arrested resists being taken into custody. If a person being arrested willingly accompanies the police officer, that officer will have no need to make physical contact, but at the same time the arrested person must acknowledge being in custody. If there is no such acknowledgment, a police officer has to make contact with the suspect. Section 10(a) of the Charter of Rights and Freedoms stipulates that "everyone has the right on arrest or detention to be informed promptly of the reasons thereof."

A police officer must inform an individual of his or her rights the moment that individual becomes a suspect in the crime under investigation. If the suspect is not informed of those rights, any evidence obtained from the suspect will be inadmissible because admitting it would not stand the test of the Charter and would place the administration of justice in disrepute. On detaining or arresting a suspect, the police must read the following:

1. Notice on arrest: "I am arresting you for . . . [briefly describe reasons for arrest]."
2. Right to counsel: "It is my duty to inform you that you have the right to retain and instruct counsel without delay. Do you understand?"
3. Caution to charged person: "You [are charged, will be charged] with . . . Do you wish to say anything in answer to the charge? You are not obligated to say anything unless you wish to do so, but whatever you say may be given in evidence."
4. Secondary caution to charged person: "If you have spoken to any police officer or anyone with authority, or if any such person has spoken to you in connection with this case, I want it clearly understood that I do not want it to influence you in making any statement."

CUSTODIAL INTERROGATION

According to s. 7 of the Charter, everyone has the right to life, liberty, and security of the person, and the right not to be deprived thereof except in accordance with the principles of fundamental justice. Once arrested, many suspects choose to remain silent, and since both oral and written statements are admissible in court, police officers sometimes stop their questioning until defence counsel are present. If the accused decides to answer the questions, he or she may decide to stop at any time and refuse to answer more questions until a lawyer arrives.

Suspects may waive this right only if they are aware of what they are doing and are able to contact a lawyer at any time if they so wish.

The police can place a suspect into custody at the time of arrest, whether the arrest occurred on the street, in a house, in a police station, or in a police vehicle. It is recommended procedure that the police inform the suspect of the right to silence and counsel before starting their questioning.

The purpose of interrogating a suspect is to obtain information—in these cases, the investigators probably don't have enough information to arrest someone. In **custodial interrogations,** the interrogation of a suspect is of primary importance because it may provide the police with incriminating evidence that can lead to a determination of guilt at the end of a court trial (Vrij 1998). Custodial interrogations may also unearth stolen property, point to the whereabouts of accomplices, and perhaps indicate the involvement of the suspect in other unsolved crimes. However, the primary goal of a custodial interrogation is to solicit a confession from the suspect (McConville and Baldwin 1982). The importance of a confession by the suspect cannot be underestimated, as Wigmore (1970) notes that nothing has a greater impact on a judge and/or jurors than a confession made by a suspect. This is because voluntary confessions are readily admitted into court as evidence.

Traditionally, Canadian courts have held that an out-of-court statement by an accused person constitutes appropriate evidence as long as the statement was given voluntarily. In *R. v. Rickett* (1975) it was determined that when an issue arises over the voluntariness of a statement, it must be proved beyond a reasonable doubt that the statement was voluntary. In essence, s. 7 of the Charter seeks to impose limits on the powers the state and its agents (such as the police) have over the detained individual. This protects the accused against the superior resources of the police; however, the police have the power to deprive an individual of his or her life, liberty, or security as long as they respect the fundamental principles of justice.

Questions are sometimes raised about interrogations when a suspect confesses to a crime. Issues surrounding the voluntariness of a confession can be raised, specifically the issue of an involuntary confession. In contrast to the importance placed on statements made during a voluntary confession by the court, involuntary confessions are most likely to be excluded as they may have been illegally obtained. This raises questions about why people confess; in particular, why do they confess to a crime they never committed? Concerns about false confessions have been raised in recent decades, particularly as they have been shown to lead to wrongful convictions and imprisonments.

Another reason why civil libertarians, defendants, and defence lawyers are concerned about police interrogations has to do with the techniques used by police investigators to obtain information from a suspect and/or accused. If the police inform the person they are going to question about his or her right to contact a lawyer (see below) and the offer is refused, the investigators are permitted to use a variety of strategies to get the suspect to provide the relevant information. Police are trained in psychological techniques for reducing a suspect's reluctance to state the truth (Macdonald and Michaud 1987). While the possibility exists that the police will be able to make the suspect confess to a crime, there is also the possibility that if police use their superior psychological interrogation techniques, some suspects will falsely confess to crimes they did not commit, and thus be wrongfully convicted (Leo 1992).

During custodial interrogations, the police follow a number of strategies to obtain information. They have devised these strategies to persuade suspects to volunteer information that could implicate them in crimes (Leo 1996). The first is referred to as the "conditioning strategy"; here, the officers provide an environment in which the suspect is encouraged to think positively of the interrogator(s) and subsequently cooperate with the authorities. By providing coffee and cigarettes, police lower the suspect's anxiety level and achieve a sense of trust. A second technique is the "de-emphasizing" strategy, which involves interrogators informing the suspect that rights are unimportant and that the most important task at hand is to empathize with the victims and their families. When this technique is used, the suspect rarely if ever thinks of stopping the interrogation in order to contact a lawyer for advice. A third technique, the "persuasion strategy," involves investigators informing suspects that if they don't tell their side of the story at that time, only the victim's will be heard during the trial.

According to Williams (2000), while the Charter has significantly increased the rights of the accused in our criminal justice system, this has not led to significant changes in police interrogations. This is largely because suspects do not appreciate "the nature and significance of their rights given problems with the clarity and adequacy of their communication" (ibid., 224). Another reason is that interrogations fall within the workings of the informal criminal justice system. Thus the police use a number of techniques that, while legal, are innovative in the sense that they are designed specifically to get the suspect to confess to the crime (see Exhibit 7.1). These techniques are sometimes successful, but they are not always so, as is evident in the case of Guy Paul Morin, who was charged and wrongfully convicted of murdering a young girl at the end of an interrogation (Makin 1992, 184–208).

In one expert's opinion, false confessions are made and typically videotaped after hours and hours of intense interrogation. It's "a myth to think that getting a suspect to recap a confession on videotape after dozens of hours of intense interrogation is putting the truth before a jury, because one can't evaluate a confession without seeing the context in which it was taken" (Drizin, in Saulny 2002, 5). Another expert, Saul Kassin, points out that time is the "invisible force" operating during interrogations. Kassin (in Saulny 2002, 5) points out that what happens over time "is that the suspect gets tired, and there is an intensification of techniques. The suspect is getting the message that denial is not escape, so they offer something else." Kassin points out that when people are later asked why they falsely confessed, the main reason they give "is something like 'I just wanted to go home.'" According to Gudjonsson and MacKeith (1982), the conditions that exist when a person tells the truth during a police interrogation are the same as those that result when a false confession is made. Kassin and Wrightsman (1985) identified three types of false confessions:

- *Voluntary false confessions.* In these situations, an individual voluntarily confesses to a crime he or she did not commit. These people may be giving a false confession to protect someone else; or establishing an alibi for another crime that is more serious; or they may be in physical fear of the person who is actually guilty.
- *Coerced-complaint false confessions.* Coerced-complaint confessions usually are the result of an intense custodial interrogation. Suspects may finally agree with police statements that falsely implicate them in a crime in order to end an extremely uncomfortable situation, or in order to receive a promised benefit for admitting (falsely) to involvement in the crime.
- *Coerced-internalized false confessions.* In this type of false confession, the suspect, who may be anxious, emotional, and/or tired of being repeatedly interrogated, may come to falsely recall an involvement in a crime and confess to it, though having had nothing to do with it. According to Kassin (1997), false confessions of this type share two elements: (1) a vulnerable suspect, such as a person whose memory is malleable because of "youth, interpersonal trust, naivete, suggestibility, lack of intelligence, stress, fatigue, alcohol or drug use"; and (2) the presentation of false evidence (such as false conclusions of polygraph tests or what accomplices have said by the police in order to convince the suspect that they are, in fact, guilty).

What happens when a confession is introduced during a trial? In Canada, a rule of criminal evidence is that no statement made by the accused to the police is admissible in court on behalf of the prosecution unless it is first shown that it was made voluntarily. Furthermore, it must be shown that the confession was the result of the accused's conscious operating mind. When the prosecution offers to place into evidence any statement made by the accused to the police, a hearing known as a *voir dire* is held in the absence of the jury, in order to ascertain whether these conditions have been met. The trial judge who conducts the hearing must determine whether the statement was made voluntarily and that there weren't any threats or promises that made the accused confess to the police.

The Charter of Rights and Freedoms is also relevant here. Mewett and Nakatsuru (2000, 171) state that "the first and prime point to bear in mind is that even if there has been a Charter violation in the obtaining of a confession, s. 24(2) does not necessarily exclude it from the trial." They add that the exclusion of evidence is not automatic, in that evidence shall be excluded only if it can be established that it violates s. 24(2) of the Charter; that is, "having regard to all the circumstances, the admission of it in proceedings would bring the administration of justice into disrepute."

Other sections of the Charter have an influence on the admissibility of evidence, including ss. 10(a) and 10(b). In addition, s. 7, which bears on the right not to be deprived of liberty except in accordance with the principles of fundamental justice, may be relevant since the Supreme Court of Canada has ruled that there is a right to silence protected by s. 7. Under the Charter, the Supreme Court has looked carefully at how the police have obtained confessions from the accused and whether or not their actions were in accordance with the principles of fundamental justice. In *R. v. Hebert* (1990), the accused had been arrested, informed of his right to counsel (which he exercised), and told by his legal counsel to exercise his right to silence. After stating to the police that he had nothing to say, he was placed in a cell with an undercover police officer who was pretending to be a person accused of a crime. Over a period of time, the undercover police officer succeeded in getting Hebert to make an incriminating statement. The Supreme Court held that when an individual chooses not to speak to the police, the police cannot then engage in actions that subvert that freedom to remain silent by trickery or by other means. The following year, in *R. v. Broyles* (1991), the Supreme Court held that an accused's right to silence had been infringed on by the police after they arranged a prison visit between an accused and his friend who was wearing a wiretap. In the course of the visit, incriminating statements by the accused were recorded.

EXHIBIT 7.1 Police Interrogations

Controversy is sometimes directed at the techniques used by the police during their interrogations in order to gain information from individuals. Supporters of the police believe that the methods they use during interrogations to obtain information from suspects not only convict the guilty but also exonerate the innocent. They also point out that the police need to find out about criminal activities in order to make society safer. Critics point out that the police sometimes use questionable techniques and that there aren't enough measures to insure the police don't coerce confessions out of suspects. The police themselves point out that interrogations are oftentimes the result of many hours of painstaking investigation and that they are not to be viewed as conversations between friends. As such, they sometimes need to place pressure on suspects in order to obtain the truth.

Empirical studies of police interrogation techniques are not common, largely due to the fact that what goes on in police interrogation rooms is usually not available to outsiders. It wasn't until 1992–93 that sociologist Richard Leo was able to personally observe 122 police interrogations (totalling more than 500 hours) in an urban California police force; in addition, he also analyzed videotaped custodial interrogations from two other police departments. Leo was particularly interested in how the police induced suspects to waive their rights, how they interrogated suspects following a waiver, and how the exercising of their legal rights affected the suspects' subsequent case processing. Leo (1996, 266, 302) concluded the following:

- Very few interrogations are coercive.
- One in five suspects invoked one or more of their rights to avoid cooperating with the police.
- Police interrogators use tactics recommended in police training manuals in order to undermine the confidence of suspects and overbear their rational decision-making.
- Police interrogators have become increasingly sophisticated in obtaining incriminating evidence during custodial interrogations.
- The majority of custodial interrogations last less than one hour.

(Continued)

EXHIBIT 7.1   Police Interrogations . . . Continued

- Suspects who provide incriminating information tend to be treated differently at every stage of the criminal process compared to those suspects who don't.

Feld (2006) published the next empirical study in his study of police interrogations of juveniles in the Minneapolis-St. Paul, Minnesota, area. Similar to Leo's findings, he found that the police conducted most of their interrogations in relatively short periods of time and under relatively non-coercive circumstances. In addition, Feld reported that juveniles provided incriminating evidence to the police at about the same rate as did the adults in Leo's study.

In the first Canadian study of this kind, King and Snook (2009) analyzed 44 videotaped police interrogations of adult suspects conducted between December 1996 and January 2008 in criminal cases in a jurisdiction located in Newfoundland. Fifty percent of the suspects interrogated by the police confessed—12 (or 27 percent) of the suspects gave a full confession while 10 suspects (23 percent) gave a partial confession. Seventeen suspects (39 percent) denied any involvement in the crime while the remaining five suspects (11 percent) gave the police no comment.

The conclusions reached by King and Snook approximated the findings found by Leo. Specifically, they discovered that the number of

individuals who waived their legal rights was almost the same (80 percent compared to 78 percent for Leo), as was the total number of individuals who provided the police with confessionary evidence (50 percent compared to 64 percent). In addition, the interrogations studied by King and Snook typically took less than an hour to complete, a finding similar to what Leo reported. The influence tactics used by the police in both studies were similar such as confronting the suspect with evidence of guilt and identifying contradictions in the suspect's account (King and Snook 2009, 691). Other interrogation techniques, such as the use "of the good cop-bad cop routine, yelling at suspects, accusing suspects committing other crimes, attempting to confuse suspects . . . " were not commonly used.

One difference between these two studies involved the use of coercive strategies by the police during their interrogations. Leo reported that such approaches were used in only 2 percent of the cases he studied, while King and Snook found that they were used by the police in 25 percent of their cases. Some researchers (e.g., Kassin 2008) have raised concerns about the use of coercive strategies by the police during interrogations and false confessions.

Source: Courtesy of Meghann McLachlan.

JAILHOUSE INTERROGATIONS

Over the past two decades there have been a number of inquiries into the wrongful convictions of individuals who were convicted of murder but later exonerated when it was discovered that they had not committed these crimes. In two of these inquiries (Ontario's *Commission of Proceedings Involving Guy Paul Morin* [1998] and Manitoba's *Inquiry Regarding Thomas Sophonow* [2001]), much attention focused on the role of jailhouse informants and the evidence they supplied to the police—evidence that was instrumental in gaining convictions later proved to be wrongful. Both inquiries criticized the use of jailhouse informants, raising questions about their reliability and the fact that they were willing, with some persuasion, to say anything in order benefit from their cooperation. In the Sophonow case, for example, before

the third trial at least 11 jailhouse informants volunteered to assist the prosecution. The Crown and the police scrutinized the volunteers and selected three of them, largely on the basis of their "credibility" and "reliability."

A jailhouse informant has been defined as "an inmate, usually awaiting trial or sentencing, who claims to have heard another prisoner make an admission about his case" (Winograde 1990, 755). Jailhouse informants typically offer the authorities information about another inmate in exchange for some benefit, such as a more lenient sentence. However, this sort of benefit from the authorities is not necessarily a prerequisite for being a jailhouse informant (Sherrin 1996, 197). Why has the testimony of jailhouse informants been used in the courts when it is acknowledged that their testimony may not be truthful and may lead to false convictions? In the Anglo-American criminal justice system, various types of informants have been used for centuries. As early as the thirteenth century, the English common law was using the "Approver System," whereby an individual charged with a capital offence could obtain a pardon by formally accusing other persons of a serious crime. If the accusation turned out to be correct (as determined by whether or not the individual named was found guilty), the approver would be granted freedom. However, if the accusation failed, the approver would be put to death. This system created a number of problems; for example, it encouraged blackmail, and individuals who became approvers came to be seen as "manipulative, abusive and desperate" (Zimmerman 1994, 155).

Despite the pitfalls of using jailhouse informants in criminal cases, it is accepted practice. There are no statistics to indicate how often evidence obtained from jailhouse informants is used in Canada; usually the public becomes aware that informants have been used only after a formal inquiry has been called to investigate a wrongful conviction or after a released informant later reveals to the press how many times, and for which cases, he or she has supplied evidence to the prosecution. In the United States, it has been estimated that in 20 percent of cases in which individuals were wrongfully convicted, the prosecution used jailhouse informants (Scheck et al. 2000). The *Inquiry Regarding Thomas Sophonow* (2001, 71) noted some of the dangers of using jailhouse informants:

- Jailhouse informants are polished and convincing liars.
- All confessions of an accused will be given great weight by the jurors.
- Jurors will give the same weight to "confessions" made to jailhouse informants as they will to a confession made to a police officer.
- Jailhouse informants rush to testify, particularly in high-profile cases.
- They always appear to have evidence that could only have come from someone who committed the offence.
- Their mendacity, and their ability to convince those who hear them, make them a threat to the principle of a fair trial as well as to the administration of justice.

Much of the concern here focuses on the impact on juries of statements by jailhouse informants. The leading Canadian case in this matter is *R. v. Vetrovec* (1982). The defendants had been convicted on a charge of conspiracy to traffic in heroin. The trial judge had warned the jury about the issues relating to convicting the defendants on the basis of the uncorroborated testimony of an accomplice. On appeal, the Supreme Court of Canada rejected any suggestion that jailhouse informants not be allowed to testify. Instead, the focus was to be on the credibility of the witnesses and whether their

testimony could be corroborated (as opposed to the quality of the evidence). The Supreme Court cautioned against placing informants in different categories, with only some categories requiring that warnings about their testimony be given to the jury. However, in its decision, the Supreme Court did offer trial judges guidance regarding how to warn jurors about the evidence supplied by jailhouse informants by noting that they should warn the jury about such evidence. In *Vetrovec*, the Supreme Court stated that it was to be left to the discretion of the trial judge whether to give "a clear and sharp warning to attract the attention of the juror to the risks of adopting, without more information, the evidence of the witness." This "clear and sharp warning" is now commonly referred to as the "Vetrovec warning." The Supreme Court of Canada, in *R. v. Sauve* (2004), adopted the framework for the Vetrovec warning from the Ontario Court of Appeal, stating that the warning has to contain the following four elements:

- Drawing the attention of the jury to the testimonial evidence requiring special scrutiny.
- Explaining why this evidence is subject to special scrutiny.
- Cautioning the jury that it is dangerous to convict on unconfirmed evidence of this sort, though the jury is entitled to do so if satisfied that the evidence is true.
- That the jury, in determining the veracity of the suspect evidence, should look for evidence from another source tending to show that the untrustworthy witness is telling the truth as to the guilt of the accused.

In 2000, the Supreme Court heard another case having implications for evidence supplied by jailhouse informants as well as for the "Vetrovec warning." In *R. v. Brooks* (2000), the defendant was accused of murdering his girlfriend's 19-month-old daughter. Part of the evidence used to convict Brooks was given by two jailhouse informants, who said they had heard the defendant say he killed the child to stop her crying. The trial judge, however, decided that the jury did not have to hear the "Vetrovec warning," and defence counsel did not ask that the warning be given to the jury. Brooks was found guilty of first degree murder. The Ontario Court of Appeal overturned the lower court's decision and ordered another trial, having ruled that the jury should have been warned that the jailhouse informants who supplied evidence to the prosecution had lengthy records of dishonesty and psychiatric disorders. When it heard the case, the Supreme Court, in a 4–3 decision, restored Brooks's conviction, having also concluded that trial judges have a significant obligation to caution jurors about the unreliability of jailhouse informants' testimony.

Thomas Sophonow was awarded $2.6 million after DNA evidence cleared him of the 1981 murder of a waitress. He had spent four years in prison. (CP PHOTO/ Pool-Winnipeg Free Press/Wayne Glowacki)

The Morin Inquiry criticized the Crown's use of two jailhouse informants. The commissioner concluded that both informants were liars who would say anything to further their own ends. The Sophonow Inquiry noted a number of factors involving the prosecution and police. Sophonow had been tried three times and convicted twice of murdering a young woman in Winnipeg. It also noted that there had been questionable police interrogations of Sophonow and that the Crown had failed to disclose relevant evidence to the defence. The commissioner also strongly criticized the Crown for relying on evidence supplied by jailhouse informants. One of the informants had 26 fraud charges dropped in exchange for his testimony that he had heard Sophonow confess. Another jailhouse informant, who received cash, had been a prosecution witness in at least eight other cases. According to the commissioner, former Supreme Court Justice Peter Cory (Inquiry regarding Thomas Sophonow 2001, 71), jailhouse informants are "a dangerous group" as "their testimony can all too easily destroy any hope of holding a fair trial and severely tarnish the reputation of Canadian justice."

As a result of the findings of these two commissions, several provinces have introduced reforms to ensure that jailhouse informants are carefully scrutinized. In Alberta, for example, Crown prosecutors are required to get a second opinion from their peers before using evidence supplied by jailhouse informants, and in British Columbia, regional Crown counsels must consult with the local Crown before deciding whether a jailhouse informant will be allowed to testify. Ontario requires jailhouse informants to be vetted by a special committee consisting of senior ministry lawyers (Joyce

2000). After the Ontario guidelines were established, between 1998 and 2004, of the 56 potential jailhouse informants, 30 were approved to testify and 26 were denied. In 13 other cases during the same time period, no recommendation was issued because a defendant either pleaded guilty or the police themselves recognized independently that an informant was unreliable. By 2009, Ontario "had effectively ended the use of jailhouse informants . . . " (Makin 2009).

RIGHT TO COUNSEL

According to s. 9 of the Charter of Rights and Freedoms, everyone has the right not to be arbitrarily detained or imprisoned. But even if detention is justified, the right to legal counsel found in s. 10 of the Charter "emerges in the face of any detention" (Abell and Sheehy 1993, 269). Section 10(b) of the Charter states:

10. Everyone has the right on arrest or detention
(b) to retain and instruct counsel without delay and to be informed of that right

Section 10(b) of the Charter gives an arrested individual the right to contact a lawyer without delay. This means that when an accused requests counsel, that request must be allowed. The right to legal advice and assistance is fundamental to ensure fairness in our criminal justice system. It is important for the accused to be able to access legal counsel as soon as possible after being arrested. Numerous issues have been raised over s. 10(b), including what the right to counsel encompasses, when and how the police must inform the accused of the right to counsel, what the accused must do to assert the right to counsel, and when it is reasonable to limit the right to counsel under s. 1 of the Charter (ibid., 269).

The accused must be given a reasonable opportunity to consult a lawyer. The accused must also have the right to talk to legal counsel privately. However, the accused cannot delay the investigation by deciding to contact counsel after several hours. The burden is on the accused to prove that it was impossible to contact a lawyer at the time the police offered him or her the opportunity to do so (R. v. Joey Smith [1989]).

The right to counsel in Canada is not absolute. It is available only to someone who is under arrest or being detained. In R. v. Bazinet (1986), the suspect voluntarily agreed to accompany the police to the police station. While answering questions about a murder, the suspect confessed to committing the crime. At this point, the police informed him of his right to counsel. On appeal, the court ruled that the police had followed proper procedure, since there was no evidence to indicate that the accused felt he had been deprived of his liberty and that he had to accompany the police.

But what happens once a suspect asks to see a lawyer? Can the police continue to interrogate that person while waiting for the lawyer to appear? The answer depends on the types of questions the police are asking. If the questions are "innocuous" (e.g., requests for the accused's name and address), they are allowed. However, questions about the facts of the case are not allowed until legal counsel has talked with the suspect.

In *R. v. Manninen* (1987), the accused had asked to see his lawyer. However, a police officer continued to question him, asking the accused for the location of a knife that had allegedly been used to rob a store. The accused then told the officers that he only had a gun while committing the robbery. The Ontario Court of Appeal ruled that this question was in violation of Manninen's rights, because it was "based on a presumption of guilt and the answer was devastating to the defence" and because it was asked "as if the appellant had expressed no desire to remain silent." As a result, the accused's admission of guilt was excluded.

However, the right to a lawyer is not a continuing right. Once the right has been complied with, that is the end of the right under s. 10(b). There is no right to have legal counsel present at any subsequent interviews between the accused and the police, as it is assumed that the lawyer will have given the appropriate information to the client in terms of what to say (or not say) to the police. However, at a later stage, the police cannot engage in trickery in order to obtain information that violates the accused's right to silence. If that happens, it may be held that this is a violation of s. 7 of the Charter.

The Supreme Court of Canada has established a high threshold for an accused to waive the Charter right to legal counsel. Individuals who elect to give up the right to counsel must first appreciate the consequences of doing so. If they do not—that is, if the police do not explain the consequences to them—anything they tell the police will be excluded. In *R. v. Clarkson* (1986), a woman confessed to the police that she murdered her husband, even though her aunt, who was present during the questioning, told her to contact a lawyer. The accused was intoxicated at the time of the questioning. The Supreme Court held that the statements of the accused were inadmissible, saying the police should have waited until she was sober to question her, since everyone must be fully aware of the consequences of waiving the right to counsel. A similar issue arose when the police obtained a statement from an intoxicated individual known to the police as an alcoholic with a Grade 4 education. In this case, *R. v. Black* (1989), the accused was originally charged with the attempted murder of another woman. She contacted her lawyer by telephone, and a few hours later the victim died. Then the police advised her that she was being charged with first degree murder. The accused asked to speak to her lawyer again, but the lawyer could not be reached. The officers then suggested she speak to another lawyer, a suggestion she refused. Shortly after this, the police questioned the accused again and she confessed to the crime. The Supreme Court ruled that since the accused had not waived her right to a lawyer, the police had violated her right to legal counsel, and consequently her statement was excluded from the evidence.

How long does an accused have to make a call? It depends on the seriousness of the charge. In *R. v. Joey Smith* (1989), the accused was arrested for robbery. After 9 p.m., he asked to contact a lawyer. Finding only a business telephone number, he decided to try again in the morning, despite police recommendations that he call that evening. The accused refused. When the police questioned him later, he made a statement "off the record" that was later used as evidence to convict him. On appeal, the Supreme Court of Canada ruled the statement to be admissible, because the crime was not considered a serious offence. Had it been a serious offence, he should have been granted an additional opportunity to contact legal counsel.

Since 1982, the Supreme Court of Canada has been interpreting the accused's right to legal counsel and silence as essential for a fair trial, and it has "been vigilant in excluding evidence that would undermine the reputation of justice" (Kelly 2005, 120). However, the Supreme Court has not simply favoured the accused at the expense of the police. According to Kelly (ibid., 120), the Supreme Court has "approached Section 10(b) in a fair and balanced manner that has placed important due process rights constraints on the police." The Supreme Court has heard numerous cases concerning this right and has held that the police have generally attempted to ensure that accused persons are informed of their legal rights. In many cases, the justices have supported police actions through s. 24(2) of the Charter by rejecting requests by the defence to exclude evidence.

COMPELLING APPEARANCE, INTERIM RELEASE, AND PRETRIAL DETENTION

An individual who has just been arrested without a warrant may be taken to the police station, where the police record the criminal charges and obtain other information relevant to the case. This process is commonly referred to as "lodging a complaint," and it usually includes a description of the suspect and, if necessary, circumstances relating to the offence. What actually happens next to the accused depends on the charge. If the charge is for a lesser offence, in all likelihood the accused will be released immediately by the officer in charge; after this, the police will lay an information and have a summons issued against the accused. (See the section titled "Arrest" in this chapter.) If the accused lives more than 200 kilometres away or is not a resident of the province, that person may be required to deposit a sum of not more than $500. This is standard operating procedure in Canada, and it expedites the processing of such cases and saves the police from having to search for the accused to serve an arrest warrant or summons. The purpose of this process is to allow as many accused as possible to leave the police station as soon as possible (s. 497 of the Criminal Code).

Since often there has been no judicial intervention in these cases (e.g., the police have arrested the accused while the crime was in progress), it is important for the police to swear an information and present it to a justice of the peace as soon as possible. If an arrest warrant has been issued after a justice of the peace signs an information, it may contain an "endorsement" authorizing the officer in charge at the police station to release the accused on similar grounds to those for being arrested without a warrant.

Those charged with indictable offences punishable by more than five years' imprisonment, those charged who the police believe will not appear at their trial, and those arrested with an arrest warrant that has not been endorsed by a justice of the peace that would allow the accused to be released, are usually processed at the police station. This processing may involve fingerprinting and photographing the accused.

What happens to people who are not released by the officer in charge at a police station? The Criminal Code (s. 503) requires that all such individuals be brought before a justice of the peace:

- when a justice of the peace is available within a period of 24 hours after the arrest, without unreasonable delay and, in any event, within that 24 hour period; and
- when a justice of the peace is not available within a 24 hour period, as soon as possible.

The purpose of the above provisions is to ensure that individuals remain in custody for as short a time as possible.

If the accused is charged with a "Section 469 crime"—murder, for example—a superior court justice decides whether the accused will be placed in a detention facility (see Chapter 8). Here, a reverse onus applies—that is, it is up to the accused to show why he or she should be released. Among the reasons for detention are these:

- The accused is charged with an indictable offence while already on judicial interim release or is in the process of appealing another indictable offence.
- The accused commits an indictable offence but is not a resident of Canada.
- The accused allegedly has broken a previous interim release order.
- The accused has committed or conspired to commit an offence under ss. 4 and 5 of the Controlled Drug and Substance Act (i.e., trafficking, exporting, or importing).

The prosecutor almost always has to show cause—that is, demonstrate that detaining the accused is justified (s. 515 of the Criminal Code). Our criminal justice system presumes that the accused should be released, and released without conditions, unless the Crown can show that it is necessary to hold that person. However, certain conditions—for example, an obligation to report to a police officer—may be imposed when the accused is released. The prosecutor may want the accused to enter into some form of recognizance. An accused who is released may be requested to deposit an amount of money with the court. A cash deposit is preferred, since the accused may disappear after paying.

Our criminal justice system prefers that a surety (an individual who will monitor the accused until the trial) be found who will agree to be indebted to the court for a specified amount of money if the accused does not appear on the appointed date. The surety may have to provide a cash deposit if the accused fails to appear.

Alternatively, the accused may be requested to deposit an amount of money with the court. Both a surety and a cash deposit may be required if the accused is not a resident of the province or lives more than 200 kilometres away from where he or she is being held. Of course, the accused may be detained if the justice of the peace feels it is necessary, but the reasons must be recorded.

The continued detention of the accused in custody can be justified only on one or more of following conditions found in s. 515(10) of the Criminal Code:

- Where the detention is necessary to ensure his or her attendance in court in order to be dealt with according to law.
- Where the detention is necessary for the protection or safety of the public, having regard to all the circumstances, including any substantial likelihood that the accused will, if released from custody, commit a criminal offence or interfere with the administration of justice.

- On any other just cause being shown and without limiting the generality of the foregoing, where the detention is necessary in order to maintain confidence in the administration of justice, having regard to all the circumstances, including the apparent strength of the prosecution's case, the gravity of the offence, the circumstances surrounding its commission, and the potential for a lengthy term of imprisonment.

Often the suspect will be released only after agreeing to certain conditions set by the court—for example, to reside at a particular residence or not to communicate with certain witnesses (s. 515[2] of the Criminal Code).

Most bail hearings are quick. The officer in charge of the investigation makes a recommendation to the Crown prosecutor concerning whether the accused should be released and, if so, whether any conditions should be placed on the release order. Depending on the seriousness of the charge, the background of the offender, and/or the attitude and circumstances of the accused, the bail hearing may take longer. Sometimes it develops into a formal hearing. When there is a debate at a bail hearing about releasing the accused, it typically involves issues relating to the conditions of release rather than whether or not the accused should be released.

BAIL REFORM

The Bail Reform Act (1972) established the system of judicial interim release described above. As amended four years later, the Act is the basis for bail in Canada today. Its creation was largely the result of the Ouimet Committee, which recommended that suspects not be placed in detention unless detention was thought to be the only means to ensure that the accused would appear in court. This recommendation was based on a Canadian study on pretrial detention and an American study on how bail discriminates against the poor. In the Canadian study, Milton Friedland (1965) reported that most of those charged with a criminal offence were arrested as opposed to being issued a summons. In the 6,000 cases he studied, he found that the accused was arrested in 92 percent of the cases and that 84 percent of those arrested remained in custody until their first court appearance.

The American study, referred to as the Manhattan Bail Project, was conducted in New York City in the early 1960s. The Vera Institute, a private, non-profit research organization dedicated to improving the criminal justice system, designed an experimental pretrial program that investigated arrested individuals who could not afford bail in order to see how many would appear in court for trial after being released back into the community following their initial court appearance. The researchers found that the appearance rate of those released on their own recognizance was consistently the same as or better than the rate of those released on monetary bail. As a result of these findings, release-on-recognizance programs were developed, and did much to change the nature of the bail process across North America.

The Manhattan Bail Project also led to the introduction of different types of pretrial release. One such innovation became known as station house release, which involves issuing a suspect a citation to appear in court at a later date and thus bypasses the costly exercise of pretrial detention. This experiment found that most suspects released back into the community appeared in court on the duly appointed date. As a result of these studies, "the prevailing view became that release should be available, regardless of financial circumstances, unless overwhelming factors preclude it" (Anderson and Newman 1993, 216).

The Bail Reform Act prefers that most offenders be released into the community pending trial. This legislation instructs police officers to issue an appearance notice to the accused rather than make an arrest unless officers feel that the public would be placed in jeopardy or the accused has committed a serious indictable offence. In addition, for most offences, the officer in charge of the lockup must release the person charged and compel that person to appear in court by a summons, by promise to appear, or on his or her own recognizance.

In addition, the legislation requires the magistrate to release the accused unless the prosecutor shows cause why the release should not occur. A process known as the "ladder effect" determines whether the accused should be released. This means that in any given case, a prosecutor must, for most offences, convince the magistrate that a less severe release mechanism is not appropriate. The ladder is found in s. 515(2) of the Criminal Code, which establishes that almost every individual can be released on recognizance provided that he or she promises to appear for trial on a designated date. Unsecured bail does not require the defendant to pay money to the court, but that person remains liable for the full amount on failure to appear at the trial. Fully secured bail requires the defendant to post the full amount of bail with the court. The amount of bail cannot be fixed so high that it becomes, in effect, a detention order.

A number of criticisms have been levelled against the bail process in Canada in the recent past (see Exhibit 7.2). Hamilton and Sinclair (1991) reported that

Every day, police vans enter the gated entrance to Toronto's Old City Hall, taking accused persons to their bail hearings. (CP PHOTO/Aaron Harris)

Aboriginal people accused of a crime in Manitoba were more likely to be denied bail than non-Aboriginal people and that they also spent longer periods of time in pretrial detention. The Ontario Commission on Systemic Racism in the Ontario Criminal Justice System found that accused who were Black were more likely to be remanded to custody than if they were not Black. Kellough and Wortley's (2002) study of bail hearings in Toronto revealed that those who received negative personality assessments from the police were more likely to have their applications for bail denied. Furthermore, these police decisions helped explain racial differences in the area of pretrial detention.

Sometimes the quality of information placed before the court in a bail hearing is insufficient in order for an in-depth consideration of risk of further violence. And even if the court orders the alleged offender to sign a peace bond, they may still violate the order and contact the victim at a later date, with tragic results. This system, according to some, "appears too cursory, too prone to error, delay and information falling through the cracks" ("Tragedies Are . . ." 2008, A12).

One such case occurred in British Columbia in 2007 and 2008. On April 4, 2008, Allan Dwayne Schoenborn appeared in a court hearing in Merritt, B.C., a community of about 8,000 residents 270 kilometres northeast of Vancouver, asking to be released on bail so that he could continue to pursue reconciliation with his estranged family. The bail hearing was conducted over the phone with a justice of the peace in Burnaby, B.C. Mr. Schoenborn was facing charges after he was arrested at a local elementary school where his children attended and charged with two counts of uttering threats against the principal and a nine-year-old girl. He informed the court during his bail hearing that he was simply being a protective father and the whole incident was "just a big mix-up." He also expressed remorse for shouting at both the principal and student. Throughout the bail hearing, Mr. Schoenborn was apologetic and meek, expressing a strong interest to be reunited with his family. The RCMP opposed his bail, requesting that he be kept in custody until the following Monday, when Mr. Schoenborn could appear before a judge in person. The RCMP officer who was present stated that Mr. Schoenborn had a prior history of resisting arrest and failing to appear for court dates, and had tried to escape from the RCMP detachment building earlier that afternoon while the police were booking him on two charges arising from the schoolyard incident. Mr. Schoenborn responded by informing the court that he was "a responsible person trying to work my way back home . . . I don't understand how (the police) could come to that conclusions that I may flee from my family" (Hunter 2008, A6).

Although the justice of the peace was informed that Mr. Schoenborn was subject to a peace bond application in Vancouver, it was not made clear in the hearing that the protection order had been put into place after an alleged incident of domestic violence against his wife. The justice of the peace asked the RCMP officer if there was any conflict between the accused and his wife and was told there was none. There was no mention of the fact that Mr. Schoenborn had pleaded guilty to violating that order some five weeks earlier. However, the RCMP spokeswoman said the justice of the peace did have access to all of the relevant information for the case. The RCMP investigator said that all of the documents were faxed to the justice of the peace. Regarding domestic violence, the RCMP stated that these "were not pertinent to the alleged threats that we were investigating. The no-contact order had nothing to do with him uttering threats to the principal or the student, and the only no-contact order was with the wife" (Hunter and Hume 2008, A6).

One major concern among the judiciary is that preventive detention is based on the prediction that the accused will do something wrong in the future. In this sense, the concerns over detention are much like the concerns raised over selective incapacitation (see Chapter 3). Such factors as a previous criminal record and the seriousness of the current offence may lead a Crown prosecutor to request preventive detention. This is at best problematic, since prosecutors may look past the current domestic abuse incident and predict on the basis of the perpetrator's prior record that the accused will obey a bail order, with a condition to stay away from his or her partner and residence.

Our legal system sometimes makes special provisions in connection with judicial interim release. One such instance involves spousal or domestic abuse. Because of zero tolerance laws on these types of abuse, the police cannot simply release the accused on an appearance notice. Usually they require a recognizance with certain conditions, such as the following:

- The accused must have no contact or communication with the complainant.
- The accused must not attend at the residence of the complainant.
- The accused must satisfy the court that he or she has another address at which to live.
- The accused must not possess firearms, ammunition, or explosives (or sometimes weapons such as knives).
- The accused must surrender any firearms acquisition certificate.

JUDICIAL RECOGNIZANCE ORDERS (PEACE BONDS)

But these restrictions are not always a deterrent to continued threats, fear of retaliation, and more violence. In a study of women in shelters across Canada conducted in April 1998, less than one-third of all women had contacted the police or sought a restraining order. In an attempt to ensure that recognizance conditions are followed, the complainant can ask that a peace bond (formally known as a judicial recognizance order) be ordered under s. 810 of the Criminal Code. If a defendant is found in violation of the peace bond, the defendant may be found guilty of a summary conviction offence, with a maximum penalty of 12 months in jail and a $2,000 fine.

According to the peace bond provisions of the Criminal Code:

810(1) any person who fears that another person will cause personal injury to him or his spouse and child or will damage his property may lay an information before a justice . . .

(3) The justice or the summary conviction court . . . may, if satisfied by the evidence adduced that the defendant has reasonable grounds for his fears,

(a) order that the defendant enter into a recognizance, with or without sureties, to keep the peace and to be of good behaviour for any period that does not exceed twelve months, and comply with other such reasonable conditions prescribed in the recognizance the court considers desirable for securing the good conduct of the defendant; or

(b) commit the defendant to prison for a term not exceeding twelve months if he fails or refuses to enter into the recognizance.

Mr. Schoenborn informed the court that he had been staying with his wife for the past three nights, following a year long separation, saying that "We're working hard on trying to have it all—we're working hard, we really are" (Hunter 2008, A6). The justice of the peace decided to give Mr. Schoenborn a "break" and release him after he posted $500 bail despite his own "grave" reservations. Mr. Schoenborn then gave a "God bless" to the justice of the peace at the end of the hearing, which was conducted over the telephone from Burnaby, B.C. He then returned to the trailer home where his wife lived with their three children.

Mr. Schoenborn already had a lengthy criminal record prior to his arrival in Merritt. In May 2007, he was

charged with sexual assault and uttering threats against his wife while she resided in Vancouver. On July 10, 2007, she swore that she had reasonable grounds of fear that Mr. Schoenborn would cause her personal harm. The court placed certain restrictions on Mr. Schoenborn, including that he could not be at any residence of his wife if he had consumed alcohol during the past 12 hours, and that he had to leave her presence or if a police officer requested him to do so. At the end of August 2007, he was later charged with a breach of recognizance from those charges, which resulted in a peace bond against him to have no contact with his wife and to stay away from her residence because he might cause "personal injury" to her. The original charges ended in a stay of proceedings on July 20, 2007, but Mr. Schoenborn admitted to causing fear of injury and was fined $500.00. The following month, he was charged with breaching the peace bonds and in February 2008, he was fined $200.00. In November 2007, he pleaded guilty to impaired driving, was fined more than $1,000 and was prohibited from driving for one year. Then, in December 2007, he was charged with driving while prohibited in the lower mainland of British Columbia (Hume 2008, A6).

On Sunday, April 6, Mr. Schoenborn's three children were found dead by their mother in her trailer in Merritt. The mother, who had left the children in the care of their father, returned home from the local store to find her three children—ages 10, 8, and 5—dead and Mr. Schoenborn gone. He was found ten days later by a local trapper and arrested and charged with three counts of first degree murder. His trial date is scheduled for October 5, 2009.

SEARCH AND SEIZURE

Two sections of the Charter of Rights and Freedoms relate specifically to search and seizure. Section 8, which states that "everyone has the right to be secure against unreasonable search and seizure," is intended to protect an individual's reasonable expectation of privacy. When an investigative technique is classified as a "search" or "seizure," the constitutional requirement of "reasonableness" applies. The Supreme Court has found that a reasonable expectation exists in, for example, a person's home (*R. v. Feeney* [1997]), with regard to information held by a doctor or hospital as a result of medical treatment (*R. v. Dersch* [1991]), and also with regard to an individual's body and bodily fluids "harvested from the individual" (*R. v. Stillman* [1997]). A reduced expectation of privacy has been found in offices and/or workplaces (*R. v. Rao* [1984]) and at border crossings (*R. v. Simmons* [1988]), as well as in prison cells housing inmates (*R. v. Wise* [1992]). There is no expectation of privacy for things in plain view in places where the public is ordinarily invited (*R. v. Fitt* [1996]), for utility billings where no special contractual provisions apply (*R. v. Plant* [1993]), and in the use of infrared overhead technology (*R. v. Bryntwick* [2002]). All unreasonable searches will breach s. 8 of the Charter, but not every unreasonable search will lead to the exclusion of evidence. Section 24(2) points out that when evidence "was obtained in a manner that infringed or denied any rights or freedoms guaranteed by the Charter, the evidence shall be excluded if it is established that . . . the admission of it in the proceedings would bring the administration of justice into disrepute."

The constitutional standards governing searches and seizures in Canada were determined in *Hunter v. Southam* (1984) (see the introduction to this chapter). In this case, the Supreme Court held that a police search without a warrant was unreasonable and that the onus was on the party wishing to uphold the search to prove otherwise. The minimal constitutional standard for a search was determined to include a prior authorization, granted by an independent person acting judicially, based upon reasonable grounds for believing in the existence of facts justifying the search and sworn by oath by the individual seeking the authorization. The Supreme Court did *not* rule that searches not meeting these minimum requirements would automatically be struck down. In essence, the test is whether a warrant is feasible for any type of search of a place, person, or motor vehicle. This ruling protects citizens from unreasonable searches and seizures through a minimum standards approach.

One of the most fundamental rights of Canadians is the right to protection against unreasonable search and seizure. In other words, a citizen has the right to be left alone by the government and its agents unless there are grounds for allowing such intrusion. A *search* is the intrusion of a government representative into an individual's privacy. A *seizure* is the exercise of control by a government representative over an individual and/or item. Generally, a search warrant is required before a search of an individual or a place can be legally conducted. Three different legal areas govern searches and seizures in Canada: common law, the Criminal Code, and the Charter of Rights and Freedoms.

The common law is concerned with the search of persons as well as places. Generally, the police must have a search warrant granted by the judiciary in order to search an individual. However, the common law gives police the right to conduct general body searches and searches of the immediate surrounding area when arresting a suspect (see the doctrine of plain view, below). A body search includes combing out hair samples for forensic evidence but does not include the taking of blood samples, which is considered to be an invasive search. For an invasive search, special statutory authorization is required, and this is usually found in the Criminal Code.

Most of what the police do in this area of law is regulated by s. 487 of the Criminal Code. All police officers must obtain a search warrant by swearing an information in front of a justice of the peace. Before issuing a warrant, the justice of the peace must decide whether there are reasonable grounds for believing that the objects in question will be found at the location in question and that these objects will prove to have been involved in the commission of an offence. The search warrant provides police officers with the power to search places but not individuals (the latter is covered by common law). Currently, a warrant can be obtained for the following:

- Any items on or in respect of which an offence under any federal Act has been committed.
- Anything that will provide evidence of any offence under federal legislation.
- Anything intended to be used to commit an offence against the person for which an arrest without a warrant may be made.

The police officer must specify the offence, describe the items as well as the place (or places) that will be searched, and explain how the search will turn up the items mentioned in the warrant application (ss. 488, 488.1, and 489 of the Criminal Code). The information provided to the justice of the peace by the police may be based on hearsay evidence and it may come from an unnamed source as long as there is evidence to support the reliability of the individual's evidence. As noted below, not all evidence is physical in the way that a weapon or stolen property is physical. For example, the Criminal Code also authorizes a search warrant allowing the police to obtain DNA samples from a suspect. Despite the legal restrictions governing searches and the seizure of evidence, the Law Reform Commission of Canada (1991) maintains that the Criminal Code contains only minimal regulations covering search and seizure and therefore that a lack of certainty exists within the law itself.

Searches usually involve places and people. The Criminal Code has a number of specific provisions regarding the searches of places; there are fewer provisions concerning the searches of persons. The purpose of a search is not to allow the police to "fish" or look around for something that may be important to their investigation; rather, it is to collect evidence. Most often, the police obtain a search warrant from a justice of the peace allowing them to search any building, receptacle, or place named in the warrant. A search warrant is not automatic. A justice of the peace will issue one only if satisfied that there are reasonable grounds to believe that in the mentioned building, receptacle, or place one of the following four items will be found:

- Anything on or in respect of which an offence has been committed or is suspected to have been committed.
- Anything that there is reasonable grounds to believe will be evidence of an offence having been committed or that will reveal the whereabouts of a person believed to have committed an offence.

- Anything that there are reasonable grounds to believe is intended to be used in the commission of an indictable offence.
- Any property used or intended for use in any way with the commission of a criminal organization offence.

A search warrant must specify for what the police are looking. However, the police may seize not only what is mentioned in the warrant but also anything that they find and believe on reasonable grounds has been obtained or used in the commission of an offence.

Can a search warrant be used to search a person? Generally, no. Do the police have the right to collect DNA samples anytime they please or whenever they conduct strip searches? Regarding these questions, see Exhibits 7.3 and 7.4. Can they conduct frisk searches whenever they want once an individual has been lawfully arrested? Should the police be able to use physical force or psychological intimidation beyond what is "reasonable" in order to accomplish the search? The answers to these questions are found in the laws governing search and seizure in Canada. Because the issue of search and seizure encompasses a variety of situations throughout the criminal justice process—notably the right to privacy and physical integrity of private citizens—there has been much debate over appropriate behaviour by the police and other government agents when it comes to searching individuals. In the case of DNA, a search warrant can now be obtained from a provincial court judge to obtain such samples from a suspect for a number of specific offences, including murder and sexual assault (s. 487.5 of the Criminal Code).

REQUIREMENTS FOR SEARCH WARRANTS

The "Reasonableness" Test

This test, as it applies to searches and seizures, generally refers to the question of whether the police have overstepped their authority. Most searches are judged to be unreasonable if an officer lacks sufficient information to justify the search. The appropriate standard of proof is one of "reasonable and probable grounds" rather than proof beyond a reasonable doubt; in other words, a search warrant can be granted only if the request for it is accompanied by facts that indicate to the court that a crime has been committed or is being committed.

Particularity

Particularity refers to the search warrant itself. A search warrant must specify the place to be searched and the

EXHIBIT 7.3 The Seizing of DNA Samples: *R. v. Stillman* (1997)

Early decisions by the courts across Canada took conflicting positions on the taking of DNA samples by the police. In Ontario, the Court of Appeal ruled in *Alderton v. R.* (1985) that the police could take hair samples for DNA testing as part of their powers of search incident to an arrest. But the New Brunswick Court of Appeal, in the case of Alan Legere, a serial killer, held that the police violated s. 8 of the Charter of Rights and Freedoms when they took hair and bodily samples without a warrant or the consent of the accused. However, they admitted the evidence into court under s. 24(2) of the Charter. And in *Borden v. R.* (1994), the Supreme Court of Canada excluded DNA evidence that had led to the accused being convicted of sexual assault (the samples in question did not involve semen). The police in that case had not informed the accused that the samples would be used in their investigation and possibly be used as evidence. The Supreme Court decided that the accused had not waived his rights or consented to the taking of the samples by the police.

Following this case, legislation authorizing the seizure of bodily samples for DNA testing was quickly approved by Parliament. Authorization involves a judge's hearing an application and granting a warrant if probable cause is present. But how far can the police go in terms of seizing a person's bodily samples? Can the police "conscript" an individual into providing them with self-incriminating evidence?

The Supreme Court then heard an appeal involving DNA used to secure a conviction of murder (R. v. *Stillman* [1997]). In this case, a 17-year-old New Brunswick youth had been convicted of the murder of a young woman. The victim had disappeared after a party she had left in the company of Stillman. Six days later, her body was recovered. She had been raped and bitten on her abdomen and had died from blows to the head. Arrested just hours after the discovery of the body, Stillman met his lawyers at the police station. They advised Stillman not to cooperate with the authorities if they wanted to take any bodily samples or to submit to an interrogation. After the lawyers left, the police proceeded to violate this directive. They took the bodily samples they wanted from the accused and then interrogated him for an hour. When the police took a break in their questioning, they agreed to contact Stillman's lawyers and request their presence at the interrogation. In the meantime, the accused went to the washroom, blew his nose, and threw the used tissue into the wastebasket. The police seized the tissue for DNA testing.

When the police took their evidence to a Crown prosecutor to receive approval for a charge, the prosecutor refused, telling them the evidence was still insufficient. Stillman was released, only to be rearrested a few months later. This time, the police obtained teeth impressions and an oral swab, a process that took about two hours to complete. This time the evidence was considered sufficient, and Stillman was subsequently found guilty of murder and sentenced in adult court to life imprisonment. As a 17-year-old, however, he could apply for parole after eight years. His conviction was upheld by the New Brunswick Court of Appeal.

On appeal to the Supreme Court, the defence argued that the teeth impressions and oral swabs had been obtained improperly by the police. The Supreme Court ruled that the police had reasonable and probable grounds to suspect Stillman of the crime. However, they also ruled that the seizures could not be justified by the police as necessary because they could be thrown away or hidden. The majority of the justices viewed the taking of the teeth impressions as especially offensive, although they had been taken by a dentist. In the court's final decision, the hair and dental seizures were deemed the result of "the abusive exercise of raw physical authority by the police." The court also wrote that "if there is not respect for the dignity of the individual and the integrity of the body, then it is but a very short step to justifying the exercise of any physical force of the police if it is undertaken with the aim of solving crimes." In addition, the court felt that while the seizure of the discarded tissue had violated Stillman's right not to be subject to unreasonable search and seizure, it could be admitted as evidence. Parliament responded to the Supreme Court decision by allowing for warrants to obtain bodily impressions if there are reasonable grounds for believing that an offence had been committed and that it would be in the best interests of the administration of justice to serve such a warrant (see s. 487.091 of the Criminal Code).

reasons for searching it. When the police request a search warrant, the warrant must identify the premises and the personal property to be seized, and it must be signed by a police officer. The facts and information justifying the need for a search warrant are set out in an affidavit requesting the warrant.

Searches Needing a Warrant

The power to issue a search warrant is located in s. 487 of the Criminal Code. Before issuing a warrant, a justice must decide whether there are reasonable grounds for believing that the objects in question will be found at the location specified and that the objects will prove to have been used during the commission of an offence.

The issue of whether the police are required to obtain a warrant as a prerequisite to a search or seizure has been a key component of the Supreme Court of Canada's interpretation of s. 8 of the Charter. During the early years of the Charter, the courts took two different positions on the need for warrants. First, some judges and justices of the peace focused on the issue of the reasonableness of police conduct, meaning that a critical evaluation of the "reasonableness" of the search can, if the issue arises, be determined after the search or seizure takes place. The presence or absence of a warrant, or the information found in the warrant, is not always considered the most important criterion in determining whether the search or seizure was reasonable. The Law Reform Commission (1983, 83), in its study of search warrants in seven Canadian cities, concluded that "there is a clear gap between legal rules for issuing and obtaining search warrants and the daily realities of practice." In some locations, police were giving only minimal information to support their request for a warrant and, as a result, were providing the "adjudication no objective basis for making a judicial determination as to whether or not to issue a warrant." This did not mean that the police were involved in illegal searches but, rather, that proper procedures had not been followed, which raised concerns about the reasonableness of a search. The Law Reform Commission (ibid., 86) concluded, after an analysis of all the documents, that

> no decisive relationship [exists] between the legality of the search and the eventual seizure of the specified item. This argues against the possibility that the widespread illegality of warrants is attributable to police decisions to search in inappropriate cases. Rather the indication is that the problem resides with adherence to procedures. In other words, the necessary factual basis for a search may well exist, but the warrant is nonetheless being issued improperly.

The second position was taken by judges and justices of the peace who interpreted s. 8 of the Charter differently. They emphasized that failure to obtain a warrant with all pertinent information is unreasonable except in the most extraordinary situations. In other words, the Charter exists to prevent unreasonable searches and seizures from taking place at all, not to determine whether they were reasonable or unreasonable after the fact.

Invoking strict standards for warrants involving searches and seizures promotes adherence to the law in three ways. First, it requires police officers to make an objective assessment of the "reasonableness" of their evidence before they act. Second, it provides judges with the exact information a police officer has obtained to date, which in turn gives judges the basis for making more informed decisions on the legality of warrants. Third, it provides a neutral and objective assessment of the evidence by a disinterested individual rather than the possibly more subjective view of a police officer "in the heat of the chase." According to advocates of the third position, a proper system for issuing search warrants can be established only in a system of prior authorization, not one that uses subsequent validation.

Warrantless Searches in Exigent Circumstances

A case involving a warrantless search is liable to be deemed illegal and thrown out of court. However, in Canada, a warrantless search can be considered reasonable under some exigent (that is, immediate) circumstances. But what are those circumstances in Canada? When can a police officer conduct a search without a warrant? After all, the Canadian courts have ruled that the police cannot go on "fishing expeditions" for evidence. What is important here are the circumstances of the case and how the police conduct their activities.

After *R. v. Feeney* in 1997 (see above), Bill C-16 was introduced by the federal government to address that ruling, they established two more exceptions to the requirement that a police officer obtain a search warrant before entering a dwelling (an existing exception allowed the police to enter a dwelling while in "hot pursuit" of a suspect). The two new exemptions are where a police officer

- has reasonable grounds to suspect that entry into the dwelling house is necessary to prevent bodily harm or death to any person; or
- has reasonable grounds to believe that entry is necessary to prevent the imminent loss or destruction of evidence.

In addition, illegal searches are not always ruled to be unreasonable. In *R. v. Heisler* (1984), for example, the Alberta Court of Appeal ruled that searching an individual's purse when the individual entered a rock concert was not illegal even though there had been no prior reasonable grounds. And in *R. v. Harris* (1987), Justice Martin of the Ontario Court of Appeal stated that minor or technical defects in a warrant would not automatically make unconstitutional a search or seizure under s. 8 of the Charter.

Drug convictions are sometimes appealed on the issue of warrantless searches. In such cases, police officers observe possession of the drug but don't have time to obtain a search warrant prior to the use or selling of it. In *R. v. Collins* (1987), police officers in British Columbia, while conducting a heroin investigation, observed two suspects in a village pub. When one individual left to go to his car, the police approached him, searched the car, and found a quantity of heroin. Back in the pub, an officer approached the other suspect and proceeded to grab her by the throat to prevent her from swallowing any evidence. The suspect dropped a balloon containing heroin. The trial judge ruled the search unreasonable because the police had used unnecessary force. The Supreme Court of Canada, however, overturned this decision, stating that there was nothing to suggest that the collection of evidence in this manner made the trial unfair.

In determining the reasonableness of a search, the courts examine the following issues:

- Whether the information predicting the commission of a criminal offence was compelling.
- Whether the information was based on an informant's tip, and whether the source was credible.
- Whether the information was corroborated by a police investigation before the decision to conduct the search was made.

The police are permitted to take into account the accused's past record and reputation, provided that such information is relevant to the circumstances of the search.

Searches Incident to an Arrest

Another exception to the search warrant requirement involves searches incident to an arrest. This power is granted to the police by the common law and allows the police to search the suspect for weapons and evidence of a crime without first obtaining a search warrant. For a search incident to arrest to be lawful, the arrest itself must be lawful. This means there must be reasonable grounds for believing that a suspect committed an indictable offence; in other words, the police cannot make an arrest solely to assist their investigation.

The courts have allowed a search incident to arrest on a number of grounds, including the following:

- The need to protect the arresting officers.
- The need to prevent the arrestee from destroying evidence in his or her possession.
- The intrusiveness of the lawful arrest being so great that the incidental search is of minor consequence.
- The fact that the individual could in any event be subjected to an inventory search at the police station.

The Supreme Court of Canada unanimously agreed in *Cloutier v. Langlois* (1990) that most searches are to be based on reasonable grounds but that searches incidental to arrest need not be. In this case, the police stopped a motorist for making an illegal right-hand turn. The officers found that the motorist had several unpaid traffic fines. The driver became agitated and abusive toward the police, who then had him spread his legs by the car and frisked him. The motorist later sued the police officers for assaulting him. The Supreme Court ruled that reasonable grounds are not necessary for a frisk search incident to an arrest, and that such searches are necessary for "the effective and safe enforcement of the law [and] ensuring the freedom and dignity of individuals." Here, the police were justified in believing that the search was necessary for their safety. In most cases, frisk searches at the time of arrest will probably be considered constitutional. In addition, searches of the immediate vicinity of a crime scene will generally be accepted if the search can be justified on the basis of "prompt and effective discovery and preservation of evidence" (*R. v. Lim* [1990]).

However, the courts have also stated that before conducting a frisk search, the police must inform the suspect of the right to counsel. But the police do not have to wait until the suspect contacts a lawyer before a search is made.

The Supreme Court has placed the following limits on the common law and the right to search an individual incident to arrest:

- The police have discretion over whether a search is necessary for the effective and safe application of the law.
- The search must be for a valid criminal objective (e.g., to check for weapons or to prevent an escape).
- The search cannot be used to intimidate, ridicule, or pressure the accused to gain admissions.
- The search must not be conducted in an abusive way.

There are exceptions to these rights. In *R. v. Tomaso* (1989), the accused appealed his conviction for dangerous driving, arguing that the police collected blood from his bleeding ear while he was unconscious in hospital. The

EXHIBIT 7.4 Strip Searches by the Police: *R. v. Golden*

In *R. v. Golden* (2001), the Supreme Court of Canada ruled for the first time on the lawfulness of a strip search. As Dickson (2002) has pointed out, this case was significant because while the courts had ruled on the police searching private residences, the rules governing physical searches were less developed. In fact, the Criminal Code does not mention body searches. In its ruling, the justices of the Supreme Court attempted to balance the reasonable expectation of privacy held by someone who has been arrested with the requirements of the police. The issue in this case revolved around s. 8 of the Charter, which states that "everyone has the right to be secure against unreasonable search or seizure."

In this particular case, police officers entered a Toronto café to arrest Golden, whom they believed was trafficking cocaine. After arresting him, the police patted him down but did not find any weapons or drugs in his possession. Still in the café, the police then visually inspected (i.e., strip searched) Golden's underwear for drugs. He was then forced to bend over a table; the police then made him lower his pants and underwear so that his buttocks and genitalia were exposed. The police were able to seize a bag of crack cocaine weighing 10 grams. Golden was arrested for possession of a narcotic for the purpose of trafficking (the police had observed him selling a substance similar to crack cocaine during their surveillance of the café).

At his trial, Golden argued that the case should be thrown out of court because the police had conducted an illegal search. He based his contention on s. 8 of the Charter. The trial judge refused to accept this defence, found him guilty, and sentenced him to 14 months in a provincial correctional facility. Golden appealed his conviction to the Ontario Court of Appeal, which dismissed his appeal. However, the Supreme Court of Canada, in a 5 to 4 vote, overturned the conviction and acquitted him.

As a result of the Supreme Court's decision, "a strip search will always be unreasonable if it is carried out abusively or for the purpose of humiliating or punishing the arrestee" (ibid., 36). The Supreme Court also decided that even when the police conducted a routine strip search in good faith and with no violence involved, it would still violate s. 8 of the Charter if there was no compelling purpose for conducting it during an arrest.

The Court also found that the common law of search incident to arrest, which permits strip searches, does not violate s. 8 of the Charter. The common law has it that such searches are to be carried out only where the police establish reasonable and probable grounds for a strip search for the purpose of discovering weapons and seizing evidence related to the offence for which the person was arrested. However, strip searches are to be conducted in a manner that preserves the dignity and privacy of the person arrested. In *Golden*, the arrest was lawful and the strip search was related to the purpose of the arrest; but the strip search had not been carried out in a reasonable manner.

---

blood sample revealed that the accused had been impaired at the time of the accident. The Ontario Court of Appeal determined that the seizure was unreasonable—but only because the accused was not charged until two weeks later.

Warrantless Searches in Motor Vehicles

The Supreme Court of Canada has established that a warrantless search of a vehicle may be reasonable if grounds exist for believing that the vehicle contains drugs or other contraband. However, the power to search a vehicle without a warrant must be found in statute or in common law (e.g., a search can be conducted incident to a valid arrest).

The legality of searching motor vehicles has been a difficult issue for the police. Can a police officer search the interior of a vehicle? Or a locked suitcase, or a closed briefcase? In *R. v. Mellenthin* (1992), the Supreme Court of Canada ruled that the accused's rights had been violated when, at a police check stop, the accused was questioned about the contents of a bag. The suspect handed over the bag, which was found to contain narcotics. However, the officer had not suspected that the accused was in possession of illegal drugs when he asked to search the bag. The Supreme Court has ruled that the purpose of a police check stop is to detect impaired drivers or dangerous vehicles, not to conduct unreasonable searches. In *Mellenthin*, there was no informed consent.

Other Types of Warrantless Searches

The Doctrine of Plain View

The police can search for and seize evidence without a warrant if the illegal object is in plain view. For example, if a police officer arrives at a home in response to an incident of domestic violence and notices marijuana on the coffee table, the officer can seize the evidence and arrest the suspect. However, if the officer suspects that more drugs are in the house, the officer will have to apply for and receive an authorized search warrant before investigating further. Also, if an officer arrests a suspect in a kitchen, the kitchen cupboards can be looked into, but only if it can be shown later that the search was more than a "fishing expedition." Justification clearly exists when there is a report of a weapon but no weapon is visible. A police officer who suspects that the weapon was placed in a cupboard just before he or she arrived may decide to check all the cupboards.

Reasonable Grounds

If a police officer stops a motor vehicle because of a defective taillight and the driver leans over, the officer may become suspicious that an illegal item is being hidden. Nothing in the act of leaning over can, by itself, make a police officer suspicious, but when the officer talks to the motorist and the motorist appears nervous and says nothing, an experienced officer can come to the reasonable conclusion that the motorist is hiding something. This may give the officer reasonable cause to search the vehicle (Salhany 1986).

The provision for "reasonable grounds" is found in s. 101(1) of the Criminal Code. It allows a police officer to search without a warrant when the officer believes he or she has reasonable grounds for believing that an offence is being committed or has been committed. The section also deals with prohibited weapons, restricted weapons, firearms or ammunition, and evidence of an offence that is likely to be found on a person, in a vehicle, or in any place or premises other than a dwelling place. In *R. v. Singh* (1983), the accused fit the description of a suspect wanted for interrogation about a multiple shooting. The incident had occurred just a few minutes before, when the suspect was seen in the same vicinity. When stopped by police, the suspect had a noticeable bulge in his pocket and refused to make eye contact with the police. The police then searched the suspect and found the weapon used in the crime. In this case, the Ontario Court of Appeal ruled that there had been no unreasonable search and seizure as specified by s. 8 of the Charter of Rights.

Similarly, in *R. v. Ducharme* (1990), police officers noticed a man running into a lane with a full garbage bag at 3 a.m. When they stopped the individual, they noticed that the man's hands were cut and bleeding. An officer searched the bag, without consent, and found 32 cartons of cigarettes. It was later reported that the glass door of a store had been broken and that cigarettes had been stolen from inside. The accused was convicted, but the defence lawyer appealed the case, arguing that the officer had performed an improper search. However, the British Columbia Court of Appeal ruled that since the search occurred peacefully in a public place, no invasion of the body occurred; under incriminating conditions it was "reasonable" for the officer to search the garbage bag. It was not necessary to arrest the accused before looking into the bag. In this case and in *Ducharme,* the courts ruled that police officers can search if they have reasonable grounds for suspicion.

Section 489 of the Criminal Code also permits police officers to seize items not mentioned on a warrant. The key issue here is that the officer must believe on reasonable grounds that the item in question has been obtained by, or has been used in, the commission of an offence.

Consent Searches

Police officers may also make a warrantless search when an individual voluntarily consents to the search. Those individuals who choose to consent to a search are waiving their constitutional rights. Thus, the police may have to prove in court that the consent was voluntarily given to them.

The major legal issue in most consent searches is whether the police can prove that consent was given to them voluntarily. In *R. v. Wills* (1992), the Supreme Court of Canada provided guidelines for establishing whether voluntary consent was given:

- The giver of the consent had the authority to give the consent in question.
- The consent was voluntary in the sense that it was free from coercion and not the result of police oppression, coercion, or other external conduct that negated the freedom to choose whether the police should continue.
- The giver of the consent was aware of the right to refuse to give consent to the police to engage in search.
- The giver of the consent was aware of the potential consequences of giving the consent.

ELECTRONIC SURVEILLANCE

The use of wiretaps to listen to conversations between individuals has had a significant impact on police work. These electronic devices allow the authorities to listen to and record private discussions between people over telephones as well as through the walls and windows of houses. Using a variety of techniques, police are able to listen to private discussions and obtain information on criminal activities.

The oldest and most commonly used type of electronic surveillance is wiretapping. With a search warrant from the courts, police officers can listen to and record conversations over telephone lines. This evidence is considered admissible and has often led to convictions.

The Law of Electronic Surveillance

In Canada, the judiciary can authorize the interception of private communications and admit the information obtained as evidence. It seems that most applications for authorizations for electronic eavesdropping are accepted. Between 1985 and 1989, only three applications out of a total of 2,222 were rejected. According to the Solicitor General of Canada (1991), this low rejection rate reflects two facts: (1) strict procedures are being followed; and (2) judges return an unknown number of applications to the police with the requirement that they provide more information about the case before any authorization is granted. The Solicitor General points out that almost all of the 408 authorizations granted in 1989 involved a conspiracy to commit a serious drug offence. Electronic surveillance seems to be a vital tool in the fight against organized drug rings.

Drug offenders have resorted to Charter defences, their argument being that electronic surveillance by the police brings the administration of justice into disrepute. However, the Supreme Court has ruled that if the police act in good faith—that is, act in accordance with what they understand the law to be—the evidence should be admitted. In *R. v. Duarte* (1990), the Supreme Court of Canada ruled on the issue of the police acting in good faith. In this case, OPP officers and the Toronto police were conducting a joint investigation involving large quantities of cocaine. The investigation also involved a police informant and an undercover police officer. Both of them consented to having electronic surveillance equipment placed in the walls of the apartment, which was occupied by the informant and paid for by the police. In this situation, a court authorization was not required by law, since both the informant and the undercover operator had agreed to the use of such equipment. The lower court judge agreed with the defendant that when the police conducted electronic surveillance without judicial authorization, even when one of the

individuals had consented to the surveillance, they had violated s. 8 of the Charter.

Two other cases, both heard in 1990 by the Supreme Court of Canada, had a significant impact on the laws governing electronic surveillance. In *R. v. Wong* (1990), the Court determined that video surveillance of a location in which there is a reasonable expectation of privacy without prior judicial authorization is contrary to s. 8 of the Charter. And in *R. v. Garofoli* (1990), the court ruled that s. 7 of the Charter entitled the accused access to materials used to obtain an authorization of electronic surveillance, subject to editing.

Electronic surveillance has become a prominent issue over the past few years. A number of Western countries, including the United Kingdom, the United States, and New Zealand, have updated their legislation in this area. In Canada, the authorities feel that Canadian laws governing electronic surveillance have not kept up with the techniques used by criminals to communicate. Currently, the police need court permission to listen in on telephone conversations. Also, it is illegal to intercept and open letter mail, but it is unclear whether e-mails are in the same category. And the Defence Department's Communications Security Establishment has the ability to intercept all telephone communications within Canada and calls across the border, but it must obtain ministerial permission to intercept and record telephone calls in which at least one Canadian citizen is involved (Naumetz 2005). Currently, about 2,000 wiretap warrants are issued each year, and they must be renewed every 60 days (Clark 2005).

One of the issues surrounding the laws governing electronic surveillance in Canada is that they were introduced more than 30 years ago. Today, the police have a difficult time monitoring e-mails and Internet

Electronic surveillance devices are much more common in public spaces, especially in large cities. Do you think they help prevent crimes and identify suspects after a crime has been committed? (© iStockphoto/Maciej Korzekwa)

surfing; sometimes they are able to conduct surveillance only by accessing service providers' facilities. The police and intelligence officials are now pointing out that their technological capabilities have not kept pace with the new technologies being used by terrorists as well as by organized criminal groups (Clark 2006). They want the federal government to introduce a law that would force telephone and Internet networks to build in access for wiretaps and surveillance capabilities as well as to keep more client records that could be accessed by the police.

In the fall of 2005, the then-Liberal federal government introduced Bill C-74 (also known as the Modernization of Investigative Techniques Act), which was designed to increase the powers of surveillance of the authorities by making the telecommunications industry build wiretapping capabilities into their networks. The intent here was to launch a system capable of conducting around-the-clock surveillance on the e-mails and Internet and phone use of more than 8,000 people at a time. The bill would require all telecommunication providers to install equipment that is "intercept capable." A draft version of the legislation did not require the police to receive court authority to intercept communications or to demand information from Internet service providers (Naumetz 2005). When the minority Liberal government lost the federal election at the end of 2005, the bill essentially "died."

The Conservative federal government decided to revive the bill and proposed new legislation in June 2009. On June 18, 2009, two new bills were introduced into Parliament: the Investigative Powers for the 21st Century Act and the Technical Assistance for Law Enforcement in the 21st Century Act. In the proposed legislation, the federal government is attempting to amend the Criminal Code to allow police to collect digital evidence during their investigations. Some of the issues addressed by this proposed legislation include updating the offence of child sexual exploitation. While the Criminal Code now prohibits anyone from using the Internet to communicate directly with a child for the purpose of facilitating child sexual exploitation, it does not prohibit someone from agreeing or making arrangements with another person to sexually exploit a child. Under the proposed legislation, a new offence would be created that prohibits anyone from using a computer system to agree or make arrangements with any individual for the purpose of sexually exploiting a child. The new offence would have a maximum punishment of 10 years' imprisonment. The new legislation would also permit the police to obtain data from the Internet, through the creation of something referred to as "transmission data." This data, which does not include the content of a private communication, could be obtained from two different types of judicial order: (1) a warrant when the data is acquired in real-time, and (2) a production order for historical data. In addition, the proposed legislation wants to ensure that communication data can be traced to the initial service provider. This would allow the police to request the disclosure of enough transmission data to trace all the service providers involved in the transmission of specific data.

Some individuals worry about the impact of the proposed bill, and contend that it will give the police and other authorities too much power in the lives of Canadians. Police and security officials counter that the bill would simply allow them to identify information that might be crucial to their time-sensitive investigations. They point out that Internet surveillance led to the June 2006 arrest of 18 terror suspects who allegedly had been planning attacks on Toronto and Ottawa (Clark 2006). Others, however, point to the same arrests and note that the police were able to work within the existing laws respecting civil liberties while tracking security threats ("Big Brother . . ." 2006; Hartley and El Akkad 2009). As early as June 15, 2006, Bell Sympatico began informing its customers through its service agreement that it was planning to "monitor or investigate content or your use of your service provider's networks and to disclose any information necessary to satisfy any laws, regulations or other governmental request" (ibid.). Lawyers concerned about legislation in this area want the federal government to "ensure Canadians' private information is appropriately protected" and that police investigations should not proceed "without a demonstrated need, just like telephone wiretaps" (Tibbetts 2006).

STAY OF PROCEEDINGS

What happens when an individual commits a crime a number of years before charges are laid? Judges in Canada have the discretion to stay the proceedings when they believe such a situation abuses the rights of the accused. A delay in the charging and prosecution of an accused for a sexual offence cannot justify a stay of proceedings, however. Sometimes the information concerning a sexual offence will come to the attention of the police years after the reported incident occurred. The police may take months or years to decide that they have the reasonable and probable grounds to lay charges.

In *R. v. L. (W.K.)* (1991), the accused was charged in 1987 with 17 counts of sexual assault, gross indecency, and assault involving his two daughters and stepdaughter. The victims complained to the police in 1986, although the first incident had reportedly occurred in 1957 and the last in 1985. The trial judge stayed the proceedings, since to do otherwise would have violated the right of the accused to fundamental justice. Both the British Columbia Court of Appeal and the Supreme Court of Canada ruled that the trial should not have been stayed. The Supreme Court ruled that the fairness of a trial is not automatically jeopardized by a lengthy pre-charge delay. In fact, such a delay may favour the accused, since the police may find it more difficult to find witnesses and corroborating evidence, if needed.

In some cases, the complainant may make charges of illegal sexual activity on the part of the accused but not wish the case to proceed to court and give evidence. This is what happened in *R. v. D.(E.)* (1990), and the police decided not to proceed with the charges on the condition the accused agree to have no more contact with the family. Four years later, the victims decided to press charges against the accused, and charges were laid by the police. The accused argued that his rights had been violated. The judge agreed that this case would constitute an abuse of process and ordered a stay of proceedings. The Crown appealed and won. The Court of Appeal rested its decision on the fact that the accused had given no formal statement to the police in 1984 and had talked to them on a "non-caution, no-charge basis." The appeal court stated that an abuse of process would have occurred only if the prosecution had unfairly reneged on the expectations it expressed to the accused.

LEGAL AID

Section 10(b) of the Charter of Rights and Freedoms states that all Canadians have the "right to retain counsel without delay" for criminal cases. This right may involve the use of legal aid lawyers for those who cannot afford to retain private counsel and who earn under a certain income. In the earliest days of our criminal justice system, defence lawyers played an important role in the protection of the accused by providing free (pro bono) **legal aid** as an expression of social responsibility. In recent decades, however, formal legal aid programs have been developed, with the result that legal aid systems across Canada are "viewed both as an aspect of social welfare and an important component of an effective justice system" (Johnstone and Thomas 1998, 2).

Since the introduction of the Charter of Rights and Freedoms, the role of legal aid has changed. In *R. v. Manninen* (1987), the accused person had the impression that the right to legal counsel was based on his ability to afford this service. Because that view was not corrected by the police, the Supreme Court held that the accused had not been able to use his right to counsel. It followed that s. 10(b) of the Charter had been violated. Today, s. 10(b) has been judicially interpreted to mean that any person arrested must be informed by the police of the existence and availability of duty counsel and legal aid in the jurisdiction (*R. v. Brydges* [1990]). In *Brydges* (at 43), the Supreme Court held that s. 10(b) imposed two duties on the police. "First, the police must give the accused or detained person a reasonable opportunity to exercise the right to retain and instruct counsel," and second, "the police must refrain from questioning or attempting to elicit information from the detainee until the detainee has had that reasonable opportunity." This right was expanded in *R. v. Pozniak* (1994), when the Supreme Court ruled that when a toll-free number had been established by local or provincial authorities, the police had to inform the detained individual that it could be used to contact duty counsel or a legal aid lawyer.

In recent years, Charter decisions have extended the use of legal aid in our criminal justice system. In *R. v. Prosper* (1994), the Supreme Court decided on the issue of whether or not s. 10(b) of the Charter imposed a substantive constitutional obligation on governments to provide free and immediate legal counsel to individuals detained by the authorities. The Supreme Court ruled unanimously that this obligation did not exist. Its decision was based on the reasoning that the original drafters of s. 10(b) of the Charter had turned down the idea of free duty counsel as part of the protections given to detainees and that "such an obligation would almost certainly interfere with governments' allocation of limited resources by requiring them to expend public funds on the provision of a service" (*R. v. Prosper* [1994], at 267).

Some, however, consider legal aid such an important part of our criminal justice system they feel its provision should become a Charter right. The approach established in *Prosper* was modified somewhat in 1999 when the Supreme Court held that government-funded legal counsel must be provided, although only in limited circumstances in order to ensure that s. 7 and the principles of fundamental justice are met. In *New Brunswick v. G.(J.)* (1999), the Supreme Court held that a constitutional obligation exists when a province removes a child from the family home and a parent seeks to challenge the court order. While the ruling in this case in effect extended s. 7 beyond the criminal law to family law and custody hearings, the justices made it clear that this obligation on provincial authorities existed only to ensure a fair trial under s. 7 when the parents lacked the financial and mental capacity to serve as their own counsel.

Others argue that this right should be extended in certain criminal cases, so that a judge can order legal aid for an accused who will serve time in a federal or provincial correctional facility if convicted. In addition to rights granted to the accused during their initial appearance in the Canadian criminal justice system, the rights of the defendant are recognized as well, including the right to a legal aid lawyer in certain conditions—for example, when an appeal of the case is heard or during parole revocation hearings. The right to legal aid continues to be expanded. In September 1999, the Supreme Court of Canada ruled that prisoners who face solitary confinement have a right to legal aid (Makin 1999).

Before a system of legal aid was introduced into our criminal justice system just a few decades ago, defendants who could not afford their own lawyers were susceptible to local provisions for free legal representation. This system was obviously problematic, with many of its critics arguing that it discriminated against the poor. An important legal decision in the United States illustrated the problem of insufficient access to free legal counsel and led to the development of formal legal aid systems in Canada. The case in question was *Gideon v. Wainright* (1963), which led to a U.S. Supreme Court decision now seen as having had a greater impact on the criminal court process than any other Supreme Court case. Gideon was charged in a Florida state court with breaking and entering a poolroom. While giving his plea, Gideon asked the court to appoint a lawyer to represent him. The court refused, since free legal representation was available only to those charged with a capital crime. Gideon argued that it was his constitutional right to be represented by a lawyer, citing the Sixth Amendment to the U.S. Constitution, which states, in part, that "in all criminal prosecutions, the accused shall enjoy the right . . . to have the Assistance of Counsel for his defense."

The state court judge refused Gideon's request, with the result that Gideon conducted his own defence. Defending himself as best he could with his limited legal knowledge, Gideon made an opening statement to the jury, cross-examined the prosecution's witnesses, called his own witnesses, and gave a concluding statement in which he argued that he was innocent of the charge. The jury found him guilty, and the judge sentenced him to five years in prison. Gideon appealed his case to the Florida Supreme Court, arguing that the state's refusal to appoint him legal counsel denied him his constitutional rights. The Florida Supreme Court upheld the conviction. Gideon then wrote a letter to the U.S. Supreme Court, which agreed to hear his case. They appointed him free legal counsel and ultimately agreed with his argument.

In Canada, the first province to provide a legal aid system was Ontario, in 1967. The last was Yukon, in 1979. In 1973, the federal government began providing funds to provincial legal aid programs; to receive funding, a program had to offer criminal law services when an accused was charged with an indictable offence or when the accused faced the loss of liberty or livelihood in a summary conviction offence. Governments are the major source of revenue for legal aid plans. The cost of providing legal aid services has increased dramatically over the past decade. In 1987–88, the total cost of legal aid programs in Canada was approximately $260 million; by 1990–91, it had risen to $412 million, and by 1992–93, to more than $600 million, before dropping to $536 million in 1996–97. The federal government has reduced its contribution significantly over the past few years, with the result that provincial governments have had to pay more of the costs. Some provinces have stopped funding legal aid programs, thus forcing provincial bar associations to pay for them. In 2002, defence lawyers in several Ontario cities proposed that they stay away from court for one day to protest the fact that legal aid fees paid to them had been frozen in that province for 15 years. Later that same year, the premier of British Columbia inspired a controversy when he announced that legal aid in that province would be reduced by 40 percent (Tibbetts 2002b).

According to the federal government's own evaluation, the financial cutbacks to legal aid in the mid- and late 1990s have had a strong negative impact. Legal aid is now a "directionless program that is hampered by federal funding cuts, patchwork of services from province to province and no national standards to ensure poor people have access to justice." The same report states that legal aid "is only given to Canada's poorest of the poor—and only when they face jail terms if convicted" (Tibbetts 2002a). Yet legal aid is considered such an important component of ensuring access to justice for the poor that a legal aid expert at the Canadian Bar Association commented that the federal government should establish minimum legal aid standards. And the Chief Justice of the Supreme Court of Canada, Chief Justice Beverley McLachlin, stated in 2002 that governments should treat legal aid as an essential service. These statements reflect the belief that all Canadians have the right to a fair trial, and that even in times of government restraint, certain basic duties are unavoidable (Davison 2000, 16).

In 2004–05, there were 755,300 applications for legal assistance across Canada. This was a 1 percent decrease from the previous year. The number of applications was much lower than in 1994–95, when there were 1.1 million applications. The reasons for this decrease include the use of prescreening procedures, changes in legal aid coverage in various provinces, stricter eligibility requirements, and an increased use of duty counsel and of pro bono services provided by private lawyers (Besserer 2006). Between 1998–99 and 2001–02, the number of legal aid applications increased slightly (to 850,000 in 2001–02). The number of applications has declined in each of the years since. In 2004–05, most legal aid applications across Canada were for criminal matters rather than civil ones. Eighty-three percent of all legal aid applications in New Brunswick were for criminal matters, as were 73 percent of all applications in Saskatchewan. In Ontario and Quebec, most legal aid applications were for civil matters (76 percent and 56 percent, respectively). These differences are consistent with the ratio of direct legal service expenditures on criminal as opposed to civil matters.

Three models for providing legal aid for those who qualify are used in Canada: **judicare,** the staff system (also referred to as the **public defender** model), and a combination of these two approaches, referred to as the mixed or combined approach. The judicare model operates in British Columbia, Ontario, and Alberta. In this program, a qualified legal aid recipient receives a certificate to that effect. The benefits of this system include lower costs, the availability of services, and the efficiency inherent in having one lawyer handle the case from beginning to end. Usually lawyers are paid a set fee for their services, but this amount is typically too low to cover their costs. Rural areas are better served by this system, since the population base is too small to justify the maintenance of a permanent legal aid office funded by the government. It is far less costly to allow clients to select legal counsel from those already in the area. Other benefits of this system are as follows: (1) legal aid recipients can select their own lawyer; (2) normal lawyer–client relationships can be maintained for poor defendants; and (3) clients can select lawyers whom they feel will best serve their interests (Burns and Reid 1981).

The staff system operates in Saskatchewan, Newfoundland and Labrador, Nova Scotia, and Yukon. In this system, the lawyers are in effect employees of the provincial government. One benefit of this system is that the lawyers involved are salaried—which ensures that the client receives competent legal counsel—and take no money for their services from their clients or their clients' families. Another advantage is that the public defenders representing a legal aid case are able to contact other public defenders; this allows them to benefit from group resources and expertise. Private-practice lawyers can also be used in this model, especially when a conflict of interest arises or if a staff lawyer is unavailable for the case.

According to Burns and Reid (ibid., 414–16), the benefits of this approach include the following:

- Better representation, because lawyers are specialists, with some becoming spokespersons for the poor.
- Lower costs.
- Greater efficiency, because the system is centralized.
- Better service of the interests of clients, because lawyers are salaried and therefore do not need to use legal tactics that benefit them.

The mixed system is practised on Prince Edward Island as well as in Manitoba, Quebec, New Brunswick, the Northwest Territories, and Nunavut. In these jurisdictions, the legal aid recipient has the right to choose legal counsel, either staff or private, from a panel of lawyers providing legal aid services (Johnstone and Thomas 1998).

Does a person receiving legal aid have a greater chance of being convicted? In a study comparing judicare legal counsel and public defenders in British Columbia, Brantingham (1985) found no difference in terms of conviction rates (guilty outcome rates) and sentence severity (the amount and length of jail term). However, she did find that these two types of legal aid varied substantially with regard to sentencing outcomes. Specifically, judicare clients received more jail sentences or absolute discharges, while the clients of public defenders were given more sentences involving probation orders, restitution, community work orders, and fines. Brantingham (ibid., 77) attributed these differences to the fact that clients of public defenders were sentenced after guilty pleas, "particularly guilty pleas following discussions between the public defenders and the Crown counsel."

Morse and Lock (1988, 36), interviewing Aboriginal offenders on their perceptions of the criminal justice system, heard considerable criticism of legal aid lawyers. They pointed to the fact that legal aid "is overworked so lawyers tell 75 percent–90 percent of accused to plead guilty," and that there "is no real choice in who gets to act as your lawyer." Native offenders also complained that legal aid lawyers did not invest much time in them and their cases and "often don't see them in custody until five minutes before appearing in court." Only 41 percent of the offenders indicated that they were satisfied with their legal representation, while 48 percent said they were dissatisfied.

HEAT EMISSIONS (FLIR) AND THE REASONABLE EXPECTATION OF PRIVACY

The purpose of s. 8 of the Charter of Rights and Freedoms is "to protect individuals from unjustified State intrusion upon their privacy (*Hunter v. Southam Inc.* [1984]) by granting individuals "a reasonable expectation of privacy" (*R. v. Evans* [1996]). In both of these cases, the Supreme Court of Canada decided that individuals can establish that a search or seizure violated their s. 8 rights if they can show that they had a reasonable expectation of privacy in the item seized, the place searched, or both. If an individual is unable to demonstrate a reasonable expectation of privacy, and that the expectation of privacy was unjustifiably intruded upon, then the state or its representatives cannot have violated the individual's rights under s. 8.

However, emerging technologies can potentially test the limits of a person's privacy in our society. Some of these emerging technologies may be used by the police in their investigation of criminal activity. One of the problems associated with emerging technologies "has been the degree to which they create novel privacy concerns by making knowable and meaningful information and data that previously existed but weren't susceptible to being captured or conclusively comprehended through ordinary human senses" (Bailey 2008, 283). One such example of this is the forward looking infra-red camera (FLIR). This technology allows the police to monitor the heat emissions emerging from a residence and which may indicate that an excessive amount of electricity is being used, perhaps for a marijuana grow operation.

What is the relationship between new technologies, police powers, and the expectation of privacy by citizens? While the right to privacy in Canada is not explicitly protected by the Charter of Rights and Freedoms, it is protected indirectly through other constitutional provisions, most notably the s. 8 protection against unreasonable search and seizure. The issue for s. 8 is the determination of whether or not the "expectation of privacy should be considered reasonable in the circumstances of a challenged search and seizure by state agents" (ibid.).

This relationship was considered by the Supreme Court of Canada in *R. v Tessling* (2004). In this case, the police received a tip that Mr. Tessling was growing a large amount of marijuana in his home. Since a tip alone is not enough to establish "reasonable and probable grounds" for a search warrant, the police decided to look for other evidence that Mr. Tessling was involved in a marijuana grow operation. They decided that since grow operations use a great deal of artificial light and emanate a large amount of heat, they flew over the house and took a picture of the heat energy coming from the house using a forward-looking infrared (FLIR) camera in order to determine whether or not a large amount of electricity was being used. The tip, together with the FLIR picture, was used to obtain a search warrant. When the police entered Mr. Tessling's house, they found large amounts of marijuana, drug-trafficking paraphernalia, as well as some weapons.

The case revolved around the issue of whether or not heat produced from within a residence entitled to a high level of privacy after the heat was emitted outside? Mr. Tessling was found guilty in the lower courts for possessing 120 marijuana plants and was handed an 18-month sentence. Mr. Tessling then appealed the verdict to the Ontario Court of Appeal. During the hearing, the Crown admitted that without the FLIR images, there was insufficient evidence to support a search warrant. A key question in this case was whether or not the use of the FLIR device constituted an unreasonable search within the meaning of s. 8 of the Charter of Rights and Freedoms.

The Court of Appeal ruled in favour of Mr. Tessling, holding that individuals have a reasonable expectation of privacy in the heat energy that emits from their residence and, as such, FLIR "merits a warrant because the detected heat may come from 'perfectly innocent' private activities, such as taking a bath or using lights at unusual hours" (Tibbetts 2004, A13). Their decision was based on the view that escaping heat is a product of activity occurring within a home—and that an individual's home is viewed as his castle. Furthermore, they noted a growing consensus in society that marijuana is not a particularly harmful drug, making it more palatable to exclude the evidence (Makin 2004, A12).

The Ontario Court of Appeal decision "was based on two basic premises: (1) despite the fact that the imaging takes place outside the home, FLIR technology reveals information about activities taking place within the home and that (2) the FLIR device reveals information that could not be otherwise be observed or quantified" (Boucher and Landa 2005, 70). The court held that the use of FLIR was a significant intrusion into the privacy of the home and should be unlawful in the absence of a warrant. They also noted that the intrusion was "almost Orwellian in its theoretical capacity" and disproportionate to the seriousness of producing marijuana. In addition, the breach of privacy in the heat emission "was deemed by the Court of Appeal to be so serious that it could not survive the test for exclusion under section 24(2) of the Charter" (ibid., 71).

The Supreme Court of Canada, in a 7–0 decision, upheld Mr. Tessling's conviction, rejecting the concerns noted by the Ontario Court of Appeal. The Supreme Court held that Mr. Tessling did not have a reasonable expectation of privacy as the information disclosed by the FLIR camera was meaningless. The Supreme Court justices took the view that such technology was both non-intrusive in its operations and mundane in the data it is capable of producing. It is clear, to repeat, that at present no warrant could ever be granted solely on the basis of a FLIR image. According to the decision by the Supreme Court,

> . . . external patterns of heat distribution on the external surfaces of the house is not information in which the respondent had a reasonable expectation of privacy. The heat distribution, as stated, offers no insight into his private life, and reveals nothing of "biographical core of personal information." Its disclosure scarcely affects the "dignity, integrity, and autonomy" of the person whose house is subject of the FLIR image. (*R. v. Tessling* [2004], para. 63)

The Supreme Court of Canada also chose not to focus on the theoretical capacity of the technology as the Ontario Court of Appeal did, but rather on its actual capacity. According to the Supreme Court,

> . . . the reasonableness line has to be determined by looking at the information generated by existing FLIR technology, and then evaluating its impact on a reasonable privacy interest. If, as expected, the capability of FLIR and other technologies will improve and the nature and quality of the information hereafter changes, it will be a different case, and the courts will have to deal

with the privacy implications at that time in light of the facts as they then exist.

In its decision, the Supreme Court identified a set of criteria it considered to be appropriate to determining whether or not privacy interests had been violated in this particular instance:

1. What was the subject matter of the FLIR image?
2. Did the respondent have a direct interest in the subject matter of the FLIR image?
3. Did the respondent have a subjective expectation of privacy in the subject matter of the FLIR image?
4. If so, was the expectation objectively reasonable? In this respect, regard must be had to:
   a. the place where the alleged "search" occurred;
   b. whether the subject matter was in pubic view;
   c. whether the subject matter had been abandoned;
   d. whether the information was already in the hands of third parties; If so, was it subject to an obligation of confidentiality?
   e. whether the police technique was intrusive in relation to the privacy interest;
   f. whether the use of surveillance technology was itself objectively unreasonably;
   g. whether the FLIR heat profile exposed any intimate details of the respondent's lifestyle, or information of a biographical nature.

The impact of this decision, according to Boucher and Landa (2005, 73), is that it appears that the police are free to use FLIR technology in its current format, and probably other versions of the technology, without a warrant, provided that the investigative technique does not reveal core biographical information about a person and so long as the technology does not permit the police to "see" inside a person's home. Prior to this decision, the jurisprudence on whether the police could use certain investigative technologies without a warrant was inconsistent. Certain decisions severely restricted the use of advanced technology without a warrant . . . Others took a narrower view of how far privacy interests extend, particularly in the information captured was exposed to the public at some level, and did not reveal intimate details. The latter approach is the one adopted by the Supreme Court in *Tessling* (ibid., 68).

Continued on next page

CRITICAL ISSUES IN CANADIAN CRIMINAL JUSTICE   (*Continued*)

Questions
1. Do you agree with the Supreme Court of Canada that the use of FLIR is "non-intrusive" and therefore does not violate the reasonable expectation of privacy?
2. The decision by the Supreme Court stated that since FLIR imagery does not allow the police to see inside a person's home it does not violate a person's reasonable expectation of privacy. Do you agree with this statement?

3. Do you believe that the police should be free to use FLIR and other technology whenever they choose to without a warrant? What restrictions, if any, will this place on an individual's guaranteed Charter rights?
4. With technology constantly evolving at a very quick pace, what implications does this have for the future of people's expectation of privacy in Canada?

SUMMARY

Police officers have the power to apply many different techniques when investigating and apprehending suspects. These include searches, electronic surveillance, interrogation, and the use of informants. Since the introduction of the Charter of Rights and Freedoms, the Supreme Court of Canada has placed many constitutional limits on the police. For example, the police must now obtain properly authorized warrants to conduct searches except in clearly defined circumstances. The police must follow these legal procedures precisely or risk losing the case for technical reasons.

Police interrogation procedures are carefully controlled. However, a number of issues continue to affect police conduct during interrogations, such as what types of procedures are used to obtain statements from suspects during this stage of evidence gathering.

A significant issue for the accused is whether he or she receives interim release or is detained for part or all of the time preceding the trial. Over the past 25 years, bail provisions have been loosened, allowing most individuals charged with a crime to be free while awaiting trial. However, recent crimes involving individuals released on bail have led to a reappraisal of the rules regarding bail, with the result that offenders charged with certain types of crimes are now refused any type of pretrial release.

Discussion Questions

1. Should guilty individuals go free because the police did not follow established legal procedures when they arrested them?

2. Should evidence that is obtained illegally always be excluded from trial? Explain.

3. Do you think that all evidence the police collect should be thrown out of court if it is ruled that they obtained it illegally?

4. Should suspects have fewer constitutional rights? If so, what rights should be curtailed? Should the courts be more concerned about the rights of victims?

5. When can the police legally search a dwelling or person without a search warrant?

6. What would happen if police officers were required without exception to obtain a search warrant before searching any person or dwelling except in cases of hot pursuit?

7. Should legal aid be available to all individuals accused of a crime? Give reasons for your answer.

8. When should an individual be denied interim release?

9. What types of inequities, if any, exist in the bail system in Canada? In the legal aid system?

10. Should all police interrogations be videotaped?

11. Should testimony from jailhouse informants be barred in criminal cases?

Suggested Readings

Cameron, J. *The Charter's Impact on Criminal Justice*. Toronto: Carswell, 1996.

Doob, A.N., P.M. Baranek, and S.M. Addario. *Understanding Justices: A Study of Canadian Justices of the Peace*. Toronto: Centre of Criminology, University of Toronto, 1991.

Mewett, A.W. and S. Nakatsuru. 2000. *An Introduction to the Criminal Process in Canada*, 4th ed. Toronto: Thomson Canada.

Pink, J.E., and D. Perrier. *From Crime to Punishment: An Introduction to the Criminal Law System*. Toronto: Carswell, 1988.

Stuart, D. *Charter Justice in Canadian Criminal Law*. Toronto: Carswell, 1996.

Velverde, M., L. MacLeod, and K. Johnson, eds. *Wife Assault and the Canadian Criminal Justice System*. Toronto: Centre for Criminology. 1995.

References

Abell, J., and E. Sheehy, eds. 1993. *Criminal Law and Procedure: Cases, Context, Critique*. North York, ON: Captus Press.

Anderson, P.R., and D.J. Newman. 1993. *Introduction to Criminal Justice*, 5th ed. Toronto: McGraw-Hill Ryerson.

Bailey, J. 2008. "Framed by Section 8: Constitutional Protection of Privacy in Canada." *Canadian Journal of Criminology and Criminal Justice*: 279–306.

Besserer, S. 2006. *Legal Aid in Canada: Resource and Caseload Statistics 2004/05*. Ottawa: Minister of Industry.

"Big Brother Wants to Watch You (Again)." 2006. *National Post*, June 29, A12.

Bilodeau, S. 2001–02. "Investigative Detention." *LawNow* 26, no. 3, 42–43.

Boucher, S., and K. Landa. 2005. *Understanding Section 8: Search, Seizure, and the Canadian Constitution*. Toronto, Ontario; Irwin Law.

Brantingham, P. 1985. "Judicare Counsel and Public Defenders: Case Outcome Differences." *Canadian Journal of Criminology* 27: 67–81.

Burns, P., and R.S. Reid. 1981. "Delivery of Criminal Legal Aid Services in Canada: An Overview of the Continuing 'Judicature versus Public Defender' Debate." *UBC Law Review* 15: 403–29.

Clark, C. 2005. "Ottawa Demands Greater Wiretap Access." *The Globe and Mail*, October 11, A1, A5.

———. 2006. "Wiretap Access Bill to Be Revived." *The Globe and Mail*, June 9, A8.

Commission on Proceedings Involving Guy Paul Morin. 1998. Toronto: Ontario Ministry of the Attorney General.

Coughlan, S.G. 1998. "Developments in Criminal Procedure: The 1996–97 Term." *Supreme Court Law Review* (2d): 285.

Davison, C. 2000. "A Right to Fairness: Legal Aid." *LawNow* 24: 14–16.

Dickson, G. 2002. "Strip Searches." *LawNow* 26: 36.

Feld, B. 2006. "Police Interrogation of Juveniles: An Empirical Study of Policy and Practice." *Journal of Criminal Law and Criminology* 97: 219–316.

Friedland, M.L. 1965. *Detention before Trial*. Toronto: University of Toronto Press.

Gudjonsson, G.H., and J.A.C. MacKeith. 1982. *False Confessions: Psychological Effects of Interrogation*. In A. Trankell, ed., *Reconstructing the Past*. Deventer, the Netherlands, pp. 253–69.

Hamilton, A.C., and C.M. Sinclair. 1991. *Report of the Aboriginal Justice Inquiry of Manitoba*, vol. 1. Winnipeg: Queen's Printer of Manitoba.

Hartley, M. and O. El Akkad 2009. "Bill proposes new powers to monitor Internet users." *The Globe and Mail*, June 19, A4.

Hiebert, J.L. 2002. *Charter Rights: What Is Parliament's Role?* Montreal and Kingston: McGill-Queen's University Press.

Hume, M. 2008. "Police Hunt for Father of Three Children Slain in B.C." *The Globe and Mail*, April 8, A6.

Hunter, J. 2008. "B.C. Father 'Got a Break' on Bail." *The Globe and Mail*, April 11, A1, A6.

Hunter, J., and M. Hume. 2008. "Official who Freed B.C. Suspect Wasn't Told of Domestic Troubles." *The Globe and Mail*, April 9, A1, A6.

Inquiry Regarding Thomas Sophonow. 2001. Winnipeg: Government of Manitoba.

Johnstone, R., and J. Thomas. 1998. *Legal Aid in Canada: 1996–97*. Ottawa: Juristat.

Joyce, G. 2000. "Prison Snitches in Spotlight." *Winnipeg Free Press*, June 18, B2.

Kassin, S.M. 2008. "False confessions: Causes, Consequences, and Implications for Reform." *Current Directions in Psychological Science* 17: 249–53.

———. 1997. "The Psychology of Confession Evidence." *American Psychologist* 52: 221–23.

Kassin, S.M., and L.S. Wrightsman. 1985. "Confession Evidence." In S.M. Kassin and L.S. Wrightsman, eds., *The Psychology of Evidence and Trial Procedure*. New York: Hemisphere.

Kellough, G., and S. Wortley. 2002. "Remand for Plea: Bail Decisions and Plea Bargaining as Commensurate Decisions." *British Journal of Criminology* 42: 186–210.

Kelly, J.B. 2005. *Governing with the Charter: Legislative and Judicial Activism and Framers' Intent*. Vancouver: UBC Press.

King, L., and B. Snook. 2009. "Peering Inside a Canadian Interrogation Room: An Examination of the Reid Model of Interrogation, Influence Tactics, and Coercive Strategies." *Criminal Justice and Behavior* 36: 674–94.

Law Reform Commission of Canada. 1991. *Police Powers*. Report 33. Ottawa: Law Reform Commission of Canada.

———. 1983. *Police Powers: Search and Seizure in Criminal Law Enforcement*, Working Paper 30. Ottawa: Law Reform Commission of Canada.

Leo, R.A. 1996. "The Impact of Miranda Revisited." *Journal of Criminal Law and Criminology* 86 (Spring): 621–92.

———. 1992. "From Coercion to Deception: The Changing Nature of the Police Interrogation in America." *Crime, Law and Social Change* 18: 35–39.

Macdonald, J.M., and D.L. Michaud. 1987. *The Confession: Interrogation and Criminal Profiles for Police Officers*. Denver, CO: Apache.

Makin, K. 2009. "Jailhouse Informants Virtually Phased Out." *The Globe and Mail*, April 14, A5.

———. 2004. "Top Court Frees Police to use Infrared Devices." *The Globe and Mail*, October 30, A12.

———. 1999. "Punished Prisoners Win Access to Legal Aid." *The Globe and Mail*, September 16, A3.

———. 1998. "Police Allowed to Enter if 911 Called, Top Court Says." *The Globe and Mail*, December 4, A6.

———. 1992. *Redrum the Innocent*. Toronto: Penguin.

McConville, M., and J. Baldwin. 1982. "The Role of Interrogation in Crime Discovery and Conviction." *British Journal of Criminology* 22: 165–75.

Mewett, A.W., and S. Nakatsuru. 2000. *An Introduction to the Criminal Process in Canada*, 4th ed. Scarborough, ON: Carswell.

Morse, B., and L. Lock. 1998. *Native Offenders' Perceptions of the Criminal Justice System*. Ottawa: Minister of Supply and Services.

Naumetz, T. 2005. "New Law Would Allow Net Spying." *Winnipeg Free Press*, August 19, A3.

Nicol, J.A. 2002. "'Stop in the Name of the Law': Investigative Detention." *Canadian Criminal Law Review* 7, 2: 223–52.

Rigakos, G. 2002. *Peace Bonds and Violence Against Women: A Three-Site Study of the Effect of Bill C-42 on Process, Application, and Enforcement*. Ottawa: Department of Justice.

_____. 1997. "Constructing the Symbolic Complainants: Police Subculture and the Nonenforcement of Protection Orders for Battered Women." *Violence and Victims* 10: 235–47.

Salhany, R.E. 1986. *Arrest, Seizure, and Interrogation*, 3rd ed. Toronto: Carswell.

Saulny, S. 2002. "Why Confess to What You Didn't Do?" *New York Times,* December 8, 5.

Scheck, B., P. Neufeld, and J. Dwyer. 2000. *Actual Innocence: Five Days to Execution, and Other Dispatches From the Wrongfully Convicted.* New York: Doubleday.

Sherrin, C. 1996. "Jailhouse Informants, Part I: Problems With Their Use." *Criminal Law Quarterly* 40: 106–22.

Solicitor General of Canada. 1991. *Annual Report on Electronic Surveillance as Required under Subsection 195(1) of the Criminal Code 1989.* Ottawa: Minister of Supply and Services Canada.

Steeves, V., and V. Pinero. 2008. "Privacy and Police Powers: Situating the Reasonable Expectation of Privacy Test." *Canadian Journal of Criminology and Criminal Justice*: 263–69.

Tibbetts, J. 2006. "Action Urged to Curb Internet Cyber Spying." *Winnipeg Free Press,* July 7, A11.

———. 2004. "Infrared Cameras no Threat to Privacy." *Winnipeg Free Press*, October 30, A13.

———. 2002a. "Legal Aid System Falling Apart, Justice Department Report Says." *National Post,* February 19, A5.

———. 2002b. "Lawyers Hope to Make Legal Aid a Charter Right." *National Post,* March 7, A9.

"Tragedies Are All Too Foreseeable." 2008. *The Globe and Mail,* April 29, A12.

Vrij, A. 1998. "Interviewing Suspects." In A. Memon, A. Vrij, and R, Bull., eds., *Psychology and Law: Truthfulness, Accuracy, and Credibility.* London: McGraw-Hill, pp. 124–46.

Wigmore, J.H. 1970. *Evidence (Vol. 3).* (Revised by J.H. Chadbourn). Boston: Little, Brown.

Williams, J.W. 2000. "Interrogating Justice: A Critical Analysis of the Police Interrogation and Its Role in the Criminal Justice System." *Canadian Journal of Criminology*, April: 209–40.

Winograde, J. 1990. "Jailhouse Informants and the Need for Judicial Use Immunity in Habeas Corpus Proceedings." *California Law Review* 78.

Zimmerman, C. 1994. "Toward a New Vision of Informants: A History of Abuses and Suggestions for Reform." *Hastings Constitutional Law Quarterly* 22.

Court Cases

Alderton v. R. (1985), 17 C.C.C. (3d) 204

Borden v. R. (1994), 92 C.C.C. (3d) 321

Brown v. Durham Regional Police Force (1998), 131 C.C.C. (3d), 21 C.R. (5th)

Caslake v. R. (1998), 1 S.C.R. 51

Cloutier v. Langlois (1990), 53 C.C.C. (3d) 257

Gideon v. Wainright, 372 U.S. 335 (1963)

Hunter v. Southam Inc. (1984), 14 C.C.C. (3d) 97

New Brunswick (Minister of Health and Community Services) v. G.(J.) (1999), 3 S.C.R. 46

Stillman v. R. (1997), 113 C.C.C. (3d) 321

R. v. Bazinet (1986), 25 C.C.C. (3d) 273

R. v. Black (1989), 50 C.C.C. (3d) 1

R. v. Brooks (2000), 1 S.C.R. 270

R. v. Broyles (1991), 3 S.C.R. 595

R. v. Brydges (1990), 53 C.C.C. (3d) 330

R. v. Bryntwick (2002), O.J. No. 3618 (Ont. S.C.J.)

R. v. Charles (1987), 36 C.C.C. (3d) 286

R. v. Clarkson (1986), 25 C.C.C. (3d) 207

R. v. Collins (1987), 1 S.C.R. 265

R. v. D.(E.) (1990), 57 C.C.C. (3d) 151

R. v. Dersch (1991), 3 S.C.R. 768

R. v. Duarte (1990), 1 S.C.R. 30

R. v. Ducharme (1990), Unreported, British Columbia Court of Appeal

R. v. Evans (1996), 1 S.C.R. 8

R. v. Feeney (1997), 2 S.C.R. 117

R. v. Fitt (1996), 267 S.C.C.

R. v. Garofoli (1990), 2 S.C.R. 1421

R. v. Godoy (1997), 7 C.R. (5th) 216

R. v. Golden (2001), S.C.C. 83

R. v. Golub (1997), 34 O.R. (3d) 743

R. v. Harris (1987), 57 C.R. (3d) 356

R. v. Hebert (1990), 2 S.C.R. 151

R. v. Heisler (1984), 11 C.C.C. (3d) 97

R. v. L (W.K.) (1991), 64 C.C.C. (3d) 321

R. v. Lim (1990), 1 C.R.R. (2d) 136 (Ont. H.C.J.) 145

R. v. Manninen (1987), 34 C.C.C. (3d) 385

R. v. Mellenthin (1992), 3 S.C.R. 615

R. v. Moran (1987), 21 O.A.C. 257 (C.A.)

R. v. Plant (1993), 3 S.C.R. 281

R. v. Pozniak (1994), 92 C.C.C. (3d) 472

R. v. Prosper (1994), 3 S.C.R. 236

R. v. Rao (1984), 12 C.C.C. (3d) 97

R. v. Rickett (1975), 28 C.C.C. (2d) 297

R. v. Sauve (2004), 182 C.C.C. (3d) 321

R. v. Simmons (1988), 297 S.C.C.

R. v. Singh (1983), 8 C.C.C. (3d) 38

R. v. Joey Smith (1989), 50 C.C.C. (3d) 97

R. v. Stillman (1997), 97 C.C.C. (3d) 97

R. v. Storey (1990), 53 C.C.C. (3d) 316

R. v. Tessling (2004), 3 S.C.R. 432

R. v. Tomaso (1989), 70 C.R. (3d) 152

R. v. Vetrovec (1982), 1 S.C.R. 811

R. v. Wills (1992), 70 C.C.C. (3d) 529

R. v. Wise (1992), 253 S.C.C.

R. v. Wong (1990), 60 C.C.C. (3d) 460

Weblinks

Some of the most important decisions made by the Supreme Court of Canada have dealt with search and seizure. To read its decisions in two landmark cases, go to http://scc.lexum. umontreal.ca/en/index.html and read the Court's decisions on *Borden* (1994, Volume 3, September 30) and *Stillman* (1997, Volume 1, March 20). *Feeney* also had a strong impact on the search and seizure policies of Canadian police; visit the same website (1997, Volume 2, May 22). The application to have the Supreme Court of Canada's decision in this case delayed for six months can be found in the *Feeney* decision—see June 27, 1997.

The Courts and Criminal Trial Procedure

CHAPTER OBJECTIVES

✓ Understand the organization of our court system.

✓ Identify the roles of the defence lawyer, Crown prosecutor, and judge.

✓ Understand that the court is designed to provide an impartial forum for the facts of the case.

✓ Discuss the role of plea bargaining in the Canadian criminal justice system.

✓ Understand the fundamental rights of the accused.

✓ Discuss the ways that trials can vary and the implications of these differences for the accused as well as for the legal system.

The criminal courts play an important role in our criminal justice system. As discussed in the previous chapter, the Supreme Court has held that the police have a constitutional obligation to inform suspects of their right to retain legal counsel. But assuming that a case goes to trial, is it possible for legal aid to represent the defendant? Legal aid has been established in all provinces and territories with the goal of helping lower-income Canadians retain legal counsel. All provinces therefore have some system for identifying those individuals who are eligible for legal aid. This eligibility assessment generally considers the individual's income, assets, and number of dependants; these factors are assessed against a set of financial guidelines established by each particular jurisdiction. Other considerations include the legal merit and urgency of the case, the cost of the proceedings, the chances of winning the case, and the client's history. Successful applicants may receive free legal aid to assist them in their trial, or they may have to repay some of the legal fees incurred.

Regarding criminal matters, legal aid is available for successful applicants charged with an indictable offence. Applications for legal aid by individuals charged with summary conviction offences are typically limited to those cases where there is a likelihood of imprisonment or the possibility of loss of livelihood. Certain provinces, most notably British Columbia and Ontario, provide legal aid only for indictable and summary conviction cases when there is the possibility of imprisonment. Legal aid plans may also factor in special circumstances; for example, the province of Alberta allows cases involving mental health or language issues (Besserer 2006).

But what happens if a case is going to trial and the defendant's legal aid application has failed? These people may qualify for other services, such as assistance from duty counsel, student legal clinics, or community legal clinics. Because of the increasing costs of litigation, more and more Canadians have been representing themselves instead of hiring lawyers to look after their cases as they progress through all the stages of the criminal justice system up to and including a trial in criminal court. In March 2006, Madam Justice Marvyn Koenigsberg of the Supreme Court of British Columbia commented during a Toronto conference on access to justice that lawyers' fees "are completely beyond the reach" of most Canadians (Blackwell 2006, A6).

Sometimes defendants fire their lawyers and end up representing themselves in criminal court even though the charges against them are serious. In *R. v. Phillips*

(2003), for example, the defendant, who was charged with attempted murder and other serious offences, fired several of his lawyers before the trial. He represented himself during the trial, during which he refused to cross-examine witnesses, presented no evidence in his own defence, and failed to follow the judge's instructions about possible defences. Upon his conviction, he appealed to the Alberta Court of Appeal, which dismissed his case. The appeal court judges noted that the trial court judge had considered a number of relevant factors pertaining to the defendant, including the fact that he could have afforded to pay a lawyer to represent him, his attempts to delay the trial, his ability to conduct his own defence, and the nature of the charges. The majority on the appeal court decided that "while an accused person has a constitutional right to a fair trial, there is no constitutional right to funded legal counsel in every case, nor is representation by a lawyer a prerequisite to a fair trial." These judges held that the defendant had been capable of defending himself and thus had received a fair trial.

In Canada, the right to legal representation is based on the need for fairness, and this applies to representation at trial. Most cases, however, are completed before a court trial. During 1999–2000, for example, cases in the criminal courts made up just 9 percent of all cases, compared to cases where the accused was convicted with a guilty plea (53 percent) and those otherwise terminated by the court without a trial (Pereira and Grimes 2002). Even for those cases that do reach a formal court trial, the early stages of the legal process are important; research indicates that critical decisions about cases are made at all stages of the criminal justice process (Hann et al. 2002). Many important decisions are made during the earliest stages of case processing. As Currie (2003, 10) has noted, while "criminal trials may be more demanding than the pre-trial stages with respect to legal technicalities, the earlier stages are, nevertheless, adversarial, formal and complex." But what factors should be taken into account when considering whether legal counsel is necessary for a fair trial? In *R. v. White* (1977), the trial judge gave the following list:

- The characteristics of the accused such as financial situation, language skills, and education.
- The complexity of legal and evidentiary matters.
- The possible outcome—for example, the possibility of imprisonment.

The extent of self-representation at all stages in the criminal process is significant. In their study of nine provincial courts across Canada, Hann and colleagues (2002) found that significant percentages of the criminally accused were being convicted without ever being represented by legal counsel. For example, they found that the rate of not having legal representation varied among the courts studied. At the first appearance, for example, the percentage of individuals charged with a criminal offence not represented by legal counsel varied between 5 and 61. For the second appearance, that percentage was between 2 and 38, while for the third court appearance it was between 1 and 32 percent. For bail hearings, the percentage of unrepresented accused varied between 3 and 72. When the accused entered a plea, between 6 and 41 percent were unrepresented, while at the final appearance, 6 to 46 percent of all accused were unrepresented.

This has led to the development of the "burden of the court" hypothesis, which has two components. The first posits that the rising number of legally unrepresented accused is placing considerable pressure on other court actors (i.e., prosecutors and judges) who must then assist the accused. For example, our system of disclosure obligates the defence counsel to request disclosure from the prosecution. However, in those cases where the accused is "self-representing," the prosecutor is obligated to ensure that the accused is informed of the right of disclosure and to assist the accused in determining how the disclosure process will proceed. According to Hann and colleagues (2002), the perception of the various court officials interviewed was that the sheer numbers of legally unrepresented were leading to "a greater burden on and increased workloads for the court" (Currie 2003, 15). For example, over a 10-day period in March 2003, court workers in Winnipeg helped 764 self-representing individuals file documents (this number of hours included both criminal and non-criminal matters). Court workers invested 67 hours of their time in person and 14 hours on the telephone to help people going to court without a lawyer. This increase in the number of people representing themselves in court is undermining the basic principle of the adversarial court process (O'Brien 2004, A5).

The second component of the "burden of the court" hypothesis is that the self-representing accused will slow down the court process because judges, in order to ensure fair process, will have to intervene in order to help the accused. In their study, Hann and colleagues concluded that the "burden of the courts" hypothesis is not supported. These researchers, however, also concluded that the data support a "burden on the accused" hypothesis. For example, the accused often self-represent themselves for ill-advised reasons—perhaps they believe that they cannot wait for a lawyer to argue the case. This can lead to worse consequences when a sentence is determined.

THE FUNCTIONS OF THE COURTS

In Chapter 1, the underlying values of our criminal justice system, which includes the court system, were discussed in terms of two models: crime control and due process. A third model has been developed recently, which is based on the values found in the informal nature of our criminal justice system.

The Due Process Model

The primary focus of our court system is to protect individual citizens from the unfair advantages held by the agents of the state. Rights guaranteed to individuals by the Charter of Rights and Freedoms, such as the right to a jury trial, the right to defence counsel, and the right to face the accuser in the courtroom, are viewed as "equalizers" which ensure that the various parties in a court trial enjoy as equal a footing as possible. This model also emphasizes the adversarial nature of our court system (see Chapter 1): (1) a neutral and impartial judge makes the decisions; (2) the prosecution and the defence have an equal chance to present relevant evidence; and (3) a highly structured set of procedures (e.g., constitutional safeguards) must be followed during the trial. It is through this system, due process advocates argue, that truth is discovered and upheld by the courts.

The Crime Control Model

This approach stands in contrast to the due process model by arguing that while safeguarding individual liberties is important, it is secondary to protecting society (and law-abiding citizens) from criminals. The police are not allowed to engage in abusive behaviour, but the courts do allow them to utilize devious techniques to outwit offenders. With regard to the courts, this model emphasizes punishment; it is the courts' responsibility to ensure that offenders are punished for their actions and for the harms they have inflicted. The main goal of the courts is not to ensure that the accused is given a "fair" chance, but rather to achieve justice through deterrence and harsh punishments. Constitutional rights are there to protect the law-abiding citizen, not the accused.

The Bureaucratic Function Model

In this model, there is a stronger focus on the day-to-day operations of the courts. While punishing criminals and protecting their constitutional rights is still a concern, the main focus is on the bureaucratic process—in particular, on the speed at which the courts can work. The length of court trials is a paramount factor here, and so is the number of appearances the accused has to make (thereby taking up valuable court resources, including time). As we saw at the beginning of this chapter, the authorities are deeply concerned about the length of court trials and about backlogs as well (a number of individuals each year are sentenced to serve their punishment in a correctional facility, but then released because they have already served a considerable amount of time waiting for the trial to start). In this model, success for judges and the court system is measured in terms of the speed at which cases are moved along rather than whether or not justice has been served. According to some observers, the adversarial nature of our courts is reflected less in the confrontation between the accused and the accuser, than in the tension between the ideals of justice and the realities of the bureaucracy (Feeley 1981).

THE ORGANIZATION OF CANADIAN CRIMINAL COURTS

The Canadian criminal justice system encompasses a variety of provincial and federal courts. In fact, there are in effect 14 different court systems at work in Canada: 13 provincial/territorial and 1 federal. These systems all differ from one another other in certain ways (see Figure 8.1).

An overview of the basic principles of our court systems is necessary in order to understand how the courts in Canada are organized. Each court has a geographical jurisdiction: provincial and territorial courts are responsible for cases arising within their boundaries, and the Supreme Court of Canada has jurisdiction over the entire country. The provinces and territories vary in how they provide court services. Generally, however, in larger cities and towns there are permanent courts (provincial/territorial courts and provincial/territorial superior courts) while in rural areas, if there is no permanent court, services are offered by circuit courts.

Provincial courts are divided into courts of limited jurisdiction and courts of general jurisdiction. Courts of limited jurisdiction (in the bigger centres there are usually a number of these) "specialize" in certain areas, such as motor vehicle violations. The proceedings are presided over by a single judge, who makes the decisions. Most minor criminal cases are decided in these courts. Justices of the peace (or magistrates, as they are known in some provinces) are part of this level of courts. In

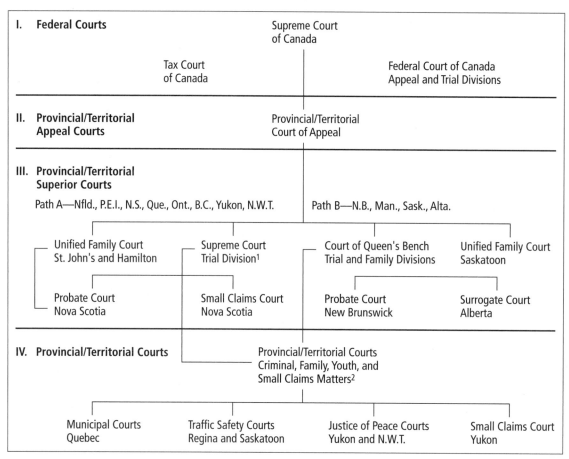

FIGURE 8.1

The Organization of the Canadian Courts

[1]Known as Superior Court of Justice in Ontario and the Superior Court in Quebec.

[2]Known as Ontario Court of Justice in Ontario and the Court of Quebec in Quebec. Small claims matters in P.E.I., New Brunswick, and Manitoba are heard in Superior Court. In Quebec, family matters are heard in Superior Court, Family Division.

Source: Besserer and Grimes 1996, 274.

most jurisdictions, these individuals provide law enforcement agents with search and seizure warrants, summonses, and subpoenas, as well as remand warrants (i.e., they conduct bail hearings).

Courts of general jurisdiction deal with the most serious criminal offences. Depending on the type of offence, the case may be decided by a judge and jury or by a judge sitting alone. To take the caseload pressure off these courts, some provinces have introduced what are referred to as special subject-matter courts. For example, a number of provinces now have courts that specialize in family violence and drug offences. Each province/territory also has **appeal courts**. In these, a number of judges hear and decide on cases where the convicted individual or the Crown prosecutor is appealing a decision made by the lower courts.

The Supreme Court of Canada is essentially an appeal court, in the sense that it has authority over all provincial/territorial appeal courts as well as those cases originally heard by the federal court system. The Supreme Court has final authority over all public and private law in Canada. This includes all federal, provincial, and municipal laws, as well as all common law, legislation, and constitutional interpretation (Bowal 2002). It hears between 105 and 140 cases a year, and more than half these cases are "hand-picked by subcommittees of three Supreme Court judges because they involve legal issues of general importance" (Greene et al. 1998, 100). The remaining cases are serious criminal cases that either the accused or the Crown has a right to have heard by the Supreme Court; these are known as "as-of-right" appeals. In these, there has been a dissent over the case in a provincial/territorial appeal court concerning a question of law, or a provincial/territorial appeal court has overturned a trial court acquittal.

The Supreme Court "creates" criminal justice policy in two different ways. The first is known as judicial review, which refers to the Court's power to decide whether a law or policy created by a province/territory is constitutional. This is also referred to as the "lawmaker" role. Many of the cases discussed in this text have involved appeals to the Supreme Court; if they are heard there, a judgment (i.e., a judicial review) will be made of the province's right to establish the law on which the case was based. The second area is the Supreme Court's authority to interpret the law, also referred to as the "law interpreter" role. Here, the Supreme Court interprets statutory laws as they have been applied to specific situations. Many of the cases discussed or mentioned in this text involve the Supreme Court interpreting a specific piece of legislation or ruling on a specific law enforcement issue—for example, the granting of search warrants (e.g., the *Feeney* decision on search warrants). Seven Supreme Court justices were recently asked whether they saw one of these two areas as more important than the other; all of them indicated that both were important (Greene et al. 1998).

It is common practice to refer to the "lower" and "higher" courts in Canada. The former refers to provincial courts, which try all provincial and summary conviction offences; superior, or higher, courts hear only indictable offences. The higher courts also encompass the provincial appeal courts, such as the Ontario Court of Appeal. Appeal courts are also known as the courts of last resort, meaning that they are the final authority in cases under their jurisdiction. Nonetheless, all individuals have the right to apply for leave to appeal to the Supreme Court of Canada, even if the provincial appeal court denies their application for an appeal.

The Supreme Court of Canada building, located in Ottawa. (Philippe Landreville/Supreme Court of Canada. Copyright © Supreme Court of Canada)

THE COURT SYSTEM

The word "court" refers to a complex part of the criminal justice system. Before a case enters the courts, the only elements of it that exist are suspected criminal offences, allegations of wrongdoing, police investigations, charges, and issues concerning bail. The only proof required prior to a criminal trial is probable cause; in order to convict a defendant in a criminal case, a higher standard of proof—beyond a reasonable doubt—must be met. This higher standard is meant to ensure that only those individuals who are found guilty (also referred to as legal guilt) are punished, not those who are thought to be guilty (also known as factual guilt). Higher standards of proof also contribute to higher levels of public confidence in both the fairness and the accuracy of the criminal justice system.

An individual who has been arrested and who has entered a plea then faces a number of decisions that have a significant impact on the determination of guilt and innocence—as well as on any punishment in the event of a finding of guilty. Besides the defendant, four other key participants emerge during the court proceedings: Crown prosecutors, defence counsel, judges and juries, and victims and witnesses. Only a court or a court-appointed official can decide whether to detain an accused prior to trial, and only the courts can decide on a defendant's guilt or innocence. In addition, the court must decide on the appropriate type and length of sanction. Note that the word "court" is used here in reference to a number of different places or individuals. It can be a room where a case is being heard, or a group of judges (e.g., the Supreme Court of Canada), or a single judge.

A judge is an officer of the government who is in charge of a court of law. The duties of a judge include deciding which evidence can be admitted in trial, which questions are appropriate to ask, and how procedural issues are to be settled. In a jury trial, the judge also has to *charge* (i.e., instruct) the members of the jury about the evidence and charges before they adjourn to the jury room to decide on the guilt or innocence of the accused. If the trial is to be decided by judge alone, he or she determines the guilt or innocence of the accused.

THE COURT SYSTEM IN CANADA

Court procedures are controlled by law, tradition, and judicial authority. These procedures govern, among other things, who may speak, when they may speak, and in what order they may speak. In addition, what can and cannot be said in court is dictated by the rules of evidence, and any questions about the admissibility of evidence are settled by the judge.

The Daily Business of the Courts

Studies of Canada's provincial courts have consistently found that in most cases the accused pleads guilty, on first appearance in court, to the charge as laid (Griffiths, et al. 1980; Hann 1973; Wheeler 1987). For example, Ericson and Baranek (1982) found that 91 of 131 accused individuals (70 percent) pleaded guilty to at least one charge when they appeared in court. Only 21 pleaded not guilty; 15 were found guilty on at least one criminal charge; and 6 were acquitted. Seventeen had their charges withdrawn or dismissed. In the remaining two cases, the accused did not appear in court to face the charges. A study by the Ontario government of cases in process during 1998 found that 91.3 percent of all criminal cases were resolved without a trial. Just over 75 percent of these cases were resolved prior to the trial, while the remaining 15 percent were resolved on the actual date of the trial (Ontario Ministry of the Attorney General 1999).

In the lower courts, the police may play an important role in prosecutorial discretion. Crown prosecutors often have little time to prepare for a case; for the sake of expediency they must then rely on information provided by the police. Prosecutors sometimes follow the suggestions of the police officer involved in the investigation (Ericson 1981). Desroches (1995, 244) found that the police work closely with Crown prosecutors "to avoid lengthy trials that tie up courts, judges, police officers, prosecuting attorney, and witnesses." If the police have succeeded in obtaining a statement of guilt from the accused, they can bargain with the defence counsel from a position of strength. In most of these cases (about 60 percent), offenders are offered no concession for their guilty pleas. And those who are able to reduce the number of charges against them in return for a guilty plea are given no guarantee of a shorter sentence.

Prosecutors can of course use their own discretion to stay proceedings, withdraw charges, or dismiss the charges altogether. For example, they may decide, given the circumstances of a case, to use their discretion to expedite matters for the victims. Prosecutors have been known to use their discretion to settle cases before the trial in order to speed up the decision-making in the criminal justice system and to protect child victims from the trauma of appearing and testifying in court (Campbell Research Associates 1992). Other reasons for prosecutors' deciding not to prosecute a case include insufficient evidence, witness problems, due process problems, a plea on another charge, and referral to another jurisdiction for prosecution. For example, Vinglis and colleagues (1990) found that Crown prosecutors in Ontario withdrew charges in drunk driving cases because witnesses were not available, errors were found by prosecutors in the technical requirements of the Criminal Code, the police failed to collect available evidence, the evidence did not substantiate the charge, and/or the information was improperly worded. Cases were also dismissed because the accused was charged in a number of different cases, the prosecutor decided to dismiss charges in exchange for a guilty plea, the accused agreed to attend a diversion program, or the accused was wanted for a more serious crime in another jurisdiction.

The Defence Lawyer

Defence counsel represents the legal rights of the accused in criminal proceedings and tries to ensure that the criminal justice system operates fairly. Some people believe that the defence lawyer's goal is to work out the best deal for the client with the prosecutor; in fact, an important part of the defence lawyer's role is to ensure that the client's legal rights are protected. To achieve this goal, defence lawyers typically examine all the evidence collected by the police—the evidence that will be used by the prosecutor in the case as per the Stinchcombe rule (see Chapter 2)—in order to assess the strength of the Crown's case in the proving of the defendant guilty beyond a reasonable doubt. This examination can, of course, lead a defence lawyer into conflict with the police, prosecutors, witnesses, and victims, who may feel that they are being attacked. But the role of the defence lawyer is not to criticize anyone as an individual; rather, it is to assess the validity and reliability of the evidence and testimony being used by the prosecutor. Defence lawyers, then, are "a check brake upon the vast machinery of the state—police officers, Crown prosecutors, and judges—as it seeks to deprive individual citizens of their liberty and freedom" (Davison 2006, 39–40).

The defence lawyer is also responsible for preparing the case, as well as for selecting a strategy for attacking and questioning the prosecutor's case. Since most defendants are not trained in the operation of the law, they are unsure of how to proceed. A defence lawyer ideally helps his or her client understand what is happening in court and the consequences of the charges if the client is found guilty. The defence lawyer sometimes hires individuals to investigate certain aspects of the case or contact other experts in the field to get a second opinion.

Some of the most significant work of the defence lawyer relates to his or her discussion of the case with the police and the prosecutor. The defence has probably worked with the investigating officers and the prosecutors on past occasions. Usually, they discuss the strength of their client's case and assess the chances of gaining a satisfactory plea bargain.

The defence lawyer represents the accused at all stages of the criminal justice process, including bail hearings, plea negotiations, and preliminary inquiries. If the trial is to be decided by a jury, defence lawyers question prospective jurors. If the client is convicted, he or she will argue for the lightest possible sentence. A defence lawyer who loses a case and who is dissatisfied with the sentence or with a legal issue may file an appeal in the hope that the appeal court will either reverse the lower court's decision or reduce the sentence.

Throughout the trial process, the formal function of the defence lawyer is to "exercise his professional skill and judgment in the conduct of the case . . . [and] fearlessly uphold the interest of his client without regard to any unpleasant consequence to himself or any other person" (Martin 1970, 376). If the accused admits to the defence lawyer that she or he committed the crime in question, the lawyer, if convinced that the admission is true, can contest the case by objecting to such legal issues as the form of the indictment and the admissibility or sufficiency of the evidence. However, that lawyer cannot suggest that another individual committed the crime, nor can he or she introduce any evidence believing it false or for the purpose of establishing an alibi for the accused.

Criminal defence lawyers are commonly asked how they can defend someone they know is guilty. According to the Canadian Bar Association's (1987) *Code of Professional Conduct*, defence lawyers are required—even when they know the client is guilty as charged—to protect that client as much as possible. Our legal system insists that accused individuals have the legal right to use every legitimate resource to defend themselves. This means that defence lawyers are required to question the evidence given by witnesses called by the prosecution and attempt to point out that the evidence taken as a whole "is insufficient to amount to proof that the accused is guilty of the offence charged"; however, "the lawyer should go no further than that" (Martin 1970, 376). Some view the role of defence lawyers as necessary to protect the integrity of our legal system; if they refuse to protect the guilty, "the right of a defendant to be represented by counsel is eliminated and with it the entire traditional trial" (Swartz 1973, 62).

The Crown Prosecutor

Crown prosecutors play a pivotal role in the courts, as it is they who present the state's case against the defendant. According to the CBA's *Code of Professional Conduct*, the primary duty of Crown prosecutors is not to gain a conviction but rather to enforce the law and maintain justice by presenting all the evidence relevant to the crime being tried in criminal court. Thus, for example, the prosecutor must disclose "to the accused or defence counsel . . . all relevant facts and known witnesses" that could influence "the guilt or innocence, or that would affect the punishment of the accused." As such, the role of the Crown prosecutor differs significantly from that of defence counsel. This role was articulated by a member of the Supreme Court of Canada, who stated in *Boucher v. The Queen* (1955):

> [i]t cannot be over-emphasized that the purpose of a criminal prosecution is not to obtain a conviction, it is to lay before a jury what the Crown considers to be credible evidence relevant to what is alleged to be a crime. Counsel have a duty to see that all available legal proof of the facts is presented: it should be done firmly and pressed to its legitimate strength but it must also be done fairly. The role of the prosecutor excludes any notion of winning or losing; this function is a matter of public duty. In civil life there can be none charged with greater personal responsibility. It is to be efficiently performed with an ingrained sense of the dignity, the seriousness and the justness of judicial proceedings.

Many prosecutors are torn between maintaining an impartial role in the courts and attempting to find the defendant guilty as charged. Grosman (1969, 63) says there is pressure on prosecutors to gain as many convictions as possible. This pressure to succeed at trial stems from two factors. The first is that in order to "maintain his administrative credibility and to encourage guilty pleas the prosecutor must demonstrate that he is able [to] succeed consistently at trial." If he failed to demonstrate this ability, more cases would be taken to court, because the defence would feel that it had a good chance to gain a favourable result for its client. The second consideration is that "confidence in present administrative practices is maintained only if the acquittal rate is not substantial." So to maintain their credibility, prosecutors attempt to gain as many guilty verdicts as possible. As a result, caseload pressure forces prosecutors to decide on the outcome of a case more on the basis of expediency than on that of justice. This has led to criticisms that the justice system provides little more than an **assembly line justice** (see Chapter 1).

Some argue that this role makes prosecutors more powerful by enabling them to define the parameters of a court case. For example, the prosecutor presents the Crown's side of the case in an opening address to the judge before the jury has heard anything else. While the opening address may be criticized in court, it makes a significant first impression. Karp and Rosner (1991, 74) have argued that in the David Milgaard case, the Crown prosecutor gave a "damning and convincing argument" to the jury, taking "full advantage" of the tradition that allows the Crown to speak first, and providing "a lengthy exposition of what he expected the forty-two witnesses to say when called to the stand."

The Responsibilities of the Crown Prosecutor

Crown prosecutors can be viewed as the chief law enforcement officers in the provincial and federal court systems. They represent provincial or federal attorneys general and ministers of justice in all phases of their work, from discussing a case with the police to making sentencing recommendations to the judge and sometimes filing appeals. The most obvious responsibility faced by Crown prosecutors is to try indictable and summary conviction offences in a court of law. A large number of responsibilities are associated with the trying of cases, such as examining court documents sent by a variety of individuals—including coroners and the police—in order to determine whether further evidence is required. Crown prosecutors can be held civilly liable if their decisions are malicious or an abuse of process (Exhibit 8.1).

Crown prosecutors also interview victims and subpoena witnesses to give testimony during the court trial. They also decide when not to try a case, even after the police have laid charges, by requesting an adjournment of the case until a future date, by withdrawing the charges, or by deciding to offer no evidence so that the court will dismiss the charges and the case (Law Reform Commission 1990; Osborne 1983).

Crown prosecutors try a wide spectrum of cases involving a variety of charges, including child sexual assault, domestic violence, and white-collar and property crimes. Because a Crown prosecutor may be assigned to one particular courtroom, as opposed to a specific case, a number of Crown prosecutors may work on a single case as it progresses through the court system. In recent years, however, there has been a trend toward specialization, in which special prosecution units try only cases involving specific charges, such as financial or economic crimes and domestic violence.

For a variety of reasons, a prosecutor may decide not to proceed with a case even though the police have already laid charges or feel they should be laid. In three provinces (British Columbia, Quebec, and New Brunswick), the police are required to allow prosecutors to review and approve evidence before charges are laid. In all other jurisdictions in Canada, charges can be laid

EXHIBIT 8.1   Malicious Prosecution

As the common law developed, an important issue was raised: Can the Crown be held liable for any of its actions if they were maliciously pursued or were an abuse of process? The answer was "no," because it was held that the King could do not wrong. Today, it is widely believed that our legal system is designed and operates in such a way as to prevent innocent people from being wrongfully harmed as they are investigated and/or processed by the justice system. In addition, the right to a fair trial has been repeatedly supported by the courts and legislatures. In recent decades, however, a number of mistakes, including wrongful convictions, have occurred as a result of errors made by representatives of the Crown (i.e., Crown prosecutors and the police). These errors had a serious impact on the lives of the citizens involved.

In 1989, the Supreme Court of Canada, in *Nelles v. Ontario* (1989), rejected the idea that Crown prosecutors are immune from civil liability. Susan Nelles was a nurse at the Toronto Hospital for Sick Children. After a number of infant deaths, she was charged with four murders. Her case was discharged after the preliminary inquiry because of the absence of evidence. She then successfully started a civil action against the police and the Attorney General of Canada. In its decision, the Supreme Court developed a four-part test to determine whether the Crown should be held liable for malicious prosecution.

The Supreme Court ruled that the plaintiff must prove the following four elements before the courts can decide that a Crown's prosecution was malicious. This test does not make it easy for the plaintiff, since "the last thing society needs are police and prosecutors afraid do their respective jobs" (Hughson 2004, 34):

- The proceedings must have been initiated by the defendant.
- The proceedings must have terminated in favour of the plaintiff.

- Reasonable and probable grounds must have been absent.
- There must have been malice, or a primary purpose other than that of carrying the law into effect.

The Supreme Court has had to deal with the issue of malicious prosecution in a number of cases since *Nelles*. In *Proulx v. A.G. of Que.* (2001), for example, it ordered the Quebec Crown to pay Benoit Proulx $1.1 million, "saying that it perverted the man's murder prosecution to obtain a wrongful conviction" (Makin 2001, A11). Proulx successfully sued the Quebec government for malicious prosecution after the Quebec Court of Appeal acquitted him of his jury conviction for murder and was critical of the evidence used against him at trial, "saying the case was built on flimsy evidence and conjecture, bolstered by unlawful interrogations and unfair traps" (ibid.). In addition, the Supreme Court modified the third element of the Nelles test by stating that this test is to be met on the basis of whether or not there is a reasonable likelihood of conviction based on admissible evidence.

In *Dix v. Canada (A.G.)* (2002), Dix successfully sued the Attorney General of Canada on behalf of the RCMP as well as the Crown prosecutor involved in the case. He had been charged for a double homicide. His charges were stayed after allegations of misconduct were made against the Crown prosecutor. The police had used evidence from "questionable" jailhouse informants; the case then fell apart when Dix's lawyer suggested that the Crown prosecutor "had misrepresented evidence at one of Mr. Dix's bail hearings in January, 1997" (Powell and Rusnell 1999, A8). The Court of Queen's Bench judge immediately halted the trial and appointed a new prosecutor. On reviewing the evidence, the new prosecutor reported that there was no reasonable likelihood of conviction. At his request, the judge dismissed the charges against Dix.

without prosecutorial approval, although prosecutors may decide not to pursue the case at a later date. For indictable offences, defence counsel may decide to contest the evidence at a preliminary inquiry in order to determine whether sufficient evidence exists to proceed to criminal trial. In such cases, the prosecutor attempts to show a judge that sufficient evidence does exist by reviewing the physical evidence and questioning and cross-examining witnesses.

The scope of prosecutorial work is extensive. Prosecutors' duties encompass the entire criminal justice system from investigation and arrest through bail and trial sentencing to appeals. One possible result of this involvement is overload. Gomme and Hall (1995) studied Crown prosecutors in one Canadian province between 1990 and 1992 to find out whether prosecutors are prone to work-related stress. They found that prosecutors routinely prosecuted six to ten trials each day in provincial court five days each week. The number of trials increased to between 12 and 14 during peak periods. The impact of this workload "severely constrains the time available to undertake the careful preparation required to ensure that the quality of legal work meets prosecutors' personal and professional standards" (ibid., 193). They found that prosecutors were susceptible to work overload and excessive strain, leading to questions about their professional effectiveness and whether justice is compromised.

Judges

The role of judges in our criminal justice system includes upholding the rights of the accused and arbitrating any disagreements that arise between a prosecutor and defence lawyer during a trial. In addition, judges who act as triers of fact in cases decide whether the defendant is guilty or innocent; in such cases, they also determine the type and length of sentence. It is important that judges be viewed as objective; only when they are seen as impartial will their decisions on rules of law and procedure be viewed as acceptable by all the parties involved.

In 2000, Beverley McLachlin was sworn in as the first female Chief Justice of the Supreme Court of Canada. (Philippe Landreville/Supreme Court of Canada. Copyright © Supreme Court of Canada.)

Canada's constitution gives the federal Cabinet the power to appoint provincial superior trial court judges, provincial and territorial court of appeal judges, federal court judges, tax court judges, and the judges of the Supreme Court of Canada. Provincial Cabinets have the power to appoint judges to the provincial court system below the level of the superior court. Appointments of provincial court judges are determined by three distinct non-partisan appointment procedures. In Ontario and Quebec, judicial nominating committees seek out the best candidates and recommend them to the Attorney General for review and appointment; in Alberta and British Columbia, provincial judicial councils screen applicants, who are then recommended to the Attorney General; and in Saskatchewan and Newfoundland and Labrador, judicial councils comment on the qualifications of candidates proposed to them by the Attorney General (Greene 1995). In the remaining provinces, patronage continues to be evident in judicial appointments; in 1985, the Canadian Bar Association reported that patronage remained an important criterion in provincial court appointments (McCormick and Greene 1990). Russell (1987) points out that though many good lawyers have been appointed to judgeships in return for their favours, some inappropriate appointments have been made as well.

CRIMINAL TRIAL PROCEDURE

The criminal trial is the start of the **adjudication** stage of the criminal justice system (see Exhibit 8.2). It is also the centrepiece of our court system. If the accused pleads guilty, a date is set for the sentencing (see Chapter 9). However, if the accused elects to be tried in court, various alternatives are open, depending on the charge. One choice the defendant can make is trial by judge and jury. Jury trials are relatively rare in Canada; Thomas (2004) found that during 2003–04, only about 2 percent of all cases were heard at the superior court level in the six reporting jurisdictions. Since these are usually high-profile cases, they usually attract much media attention; this is why so many Canadians believe they are typical of what happens in the Canadian justice system.

The Plea

In most cases an accused who appears in criminal court for an indictable offence enters what is known as a general plea—that is, a plea of guilty or not guilty. Three other pleas (referred to as special pleas) are available to the accused: autrefois acquit, autrefois convict, and pardon. An estimated 90 percent of accused plead guilty prior to trial or when they appear in a lower court for the

EXHIBIT 8.2 Case Processing

There are many paths that a criminal trial can take as it makes its way through adult criminal court in Canada. These variations in case processing depend on several factors including the seriousness of the offences being heard, and the elections made by the Crown and the accused. For most cases, the trial process in adult provincial/territorial criminal courts will include some or all of the elements listed below.

First Appearance: The first appearance in court is usually a bail hearing in a provincial court, where the court must determine if the accused should be released pending trial. Most offences require the Crown to show that the accused is either a danger to the community or a risk to flee prosecution before a remand order is given. However, several offences are classified as reverse onus offences, where the accused must show cause why his detention is not justified—*Criminal Code* s. 515(6).

Crown Elections: The Crown is eligible to elect the type of proceeding for hybrid offences, which are also known as "dual procedure" offences. The defining *Criminal Code* sections for hybrid offences specify that the Crown may try the case in one of two ways: (1) as a summary conviction offence—the least serious offence type, which also carries a lower maximum penalty; or (2) as the more serious indictable offence. If the Crown elects to try the case as an indictable offence, the accused faces the possibility of a prison sentence that, depending on the offence, ranges between no minimum sentence to life in prison.

Defence Elections: Where permitted under the *Criminal Code*, the accused may elect to be tried in adult provincial/territorial criminal court or in Superior Court—with or without a jury. If the accused elects to be tried in Superior Court, a preliminary inquiry may be held. (See Preliminary Hearings below.) The defence is not eligible to elect the mode of trial for summary conviction offences, or offences identified under *Criminal Code* s. 469 or 553. These *Criminal Code* sections identify offences that are the absolute jurisdiction of a single court level, Superior Court and provincial/territorial court respectively.

Preliminary Hearings: The purpose of the preliminary inquiry process is to determine if there is sufficient evidence in the case to proceed to trial in a higher court level, Superior Court. The provincial court judge will commit the case for trial in Superior Court if the evidence is compelling and there is a reasonable expectation of a judgment against the accused. However, if the evidence is not convincing, the judge must stop the proceedings against the accused—and the court finding will be recorded as "discharged at preliminary."

The preliminary inquiry process is a way for the accused to review all of the Crown's evidence before proceeding to the higher court. The defence is permitted to question all of the Crown witnesses and to review any prosecution exhibits related to the charges, which helps the accused's council prepare for trial.

Fitness Hearings: When the accused's mental health is brought into question, the court will order a psychiatric examination. In the fitness hearing that results, the accused will be found fit for trial or remanded in custody until the Lieutenant Governor of the province permits release.

Trial: The trial begins with the accused entering a plea of guilty, guilty of a lesser charge, not guilty, or special plea (i.e., previous conviction, previous acquittal, or pardon—*Criminal Code* s. 607). In some cases, the accused may refuse to enter a plea, and the court will enter a plea of not guilty on behalf of the accused. A guilty plea will usually result in an immediate conviction, but the court may also refuse to accept a guilty plea if that plea is given with conditions, or if the court feels that the accused does not understand that the plea is an admission of guilt.

A plea of not guilty will result in a trial, where the evidence against the accused is heard and the court will make a judgment on that evidence. The final disposition, or decision, of the court will be either (1) guilty of the offence charged, (2) guilty of an included offence, (3) not guilty of the charged offence, or (4) not guilty on account of insanity. The court may sentence the accused immediately following a finding of guilt; however, the court may also delay the sentencing to a later date so that all relevant factors can be considered prior to imposing a sentence on the accused.

Source: Statistics Canada, *Juristat*, Catalogue 85-002, Vol. 20, no. 1, March 2000, p. 6.

first time. If the accused pleads not guilty to an indictable offence (a common plea in the more serious and complex cases), a trial date is set that is acceptable to both the prosecution and the defence. In most cases, the accused is released under the same terms and conditions he or she was previously given.

The presiding judge at the initial appearance is a provincially appointed judge. What happens next is determined by the type of charge—that is, whether it is indictable, hybrid, or summary conviction. If the accused is charged with a summary conviction offence, the trial is held in a summary conviction court. The information is read to the accused, who is then asked whether he or she pleads guilty or not guilty. If the accused pleads not guilty, a date will likely be set for a trial before a provincial court judge, since it is typical in larger communities that the court docket will be full on that particular day. An accused who pleads guilty will be sentenced immediately or remanded until the judge has the opportunity to hear submissions concerning the sentence. The Criminal Code allows for remands of up to eight days, unless the accused consents to a longer adjournment. (Accused in custody generally enforce their eight-day rights.) If the charge is for an indictable offence (e.g., a gaming offence), because it is under the absolute jurisdiction of a provincially appointed judge (a Section 553 offence), trial may proceed right away (Mewett and Nakatsuru 2000) (See Exhibit 8.3).

Preliminary Hearing

A preliminary inquiry, or preliminary hearing, is held when an accused is charged with an offence that must be tried by a judge and jury, or when the accused elects to be tried by a judge and jury or by a judge alone. The purpose of this inquiry is twofold: (1) to see whether there is enough evidence collected by the Crown prosecutor (and by the defence, if it wishes to make the same determination) to proceed to a criminal trial, and (2) to protect the accused from being placed on trial unnecessarily. During the preliminary inquiry, a provincial court judge or justice of the peace examines the evidence and hears witnesses in order to determine whether a reasonable jury (or a judge when there is no jury) would find the accused guilty. The intention of the preliminary inquiry is *not* to determine guilt. In other words, the Crown prosecutor does not have to convict the accused but only to introduce sufficient evidence to make the guilt of the accused a reasonable expectation (Mewett and Nakatsuru 2000).

The preliminary inquiry is conducted in much the same way as a regular trial. It is usually open to the public. The accused can request a prohibition of the publication of the proceedings either until charges are discharged or,

if a trial is held, until the trial is over. The publication ban order is mandatory when requested by the accused at the opening of the inquiry, but discretionary when the prosecutor applies for it.

The prosecution presents its evidence as well as any witnesses. The accused has the right to cross-examine any or all witnesses and to challenge the prosecutor's evidence. It is not necessary for the prosecution to present all the evidence it has as long as it provides *sufficient* evidence to the judge that a reasonable case can be made against the accused. After the prosecutor presents the evidence, the judge informs the accused that he or she has heard the evidence and asks whether the accused wishes to reply to the charge. Rarely does a defendant decide to discuss the evidence, but, if so, whatever the accused says is written down and might be used against him or her during the actual trial. The next step allows the accused to call any witnesses he or she feels merit attention.

After all the evidence is presented to the court, the judge decides whether the prosecution has provided sufficient evidence to prosecute the accused. If the judge believes the evidence is sufficient, a trial is scheduled; if it is insufficient, the charges are dropped and the defendant is freed. The judge weighs the evidence just as if it were evidence at a criminal trial. A presiding judge who decides there is insufficient evidence to proceed will discharge the accused. This discharge does not mean the accused is acquitted; rather, it means the accused cannot be tried on that information and that the proceedings on that information are ended. If fresh evidence is brought to light about the case, the prosecution usually proceeds by way of a *direct indictment*. This allows the Crown prosecutor, after receiving the permission of the Attorney General or a Deputy Attorney General, to bypass the preliminary inquiry and indict the accused directly.

In the real world, the accused often waives the preliminary inquiry with the consent of the prosecutor, especially if he or she knows what evidence the prosecutor will be using at trial. In Canada, the accused usually has the right to waive the preliminary inquiry. A defendant is most likely to waive a preliminary inquiry for one of three reasons:

1. The accused has decided to enter a plea of guilty.
2. The accused wants to speed up the criminal justice process and have a trial date set as early as possible.
3. The accused hopes to avoid the negative publicity that might result from the inquiry.

In December 2003, a new policy (Bill C-15A) amending the operations of preliminary inquiries came into effect in Canada. Preliminary inquiries are no longer

If the accused is charged with a Supreme Court exclusive offence (a s. 469 offence), the presiding provincial court judge has no jurisdiction to try the case and so sets a date for a trial to be heard by a superior court judge. These cases must be heard by a superior court judge and jury unless, in special circumstances, the Attorney General of the province allows the case to be heard by judge alone. In all other criminal cases involving indictable offences, the accused has the right to select trial by superior court judge alone or by provincial court judge alone.

In Canada, it is possible to have a trial even if the accused pleads guilty. To the trial court judge, the Crown prosecutor usually makes a brief statement of the case's facts and of other information considered relevant to the case. At this time, the accused may disagree with certain or all aspects of the prosecutor's statement. The judge then inquires into the nature of the disagreement; if the judge decides there is substance to the disagreement, he or she advises the accused to withdraw the plea of guilty and instead enter a plea of not guilty. If the accused pleads guilty to a lesser offence, the judge may decide to proceed with the more serious charge if it arose from the same factual circumstances.

In these situations, the Crown prosecutor may decide to accept the guilty plea and not proceed on the original (and more serious) charge. The presiding judge need not accept this guilty plea; if not, the trial continues with the original charge. Mewett and Nakatsuru (2006, 117) point out that a Crown prosecutor's decision to accept a plea of guilty to a lesser charge depends on a number of factors, including "the seriousness of the charge, avoiding the necessity for witnesses to testify, the public interest, the likelihood of securing a conviction on the more serious charge, and so on." Thus, a plea bargain made between the defence and prosecution may not be accepted by the trial court judge.

An individual's plea of guilty must be a free and voluntary act. Once it is accepted, the accused gives up his or her constitutional rights, including the right to cross-examine witnesses and to have a trial by jury (if applicable). However, a judge may decide to review the evidence, and if it appears that the accused wishes to change his or her plea, the judge has the discretion to allow the change. Clearly, then, a judge must exercise caution when accepting the accused's plea of guilty. The judge must believe that the facts of the case warrant the plea and

that the accused has made it voluntarily. The accused, if not represented by defence counsel, must be informed of the right to make a plea voluntarily, and the judge may insist on the presence of a defence lawyer before the plea is accepted by the court. In addition, the judge has the right to allow the accused to withdraw a plea of guilty if he or she was "in a disturbed state of mind at the time" of the guilty plea (*R. v. Hansen* [1977]).

SECTION 469 OFFENCES

The offences listed below are the exclusive jurisdiction of superior criminal courts:

- treason
- alarming Her Majesty
- intimidating Parliament or Legislature
- inciting mutiny
- seditious mutiny
- piracy
- piratical acts
- attempting to commit any of the above offences
- murder
- conspiring to commit the above offences
- being an accessory after the fact to high treason, treason, or murder
- bribery by the holder of a judicial office

SECTION 553 OFFENCES

- theft, other than theft of cattle
- obtaining money or property on false pretences
- possession of property obtained, directly or indirectly, from the commission of an indictable offence
- defrauding the public, or any person, of any item
- mischief under subsection 430(4) of the Criminal Code
- keeping a game or betting house
- betting, pool selling, bookmaking, etc.
- placing bets
- offences involving lotteries and games of chance
- cheating at play
- keeping a common bawdy-house
- driving while disqualified
- fraud in relation to fares
- counselling, attempts to commit, or being an accessory to any of the offences listed above

Source: Besserer and Grimes 1996, 277.

automatic in this country; instead, they must be explicitly requested by either the Crown prosecutor or the defence lawyer. Those who request an inquiry must produce a list of the issues they would like covered and the witnesses from whom they would like to hear. There is also now greater scope for having written statements introduced during the preliminary hearing; thus, witnesses are no longer always obligated to appear in person.

Over the past decade, much debate had focused on the role of and need for preliminary inquiries in the Canadian criminal justice system. A number of provincial justice ministers and Attorneys General feel that preliminary inquiries should be eliminated altogether because of the costs and time delays they involve. They also argue that these inquiries place witnesses and victims in a vulnerable position as they must suffer through traumatic interrogations in addition to the questioning they would face during a criminal trial. Supporters of preliminary inquiries point out that they offer defence lawyers their only opportunity to examine witnesses prior to a client's trial. In addition, such inquiries are necessary because they ensure that cases will proceed to trial only if there are sufficient grounds. Bill C-15A represented a compromise between the two positions and was seen as guaranteeing that the rights of the defendant would not be compromised. It was an attempt to strike "a balance that would permit such functions as discovery and screening, without unduly prolonging the process or making it unfair." The amendments were also an attempt to make the preliminary inquiry "a more efficient, more effective and more limited procedure" (Baer 2005).

The Prosecutor Screening Process

Once the police arrest and lay charges against a suspect, it is not automatic that a prosecutor will try the case. For various reasons, many defendants are never brought to trial. Crown prosecutors "have virtually unfettered discretion as to when to charge, what to charge, when the charge should be reduced or dropped" (Stuart and Delisle 1994, 525). Thus the prosecutor has the power to decide between trying the case in court on the charges laid, or plea bargaining, or staying proceedings, or dismissing the charges outright. In addition, in hybrid offences, the prosecutor has the discretion to proceed by way of indictment or summary conviction. The prosecutor's discretionary powers exist at all levels of criminal trials. The courts have been reluctant to limit prosecutorial discretion—the Supreme Court of Canada ruled in *R. v. Beare* (1988) that prosecutorial discretion does not violate the principles of fundamental justice, stating that it is an essential component of our criminal justice system.

The right of prosecutors to choose whether or not to proceed with cases is a major source of case attrition (see Chapter 1). Prosecutors use a screening process to determine what to do with a given case. Several factors are often involved with case screening:

- The most important factor in the decision whether or not to prosecute is not the prosecutor's belief in the guilt of the accused, but whether there is sufficient evidence for a conviction. If prosecutors decide there is strong evidence in the case (e.g., overwhelming physical evidence, a confession, and a number of reliable and credible witnesses), the decision to prosecute is easier (Boland et al. 1992).
- Prosecutors have case priorities—that is, with all cases being hypothetically equal, the prosecutor will take a violent criminal to court before someone charged with vandalism.
- The record of the accused is also a significant factor. If the accused has committed a large number of prior offences, the prosecutor will usually decide to prosecute that offender before prosecuting a first-time offender. Sometimes prosecutors decide to pursue all cases that fall into a certain category, such as domestic violence, gang-related activity, or drunk driving.
- An important consideration can be the nature of the witnesses, that is, how cooperative they are (or are not). For example, some cases involving domestic violence are dropped because the witnesses will not cooperate with the prosecutor. A violent crime is more likely to be pursued in court when it involves strangers rather than family members.
- The credibility of victims (or witnesses) can influence the decision to proceed with a case. If the victim or witness is a prostitute or drug addict, and the defendant an upstanding citizen, prosecutors may be reluctant to have a trial, particularly a jury trial during which 12 citizens will be deciding who is more trustworthy.
- A prosecutor may decide to drop a case against the accused if that person will be testifying against someone else in another trial. For example, if the accused is a small-time drug dealer, the prosecutor may drop all charges for information leading to the arrest and conviction of a major supplier.

These case-processing decisions become integrated into a strategy for the prosecutor's office. A number of models have been developed to guide prosecutors regarding when to proceed with the case to court and when to drop or stay charges (Jacoby 1979):

- *The transfer model.* In this model, very little screening occurs and prosecutors charge most of the accused after they receive the case from the police. The key factor here is the amount of resources available to a prosecutor's office: if it has ample resources, more cases will be heard in court.

- *The unit model.* Here, individual prosecutors are given significant amounts of discretion to do as they like with each case. There is not much organizational guidance, and little specific policy given to prosecutors.
- *The legal sufficiency model.* Here, cases are screened according to their legal elements. If there are sufficient legal grounds, the case will probably be prosecuted.
- *The system efficiency model.* In this model, cases are disposed of in the quickest possible way. Only those cases where there is a high probability of success will be prosecuted; those which are not as clear cut will be rejected as too time consuming (even if they may end with a conviction) because there are not enough resources.
- *The trial sufficiency model.* Here, a case proceeds to court only if a conviction is likely. Resources are secondary, given the prosecutor's feeling that the case will end in a conviction.
- *The defendant rehabilitation model.* Here, the prosecutor's decision rests on whether it is possible to rehabilitate the defendant. Under this model, alternatives (e.g., treatment programs) are sought out before the case goes to court as long as the accused agrees to participate.

Plea Bargaining

There is no formal definition of plea bargaining in the Criminal Code. As a general definition, plea bargaining has been defined as "any agreement by the accused to plead guilty in return for the promise of some benefit" (Law Reform Commission of Canada 1975, 45). According to this definition, plea bargaining involves the idea that justice can be purchased at the bargaining table. Since the Law Reform Commission wrote this definition, however, it has been acknowledged that this practice involves more than an accused bargaining with the Crown in exchange for some reduction in punishment. To better recognize the multitude of ways in which plea bargaining takes place in our criminal justice system, Perras (1979, 58–59) defined it as "a proceeding whereby competent and informed counsel openly discuss the evidence in a criminal prosecution with a view to achieving a disposition which will result in the reasonable advancement of the administration of justice."

Plea bargaining exists because it serves a variety of purposes (Wheatley 1974):

- It improves the administrative efficiency of the courts.
- It lowers the cost of prosecution.
- It permits the prosecution to devote more time to more important cases.

In the real world, plea bargaining involves a large number of activities, including discussions about charges, sentences, the facts of the case, and procedural issues. Plea bargaining can occur before the trial starts, but it can also be done during the trial when the defendant and defence counsel perceive a benefit in pleading guilty. Plea bargaining agreements, then, can take several forms but are typically designed to expedite the trial. Most plea bargaining occurs between the accused, the defence lawyer, and the Crown prosecutor. **Charge bargaining** may involve the following activities:

- The reduction of the charge to a lesser or included offence.
- The withdrawal or stay of other charges or the promise not to proceed on other possible charges.
- The promise not to charge friends or family members of the defendant.
- The promise to reduce multiple charges to one all-inclusive charge.
- The promise to stay certain criminal counts and to proceed on others and to rely on the material facts that supported the stayed counts as aggravating factors for sentencing purposes.

A plea bargain for dropped charges involves dropping extraneous illegal actions that are contained in the complaint. For example, the prosecutor may agree to drop an auto theft charge accompanying a drug offence.

Sentence bargaining is another common form of plea bargaining. Prosecutors and defence lawyers recommend to the presiding judge an appropriate sentence for the accused. Judges do not have to accept this recommendation, but they usually do. Sentence bargaining usually includes the following:

- A promise to proceed summarily rather than by way of indictment.
- A promise from the Crown to make a particular recommendation in relation to sentence.
- A promise not to oppose defence counsel's sentence recommendation.
- A promise not to appeal against the sentence imposed at trial.
- A promise not to apply for a more severe penalty.
- A promise not to apply for a period of preventive detention.
- A promise to make a representation as to the place of imprisonment, type of treatment, and so on.
- A promise to arrange sentencing before a particular judge.
- A promise on the type of conditions to be imposed on a conditional sentence.

In sentence bargaining, the prosecutor agrees to recommend a shorter sentence to the judge or to proceed in the court trial by way of summary conviction in a hybrid offence. For example, a Crown prosecutor may agree to proceed against an individual charged with sexual assault (level 1) on the basis of a summary conviction charge rather than an indictable offence.

Procedural bargaining may include the following:

- A promise by the Crown prosecutor to proceed by way of summary conviction instead of indictment.
- A promise to dispose of the case at a specified future time if, on the record and in open court, the accused is prepared to waive the right to trial within a reasonable time.

In cases involving **fact bargaining**, the prosecutor and defence lawyer agree not to submit certain facts about the case or the background of the offender into court. In so agreeing, they hope the accused will receive a lighter sentence. Such a practice usually involves the following:

- A promise not to volunteer certain information about the accused (e.g., information on the defendant's previous convictions).
- A promise not to mention a circumstance of the offence that might be interpreted by the judge as an aggravating factor (and therefore as making the accused deserving of a more severe sentence).

Plea bargaining may also involve what is referred to as "label bargaining." This involves an attempt by defence counsel to ensure that the accused is not charged with an offence that carries a negative label (e.g., child molestation) in exchange for a less socially objectionable one (e.g., assault) by offering a plea of guilty.

As noted above, Crown prosecutors are obligated not only to serve the public interest but also to ensure that justice is done. They have a professional obligation to plea bargain with the accused, and they must do so on the basis of fairness, openness, accuracy, non-discrimination, and the public interest. Section 10(b) of the Charter of Rights and Freedoms states that plea bargaining is an essential aspect of prosecutorial discretion in criminal cases. Crown prosecutors may either initiate or respond to a plea bargain, and the plea bargain should be offered to the accused as soon as possible.

Even after a plea bargain has been agreed on among the accused, the defence lawyer, and the Crown prosecutor, the sentence must still be determined by the judge assigned to the case. A joint recommendation on sentencing by the prosecutor and the defence lawyer is not binding on a judge. Judges, however, are legally obligated not to reject a joint submission unless it is contrary to the public interest and the recommended sentence would bring the administration of justice into disrepute. If a judge decides that the recommended sentence is not lawful, the accused will not be able to withdraw the guilty plea. In Canada, it is rare for lawyers to discuss plea bargains privately with a judge. However, during a pretrial conference—that is, an informal meeting held in a judge's office—a full and free discussion of the issues raised can take place without prejudice to the rights of the parties in any of the proceedings occurring afterward (s. 625.1 of the Criminal Code). During these conferences, issues can be considered with the general goal of ensuring a fair and expeditious hearing. A pretrial conference can be held at the request of the Crown prosecutor, the accused, or the court. In the case of a jury trial, a pretrial conference is mandatory (s. 625.1[2] of the Criminal Code).

Prosecutors prefer to devote their time to serious crimes or to cases in which they have a good chance of securing a conviction, so they may agree in other cases to accept a guilty plea to a lesser charge; doing so saves the court's time and money and reduces the risk that the prosecution will lose the case should it proceed to trial. In addition, the prosecutor may gain information about other criminals that will help solve other crimes.

Plea bargaining has been both criticized and defended by a wide variety of individuals and sectors in the criminal justice system. Many of the criticisms are voiced by crime control advocates, who contend that it is unfair, that it is hidden from public scrutiny, and that it results in too much leniency. Other critics focus on the impact that plea bargaining has on the integrity of the criminal justice system. They point out that it undermines many of the system's core values because it avoids due process standards designed to protect the accused. It is also pointed out that innocent persons may feel compelled to plead guilty to crimes they never committed.

Advantages of plea bargaining include the fact that it increases the efficiency of our criminal justice system. Also, it reduces the costs of operating that system as well as the workloads of prosecutors so that they can pursue more serious criminal cases. It may also reduce the trauma felt by victims because it means they won't be cross-examined in a criminal trial.

The practice of plea bargaining will probably continue to be debated vigorously. The arguments of both supporters and critics will no doubt ensure that it stays within the bounds of the principles of our criminal justice system. That said, there will surely be cases where it is appropriate to review plea bargaining. The Law Reform Commission (1975, 14) once referred to plea bargaining as "something for which a decent criminal justice system has no place." Yet, it later changed its view, calling plea bargaining a normal practice in the criminal justice system, and in 1989, it commented that plea bargaining is not a "shameful practice" (Law Reform Commission 1989, 8).

THE JURY

The right to a jury trial has existed in Canada for almost 300 years. The right to be tried by a jury of one's peers is one of the oldest protections of individual liberty in our criminal justice system. It is designed to protect the accused from the powers of the state, from arbitrary law enforcement, and from overzealous prosecutors and biased judges (Hans and Vidmar 1986; Levine 1992). The right to trial by jury is still considered important enough in our legal system that it was included in the Charter of Rights and Freedoms for any charge in which an accused could be imprisoned for five years or more (Davison 2005). As we have seen, this does not mean that every accused selects to be tried by a jury; the bulk of the offences that go to trial are electable offences, and the accused often selects to be tried by judge alone. This right is enshrined in the Charter of Rights and Freedoms (ss. 11[d] and 11[f]). However, in comparison to other Western countries, such as the United States, the law in Canada provides for jury trials in only the more serious criminal offences.

The specific role of a **jury** in our legal system today is similar to that of a judge trying a case alone—that is, it is "to decide the facts from the trial evidence present and to apply the law (provided by the judge) to those facts to render a verdict" (Vidmar and Schuller 2001, 130). The jury must be representative of the community, be independent and impartial, and approach the trial with an open mind. Within its role, the jury is to make its decision about the guilt or innocence of the accused based on its evaluation of the evidence. Since jurors are members of the community where the alleged criminal offence occurred, it serves as the conscience of the community as opposed to the opinion of one person (i.e., the judge).

In a number of cases, the Supreme Court of Canada has identified the importance of both the representativeness and the impartiality of the jury. Individuals selected to be jurors come from the community in which the trial is being heard. The final selection of jurors may not be entirely representative of the community, but the original group of people from which they were selected (called an array) will have been more representative because they were randomly selected to be potential members of the jury. Trial court judges have held that

the selection of a jury array that excluded inhabitants of First Nations communities was not representative (*R. v. Nahdee* [1993]; neither was an array that included too few women (*R. v. Nepoose* [1991]). And in *R. v. Sherratt* (1991), the Supreme Court held that the jury must consist of individuals who are impartial.

According to Davison (2005, 38), the most basic value of the jury is that it is democratic. This means that the jury

> brings representatives of the community, with their varying life experiences, occupations, and common sense, into a setting usually (perhaps too often) occupied exclusively by lawyers and judges bound up in the legal principles and precedents and outcomes. At its heart, the jury represents society, and the prevailing views in society, about what should be penalized and what ought not.

The Right to a Jury Trial

Before a case is heard in court, the accused may have the right to decide between a trial by judge and jury or by judge alone. In Canada, the right to a jury trial is found in s. 11(f) of the Charter of Rights and Freedoms, which states that any person charged with an offence has the right to trial by jury where the maximum punishment for the offence is imprisonment for five years or more. In *R. v. D.(S)* (1992), this five-year rule was challenged by the accused, who had been charged with an offence carrying a maximum punishment of less than five years. The court held that no principle of fundamental justice had been violated, as no right exists that entitles the accused to a jury trial in every criminal case. Note also that most indictable offences are electable and that many accused persons decide not to be tried by judge and jury.

Once an accused has been convicted and further proceedings take place on the basis of the conviction, there can be no additional jury trial. For example, when convicted murderer Paul Bernardo was declared a dangerous offender, his defence lawyer made no attempt to have the case heard by both a judge and jury, since Bernardo had already been found guilty and, as such, was not an individual "charged with an offence" as specified in s. 11(f) of the Charter. This was based on a previous case heard by the Supreme Court of Canada, which ruled that it is wrong to allow an individual already convicted to have the right later on to request a jury trial (*R. v. Lyons* [1987]).

A jury usually does not have input into the sentence imposed on the accused after the finding of guilt. Juries do, however, assist in the determination of a sentence at two points in our legal system. One is when the accused is found guilty of second degree murder. Here, the jury will be asked to make a recommendation on the length of time the accused should have to wait (i.e., more than 10 years) before being eligible to apply for parole. The other is during a "faint hope" hearing (see Chapter 12).

Jury Selection

If the accused decides to be tried by a judge and jury, jury selection follows. Jury selection is a four-step procedure. Three of these occur outside the court and are a provincial responsibility; the fourth takes place inside the court and is governed by the Criminal Code. The three out-of-court stages are as follows:

1. The assembly of a source list of persons who may be qualified, under provincial law, to serve as jurors (most but not all provincial jury acts specify some or all of the sources to be consulted when the list is prepared).
2. A determination of the identity of those on the source list who are qualified to serve, according to the relevant provincial jury act, and the disqualification or exemption from service of those on the list who, for various reasons, are usually also specified in the appropriate jury act.
3. The selection from the names remaining on the source list of a jury panel, whose members are, as appropriate, summoned to appear in court in accordance with the procedures set out in each provincial jury act.

A list of initial candidates is then compiled. The ways this is done varies from province to province. This initial list, referred to as a jury array, provides the government with the names of citizens who are potential jurors. Each province has a jury act that specifies who may be selected for the jury array. Section 626 of the Criminal Code allows each province to determine the qualifications for potential selection. This section precludes discrimination on the basis of sex.

A number of individuals from the juror list appear in court (the number varies widely from jurisdiction to jurisdiction), where an in-court selection process follows. The framework for this in-court procedure is found in s. 631 of the Criminal Code. The purpose of this process is to determine which of the prospective jurors are impartial. Canadian trial judges do not have the authority to determine the impartiality of prospective jurors (in the United States, judges do have this authority). The judge can ask the assembled panel of prospective jurors whether, if selected, they might be unable to serve on the jury (because of a health problem, for example). The judge may excuse those who indicate they have concerns.

In Canada, the decision to select a jury is held by two layperson triers. To select the first juror, two individuals are randomly chosen and sworn to serve as triers. The triers listen to prospective jurors as they respond in turn to questions approved by the court. The triers must decide, after each response, whether the candidate is impartial. Once the candidate is deemed to be impartial, another prospective juror is called forward; the process continues until another impartial juror is found. When this happens, one of the original two triers is replaced. However, even if the triers decide that a juror is impartial, either the Crown prosecutor or the defendant may exercise a peremptory challenge (see below), making the triers call another prospective juror. Once the twelfth juror is called, the jury is sworn.

There are two types of challenges in Canada: the challenge for cause (where a reason must be given for, and a determination made about, the validity of the challenge) and the peremptory challenge (where no questioning of prospective jurors takes place and where no cause need be stated as to why a potential juror is being eliminated). The purpose of both challenges is to eliminate jurors considered by either side to be unqualified or not impartial. In this process, the prosecution and the defence lawyer may challenge potential jurors in order to assess their appropriateness to sit on the jury. Potential jurors may be questioned under oath about such things as their personal background, occupation, residence, interest in the case, and attitudes about certain relevant issues; typically, though, the court allows only one or two specific questions—approved by the trial judge—to be put forward. Any citizen who is thought to have a bias for or against the accused—for example, a person who is a friend of the accused or who has already formed an opinion—will be eliminated. Sometimes potential jurors are not questioned at all—the Crown prosecutor and defence lawyer may simply look at the potential juror and/or the information they have about that person (which consists of name, address, and occupation) and use a peremptory challenge.

If there is a challenge for cause, a reason must be provided and the judge must determine whether the reason has merit. For either side, the usual approach is to challenge for cause first, as the number of peremptory challenges is limited. A potential juror may be challenged if, for example, he or she was convicted of an offence and incarcerated for more than 12 months, or is physically unable to serve on the jury, or cannot speak either official language of Canada, or is a non-Canadian or a landed immigrant (Criminal Code provisions, cited by Mewett and Nakatsuru 2000). If a potential juror is challenged peremptorily, no reason need be given.

Challenges for cause are rare in Canada (Vidmar 1999). Most challenges are peremptory, but the number of such challenges is limited. Section 634(1) of the Criminal Code was changed in 1992 to allow both the prosecutor and defence to exercise 20 peremptory challenges when the accused is charged with high treason or first degree murder, 12 challenges when the accused is charged with all other offences punishable by imprisonment of five years or more, or four peremptory challenges for all other offences. Different numbers of challenges open to the Crown apply in cases where there are accused being jointly tried.

Challenges for cause are used to determine whether prospective jurors are indifferent. Canadian courts have not allowed questions that are not relevant to showing partiality—the presumption is that all potential jurors will follow their oath. Historically, questions involving the possible racial bias of jurors have not been allowed in Canada. In 1993, the Ontario Court of Appeal was the first court to acknowledge the possibility of juror racial prejudice. In this case, *R. v. Parks* (1983), a Black male was accused of murdering a White male during a cocaine transaction in Toronto. Here, the Court of Appeal held that "it was essential for the accused to be able to ask potential jurors about their racial bias." The Court of Appeal "hoped that allowing one question would legitimate the trial process as fair and nondiscriminatory" (Roach 1999, 228). Many judges, however, interpreted this ruling as being applicable only to the Toronto area. However, the Court of Appeal stated later on that one question could be asked throughout the province. The Court of Appeal also clarified what type of question could be asked: general questions related to the offence in question could not be asked. This question cannot be used for trials involving defendants who are gay or Vietnamese, because of "the lack of evidence of systemic discrimination against these groups."

This issue soon resurfaced. In *R. v. Williams* (1996), a trial judge in British Columbia refused to allow an Aboriginal male to ask a question to potential jurors relating to their potential biases. This ruling was appealed to the British Columbia Court of Appeal, which upheld the decision of the trial judge. This case was then appealed to the Supreme Court, which ruled in favour of the accused. And in *Mankwe v. R.* (2001), the Supreme Court held that the defence may question potential jurors about their views about Black people. This case involved a Black male who had been convicted by a jury of sexually assaulting a woman working for an escort agency in his apartment. The Supreme Court ordered a new trial, and ruled his lawyer could ask potential jurors whether they believed that Black people

- commit more crimes in Canada than other Canadians;
- have a greater propensity to commit crimes of violence;
- are more likely to commit crimes of a sexual nature than other races; *and*
- have a greater tendency to lie than people of other races do.

Only the trial judge has the right to "stand aside" a prospective juror, and then only in limited circumstances. A judge may ask a juror to stand aside for reasons of personal hardship or any other reasonable cause (s. 633 of the Criminal Code). Exempting a prospective juror allows the judge, in those situations where a full jury has not yet been sworn, to call back jurors in the hope that both sides can agree to allow them to serve as jurors. In these cases, however, the recalled jurors are subject to the same challenges as the other jurors (s. 641 of the Criminal Code).

In Canada, all juries consist of 12 individuals. Until 1992, courts in Yukon and the Northwest Territories were allowed to select only six individuals. However, the Court of Appeal of the Northwest Territories held that such a jury was in violation of s. 15 of the Charter. Sometimes cases are tried by a jury of 11. This is because a judge has the power to discharge a juror because of illness or any other reasonable cause. A trial may continue as long as ten jurors remain; if the number falls below 10, the jury must be discharged and the process started over, as specified by s. 634 of the Criminal Code.

LEGAL RIGHTS AND CRIMINAL TRIALS

The point of a criminal trial "is for the prosecution to prove, according to law, the guilt of the accused" (Mewett and Nakatsuru 2000, 133). This means that the prosecutor must prove that the defendant committed the act in question and had the appropriate mental element at the time the criminal offence was committed. Every trial involves certain legal principles concerning the rights of the accused; these are specified in the Charter of Rights and Freedoms and in rules of evidence. These rights were introduced to ensure that the accused would be given a fair trial. Discussed below are the most fundamental rights that accused persons possess in the Canadian legal system.

The Presumption of Innocence

According to s. 11(a) of the Charter, everyone has the right "to be presumed innocent until proven guilty according to law in a fair and public hearing." The burden of proving guilt in a court of law lies with the state (i.e., the prosecutor). Even if the accused is factually guilty, the prosecutor still has to convince a judge or jury that the defendant is legally guilty.

The Right of the Accused to Confront the Accuser

The right of the accused to confront the accuser is essential to a fair trial, since it controls the type of evidence used in court. Hearsay evidence—that is, second-hand information—is accepted as evidence only in rare circumstances, such as, for example, when it is information divulged by a dying person. This is what happened in a famous American criminal case involving the Ford Motor Company and one of its vehicles, the Pinto (Cullen et al. 1987). In this case, it was ruled that a deathbed statement made to a nurse by a victim of a traffic accident involving a Pinto could be entered into the court record, even though it could not be corroborated. This evidence proved to be a major factor in the outcome of the case.

Furthermore, the accused (usually through the defence lawyer) has the right to cross-examine all witnesses and victims who testify for the prosecution. Cross-examination allows the defence to challenge (and perhaps thus discredit) any statement or testimony given by a prosecution witness or a victim.

Child sexual assault legislation allows a child to testify outside the courtroom when the accused is charged with certain sexual offences. Judges are permitted to allow a child to testify from behind a screen or via closed-circuit television from another room in the courthouse. However, the provisions in this legislation protecting children from the sight of the alleged abuser have not always been accepted outright by members of the judiciary. In *R. v. Ross* (1989), the Nova Scotia Court of Appeal upheld the constitutionality of the provision, ruling that "the right to face one's accusers is not, in this day and age, to be taken in a literal sense . . . It is simply the right of the accused person to be present in court."

The use of videotape as the sole evidence of the victim's testimony, however, has proved to be more problematic. In *R. v. Meddoui* (1990), heard in the Court of Queen's Bench of Alberta, the trial judge accepted the videotape of the victim as evidence. However, in another case that same year (*R. v. Thompson* [1990]), the use of videotape was ruled as violating ss. 7 and 11(d) of the Charter. In the future, therefore, the use of videotape as prima facie evidence will likely be rare in Canadian courts.

The Right to a Speedy Trial

One of the most serious problems facing the courts today is delays in hearing criminal cases. Delays may arise for any number of reasons, such as plea bargaining, procedural and evidentiary issues, and court cancellations. These delays may contravene s. 11(b) of the Charter, which guarantees that any person charged with an offence has the right "to be tried within a reasonable time."

Section 7 of the Charter considers the right to a speedy trial to be part of fundamental justice. This right was clarified in *R. v. Askov* (1990) (see Exhibit 8.4). In this case, three men charged with weapons offences were denied bail in November 1983. The men were released on bail in May 1984, but their court trial was put over until September 1985, due to a backlog of cases. The lawyers for the accused argued that their clients' right to a fair trial had been unfairly violated by courtroom delays. The presiding judge agreed, but the Ontario Court of Appeal overturned that decision. However, the Supreme Court of Canada agreed with the trial judge. When the Supreme Court made its decision, it identified four factors for a judge to rule on when unreasonable delay had occurred:

1. *The length of the delay.* No absolute time limit was identified by the Supreme Court. However, it did rule that "it is clear that the longer the delay, the more difficult it should be for a court to excuse it." This factor is to be balanced with the other factors, including "the standard maintained by the next comparable jurisdiction in the country."
2. *The explanation for the delay.* Two key factors were identified: (a) the conduct of the Crown and (b) systematic or institutional delays. In addition, the accused cannot unduly cause a delay in the proceedings; if the accused were to make a deliberate attempt to delay the trial, the courts would not rule in his or her favour and the burden of proof would lie with the accused.
3. *Waiver.* An accused who permits a waiver is indicating that he or she understands the s. 11(b) guarantee to a speedy trial and is, in effect, agreeing to waive that guarantee.
4. *Prejudice to the accused.* The Crown may proceed with the case when, despite a long delay, no resulting damage was suffered by the accused.

The impact of *Askov* was enormous. Almost 50,000 criminal charges were permanently stayed in Ontario during the next 11 months, including a number of cases involving charges of sexual assault, assault, and fraud (*R. v. Morin* [1992]). Within two years, however, the Supreme Court of Canada had reconsidered the issue of speed trials. In *Morin*, it ruled that a delay of between 14 and 15 months in a case involving charges of impaired driving did not violate s. 11(b) of the Charter. In this case, the Supreme Court changed its direction by ruling that the protection of society was served by allowing "serious cases to come to trial, that administrative guidelines are not limitation periods, and the importance of evidence of prejudice" (Stuart 1995, 347). Since *Morin*, the number of cases stayed due to unreasonable delay has fallen dramatically. This change came about mainly because provincial governments provided more resources to the courts and investigated other strategies, such as diversion programs. Most cases in Canada are now heard within one year of the first court appearance. In fact, many cases are dealt with in a single appearance, usually within the first four months of the initial court appearance.

The Right to a Public (Open) Trial

Do members of the public have the right to attend criminal trials in Canada? And do the members of the media have the right not only to attend criminal trials but also to publish reports on what they heard in the case? Courts are public institutions and therefore accessible to the

---

EXHIBIT 8.4 The Right to a Speedy Trial (*R. v. Askov* [1990])

R. v. Askov (1990) illustrates how the Supreme Court of Canada interpreted the right to speedy justice for the accused. This decision relates to s. 11(b) of the Canadian Charter of Rights and Freedoms, which states that any person charged with an offence has the right "to be tried within a reasonable time."

FACTS OF THE CASE
In November 1983, Askov (along with a few associates) was charged with the possession of a prohibited weapon, possession of a weapon for a purpose dangerous to the public, pointing a firearm, and assault with a weapon. He was denied bail in November 1983 but was released on bail in May 1984 on a recognizance of $50,000. A preliminary inquiry started in July 1984 lasted until September 1984. There was enough evidence to proceed to trial, but the trial wasn't slated to start for 13 months, owing to scheduling problems. By then almost two years had passed since the charges were laid. The case was then rescheduled to be heard in September 1986.

When at last the trial started, defence counsel argued that it should be stayed because of the length of time the case had taken to come to trial (by then almost three years). The trial judge denied the request, stating that "insufficient institutional resources" were the source of the delay. This ruling was confirmed by the Ontario Court of Appeal.

DECISION
Askov appealed this decision to the Supreme Court, which heard the case in October 1990. The court ruled in favour of Askov, setting out a number of factors to be used by the courts when determining whether the delay for a case to come to trial is excessive (see above list). In addition,

the court stated that a waiting period of five to eight months for a case to come to trial was acceptable.

SIGNIFICANCE OF THE CASE
The impact of *Askov* was described by a judge on the Ontario Court of Appeal as "staggering." In the six months following the court's decision, more than 34,000 charges were stayed, dismissed, or withdrawn. This included 8,600 impaired driving charges, 6,000 cases involving theft under $1,000, a substantial number of charges involving assaults and frauds, 500 sexual assaults, more than 1,000 drug offences, and thousands of violations of provincial statutes.

UPDATE
Seventeen months later, the Supreme Court of Canada, in *R. v. Morin* (1992), changed the acceptable waiting period to eight to ten months. It also introduced a number of other tests, so that it was no longer necessary for the prosecutor to prove that the delay had been caused by the accused, that institutional delay was justified, or that the accused had waived his or her rights under s. 11(b) of the Charter. According to Kelly (2005, 130), this "fundamental shift effectively transformed the *Askov* test [from one] that largely emphasized the due process rights of the accused to one that considers the institutional pressures on the judicial system and the crime control objective of factual guilt." The immediate impact of the change introduced in *Morin* was that the median elapsed time for cases involving serious charges became longer. The longest median elapsed times for violent crimes are for cases involving, for example, homicide (451 days), sexual exploitation (370 days) and sexual assault (368 days) (Marth 2008).

---

public. But what about the ability to access and publish documents in the media related to a case? The principle of openness allows the media to access and publish such materials unless a judge considers that the application "would render the proper administration of justice unworkable" (*C.B.C. v. New Brunswick Attorney General* [1996]). In Canada, this principle of openness is not absolute as there are some federal and provincial restrictions limiting the ability of the public or media to access and publish information pertaining to a criminal case. Federal legislation, for example, gives the trial judge the discretion to order a publication ban of information that would disclose the identity of the complainant or witness in sexual offences (s. 486(3) of the Criminal Code). However, in these cases a judge has no discretion when the complainant or a witness is under the age of 18 and applies for a publication ban (in these cases, a prosecutor can also apply for a ban on publication). Section 276(3) of the Criminal Code prohibits discussions that involve the admissibility of evidence about the sexual activity of the defendant. And s. 110 of the Youth Criminal Justice Act prohibits the publication of the name of a youth if it would potentially identify a youth being dealt with under the legislation. In other cases, however, what are the rights of the media to report on the facts and identities of the individuals involved? The judicial tradition in Canada has been to "interfere as little as possible with the fundamental right of freedom of expression . . . Publicity is the burden that citizens of democratic countries must bear when they go to court" ("An Excessive Use . . ." 2004).

The right of individuals to attend a public trial and publish materials about it is referred to as the "open court principle." In the pre-Charter common-law rule concerning bans on publishing, the right to a fair trial was emphasized over the free-expression interests of those affected by the ban. This meant that the common law "required that those seeking a ban demonstrate that there was a real and substantial risk of interference with the right to a fair trial" (Eastwood 2004, 36). While this issue is not addressed explicitly by the Charter, s. 2(b) guarantees freedom of the press and other forms of the mass media. However, freedom of the press is limited by s. 1 of the Charter, where it has been held that freedom of the press is not an absolute. A discussion of the most fundamental rights that accused persons possess in the Canadian legal system follows.

Publication Bans

While most criminal trials are open to reporting by the media, a public trial is for the benefit of the accused. Section 11(b) of the Charter states that any person charged with an offence has the right "to be presumed innocent until proven guilty according to law in a fair and public hearing." This means that justice cannot be served by secret court trials.

But, as noted earlier, the accused can ask the judge to order a ban on the publication of certain evidence emerging in a preliminary inquiry. In such a case, the name of the accused can be published, but specific evidence presented in court cannot, as "this might jeopardize the ability of the accused to receive a fair trial" (Boyd 1995, 41). The rationale is that the media could give out information that biases potential jurors or judges. As a result, great care is taken to protect the accused.

These cases typically involve issues concerning the effects of pretrial publicity and whether publicity will influence the right of the accused to a fair trial. The Supreme Court ruled in *Dagenais v. CBC* (1994) that the right to a fair trial does not take precedence over the right to a free press; in this way it rejected the approach taken in the pre-Charter common law. It now requires instead "a balance to be achieved that fully respects the importance of the rights that have come into conflict" (Eastwood 2004, 35). In *Dagenais*, the members of a Catholic religious order charged with physically and sexually abusing young boys in their care applied to a superior court judge for an injunction restraining the CBC from showing the miniseries *The Boys of St. Vincent* on television. The Court of Appeal agreed, but limited the extent of the injunction to Ontario and Montreal. The Supreme Court stated that the common-law rule was inappropriate since it emphasized the right to a fair trial over the right to freedom of expression. When Charter rights come into conflict, Charter principles require a balance that respects both. The Supreme Court then set out a modified common-law rule (referred to as a "test") that would be used in future cases to establish the fairness of a trial:

A publication ban should only be ordered when:

(a) such a ban is necessary to prevent a real and substantial risk to the fairness of a trial, because reasonably available alternative measures will not prevent the risk; *and*

(b) the salutary effects of the publication ban outweigh the deleterious effects to the free expression of those affected by the ban.

The judgment in *Dagenais* "held the promise of a new era of open courts. Press freedom would no longer automatically rank behind other constitutional freedoms" (Makin 2003, A8). Yet publication bans have continued to be granted in large numbers since *Dagenais*, largely as a result of the priority given to protecting the privacy of groups in Canada. However, due to a "jurisdictional oddity," provincial appellate courts cannot hear challenges to publication bans (s. 40[1] of the Supreme Court Act). Instead, someone wanting to challenge a publication ban must obtain leave to appeal to the Supreme Court, a process that is "costly and usually doomed because the court can only hear a tiny proportion of cases" (ibid.).

In order for a publication ban to be granted by the courts, both the criteria noted in *Dagenais* must be satisfied. A question arises from this issue: Just how much does pretrial publicity influence jurors? Freedman and Burke (1996, 257) studied the effects of pretrial publicity in the Paul Bernardo case to evaluate whether it would have posed a real and substantial risk to the fairness of the trial. In their study of 155 adults who served as mock jurors in this case—a case aptly described as "one of the most sensational cases in Canadian history"—they found that pretrial publicity had only a limited negative effect on the verdict. This led the researchers to conclude "there was no relation between the amount heard and ratings of guilt or verdicts either before or after the trial account."

There are other reasons why a publication ban may be sought in Canada, such as to protect the techniques used by the police in an undercover operation. In *R. v. Mentuck* (2001) a publication ban was sought by the Crown prosecutor because it was felt that the facts of the case (which involved an undercover police operation) could jeopardize the identity of police officers as well as reveal the operational methods used by the police in similar undercover operations. The trial judge granted a one-year ban concerning the identity of the undercover police officers but refused to order a publication ban regarding the operational methods. The Crown appealed the decision to the Supreme Court of Canada. The Supreme Court stated that the protection of rights in the Charter of Rights and Freedoms, such as the right to a fair trial, was "not the only legitimate objective under which a judge can consider the common law discretion to grant a publication ban" (Eastwood 2004, 37). However, the Supreme Court noted that it could not directly apply the "test" it had established in *Dagenais* since the publication ban applied for in *Dagenais* was based on protecting the accused's right to a fair trial, whereas in *Mentuck*, the publication ban had been applied for in order to protect the safety of undercover police officers as well as to keep from public knowledge the type of police operation used. To properly assess the issue of a publication ban in *Mentuck*, the Supreme

Television cameras record the opening day of an appeal trial involving two biker club members convicted of manslaughter in 1996, Wednesday Mar. 15, 2000, at the courthouse, in Quebec City. (CP PHOTO/Jacques Boissinot)

Court replaced the "fairness of the trial" test established in the first criterion of *Dagenais* with "the proper administration of justice."

In terms of the publication ban concerning the identity of the undercover police officers, the Supreme Court accepted the one-year publication ban as decided by the trial judge. The Supreme Court decided that the one-year ban on identifying the officers was "necessary and there is no reasonable alternative." The request for a publication ban concerning the operational methods of the police was held as unnecessary by the Supreme Court, which stated that the publication of this information "does not constitute a serious risk to the efficacy of police operations, and thus to that aspect of the proper administration of justice." The reality of the risk must be "well-grounded in evidence." Furthermore, the Supreme Court stated that "the benefits this ban promises are, at best, speculative and marginal improvements in the efficacy of undercover operations and the safety of officers in the field, but the deleterious effects are substantial. Such a ban would seriously curtail the freedom of the press in respect to an issue that may merit widespread public debate."

Another important issue involving publicity and criminal cases is whether trials should be televised as a matter of right. The situation in Canada is different from that in the United States, where in 1981, the U.S. Supreme Court removed all constitutional obstacles to the use of television over the complaints of the accused. As a result, during the summer of 1995 many Canadians watched live TV coverage of the O.J. Simpson trial, though they could view only artists' sketches of the Paul Bernardo trial.

According to s. 486(1) of the Criminal Code, a judge has the right to exclude the public for all or part of the trial if he or she feels it is in the "interest of public morals, the maintenance of order, or the proper order of administration." Exclusion is most commonly ordered when a child or mentally challenged person is about to testify and the judge believes that exclusion will assist the witness.

One of the most controversial decisions a judge can make is to exclude the media. Rarely are members of the media banned from the courtroom. It is more common for a superior court judge to issue a non-publication order to protect "the integrity of the court." In addition, s. 486(3) expressly allows a trial judge to ban the publication of anything that would identify the names of the complainant or witnesses in trials involving sexual offences.

THE CRIMINAL TRIAL

A criminal trial is a formal process that strictly follows rules of evidence, procedure, and criminal law. The formality and rigidity implied by this definition stand in sharp contrast to trials shown on many television shows and in movies, which present the courtroom as a "no-holds barred" arena in which defence lawyers and prosecutors ask leading questions, act in a prejudicial manner, and win cases through courtroom trickery. The reality is that every criminal trial follows a particular procedure that must be observed by all parties involved. As a result, trials are complicated events, and the judge has to make decisions about technical questions of procedure and about what evidence is allowed to enter the court.

The key actors are the prosecutor and defence lawyer, who present their case as persuasively as they can and in a manner that they hope is most likely to lead to an adjudication in their favour. Prosecutors use police reports, testimony from witnesses and victims, and physical evidence in an attempt to persuade the court that the defendant is guilty. The defence lawyer tries to point out weaknesses in the prosecutor's case, and at the same time presents evidence beneficial to the accused. The defence lawyer tries to ensure that his or her client's constitutional rights are protected. Since only one side can win, both the prosecutor and the defence lawyer will assess the trial in order to see whether an appeal is necessary.

The Opening Statement

Once the jury has been selected and the trial begins, the criminal charges are read to the jurors by a court employee. Both the prosecutor and the defence lawyer then have the right to make opening statements to the jury. In Canada, the prosecutor presents the first opening statement. This statement usually includes a summation of the criminal charges, the facts of the case, and the Crown's plan on how it will proceed. However, the prosecutor cannot be biased or impartial in his or her opening comments, since the prosecutor's role is to assist the jury in arriving at the truth. In other words, Crown prosecutors have a duty to be impartial, and this duty precludes any notion of winning or losing. They must guard against stating information that is likely to excite and inflame the jury against the accused. Nor may they "express a personal opinion as to the guilt of the accused or state that the Crown [is] satisfied as to the accused's guilt" (Salhany 1986, 274).

The defence can choose not to make an opening statement. The defence lawyer, too, outlines the case but informs the jury of how he or she intends to show that the defendant is innocent of all charges. This plan entails describing how he or she will prove the prosecution's case to be inadequate.

Prosecutors cannot promise evidence that they will not be bringing to court. If they mention the name of a particular witness and the testimony they expect from that witness, and this individual does not appear, the judge may rule the statement was prejudicial toward the accused and subsequently set aside any verdict of guilt. In addition, the prosecutor cannot mention any evidence that he or she knows will be inadmissible and cannot mention the prior record of the accused, if one exists.

If the trial does not involve a jury, the opening statements can be brief, as the judge is probably knowledgeable about the case, the appropriate rules of law, and some of the evidence, which may already have been discussed in a preliminary inquiry.

All evidence submitted in the court in an attempt to prove the defendant innocent or guilty must meet the highest standard of proof. The standard is "guilty **beyond a reasonable doubt**," and it is viewed as the basis for reducing the risk of mistaken conviction if there are questions about certain facts presented during the trial. The standard goes hand in hand with the belief that it is better to release one hundred guilty individuals than to convict one who is innocent.

Trial Evidence

Once the opening statements have concluded, the prosecution starts its case by presenting evidence. Usually the first evidence to be presented is testimony provided by sworn witnesses (e.g., police officers, medical examiners, and victims). This type of testimony consists of reports from the witnesses on anything that they saw, heard, or touched. Sometimes it involves the opinions of witnesses; for example, an eyewitness may give an opinion as to whether the defendant seemed confused. Expert witnesses are specialists in certain areas that apply to the case. For example, a medical examiner can give expert testimony on the time of death or on how injuries occurred. No more than five expert witnesses may be used by the prosecution or defence without the approval of the judge.

When the prosecution finishes its questioning, the defence has the right to cross-examine the witness. Cross-examination can focus on the oral and written statements of the witness. Testimony is only one form of evidence that may be used during a trial. Other types of evidence are as follows:

- *Real evidence.* This type of evidence consists of exhibits such as weapons, clothing, and fingerprints. Real evidence must be original. However, photographs and duplicates may be introduced as evidence.
- *Direct evidence.* This type of evidence consists of the observations of eyewitnesses.
- *Circumstantial evidence.* This type of evidence proves a subsidiary fact from which the guilt or innocence of the accused may be inferred.

One of the most important roles of a police officer is to give expert testimony during court trials. (Courtesy of Valerie Van Brocklin and Alaska State Troopers)

All evidence presented in court is governed by the rules of evidence. The judge acts as an impartial arbitrator and rules on whether certain types of evidence are allowed into the trial. Judges may decide to exclude certain evidence. One such type of evidence that is excluded is known as hearsay evidence. This is information that a witness hears from someone else. The courts have ruled that such information represents a denial of the defendant's right to cross-examination, since witnesses do not have the ability to establish the truth of the information.

The Defence Lawyer's Presentation of Evidence

The defence lawyer has the right to introduce any number of witnesses at a trial or none at all. If he or she does introduce a witness, the prosecution has the right to cross-examine that individual. One of the most critical decisions a defence lawyer makes is whether to have his or her client give testimony under oath. During a criminal trial, the defendant has the right to be free from self-incrimination (i.e., the right to remain silent), which means that the accused has the right not to testify.

The Closing Arguments

Section 651 of the Criminal Code determines whether the prosecution or defence presents their closing argument first. If the defence presents evidence or the defendant testifies, the defence must address the jury before the prosecution does. If no defence evidence is called, the prosecutor presents his or her evidence first. During their closing arguments, both prosecution and defence are allowed to offer reasonable inferences about the evidence and to show how the facts of the case prove or disprove the defendant's guilt. However, they are not allowed to comment on evidence not used during the trial.

The Charge to the Jury

After the defence lawyer and the prosecutor make their final presentations to the court, the judge instructs the jury, or **charges the jury,** as to the relevant principles of law that they have to take into account when deciding on the guilt or innocence of the defendant. The judge includes information such as the elements of the alleged offence, the evidence required to prove each charge, and the degree of proof required to obtain a guilty verdict. It is essential for the judge to clearly explain the relevant laws and evidence requirements as well as the meaning of reasonable doubt. In addition, judges must instruct the jury on the procedures they should use when making their decision. These instructions are important, since they may prove to be the grounds for an appeal.

On paper, these instructions seem simple and reasonable. In reality, they may confuse jurors and lead them to make incorrect evaluations of the evidence or to select the wrong verdict. The final instructions given to the jury apply to issues of evidence and testimony and usually include mention of (1) the definition of the crime with which the defendant is charged, (2) the presumption of the defendant's innocence, (3) the burden of proof that lies with the prosecution, and (4) the fact that if, after discussion, there remains reasonable doubt among the jurors as to the guilt or innocence of the defendant, he or she must be acquitted.

The judge also instructs jurors about the possible verdicts they might consider. While the jury may reach a verdict on the guilt or innocence of the defendant on the original charge, it often has the option to decide on the degree of the offence (e.g., second degree murder or manslaughter).

The Verdict

After the judge reviews the case and the charges, the jury moves to a separate room to consider the verdict. The jury verdict in a criminal case must always be unanimous. Juries may take a few hours, a number of days, or many weeks to review all aspects of the case before reaching a decision.

If the jury remains deadlocked after a lengthy deliberation, it may return to the courtroom and inform the judge of this. The judge may ask the jurors to return to the jury room for a final attempt to arrive at a verdict; in most cases the judge specifies a time limit. If all reasonable attempts to reach a verdict fail, a *hung jury* results. In such cases, the judge dismisses the jury and declares a mistrial. It is then up to the prosecution to decide whether to retry the case—a decision that must be made within a specified time period. If a new trial is ordered, a new jury has to be appointed.

When the jury reaches a verdict of guilty, the judge sets a sentencing date. In the interim, the judge can request a pre-sentence report from a probation officer before imposing a sentence. In such cases, the defence lawyer can start the process of appeal. Defendants may be released while awaiting sentencing or may be held in custody.

The jury plays no role in sentencing except in cases of second degree murder. In such cases, it can make a recommendation to the judge that the length of time before parole be increased from ten years to a longer period, which cannot exceed 25 years. However, this is a recommendation only, and the trial judge is not bound to accept it.

Jury nullification has occurred when a jury does not follow the court's interpretation of the law in every situation, thereby *nullifying* (i.e., suspending) the requirements of strict legal procedure. In a typical case of nullification, a jury chooses to disregard what the judge told them about specific aspects of the law or evidence because it considers the application of the law to the defendant to be unjust.

Jury nullification can occur in two ways. The first is when a verdict of guilty is reached and the judge decides the verdict is erroneous. In such a case, the judge may refuse to abide by the verdict and may instruct the jury to acquit the defendant. The second occurs when the judge requests a jury to *arrest* its verdict of guilty and acquit the accused.

APPEALS

Canada's criminal justice system allows all those convicted of a crime a direct criminal appeal. Both the defendant and the prosecution have the right to appeal the decision in a case. The convicted individual has the right to appeal a conviction, or the sentence, or being found mentally unfit to stand trial (because of a mental disorder).

If the trial involved an indictable offence and was heard by a provincial judge, by a federally appointed judge without a jury, or by a judge and jury, the appeal is taken to the provincial court of appeal. The accused may appeal the conviction if it involves a point of law (i.e., the trial judge made an incorrect legal ruling), a question of fact (i.e., the trial judge drew the wrong inference from the facts of the case), or the length of the sentence. The prosecution may appeal an acquittal on issues involving a point of law or a sentence but not on the basis of questions of fact. In addition, the terms of an appeal for the prosecution depend on whether the trial involves an indictable or a summary conviction offence. In a summary conviction case, the prosecutor can appeal against either a dismissal or the sentence. In an indictable offence case, the prosecution can appeal the sentence if the accused was acquitted, if it was found that the accused was not criminally responsible on the basis of a mental disorder, or if the accused was found unfit to stand trial (Mewett and Nakatsuru 2000).

There are limits to the length of time that may pass before an appeal is filed. However, extensions can be obtained for a variety of reasons. During an appeal it is not uncommon for the convicted individual to apply for bail or some other form of pretrial release.

The appeal court can order a new trial, or it can acquit the convicted individual, if it finds that the trial judge made an error in law, that the verdict was unreasonable and not supported by the evidence, or that a miscarriage of justice took place. If it appears that the position of the prosecutor is no longer valid, the appeal court usually grants an acquittal. If it decides that there is still enough evidence for the prosecutor to argue the case, it will order a new trial.

If the appeal court decides that the appeal registered by the prosecution is valid, it normally grants a new trial. However, it can convict and sentence the accused if the trial was by judge alone and enough evidence was presented to the court.

For summary conviction offences, the convicted individual usually appeals a conviction or sentence to a federally appointed judge in a superior court. Again, the accused may be released pending the outcome of the appeal. It is rare for a summary conviction offence to be heard by the Supreme Court of Canada, and then only if the case involves an important legal issue.

CRITICAL ISSUES IN CANADIAN CRIMINAL JUSTICE

MENTAL HEALTH COURTS

Deinstitutionalization refers to the idea that incarceration has criminogenic effects upon individuals. As a result, there needs to be a reduction in the prison population through the establishment of community-based alternatives. Since the 1960s, there has been a deinstitutionalization of mental health cases in Canada from psychiatric and general hospitals. Some believe that one of the results of the deinstitutionalization of the mental health cases has been an increase in the number of individuals with mental illness coming to the attention of the law, being arrested and remanded and then sent to a provincial or federal correctional facility (Arboleda-Florez et al. 1996; Kellough and Wortley 2002). Schneider (2000) points out that during the 1990s in Canada, the number of mentally disordered individuals accused in the Canadian criminal justice system grew at a rate of over 10 percent a year. In a study of 790 males incarcerated in the Vancouver Pretrial Services Centre in August 1989 to July 1990, Corrado et al. (2000) reported that 16 percent had a major medical disorder (e.g., cognitive impairment, schizophrenic disorder, major mood disorder), 86 percent had a substance abuse disorder, and 88 percent had other types of mental disorders (e.g., anxiety disorders, minor mood disorders). Furthermore, mental disorders have been found to be more prevalent among incarcerated offenders in Canada (Johnson 2003). In 2007–08, 11.1 percent of offenders committed to a federal correctional facility had a mental health diagnosis at the time of admission and 6.1 percent were receiving outpatient services prior to admission (Public Safety Canada 2008).

Specialized courts focus on one type of criminal activity—for example, domestic violence or drug abuse. All cases within a jurisdiction that involve a particular type of offence are sent to the specialized court, where it is believed that the offenders will receive specialized services and prompt resolution of their needs. Mental health courts, which first emerged in the United States

Continued on next page

during the mid-1990s, are a type of specialized court. At the present time, mental health courts are operating in Ontario (which opened the first mental health court in Canada in 1998) and New Brunswick. Newfoundland and Labrador are operating a pilot project, while other jurisdictions in Canada (e.g., British Columbia, Manitoba, Nunavut, and Yukon) are developing them.

Mental health courts in the United States involve accused individuals who are eligible and consent to the choice—either they agree to participate in the court and have the criminal charges against them reduced, stayed, or dropped or return to the regular trial court. The involvement of the accused is entirely voluntary and they may decide to leave the program at any time. In Canada, however, the approach differs. The main emphasis is upon the fitness of the accused to stand trial. The participation of the accused in this part of the mental health court is not voluntary. Once fit, however, the accused may decide to "remain within the mental health court for a bail hearing, participate in diversion, or resolve the matter with a guilty plea" (Schneider et al. 2007, 6).

Mental health courts are based on the idea that law can become therapeutic by incorporating the insights of the behavioural sciences (Vandergoot 2006). Therapeutic justice provides a basis for law that attempts to combine the behavioural sciences with legal processes and procedures. According to Wexler (1994: 279–80), the focus of this approach is that, "within important limits set by principles of justice, the law ought to be designed to serve more effectively as a therapeutic agent . . . [and it] enables us to ask a series of questions regarding legal arrangements and therapeutic outcomes that would likely have gone unaddressed under other approaches." In the mental health courts, therapeutic justice sees the law as "a force for providing beneficial, rehabilitative outcomes for mentally disordered accused persons" (Reiksts 2008, 32).

The therapeutic justice approach has impacts at the individual and the court levels. At the individual level, judges are able to introduce principles from behavioural sciences by requiring offenders to participate in the process of problem solving to encourage their following of court mandated activities. At the court level, special programs and services are

introduced, representing both treatment and justice concerns.

Specialized courts differ from the traditional courts in a number of respects. According to the Center for Court Innovation (Berman and Feinblatt 2001), specialized courts have the following features:

- *Outcomes are elevated above process.* The main concern is with the reduction of recidivism.
- *Judicial monitoring is critical.* Judges closely monitor offenders.
- *Informed decision making is necessary.* Judges hand down sentences with more information about offenders' backgrounds than may be available in traditional sentencing contexts.
- *Collaboration.* Specialized courts typically collaborate with other public and private agencies, many of which are often located in the courthouse.
- *Nontraditional roles.* Specialized court personnel often assume different roles. For example, prosecutors in specialized courts are more interested in assisting defendants than seeing that they are convicted or punished.
- *Systemic change.* Specialized courts try to change the way the criminal justice system works.

Mental health courts focus their attention upon mental health treatment to assist people with emotional problems reduce their chances of re-offending. By focusing upon the need for treatment, along with providing supervision and support from the community, mental health courts provide a place for those dealing with mental health issues to avoid being incarcerated, where they will have little or no access to the treatment they need.

While mental health courts vary in their approach, most share a number of basic operating procedures:

- The theoretical basis of the court attempts to address the underlying causes of crime that traditional courts have often been unable to achieve.
- The focus is upon the mentally ill person as an individual. The first question the mental health court asks is how can the law benefit the accused in dealing with his or her mental

health issues and at the same time protect the public.

- Most demand active participation by the defendant.
- The participant must be diagnosed with a mental illness, and a direct link must be established between the illness and the crime committed.
- Intervention must occur quickly; individuals must be screened and referred to the program either immediately after arrest or within three weeks.
- Once in the program, participants are closely monitored by case managers. Mental health courts use judicially monitored programs with a multidisciplinary team approach to encourage voluntary treatment over punishment.
- The multidisciplinary approach is implemented at the court level by creating a Mental Health Court Team. These teams usually consist of specially trained judges, lawyers, psychologists, psychiatrists, specially trained nurses, community caregivers and case managers or probation officers.
- Most provide voluntary outpatient or inpatient mental health treatment, in the least restrictive manner appropriate as determined by the court, that carries with it the possibility of dismissal of charges or reduced sentencing on successful completion of treatment.
- Centralized case management involves the consolidation of cases that include the mentally ill or mentally disabled defendants (including those who violate their probation orders) and the coordination of mental health treatment plans and social services, including life skills training, placement, health care, and relapse prevention for each participant who requires such services.
- Supervision of treatment plan compliance continues for a term not to exceed the maximum allowable sentence or probation for the

charged or relevant offence, and, to the extent possible, psychiatric care continues at the completion of the supervised period.
- The goal is to satisfy the traditional criminal law function of protecting the public by dealing in individual cases with the real—rather than the apparent—causes that lead to violations of the law.

The mental health court approach appears to be beneficial to both offenders and society, but in some locations it has run into difficulties. For example, sometimes there is a lack of community support for programs and institutions treating mentally ill offenders. In addition, most programs only accept the non-violent mentally ill; those who are prone to violent behaviour still serve their sentences in correctional facilities without receiving the same quality of services as those who enter into a mental health court. It is also a problem to evaluate the success of mental health courts; in comparison, drug court outcomes can be determined by whether or not the participants are able to remain drug-free. For those involved in drug courts, however, the issue can be more difficult since they suffer from complex mental issues, and the multidisciplinary teams have to be sure that the participants have gained control over their illness, which can be a more difficult issue to establish.

Questions
1. Where would you draw the line in terms of including someone into a mental health court and protecting the public?
2. Why do you think there is sometimes little community support for these types of courts and their associated programs?
3. Do you think that individuals should only be given one chance to participate in a mental health court?
4. What positives and/or negatives do you see for a community when a mental health court is implemented in the area?

SUMMARY

Our court systems are organized at the federal and provincial levels. Because the accused is presumed innocent until proved guilty, it is up to the prosecutor to prove guilt beyond a reasonable doubt. The key actors in the courts are the judge, the prosecutor, and the defence lawyer. The prosecutor represents the interests of the state, while defence lawyers provide essential services to their clients. The prosecutor uses evidence collected by the police to convince the court that the defendant is guilty, while the defence lawyer attacks the prosecution's case.

An important part of the trial is the selection of members of the public to serve as jurors. The law allows both lawyers and prosecutors to challenge any prospective juror on the basis of cause or for peremptory reasons.

Trials are conducted in accordance with rules of evidence and criminal procedure. These rules are enforced by judges who, during trials, act as arbitrators in any issues that arise. Evidence must be reliable and relevant, otherwise it is inadmissible.

Discretion is an important issue at this stage of the criminal justice system. Since the number of cases in which individuals are charged with crimes far exceeds the actual number of available courts, plea bargaining becomes important in the day-to-day functioning of our criminal justice system. Many cases are never heard formally in a courtroom because they are plea bargained.

Discussion Questions

1. Should the prosecutor have absolute discretion over which cases are heard in court? Why or why not?

2. What are some of the undesirable features of plea bargaining?

3. Do you think the right to a jury trial should be expanded to all defendants?

4. Should criminal court trials in Canada be televised, as they are in the United States?

5. Describe the problems associated with pretrial publicity. What is the *right to know*, and should it overrule the right to a fair trial? How are jurors selected? Should factors such as the race, gender, and social class of the accused be considered when selecting jurors?

6. What are the arguments for and against the appointment of judges? The election of judges?

7. Why should a speedy trial be a legal right for defendants?

8. Should all defendants accused of a criminal offence be allowed to plea bargain for a reduced sentence in exchange for a guilty plea?

9. Should judges be formally required to participate in all plea bargains? Give your reasons.

10. What are the disadvantages for a defendant who does not receive interim release? What are the advantages for those who receive it?

11. Should victims be given more power so that their concerns are heard at all stages of the trial, not just at sentencing?

12. Do you think that a defence lawyer should be morally obliged to represent a person who may have committed a crime?

Suggested Readings

Arcaro, G. *Criminal Investigation: Forming Reasonable Grounds.* Scarborough, ON: Nelson Thomson Learning, 2000.

Balkan, J. *Just Words: Constitutional and Social Wrongs.* Toronto: University of Toronto Press, 1997.

Borovoy, A. When Freedoms Collide. Toronto: Lester, 1988.

Cairns, A. *Charter versus Federalism: The Dilemmas of Constitutional Reform.* Montreal: McGill-Queen's University Press, 1992.

Russell, P.H. *The Judiciary in Canada: The Third Branch of Government.* Toronto: McGraw-Hill Ryerson, 1987.

References

"An Excessive Use of Publication Bans." 2004. *The Globe and Mail,* September 20, A12.

Arboleda-Florez, J., H.L. Holley, and A. Cristanti. 1996. *Mental Illness and Violence: Proof or Stereotype.* Ottawa: Health Promotion and Programs Branch, Health Canada.

Baer, N. 2005. "Modern Justice: Recent Criminal Code Updates Aim to Make the Justice System Sleeker, Techno-Friendly and Fair." *Justice Canada*, 2.

Berman, G., and J. Feinblatt. 2001. *Problem-Solving Courts: A Brief Primer.* New York: Center for Court Innovation.

Besserer, S. 2006. *Legal Aid in Canada: Resources and Caseload Statistics 2004/05.* Ottawa: Minister of Industry.

Besserer, S., and R.C. Grimes. 1996. "The Courts," in L.W. Kennedy and V.F. Sacco, eds., *Crime Counts: A Criminal Event Analysis.* Scarborough, ON: Nelson Canada.

Blackwell, R. 2006. "Judges Decry Trend of Citizens Playing Lawyer." *The Globe and Mail*, March 10, A6.

Boland, B., P. Mahanna, and R. Scones. 1992. *The Prosecution of Felony Arrests, 1998.* Washington, DC: Bureau of Justice Statistics.

Bowal, P. 2002. "Ten Differences." *LawNow* 26, 6: 9–11.

Boyd, N. 1995. *Canadian Law: An Introduction.* Toronto: Harcourt Brace Canada.

Campbell Research Associates. 1992. *Review and Monitoring of Child Sexual Abuse Cases in Hamilton-Wentworth, Ontario.* Ottawa: Department of Justice.

Canadian Bar Association. 1987. *Code of Professional Conduct.* Ontario: Canadian Bar Association.

Corrado, R., I. Cohen, S. Hart and R. Roesch. 2000. "Comparative Examination of the Prevalence of Mental Disorder Among Jailed Inmates in Canada and the United States." *International Journal of Law and Psychiatry* 10, 29-39.

Cullen, F., W.J. Maakestad, and G. Cavender. 1987. *Corporate Crime under Attack: The Ford Pinto Case and Beyond.* Cincinnati, OH: Anderson.

Currie, A. 2003. *The Unmet Need for Criminal Legal Aid: A Summary of Research Results.* Ottawa: Department of Justice Canada.

Davison, C.B. 2006. "In Defence of Defence Counsel." *LawNow* 30: 39–40.

———. 2005. "The Values of a Jury Trial." *LawNow* 30: 37–38.

Desroches, F.J. 1995. *Force and Fear: Robbery in Canada.* Scarborough, ON: Nelson Canada.

Eastwood, P. 2004. "Publication Bans Since *Dagenais.*" *LawNow* 28: 35–37.

Ericson, R. 1981. *Making Crime: A Study of Detective Work.* Toronto: University of Toronto Press.

Ericson, R., and P.M. Baranek. 1982. *The Ordering of Justice: A Study of Accused Persons as Defendants in the Criminal Process.* Toronto: University of Toronto Press.

Feeley, M. 1981. *Felony Arrests: Their Prosecution and Disposition in New York Court.* New York: Vera Institute.

Freedman, J.L., and T.M. Burke. 1996. "The Effect of Pretrial Publicity." *Canadian Journal of Criminology* 38: 253–70.

Gomme, I.M., and M.P. Hall. 1995. "Prosecutors at Work: Role Overload and Strain." *Journal of Criminal Justice* 23: 191–200.

Greene, I. 1995. "Judicial Accountability in Canada." In P.C. Stenning, ed., *Accountability for Criminal Justice: Selected Essays.* Toronto: University of Toronto Press, pp. 355–75.

Greene, I., C. Baar, P. McCormick, G. Szablowski, and M. Thomas. 1998. *Final Appeal: Decision-Making in Canadian Courts of Appeal.* Toronto: Lorimer.

Griffiths, C.T., J. Klein, and S.N. Verdun-Jones. 1980. *Criminal Justice in Canada.* Vancouver: Butterworths.

Grosman, B. 1969. *The Prosecutor: An Inquiry into the Exercise of Discretion.* Toronto: University of Toronto Press.

Hann, R.G. 1973. *Decision Making in the Criminal Court System: A Systems Analysis.* Toronto: Centre of Criminology.

Hann, R.G., J. Nuffield, C. Meredith, and M. Svoboda. 2002. *Court Site Study of Adult Unrepresented Accused in the Provincial Criminal Courts: Part I—Overview Report.* Ottawa: Department of Justice Canada.

Hans, V.P., and N. Vidmar. 1986. *Judging the Jury.* New York: Plenum.

Hughson, B.F. 2004. "Malicious Prosecution." *LawNow* 28: 32–34.

Jacoby, J. 1979. "The Charging Policies of Prosecutors." In W. McDonald, ed., *The Prosecutor.* Beverly Hills, CA: Sage, pp. 75–97.

Johnson, S. 2003. *Custodial Remand in Canada, 1986/87 to 2000/01.* Ottawa: Canadian Centre for Justice Statistics.

Karp, C., and C. Rosner. 1991. *When Justice Fails: The David Milgaard Story.* Toronto: McClelland and Stewart.

Kellough, G., and S. Wortley. 2002. "'Remand for Plea': Bail Decisions and Plea Bargaining as Commensurate Decisions." *British Journal of Criminology* 42: 186–210.

Kelly, J.B. 2005. *Governing with the Charter: Legislative and Judicial Activism and Framers' Intent.* Vancouver: UBC Press.

Law Reform Commission of Canada. 1990. *Controlling Criminal Prosecutions: The Attorney General and the Crown Prosecutor.* Ottawa: Law Reform Commission of Canada.

———. 1989. *Plea Discussions and Agreements.* Ottawa: Law Reform Commission of Canada.

———. 1975. *Criminal Procedure: Control of the Process.* Ottawa: Minister of Supply and Services Canada.

Levine, J.P. 1992. *Juries and Politics.* Pacific Grove CA: Brooks/Cole.

Makin, K. 2003. "Lawyer Laments Rise in Publication Bans." *The Globe and Mail,* October 31, A8.

———. 2001. "Innocent Man Wins in Top Court." *The Globe and Mail,* October 19, A11.

Marth, M. 2008. *Adult Criminal Court Statistics, 2006/07.* Ottawa: Canadian Centre for Justice Statistics.

Martin, J. 1970. "The Role and Responsibility of the Defence Advocate." *Criminal Law Quarterly* 12.

McCormick, P., and I. Greene. 1990. *Judges and Judging: Inside the Canadian Judicial System.* Toronto: Lorimer.

Mewett, A.W. and S. Nakatsuru. 2000. *An Introduction to the Criminal Process in Canada,* 4th ed. Scarborough, ON: Carswell.

O'Brien, D. 2004. "More Representing Selves in Court." *Winnipeg Free Press.* January 31, A5.

Ontario Ministry of the Attorney General. 1999. *Report of the Criminal Justice Review Committee.* Toronto: Ministry of the Attorney General.

Osborne, J.A. 1983. "The Prosecutor's Discretion to Withdraw Criminal Cases in the Lower Courts." *Canadian Journal of Criminology* 25: 55–78.

Pereira, J., and C. Grimes. 2002. *Case Processing in Criminal Courts, 1999/00.* Ottawa: Canadian Centre for Justice Statistics.

Perras, D.W. 1979. "Plea Negotiations." *Criminal Law Quarterly* 22: 58–73.

Powell, K., and C. Rusnell. 1999. "To Tell the Truth." *National Post,* January 18, A8.

Public Safety Canada. 2008. *Corrections and Conditional Release Statistical Review.* Ottawa. Public Safety Canada.

Reiksts, M. 2008. "Mental health courts in Canada." *LawNow,* 33, 31–34.

Roach, K. 1999. *Due Process or Victims' Rights: The New Law and Politics of Criminal Justice.* Toronto: University of Toronto Press.

Roberts, J.V., and C. Grimes. 2000. *Adult Criminal Court Statistics,* 1998/99. Ottawa: Canadian Centre for Justice Statistics.

Russell, P. 1987. *The Judiciary in Canada: The Third Branch of Government.* Toronto: McGraw-Hill Ryerson.

Salhany, R.E. 1986. *Arrest, Seizure, and Interrogation,* 3rd ed. Toronto: Carswell.

Schneider, R.S. 2000. *A Statistical Survey of Provincial and Territorial Review Boards.* Ottawa: Department of Justice.

Schneider, R.S., H. Bloom, and M. Heerma. 2007. *Mental Health Courts: Decriminalizing the Mentally Ill.* Toronto: Irwin Law.

Stuart, D. 1995. "Prosecutorial Accountability." In P.C. Stenning, ed., *Accountability for Criminal Justice: Selected Essays.* Toronto: University of Toronto Press, pp. 330–54.

Stuart, D., and R.J. Delisle. 1995. *Learning Canadian Criminal Law.* Scarborough, ON: Carswell.

Swartz, M.A. 1973. Quoted in J. Caplan, *Criminal Justice.* Mineola, NY: Foundation Press.

Thomas, M. 2004. *Adult Criminal Court Statistics, 2003/04.* Ottawa: Canadian Centre for Justice Statistics.

Vandergoot, M.E. 2006. *Justice for Young Offenders.* Saskatoon, SK.: Purich.

Vidmar, N. 1999. "The Canadian Criminal Jury: Searching for a Middle Ground." *Law and Contemporary Problems* 62: 141–72.

Vidmar, N., and R. Schuller. 2001. "The Jury: Selecting Twelve Impartial Peers." In R.A. Schuller and J.R.P. Ogluff, eds., *Introduction to Psychology and the Law.* Toronto: University of Toronto Press, pp. 126–56.

Vinglis, E., H. Blefgen, D. Colbourne, P. Culver, B. Farmer, D. Hackett, J. Treleaven, and R. Solomon. 1990. "The Adjudication of Alcohol-Related Criminal Driving Cases in Ontario: A Survey of Crown Attorneys." *Canadian Journal of Criminology* 32: 639–50.

Wexler, D.B. 1994. "Therapeutic Jurisprudence and the Criminal Justice Courts." *William and Mary Law Review,* 35: 278–99.

Wheatley, J.R. 1974. "Plea Bargaining: A Case for Its Continuance." *Massachusetts Law Quarterly* 59: 31–41.

Wheeler, G. 1987. "The Police, the Crowns, and the Courts: Who's Running the Show?" *Canadian Lawyer.* February.

Court Cases

Boucher v. The Queen (1955)

C.B.C. v. New Brunswick (Attorney General) (1996), 3 S.C.R.

Dagenais v. Canadian Broadcasting Corp. (1994), C.C.C. (3d) 289

Dix v. Canada (A.G.) (2002), A.J. 784

Mankwe v. R. (2001), O.J. S.C.C.

Nelles v. Ontario (1989), 2 S.C.R. 170

Proulx v. A.G. of Que. (2001), 3 S.C.R. 9

R. v. Askov (1990), 59 C.C.C. (3d) 449

R. v. Beare (1988), 45 C.C.C. (3d) 57 (S.C.C.)

R. v. D.(S.) (1992), 72 C.C.C. (3d) 575

R. v. Hansen (1977), 37 C.C.C. (2d) 371

R. v. Lyons (1987), 37 C.C.C. (3d) 1

R. v. Meddoui (1990), 61 C.C.C. (3d) 345

R. v. Mentuck (2001), 3 S.C.R. 442

R. v. Morin (1992), 71 C.C.C. (3d) 1

R. v. Nahdee (1993), 26 C.R. (4th) 109 (Ont. Ct. Gen. Div.)

R. v. Nepoose (1991), 85 Alta. L.R. (2d) 8 (Q.B.)

R. v. Parks (1993), 15 O.R. (3d) 324, 24 C.R. (4th) 81

R. v. Phillips (2003), ABCA 4

R. v. Ross (1989), 49 C.C.C. (3d) 475

R. v. Sherratt (1991), 1 S.C.R. 509

R. v. Thompson (1990), 59 C.C.C. (3d) 225

R. v. White (1977), 32 C.C.C. (2d) 478

R. v. Williams (1996), 106 C.C.C. (3d) 215 BCCA

Weblinks

For an influential decision by the Supreme Court of Canada regarding the speed of trials, go to http://scc.lexum.umontreal.ca/en/index.html and read *R. v. Askov* by clicking on 1990, then Volume 2. The decision was announced on October 18, 1990. For the Supreme Court's decision in *R. v. Lyons,* go to 1987, Volume 2 (October 15). For *R. v. Mentuck,* go to 2001, Volume 3 (November 15).

CHAPTER 9

Sentencing and Punishment

CHAPTER OBJECTIVES

✓ Explain and contrast the four main goals of criminal sentencing.

✓ Outline the various sentences available to a judge.

✓ Know the recent changes to sentencing in Canada.

✓ Explain why there is a difference between the sentence handed out by a judge and the actual sentence served by the offender.

✓ Explain why alternatives to sentencing in Canada appeared, such as Aboriginal healing circles.

✓ List the major forms of punishment available to judges.

✓ Discuss the impact of mandatory minimum sentences on gun-related crimes.

✓ Identify and explain the causes of wrongful convictions.

Once an accused person is convicted at the end of a criminal trial, the court must adjudicate an appropriate sentence. Our criminal justice system operates on the belief that justice at sentencing must prevail; that is, guilty people must be punished for the crime. This stage is one of the most controversial, since the public is concerned about the type and length of punishment. Some people argue that sentences are too short; others believe they are too long.

Sentencing is the process by which a judge imposes a punishment on a convicted criminal. The punishments available to the sentencing judge depend on the offence committed by an offender, but there are a wide variety of punishments available from which a judge can select. Sentences can include incarceration, fines, community service orders, or probation. Allegations about **disparity** and discrimination in sentencing have led to demands that judicial discretion be controlled and that alternative sanctions be introduced. When an individual is convicted, a punishment must be handed out. The question then becomes, "What is the appropriate sentence that indicates the disapproval of society?"

Judges' sentencing decisions can be based on a number of factors, most commonly the objective factors involved in an offence (e.g., the seriousness of the offence) and the characteristics of the offender (e.g., prior criminal record). But they can also be based on other documents that focus upon the convicted offender and his or her prior record, notably the **pre-sentence report.** Pre-sentence reports are prepared for judges by probation officers in order to help judges determine an appropriate sentence. Hogarth (1971) conducted a study of judges' sentencing practices and reported that most judges were satisfied with the information about offenders they obtained from pre-sentence reports. He also found that they were most generally used for serious offences such as assaults causing bodily harm and robbery, that the family background of offenders was considered by judges to be an essential piece of information in 61 percent of the cases, compared to an offender's attitude toward rehabilitation, the mental condition of the offender, and the use of alcohol and other drugs—all of which were cited by the judges as essential less than 20 percent of the time. Later studies by Hagan (1975) and Boldt et al. (1983) found that judges in Canada followed the recommendations by probation officers in approximately 80 percent of the cases. In contrast, Gabor and Jayewardene (1978) reported that only 43 percent of the judges they studied followed a probation officer's recommendation for a community-based penalty.

Section 721 of the Criminal Code gives the legislative authority for the pre-sentence report. Probation officers prepare a report when requested by the court "for the purpose of assisting the court in imposing a sentence or in determining whether the accused should be discharged pursuant to s. 730." The court can request a pre-sentence report only after an offender has been found guilty or enters a plea of guilty.

A significant amount of discretion is given what a pre-sentence report may contain in Canada. However, the Criminal Code specifies that the following information will be included:

(3)(a) . . . offender's age, maturity, character, behaviour, attitude and willingness to make amends;

(3)(b) . . . history of previous dispositions under the *Youth Criminal Justice Act* and of previous findings of guilt under this Act and any other Act of Parliament;

(3)(c) . . . history of any alternative measures used to deal with the offender, and the offender's response to those measures; and

(3)(d) . . . any matter required by any regulation made under subsection (2), to be included in the report.

Subsection 2 refers to the type of offence that may require a report and the content of the form. While there is some mandatory content in to be included in each pre-sentence report, there is also considerable discretion in the Criminal Code to allow each province to determine what the other information should be included.

A study of 11 cities as well as Prince Edward Island and Nunavut by Bonta et al. (2005) sought to determine the views of judges, probation officers, Crown prosecutors, and defence counsel on pre-sentence reports. One of their key interests was to evaluate the impact of these reports upon a judge's determination of a sentence. They reported that 60 percent of the judges would prefer to see pre-sentence reports to include sentencing recommendations. Almost all judges (94 percent) indicated that they would follow a recommendation of a community placement (especially a conditional sentence). In addition, judges held positive attitudes toward offender rehabilitation. According to Bonta and his colleagues, information on treatment needs "were valued by all the key actors in the sentencing process and judges were particularly interested in treatment recommendations" (ibid., 23).

THE PHILOSOPHICAL RATIONALE OF SENTENCING

In Chapter 3, the six major crime control philosophies were identified. These philosophies include the goals of criminal punishment. But how should society try to attain these goals? It is governments that determine what the criminal sanctions will be in general, and it is judges who make sentencing decisions in individual cases. Support for the possible approaches to sentencing vary among the public. According to Roberts (2001, 206), a consistent finding concerning public opinion of sentencing in Canada, the United States, and the United Kingdom is that sentences are not harsh enough. However, when confronted with the details of a specific criminal case, the public "are less punitive than many politicians believe." In the United States, researchers have discovered that most Americans (53 percent) are of the opinion that the most important goal of sentencing is to punish the offender appropriately for the crimes for which he or she has been convicted (i.e., the justice model), while 21 percent think it should be rehabilitation and another 13 percent feel it should be deterrence or incapacitation. While the majority of Americans support the justice model over rehabilitation, 61 percent also felt that most or some offenders could be rehabilitated "given early intervention with the right program." Only 9 percent of Americans feel that no offenders can be rehabilitated (Flanagan 1996, 78).

Many Canadians view sentencing as the most important stage in the criminal justice system, since it is at that point that the offender is punished. But punishment in Canada can mean a fine, probation, community service, imprisonment, an intermittent sentence, or a recognizance to keep the peace. As well, a judge may combine certain of these punishments—for example, a fine and a probation order—into what is known as a split sentence. Perhaps because of the number of sentencing options open to judges, sentences have come under heavy criticism. Critics argue that sentences are too lenient or too long. It is rare that everyone agrees on their appropriateness in any given criminal case.

Sentencing involves handing out a punishment to the convicted offender. It has been argued that punishing criminals serves two ultimate purposes: (1) the "deserved infliction of suffering on evil doers"; and (2) the "prevention of crime" (Packer 1968, 36–37). Although this statement seems straightforward, it raises many questions. For example, how do we determine what is a "deserved" punishment? How can we be certain that punishment will "prevent" crimes? How can we know that convicted offenders are "rehabilitated"?

Should sentences of incarceration be shorter than longer? And what is the overriding purpose of sentencing: to protect society or to benefit offenders? To answer these questions, we need to consider the six basic goals of sentencing. While these goals are presented as separate and distinct from one another, sentences in Canada can reflect a combination of them (Doob 1992). Traditionally, four rationales have been given for a punishment imposed by the courts: deterrence, rehabilitation, selective incapacitation, and justice. As we have seen (Chapter 3), two newer rationales, restoration and healing, have received greater attention in recent years.

Deterrence

By punishing an offender, the state indicates its intent to control crime and deter potential offenders. Deterrence, the oldest of the four main sentencing goals, refers to the protection of society through the prevention of criminal acts. This is accomplished by punishing offenders in accordance with their offence. Too lenient a sentence might encourage more people to engage in criminal activity because they would not fear the punishment for their offence; too severe a sentence might reduce the ability of the criminal justice system to impose punishment that is regarded as fair and impartial, and might actually encourage more criminal activity. For example, if all convicted robbers were to receive a minimum of ten years for their crimes, they might kill their victims if those victims are the only witnesses able to identify them. For the deterrence approach to work, it must strike a balance between fear and justice among both offenders and law-abiding citizens.

There are two types of deterrence: specific and general. Specific deterrence attempts to discourage, through punishment, an individual offender from committing another crime (or recidivating) in the future. General deterrence refers to a sentence that is severe enough to stop people from committing crimes. To date, there is some evidence that specific deterrence works, but only in certain instances, such as in domestic violence (Sherman and Berk 1984). However, many more studies have found that specific deterrence does not stop people from committing a second crime once they serve their sentence for a first offence (Fagan 1989; Wheeler and Hissong 1988). General deterrence, by punishing an offender, is intended to have an impact on the members of society. Specific deterrence is intended to discourage individuals from engaging further in the behaviour that led to their conviction and sentencing; it is predicated on an individual's wish to avoid the pain of punishment in the future.

The objectives of general and specific deterrence may be incompatible. For example, a man who assaults his wife may best be deterred from spousal assault by participating in anger management therapy. This sentence may not be in the best interests of general deterrence, however, if the punishment is not perceived as adequate to deter members of society from engaging in the same behaviour. Another reason why deterrence can be difficult to achieve is that it relies on the certainty and speed of punishment. If the punishment for a crime is harsh but the risk of being apprehended is low, it is doubtful that potential offenders will be deterred.

Selective Incapacitation

Incapacitation is the removal or restriction of the freedom of offenders, making it almost impossible for them to commit another crime during their period of incarceration. An offender who is considered a significant risk to society may be sentenced to a long term in prison. Incarcerating those individuals (referred to as "chronic" offenders) who commit the most heinous and/or the greatest number of criminal offences is thought to reduce the crime rate. In essence, the goal of incapacitation is to prevent future crimes by imprisoning individuals on the basis of their past criminal offences. At the present time, incapacitation is achieved mainly by imprisoning offenders for very lengthy periods of time, by implementing punishments such as the "three strikes" laws in the United States.

The incapacitation and deterrence approaches both focus on punishing criminals for the express purpose of protecting society. However, incapacitation differs from deterrence in that it favours much longer sentences. Supporters of incapacitation argue it is an effective crime prevention approach. Ehrlich (1975) declared boldly that a 1 percent increase in sentence length leads to a 1 percent decrease in the crime rate. Zedlewski (1987) concluded that for every $1 spent on

This is a view of the men's maximum security unit of the Saskatchewan Penitentiary in Prince Albert, Saskatchewan. (CP PHOTO/Thomas Porter)

incarcerating an offender, there is a $17 saving to society in terms of social costs. Critics of this approach believe it is flawed since it does not include proportionality (see Chapter 3) for specific types of criminal offences. That is, how can we be sure that punishing a robber to life imprisonment will reduce the crime rate? Perhaps a much shorter punishment would ensure that that offender would not commit another robbery on release from prison. Another argument is that incapacitating criminals only protects society while the offender is in prison. Some argue that after offenders have served their prison terms, they may actually be more predisposed to committing more crime (Clear 1980).

Rehabilitation

A sentencing approach that emphasizes rehabilitation is based on the belief that many (but not all) offenders can be treated in such a way that, once released, they will live crime-free lives in their communities. Attempts are therefore made to "correct" the behaviour and/or personality of offenders through a variety of programs. Supporters of rehabilitative sentences argue it is fairer and more productive to treat certain offenders rather than punish them without treatment. The purpose of this sentencing approach is to treat the social and psychological problems of offenders in the hope of returning them to society as law-abiding citizens. Since every offender is potentially different in the type and length of treatment he or she needs, supporters of this approach argue that a variety of programs should be available to assist in the treatment. Rehabilitation-based sentencing is predicated on reform in the future rather than on the criminal act committed.

The success of rehabilitation programs has been strongly contested. Many argue that a "get tough" approach (i.e., a deterrence or incapacitation approach) to sentencing and punishment is more successful in controlling crime. But others point to recent findings that the rehabilitation approach does succeed, especially when treatment programs and offender needs are matched effectively (Andrews et al. 1990). Rehabilitative sentences, in contrast to those based on the deterrence and incapacitation approaches, do not always include imprisonment. In fact, offenders may be sentenced to serve their punishment in the community if more appropriate services are available to them.

The Justice Model

According to the justice model, offenders should be punished no more or less severely than their actions warrant. Specifically, the severity of the sentence should depend on the severity of the crime—that is, the essence of punishment should be to punish offenders with fairness and justice and in proportion to the gravity of their criminal offences. Offenders are to be punished because they deserve to be: "their punishment should fit the crime" (Durham 1988). This approach specifies that all punishments should be equally and fairly given to those with the same number of prior criminal convictions and who have committed the same crime. The focus is on the crime committed rather than on any attributes of the individual. Extralegal factors such as race, gender, and social class are not to be considered. Different individuals who commit the same offence may receive different sentences, but only because of mitigating or aggravating factors. The actual sentence imposed should be based on the crime committed. This model is not concerned with the likelihood of treatment success or a reduction in the crime rate.

The justice model differs from the deterrence and incapacitation approaches in that (1) it focuses on an offender's past behaviour as the rationale for sentencing rather than on his or her future criminality and the protection of society; and (2) it believes that sentences, while determinate, should be more shorter than longer. This means that for a specific criminal offence, justice model advocates would support a sentence of five years (with no parole); in contrast, supporters of the deterrence and incapacitation approaches would prefer a longer sentence (also with no parole). In theory, then, the justice model favours a sentencing approach with shorter periods of punishment (including community-based punishments).

Restoration

Restorative justice focuses mainly on repairing the harm that has been done as the result of a crime. Responses to crime "should not, primarily, punish or rehabilitate the offender but set the conditions for repairing as much harm as possible the harm caused" (Walgrave 2005, 5). This is to be accomplished by examining the harm done to both the victim and the community. And while a maximum punishment should be listed for all offences, there shouldn't be a minimum punishment. Preference is given to a wide range of sentences available to a judge at the lower limits. This means that fines, community service, compensation, reconciliation, and apologies are to be preferred over imprisonment for many crimes.

According to White and Haines (2002), the restoration approach encompasses the following elements:

- *Parsimony*—that is, the criminal justice authorities must be able to justify the sentences handed out.

- *Control*—that is, over those who have power by virtue of their positions within the criminal justice system.
- *Reprobation*—specifically, the criminal justice system should place offenders in positions where they can experience community disapproval.
- *Reintegration* of offenders back into society.

In addition, sentences under this model would be shorter than those imposed under the incapacitation model.

Healing

Healing is multifaceted. It can mean different things to different people depending on the context in which it is used. Healing, "for many Aboriginal people, is the objective of justice, and justice derives from the restorative/transformative processes of healing. Hence, healing is a broad notion that encompasses restorative justice" (Proulx 2005, 35). Proulx also points out that healing encompasses such activities as the reintegration of victims and offenders at the individual *and* community levels.

Justice is an essential component of healing, but the type of justice envisioned differs from that of the dominant society. According to Henderson and McCaslin (2005, 6), justice as healing is "concerned with equitable processes or ceremonies to resolve conflicts with more than substantive rules." Healing can also involve justice as a "lived experience." The Law Reform Commission of Canada (1999, 22–23), points out that justice viewed in this way involves "a process of negotiation and agreement between parties to a conflict. By searching for truth in this sense, parties are better able to comprehend each other's position. In turn, this encourages a better understanding of their own behavior."

Sentencing circles provide the offender, the victim, and the community with the opportunity to start the healing process. The Native Law Centre (2006) identifies various options available to sentencing circles, including these:

- Peer counselling.
- Community service work.
- Mediation.
- Aboriginal spiritual activities such as sweat lodges, as well as forgiveness/sacrifice ceremonies.
- Aboriginal cultural activities, such as powwows.
- Talking and healing circles.
- Curfew rules and regulations respecting residency.
- "Western" sentences, such as fines, incarceration, probation, house arrest, and electronic monitoring (usually for six months).

HOW DO JUDGES DECIDE ON A SENTENCE?

Many people argue that those who commit serious crimes should receive lengthy sentences. When this doesn't happen, judges are often criticized for being too lenient. Judges do not reach their sentencing decisions in an arbitrary way, however. Their options are restricted by law (these restrictions are referred to as the "structure of sentencing"). For example, it is impossible for a judge to sentence an offender to life imprisonment for a summary conviction offence, since that sentence is outside what is allowed by law. But judges do have certain parameters within which they can individualize sentences on the basis of the offender's characteristics (e.g., prior record) as well as on **mitigating circumstances** or **aggravating circumstances** surrounding the crime itself. They cannot, however, use unfettered discretion in every case. In some instances, such as first and second degree murder and manslaughter, fixed minimum sentences apply that the judge cannot change.

There are, however, a number of sentencing principles (see below) that judges are required to follow when deciding on an appropriate sentence. In *R. v. Priest* (1996), the Ontario Court of Appeal listed a number of principles that the trial judge in that case had broken. This case involved a 19-year-old first-time offender who had pleaded guilty to a charge of breaking and entering. The accused had cooperated fully with the authorities after he was caught and had returned to the owner all the items stolen. The Crown prosecutor requested a sentence of 30 to 60 days with probation. The trial judge, without discovering anything new about the accused (but noting the large number of break and enter charges on the court docket), sentenced the accused to one year on the basis of general deterrence. According to Edgar (1999), the Ontario Court of Appeal noted some of the principles that the judge had broken in this case:

- Prevalence of crime in an area is not to be the primary consideration in sentencing. It can only be one consideration among many.
- A custodial sentence on a first-time offender should not be imposed without either a pre-sentence report or some other very clear information about the accused's background and circumstances.
- Proportionality requires the sentence to reflect the seriousness of the offence, the culpability of the offender, and the harm occasioned by the offence.
- The role of the courts requires the imposition of appropriate sentences, not unduly harsh ones. A just society is not promoted by sentences that are far beyond those imposed for similar offences in other parts of the province.

If certain principles govern the sentencing decisions of judges in a province, what is the source of judicial discretion? Is it the personal preferences of a particular judge, the seriousness of the crime, the defendant's race, the quality of the arguments made by the defence attorney and Crown prosecutor during the trial, or perhaps the impact of the crime on the victim(s)? All of these factors may in some way contribute to the judge's decision.

If you were a judge with the responsibility for deciding which offenders are to be incarcerated and which are to stay in the community, how would you decide? What criteria would you use? Criminal sentences in Canada vary widely, from a discharge to life imprisonment. This variation originates in the Criminal Code, which sets out the maximum punishment for each offence. When you make your sentencing decision, it is of concern not only to the offender but also to the community, the police, and the victims. And of course your decision may be a mistake. What happens, for example, if you decide to sentence a convicted offender to probation and while that person is serving that sentence he or she commits a series of violent crimes? Would you change your sentencing approach in the future, or would you view the probation order and its consequences as an aberration?

In Canada, judges enjoy a substantial amount of discretion in terms of both the type and the severity of the sentences they can hand down. Only a few offences specify a minimum or a mandatory punishment. For most offences, the Criminal Code specifies a maximum punishment and then allows judges the discretion to select the appropriate sentence. This does not mean that judges can select any punishment they wish, for they are governed by three factors that are integral to the sentencing process in Canada. The first two determine the sentencing options available to the judge; the third frames the options from which a judge selects a sentence:

- The direction given in the statutes (generally the Criminal Code) in relation to the particular offence.
- Rules and principles that offer guidance to the judge as to which dispositions should be used.
- The personal characteristics of the judge (ibid., 112).

Judges in Canada are able to individualize sentences in other ways as well; for example, they can select a sentence from a wide range of purposes "whereby any sentence can be justified" (Doob and Webster 2006, 351). Since judges have a number of sentencing options available to them, as we've seen, they must first determine what they hope to accomplish with the sentence. Sentencing always has at least one of the following objectives: deterrence, selective incapacitation, justice, or rehabilitation. These are important to sentencing because our system of justice is supposed "to accomplish some social utility beyond merely solving crimes and catching criminals" (Anderson and Newman 1993, 288). Two factors are important here: sentencing and dispositions.

Sentencing has been defined as "the judicial determination of a legal sanction to be imposed on a person found guilty of an offence" (Canadian Sentencing Commission 1987, 153). According to Roberts and Cole (1999, 4), this brief definition includes "all the traditional elements, namely that the sanction must be legal, it must be imposed by a judge, and it can follow a criminal conviction." This needs to be distinguished from the actual sentence (the disposition) imposed on the offender. A disposition refers to "the actual sanction imposed in sentencing" (Law Reform Commission of Canada 1974, 4) or "the judicial determination of legal sanction to be imposed on a person found guilty of an offence" (Canadian Sentencing Commission 1987, 153).

Of course, before someone receives a disposition, they must plead guilty or be found guilty in a court of law. One can assume that a person who admits to having committed an offence will be found guilty. The issue then becomes the type and length of the disposition. If the crime involves a serious, violent act, is it not reasonable to expect a lengthy period of imprisonment as the disposition? One would think so, yet the events of the court trial and the factors surrounding the commission of the offence may have significant weight in determining the final disposition.

Punishments vary widely across Canada, from probation to life imprisonment (see Figure 9.1). The highest rate of imprisonment in Canada during 2006–07 was on Prince Edward Island, where 55 percent of all guilty cases resulted in a period of incarceration. The lowest rates of imprisonment were in New Brunswick (25 percent), Nova Scotia (25 percent), Saskatchewan (26 percent), and Ontario (33 percent). This variation has been attributed to several factors. One is the combination of offences found in a given jurisdiction. This means that if "a particular jurisdiction has a higher than average percentage of the more serious crimes, it may also have a higher than average overall percentage of cases being sent to prison" (Marth 2008, 6). Another is that courts across Canada may use punishments differently. For example, Marth (ibid.) points out that on Prince Edward Island, individuals convicted of an impaired driving offence (including first-time offenders) commonly receive a punishment involving a period of incarceration. And since this category of offences accounts for almost 30 percent of all guilty cases in the province, the overall number of cases where there is a sentence involving incarceration will be higher than the national average.

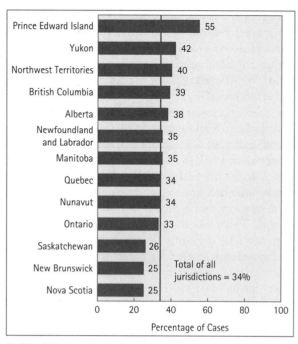

FIGURE 9.1

Cases Sentenced to Prison for the Most Serious Offence in the Case, Canada, 2006–2007

Note: Information from Quebec's municipal courts (which account for approximately 20% of federal statute charges in that province) are not yet collected. Coverage for Adult Criminal Court Survey data as of 2006/2007 is estimated at 98% of adult criminal court caseload.

Source: Michael Marth "Adult Criminal Court Statistics, 2006/2007" *Juristat*, Vol. 28, no. 5, p. 6. Statistics Canada catalogue no. 85-002-XIE.

Although almost everyone agrees that offenders "should be punished in some way, there is far less consensus about the purpose of punishment" (Roberts and Cole 1999, 5). These purposes are embedded in the principles that guide our criminal justice system (see Chapter 3). Any sentence can reflect one of these purposes or a combination of them. If any specific purpose of sentencing can be said to exist, it is closest to specific deterrence—that is, to reduce "the crime rate by stopping the criminal activities of apprehended offenders and deterring others from committing crimes" (Anderson and Newman 1993, 288). The best way to achieve this is, of course, open to opinion and debate.

Sentencing Options

Judges in Canada have a number of dispositions available to them when punishing a convicted offender. These include the following:

- *Imprisonment.* Canada has always imprisoned offenders, be it for the purpose of deterrence, incapacitation,

rehabilitation, or justice. A sentence of imprisonment can be served in either a federal or a provincial correctional facility (see Chapter 11). In recent years, governments have been trying to limit the use of imprisonment except for the most serious offences.
- *Intermittent sentences.* These sentences allow offenders to serve their time on an intermittent basis (such as weekends) so that they can continue to engage in other activities (e.g., employment). By law, such sentences are limited to a maximum of 90 days.
- *Fines.* These can be levied by judges in combination with incarceration and probation or independently of other types of punishments. When a judge chooses to punish an offender with a fine only, it indicates that the judge considers the offender not to be a threat to the community and thus not in need of supervision.
- *Restitution and community service.* While fines are payable to a government, restitution and community service are paid to injured parties. These punishments are also referred to as "reparations." Restitution is a payment made directly to the victim; community service is an attempt to make the offender do something that will benefit the community.
- *Probation.* With this criminal sanction, offenders are allowed to spend their sentence (or part of it) in the community under supervision, provided that they follow certain conditions set by the court (see Chapter 10).
- *Restorative justice.* Some judges feel that when an offender has committed a non-serious crime, the relationship between the offender and the victim can be "healed" by having them meet and discuss the offence.
- *Absolute and conditional discharges.* An offender who receives an absolute or conditional discharge is not considered to have been convicted of an offence. A conditional discharge means that an offender is discharged with conditions and will be supervised as if on probation. An absolute discharge means that the offender does not need any supervision.
- *Community-based sanctions.* This approach emphasizes non-criminal alternatives to traditional punishments. These include referral to substance abuse or behavioural modification programs.
- *Conditional sentence.* A conditional sentence of imprisonment means that the execution of the prison sentence is suspended. A conditional sentence is more serious than probation but less serious than imprisonment.

The Sentencing Process

In sentencing a convicted offender, the judge relies on information provided by others. As noted earlier in this chapter, a pre-sentence report is a valuable document for judges. Compiled by a probation officer, these reports provide relevant information about the crime and its impact on the victim(s), as well as a large amount of information about the offender. This personal information, which had not been admissible at trial, tells the judge (among other things) whether the individual is employed and how much family support he or she has.

In addition, a joint submission (i.e., by the Crown prosecutor and the defence lawyer) recommending a sentence may be handed to the judge. This is usually the result of a plea bargain struck between the prosecution and the defence. The judge does not have to accept the recommendation in the joint submission; however, judges usually follow such submissions as long as doing so is in the public interest and will not bring the administration of justice into disrepute. Judges may reject such submissions if they consider the proposed sentence to be too far removed from the normal sentences handed out for similar cases.

A judge will also consider other factors when deciding on a sentence. The most important of these are the seriousness of the offence and whether or not there were any mitigating or aggravating factors (see Exhibit 9.1). Usually, the more serious the offence is, the longer the sentence. Mitigating circumstances permit a shorter sentence to be handed down; aggravating circumstances include such things as a prior criminal record, the resort to violence during the crime, and the use of a weapon during the crime. A judge who determines that aggravating factors were involved in a crime may decide to make the offender serve a longer term in a correctional facility before being allowed to apply for parole.

SENTENCING LAW IN CANADA

In 1994, then-Justice Minister Allan Rock introduced Bill C-41, which proposed to reform the sentencing system as well as intermediate punishments (see Chapter 10). On September 3, 1996, Bill C-41 (known as the Sentencing Reform Bill) was proclaimed, bringing about a significant change in the sentencing system in Canada. The bill had three objectives: "(1) to provide a consistent framework of policy and process in sentencing matters; (2) to create a system of sentencing policy and process approved by Parliament; and (3) to increase public accessibility to the law relating to sentencing" (Daubney and Parry 1999, 33). It also introduced conditional sentences as an option for judges (see Chapter 10). Bill C-41 was an attempt to achieve a "balanced approach" to criminal justice by giving judges direction when considering community alternatives for offenders in appropriate situations while also permitting longer periods of incarceration for high-risk, violent offenders.

This bill included a statement about the purpose and principles of sentencing (s. 718). The following are excerpts:

> The fundamental purpose of sentencing is to contribute, along with crime prevention initiatives, respect for the law and the maintenance of a just, peaceful and safe society by imposing just sanctions that have one or more of the following objectives:
>
> - to denounce unlawful conduct;
> - to deter the offender and other persons from committing offences;
> - to separate offenders from society, where necessary;
> - to assist in rehabilitating offenders;
> - to provide reparations for harm done to victims or the community; and
> - to promote a sense of responsibility in offenders, and acknowledgment of the harm done to victims and to the community.

Other key principles from Bill C-41 that guide Canada's sentencing approach are these:

- An offender should not be deprived of liberty, if less restrictive sanctions may be appropriate in the circumstances.

EXHIBIT 9.1 Aggravating and Mitigating Circumstances

AGGRAVATING CIRCUMSTANCES	MITIGATING CIRCUMSTANCES
• Previous convictions of the offender • Gang activity • Vulnerability of the victim • Planning and organization • Multiple criminal incidents • Use or threatened use of a weapon • Brutality	• First-time offender • Employment record • Rehabilitative efforts since the offence was committed • Disadvantaged background • Guilty plea and remorse • The length of time it took to prosecute or sentence the offender • Good character

- All available sanctions other than imprisonment that are reasonable in the circumstances should be considered for all offenders, with particular attention to the circumstances of Aboriginal offenders.

These objectives include all of the traditional purposes of sentencing such as deterrence, justice, incapacitation, and rehabilitation. Significantly, s. 718(e) highlights the federal government's interest in restorative justice as it relates to the "reparation for harm done to victims and the community and in promoting a sense of responsibility in offenders and acknowledgment of the harm done to the victims and to the community" (Daubney and Parry 1999, 34). In addition, the bill's emphasis on "least restrictive measures" directs sentencing judges to use incarceration only when other sentencing alternatives (e.g., community penalties) are inappropriate. This is consistent with Parliament's decision to emphasize restorative justice.

Ten objectives of "just sanctions" are identified in s. 718 of the Criminal Code. Since judges can typically sentence an offender by "selecting" one of the following objectives, and since most of these sentencing objectives have existed for years, "the result is little more than a legislated statement of the status quo. To this extent, s. 718 codifies current judicial practice" (Roberts and von Hirsch 1999, 53). The ten objectives are:

- denunciation
- individual deterrence
- general deterrence
- incapacitation
- reparation to the individual
- restitution to the community
- the promotion of a sense of responsibility in offenders
- acknowledgment of the harm done to victims
- acknowledgment of the harm done to communities
- the creation of opportunities to assist in the offender's rehabilitation

A statement concerning the fundamental principle of sentencing is found in s. 718.1, which declares that a sentence must be proportionate to the seriousness of the offence and the degree of responsibility of the offenders. According to the Department of Justice (2005, 2), it is the combination of the "principle of proportionality and the emphasis on the facts relating to both the offence and the offender" that sets Canada's sentencing approach apart from those of other countries. This section has introduced a number of other sentencing principles as well (see Exhibit 9.2). Overall, these principles provide a general framework for guiding sentencing judges and courts and for encouraging flexibility by judges. Over time, provincial courts of appeal and the Supreme Court of Canada "are providing more detailed guidance as to how the various principles should be applied to categories of offence and offenders" (ibid.).

One of the most controversial cases in recent Canadian sentencing history is *R. v. Gladue* (1999). This case involved s. 718.2(e) of the Criminal Code (see below), which states "all available sanctions other than imprisonment that are reasonable in the circumstance, should be considered for all offenders, with particular attention to aboriginal offenders." Jamie Tanis Gladue, an Aboriginal woman, was charged with the second degree murder of her husband. She had reason to believe that he was having an affair, and an argument ensued, during which Ms. Gladue stabbed him in the heart with a knife. Following the preliminary inquiry and the selection of the jury, she pleaded guilty to the charge of manslaughter. She was then sentenced to three years in prison with a ten-year firearms prohibition, a sentence typically handed out to those convicted of manslaughter in Canada.

The trial judge noted a number of mitigating factors in this case. These included her supportive family, the treatment for alcoholism she had been undergoing since the incident, her remorse, and her guilty plea. Aggravating factors included the fact that she had stabbed her husband twice, had intended to seriously harm him, and had committed a serious crime (Lash 2000).

When handing down the sentence, the trial judge noted that Ms. Gladue was Cree but that she lived "off reserve" and was therefore not entitled to the special consideration due to her on account of her Aboriginal status as stipulated in s. 718.2(e). The case was appealed to the British Columbia Court of Appeal on the basis of her attempts to "rehabilitate herself" since the offence, the 17 months she had waited prior to her trial to start, and the fact that the trial judge failed to consider her Aboriginal status. Again Ms. Gladue lost. She then appealed the verdict to the Supreme Court of Canada. The Supreme Court considered only one factor in her appeal—whether or not the trial judge had given appropriate attention to her Aboriginal status. It was decided that Ms. Gladue was to receive a conditional sentence (see Chapter 10) of two years less a day, to be served in the community. The Supreme Court justices, in reaching their judgment, commented on the discrimination experienced by Aboriginal people in the criminal justice system, noting also "the excessive imprisonment of Aboriginal people is only the tip of the iceberg insofar as the estrangement of the Aboriginal peoples from the Canadian justice system is concerned."

This decision was quickly followed by two similar cases, also in British Columbia. In the first, a Métis

Section 718.2 of the Criminal Code specifies a number of sentencing principles:

(a) a sentence should be increased or reduced to account for any relevant aggravating or mitigating circumstances relating to the offence or the offender, and, without limiting the generality of the foregoing,
   (i) evidence that the offence was motivated by bias, prejudice or hate based on race, national or ethnic origin, language, colour, religion, sex, age, mental or physical disability, sexual orientation, or any other similar factor; or
   (ii) evidence that the offender, in committing the offence, abused the offender's spouse or child;
   (iii) evidence that the offender, in committing the offence, abused a position of trust or authority in relation to the victim

shall be deemed to be aggravating circumstances; or
   (iv) evidence that the offence was committed for the benefit of, at the direction of or in association with a criminal organization;

(b) a sentence should be similar to sentences imposed on similar offenders for similar offences committed in similar circumstances;
(c) where consecutive sentences are imposed, the combined sentence should not be unduly long or harsh;
(d) an offender should not be deprived of liberty, if less restrictive sanctions may be appropriate in the circumstances; and
(e) all available sanctions other than imprisonment that are reasonable in the circumstances should be considered for all offenders, with particular attention to the circumstances of aboriginal offenders.

woman who had stabbed her common-law husband to death was given a conditional sentence, enabling the defendant to look after her five-year-old daughter. And in July 1999, the British Columbia Supreme Court used the same section to reduce a life sentence to 20 years' imprisonment for a 37-year-old Métis man.

However, applications for a reduced sentence based on s. 718.2(e) are not always accepted by the courts. For example, in 2000, a judge in Nanaimo, British Columbia, rejected a defendant's Aboriginal status as a reason for reducing her 10-year sentence for fatally abusing her stepdaughter (Bailey 2000). This sentencing provision has been criticized since its introduction ("Equal under the Law" 1998; Humphreys 2001; Seeman 2001). Some critics contend that this provision violates the principles of proportionality and equality introduced in Canada's sentencing law in 1996 (e.g., Brodeur and Roberts 2002).

SENTENCING PATTERNS IN CANADA

What sentences do convicted people receive for their criminal actions? A recent analysis of sentencing practices used information from all jurisdictions in Canada during 2006–07. The adult provincial criminal courts heard 372,084 cases involving 1,079,062 charges in 2006–07, a figure virtually unchanged from 2005–06

(see Figure 9.2). Most cases (88 percent) had a Criminal Code charge as the most serious offence in the case. The remaining 12 percent involved federal statutes. Of the cases involving the Criminal Code, the "crimes against person" category accounted for 25 percent, while the "crimes against property" and "Other Criminal Code" categories represented 24 and 8 percent, respectively; "administration of justice" accounted for 17 percent and "Criminal Code traffic" accounted for 14 percent (Marth 2008).

During 2006–07, the most frequently occurring offences were impaired driving (11 percent), common assault (11 percent), theft (10 percent), failure to comply with a court order (7 percent), and breach of probation (7 percent). Cases involving sexual assault and other sexual offences accounted for less than 2 percent of all cases, while homicide and attempted murder accounted for approximately 0.2 percent. Of all the adult criminal court cases, 78 percent involved a male accused while 16 percent involved a female accused. (The sex of the accused was not recorded in less than 2 percent of the cases.) The remaining cases (less than 1 percent) involved a company. Males were overrepresented, but this finding varied by type of offence. For example, males accounted for the majority of all sexual assaults (91 percent), unlawfully at large (86 percent) and break and enter (85 percent). In addition, younger adults were overrepresented relative to older adults. In 2006–07, 18- to 24-year-olds were 12 percent of the Canadian population but accounted for 31 percent of

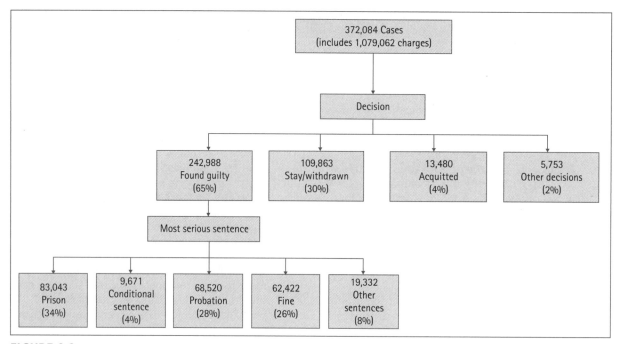

FIGURE 9.2

Adult Court Processing of Federal Statute Cases in Provincial and Selected Superior Courts, Canada, 2006–2007

Notes: Found guilty decisions include absolute and conditional discharges. Stay/Withdrawn includes cases stayed, withdrawn, dismissed, and discharges at preliminary inquiry. Other decisions include final decisions of not criminally responsible, waived in province/territory, and waived out of province/territory. This category also includes decisions where a conviction was not recorded, the court accepted a special plea, cases which raised Charter arguments or cases where the accused was found unfit to stand trial. The sentence was not known in less than 1% of convicted cases in 2006/2007. Conditional sentencing data was not collected in Quebec for 2006/2007, resulting in an undercount of conditional sentences. Coverage for Adult Criminal Court Survey data as of 2006/1007 is estimated at 98% of national adult criminal court caseload.

Source: Michael Marth "Adult Criminal Court Statistics, 2006/2007" *Juristat*, Vol. 28, no. 5, p. 4. Statistics Canada catalogue no. 85-002-XIE.

all cases in adult criminal courts. Persons aged 25 to 34 accounted for 18 percent of all cases in those courts but 27 percent of the total cases disposed in adult criminal court (ibid.).

During 2006–07, the accused was found guilty in 65 percent of the cases disposed of in the adult criminal courts (see Figure 9.2). In 30 percent of the cases, the most serious offence was resolved by a decision to stay or withdraw charges, and 4 percent of all cases resulted in an acquittal. The remaining cases involved other decisions (e.g., the accused was found unfit to stand trial, or a finding of guilt was not recorded) (ibid.). The crime against the person with the highest "guilty" percentage was robbery (69 percent), followed by major assault (54 percent) and common assault (53 percent) (see Figure 9.3). For crimes against property, the highest "guilty" percentage was for break and enter (72 percent) and theft (68 percent) (see Figure 9.4). The sentences for those cases disposed of during 2006–07 included incarceration (34 percent), probation (28 percent), a fine

(26 percent), other sentences (8 percent), and conditional sentences (4 percent). The provinces of New Brunswick (80 percent) and Newfoundland and Labrador (77 percent) and had the highest percentage of cases found "guilty" in 2006–07; Ontario (59 percent), Manitoba (62 percent), and the Yukon (63 percent) had the lowest (ibid.).

The findings of this study of the adult provincial criminal court caseload during 2006–07 also included the following:

- Probation was the most common sentence, imposed in 43 percent of all guilty cases. Incarceration in either a provincial or federal correctional facility accounted for 34 percent of all guilty cases.
- Fines were imposed in 30 percent of all cases.
- Thirty-one percent of all cases where the accused was found guilty of an offence in the category of "crimes against the person" were sentenced to prison.
- The violent crime category was the most likely to include a sentence of probation (73 percent).

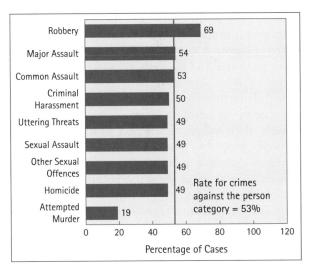

FIGURE 9.3

Cases Found Guilty with a Crime Against the Person as the Most Serious Offence in the Case, Canada, 2006–2007

Notes: Found guilty cases include absolute and conditional discharges. Coverage for Adult Criminal Court Survey data as of 2006/2007 is estimated at 98% of caseload.
Source: Michael Marth "Adult Criminal Court Statistics, 2006/2007" *Juristat*, Vol. 28, no. 5, p. 5. Statistics Canada catalogue no. 85-002-XIE.

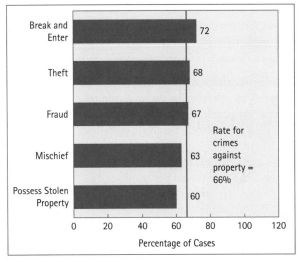

FIGURE 9.4

Cases Found Guilty with a Crime Against Property as the Most Serious Offence in the Case, Canada, 2006–2007

Notes: Found guilty cases include absolute and conditional discharges. Coverage for Adult Criminal Court Survey as of 2006/2007 is estimated at 98% of adult criminal caseload.
Source: Michael Marth "Adult Criminal Court Statistics, 2006/2007" *Juristat*, Vol. 28, no. 5, p. 5. Statistics Canada catalogue no. 85-002-XIE.

- Of the 35,126 individuals who were found guilty of crimes against the person and who received probation, 31 percent also received a prison sentence.
- The most common length of a probation order was 6 to 12 months (51 percent); 31 percent were for greater than one month to two years.
- The mean amount for fines was $758.
- Fines were most frequently imposed when the accused was found guilty of impaired driving (86 percent) or drug possession (50 percent).
- Multiple-charge cases represented 60 percent of the caseload.
- The average number of court appearances was 5.1. In 1994–95, the number had been 4.1.
- Thirty-four percent of all guilty individuals received a sentence involving a period of incarceration in a provincial or federal correctional facility.
- The mean period of incarceration was 117 days.
- The mean prison sentence for attempted murder was 1,877 days, while for break and enter it was 160 days.

During 2006–07, data on superior courts were collected in seven jurisdictions. There were 1,406 cases completed in the superior courts in seven jurisdictions. The criminal offences heard most often in the superior courts involved crimes against the person (39 percent), other federal statute crimes (35 percent), and crimes against property (12 percent). Fifty-five percent of all cases heard in the superior courts resulted in a guilty finding. The accused was acquitted in 10 percent of cases. Most guilty findings (47 percent) resulted in a prison sentence; 22 percent of those convicted received a conditional sentence. The average sentence length for those sentenced to a period of incarceration after a trial in superior court was 989 days (nearly three years) (ibid.).

SENTENCING AND HEALING CIRCLES

In recent years, much attention has been paid to the overrepresentation of Aboriginal people in the federal and provincial correctional systems. Quigley (1994, 270) has summarized the implications of this:

- Aboriginal accused persons are more likely to be denied bail. This likelihood in turn tends to increase the likelihood of incarceration on conviction.
- Aboriginal offenders are more likely to be committed to jail for non-payment of fines. In Saskatchewan

during 1992–93, almost 75 percent of admissions to jails for fine default were Aboriginal people.

• Aboriginal offenders are less likely to receive probation as a sentence than are non-Aboriginal offenders.

From this evidence, Quigley (ibid., 271) recommended an attempt "to decrease the preponderance of Aboriginal people within the prison system." One proposal has been to reintroduce sentencing and healing circles, in which a group of Elders participate with a judge in the sentencing process in an attempt to heal the accused, the victim, and the community.

The nature of sentencing circles varies across Canada, but some features are common to all. Quigley (ibid., 288) notes that modern sentencing circles are a hybrid of traditional Aboriginal community justice and the Western legal system: "sentencing circles are a variation in procedure, not necessarily a change in the substance of sentencing." Judges retain the right to give final approval to a sentence imposed by a sentencing circle. What is different is the process. In some ways, a sentencing circle operates much like the Western legal system. For example, any dispute on a factual matter is resolved by calling for evidence and through the examination and cross-examination of witnesses. The difference is

that, through discussions within the sentencing circle, "respected members of the community, the victim, the police, the accused, the family of the accused, Crown and defence counsel, and the judge try to jointly arrive at a decision that is acceptable to all."

Jurisdictions vary regarding which types of offences can be heard by sentencing circles. Generally, though, these offences are minor in nature, typically involving property crimes. Serious violent crimes are usually not allowed to be heard by a sentencing circle, although there are exceptions (see the discussion of Hollow Water in Chapter 3).

A number of other criteria are considered in determining whether a sentencing circle will be held. In *R. v. Joseyounen* (1995), the following criteria were set out:

• The accused must agree to be referred to the sentencing circle.
• The accused must have deep roots in the community in which the sentencing circle is held and from which the participants are to be drawn.
• There are Elders or respected non-political community leaders willing to participate.
• The victim is willing to participate and has not been coerced into participating.

Sentencing circles bring offenders, victims, their families, community members and Elders together to discuss the impact of a crime. The meeting is conducted in a circle, which is designed to reduce hierarchy and promote the sharing of ideas. (CP PHOTO/Winnipeg Free Press/Joe Bryksa)

- The court should determine beforehand whether the victim is suffering from the battered woman syndrome. If she is, she should receive counselling and be accompanied by the support team in the circle.
- Disputed facts must be resolved in advance.
- The case must be one in which the court is willing to depart from the usual range of sentencing.

There are a number of circumstances where the sentencing circle is not appropriate, such as the following:

- A term of incarceration in excess of two years is realistic.
- There have been frequent repeat offences or the offence is indictable.
- The attitude of the offender prohibits his or her involvement.
- There are no community sentencing options available to the circle.
- The community is not prepared to be involved in the circle (Native Law Centre 2006).

Once a sentence has been agreed on, it is not automatically accepted by the Western legal system. For example, the Saskatchewan Court of Appeal overturned the sentence handed down by a sentencing circle to Ivan Morin (*R. v. Morin* [1995]). Morin, a 34-year-old Métis, was convicted in 1992 of robbing a gas station of $131 and choking a female attendant. He was sentenced to jail for 18 months instead of the 6 to 8 years requested by the Crown. The Crown had proposed its sentence based on Morin's 34 prior criminal convictions, which ranged from drunk driving and small-time break-ins to attempted murder and kidnapping. Even so, the trial judge accepted the recommendation of the sentencing circle. The Crown appealed the case, largely on the basis that Morin was using the sentencing circle to receive the lightest sentence possible and showed neither real remorse nor interest in rehabilitation. The Saskatchewan Court of Appeal, in its review of the case, noted that judges should accept the decisions of sentencing circles in cases where (1) the accused agrees to be referred to a sentencing circle; (2) the accused has deep roots in the community in which the circle is held; (3) the Elders are willing to support the offender; and (4) the victim voluntarily participates. Since Morin appeared to be trying to take advantage of the lighter sentences associated with sentencing circles, the appeal court accepted the argument presented by the Crown and increased the sentence. Such appeals, however, are rare.

The benefits of sentencing circles are many. According to a Yukon court, they include these:

1. The monopoly of professionals is reduced.
2. Lay participation is encouraged.
3. Information flow is increased.
4. There is a creative search for new options.
5. The sharing of responsibility for the decision is promoted.
6. The participation of the accused is encouraged.
7. Victims are involved in the process.
8. A more constructive environment is created.
9. There is greater understanding of the limitations of the justice system.
10. The focus of the criminal justice system is extended.
11. There is greater mobilization of community resources.
12. There is an opportunity to merge the values of Aboriginal nations with those of the larger society (*R. v. Moses* [1992]).

Healing circles have both supporters and detractors. Some offer only cautious support (Clairmont 1996; LaPrairie 1998; Roberts and LaPrairie 1996). Clairmont studied three such programs in three different communities and concluded that "in all programs the objectives relating to victims and community reconciliation have proven elusive to date." Clairmont notes that it is especially important for these programs to involve the community at large. LaPrairie (1998) reports that victims often find healing programs to be less positive experiences than do the offenders. In addition, only about 30 percent of the families of offenders and victims considered that offenders had been dealt with appropriately. As LaPrairie notes, "these findings are not . . . to suggest a lack of merit in the projects identified above or in pursuing local justice in aboriginal communities . . . [but] to identify the need for greater clarity in the development and delivery of local justice services."

ISSUES IN SENTENCING

Some Canadians believe that judges are too lenient when punishing offenders. This has led researchers to study public opinion about sentencing. Another key issue is variations in sentencing. Should sentence severity depend on the judge who hears a case or on the jurisdiction in Canada in which the case is heard? Finally, what are other jurisdictions doing to control judicial variation in sentencing? Is it possible to eliminate sentencing variation by implementing different sentencing laws? When differences in sentences are found (especially when they involve sentencing disparities and sentencing discrimination), it is common to blame judicial discretion.

Sentencing Disparity

Sentencing disparity arises when similar crimes do not receive similar punishments. A certain amount of variation in sentencing must be expected, since a number of factors in a particular case can lead a judge to decide on a longer (or shorter) sentence. As Roberts (2001, 200) points out, sentencing "without any variation would be sentencing without justice." But how extensive are sentencing variations? And do these variations result in disparities in sentencing decisions?

The Canadian Sentencing Commission (1987) identified three types of sentencing variation:

1. From case to case, where the same judge imposes different sentences for similar offenders convicted of the same offence committed in similar circumstances.
2. From judge to judge, where different judges impose different sentences in similar cases.
3. From court to court, where different courts in a particular jurisdiction use different standards for what is considered an appropriate sentence in specific cases.

The Sentencing Commission interviewed 400 judges, who indicated that they felt variation existed among their sentencing practices, largely owing to differences in personal attitudes. In addition, over 80 percent of approximately 700 Crown prosecutors and defence lawyers believed that unwarranted variation existed in sentences within their jurisdictions, and almost 90 percent said they felt there was unwarranted variation across Canada. This was the result of the Canadian approach to sentencing, which gives judges a significant amount of discretion in their sentencing decisions. The inevitable result is "unwarranted disparity in sentencing" (Roberts 2001, 204).

A few studies have reported sentencing variations based on individual judges rather than on the objective legal facts of cases. An early study, by Hogarth (1971), examined the sentencing patterns of 71 magistrates in Ontario to see whether variations existed in sentences and, if they did, whether sentencing differences could be explained by either the facts of the case (e.g., the seriousness of the offence, or whether the accused pleaded guilty), or characteristics of the offender (e.g., a prior criminal record), or characteristics of the sentencing judges. According to Hogarth, if sentencing disparity didn't exist, the facts of the case and the characteristics of the offender would explain any variations in sentencing. He found that judges' penal philosophies and attitudes determined what they considered important during a trial, and that this ultimately influenced both the type and length of sentences imposed. Hogarth concluded that "one can explain more about sentencing by knowing . . . about the judge than by a great deal about the facts of the case"; while 9 percent

of the sentencing variation could be explained by the objective facts of a case, over 50 percent could be explained by facts about judges.

The most notable study in this area was conducted by Palys and Divorski (1986), who presented five hypothetical cases to 206 Canadian provincial court judges and asked them to indicate what sentence they would impose on the offender. While judges were found to vary in their sentencing decisions in all five cases, the greatest differences were discovered in a case involving assault causing bodily harm. The judges' sentences varied from a $500 fine plus six months' probation to five years in a federal correctional facility. Not all offences resulted in significant variations in sentencing. For example, for the offence of break and enter, the sentences varied from a **suspended sentence** to one year in a provincial correctional facility.

Roberts and Birkenmayer (1997) later found significant variation in sentencing patterns among provinces after controlling for the seriousness of the offence. The amount of variation depended on the type of offence under study. They found that the rate of incarceration for the offence of "theft under" ranged from a low of 4 percent in Newfoundland to a high of 26 percent in Yukon. Relative to the variation discovered in offences of other types, the variation in this offence was fairly slight, due largely to "legally relevant factors as well as the fact that the monetary limit of this criminal offence places a constraint on the variability in offence seriousness" (ibid., 6). Other offences were found to have a greater sentencing range. For example, incarceration rates for breaking and entering ranged from 26 percent in the Northwest Territories to 78 percent on Prince Edward Island.

Courthouse Norms

Another explanation for sentencing disparity focuses on individual **courtroom work groups.** The norms established by such groups can lead to sentencing disparities. These norms arise from structural factors in the courthouse, such as case backlogs, which to many "have become the force that drives the modern court system" (Makin 2004, F6). Many pretrial conferences are held between Crown prosecutors and defence lawyers, with the goal of reaching an agreement prior to the trial. And some judges feel that if they "don't agree to precise plea bargains," the courts "will likely become more backlogged." They believe that pretrial negotiations "are fine when they are properly conducted." Some, however, question how often the proper procedures are followed. According to one provincial court judge, one result of this system is that "justice is becoming less and less visible" (ibid.).

Sentencing Discrimination

Sentencing discrimination occurs when the length of a sentence is influenced by extralegal factors, such as the defendant's race, gender, or social class, or by any other factor not directly related to the criminal offence (see Chapter 1). Canadian studies that have investigated the possibility of discrimination in sentencing have focused on two minority groups: Aboriginal people and Black people. They have reached differing conclusions. LaPrairie (1990), in her study of the overrepresentation of Aboriginal people in correctional facilities in Canada, reported that while they are overrepresented in Canadian correctional facilities, this is not due to discriminatory sentencing practices. And when differences are found, researchers have reported that these can be explained to a certain degree by the differences in the seriousness of the offences and the prior records of Aboriginal and non-Aboriginal offenders (Hann and Harman 1992; York 1995). However, other researchers (e.g., Clairmont 1989; Clairmont et al. 1989; Renner and Warner 1981) report finding some degree of sentencing discrimination. Williams (1999, 212) found that the variables of unemployment and detention before trial "did have a discernable effect in that both were associated with higher imprisonment rates." That is, judges who use extralegal factors such as unemployment and being held in detention before trial as reasons for incarcerating convicted offenders "are likely to discriminate against black men without ever intending to do so." And the Aboriginal Justice Inquiry (Hamilton and Sinclair 1991) found that more Aboriginal people than non-Aboriginal people were given a sentence of incarceration.

Public Opinion and Public Confidence in Sentencing

Research conducted in a number of Western countries in recent years indicates that members of the public select harsher sentences than judges do. Studies have long pointed out the wide gap that exists between the sentences imposed by judges and those the public would have handed down in the same cases. However, research comparing the relative punitiveness of public and judicial attitudes toward the punishment of offenders has come to a different conclusion (Roberts 1988; Roberts and Doob 1989; Zamble 1990). Roberts and Doob (1989) found that 62 percent of the public and 63 percent of the judiciary agreed on which offenders should be incarcerated. These same researchers found that when they presented the public with sufficient information about different sentencing options available to judges, the former became *less* punitive than the latter. The public recommended

incarcerating a total of 81,863 offenders in the study, whereas judges had incarcerated a total of 92,415.

But does the public agree with judges about which offences should lead to incarceration? When Roberts and Doob (ibid.) compared the rank orderings of the public with the actual actions of the judiciary on ten offences, they found substantial differences between the two groups. Of the ten offences, the public suggested more punitive sentences for five (arson, assaulting a police officer, forgery, theft over $5,000, and fraud over $5,000) and gave virtually the same response for two offences (possession of dangerous weapons and kidnapping). Those offences for which the judiciary gave more punitive responses were robbery, perjury, and break and enter.

So it seems that the public may be more punitive than judges when sentencing offenders. Yet the same public tends to support a variety of sentencing goals. For example, one Canadian study found that when a crime was judged relatively minor, the sentencing goal supported by most of the public was deterrence. However, the public responded differently when presented with serious violent crimes. For violent crimes such as robbery and sexual assault, the public showed little approval for deterrence; selective incapacitation received the most support (Canadian Sentencing Commission 1987). Kaukinen and Colavecchia (1999), using data collected by the 1993 General Social Survey (GSS), found that the socioeconomic status of individuals is an important predictor of public attitudes toward sentencing. Higher status respondents were dissatisfied with the ability of the courts to assist victims of crime (see below), while dissatisfaction with the ability of the courts to protect the legal rights of the accused was most often expressed by individuals belonging to lower socioeconomic groups.

In the 2007 National Justice Survey, researchers attempted to document the level of confidence held by Canadians toward the criminal justice system. Less than 15 percent of Canadians sampled indicated they possessed "high confidence" in the criminal justice system compared to the health system, the education system, and social welfare system. Respondents were more likely to indicate lower confidence as they further along the criminal justice system from police to parole. Respondents indicated that they had more confidence that the police will solve a crime after it has been committed compared to preventing a crime from occurring in the first place. In terms of the courts, respondents expressed more confidence that they will determine an individual's guilt or innocence compared to their ability to hand down an appropriate sentence. While respondents were relatively confident that the correctional system would prevent offenders from escaping, they were less confident that this system rehabilitated offenders. Finally, respondents were equally concerned with the ability of the parole system to safely release and supervise offenders within the community (Latimer and Desjardins 2007).

MANDATORY MINIMUM SENTENCES FOR GUN-RELATED CRIMES

In Chapter 1, it was pointed out that some politicians and political parties as well as police organizations want to increase the mandatory minimum penalties (MMP) as a way to deter gun-related crimes in Canada. A mandatory minimum sentence is a statutorily determined punishment that must be applied to all of those who are convicted of a specific crime. An MMP is one form of **determinate sentence;** another type is referred to as "truth in sentencing." Truth-in-sentencing laws require offenders to serve at least 85 percent of their sentence. They usually focus on violent offenders and limit or eliminate altogether parole eligibility for these designated offenders.

MMP for gun-related crimes became an issue in the 2006 federal election, even though some of the existing offences in the legislation governing gun-related crimes already utilize MMP (see Exhibit 9.3). The new

---

EXHIBIT 9.3   Mandatory Minimum Penalties for Gun-Related Crimes

The criminal use of firearms is prohibited by the Criminal Code (Part III, Firearms and Other Weapons). Some of the offences and their associated penalties are as follows:

USE OF FIREARMS

- Use of a firearm in the commission of criminal negligence causing death, manslaughter, attempted murder, aggravated sexual assault, kidnapping, hostage taking, robbery, or extortion (minimum of four years, with a maximum of life).
- Causing bodily harm with intent using a firearm or sexual assault with a weapon (using a firearm) (minimum of four years, maximum of 14 years).
- Use of a firearm or imitation in the commission of an indictable offence (minimum of one year, three years consecutive on a second or subsequent offence, maximum of 14 years).

POSSESSION OF FIREARMS OFFENCES

- Possession of restricted or prohibited firearms with ammunition (if on indictment, to a minimum of one year, and a maximum of ten years; if by summary conviction, to a maximum of one year).
- Possession of a weapon obtained by crime (by indictment, minimum of one year and a maximum of ten years; if by summary conviction, a maximum of one year).
- Possession of a firearm knowing that it is unauthorized (minimum of one year on second offence, minimum two years less a day on a third or subsequent offence, maximum of ten years).

IMPORT AND EXPORT FIREARM OFFENCES (SMUGGLING)

- Importing or exporting a firearm knowing it is unauthorized (minimum of one year, maximum of ten years).

TRAFFICKING OF FIREARM OFFENCES

- Weapons trafficking (minimum of one year, maximum of ten years).
- Possession for the purpose of trafficking (minimum of one year, maximum of ten years).

In May 2006, the federal justice minister introduced legislation increasing the mandatory minimum penalty provisions of the Criminal Code. Under the proposed legislation, the use of a firearm in committing a serious offence will be subject to an increased minimum sentence. If, for example, an offence is gang-related, or if a restricted or prohibited firearm such as a handgun is used, the minimum penalty will be as follows:

- Five years on the first offence.
- Seven years if the accused has one prior conviction involving the use of a firearm to commit an offence.
- Ten years if the accused has more than one prior conviction for using a firearm to commit an offence.

Other firearms-related offences, such as firearms trafficking and smuggling, and the new offence of robbery where a firearm is stolen, will also have higher mandatory minimum sentences:

- Three years for the first offence.
- Five years if the accused has a serious prior firearm-related conviction.

legislation proposed by the federal government in May 2006 called for stronger penalties for the use of firearms. At the core of the new legislation was "tougher" MMP; the hope was that it would deter these types of offences. According to these Federal Justice Minister and Attorney General of Canada Vic Toews, by "ensuring that tougher mandatory minimum sentences are imposed for serious and repeat firearms crime, we will restore confidence in the justice system, and make our streets safer." He added that there would be "clear consequences for gun crime—prison sentences that are in keeping with the gravity of the offence" (Department of Justice 2006). He also "insisted that mandatory minimum sentences have reduced crime in the United States" (Clark 2006, A1). However, his comments about reducing crime were countered by the chair of the criminal law section of the Canadian Bar Association, who said that such laws "limit a judge's discretion to apply the fairest sentence," and who added that the "best available data seem to suggest that a high sentence does not deter, and more likely it is the probability of being caught that will deter . . . you increase the probability of someone being caught by increasing resources to police agencies" (ibid.).

Canada already had already introduced mandatory minimum sentences for firearms-related offences. Nineteen of these offences were established in 1995 when Bill C-86, which contained new firearms legislation, was passed (Gabor 2002). Stronger sanctions were added to these existing laws on December 1, 1998. One of the new sections (s. 109 of the Criminal Code) identifies four offence categories for which, on conviction, the judge must prohibit the possession of a wide range of weapons, including firearms and crossbows. These categories include (1) serious offences (i.e., those with a maximum term of incarceration of ten years or more), (2) several listed weapons offences and criminal harassment (stalking), and (3) offences involving weapons while the individual was under a previous prohibition order. In addition, a person convicted of a listed offence for the first time, the prohibition order must be for at least ten years after release from a correctional facility (or after the trial, if that person was not sentenced to a period of incarceration). Any subsequent order involving the same person has to be for life. The second new section (s. 110 of the Criminal Code) allows judges to impose a prohibition order for the following: (1) crimes involving violence with a maximum sentence of less than ten years, and (2) crimes involving weapons while the accused is not under a prohibition order. Once again, the order must be for a minimum of ten years, and the judge must give reasons for not imposing this sentence (Edgar 1999).

On May 4, 2006, then-Minister of Justice and Attorney General of Canada Vic Toews introduced legis-lation (Bill C-10) intended to toughen sentencing for crimes involving firearms by enhancing the mandatory minimum penalty provisions of the Criminal Code. Under the proposed legislation, the use of a firearm during the commission of a serious offence would be subject to an escalating mandatory minimum penalty sentences. If, for example, an offence is related to gang activity, or if a restricted or prohibited firearm such as a handgun is used in the commission of an offence, the proposed legislation would establish a minimum penalty of five years on the first offence; seven years if the accused has one prior conviction for using a firearm to commit an offence; and ten years if the accused has more than one prior conviction for using a firearm to commit an offence.

The other significant changes proposed by Bill C-10 in its original form included the following:

- Adding the new offence of "breaking and entering to steal a firearm" with a mandatory minimum penalty of one year for a first offence, three years for a second offence, and five years for a third or subsequent offence.
- Adding a new offence of "robbery to steal a firearm" with a mandatory minimum penalty of three years for a first offence, and five years for a second or subsequent offence.
- Escalating the mandatory minimum penalties for several firearm related offences in the Criminal Code that already have an existing minimum term of imprisonment of one year, such as possessing a prohibited or restricted firearm with ammunition, possessing a firearm obtained through the commission of an offence, trafficking in a firearm, and importing or exporting a firearm without authorization. Bill C-10 proposed an increase of the mandatory minimum penalties for these offences to three years for a first offence, and five years for a second and subsequent offence.
- Escalating the mandatory minimum penalties for several firearm offences in the Criminal Code that have already have a current minimum term of imprisonment for four years, such as the use of a firearm in the commission of an attempted murder, aggravated sexual assault, kidnapping, and robbery. Bill C-10 would increase the mandatory minimum penalties for these offences to five years for a first offence, seven years for a second offence, and ten years for a third or subsequent offence.

At the end of May 2007, the proposed two new offences,—breaking and entering to steal a firearm and robbery to steal a firearm—were removed from the original version of the bill and are not subject to any mandatory minimum term of imprisonment. In addition, for the remaining offences contained in Bill C-10, the mandatory minimums for a third or subsequent offence were not placed back into the bill. In addition, for those offences that currently have a mandatory minimum sentence of one year, the new mandatory minimums would be three years for the first offence, and five years for the second and subsequent offences.

As noted in Chapter 1, Bill C-10 was later combined with four other bills to form Bill C-2—the *Tackling Violent Crime Act*. On February 27, 2008, the Senate passed the new bill.

WRONGFUL CONVICTIONS

One of the most important principles in our criminal justice system is that a person is innocent until proven guilty. A number of cases have emerged over the past two decades that have raised the issue of wrongful accusations and convictions in Canada. A number of American researchers have estimated the number of wrongfully accused and executed. For example, Scheck and his colleagues (2000) reported that more than 25 percent of all prime suspects were excluded prior to trial as a result of DNA testing conducted in 18,000 criminal cases in the United States. In other words, 4,000 of the prime suspects in cases were wrongly accused. Radelet et al. (1992) estimated that at least 23 individuals had been wrongfully executed in the United States. And, again in the United States, Liebman and colleagues (2000) found serious, reversible errors in almost 70 percent of the thousands of capital cases they studied over a 23-year period (1973–95). A study of the 200 individuals in the United States to be exonerated by DNA evidence found that they served an average of 12 years in prison, 176 were convicted of sexual assault, and 14 were on death row (Conway 2007, 14).

There is no systematic record of the number of wrongful convictions, but in the United States, Huff et al. (1986) attempted to empirically estimate the number of wrongful convictions by surveying all the Attorneys General in the United States as well as the following in the state of Ohio: all presiding judges of the common plea courts; all county prosecutors, public defenders, and sheriffs; and the chiefs of police of seven large cities. They defined wrongful convictions as "cases in which a person (is) convicted of a felony but later . . . found innocent beyond a reasonable doubt, generally due to a confession by the actual offender, evidence that had been available but was not sufficiently used at the time of the conviction, new evidence that was not previously available, and other factors." The results were startling— based on the surveys, the researchers conservatively estimated that about 0.5 percent of all felony convictions were incorrect. That is, of every 1,000 individuals convicted of a serious crime, 5 are actually innocent of the charge(s). Huff (2004) points out that while a percentage of less than 1 may not seem high, in 2000, in the United States an average of 7 million people were convicted of serious crimes, meaning that there could have been 34,250 persons wrongfully convicted in that year!

What causes wrongful convictions? According to research in the United States, a number of factors consistently appear in almost all cases of wrongful conviction. These include relying on jailhouse informants for evidence (see Chapter 7), perjury, misleading police line-ups, forensic errors, false or coerced confessions, police and prosecutor misconduct (including the withholding of evidence), eyewitness error, community pressure for a conviction, ineffective legal counsel, and the "ratification of error" (i.e., the tendency of individuals working in the criminal justice system to "rubber-stamp" decisions made at the lower levels as cases move through the next stages of the system). In most cases, more than one factor has been found that contributed to a wrongful conviction— in some cases, most of the above-noted reasons may have been in play. A number of these reasons are discussed below.

Eyewitness Error

Eyewitness error is viewed as the main cause of wrongful convictions. For example, Huff and colleagues (1986) reported that 79 percent of their respondents ranked witness error as the most frequent type of error resulting in a wrongful conviction. Scheck et al. (2000) point out that in 84 percent of the DNA exonerations they studied, charges ultimately proved to be incorrect were laid against the accused on the basis of mistaken eyewitness identification. A number of researchers, such as Loftus (1979), Loftus and Doyle (1991), and Penrod (2003), have studied eyewitness identification extensively and how it can be "significantly affected by psychological, societal, cultural, and systemic factors, and how police line-ups should and should not be conducted to ensure fairness to suspects" (Huff 2004, 110). In the United States, 75 percent of the cases in which the first 200 individuals were exonerated by DNA were found to include eyewitness error identification (Conway 2007, A14).

Forensic Errors

DNA analysis has resulted in the exoneration of many wrongfully convicted individuals (Scheck et al. (2000)). But in some cases, faulty evidence submitted by forensic scientists has led to wrongful convictions. An analysis of the first 200 individuals in the United States exonerated by DNA discovered that in 110 of them,

Overzealous or Unethical Police and Prosecutors

Based on their study of post-conviction DNA exonerations of the wrongfully convicted, Scheck and colleagues (2000) concluded that 63 percent involved police and/or prosecutorial misconduct. An inquiry into three wrongful conviction murder cases in Newfoundland found that these cases had been "botched largely because of a dysfunctional Crown 'culture' that was overzealous and unquestioningly accepted police theories." The report's author added that "by failing to view evidence objectively and becoming over aggressive in their pursuit of legal victories . . . prosecutors played an instrumental role in the wrongful convictions" (Makin 2006, A7). Other concerns in this category relate to the use of false or misleading evidence, tampering with witnesses, and failing to disclose exculpatory evidence (Huff 2004).

PRESUMPTIVE SENTENCES (SENTENCING GUIDELINES)

Another type of determinate sentence is referred to as a presumptive sentence. Presumptive sentences are developed by either the legislature or a designated committee (usually referred to as a sentencing commission) to give judges guidance on selecting a sentence between a minimum and maximum sentence length (referred to as a "range"). Judges are required to sentence an offender within a specific range unless there are mitigating or aggravating factors. Judges who deviate from the designated sentencing range must usually give reasons why.

Sentencing guidelines are an attempt to control judicial variation in sentencing. Supporters of guidelines have argued that sentencing systems that leave unchecked the discretionary powers of judges lead to disparity in sentencing decisions, and that sentencing guidelines can eliminate sentencing disparity by controlling this discretion. Such guidelines typically state that sentencing should be done without regard to the race, gender, or social or economic status of the defendant. Also, they allow judges to make sentencing decisions based solely on two factors: (1) the severity of the crime for which the offender was convicted; and (2) the prior record of the offender. In this way, guidelines regulate both the decision to commit an offender to prison and the length of the prison term. They are constructed to imprison those convicted of serious violent crimes as well as those who have long criminal records. Most property offenders would not be imprisoned until they

In his report, Judge Goudge accused Dr. Charles Smith of making "false and misleading statements" in criminal cases. At least twelve people were wrongfully convicted and went to jail, while another eight were wrongly accused on the basis of Dr. Smith's reports. (CP PHOTO/Frank Gunn)

mistakes or other problems with forensic science was found (Conway 2007, A14). Three wrongful conviction cases involved experts testifying in misleading ways or misstating what was in the lab reports. The Manitoba Justice Department established a committee to review potential murder convictions on the basis that flawed hair analysis had tainted two murder convictions in that province; this has led to a further review of both cases (Smith 2004). This committee was established after James Driskell won his freedom after serving more than 13 years in prison. DNA evidence proved that he had been wrongfully convicted on the basis of forensic hair analysis, which until the mid-1990s had been a commonly used scientific approach in Canadian courts. After a review of 492 convictions during the previous 15 years, it was concluded that none warranted retesting hair samples using DNA samples to see whether mistakes were made (MacAfee 2005, A5). In addition, the investigation of the practices of pathologist Dr. Charles Smith by the Goudge Commission reported that he had made significant errors in at least 20 cases he handled for the Ontario Chief Coroner's Office (Makin 2008a, A4).

had been convicted of a number of offences; instead, they would be given alternative sanctions, to be served in the community.

Sentencing guidelines have four purposes:

- *Uniformity*. Improving the chances that similar offenders who have committed similar offences will receive similar sentences.
- *Neutrality*. Reducing the chances that race, gender, ethnicity, age, and class affect sentencing by restricting the criteria for sentencing to the seriousness of the crime and the criminal history of the offender.
- *Truth*. Ensuring that the type and length of sentences that offenders actually serve nearly equal the sentence lengths judges impose.
- *Control*. Preventing rapidly growing prison populations from overtaking prison spaces or resources.

Sentencing guidelines are particularly popular in part because they ignore all characteristics of the offender and focus solely on the act for which the offender has been convicted in court. Because the gender, race, age, and social class of the offender are irrelevant to the sentence, advocates of this approach contend that it is fair and equal to all.

Sentencing guidelines were recommended by the Canadian Sentencing Commission (1987) as an approach to eliminating some of the problems associated with sentencing in Canada at the time. Some of the problems identified by the commission were these:

- Maximum penalties were unrealistically severe and did not always reflect the relative seriousness of offences.
- Mandatory minimum sentences were creating injustices by unnecessarily restricting judicial discretion without achieving other purposes assigned to them.
- Systematic information about current sentencing practice was lacking. For policymakers and sentencing judges alike, easily accessible information did not exist (Stuart and Delisle 1995, 903).

Because of these problems, in 1987, the commission recommended a "fundamental overhaul" of sentencing practices in Canada. The recommended changes were as follows:

1. A new rationale for sentencing (which was achieved through the introduction of Bill C-41).
2. Elimination of all mandatory minimum penalties (other than for murder and high treason).
3. Replacement of the current penalty structure for all offences other than murder and high treason with maximum penalties of 12 years, 9 years, 6 years, 3 years, 1 year, or 6 months. In exceptional cases, for the most serious offences that carry a maximum

sentence of either 12 or 9 years, provision would be made to exceed these maximums.
4. Elimination of full parole release (other than for sentences of life imprisonment).
5. Provision for a reduction of time served for those inmates who display good behaviour while in prison. The portion that could be remitted would be reduced from one-third to one-quarter of the sentence imposed.
6. An increase in the use of community sanctions. The commission recommended greater use of sanctions that do not imply incarceration (e.g., community service orders, compensation to the victim or community, and fines, which do not involve any segregation of the offender from the community).
7. Elimination of "automatic" imprisonment for a fine default, to reduce the likelihood that a person who cannot pay a fine will go to jail.
8. Creation of a presumption for each offence respecting whether a person should normally be incarcerated or not. The judge could depart from the presumption by providing reasons why.
9. Creation of a "presumption range" for each offence normally requiring incarceration (again, the judge could depart by providing reasons).
10. Creation of a permanent sentencing commission to complete the development of guideline ranges for all offences, to collect and distribute information about current sentencing practices, and to review and (in appropriate cases) modify (with the assent of the House of Commons) the presumptive sentences in light of current practice and appellate decisions.

Federal Justice Minister Nicholson announces legislation that would limit the two-for-one credit at the time of sentencing. Do you think this new legislation, if passed, will limit the sentencing discretion of judges? (CP Photo/Adrian Wyld)

Do sentencing guidelines actually achieve their goals of fairness and equity? In the United States, sentencing guidelines have been analyzed by the federal government and by a number of states that have introduced them. (The Canadian Sentencing Commission used the approach taken by Minnesota as a guide for many of its policy recommendations.) Miethe and Moore (1985) studied the impact of defendants' social class on sentences during the first year of the Minnesota sentencing guidelines. They found that judges were following the guidelines by giving greater weight to offence-based characteristics, such as the use of a weapon and the severity of the criminal action. There was a decline in differential treatment of offenders on the basis of race, employment status, and gender; and likewise, a decline in sentencing variations among jurisdictions. Miethe and Moore also found that tighter controls on judicial discretion were not leading to greater discretion upstream in the criminal justice system—as in, for example, increased prosecutorial discretion. They also found that there was a shift in prison populations from property offenders to violent criminals. Four years later, in a follow-up study, they found that judges had substantially reduced sentence disparities. But they also reported that some variations had arisen—for example, they found that judges and prosecutors were "bending" the structure of the guidelines. Judges were sometimes departing from the guidelines (about 10 percent of the time), and prosecutors were changing their charging and plea-bargaining practices to circumvent guidelines they perceived as unreasonable. Other researchers (e.g., Kramer et al. 1989) confirmed these research findings.

However, studies conducted during the 1990s found considerable variation emerging with regard to how guidelines were being applied. D'Alessio and Stolzenberg (1995) found more deviation from sentencing guidelines the longer they were in effect. They also found that judges were not giving first-time violent offenders prison terms, even when the guidelines stipulated a period of incarceration. In his 25-year evaluation of the Minnesota Sentencing Guidelines, Frase (2005) reported that sentences ultimately became more uniform, at least relative to conviction offence and prior record of the offender. He also found that sentences are now more proportional and that they are largely parsimonious (i.e., judges are selecting the least restrictive alternative). He identified a number of unintended consequences of the sentencing guidelines in Minnesota, including that: they may reflect racial bias; there are too many people serving their sentences in prison for breaking minor technical rules while on parole; and judges are underusing intermediate sanctions, preferring

to send offenders to jail rather than back into the community (ibid., 206–7).

These studies tell us that it is very difficult to eliminate disparity and discrimination at the sentencing stage, at least to date. Section 718.2 of the Criminal Code instructs judges to "take into consideration" a number of principles, including that "a sentence should be similar to sentences imposed on similar offenders for similar offences committed in similar circumstances." As Brodeur and Roberts (2002, 82) suggest, since "this is a codified sentencing principle—one of just a few—in our view judges should take it seriously indeed."

Victim Participation in Sentencing

In the 1980s, a significant issue was raised in Western legal systems: the right of victims to participate in the trial, typically through **victim impact statements.** Proponents of this reform argued that integrating victims into the court system and guaranteeing their right to that involvement would recognize victims' wishes for status in court proceedings (Hall 1991). Others added that recognizing victims would increase their dignity, underscore that real individuals had suffered at the hands of a criminal, and promote fairness by giving victims the right to be heard in court (Henderson 1985; Kelly 1984; Sumner 1987).

Opponents of this reform argued that establishing victims' rights would challenge the very basis of the adversarial legal system—in particular, the idea that crime is a violation against the state rather than against an individual (Ashworth 1993). Others pointed out that recognizing victims in our legal system would place too much pressure on the judge, promote vindictiveness on the part of the victims, and lead to more court delays, longer trials, substantial increases in legal costs to the state, and disparity in sentencing. Some noted that judges themselves are reluctant to consider the feelings and concerns of victims when it comes to sentencing offenders. The courtroom is their domain, and while outsiders can inform the judiciary of their experiences, there is no guarantee that the victims will have any influence on its decisions (Grabosky 1987; Miers 1992; Rubel 1986).

Since 1989, when the federal government enacted Bill C-89, victims in Canada have had the right to file a victim impact statement (see Exhibit 9.4). In this document, they detail the effects of the crime on them. This statement is forwarded to the judge for consideration in sentencing. These forms are an attempt to bring victims into the criminal justice system by allowing them an

In May 1988, Parliament passed Bill C-89, which addressed victims' rights. These rights are defined as follows:

1. A victim has the right to be treated with courtesy, compassion, dignity and respect for the privacy of the victim;

    • the right to access social, legal, medical, and mental health services that are responsive to the needs of the victims' dependants, spouse or guardian; and
    • the right to have property stolen from a victim returned to the victim as soon as possible.

2. Subject to the limits imposed by the availability of resources and to any other limits that are reasonable in the circumstances of each case, a victim has the right to be informed of:
    (i)   the name of the accused,
    (ii)   the specific offence with which the accused is charged,
    (iii) the scope, nature, timing and progress of prosecution of the offence,
    (iv)   the role of the victim and other persons involved in the prosecution of other offence and of any opportunity to make representations on restitution and the impact of the offence on the victim,
    (v)   court procedures, and
    (vi)   crime prevention measures;

    • the right to be informed by law enforcement, court, health and social services personnel, at the earliest possible opportunity of the services, remedies and mechanisms to obtain remedies available to a victim and;
    • while waiting to give evidence at a proceeding in respect to an offence, the right to be kept apart, where necessary, from the accused and the accused's witnesses to ensure the safety of the victim, and the victim's family and to protect them from intimidation and retaliation.

On April 15, 1999, amendments were tabled to the Criminal Code that strengthened the rights of victims of crime in the criminal justice system:

• ensure that victims are informed of their opportunity to prepare a victim impact statement at the time of sentencing;
• ensure that victims have the choice to read the victim statement aloud;
• require that victim impact statements be considered by courts and Review Boards following a verdict of not criminally responsible on account of mental disorder;
• extend to victims of sexual or violent crime up to age 18 protections that restrict personal cross-examination by self-represented accused persons;
• require police officers and judges to consider the victim's safety in all bail decisions;
• allow victims and witnesses with a mental or physical disability to have a support person present when giving testimony; and
• make it easier for victims and witnesses to participate in trials by permitting the judge to ban publication of their identity where it is necessary for the proper administration of justice.

opportunity to influence sentencing, either through a written statement or by speaking before a judge in the courtroom. By this means, a victim can tell the court about the impact of the crime and in some cases recommend a sentence.

The impact of such statements on sentencing is largely unknown, since judges rarely allude to them. However, some judges have made it a habit to mention them in certain cases, especially when there were aggravating circumstances in the offence that severely traumatized the victim. In this situation, some judges have handed down tougher sentences.

During the 1980s and 1990s, provincial governments across Canada passed victims' rights legislation.

The first jurisdiction in Canada to introduce a Victims' Bill of Rights was Manitoba, in 1986. Since then, all other provinces and the federal government have passed victims' rights legislation. In June 1996, Ontario proclaimed Bill C-23, known as the Victims Bill of Rights. This bill outlined the principles and standards for the treatment of victims in the criminal justice system—for example, it allowed for greater access to information for the victim, for the right to have property involved in a criminal offence returned as quickly as possible, and for the victim's right to input during sentencing. The federal government expanded its legislation on victims in September 1996, when it passed Bill C-41. Amendments were made to the Criminal Code in 1999 that specifically codified the rights of victims of crime in order to increase their participation. This bill also made it possible for victim impact statements to be admitted during sentencing, provided for restitution to the victims, and enabled victims to attend some parole hearings (Bacchus 1999).

Prior to the 1999 amendments, researchers discovered that victim impact statements were not being used by victims in many cases. In 1988, a two-year study evaluating the use of victim impact statements in Winnipeg was published. The findings "revealed little of great significance, save for the opposition demonstrated by law enforcement and judicial officials to the introduction to these statements" (Young 2001, 24). Also in 1988, the federal justice department conducted a series of studies exploring their use in five Canadian cities. This report found that the use of victim impact statements varied hugely among cities, from a low of 14 percent of cases to a high of 83 percent. Around this time, Giliberti (1990) conducted a six-city study that examined various aspects of victim impact statements and their use in the courts.

Part of Giliberti's study evaluated the effect of victim impact statements on victims. To their surprise, the researchers found that these statements made no difference to victims' degree of satisfaction with the justice system. According to the victims, the most important feature of the program was that it enabled them to discuss the offence and its effects and to have this information given to the court. The program also provided them with useful feedback about the case as it progressed through the system, and allowed them to contact someone should they experience any difficulties. But it was also reported that the impact of this program was the same for participants and non-participants in terms of the level of their participation in the criminal justice system. Involvement in the program made no difference regarding satisfaction with how the case was handled or the likelihood of reporting future incidents to the police. It was found that most victims held negative attitudes toward sentencing both before and after their cases were heard.

The effect of victim impact statements on the criminal justice system varied across the six cities that Giliberti studied. For example, in Victoria, British Columbia, few victim impact statements were used in court when their use was controlled by prosecutorial discretion. Prosecutors indicated that they did not use them because they contained no new information, because too many were vague or contained largely irrelevant information, because they were of doubtful accuracy, and because they contributed to higher operating costs of the criminal justice system. In Toronto, prosecutors felt that victim impact statements could play a significant role in court,

and as a result two-thirds of the victim impact statements in Toronto were entered into court trials as exhibits and one-third were used as Crown submissions.

For all Crown prosecutors, victim impact statements had the greatest impact in sexual assault and sexual abuse cases. Also, these statements were considered helpful in raising prosecutors' awareness of the long-term emotional impact on victims—an impact that had not been captured in other documents available to prosecutors (Roberts 1992, 67). Victim statements had some impact on judges. Thirteen judges responded to the question "Have victim impact statements actually affected sentences that you have passed?" Seven of them said yes, six answered no. However, in British Columbia, Roberts (ibid., 77) reported a "minor change" in sentences imposed by judges in cases where a victim impact statement was used, while "occasionally sentences have been dramatically higher." According to Roach (1999, 291), these low rates of victim participation indicated that victim impact statements "have not emerged as a major criminal justice issue" in this country and that these low rates of participation may be the result of victims' reluctance "to expose their suffering to adversarial challenge."

Roberts and Edgar (2006) researched the perceptions and experiences of judges in three Canadian provinces concerning victim impact statements in their courtrooms. Their survey focused upon two questions relating to the use of victim impact statements in Canada: (1) do victim impact statements serve a useful purpose at sentencing? and (2) have the reforms made in the late 1990s had an impact on the participation of the victim in the sentencing process? The researchers reported that judges had responded positively to both of these questions. According to Roberts and Edgar (ibid., 27), there is little doubt that judges "found victim impact statements to represent a unique source of information that is relevant to the principles of sentencing." In addition, the researchers found that victim impact statements were used only in a minority of case proceeding to sentencing. They were unable to conclude that these low participation rates were the result of decisions made by the victims or for reasons related to the administration of justice. It is clear, however, that judges do not need victim impact statements in minor cases in order to determine the impact of a crime upon a victim (D'Avignon 2001) A minority of the participating judges indicated were not supportive of victims attempting to influence their sentencing decisions. Any recommendations made by victims about sentencing are to be through the Crown prosecutor's sentencing recommendations rather than the victim impact statement itself.

MANDATORY MINIMUM SENTENCING LAWS: DO THEY ACHIEVE THEIR GOALS?

At the present time in Canada, there are approximately 40 to 45 mandatory minimum sentences. They can be placed into four different categories: first and second degree murder (first introduced in 1976), firearms offences (originally introduced in 1995), sexual offences involving children (first enacted in 2005), and breaking and entering (originally introduced in 2008). In addition, there are a number of other offences, such as impaired driving, child prostitution, and betting, that have mandatory minimum sentences if the offender has a prior conviction for the same offence.

Under mandatory minimum sentencing laws, offenders are required to spend some time (the mandatory minimum amount of time specified by law) incarcerated in a correctional facility. Under mandatory minimum sentences, the laws remove both judges' and correctional officials' discretionary powers. Judges are unable to hand out a sentence that doesn't include the length of time to be served by the law (e.g., probation). In *R. v. Ferguson* (2008), the Supreme Court of Canada, in a 9–0 ruling, upheld Parliament's right to create mandatory minimum sentences and to have them enforced by judges (Foot 2008, A4). According to Chief Justice Beverley McLachlin, the law "mandates a floor below which judges cannot go. To go below this floor on a case-by-case basis runs counter to the clear wording of the sections and the intent that it evinces" (Makin 2008b, A9). This decision continues previous rulings made by the Supreme Court and provincial courts of appeal. In *R. v. Morrissey* (2000), the Supreme Court also upheld the mandatory minimum sentence of four years' imprisonment for a death caused by criminal negligence and a firearm. In 2007, a special five-judge panel of the Ontario Court of Appeal ruled in *R. v. Panday* (2007) that judges cannot undercut mandatory minimum sentences by showing leniency to the accused who "lived under virtual house arrest awaiting their trials" (Makin 2007, A11). Not everyone is supportive of these decisions, as one observer stated that they may lead to unjust decisions by the courts in exceptional cases (Roach 2008: 4).

According to the U.S. Sentencing Commission (1991), the principles of mandatory minimum sentences include the following:

- *Equality.* Similar offences receive similar sentences.
- *Certainty.* Offenders and the public know that offenders will serve the minimum prison time that the law prescribes.

- *Just deserts.* Dangerous offenders and criminals who use guns deserve mandatory long prison terms.
- *Deterrence.* Mandatory prison sentences deter crime by sending the strong message that those who "do the crime" really will "do the time."
- *Incapacitation.* Mandatory prison terms protect public safety by locking up dangerous offenders and criminals who use guns.

One goal of mandatory minimum sentences is that designated crimes will receive harsher punishments in order that selected offenders (e.g., dangerous offenders and criminals who use guns) can't harm law-abiding members of society when they are locked up in a prison. Another goal is deterrence: the knowledge that committing a crime with a mandatory minimum sentence will lead to a certain and severe punishment that will deter individuals from committing a crime.

Do mandatory minimum sentences achieve these goals? It seems logical that they would, and such laws have been extremely popular in the United States. Most of these laws were introduced in the United States starting in the 1970s, and some of the original statutes dealt with the use of selling drugs. Perhaps the best known mandatory minimum sentencing law is New York's drug law, introduced in 1972. Under these laws, the possession of or sale of heroin or other narcotics was punished by mandatory minimum prison sentences of one to fifteen years, with maximum sentences ranging up to life imprisonment. If they were released, offenders were placed on parole for the rest of their lives, and pleas to lesser charges were not allowed. The New York City Bar Association studied the impact of this law on drug offences. Researchers compared arrests, indictments, and convictions in 1973 (a year prior to the law being passed) with 1975 (more than a year after the law had taken effect). Arrests had fallen by 20 percent, the rate of indictments had dropped from 39 percent to 27 percent, and the number of convictions had gone from 6,033 to 3,147 (Association of the Bar of the City of New York, 1977). It was not until March 2009 that these laws were repealed. (Peters 2009).

It is also argued that mandatory minimum sentencing laws have an incapacitation effect, specifically by removing from the streets those criminals who use guns. According to Tonry (1996), most of the mandatory minimum sentencing laws in the United States were introduced during the 1980s and early 1990s, and many of these statutes dealt with the use of firearms in serious crimes. Following is a review of selected American research into the use of mandatory minimum sentencing laws for gun-related crimes and the impact of those laws on crime.

Loftin and McDowell (1981) studied the effects of the Michigan firearms law, which required a two-year mandatory sentence for serious crimes committed with a firearm. In particular, they were interested in the impact of the new law on the certainty and severity of sentences as well as on the number of serious violent crimes in Detroit. As part of this new law, the Detroit prosecutor announced that the new policy would include a strictly enforced ban on plea bargaining in these cases. In their study of cases processed between 1976 and 1978, Loftin and McDowell found little change in either the certainty or the severity of sentences for firearms-related murders and armed robberies. However, they did find that the law significantly increased the expected sentences for firearms-related assault cases.

According to Loftin and McDowell, two factors explain their findings. First, the expected minimum sentence for murders and robberies did not increase because offenders convicted of these crimes were already receiving longer sentences. Second, the sentences increased for assaults because the sentences handed out prior to the new law had been lighter—probation and suspended sentences were typical. These shorter sentences were explained as the result of the relationship between the offender and victim. In many cases, the offender and victim knew each other, and as a result prosecutors regularly settled these cases with a plea bargain to a lesser offence. Based on their data, Loftin and McDowell concluded that the mandatory minimum sentencing laws associated with the new gun law did not significantly change the number or type of violent offences committed in Detroit.

Three years later, Loftin and McDowell (1984) published their study of the Florida felony firearm law, which mandated a three-year prison sentence for anyone possessing a firearm or attempting to commit any of 11 specified serious crimes. After analyzing the data for three Florida cities (Miami, Tampa, and Jacksonville), they concluded that the new law did not have a measurable deterrent effect on violent crime. These same two researchers studied the effect of a mandatory minimum sentencing law in Philadelphia and Pittsburgh, Pennsylvania, and reported that the new sentencing laws had reduced the number of homicides but that their effect on assaults and robberies was inconclusive.

Further analyses of the nationwide effects of mandatory minimum sentencing law in the United States have not reported any effects on crime prevention. Kleck (1991), in his study of 170 cities in 1980, found that the new laws were not related to the rates of homicide, assault, or robbery. And Marvell and Moody (1995) studied the effects of mandatory minimum sentencing laws on crime and prisons and reported little evidence to support the contention that such laws have any effects on either crime rates or firearm use. On the basis of these and other studies, the best that can be said about the impact of mandatory minimum sentencing laws on gun-related crime is that the findings are mixed, with some effects being found for certain offences but minimal effects for most crimes.

Evaluations of mandatory minimum sentencing laws have reported that their potential impacts are not as significant as supporters think they will be. This has been attributed to that fact that these laws, once passed, are generally altered by implementation practices, reinterpretation, changes in the legal statutes, court rulings, and the passage of subsequent legislation. Of these, most evaluations have pointed to adaptations to implementation practices by significant criminal justice actors as being the most common mechanism that alters the goals of mandatory minimum sentencing laws.

This process of adaptation is commonly referred to as "the law of criminal justice thermodynamics." Walker (2007, 62) refers to this as "an increase in the severity of the penalty will result in less frequent application of that penalty." An important corollary of this law is that "the less often a severe penalty is applied, the more arbitrary will be the occasions when it is applied." Walker uses the death penalty as an example, pointing out that since it is a severe penalty, it exerts "an enormous amount of pressure" on courtroom actors to avoid its application e.g., plea bargaining, reducing a charge, and appealing every possible issue.

Others have referred to another aspect of this process which they refer to as the "hydraulic displacement of discretion" or "system hydraulics"

Continued on next page

(Heumann and Loftin 1979; Miethe 1987). This refers to the fact that any change made within the criminal justice system will have an effect on the other components of the system. That is, the introduction of a sentencing reform such as a mandatory minimum sentencing law potentially affects not only the operation of the courts but the police and the correctional systems as well. Feeley (1983) points out that reforms in one area of the criminal justice system is likely to alter the operations in other areas of the system, leading to results other than those that were originally intended.

Three inter-related system-level effects have been found to be associated with the introduction of mandatory minimum sentences. These include a shift in the balance of courtroom power, increased prosecutorial authority, and changes in how plea bargains are made. It has been found that when mandatory sentencing laws are introduced, prosecutors find themselves with greater authority than all other system participants. In particular, prosecutors are now in a position to determine which cases will be prosecuted while judges lose much of their authority over sentencing. Some of the implications of this shift to greater prosecutorial authority include "decisions are no longer as public as was previous when judges were in authority; their decisions are rarely subject to review and do not occur in open court." The introduction of mandatory sentencing laws have also been found to give prosecutors enhanced plea bargaining powers, providing them "with a valuable tool with which to ensure that severe sanctions are imposed in appropriate cases" (Merritt et al., 2006, 12).

According to Feeley (1983), some of the important issues to consider when implementing mandatory minimum sentencing laws include the following:

- The importance of understanding and accepting the limitations of mandatory minimum sentencing law reforms—what can and cannot be accomplished.
- The need to understand the limitations of mandatory minimum sentencing laws that are inadequate in dealing with complex situations to which they must be applied.
- The dangers of creating laws for symbolic appeal than for actual effect.
- The importance of understanding criminal justice system dynamics and the interrelationships between the various actors before implementing reforms.

Questions

1. What plausible effects may result from removing sentencing discretion from judges in cases involving mandatory minimum punishments? What effects do you predict will happen?
2. Do you believe prosecutors should have more power to determine the outcome of cases than judges?
3. By removing discretionary powers from the courts in terms of mandatory minimum sentences, what might be the impact on prison populations?
4. Do you agree with the statement that mandatory minimum sentences are created for "show" in order to create a false sense of security for citizens?

SUMMARY

The sentencing of a convicted person is one of the most crucial decisions made in our criminal justice system. Canadian judges have considerable discretion in determining the length of a sentence, and their decisions reflect how they wish the accused to be punished. However, in most cases the decision of the judge is not final, since a parole board often decides to grant full parole before the sentence is completed.

Whatever the reason for a sentence, the objective is to reduce crime by incarcerating criminals and deterring others from committing crimes. The deterrence, selective incapacitation, rehabilitation, and justice models all differ from one another in terms of their approaches to dealing with offenders through sentencing.

The Canadian government has recently been attempting to emphasize the justice model. The Canadian Sentencing Commission was formed in 1987 to investigate problems with the current sentencing approach and to suggest alternative approaches that are both coherent and consistent. A number of significant problems have been identified in the sentencing patterns of judges. These problems include discrimination and disparity. This suggests why a structured approach to sentencing is favoured by some. In addition, alternative sanctions for Aboriginal people have been introduced in the hope that they will reduce the overrepresentation of Aboriginal people in correctional systems across Canada.

Discussion Questions

1. Why is sentencing considered by many to be the most critical phase in our system of justice?
2. What are some of the arguments for and against using factors other than the crime itself in deciding an appropriate sentence for a convicted offender?
3. Compare the different types of sentences affiliated with each of the different models of criminal justice. What are the benefits and disadvantages of each?
4. Are there any crimes for which the Canadian government should pass mandatory sentencing laws?
5. Should public opinion affect sentencing decisions made by judges?
6. Should Canada have a well-defined sentencing policy? If so, what would be the impact of such a policy?
7. Should victims play a larger role in the sentencing of offenders? How could victims be given a greater role?
8. What are the benefits and drawbacks of Aboriginal sentencing circles?
9. Should Canada reintroduce the death penalty as a sentence for first degree murder? Using the United States as your example, do you think that the death penalty deters crime? Explain your answer.
10. Why should compensation systems be developed to help victims of wrongful convictions?
11. What aspects of the criminal justice system would you change in an attempt to decrease wrongful convictions?

Suggested Readings

Makin, K. *Redrum the Innocent*, rev. ed. Toronto: Penguin, 1998.

Roberts, J., and D.P. Cole, eds. *Making Sense of Sentencing*. Toronto: University of Toronto Press, 1999.

Roberts, J., and L. Stalans. *Public Opinion, Crime and Criminal Justice*. Boulder, CO: Westview Press, 1997.

Sher, J. *"Until You Are Dead": Steven Truscott's Long Ride into History*. Toronto: Knopf Canada, 2001.

Tonry, M. *Sentencing Matters*. New York: Oxford University Press, 1996.

Walker, N. *Why Punish?* Oxford: Oxford University Press, 1991.

References

Anderson, P.R., and D.J. Newman. 1993. *Introduction to Criminal Justice*, 5th ed. Toronto: McGraw-Hill Ryerson.

Andrews, D.A., I. Zinger, R. Hoge, J. Bonta, P. Gendreau, and F. Cullen. 1990. "Does Correctional Treatment Work? A Clinically Relevant and Psychologically Informed Meta- Analysis." *Criminology* 28: 393–404.

Ashworth, A. 1993. "Victim Impact Statements and Sentencing." *Criminal Law Review:* 498–509.

Association of the Bar of the City of New York. 1977. *The Nation's Toughest Drug Law: Evaluating the New York Experience.* Washington, D.C.: Drug Abuse Council.

Bacchus, S. 1999. "The Role of Victims in the Sentencing Process." In J.V. Roberts and D.P. Cole, eds., *Making Sense of Sentencing.* Toronto: University of Toronto Press, pp. 217–29.

Bailey, I. 2000. "Woman Gets 10 Years for Death of Stepdaughter." *National Post,* August 12, A4.

Boldt, E.D., L. Hursch, S.D. Jonson, and K.W. Taylor. 1983. "Presentence Reports and the Incarceration of Natives." *Canadian Journal of Criminology,* 25: 269–76.

Bonta, J., G. Bourgon, R. Jesseman, and A.K. Yessine. 2005. *Presentence Reports in Canada 2005-03.* Ottawa: Public Safety and Emergency Preparedness Canada.

Brodeur, J.P., and J.V. Roberts 2002. "Taking Justice Seriously." *Canadian Criminal Law Review* 7: 77–91.

Canadian Sentencing Commission. 1987. *Sentencing Reform: A Canadian Approach.* Ottawa: Minister of Supply and Services.

Clairmont, D. 1996. "Alternative Justice Issues for Aboriginal Justice." *Journal of Legal Pluralism and Unofficial Law* 36: 125–58.

———. 1989. *Discrimination in Sentencing: Patterns of Sentencing for Assault Convictions.* Halifax: Royal Commission on the Donald Marshall, Jr., Prosecution.

Clairmont, D., W. Barnwell, and A. O'Malley. 1989. *Sentencing Disparity and Race in the Nova Scotia Criminal Justice System.* Halifax: Royal Commission on the Donald Marshall, Jr., Prosecution.

Clark, C. 2006. "Crackdown Takes Aim at Guns, Sentencing." *The Globe and Mail,* June 6, A1, A5.

Clear, T. 1980. *Harm in Punishment.* Boston, MA: Northeastern University Press.

Conway, C. 2007. "The DNA 200." *The New York Times,* May 20, 2007, A14.

D'Alessio, S.J., and L. Stolzenberg. 1995. "The Impact of Sentencing Guidelines on Jail Incarceration in Minnesota." *Criminology* 33: 283–302.

D'Avignon, J. 2001. *Victim Impact Statements: A Judicial Perspective.* Winnipeg: University of Manitoba.

Daubney, D., and G. Parry. 1999. "An Overview of Bill C-41 (The Sentencing Reform Act)." In J.V. Roberts and D.P. Cole, eds., *Making Sense of Sentencing.* Toronto: University of Toronto Press, pp. 31–47.

Department of Justice. 2006. *Minister of Justice Proposes Tougher Mandatory Minimum Prison Sentences for Gun Crime.* Ottawa: Department of Justice Canada. www.justice.gc.ca. Retrieved May 17, 2006.

———. 2005. *Fair and Effective Sentencing—A Canadian Approach to Sentencing Policy.* Ottawa: Department of Justice Canada. www.justice.gc.ca. Retrieved February 15, 2006.

Doob, A.N. 1992. "Community Sanctions and Imprisonment: Hoping for a Miracle but Not Bothering Even to Pray for It." *Canadian Journal of Criminology* 32: 415–28.

Doob, A.N., and C.M. Webster. 2006. "Countering Punitiveness: Understanding Stability in Canada's Imprisonment Rate." *Law & Society Review* 40: 325–65.

Durham, A. 1988. "The Justice Model in Historical Contexts: Early Law, the Emergence of Science, and the Rise of Incarceration." *Journal of Criminal Justice* 16: 331–46.

Edgar, A. 1999. "Sentencing Options in Canada." In J.V. Roberts and D.P. Cole, eds., *Making Sense of Sentencing*. Toronto: University of Toronto Press, pp. 122–36.

Ehrlich, I. 1975. "The Deterrent Effect of Capital Punishment: A Question of Life and Death." *American Economic Review* 65: 397–417.

"Equal under the Law." 1998. *National Post.* December 14, A15.

Fagan, J. 1989. "Cessation of Family Violence: Deterrence and Dissuasion." In L. Ohlin and M. Tonry, eds., *Crime and Justice: A Review of Research*, vol. 11. Chicago: University of Chicago Press, pp. 100–51.

Feeley, M. 1983. *Court Reform on Trial: Why Simple Solutions Fail*. New York: Basic Books, Inc.

Flanagan, T.J. 1996. "Reform or Punish: Americans' Views of the Correctional System." In T.J. Flanagan and D.R. Longmire, eds., *Americans View Crime and Justice: A National Public Opinion Survey*. Thousand Oaks, CA: Sage.

Foot, R. 2008. "Court Backs Minimum Sentences." *National Post*, March 1, A4.

Frase, R.S. 2005. "Sentencing Guidelines in Minnesota." In M. Tonry, ed., *Crime and Justice: A Review of Research*. Chicago: University of Chicago Press, pp. 131–219.

Gabor, T. 2002. *Mandatory Minimum Penalties: Their Effects on Crime, Sentencing Disparities, and Justice System Expenditures*. Ottawa: Department of Justice Canada.

Gabor, T., and C. H. S. Jayewardene. 1978. "The Pre-sentence Report as a Persuasive Communication." *Canadian Journal of Criminology*, 20, 18–27.

Giliberti, C. 1990. "Study Probes Effectiveness of Victim Impact Statements." *Justice Research Notes* 1: 1–8.

Grabosky, P.N. 1987. "Victims." In G. Zdenkowski, C. Ronalds, and M. Richardson, eds., *The Criminal Injustice System*, vol. 2. Sydney, Australia: Pluto Press, pp. 143–57.

Hagan, J. 1975. "The Social and Legal Construction of Criminal Justice: A Study of the Presentencing Process." *Social Problems*, 22, 620–37.

Hall, D.J. 1991. "Victim Voices in Criminal Court: The Need for Restraint." *American Criminal Law Review* 28: 233–66.

Hamilton, A., and C.M. Sinclair. 1991. *Report of the Aboriginal Justice Inquiry of Manitoba, vol. 1. The Justice System and Aboriginal People*. Winnipeg: Queen's Printer.

Hann, R., and W. Harman. 1992. *Predicting General Release Risk for Canadian Penitentiary Inmates*. Ottawa: Ministry of the Solicitor General.

Henderson, J.S.Y., and W.D. McClasin. 2005. "Exploring Justice as Healing." In W.D. McClasin, ed., *Justice as Healing: Indigenous Ways*. St. Paul, MN: Living Justice Press, pp. 3–9.

Henderson, L.N. 1985. "The Wrongs of Victims Rights." *Stanford Law Review* 37: 937–1021.

Heumann, M. and C. Loftin. 1979. Mandatory Sentencing and the Abolition of Plea Bargaining." *Law and Society Review* 13: 393–430.

Hogarth, J. 1971. *Sentencing as a Human Process*. Toronto: University of Toronto Press.

Huff, C.R. 2004. "Wrongful Convictions: The American Experience." *Canadian Journal of Criminology and Criminal Justice* 46: 107–20.

Huff, C.R., A. Rattner, and E. Sagarin. 1986. "Guilty until Proven Innocent: Wrongful Conviction and Public Policy." *Crime and Delinquency* 34: 518–44.

Humphreys, A. 2001. "Going Easy on Native Criminals a Mistake." *National Post*, March 28, A4.

Kaukinen, C., and S. Colavecchia. 1999. "Public Perceptions of the Courts: An Examination of Attitudes Toward the Treatment of Victims and Accused." *Canadian Journal of Criminology* 41: 365–84.

Kelly, D.P. 1984. "Victims' Perceptions of Criminal Justice." *Pepperdine Law Review* 11: 15–22.

Kleck, G. 1991. *Point Blank: Guns and Violence in America*. New York: Adline de Gruyter.

Kramer, J.H., R.L. Lubitz, and C.A. Kempinen. 1989. "Sentencing Guidelines: A Quantitative Comparison of Sentencing Policy in Minnesota, Pennsylvania, and Washington." *Justice Quarterly* 6: 565–88.

LaPrairie, C. 1998. "The 'New' Justice: Some Implications for Aboriginal Communities." *Canadian Journal of Criminology* 40: 61–79.

———. 1990. "The Role of Sentencing in the Overrepresentation of Aboriginal People in Correctional Institutions." *Canadian Journal of Criminology* 32: 429–40.

Lash, J. 2000. "Case Comment: *R. v. Gladue*." *Canadian Woman Studies* 20: 85–91.

Latimer, J., and N. Desjardins. 2007. *The 2007 National Justice Survey: Tackling Crime and Public Confidence*. Ottawa: Department of Justice.

Law Reform Commission of Canada. 1999. *From Restorative Justice to Transformative Justice*. Ottawa: Law Commission of Canada.

———. 1974. *Studies on Sentencing: Working Paper 3*. Ottawa: Information Canada.

Liebman, J.S., J. Fagan, V. West, and J. Lloyd. 2000. "Capital Attrition: Error Rates in Capital Cases, 1973–1995." *Texas Law Review* 78: 1839–65.

Loftin, C., and D. McDowell. 1984. "The Deterrent Effects of the Florida Felony Firearms Law." *Journal of Criminal Law and Criminology* 75: 250–59.

———. 1981. "'One with a Gun Gets You Two': Mandatory Sentencing and Firearms Violence in Detroit." *American Academy of Political and Social Sciences* 455: 150–67.

Loftus, E.F. 1979. *Eyewitness Testimony*. Cambridge, MA: Harvard University Press.

Loftus, E.F., and J. Doyle. 1991. *Eyewitness Testimony: Civil and Criminal*, 3rd ed. New York: Klouwer.

MacAfee, M. 2005. "Manitoba Review of Hair Evidence Turns up Little." *The Globe and Mail*, September 21, A5.

Makin, K. 2008a. "Deeply Flawed Coroner's Office Condemned." *The Globe and Mail*, October 2, A4.

———. 2008b. "Ruling Deals Blow to Mandatory Sentencing Exemption." *The Globe and Mail*, March 1, A9.

———. 2007. "'Bail Is Not Jail,' Ontario Appeal Court Rules." *The Globe and Mail*, September 12, A11.

———. 2006. "Prosecutors Must Share Blame for Botched Cases, Report Says." *The Globe and Mail*, June 22, A7.

———. 2004. "In the Back Halls of Justice." *The Globe and Mail*, April 26, F6, F7.

Manson, A. 2001. *The Law of Sentencing*. Toronto: Irwin Law.

Marth, M. 2008. *Adult Criminal Court Statistics 2006/07*. Ottawa: Canadian Centre for Justice Statistics.

Marvell, T., and C. Moody. 1995. "The Impact Study of the Enhanced Prison Terms for Felonies Committed with Guns." *Criminology* 33: 247–81.

Merritt, N., T. Fain, and S. Turner. 2006. "Oregon's Get Tough Sentencing Reform: A Lesson in the Justice System." *Criminology & Public Policy* 5: 5–36.

Miers, D. 1992. "The Responsibilities and the Rights of Victims of Crime." *Modern Law Review* 55: 482–505.

Miethe, T. 1987. "Charging and Plea Bargaining Practices under Determinate Sentencing: An Investigation of the Hydraulic Displacement of Discretion." *Criminology* 25: 155–76.

Miethe, T.D., and C.A. Moore. 1985. "Socioeconomic Disparities under Determinate Sentencing Systems: A Comparison of Preguideline and Postguideline Practices in Minnesota." *Criminology* 23: 337–64.

Native Law Centre. 2006. "Sentencing Circles: a General Overview and Guidelines." Saskatoon: University of Saskatchewan. www.usask.ca/nativelaw/publications. Retrieved January 15, 2006.

Packer, H.L. 1968. *The Limits of the Criminal Sanction*. Palo Alto, CA: Stanford University Press.

Palys, T.S., and S. Divorski. 1986. "Explaining Sentencing Disparity." *Canadian Journal of Criminology* 28, pp. 347–62.

Penrod, S. 2003. "Eyewitness Identification Evidence: How Well Are Witnesses Police Performing? *Criminal Justice* 18: 36–47.

Peters, J.W. 2009. "Legislation to Overhaul Rockefeller Drug Laws Moves Ahead Swiftly." *The New York Times*, March 1, 19.

Proulx, C. 2005. *Reclaiming Aboriginal Justice, Identity and Community*. Saskatoon, SK: Purich.

Quigley, T. 1994. "Some Issues in the Sentencing of Aboriginal Offenders." In R. Gosse, J.Y. Henderson, and R. Carter, eds., *Continuing Poundmaker and Riel's Request*. Saskatoon: Purich, pp. 269–98.

Radelet, M.L., H.A. Bedau, and C. Putnam. 1992. *In Spite of Innocence*. Boston, MA: Northeastern University Press.

Renner, K., and A. Warner. 1981. "The Standard of Social Justice Applied to an Evaluation of Criminal Cases Appearing before the Halifax Courts." *Windsor Yearbook of Access to Justice* 1: 62–80.

Roach, K. 2008. "The Future of Mandatory Minimum Sentences after the Death of Constitutional Exceptions." *The Criminal Law Quarterly*, 54: 1–4.

———. 1999. *Due Process and Victim's Rights: The New Law and Politics of Criminal Justice*. Toronto: University of Toronto Press.

Roberts, J.V. 2001. "Sentencing, Parole and Psychology." In R.A. Schueller and J.R.P. Ogloff, eds., *Introduction to Psychology and Law: Canadian Perspectives*. Toronto: University of Toronto Press, pp. 188–213.

———. 1988. "Public Opinion about Sentencing: Some Popular Myths." *Justice Report* 5: 7–9.

Roberts, J.V., and A. Birkenmayer. 1997. "Sentencing in Canada: Recent Statistical Trends." *Canadian Journal of Criminology* 39: 459–82.

Roberts, J.V., and D.P. Cole. 1999. "Introduction to Sentencing and Parole." In J.V. Roberts and D.P. Cole, eds., *Making Sense of Sentencing*. Toronto: University of Toronto Press, pp. 3–30.

Roberts, J.V., and A.N. Doob. 1989. "Sentencing and Public Opinion: Taking False Shadows for True Substances." *Osgoode Hall Law Journal* 27: 491–515.

Roberts, J.V., and A. Edgar. 2006. *Victim Impact Statements at Sentencing: Judicial Experiences and Perceptions: A Survey of Three Jurisdictions.* Ottawa: Department of Justice.

Roberts, J.V., and C. LaPrairie. 1996. "Circle Sentencing: Some Unanswered Questions." *Criminal Law Quarterly* 39: 319–55.

Roberts, J.V., and A. von Hirsch. 1999. "Legislating the Purpose and Principles of Sentencing." In J.V. Roberts and D.P. Cole, eds., *Making Sense of Sentencing.* Toronto: University of Toronto Press, pp. 48–62.

Roberts, T. 1992. *Assessment of the Victim Impact Statement Program in British Columbia.* Ottawa: Department of Justice, Research and Sentencing Directorate.

Rubel, H.C. 1986. "Victim Participation in Sentencing Proceedings." *Criminal Law Quarterly* 28: 226–50.

Scheck, B.C., P.J. Neufeld, and J. Dwyer. 2000. *Actual Innocence.* New York: Doubleday.

Seeman, N. 2001. "Two Kinds of Justice Is No Justice at All." *The Globe and Mail,* December 6, A23.

Sherman, L.W., and R. Berk. 1984. "The Specific Deterrent Effects of Arrest for Domestic Assault." *American Sociological Review* 49: 261–72.

Smith, G. 2004. "Faulty Hair Analysis of Hair Samples Sparks Calls for Case Reviews." *The Globe and Mail,* September 16, A7.

Stuart, D., and R.J. Delisle. 1995. *Learning Canadian Criminal Law,* 5th ed. Toronto: Carswell.

Sumner, C.J. 1987. "Victim Participation in the Criminal Justice System." *Australian and New Zealand Journal of Criminology* 20: 195–217.

Tonry, M. 1996. *Sentencing Matters.* New York: Oxford University Press.

U.S. Sentencing Commission. 1991. *Mandatory Minimum Penalties in the Federal Criminal Justice System.* Washington, D.C.: U.S. Sentencing Commission.

Walgrave, L. 2005. "Towards Restoration as the Mainstream in Youth Justice." In E. Elliott and R. Gordon, eds., *New Directions in Restorative Justice: Issues, Practice, Evaluation.* Cullompton, Devon: Willan, pp. 3–25.

Walker, S. 2007. *Sense and Nonsense about Crime and Drugs: A Policy Guide,* 6th ed. Belmont, CA: Wadsworth.

Wheeler, G., and R. Hissong. 1988. "Effects of Sanctions on Drunk Drivers: Beyond Incarceration." *Crime and Delinquency* 34: 29–42.

White, R., and F. Haines. 2002. *Crime and Criminology: An Introduction.* New York: Oxford University Press.

Williams, T. 1999. "Sentencing Black Offenders in Ontario." In J.V. Roberts and D.P. Cole, eds., *Making Sense of Sentencing.* Toronto: University of Toronto Press, pp. 200–16.

York, P. 1995. *The Aboriginal Federal Offender: A Comparative Analysis between Aboriginal and Non-Aboriginal Offenders.* Ottawa: Correctional Services Canada.

Young, A.N. 2001. *The Role of the Victim in the Criminal Process: A Literature Review—1989 to 1999.* Ottawa: Department of Justice Canada.

Zamble, E. 1990. "Public Support for Criminal Justice Policies: Some Specific Findings." *Forum on Corrections Research* 2: 14–19.

Zedlewski, E.W. 1987. *Making Confinement Decisions.* Washington, DC: Government Printing Office.

Court Cases

R. v. Ferguson (2008), S.C.C. 6

R. v. Gladue (1999), 1 S.C.R. 688

R. v. Joseyounen (1995), 6 W.W.R. 438

R. v. Morin (1995), 9 W.W.R. 696

R. v Morrissey (2000), S.C.R. 90

R. v. Moses (1992), 11 C.R. (4th) 357

P. v. Panday (2007), Ont. C.A. 597

R. v. Priest (1996), 110 C.C.C. (3d) 289 (Ont. C.A.)

Weblinks

For one of the most controversial cases in Canada dealing with the issue of whether an accused could sue the government for malicious prosecution, read the Supreme Court's judgment in *Nelles v. Ontario* (1989). Go to http://scc.lexum.umontreal.ca/en/index.html, then click on 1989, Volume 2. This decision was announced on August 14, 1989. To read about the cases concerning circle sentencing mentioned in the text, specifically about *R. v. Morin* (1995), go to http://www.usask.ca/nativelaw/publications/jah/morin.html. To read the judgment in *R. v. Moses*, go to http://www.usask.ca/nativelaw/factums/moses.html.

CHAPTER 1

Alternatives to Prison: Probation, Conditional Sentences, and Intermediate Sanctions

CHAPTER OBJECTIVES

✓ Outline the major forms of intermediate sanctions: intensive supervision programs, home confinement and electronic monitoring, and day fines.

✓ Evaluate whether the goals of intermediate sanction programs—reducing prison populations and prison costs and increasing safety—are being achieved.

✓ Discuss whether deterrence-based programs work.

✓ Consider whether intermediate punishment sanctions would be beneficial if introduced in Canada.

✓ Discuss the importance of alternatives to prisons and how they affect the number of individuals incarcerated in Canada.

✓ Discuss why drug treatment courts have been introduced, and some of the obstacles they face.

T his chapter reviews the main alternatives to imprisonment used in Canada and in other Western nations today: probation, conditional sentences, and three types of intermediate punishment—intensive supervision probation, home confinement and electronic monitoring, and day fines. The main purpose of community correctional services is to administer and monitor diversion programs, pretrial supervision, and community-based sentences. Community correctional services are also responsible for a number of additional justice activities that best fit within the community corrections context; these include drafting pre-sentence reports and operating fine option programs (Calverley and Beattie 2005). Many of these programs are available across Canada, but in some jurisdictions a number of these programs are either not available or of limited availability.

Both probation and conditional sentences are forms of community-based sanctions. Probation has existed in Canada for more than a century; conditional sentences were not implemented until 1996 as part of the package of reforms proclaimed when Bill C-41 was passed (see Chapter 9). Intermediate punishments have been used in the United States for quite some time and are starting to appear (or to be considered) in Canada. For example, most provinces now have some form of intensive supervision probation, and three provinces have published the results of their pilot projects on home confinement and electronic monitoring. This chapter also reviews intermediate punishment programs in the United States, providing us with some basis for judging them and for deciding whether they are appropriate for Canada.

On August 12, 2008, the then-Minister of Public Safety, Stockwell Day, announced a pilot electronic monitoring (EM) program that would monitor 30 federal offenders in Ontario after they were paroled from a federal correctional facility. Mr. Day announced that the parolees would wear ankle bracelets equipped with Global Positioning System (GPS) receivers, and would be used on "high-risk" parolees who pose a threat of violence. He also stated that the federal government wanted "to make sure that people who have a history of violent reoffending or reoffending of sexual offences are properly monitored" (Tibbetts 2008, A41). This new program represents a change of federal policy towards the use of EM. In the past, EM had been rarely used by federal authorities. One example when it was used was when Adil Charkaoui, a terror suspect, was fitted with an EM device as per a court-ordered condition.

The GPS system would alert federal officials monitoring the program when an offender violates conditions of parole, such as curfews, restraining orders, or being too close to certain designated places, such as a school. The federal program is modelled on the Province of Nova Scotia's EM system.

PROBATION

Probation is based on the idea that some offenders are not actually dangerous criminals who threaten society. A judge gives probation at the sentencing, after suspending the offender's sentence; however, a judge cannot suspend a sentence for an offence that has a specified minimum punishment. A probation order can be imposed either as a single sentence or as a "split sentence." With the latter, an offender is required to complete another punishment (e.g., pay a fine or serve a period of time not exceeding two years) before going on probation. In Canada, probation is a required accompaniment to a suspended sentence or conditional discharge.

For adult offenders, the maximum length of a probation order is three years. Marth (2008) reports that the proportion of offenders receiving probation as part of their sentence has increased over the past decade. In 2006–07, 43 percent of all guilty persons received probation; ten years ago that figure was only 37 percent. He also notes that the mean length of probation orders stayed relatively stable over time, at about 455 days. Belanger (2001) found that during 1999–2000, probation was used in 40 percent of all single-conviction cases and 49 percent of all multiple-conviction cases (i.e., cases resulting in two or more sentences). At that time in cases involving a single conviction, the average sentence length was 434 days. When probation was used for cases involving more than one conviction, the average sentence length was longer (556 days).

Probation typically involves an offender being released into the community under the supervision of a provincial probation service. It is, in essence, a contract between an offender and the state in which the former promises to abide by the conditions mandated by the court. If the offender breaks the conditions of probation, a federal statute, or the Criminal Code, a breach of probation has occurred and he or she is guilty of an offence (s.733 [1] of the Criminal Code). Mandatory conditions of probation include remaining within a particular jurisdiction, reporting to a probation officer as required, keeping the peace, keeping authorities informed about changes of residence, refraining from contact with criminal associates, and notifying the court or probation officer of any change in employment or occupation (s. 732.1[2] of the Criminal Code). The court may impose other conditions deemed reasonable "for protecting society and for facilitating the offender's successful reintegration into the community" (s. 732.1[3][h]). Optional conditions may include drug counselling, avoiding contact with children (e.g., if a child molester is placed on probation), or performing a specified community service order. It is noteworthy that reporting to a probation officer is also an optional condition of probation (s. 732.1 [3][a] of the Criminal Code). In the event of a new offence, the court may revoke the probation order and, in the case of a suspended sentence, impose any sentence that could have been handed out if the sentence had not been suspended. Alternatively, the court may make changes to the optional conditions as deemed by the court (s. 733.2[5][d][e]).

Judges have considerable discretion when determining whether to give probation. Section 731 of the Criminal Code states:

> Where an accused is convicted of an offence, the court may, having regard to the age and character of the accused, the nature of the offence and the circumstances surrounding the commission
>
> (a) . . . suspend the passing of sentence and direct that the accused be released on the conditions prescribed in a probation order.

Probation has been the most common community-based punishment, and it is constantly being revised. For example, when Bill C-41 (see Chapter 9) was proclaimed, it included probation as a punishment for firearm offences. Section 100 of the Criminal Code provides for prohibition orders against the possession of firearms, ammunition, or explosive devices. These orders are imposed on offenders who have been convicted or discharged in connection with offences involving violence, threats of violence, or firearms. Courts are now required (s. 731.1) to consider Section 100 of the Criminal Code before imposing a probation order (Daubney and Parry 1999).

Bill C-41 also made allowances for the long-term supervision (sometimes referred to as "super-probation") of certain offenders in the community (see Chapter 3). Section 753.1 of the Criminal Code focuses on individuals whom the courts find to be dangerous offenders. A judge who decides that there is a possibility that an offender will be a high-risk threat to the safety of a community, or that they might re-offend once released, can order the offender to be placed on probation while in the community for a period of up to ten years. The supervision may be attached to parole, and would begin after parole has been successfully completed.

The Use of Probation as a Sanction

Probation is the most common form of community sanction in Canada. Of the 242,988 accused found guilty in adult criminal court during 2006–07, 105,415 (43 percent) were handed down sentences involving probation. Probation was most likely to be part of a sentence in the category of crimes against the person (73 percent), compared to 54 percent of offenders in the category of crimes against property and 49 percent in the category of "other" Criminal Code. As Table 10.1 indicates, the most common offence in the category of crimes against the person where probation was used was criminal harassment (stalking), at 87 percent; common assault and uttering threats had probation orders attached to the sentence 78 percent and 76 percent of the time, respectively. The most common offences in the category of crimes against property in which a probation order was used were mischief (66 percent) and break and enter (61 percent). In the category of "other" Criminal Code, the most common use of probation was for weapons possession (52 percent). During 2006–07, the most common length of probation was 6 to 12 months (51 percent of guilty cases with probation) (Marth 2008) (see Figure 10.1).

Eligibility for Probation

Many people believe that probation is granted to first-time offenders who commit minor property offences. However, probation is commonly given to individuals convicted of violent offences. There are two reasons why most violent criminals are given a sentence of probation: (1) the violent crimes that most commonly receive probation are less serious and therefore warrant a lenient response, and (2) the offender's prior criminal record suggests this is appropriate. Regarding (1), according to Roberts (1999), over 67 percent of all violent crimes are considered relatively minor. Regarding (2), the accused's prior criminal record has a strong impact on sentencing patterns. Roberts (ibid., 95) points out that "property offenders are more likely to have prior convictions than violent offenders [and] are more likely to have been sentenced to probation in the past. This may discourage judges from imposing probation on this second (or third) occasion."

Studies of probation orders indicate that offenders are increasingly being sentenced to probation and that probation terms are growing longer. In 2006–07, for example, nine offences had a median probation sentence of 18 months or longer, almost the same number for each year since 2002–03 (see Table 10.2). The offences that led to long probation orders tended to be serious, and probation was usually imposed in combination with incarceration. Certain violent crimes (e.g., attempted murder, robbery, sexual assault, and sexual abuse) are given the longest probation terms, usually around two years. Two other violent offences—criminal harassment and

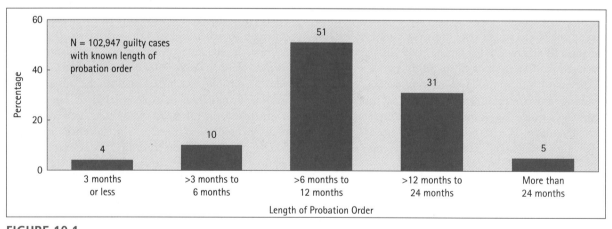

FIGURE 10.1

Guilty Cases by Length of Probation for the Most Serious Offence in the Case, Canada, 2006–2007

Notes: Due to rounding, percentages may not add to 100. Excludes cases where the length of probation sentence was unknown (2% or 2,468 cases). Coverage for Adult Criminal Court Survey data as of 2006/2007 is estimated at 98% of caseload. *Source:* Michael Marth "Adult Criminal Court Statistics, 2006/2007" *Juristat*, Vol. 28, no. 5, p. 8. Statistics Canada catalogue no. 85-002-XIE.

TABLE 10.1 Convicted Cases by Type of Sentence for the Most Serious Offence in the Case, Canada, 2006/2007

Offence Category	Guilty Cases	Type of Sentence for Most Serious Offence							
		Prison		Conditional Sentence[1]		Probation		Fine	
	number	number	percent	number	percent	number	percent	number	percent
Total offences	**242,988**	**83,043**	**34.2**	**9,878**	**4.1**	**105,415**	**43.4**	**73,513**	**30.3**
Criminal Code total	214,163	75,460	35.2	8,008	3.7	96,967	45.3	60,218	28.1
Crimes against the person	**48,329**	**15,111**	**31.3**	**2,581**	**5.3**	**35,126**	**72.7**	**4,160**	**8.6**
Homicide	140	115	82.1	3	2.1	12	8.6	0	0.0
Attempted murder	43	30	69.8	1	2.3	7	16.3	1	2.3
Robbery	2,900	2,249	77.6	245	8.4	1,322	45.6	15	0.5
Sexual assault	1,519	753	49.6	244	16.1	999	65.8	52	3.4
Other sexual offences	722	448	62.0	100	13.9	483	66.9	12	1.7
Major assault	10,536	4,485	42.6	937	8.9	7,119	67.6	925	8.8
Common assault	21,837	3,519	16.1	661	3.0	16,953	77.6	2,227	10.2
Uttering threats	8,021	2,623	32.7	257	3.2	6,131	76.4	786	9.8
Criminal harassment	1,459	392	26.9	59	4.0	1,264	86.6	82	5.6
Other crimes against the person	1,152	497	43.1	74	6.4	836	72.6	60	5.2
Crimes against property	**59,318**	**24,273**	**40.9**	**3,112**	**5.2**	**31,991**	**53.9**	**9,329**	**15.7**
Theft	25,119	9,940	39.6	1,100	4.4	12,219	48.6	4,980	19.8
Break and enter	8,293	5,031	60.7	691	8.3	5,015	60.5	340	4.1
Fraud	10,001	3,580	35.8	870	8.7	6,030	60.3	1,207	12.1
Mischief	7,665	1,624	21.2	109	1.4	5,057	66.0	1,387	18.1
Possess stolen property	7,768	3,877	49.9	283	3.6	3,404	43.8	1,354	17.4
Other property crimes	472	221	46.8	59	12.5	266	56.4	61	12.9
Administration of justice	**46,415**	**22,270**	**48.0**	**917**	**2.0**	**14,045**	**30.3**	**11,213**	**24.2**
Fail to appear	2,646	1,136	42.9	50	1.9	587	22.2	774	29.3
Breach of probation	21,750	11,235	51.7	563	2.6	7,489	34.4	4,659	21.4
Unlawfully at large	1,969	1,579	80.2	24	1.2	305	15.5	170	8.6
Fail to comply with order	18,476	7,833	42.4	195	1.1	4,864	26.3	5,282	28.6
Other administration of justice	1,574	487	30.9	85	5.4	800	50.8	328	20.8
Other *Criminal Code*	**19,608**	**7,030**	**35.9**	**626**	**3.2**	**9,676**	**49.3**	**4,495**	**22.9**
Weapons	5,440	2,092	38.5	240	4.4	2,815	51.7	1,117	20.5
Prostitution	774	159	20.5	16	2.1	357	46.1	208	26.9
Disturbing the peace	1,344	182	13.5	4	0.3	629	46.8	484	36.0
Residual *Criminal Code*	12,050	4,597	38.1	366	3.0	5,875	48.8	2,686	22.3
Criminal Code traffic	**40,493**	**6,776**	**16.7**	**772**	**1.9**	**6,129**	**15.1**	**31,021**	**76.6**
Impaired driving	32,594	3,319	10.2	296	0.9	3,664	11.2	27,904	85.6
Other *Criminal Code* traffic	7,889	3,457	43.8	476	6.0	2,465	31.2	3,117	39.5
Other federal statute total	**28,825**	**7,583**	**26.3**	**1,870**	**6.5**	**8,448**	**29.3**	**13,295**	**46.1**
Drug possession	7,628	1,210	15.9	81	1.1	2,342	30.7	3,818	50.1
Drug trafficking	6,051	2,896	47.9	1,733	28.6	1,693	28.0	535	8.8
Youth Criminal Justice Act/Young Offenders Act	817	263	32.2	11	1.3	273	33.4	264	32.3
Residual federal statutes	14,329	3,214	22.4	45	0.3	4,140	28.9	8,678	60.6

0 true zero or a value rounded to zero

1 in 2006/2007, conditional sentencing data were not available for Quebec.

Notes: The sentence types presented are not mutually exclusive and will not add to 100. Probation tools include mandatory probation for cases given a conditional discharge (C.C.C. s.730(1)) or a suspended sentence (C.C.C. s.731(1)(a)). In Quebec, most drug offences are recorded under residual federal statutes, resulting in an undercount of drug possession and drug trafficking cases and an overcount of residual federal statute cases. Coverage for Adult Criminal Court Survey data as of 2006/20007 is estimated at 98% of adult court caseload.

Source: Michael Marth "Adult Criminal Court Statistics, 2006/2007" *Juristat*, Vol. 28, no. 5, p. 15. Statistics Canada catalogue no. 85-002-XIE.

TABLE 10.2 Guilty Cases by Mean and Median Length of Probation Sentence, Ten Provinces and Territories, 2002/2003 to 2006/2007

Offence Category	2002/2003 Mean	2002/2003 Median	2003/2004 Mean	2003/2004 Median	2004/2005 Mean	2004/2005 Median	2005/2006 Mean	2005/2006 Median	2006/2007 Mean	2006/2007 Median
					days					
Total offences	**451**	**365**	**452**	**365**	**453**	**365**	**455**	**365**	**453**	**365**
Criminal Code total	**452**	**365**	**451**	**365**	**454**	**365**	**454**	**365**	**453**	**365**
Crimes against the person	**483**	**365**	**482**	**365**	**486**	**365**	**484**	**365**	**482**	**365**
Homicide	802	730	760	730	902	1,095	718	730	829	730
Attempted murder	760	730	732	730	834	1,095	867	730	991	1,095
Robbery	651	730	674	730	682	730	687	730	679	730
Sexual assault	634	540	645	720	652	730	657	730	679	730
Other sexual offences	760	730	761	730	767	730	786	730	784	730
Major assault	507	365	500	365	516	365	518	365	516	365
Common assault	410	365	407	365	412	365	410	365	409	365
Uttering threats	506	365	507	365	503	365	501	365	499	365
Criminal harassment	640	720	629	545	621	545	626	545	602	545
Other crimes against the person	599	540	611	545	601	545	618	545	608	545
Crimes against property	**448**	**365**	**447**	**365**	**448**	**365**	**448**	**365**	**447**	**365**
Theft	402	365	405	365	406	365	407	365	403	365
Break and enter	555	540	551	540	559	540	560	540	559	540
Fraud	492	365	492	365	489	365	483	365	490	365
Mischief	384	360	382	365	386	365	393	365	396	365
Possess stolen property	426	365	425	365	433	365	434	365	429	365
Other property crimes	569	540	524	365	529	365	501	365	569	540
Administration of justice	**393**	**365**	**391**	**365**	**392**	**365**	**395**	**365**	**390**	**365**
Fail to appear	318	360	334	360	320	365	346	365	335	365
Breach of probation	399	365	397	365	407	365	409	365	404	365
Unlawfully at large	375	365	393	365	408	365	387	365	394	365
Fail to comply with order	382	360	376	360	364	365	366	365	364	365
Other administration of justice	446	365	442	365	440	365	472	365	457	365
Other *Criminal Code*	**464**	**365**	**462**	**365**	**465**	**365**	**476**	**365**	**484**	**365**
Weapons	469	365	479	365	486	365	488	365	491	365
Prostitution	354	360	367	360	355	365	367	365	350	365
Disturbing the peace	321	360	316	360	309	365	310	363	320	365
Residual *Criminal Code*	489	365	482	365	484	365	497	365	507	365
***Criminal Code* traffic**	**390**	**365**	**397**	**365**	**409**	**365**	**411**	**365**	**413**	**365**
Impaired driving	383	360	391	365	403	365	402	365	400	365
Other *Criminal Code* traffic	404	365	407	365	421	365	424	365	434	365
Other federal statute total	**434**	**365**	**457**	**365**	**452**	**365**	**458**	**365**	**456**	**365**
Drug possession	282	270	301	360	306	365	308	365	318	365
Drug trafficking	416	365	415	365	422	365	432	365	439	365
Youth Criminal Justice Act/Young Offenders Act	303	360	311	360	293	360	347	365	328	365
Residual federal statutes	541	540	541	540	552	540	555	540	549	540

Notes: Excludes cases where length of probation was not known. Maximum probation term is 1,095 days. Probation totals include mandatory probation for cases given a conditional discharge (CCC s.730(1)) or a suspended sentence (CCC s.731(1)(a)). In Quebec, most drug offences are recorded under residual federal statutes, resulting in an undercount of drug possession and drug trafficking cases and an overcount of residual federal statute cases. This trend analysis table does not include data from Manitoba, Northwest Territories, and Nunavut. Coverage for Adult Criminal Court Survey data for five-year trend analysis (ten jurisdictions) is estimated at 90%.

Source: Michael Marth "Adult Criminal Court Statistics, 2006/2007" *Juristat*, Vol. 28, no. 5, p. 19. Statistics Canada catalogue no. 85-002-XIE.

"other crimes against the person"—have a median probation length under two years (Marth 2008). In 2006–07, there were two property offences where the median length of the probation order exceeded one year—break and enter and "other property crime," both of which had a median length of 540 days. During the same year, 15 percent of all probation orders for violent crimes were for more than two years, an increase of 7 percent from 1999–2000 (ibid.).

Breaches of Probation

Breaches of probation are common and have increased over the past few years. In 1997–98, more than 30,139 breach-of-probation cases were heard in adult criminal courts in eight provinces and territories. This increased to 41,947 cases in 2002–03 and to 43,340 in 2003–04 (Taillon 2006). Unemployed young men with a low income, a criminal record, and a history of instability are most at risk for rearrest while on probation (Morgan 1994). Female probationers with stable marriages, higher levels of education, and either part- or full-time employment are most likely to succeed while on probation. A number of factors are consistently associated with a sentence of probation: prior record, a previous probation sentence, and a prior period of incarceration (ibid.).

The high number of breaches of probation became a major issue in the early 1990s during debates about sentencing reform. Many felt that changes were necessary to those sections of the Criminal Code pertaining to probation, in that the sanctions available for breach of probation were ineffective and commonly led to plea bargains. Daubney and Parry (1999, 36) point out that the issues associated with probation included concerns that "supervision was too often ineffective, due to a lack of ability to change conditions of probation to suit the case, and the overall authority of the probation officer." Bill C-41 took these problems into account and revised some of the provisions relating to the enforcement and administration of probation.

THE CONDITIONAL SENTENCE OF IMPRISONMENT

One of the most controversial sections of Bill C-41 was the creation of the conditional sentence. This sentence was created in order to inject restorative considerations into the sentencing process (Roach 2000b). The conditional sentence is a sentence of imprisonment of less than two years that the offender serves in the community under both optional and mandatory conditions.

Section 742.2 states that a conditional sentence may be imposed under the following conditions:

(a) the Criminal Code does not set a minimum term of imprisonment;
(b) the court imposes a sentence of less than two years; and
(c) the court is satisfied that allowing the offender to serve the sentence in the community would not endanger the safety of the community and would be consistent with the fundamental purpose and principles of sentencing as set out in s. 718 to 718.2 of the Criminal Code. The court may, for the purposes of supervising the offender's behaviour in the community, order that the offender serve the sentence in the community, subject to an offender's complying with the conditions of a conditional sentence order under s. 742.3.

A conditional sentence is meant to be an alternative to imprisonment. The hope is that such sentences will reduce the number of incarcerated individuals (Daubney and Parry 1999; Reed and Roberts 1999). When a court imposes a conditional sentence, it "has essentially substituted the community for jail as the place where the sentence is to be served, as long as conditions set out in its order are respected" (Daubney and Parry 1999, 42). Roach (2000a, 26) points out that conditional sentences "were defined as sentences of imprisonment that should be served under strict conditions in the community."

Mandatory conditions include law-abiding behaviour, appearing before the court when ordered, remaining within a specific set of boundaries unless the court grants permission to leave, and informing the court or supervisor of any change in address or occupation. Optional conditions include those which are possible in most probation orders, such as attending a treatment program and providing support and care for dependants. The most common options used to date include curfews, mandatory medical or psychiatric treatment, and orders preventing offenders from contacting other persons. The least used option is home confinement and electronic monitoring (Roberts et al. 2000).

In terms of punishment, sentencing judges have situated conditional sentences between incarceration and probation. This means that conditional sentences "can and should reflect aims of penal policy that are appropriate to both incarceration and probation" (Roberts and Healy 2000, 309). In *R. v. Proulx* (1999), the Supreme Court clarified the differences between conditional sentences and probation. While the terms of a conditional sentence may appear to be similar to those available under probation, there are differences in purposes as well as in enforcement procedures. Conditional sentences should be more punitive than probation with regard to restrictions on liberty, such as house arrest. Besides restrictions on movement, tougher conditions than those imposed under probation may be used. Rehabilitation is the primary objective of probation; conditional sentences are intended to fulfill the principles of denunciation and rehabilitation (Lonmo 2001). A conditional sentence does not have to be the same length as a period of incarceration—for example, a six-month period of incarceration can mean a one-year conditional sentence. In addition, the Supreme Court also ruled that when an offender breaches a conditional sentence without a reasonable excuse, he or she will presumably serve the rest of the sentence incarcerated.

In 2006, as part of its Speech from the Throne, the Liberal-controlled federal government introduced legislation that would end the use of conditional sentences for serious offences. Under the proposed reforms, a conditional sentence would no longer be an option for anyone convicted of an offence prosecuted by indictment and that carries a maximum prison sentence of ten years or more. Those who committed serious crimes, such as designated violent and sexual offences, major drug offences, crimes against children, and impaired driving causing death or bodily harm, would be ineligible for a conditional sentence. In addition, select weapons offences, such as an assault with a weapon causing bodily harm, would be ineligible when prosecuted by indictment. When they were elected, the new Conservative-led federal government reintroduced legislation and on December 1, 2007, it came into force. It amended s. 742.1 of the Criminal Code in order that indictable offences punishable by ten years or more that qualify as either serious personal injury offences (e.g., sexual assault, aggravated sexual assault, or sexual assault with a weapon), terrorism offences, or criminal organization offences be ineligible from receiving conditional sentences.

On June 15, 2009, the Conservative-led federal government proposed more legislation aimed at amending the Criminal Code that would further restrict the use of conditional sentences for a number of serious property and violent crimes. The proposed legislation stipulates that conditional sentences are not available when the offence is prosecuted by indictment; when the law prescribes a maximum sentence of ten years for an offence; and the offence results in bodily harm; involves the importing or exporting, trafficking, and production of drugs; or involves the use of a weapon. Some observers commented that "if the (federal government) cared about public safety they would . . . abandon discredited ideas for people who are no risk to the community" and that the announcement was "ideologically and politically driven, not evidence-based, and smacking of everything that is wrong with our criminal justice system" (Makin 2009, A4).

The proposed legislation would further restrict and eliminate the use of conditional sentences for the following:

- Offences for which the law prescribes a maximum sentence of 14 years or life.
- Offences prosecuted by indictment and for which the law prescribes a maximum sentence of imprisonment of 10 years that
  - result in bodily harm;
  - involve the import/export, trafficking, and production of drugs; or
  - involve the use of weapons.

- Offences specified below when prosecuted by indictment:
  - Prison breach
  - Luring a child
  - Criminal harassment
  - Sexual assault
  - Kidnapping, forcible confinement
  - Trafficking in persons—material benefit
  - Abduction
  - Theft over $5,000
  - Auto theft
  - Breaking and entering with intent
  - Being unlawfully in a dwelling-house

The Use of Conditional Sentences

In the 43 months between the proclamation of Bill C-41 on September 6, 1996—when the conditional sentence became one of the courts' sentencing options—and March 31, 1999, judges imposed conditional sentences against 58,734 offenders. In 2006–07, there were 9,878 conditional sentences handed out (see Table 10.1). The median length of conditional sentences alone granted during this period was eight months. Across Canada, conditional sentences were most often ordered for crimes against property (32 percent), followed by violent crimes (26 percent), drug offences (18 percent), administration of justice offences (9 percent), and driving offences (8 percent). A study by Roberts et al. (2000) of judges' views on conditional sentencing found that they would impose conditional sentences more often if greater support services were available in the community, although 67 percent of the judges felt that conditional sentences were less effective than jail in deterring crime.

In the first five years of their availability, almost 19 percent of all conditional sentences were imposed on women. Offenders between the ages of 31 and 40 received the greatest number of conditional sentences (33 percent); 70 percent of those who were given a conditional sentence had a prior record. Just over 17 percent of all such orders were given to Aboriginal offenders. Aboriginal people received just over 67 percent of all conditional sentences imposed in Saskatchewan in that two-year period; the equivalent figure for Manitoba was 45 percent. This is was keeping with s. 718(2)e of the Criminal Code, which states in part that "all available sanctions other than imprisonment that are reasonable in their circumstances should be considered for all offenders, with particular attention to the circumstances of aboriginal offenders" (see Chapter 9) (LaPrairie 1999).

The first study of the success rates of conditional sentences was conducted by LaPrairie (ibid.). Relying on information provided by seven jurisdictions, she reported that the overall breach rate was 18 percent, with a high of 26 percent in British Columbia to a low of 15 percent in Ontario. Fifty-six percent of these breaches were for violating a mandatory condition, 36 were for new offences, and the remaining 8 percent were for breaches of an optional condition. Forty-four percent of these breaches resulted in either imprisonment or partial imprisonment for the rest of the order; 26 percent resulted in nothing being done to the offender; 20 percent led to "amending conditions"; the remaining 7 percent of cases involved an "unknown" response.

Roberts and Gabor (2004) report that the success rate for conditional sentences during the four years between 1997–98 and 2000–01 was 89 percent. But they also note that in two provinces—Manitoba and Saskatchewan—the rate of successfully completed conditional sentences declined. They offer two possible reasons for this decline with the first being that, as a result of technical amendments involving breach hearings introduced in 1999, probation officers may have reported more breaches, and, in turn, prosecutors may have decided to proceed with more hearings. The second is that the Supreme Court of Canada produced guidelines in 2000 that encouraged judges to use more conditional sentences and, at the same time, to use tougher conditions on offenders receiving conditional sentences. As a result, "courts are going to increase the risk level of offenders on conditional sentences" (ibid., 104).

Roberts (1999) raises the issue of disparity in the use of conditional sentences. He argues that the broad discretionary powers granted to judges may lead some of them to view the same case in different terms. One judge may decide that placing the offender on a conditional sentence would pose a threat to the community and therefore give the offender a prison sentence; another judge may not interpret the case in the same way, and

reason that the offender should be given a conditional sentence. He also notes that the provinces have taken different approaches to the issue of conditional sentences, and as a result, disparities have emerged among the provinces. For example, the Saskatchewan Court of Appeal has ruled in support of conditional sentences, while the Court of Appeal in Alberta has treated the role of conditional sentences in a more conservative manner.

The Impact of Conditional Sentences

Have conditional sentences reduced the number of offenders sentenced to a period of imprisonment? The issue here, as it is for all alternative sanctions, is that conditional sentences may lead to "net-widening." Net-widening occurs when offenders are diverted into a new program (such as conditional sentencing) even though they are not really the individuals for whom the program was originally intended. As a result, those individuals placed in the new program are given harsher sanctions than they would have received had the program never been launched in the first place. In other words, the argument is that people who receive conditional sentences would normally have received probation—and since a large number of people are now receiving conditional sentences, more people need to be placed on probation. The end result is that more people are placed under the supervision of the authorities.

Supporters of conditional sentences believed that incarceration rates would decrease after they were introduced. Critics argued that the opposite would happen—that judges would hand down the "more severe" conditional sentence to those offenders who in the past would have received probation. Reed and Roberts (1999) conducted an analysis of conditional sentences, which on the surface suggested that they were helping bring down incarceration rates; however, they were reluctant to attribute this decrease to conditional sentences. In fact, they felt that this decline in custodial admissions "cannot be attributable to the introduction of conditional sentence, since . . . admissions to custody had been declining for several years before conditional sentences were introduced." In other words, fewer offences were being committed, and as a result fewer charges were being laid; therefore fewer offenders were being admitted to correctional facilities. They went on to point out that the best way to assess the impact of conditional sentences would be to compare sentences of admission to both federal and provincial correctional facilities, since the percentage of these admissions "should have declined by the number of conditional sentences imposed" (ibid., 9).

Reed and Roberts's analysis indicates that the total number of sentences of imprisonment handed down has changed little since conditional sentences were introduced in late 1996. They found that in the year prior to the establishment of conditional sentences, 35 percent of sentences imposed in eight jurisdictions across Canada involved a term of imprisonment; in 1997–98, with more than 22,000 conditional sentences imposed, the proportion of terms of imprisonment remained at 35 percent. Roach (2000a, 26), after looking at the first two years of the use of conditional sentences, commented that the data "strongly suggests conditional sentences have resulted in net widening." However, Belanger (2001), after examining data on the types of sentences (e.g., custody, probation, a conditional sentence) that offenders were receiving, reported that the number of sentences involving a term of custody had dropped from 60 percent to 49 percent, while probation orders had increased from 40 percent to 42 percent. This led Belanger (ibid., 13) to conclude that "these data would imply that net widening is not occurring at the national level." Roberts and Gabor (2004, 102) found that there had been net widening in five of the nine provinces studied and that the national effect of this was "a very small degree of net widening (1 percent)." They also found that while there was "a significant negative correlation between changes in the rate of custody and the volume of conditional sentences," a considerable proportion of the drop in custody rates could be explained "by variables other than the introduction of conditional sentencing." In other words, judges were using other alternatives to imprisonment besides conditional sentences (ibid., 100).

INTERMEDIATE SANCTIONS

Community corrections have traditionally used rehabilitation as an approach to dealing with offenders. Probation officers have been regarded as caseworkers or counsellors whose primary task is to help offenders adjust to society. Surveillance and control are minimal compared to what offenders encounter elsewhere in the criminal justice system. Over the past two decades, **intermediate sanctions** have been introduced in an attempt to introduce more control over offenders who have been released into the community.

Intermediate sanctions include programs usually administered by probation departments, such as intensive supervision probation, home confinement, fines, electronic monitoring, and restitution orders. These sanctions are also referred to as "judicially administered sanctions," because most often it is judges who sentence offenders to these programs. Intermediate sanctions are an outgrowth of justice model–based policies; it is this model that first

stirred interest in alternative sanctions (see Chapter 3). A major concern relating to these programs is that a large number of offenders serving these types of sentences might recidivate and subsequently be placed in a correctional setting. If intermediate sanctions are to succeed, care must be taken to maintain high-quality programs and to screen the offenders who participate in them.

Intermediate sanctions were first introduced in the belief that they would reduce prison overcrowding and substantially reduce the costs of placing offenders in the correctional system. Early advocates also believed that such programs would protect the community by exerting more control over offenders than traditional probation services. It was also hoped that these new forms of punishment would discourage potential offenders from committing crimes and help rehabilitate offenders through mandatory treatment orders reinforced by mandatory substance-abuse tests and the firm revocation of violators (Byrne et al. 1992).

The idea of intermediate punishments is popular for several reasons. First, there is the strong belief that the costs associated with these programs are somehow lower. The direct costs of administering and supervising an intermediate punishment program are generally thought to be much less than those of running a prison. Indirect cost savings result when offenders on intermediate sanctions are required to find employment, thus generating income, paying taxes, and participating in community service projects and other such activities— activities that would not be possible if they were imprisoned (Rackmill 1994).

Second, some jurisdictions require participants to help pay for the costs of the program. Byrne et al. (1989) point out that intensive-supervision probationers usually have to pay a probation supervision fee of $10 to $50 per month, as well as any court-ordered fines and restitution payments. Intermediate punishments also save money by diverting large numbers of offenders away from prison. Collectively, this should save millions of dollars each year, provided that a substantial number of intermediate punishment programs are in place.

Third, intermediate punishments can result in sentences that are seen as fair, equitable, and proportional (Morris and Tonry 1990). Sending violent criminals to prison makes sense, but shouldn't those convicted of fraudulent offences be given a lighter punishment, albeit one that maintains some degree of control? Such a system, Tonry and Will (1990) argue, establishes fairness and equity in sentences not involving incarceration, as it can increase the punishment for those who are reconvicted of an offence but for whom a prison sentence is inappropriate. Intermediate punishments also provide stronger control than normal community supervision. In theory, they also lead to greater deterrence, because the greater amount of surveillance makes it likely that anyone violating the terms of the program will be caught and punished. Furthermore, offenders under intermediate punishment should also commit fewer offences, because the conditions of the program limit their opportunities to engage in such activities. According to Petersilia and Turner (1993), closer surveillance will likely uncover more technical rule violations.

Critics argue that the benefits of intermediate punishments have not been achieved. Instead, they argue that these programs have brought about a new era of punitive punishments that simply incarcerate more offenders than before (Morris and Tonry 1990). Clear (1994) believes that these new punishments reflect the "penal harm movement"—a series of seven interrelated components based on the assumption that crime rates can be reduced if more offenders are punished and placed under the control of criminal justice agencies. His argument is related to net-widening in the sense that it contends that more, not fewer, offenders will be placed in these programs.

The components of the "penal harm movement," when combined, create what Clear refers to as the punishment paradigm. The components in this paradigm are as follows:

1. The "root causes" of crime, such as social inequality, racism, and poverty, cannot be changed or have no relevance to the causes of crime.
2. Any programs developed and implemented to combat the root causes of crime are misplaced and will not reduce the crime rate.
3. Criminals will only be deterred if the criminal justice system ensures that they receive enough pain for their wrongs.
4. Prisons are an effective means of reducing crime because they keep criminals off the street.
5. Society will be much safer with large numbers of criminals in prison.
6. Offenders in the community should be controlled, not incarcerated, through a variety of programs known as intermediate punishments, such as house confinement, electronic monitoring, and intensive probation supervision.
7. If crime rates do not decrease, more punishment, community control, and prisons will be needed.

Intensive Supervision Probation

Intensive supervision probation (ISP) is the most common form of intermediate punishment today (Petersilia 2004). It can be used across jurisdictions or for a specific program.

For example, when Manitoba instituted its high-risk probationer program, it contained an intensive supervision component. The popularity of ISPs stems from the notion that they can reduce prison populations, eliminate the need to build costly new prisons, and prevent the negative impact of imprisonment on offenders. They are also seen as promoting public safety by ensuring that all offenders are subject to intensive surveillance; in this way, they reduce the opportunities for involvement in criminal activities (Petersilia 1987b).

How is ISP different from regular probation? The most commonly cited advantage to ISP is that probation officers in these programs have fewer clients—usually between 15 and 40. According to Thompson (1985), ISP programs are also unique in the following ways:

1. *Supervision is extensive.* Probation officers have multiple weekly face-to-face contacts with offenders, as well as collateral contacts with employers and family members.
2. *Supervision is focused.* Monitoring activities focus on specific behavioural regulations governing curfews, drug use, travel, employment, and community service.
3. *Supervision is ubiquitous.* Offenders are frequently subjected to random drug tests and unannounced curfew checks.
4. *Supervision is graduated.* Offenders commonly proceed through ISP programs in a series of progressive phases—each of which represents a gradual tempering of the proscriptions and requirements of ISP—until they are committed to regular supervision as the final leg of their statutory time on probation.
5. *Supervision is strictly enforced.* Penalties for new arrest and non-compliance with program conditions are generally swift and severe.
6. *Supervision is coordinated.* ISP offenders are usually monitored by specially selected and trained officers who are part of a larger specialized, autonomous unit.

ISP programs are not designed for leniency but rather for punishment. As one policymaker stated in reference to these programs, "We are in the business of increasing the heat on probationers . . . to satisfy the public's demand for just punishment . . . Criminals must be punished for their misdeeds" (Erwin 1986, 24).

Offenders do not have an easy time in ISP programs; usually, ISP involves several contacts with a probation officer every week, residence only in approved locations, random drug and alcohol tests, and one year's minimum involvement. In fact, because of the intrusive nature of these programs, many offenders choose not to participate when given the chance, even if the alternative is prison. Petersilia and Turner (1993) report that in Oregon, 25 percent of the offenders they studied who were eligible for an ISP program preferred prison instead.

Evaluations of ISPs

Early evaluations of two ISP programs in the United States led to the rapid spread of ISPs across that country and, to a lesser degree, Canada. Expectations were high. As Petersilia (1993) points out, the rapid expansion of ISP programs was based on a number of hopeful assumptions. The first assumption was that many offenders present only a medium risk and should neither be placed on routine probation nor sent to prison. Instead, they should be placed in the community, but under more stringent conditions than those enforced by regular probation programs. The second assumption was that ISPs are cost-effective because they mean that fewer people are sentenced to prison. The third assumption is that ISPs provide stronger crime control than regular probation but less control than prison. Once judges understand that ISP offers stricter control than regular probation, they will show more willingness to apply this form of community sentencing.

Three key findings appeared over and over in evaluations of ISPs. First, most ISP participants were not prison-bound offenders. In fact, many of the offenders who ended up in ISPs should have been placed in regular probation programs. From the perspective of those who created ISPs, this problem was caused not by the original guidelines but rather by judges who ignored those guidelines. Judges were placing lower-risk offenders on ISPs, and as a result, ISPs were "widening the net," since the number of people assigned to regular probation programs and prison remained the same.

Second, the re-arrest rates for ISP participants increased after they were placed under tighter supervision. Instead of reducing criminal activity, ISP programs were actually *increasing* it, leading to higher incarceration rates and system costs. Petersilia and Turner (1993) found little difference in re-arrest rates after one year (38 percent for ISP participants and 36 percent for regular probationers). The study also indicated that a much higher percentage of ISP participants were being arrested for technical violations (70 percent versus 40 percent of regular probationers). As a result, 27 percent of ISP participants had been sent to a correctional facility after one year, compared to 19 percent of regular probationers.

Third, recidivism rates were lower in ISP programs that included a rehabilitative component. Byrne and Kelly (1989, 37), for example, found that "58 percent of

the offenders who demonstrated improvement in the area of substance abuse successfully completed the one-year at risk, as compared with only 38 percent of those who did not improve." These researchers concluded that crime control could be achieved, but only through the use of rehabilitation measures.

Jolin and Stipak (1992) reported that drug treatment programs led to a significant reduction in offenders' drug use (from 95 percent at the time they started the program to 32 percent at the completion of the program). Latessa (1995) found that high-risk clients fared no worse, and sometimes better, than random samples of regular probationers when they participated in ISPs with a treatment component. Finally, offenders sentenced to treatment-based ISPs were found to have lower recidivism rates than a matched group of regular probationers (21 percent versus 29 percent)—a finding attributed to the fact that ISP participants received "significantly more treatment services" (Gendreau et al. 1994, 34). Gendreau and Little (1993), after systematically reviewing 175 evaluations of intermediate sanction programs, concluded that "in essence, the supervision of high-risk probationers and parolees must be structured, [be] intensive, maintain firm accountability for program participation, and connect the offender with prosocial networks and activities."

HOME CONFINEMENT AND ELECTRONIC MONITORING

Home confinement (HC) and **electronic monitoring** (EM) are designed to restrict offenders to their place of residence. In this way, the offender can maintain family ties and continue to work and to use community programs and resources.

But how can correctional officials be sure that offenders are following their probation orders and remaining at home during the designated times? This issue has been solved by electronic monitoring, which tells officials at a central location whether the offender is ignoring the home confinement agreement by violating a curfew order. The hope is that by increasing the certainty of detection, EM will deter those sentenced to HC from re-offending.

Just as with ISP, HC and EM started slowly but became popular within a few years. In 1986, only 95 offenders were on EM programs in the United States. Within a year, however, this number had increased to 2,300. By 2007, more than 130,000 monitorees were being controlled by 1,200 or so different agencies. The interest in EM is based largely on the assumption that it saves money while ensuring effective surveillance.

Canada has been slow to introduce house arrest and EM, even though the Supreme Court of Canada ruled in *R. v. Proulx* (2000) that conditional sentences should include house arrest as the "norm, not the exception." In the same ruling, the Court "virtually mandated the use of electronic monitoring as part of many conditional sentences" (Makin 2000, A8). The federal and provincial governments have been criticized for introducing EM too slowly. In 1999, the Ontario Court of Appeal commented that EM could be used more often—a comment apparently not embraced by provincial authorities (Makin 1999).

Electronic Monitoring Technology

Until recently, the most common form of EM technology did not involve any interaction or communication between those being monitored and those controlling the equipment. This system, referred to as a "continuously signalling system," has three components. The offender wears a transmitter (usually on the ankle) that emits a constant signal, which is monitored by personnel in a central office. A receiver/dialer is attached to the telephone at the monitored location, usually the offender's place of residence. This device receives the signal from the transmitter and dials the central computer at the monitoring centre, where a computer records the absence or presence of an offender in his or her home during a designated time period. If the central computer notices that the offender is not at home at the designated time, it prints out a message. A supervising officer is then contacted and the authorities called (Ball et al. 1988; Schmidt 1998).

In the second major form of EM, periodic calls are made to the offender's residence, and the offender's presence is verified using what is known as "programmed contact equipment." A wide variety of equipment can be used for verification. In the system known as an "electronic handshake," the offender wears a device that is to be inserted into a piece of equipment attached to the telephone. Voice verification technology requires the offender to repeat certain words for which a voice-print was made when the offender entered the program. Another device is similar in design to a wristwatch, and beeps when the monitoring agency decides to randomly call the offender on the program. When the offender receives the call, he or she calls a special telephone number and establishes his or her "caller ID" by pressing a button attached to the equipment. Other types of systems are used, including a drive-by system and a system that can track the offender through a global positioning system (GPS).

Evaluations of Electronic Monitoring Programs

Low-risk offenders have been the most common target group for HC and EM programs (Brown and Roy 1995). When these programs were first introduced on a large scale in the United States, they were used almost exclusively for cases of driving while impaired (DWI) and driving under suspension (DUS). The rates of successful program completion were high—often 80 to 90 percent. For example, in their analysis of EM programs for DWI and DUS offenders over a seven-year period, Lilly and colleagues (1993) found that the rate of successful completion exceeded 97 percent. According to these researchers, this rate of success was impressive, given the higher rates of EM violations during the early months and the increased surveillance of program participants. Research has consistently found a positive relationship between the age of traffic offenders and their success rates in EM programs. Lilly et al. reported that the success rate for individuals between 17 and 40 was between 74 and 84 percent, whereas the rate for those over 40 was between 85 and 92 percent.

British Columbia was the first Canadian jurisdiction to use EM (British Columbia Department of Corrections 1995). Started as a pilot project in Vancouver in 1987, it was intended to provide a less expensive alternative to incarceration. In the initial study, 92 individuals in the Vancouver area were placed in an EM program. Only non-violent offenders were allowed to participate. Three participants had been convicted of drug trafficking, two for property offences, and one for a crime against a person; 83 of the offenders (or 90 percent) had been convicted for DWI or DUS. All had at least one prior conviction. While the EM sentences varied between 7 and 90 days, almost half the program participants were placed in the program for 10 to 15 days; others were in the program for 70 to 90 days. All offenders succeeded in completing their EM sentence. These results led to an expansion of the program, and by 1992, EM was available throughout the province except in sparsely populated areas. By 1996, about 300 offenders were participating in EM programs. Reports at that time indicated that the program was indeed cheaper than sending offenders to a correctional facility; those reports also identified a number of benefits for offenders (Mainprize 1992; 1995).

These success rates have led policymakers to experiment with placing more serious offenders on HC and EM programs. One pilot EM program for higher-risk offenders was conducted in Newfoundland. In this program, these offenders were required to attend an intensive treatment regimen. After one year, the recidivism rate (defined as re-arrest, reconviction, and imprisonment/reimprisonment) for the group was 26.7 percent, which was lower than for probationers and a group of inmates. This extra programming "may explain the lower than expected recidivism rate for this group" (Bonta et al. 2000, 72). This led the researchers to conclude that the quality of the treatment program "may explain the lower than expected recidivism rate for this group" (ibid.).

In a recent evaluation of the EM programs in British Columbia, Saskatchewan, and Newfoundland, Bonta et al. (1999) compared 262 participants in EM programs with a group of offenders who were either incarcerated or on probation. The recidivism rates were 26.7 percent for the EM participants, 33.3 percent for the probationers, and 37.9 percent for those incarcerated. However, the EM participants had lower recidivism rates because they were lower-risk offenders and were thus less likely to recidivate anyway. When the researchers introduced into their analyses the risk levels of all the offenders they studied, the differences in the recidivism rates could not be attributed to the type of sanction. The researchers concluded that EM programs do not reduce the recidivism of offenders more effectively than custody or probation. This study also raised questions about net-widening—specifically, whether EM programs were targeting low-risk offenders who would otherwise have received a community sanction. The researchers' findings led them to question whether EM programs are more cost-effective, whether they really contribute to greater public safety, and whether attempts to reduce criminal behaviour might not be served better by treatment programs.

Other concerns about EM have been raised in the United States. In an earlier study of drinking drivers on HC and EM, Baumer et al. (1990) found no significant differences in recidivism rates between high-risk probationers supervised by EM and those under "manual" supervision (20.5 percent for EM and 18.3 percent for manual supervision). They also found that 42 percent of each group had violated the terms of their programs by being absent when they should have been at home. The researchers to conclude that EM programs do not guarantee reduced recidivism rates relative to manual programs. In another study comparing EM program participants with offenders under manual supervision, Brown and Roy (1995) found that participants in the experimental group were more likely to complete their home confinement sentence, although the difference in the failure rates (18 versus 22 percent) was not substantial. This study concluded, among other things, that EM was more effective when used with offenders who were unemployed and unmarried.

The Impact of Home Confinement and Electronic Monitoring Programs

According to Clear and Hardyman (1990), early supporters of intermediate punishment programs such as ISP made exaggerated claims that these programs would revolutionize corrections—that they would result in better crime control, reduced prison populations, fiscal savings, and greater public safety. Of course, more modest claims—for example, that there are little if any cost savings, and only a minimal increase in public safety—would have led to diminished support for these programs and made them more difficult to implement.

ISP, HC, and EM programs have been viewed as "panaceas" for the control of crime. As a consequence, little attention was initially paid to what these programs hoped to accomplish, and thus researchers found it difficult to say whether these programs had achieved their goals. As Tonry (1990, 180) has commented, ISP programs have succeeded, not in terms of achieving their stated goals, but rather in serving "latent bureaucratic, organizational, political, professional, and psychological goals of probation departments and officers."

Bonta et al. (2000, 73) posit that the impact of EM varies with the intended outcomes. If such a program is designed solely to achieve program completion, then the surveillance and control nature of EM "may ensure that offenders complete a period of supervision without incident." In fact, they found that completion rates were high in the various provincial programs regardless of the amount of time offenders spent in them (from an average of 37.3 days in British Columbia

In an attempt to reduce the number of car thefts in Winnipeg, the provincial government introduced electronic anklets for young thieves identified as high-risk repeat offenders in 2008. This program, along with a number of other programs, led to the reduction of car thefts in excess of 60 percent in the following year compared to the previous year. (CP PHOTO/John Woods)

to 71.6 days in Newfoundland and 139.3 days in Saskatchewan). However, if the desired outcome of an EM program is to reduce recidivism, "EM has questionable merit" (ibid.).

FINES

Since 1996–97, fewer sentences in Canada have involved fines. In 2006–07, 30 percent of guilty cases resulted in a fine, compared to 32 percent in 2003–04, 37 percent in 2000–01, and 44 percent in 1996–97. Over these same years, there has been a trend toward higher fines: in 1994–95, the mean for all fines was $410; by 2000–01, it was $600; by 2002–03, it was $654; and during 2006–07, it was $758. In Canada, **fines** can be imposed alone or in conjunction with other sanctions, with this exception: if the offence carries a minimum or a maximum penalty of more than five years, the offender cannot receive a fine alone.

During 2006–07, the cases involving a fine as the most frequently imposed sentences were impaired driving (86 percent), drug possession (50 percent), other Criminal Code—traffic (40 percent), and disturbing the peace (36 percent). Not surprisingly, fines are rarely used as the most severe sanction in the category of crimes against the person. The offences in this category for which fines were used most often were common assault (10.2 percent), uttering threats (9.8 percent), and major assault (8.8 percent) (Marth 2008).

According to adult court statistics for 1999–2000, fines were most often imposed as a single sanction: 45 percent of offenders required to pay a fine received no other punishment. More than one-third of all fines (36 percent) were imposed in impaired driving cases. A fine was imposed in 41 percent of cases with convictions; however, only 2 percent of offenders who received a prison sentence had to pay a fine as well. Fines were used in single-conviction cases involving violence, but only 19 percent of these involved fines (the average fine was $419).

Questions about the fairness of fines have surfaced over recent decades in Canada. In most jurisdictions, judges receive little guidance on how and against whom to impose fines, but it is agreed that once the facts of a case are considered, judges use fines as a sanction in an appropriate manner. For example, low-risk offenders are more likely to receive a fine instead of incarceration. However, judges often make decisions with little information about the offender's ability to pay; as a result, a significant number of people default on the fines imposed on them and end up in a provincial or territorial correctional facility. In 1997–98, just over one-fifth (22 percent) of all

admissions to these facilities were for failing to pay a fine. While this was a 4 percent reduction from the previous year, Reed and Roberts (1999) indicate that admissions to custody for fine default had decreased in Canada only slightly over the past 15 years. In 1981–82, for example, 29 percent of all admissions to provincial and territorial facilities were for fine default. Jurisdictions in Canada vary in their use of incarceration for those who default on a fine: in 1997–98, the number of individuals incarcerated in a provincial facility for failing to pay a fine ranged from 1 percent in Newfoundland and 2 percent in Ontario to 33 percent in Alberta and 57 percent in Quebec.

In the 1970s, some provincial governments attempted to develop fine option programs as alternatives for people who could not pay the fines imposed on them by the courts. (Community service was a common option.) According to a report on fines by the Law Reform Commission (1975), fines can discriminate against poor offenders. It noted that 57.4 percent of Aboriginal admissions to provincial institutions in Saskatchewan in 1970–71 were for non-payment of fines, compared to 24.7 percent of non-Aboriginal admissions. The inability to pay fines is a significant reason why Aboriginal offenders are overrepresented in provincial and territorial correctional facilities; since Aboriginal people experience high rates of unemployment (between 60 and 90 percent) in their communities, fines are not reasonable options for them (Frideres and Robertson 1994, 110). As the Alberta Task Force on the Criminal Justice System and Its Impact on the Indian and Métis People of Alberta (Alberta 1991) stated, the use of custody for fine defaulters does not fulfill the principle of proportionality and the purposes of sentencing, which includes the protection of the community as well as deterrence.

One approach to avoiding the incarceration of fine defaulters was to have defence counsel introduce information about the accused's ability to pay a fine into the court record, subject to cross-examination by the Crown prosecutor. It was also possible for a judge to request that this information be included in a pre-sentence report. Bill C-41 simplified the process of including this information when it introduced the provision that the court "may fine an offender under this section only if the court is satisfied that the offender is able to pay the fine." If the offender cannot pay, other alternative sanctions are to be considered, including probation, a conditional sentence, an absolute or conditional discharge, or incarceration.

Another alternative is day fines. The concept of day fines was introduced in Finland in 1921 and is based on the idea that a fine can satisfy the idea of proportionality by assessing an offender's net income as well as the seriousness of the crime. Day fines (in contrast to the current fixed-fine system) are weighted by a daily-income value taken from a chart similar to an income tax table; the offender's number of dependants is also considered. Evaluations of day fine programs in the United States have found that they are generally successful, in that they increase the amount of money collected from fines while at the same time reducing the number of arrest warrants for failure to pay. Even when the fine cannot be paid in full, most offenders pay at least some of the amount owed to the state (Hillsman 1990).

INTERMEDIATE SANCTIONS: HOW WELL DO THEY WORK?

In 1985, Sawyer called intermediate sanctions the future of corrections. But have they lived up to this? More than 20 years later, we are in a position to examine whether they have achieved their goals, particularly in the areas of reducing prison populations, saving money, and deterring crime. The results of several American evaluations are reviewed below.

Do Intermediate Sanctions Reduce Prison Crowding?

This question is perhaps the most critical of all. Advocates of intermediate sanction programs (ISPs) have long argued that they decrease the number of offenders incarcerated. However, as Morris and Tonry (1990, 223–34) point out, these advocates base their contention on the belief that most individuals convicted of a serious crime are sent to prison—an assumption that Morris and Tonry point out is incorrect in that "most felonies never were or are not now punished by imprisonment." In reality, most offenders placed in ISPs would otherwise have been placed in regular probation programs or given suspended sentences instead of being sent to prison. Also, evaluations of ISPs have found high re-arrest rates for offenders; some American states report at best a 50 percent success rate for ISPs (Erwin and Bennett 1987). Researchers have also discovered that ISPs have had only a minor impact on the total prison population. For example, Petersilia (1987a) found that Georgia's ISP "saved" 186 prison beds in a year—a number that Tonry (1990) considers unlikely to significantly reduce prison crowding. Tonry (ibid., 178) also argues that some ISPs may "fill more prison beds than they empty" because so few offenders from prison are actually placed in these programs. ISPs are generally filled by low-risk offenders who normally would have been placed on regular probation.

Petersilia (1987b), in her review of five EM programs, found that most offenders sentenced to them were not from prison, but rather were on regular probation. With few exceptions, "participants in the program had only been convicted of misdemeanors" (Johnson et al. 1989, 156–57).

Are Intermediate Sanctions a Cost-Saving Alternative?

One of the most common arguments in favour of ISPs is that they cost less than incarceration programs. Most of these arguments are based on average per-offender costs, which many have pointed out is a misleading approach to evaluating the financial savings of ISPs. One reason for this is the length of time that offenders are sentenced to prison or to an ISP. Morris and Tonry (1990) point out that it is misleading to directly compare costs because if the average offender serves 12 months in an ISP at a cost of $3,000 per month but would otherwise have served three months in prison at a total cost of $14,000 the ISP costs more, not less.

Comparing per-offender costs is misleading for another reason: it assumes that all offenders are diverted into ISPs from prison. In fact, many ISP participants (a figure that varies from 50 percent to 80 percent, depending on the jurisdiction and the type of program) have been diverted from regular probation programs. According to Tonry (1990, 182), ISPs' "costs per day are six times higher than the cost of ordinary probation." Moreover, the greater the number of individuals placed in an ISP directly from the courts, the less the savings because fewer people are being taken out of prison.

Furthermore, most cost comparisons look only at the costs of building a new prison but ignore the costs of operating an ISP, which is labour intensive. If 25 offenders in an ISP require the hiring and training of four to eight new employees, this "increases direct outlays in the form of salaries and expanded overhead expenses, but also produces longer-term financial commitments in the form of employment benefits and pensions" (U.S. General Accounting Office 1990, 27).

When all costs, both direct and marginal, are factored in, any savings may be limited. For example, Petersilia and Turner (1993, 309) studied 14 programs and reported that in "no site did intermediate sanction programs result in cost-savings during the one year follow-up period." This was due mainly to the large number of technical violations, revocations, and incarcerations and the cost of court appearances, resulting in costs up to twice as high as those for routine probation and parole supervision.

In their study of home confinement in Arizona, Palumbo and colleagues (1992) discovered that because of organizational operating problems, the actual cost of the program exceeded the cost of prison. They determined that the key factor in the higher costs was that while the ISPs were increasing the number of program participants, the prisons remained overcrowded. The same researchers reported that if "an alternative is not used as a way of reducing the total number of prison beds in use, or to eliminate some of these institutions, then alternatives to incarceration cannot be cost-effective" (ibid., 238). This reasoning is supported by Tonry (1990, 180), who analyzed the full cost-saving potential of ISPs and concluded that "only when the numbers of people diverted from prison by a new program permit the closing of all or a major part of an institution or the cancellation of construction plans will there be substantial savings."

Another argument in favour of intermediate punishments is that many of them charge a fee to the offenders participating in them. Renzema and Skelton (1990, 14) point out that in the programs they reviewed, about two-thirds of the participants paid fees. The average cost was $200 a month, with probationers paying "an average of $155 a month while inmates pay an average of $228 a month. A few programs charge clients as much as $15 a day for monitoring."

Tonry (1990) has pointed out a significant error made by those who evaluate the cost savings of ISPs: they fail to include the cost of recidivists. Since offenders in these programs may be caught for technical violations or new crimes and be sent to prison, the additional time incarcerated must also be factored into any comparison of costs. With recidivism rates at about 40 to 50 percent, taking incarceration time into account in the cost–benefit analysis would substantially increase the costs of these programs.

Can Intermediate Sanctions Control Crime?

The third point raised by advocates of ISPs relates to their effectiveness in controlling crime. It is argued that more intensive supervision cannot help but reduce crime. Basing their arguments on the recidivism rates reported in early evaluation studies, they emphasize that ISPs have the potential both to "control offenders in the community and to facilitate their growth to crime-free lives" (Morris and Tonry 1990).

However, some studies have found that many offenders released from ISPs committed serious crimes. Even low-risk offenders in ISPs have been found to re-offend at a high rate on release. For example, almost 27 percent of offenders in three provinces recidivated, although they had lower risk levels than either the inmates or the probationers to whom they were being compared. According to Bonta et al. (2000), the lower recidivism rates of those in EM programs can explain their lower risk. Many studies (Petersilia and Turner 1993; Wallerstedt 1984) have found that individuals released from ISPs often have high recidivism rates and that many of their offences are serious. In addition, many researchers have reported that these programs fail to result in any reduction in crime rates. Pearson (1986, 443–44), for example, concluded that "we can be confident that intermediate sanction programs at least did not increase recidivism rates."

In one of the most comprehensive analyses of its kind, Petersilia and Turner (1993) reported that in the 14 ISPs they studied, no participants were re-arrested less often, had a longer time before being re-arrested, or were arrested for less serious offences than those individuals on regular probation. When the researchers included technical violations in their recidivism measure, "the record for intermediate sanction programs looks somewhat grimmer" (Petersilia and Turner 1993, 310–11). About 65 percent of the offenders in these programs recorded a technical violation, compared to 38 percent of those offenders on regular probation. The researchers also found no support for the argument that offenders arrested for technical violations reduced the incidence of any future criminal acts.

Do Intermediate Sanctions Work?

The concerns raised about alternative sanctions do not mean that they should be abandoned as another failed experiment. Perhaps there was too great an expectation that these programs would somehow "save" the current correctional crisis by reducing prison populations and recidivism, besides making communities safer. As Finckenhauer (1982) has noted, the history of corrections is filled with great expectations but, at the same time, littered with one failed panacea after another. New programs are attractive because they always promise to do so much, at a minimal cost. When programs are poorly conceived and implemented and, as a result, fail to reach their goals, it is not surprising that they are labelled as another program that "didn't work."

Yet a number of important lessons can be learned by examining the rise and growth of alternative correctional programs, particularly the rapid growth in intermediate sanctions. One lesson is that the number of offenders entering the correctional system is beyond the control of criminal justice officials. Political demands for tougher penalties and a "war on crime" can have a significant impact on the operations of all facets of our criminal justice system. The police are under more pressure to arrest and charge more alleged criminals; the courts are under more pressure to deal with these alleged offenders more speedily. But when offenders enter the correctional system, often with long sentences, correctional officials have a hard time knowing where to put them.

Underlying ISPs is the justice model. The results to date have revealed not only that specific programs do not reach their objectives, but also that the justice model preference of alternative sanctions is open to question. However, evidence is emerging that some intermediate punishment programs, when merged with rehabilitation-based principles, achieve more favourable results (Gendreau et al. 1994). Researchers who have evaluated programs and who have seen the high rates of recidivism in these programs have recommended the inclusion of rehabilitation. For example, in their study of the Florida Community Control Program, Smith and Akers (1993, 228) noted that "a more persuasive model might move back in the direction of community reintegration and propose that occupation skill enhancement, education, substance abuse treatment, behavior modification and other practices be added to the principle of closely supervising home confinement." And in their analysis of the 14 sites experimenting with intermediate supervision probation, Petersilia and Turner (1993, 321) reported that in the three California locations included in their study, offenders who "received counseling, held jobs, paid restitution, and did community service were arrested 10–20 percent less often than were other offenders."

These comments are consistent with a growing literature on the importance of introducing effective rehabilitative components into ISPs. Any such program would have to identify which offenders are to receive treatment. This means that the principles of risk, need, and responsivity must be introduced (see Chapter 12) (Andrews et al. 1990). As Petersilia and Turner (1993, 320) point out, placing drug-dependent offenders into an ISP that "forbids drug use, provides frequent drug testing, and provides no assured access to drug treatment virtually guarantees high violation rates." The potential for intermediate sanctions with a strong rehabilitative component exists, but only if such programs "provide the opportunity to channel offenders into treatments that address criminogenic needs—sources of criminality that are not targeted and affected by surveillance and punishment" (Cullen et al. 1995).

SPECIALIZED COURTS: DRUG TREATMENT COURT

Drug treatment courts began to appear in the United States in 1989, when the first such court was opened in Dade County, Florida. The goal was to develop an entirely new approach to processing drug cases that did not involve incarcerating drug-dependent offenders. By May 2001, there were almost 700 drug courts in the United States with a caseload of about 225,000. A key impetus behind these courts was the Violent Crime Control and Enforcement Act of 1994, which required the federal government to fund drug treatment courts. Having succeeded in the United States, these courts were introduced in Canada. The first drug treatment court in Canada was the Toronto Drug Treatment Court, established in 1998. A second one opened in Vancouver in 2001. Since then, drug treatment courts have been opened in Edmonton, Regina, Winnipeg, and Ottawa, all as part of the national drug strategy.

Drug treatment courts are based on the idea that criminal justice can be therapeutic rather than simply punitive. They are based on both restorative justice and therapeutic jurisprudence. Therapeutic jurisprudence has been defined as "the use of social science to study the extent to which a legal rule or practice promotes the psychological and physical well-being of the people it affects" (Hora et al. 1999).

The approach taken by drug treatment courts runs directly counter to "supply-side enforcement," which is the path most often taken in the United States and Canada for preventing the selling and consumption of illicit drugs. Under the supply-side approach, law enforcement agencies are the primary criminal justice agency in the "war on drugs." They detect those individuals who produce and/or sell illicit drugs with the goal of reducing the supply. Other criminal justice agencies then become involved in the fight. The courts ensure that convicted drug offenders receive certain types of sentences; and lawmakers pass legislation to support police efforts. The Proceeds of Crime Act allows the police to confiscate monies and/or material goods (such as vehicles) obtained through the earnings from illicit drugs.

The supply-side approach has been questioned over the years by those who argue that prevention programs are a better approach than incarceration. Drug treatment courts offer a combination of active and intensive judicial supervision with treatment centres and other community resources (e.g., addiction treatment centres) that allow offenders to serve their sentences in the community, under the supervision of the courts and criminal justice system personnel.

As a movement, drug treatment courts have been most commonly introduced in the United States. This is partly because the "war on drugs" has been a high priority in that country for more than 30 years. Americans view drug use as one of their country's biggest domestic problems (Maguire and Pastore 1998). Governments in the United States tend to make drugs the main plank in their criminal justice activities (Walker 2001). Punitive responses to illegal drugs have usually been favoured. Yet at the same time, American society has generally been willing to try alternative approaches to reducing the drug problem.

Klienman and Smith (1990) report that the number of prosecutions for drug-related offences in Washington, DC, increased by 503 percent between 1983 and 1987. And by 1991, 25 percent of all inmates in the United States were either serving a sentence or awaiting trial on a drug-related offence. Many critics of the punitive approach argue that after decades of get-tough policies, drug use remains a persistent problem. They point to research that demonstrates that responses such as enhanced monitoring and longer prison sentences aren't very successful (Andrews and Bonta 1998; Fagan 1994). These factors, in conjunction with research arguing that many drug addicts do respond to treatment—especially treatment that is both long term and intensive—have led to the rapid development of drug treatment courts (Prendergast et al. 1995).

One prominent feature of drug treatment courts is that they involve the development of programs that fit local circumstances, such as the current incidence of drug use, drug arrest patterns, and the type and availability of community services. In the United States, these courts have emphasized a wide array of programs, including diversion and probation. And once a client has successfully completed the program, the court can end the case by dropping the charges, reducing the sentence, or ending a probation order.

Drug treatment courts are continuing to evolve, and differences among them exist. That said, some key components of them have been outlined by the Drug Court Programs Office (1997), an office of the U.S. Department of Justice:

- They integrate alcohol and drug treatment services with justice system case processing.
- They take a non-adversarial approach that emphasizes teamwork.
- They define eligible participants in the early stages and place them quickly in the drug court program.
- Participants are provided with access to a continuum of alcohol, drug, and related treatment and rehabilitation services.

- Abstinence is monitored through frequent alcohol and drug testing.
- A coordinated strategy governs drug court responses to participants' compliance and non-compliance.
- Strong emphasis is placed on ongoing judicial interaction with each drug court participant.

These courts also develop partnerships with public agencies and community groups in order to gain local support.

The main goal of drug treatment courts is to eliminate or reduce drug and alcohol use and the criminal activities that are related to it. Related goals are to decrease case-processing times, relieve the courts of drug-related cases, reduce jail and prison populations, increase offender accountability, and reduce the cost of controlling drug offenders (in effect, by keeping them out of jail) (Drug Court Programs Office 1997).

Drug treatment courts have significant implications for the courts. In the traditional court system, defendants and the state behave as adversaries and cases are determined by a neutral judge (or jury) on the basis of the facts presented in court. In such a system, there are always clear winners and losers. In contrast, in drug treatment courts, defence lawyers fight for their clients but do so while working *with* the court to develop a recovery plan. The prime mover of the case is the court itself, which ensures that the goals and objectives of the plan are achieved through the consistent application of appropriate rewards and sanctions. Judicial interest in these cases is strong, since drug treatment courts place much of the case management into the hands of the judges. (Most of the case management is done by the treatment team, with weekly reports being sent to the court. The court, along with the judge, oversees this process.)

The roles played by prosecutors and defence lawyers in drug treatment courts are often unconventional. For example, prosecutors have the right to reject certain cases on the basis of public safety or because they involve an offender assessed as high risk and/or violent. Generally, though, prosecutors are willing to structure a plea bargain so that it combines treatment with punishment. For their part, defence lawyers usually allow their clients to enter drug treatment court if they view them as seriously addicted, as at risk of recidivism, and/or as likely to be convicted and incarcerated on the basis of the evidence (Hora et al. 1999).

The most effective drug treatment courts have been found to base their activities on an understanding of the physiological, psychological, and behavioural realities of drug abuse, and they hand down sentences that bear those realities in mind (National Institute on Drug Abuse 1999). These courts also recognize that addiction is a relapsing disease, so they attempt to moderate sentences in light of that reality. They try to keep most if not all non-compliant offenders in the program through encouragement from the personnel involved in the program as well as through graduated sanctions, such as increased urinalysis testing. Compared to the system practised in the United States, graduated sanctions in the Canadian system does not include increased urinalysis testing; instead, testing is done on a randomized basis. Graduated sanctions in Canada include community service hours, increased court attendance, and bail revocation. Other therapeutic remands might include having clients write an essay on a particular topic, such as "Why is honesty important?" Every effort is made to match interventions to clients' needs as individually assessed (Belenko 2000; Johnson et al. 2000).

Clients are still held accountable for their actions. The defendants in drug treatment courts are required to enter into a "contingency contract" with the court. This contract holds them accountable for attending treatment programs and for complying with the rules. These rules include rewards and sanctions, both of which the offenders can control through their behaviour. (Drug treatment courts try to use the terms "sanctions" and "rewards" as opposed to "punishments" and "rewards." The term "punishment" is attached to the traditional criminal justice system; and research in this area illustrates that rewards are far more effective at empowering change for drug treatment court clients than sanctions [Marlowe and Kirby 1999; Meyer 2008].) Clients are rewarded for keeping to these rules; they can be sanctioned for breaking them (Harrell and Kleiman 2000; Inciardi et al. 1996).

Drug treatment courts have a number of common characteristics. For example, they all require the offender to do the following:

- Appear frequently in front of judges.
- Enter an intensive treatment program.
- Undergo frequent, random urinalysis.
- Accept sanctions for failure to comply with program requirements.
- Become drug-free.
- Develop vocational and other skills to promote re-entry into the community.
- Have stable housing.

The first drug court in Canada opened in Toronto on December 1, 1998. In keeping with the philosophy of this movement, it has ties with the community. Two committees govern this court: the

In drug treatment courts, defence lawyers work with the court to develop a recovery plan for their clients. (Courtesy of Centre for Addiction & Mental Health (CAMH).)

Operations Committee and the Community Advisory Committee (CAC). The former is in effect an operating committee while the latter sets community policy (LaPrairie et al., 2002). The Steering Committee was integrated into the Operations Committee a number of years ago. The Operations Committee makes operational decisions while the CAC plays an advisory role in relation to program policy, development, and community connections.)

An individual who wants to be accepted into the program is screened; those with a record of violence or who are unwilling to accept treatment will not be admitted. Not every person who applies to the program is accepted. Those who are admitted are placed on a special drug treatment court bail and begin their treatment. They have to agree to urine tests and must appear in front of a drug court judge as often as twice a week during the initial stages of treatment to discuss their progress.

All program participants must plead guilty prior to entering the drug treatment court. They are also required to sign a Rule and Waiver form by which they waive various constitutional rights such as the right to be tried within a specific time. A participant who successfully completes the program will be given a non-custodial sentence (usually a period of time on probation with a list of conditions). Those who fail to complete the program will have to appear in criminal court again for sentencing (Chiodo 2001). A unique aspect of Toronto's drug treatment court is that all participants must stay in court after they report on their progress, in order to listen to other participants talk about their addictions and treatment.

The court's target group is non-violent offenders who are addicted to crack cocaine, heroin, and/or methamphetamine. Most of those admitted to the Toronto Drug Treatment Court (80.6 percent) reported using cocaine during the previous 90 days; others reported using marijuana, alcohol, heroin, cocaine, or prescription drugs (LaPrairie et al. 2002). Individuals with substance use issues can apply for the program once they have been charged with possession or trafficking in small quantities of crack cocaine, heroin, and/or cocaine, have been charged with a prostitution-related offence or have been charged with a property-related offence.

Participants remain in the program for 12 to 16 months. Some participants graduate at the 10-month mark but this is the exception, not the rule. By the program's end, the participants who get that far are drug free, have completed employment and life skills courses, and have a stable job and home life. Of the first 75 participants admitted to the program, 42 (56 percent) were still participating a year later. Of the clients who were no longer involved in the program, 20 (27 percent) had been expelled, 4 (5 percent) had withdrawn, and 8 (11 percent) had been terminated after failing in some component of

the program (e.g., they had failed to appear for treatment court as scheduled).

By the end of its first 18 months of operation, 198 drug-dependent offenders had been asked if they wanted to enter the program. Of these, 150 had agreed to participate. Eighty-one (54 percent) of those agreeing to participate had withdrawn or been expelled from the program; 59 (39 percent) were still in the program; and 10 (7 percent) had graduated. According to the researchers, the "vast majority of those no longer with the program had been expelled and [had] not withdrawn voluntarily" (LaPrairie et al. 2002, 1543). The retention rate for the Toronto drug treatment court program over the 18 months was 46 percent, a lower figure than those found for similar groups in the United States; however, this rate of retention in the Toronto Drug Treatment Court is higher than the retention rates for some general addiction treatment programs. Preliminary data on those who graduated from the program found that the graduates "exhibit evidence of less use during the first three months [after graduating], followed by even lower levels after that" (ibid., 1551).

CRITICAL ISSUES IN CANADIAN CRIMINAL JUSTICE

THE COMMUNITY JUSTICE MOVEMENT

Canada's first community court opened in the middle of September 2008, in Vancouver. It deals with individuals who plead guilty to minor offences such as shoplifting, theft from cars, mischief, assault, and drug possession in the downtown area. It is estimated that about half of those arrested in the downtown area of Vancouver suffer from mental illness or drug addiction, or both ("Hopeful New . . . " 2008, A14). It expects to hear 1,500 cases a year and will try to deal with these cases more quickly than the traditional criminal justice system (Hume 2008).

The court will integrate social and health services including teams of social workers, drug counsellors, and other experts available to assist the clients of the court. While offenders who appear in the community court can receive jail time, the goal is to allow those offenders who plead guilty the goal is to allow those offenders who plead guilty after their arrest the option of going to the community court after their arrest of going to the community court. Those individuals who plead not guilty will enter the traditional criminal justice system. The Crown agrees to stay charges against the individuals brought to

the community court as long as they promise to return to the court a few weeks later with proof they had willingly participated in alternative programs. Once individuals sign bail conditions, they can be released immediately. Some of the individuals who appeared in the community court on the first day of its operation were told they would not be sent back to a cell but offered assistance in finding homes or placed in a drug treatment programs instead (Hume 2008; Matas 2008).

The B.C. government started the court as it was facing increased pressure to improve conditions in the Downtown Eastside area, a low-income area "dominated by open-air drug markets, back lane 'shooting' galleries where addicts inject drugs, and the mentally ill living on the street" (Matas, 2008, A6). However, on the eve of the court's opening, the provincial court judge presiding over it stated that the city of Vancouver doesn't have enough facilities and other resources for all the individuals it expects. However, he expressed optimism that the B.C. government will deliver on its promises to build more housing and increase support for drug treatment programs over the next few years.

Continued on next page

Community Justice

What is the basis for community courts? It is found in the idea of community justice, which focuses on the belief that crime not only involves an offender, an incident, or a case that needs to be processed through the criminal justice system, but also as a social problem that affects the life within the community. It appears to share a similar focus to that offered by restorative justice (see Chapter 3), but outside of a focus on community empowerment, it is quite different. Community justice is viewed by Clear and Karp (1999) as all those activities that include community in their processes, particularly neighbourhood-level operations, problem solving, decentralization of authority and accountability, and citizen involvement within the justice process.

In the past decade, a number of American cities and states have started to devise new policies to provide an alternative to the traditional criminal justice system in communities that experience high crime rates. These programs use combinations of probation officers, police officers, prosecutors, and citizens in an attempt to better deal with the prevention of crime in the community. Clear and Karp (ibid.) have documented how the police and probation officers work together in Milwaukee in order to better deal with some of the problems that exist in high-crime neighbourhoods. They also point out that in Portland, Oregon, prosecutors have gone into high-crime neighbourhoods in order to deal with problems of the citizens who live there, and also how probation staff has opened up neighbourhood centres in Phoenix, Arizona.

According to Clear and Karp, each of these initiatives includes programs involving victims, the broader community, and offenders in a process that is called "community justice." The community justice approach has been defined as "an ethic that transforms the aims of the justice system into enhancing community life or sustaining community" (Clear and Karp 2000). At the same time, it is a philosophy of justice, a strategy of justice, as well as a series of justice programs.

As a philosophy of justice, community justice is based on a view that differs from the traditional goals of criminal justice—the apprehension, conviction, and punishment of offenders. In contrast, community justice recognizes the importance of viewing crime and its resultant problems as a central problem to the quality of community life. As a result, community justice

not only attempts to respond to criminal activity but also includes as a goal the improvement of community life, particularly for those communities affected by high crime rates. Sampson and colleagues (1997) have referred to the quality of life that communities need to reduce crime as "collective efficacy." They found that neighbourhoods vary in their ability to "activate informal social control." Informal social control involves residents acting proactively when they see questionable behaviour. The likelihood that residents will do such things, however, is contingent upon whether or not there is mutual trust among them. In neighbourhoods where such cohesiveness exists, residents can depend on each other to enforce rules of civility and good behaviour. Such places have "collective efficacy, defined as social cohesion among neighbors combined with their willingness to intervene on behalf of the common good" (ibid., 918).

As a strategy of justice, two recent innovations in the area of justice are included: community policing and environmental crime prevention. Community policing uses strategies to identify alternative ways to successfully determine the root causes of crime as opposed to relying on arrests as a way to respond to crimes. The police are encouraged to form partnerships with community members as well as decentralizing decision-making to the police officers in an attempt to develop area-specific strategies for reducing crime. Environmental crime prevention involves an approach to crime prevention that starts with an analysis of why crime tends to concentrate in certain locations at certain times. These "hot spots" can include 20 percent of a city's locations but account for 70 percent of all criminal activity. Sherman et al. (1995) reported from their study in Minneapolis that more than 50 percent of all 911 calls came from only 3 percent of the city's 115,000 addresses. In addition, they found that all robberies occurred in 2.2 percent of the addresses. By analyzing these patterns, this approach attempts to look for ways to change the physical environment of crime as a means of reducing crime. The researchers devised the Minneapolis Hot Spots Experiment in which the police applied "three hours a day of intermittent, unpredictable police presence" to a random selection of the "worst" hot spots. Robberies decreased by 20 percent, and overall crime fell by 13 percent in the targeted locations.

Three major areas of community justice have emerged: community policing (see Chapter 6), community prosecution (also referred to as "community-oriented lawyering"), and community courts.

Community-Oriented Lawyering

A recent innovation in the court system involves community-based lawyering. Some lawyers have started to move away from reactively processing cases presented to them by starting to work in partnership with other criminal justice agencies and communities in order to address the problems faced by residents of neighbourhoods. This work is called community-oriented lawyering, and while it has been existence in the United States for over a decade, the first such position in Canada (referred to as "community prosecutor") started in Winnipeg in 2006 (Owen 2006).

The goals of community-oriented lawyering include the prevention and reduction of disorder and crime, restoration of victims and communities to more effective and healthier functioning, and empowerment of local citizens. And though prosecution is still an activity employed by prosecutors, for community-oriented lawyers, it is only one tactic that can be used to solve problems in neighbourhoods and communities. Prosecutors are taking a leadership role in building connections and initiatives that bring together citizens, businesses, government agencies, and other criminal justice agencies in the community for the purposes of reducing crime and increasing safety (Coles and Kelling 1998). This means they are developing accountability at the neighbourhood level by implementing tactics that include the following:

1. Refining their core capabilities in order to enhance the prosecution of violent and repeat offenders.
2. Helping set standards for the selective prosecution of offenders and offences in the context of neighbourhood priorities.
3. Relying on civil law and the use of civil initiatives as well as criminal law and criminal sanctions.
4. Using diversion and alternatives to prosecution, sentencing, and incarceration such as mediation, treatment, community service, and restitution to victims.

In the same way that community policing introduced a distinctive approach to law enforcement, community-oriented lawyers have started to redefine the role of lawyers. According to Connor (2000), the most important factor in this redefinition is that some lawyers could not help but notice the changes in policing and the positive results occurring as a result of the introduction of community policing initiatives. From the police they learned it was possible, in some cases, to change their strategy and pursue an approach that favours prevention in order that the cycle of crimes brought about by drug addiction, child abuse, and untreated mental illness can be eliminated.

To achieve the goals of community-oriented lawyering, a new approach was needed. Most significant here is that the traditional approach has been to ask, "What happened?" while the new approach attempts "to reshape what will happen" (ibid., 28). Community-oriented lawyers approach their jobs by focusing on the problems of particular people and places rather than just crimes and legal cases. As Connor (ibid.) points out, these lawyers "think beyond the individual drug sale to the drug market itself; beyond the civil action for termination of parental rights to the woman who seems trapped in a cycle of abusive relationships."

In addition, the definition of success has changed. No longer is winning the case the only desired outcome, as increasing neighbourhood safety, preventing crime, and improving the quality of life have all become important considerations. In order to achieve these goals, community-oriented lawyers listen to the victims themselves as well as to service providers, local residents, and criminal justice agents who work in the community, such as police officers who work in community storefronts. Other changes include the sharing of information and the making of decisions based on the feelings and concerns of other members of the community. Another significant change is that court case processing is a tool, not an end in itself. Instead, other types of activity are used, such as employing non-adversarial solutions and negotiating outcomes between the parties involved.

How can the effectiveness of community-oriented lawyers be measured? Like success in community policing, success in community-oriented lawyering will include traditional outcome measures—in this case, the conviction of criminals in a court of law. But it will also include several other measures, such as the degree to which certain neighbourhood problems are solved and the effectiveness of civil sanctions and negotiated agreements used in lieu of prosecution.

Continued on next page

Other possibilities include evaluating the perceptions of safety by the residents in a designated area, increasing the involvement of citizens in crime prevention and crime reduction, improving case management procedures used by the police, and improving the ability of individual citizens and neighbourhood groups to solve problems.

Community Courts

Community courts are decentralized courts that respond directly to community concerns rather than wait for serious crimes to be committed. They share certain features that create a strong connection between unruly conduct and the adjudication process. Among those features is the formation of citizens' advisory committees, the use of citizen volunteers and programs that involve the community more closely in the adjudication process. According to Rottman, community-based justice programs share certain elements. First, they all practise some type of restorative-based justice. Second, community courts treat those involved as real individuals rather than as abstract legal persons. Third, community resources are used in the adjudication of disputes.

Rottman (1996) states that three different models exist for today's community-focused courts. The first is Navajo Peacemaking, an approach that uses Navajo traditions and principles in the judicial process. The integration of Navajo customs is most evident in the Peacemaker division of the Navajo Nation judicial branch, which emphasizes non-adversarial processes in dispute resolution. The formal aspects of this process include a peacekeeper, who is a person recognized for ability and wisdom; the parties in disagreement; their extended families; and Navajo religious ceremonies. Peacemaking gains its authority from the community.

All Peacemaker sessions take a similar approach and address problems that range from marital discord to land dispute. Peacemaking is a ceremony. First, basic rules are established and prayers are made. Then, all those in attendance become involved in the questions and answers, the peacemaker develops a problem-solving statement, agreements are made, and finally, prayers are offered once again. It is important to emphasize that there are no winners or losers, but only agreed-upon decisions. Generally these sessions last two or three hours, but some have gone on for much longer (Rottman 1996; Zion 1998).

The second approach identified by Rottman involves the return of certain types of criminal cases back into communities through the use of local or "branch" courts. The Midtown Community Court (MCC), located in Manhattan, New York City, is perhaps the most famous example of this approach. In the MCC, only minor offences are heard. But this is not just another court trial using the same actors and the same rules in a criminal courtroom that just happens to be located in a community. Instead, the community plays a significant role and is viewed as having a major role to play in the process and decision. In the MCC, community groups provide opportunities and the supervision of sentences that are served in the community. In addition, they provide other resources and services, such as treatment, support, and education. Eventually a community advisory board was created and a mediation board developed in order for disputes within the community to be resolved outside the traditional legal process.

The third type of community court identified by Rottman is the community justice centre. The community justice centre "significantly expands traditional notions about the role of courts and tests the extent to which they are capable of serving as catalysts for change" (Rottman 1996, 50). The centre consists of local agencies that supervise community service sentences, local residents groups that become involved in the legal process, and administrators that coordinate and makes recommendations for programs and services to those who need them. The Red Hook Community Justice Center in Brooklyn, New York, generally hears misdemeanour criminal cases but also hears such felony cases such as domestic violence and juvenile delinquency. In addition, civil cases such as landlord–tenant disputes and small claims are heard.

Questions

1. Do you believe that community justice is a viable alternative in every community?
2. What do you think are the positive and negative aspects of the community justice movement?
3. Do you think that community prosecution will prove to be effective in lowering the crime rate and solving the root causes of crime within communities?
4. Do you believe that the community justice movement, by involving the public in decision-making, will help to increase legitimacy for the criminal justice system?

SUMMARY

Alternative sanctions to custody have developed rapidly to meet the needs of both the social control system and offenders. These types of sanctions fall between incarceration and probation. They fill a need for the state to have a significant amount of control over offenders, but at the same time, they enable offenders to live in the community. This allows governments to save money, open up spaces in prison for more violent offenders, and give the appearance that sentences are fairer.

The most common form of alternative sanction is probation. Over the past decade or so, new programs in this area have been created. One is intensive supervision probation, which is characterized by close contact between probation officers and their clients. Home confinement is increasing in popularity and is usually accompanied by electronic monitoring devices. Day fines are another alternative; these are usually directed toward offenders who are unable to pay a fixed fine because of financial constraints (i.e., poverty). Another is the conditional sentence of imprisonment; yet another is drug treatment court.

Advocates generally say that these programs have met their goals. Researchers are much more cautious, although they have identified many components of these programs as crucial factors in reducing future criminality. Whatever their successes or failures, these programs continue to be used in the hope that they will evolve into effective and low-cost alternatives to traditional approaches of punishment.

Discussion Questions

1. Is serving a sentence in the community a "real" punishment? Explain your answer.
2. Compare and contrast "regular" probation with intensive supervision probation.
3. Do intermediate punishments reduce crime? Give reasons for your answer.
4. What are the most successful aspects of intermediate punishment programs?
5. Why do you think Canada has been slower to introduce intermediate punishments than the United States?
6. Compare and contrast EM programs that use the continuously signalling system with EM programs using programmed contact equipment.
7. Do intermediate punishments really help reintegrate offenders back into society? Explain.
8. Discuss the goals of intermediate punishments. Why were they introduced?
9. Do you think that drug treatment courts can succeed? Why or why not?

Suggested Readings

Byrne, J.M., A.J. Lurigio, and J. Petersilia, eds. *Smart Sentencing: The Emergence of Intermediate Sanctions.* Newbury Park, CA: Sage, 1992.

Ellsworth, T., ed. *Contemporary Community Corrections,* 2nd ed. Prospect Heights, IL: Waveland Press, 1996.

Hartland, A.T., ed. *The Search for Effective Correctional Interventions.* Newbury Park, CA: Sage, 1995.

Morris, N., and M. Tonry. *Beyond Prison and Probation: Intermediate Punishments in a Rational Sentencing System.* New York: Oxford University Press, 1990.

Smykla, J., and W.L. Selke. *Intermediate Sanctions: Sentencing in the 1990s.* Cincinnati, OH: Anderson, 1995.

Tonry, M., and K. Hamilton, eds. *Intermediate Sanctions in Overcrowded Times.* Boston, MA: Northeastern University Press, 1995.

References

Alberta. 1991. *Report of the Task Force on the Criminal Justice System and Its Impact on the Indian and Métis People of Alberta,* vol. 1. Edmonton.

Andrews, D.A., and J. Bonta. 1998. *The Psychology of Criminal Conduct,* 2nd ed. Cincinnati, OH: Anderson.

Andrews, D.A., J. Bonta, and R.D. Hoge. 1990. "Classification for Effective Rehabilitation: Rediscovering Psychology." *Criminal Justice and Behavior* 17: 19–52.

Ball, R.A., C.R. Huff, and J.R. Lilly. 1988. *House Arrest and Correctional Policy: Doing Time at Home.* Newbury Park, CA: Sage.

Baumer, T.L., R.I. Mendelsohn, and C. Rhine. 1990. *The Electronic Monitoring of Non-Violent Convicted Felons: An Experiment in Home Detention: Executive Summary.* Washington, DC: National Institute of Justice.

Belanger, B. 2001. *Sentencing in Adult Criminal Courts 1999/00*. Ottawa: Canadian Centre for Justice Statistics.

Belenko, S. 2000. "The Challenges of Integrating Drug Treatment into the Criminal Justice System." *Albany Law Review 63: 833–76.*

Bonta, J., J. Rooney, and S. Wallace-Capretta. 1999. *Electronic Monitoring in Canada*. Ottawa: Public Works and Government Services Canada.

Bonta, J., S. Wallace-Capretta, and J. Rooney. 2000. "Can Electronic Monitoring Make a Difference? An Evaluation of Three Canadian Programs." *Crime and Delinquency* 46: 61–75.

British Columbia Department of Corrections. 1995. "British Colombia Corrections Branch Electronic Monitoring Program." In K. Schulz, ed., *Electronic Monitoring and Corrections: The Policy, the Operation, the Research*. Burnaby, BC: Simon Fraser University, pp. 53–58.

Brown, M.P., and S. Roy. 1995. "Manual and Electronic House Arrest: An Evaluation of Factors Related to Failure." In J. Smykla and W.L. Selke, eds., *Intermediate Sanctions: Sentencing in the 1990s*. Cincinnati, OH: Anderson.

Byrne, J.M., and L. Kelly. 1989. *Restructuring Probation as an Intermediate Punishment: An Evaluation of the Implementation and Impact of the Massachusetts Intensive Probation Supervision Program: Final Report*. Washington, DC: National Institute of Justice.

Byrne, J.M., A.J. Lurigio, and C. Baird. 1989. "The Effectiveness of the New Intensive Supervision Programs." *Research in Corrections 2*, no. 2: 1–48.

Byrne, J.M., A. Lurigio, and J. Petersilia. 1992. "Introduction: The Emergence of Intermediate Sanctions." In Byrne, Lurigio, and Petersilia, eds., *Smart Sentencing*. Newbury Park, CA: Sage, pp. ix–xv.

Calverley, D., and K. Beattie. 2005. *Community Corrections in Canada 2004*. Ottawa: Ministry of Industry.

Chiodo, A.L. 2001. "Sentencing Drug-Addicted Offenders and the Toronto Drug Court." *Criminal Law Review* 45: 53–99.

Clear, T. 1994. *Harm in American Penology: Offenders, Victims, and Their Communities*. Albany, NY: SUNY Press.

Clear, T., and P. Hardyman. 1990. "The New Intensive Supervision Movement." *Crime and Delinquency* 36: 42–60.

Clear, T.R., and D.R. Karp. 2000. "Toward the Ideal of Community Justice." *NIJ Journal*. Washington, DC: U.S. Department of Justice, National Institute of Justice.

———. 1999. *The Community Justice Ideal: Preventing Crime and Achieving Justice*. Boulder, CO: Westview.

Coles, C., and G. Kelling. 1998. "Prosecution in the Community: A Study of Emergent Strategies." Paper presented at J.F. Kennedy Law School, Harvard University, Program in Criminal Justice, September.

Connor, R. 2000. "Problem-Solving Lawyers." *National Institute of Justice Journal,* January: 26–33.

Cullen, F.T., J.P. Wright, and B.K. Applegate. 1995. "Control in the Community: The Limits of Reform?" In A.J. Hartland, ed., *The Search for Effective Correctional Interventions*. Newbury Park, CA: Sage.

Daubney, D., and G. Parry. 1999. "An Overview of Bill C-41 (The Sentencing Reform Act)." In J.V. Roberts and D.P. Cole, eds., *Making Sense of Sentencing*. Toronto: University of Toronto Press, pp. 31–47.

Drug Court Programs Office, Office of Justice Programs. 1997. *Defining Drug Courts: The Key Components.* Washington, DC: U.S. Department of Justice.

Erwin, B.S. 1986. "Turning Up the Heat on Probationers in Georgia." *Federal Probation* 50: 17–24.

Erwin, B.S., and L.A. Bennett. 1987. "New Dimensions in Probation: Georgia's Experience with Intensive Probation Supervision (ISP)." Research in Brief. Washington, DC: U.S. Government Printing Office.

Fagan, J.A. 1994. "Do Criminal Sanctions Deter Drug Crimes?" In D.L. MacKenzie and C.D. Uchida, eds., *Drugs and Crimes: Evaluating Public Policy Initiatives.* Thousand Oaks, CA: Sage.

Finckenhauer, J.Q. 1982. *Scared Straight! and the Panacea Phenomenon.* Englewood Cliffs, NJ: Prentice-Hall.

Frideres, J.S., and B. Robertson. 1994. "Aboriginals and the Criminal Justice System: Australia and Canada." *International Journal of Contemporary Sociology* 31: 101–27.

Gendreau, P., F.T. Cullen, and J. Bonta. 1994. "Intensive Rehabilitation Supervision: The Next Generation in Community Corrections?" *Federal Probation* 58: 72–78.

Gendreau, P., and T. Little. 1993. "A Meta-analysis of the Effectiveness of Sanctions on Offender Recidivism." Unpublished manuscript, University of New Brunswick, Saint John.

Harrell, A., and M. Kleiman. 2000. "Drug Testing in Criminal justice Settings." In C.G. Leukefeld and F. Tims, eds., *Treatment of Drug Offenders: Policies and Issues.* New York: Springer, pp. 149–71.

Hillsman, S.T. 1990. "Fines and Day Fines." In M. Tonry and N. Norris, eds., *Crime and Justice: A Review of Research,* vol. 12. Chicago: University of Chicago Press, pp. 49–98.

"Hopeful New Court." 2008. *The Globe and Mail,* September 2, A14.

Hora, P., W. Schma, and J. Rosenthal. 1999. "Therapeutic Jurisprudence and the Drug Treatment Court Movement: Revolutionizing the Criminal Justice System's Response to Drug Abuse and Crime in America." *Notre Dame Law Review* 74: 439–538.

Hume, M. 2008. "Experimental Court Offers Justice with a Clean Break." *The Globe and Mail,* September 11, A1, A7.

Inciardi, J., D. McBride, and J.E. Rivers. 1996. *Drug Control and the Courts.* Thousand Oaks, CA: Sage.

Johnson, S., D.J. Hubbard, and E. Latessa. 2000. "Drug Courts and Treatment: Lessons to be Learned from the 'What Works' Literature." *Corrections Management Quarterly* 4: 70–77.

Jolin, A., and B. Stipak. 1992. "Drug Treatment and Electronically Monitored Home Confinement: An Evaluation of the Community-Based Sentencing Option." *Crime and Delinquency* 38: 158–70.

Klienman, M.A., and K.D. Smith. 1990. "State and Local Drug Enforcement: Search of a Strategy." In M. Tonry and J.Q. Wilson, eds., *Drugs and Crime.* Chicago: University of Chicago, pp. 69–108.

LaPrairie, C. 1999. *Conditional Sentence Orders by Province and Territory.* Ottawa: Department of Justice.

LaPrairie, C., L. Glicksman, P.G. Erickson, R. Wall, and B. Newton-Taylor. 2002. "Drug Treatment Courts—A Viable Option for Canada? Sentencing Issues and Preliminary Findings from the Toronto Court." *Substance Use & Misuse* 37: 1529–66.

Latessa, E. 1995. "An Evaluation of the Lucas County Adult Probation Departments ISP and High Risk Groups." In A.T. Hartland, ed., *The Search for Effective Correctional Interventions.* Newbury Park, CA: Sage.

Law Reform Commission of Canada. 1975. *Criminal Procedure: Control of the Process.* Ottawa: Minister of Supply and Services Canada.

Lilly, J.R., R.A. Ball, G.D. Curry, and J. McMullan. 1993. "Electronic Monitoring of the Drunk Driver: A Seven-Year Study of the Home Confinement Alternative." *Crime and Delinquency* 39: 462–84.

Lonmo, C. 2001. *Adult Correctional Services in Canada 1999/00.* Ottawa: Canadian Centre for Justice Statistics.

Maguire, K., and A.L. Pastore, eds. 1998. *Sourcebook of Criminal Justice Statistics— 1997.* Washington, DC: Department of Justice, Bureau of Justice Statistics.

Mainprize, S. 1995. "Social, Psychological, and Familial Impacts of Home Confinement and Electronic Monitoring: Exploratory Research Findings from British Columbia's Pilot Project." In K. Schulz, ed., *Electronic Monitoring and Corrections: The Policy, the Operation, the Research.* Burnaby, BC: Simon Fraser University, pp. 141–87.

———. 1992. "Electronic Monitoring in Corrections: Assessing the Cost Effectiveness and the Potential for Widening the Net of Social Control." *Canadian Journal of Criminology* 34: 161–80.

Makin, K. 2009. "Tories to Propose Law Ending Conditional Sentences for Serious Crimes." *The Globe and Mail,* June 15, A4.

———. 2000. "Judge Blasts Ontario's Monitoring of Convicts." *The Globe and Mail,* January 28, A8.

———. 1999. "Fear Limits Use of Electronic Monitoring." *The Globe and Mail,* October 11, A3.

Marlowe, D.O., and K.C. Kirby. 1999. "Effective Use of Sanctions in Drug Courts: Lessons from Behavioral Research." *National Drug Court Institute Review,* 2: 1–32.

Marth, M. 2008. *Adult Criminal Court Statistics, 2006/07.* Ottawa: Canadian Centre for Justice Statistics.

Matas, R. 2008. "B.C. Judge Sets Goal of Crime-Free Downtown Eastside." *The Globe and Mail,* August 27, A6.

Meyer, W. 2008. *Incentives and Sanctions: The Informal Use of Responses to Motivate Behavior Change.* Paper presented at the Canadian Association of Drug Treatment Courts Conference, Ottawa. November.

Morgan, K. 1994. "Factors Associated with Probation Outcome." *Journal of Criminal Justice* 22: 341–53.

Morris, N., and M. Tonry. 1990. *Between Prison and Probation: Intermediate Punishments in a Rational Sentencing System.* New York: Oxford University Press.

National Institute on Drug Abuse. 1999. *Principles of Drug Addiction Treatment: A Research-Based Guide.* Rockville, MD: National Institute on Drug Abuse.

Owen, B. 2006. "She Brings Justice System to the Streets." *Winnipeg Free Press,* May 14, A3.

Palumbo, D.J., M. Clifford, and Z.D. Snyder-Joy. 1992. "From Net-Widening to Intermediate Sanctions: The Transformation of Alternatives to Incarceration from Benevolence to Malevolence." In J.M. Byrne, A.J. Lurigio, and J. Petersilia, eds., *Smart Sentencing: The Emergence of Intermediate Sanctions.* Newbury Park, CA: Sage, pp. 229–44.

Pearson, F. 1986. *Research on New Jersey's Intensive Supervision Program: Final Report.* Washington, DC: National Institute of Justice.

Petersilia, J. 2004. "Community Corrections." In J.Q. Wilson and J. Petersilia, eds., *Crime: Public Policies for Crime Control.* Oakland, CA.: Institute for Contemporary Studies.

———. 1993. "Measuring the Performance of Community Corrections." *Performance Measures for the Criminal Justice System.* Washington, DC: U.S. Department of Justice.

———. 1987a. "Georgia's Intensive Probation: Will the Model Work Elsewhere?" In B. McCarthy, ed., *Intermediate Punishments: Intensive Supervision, Home Confinement and Electronic Monitoring.* Monsey, NY: Criminal Justice Press, pp. 15–30.

———. 1987b. *Expanding Options for Criminal Sentencing.* Santa Monica, CA: Rand.

Petersilia, J., and S. Turner. 1993. "Intensive Probation and Parole." In M. Tonry, ed., *Crime and Justice: A Review of Research,* vol. 17. Chicago: University of Chicago Press, pp. 281–336.

Prendergast, M., M.D. Anglin, and J. Wellisch. 1995. "Up to Speed: Treatment for Drug-Abusing Offenders under Community Supervision." *Federal Probation* 59: 66–75.

Rackmill, S.J. 1994. "An Analysis of Home Confinement as a Sanction." *Federal Probation* 58: 45–52.

Reed, M., and J.V. Roberts. 1999. Adult Correctional Services in Canada, 1997–98. Ottawa: Juristat.

Renzema, M., and D. Skelton. 1990. "Trends in the Use of Electronic Monitoring: 1989." *Journal of Offender Monitoring* 3: 14–19

Roach, K. 2000a. "Conditional Sentences, Restorative Justice, Net-Widening and Aboriginal Offenders." In *The Changing Face of Conditional Sentencing: Symposium Proceedings.* Ottawa: Department of Justice, pp. 25–38.

———. 2000b. "Changing Punishment at the Turn of the Century: Restorative Justice on the Rise." *Canadian Journal of Criminology* 42: 249–80.

Roberts, J.V. 1999. "Conditional Sentencing: Issues and Problems." In J.V. Roberts and D.P. Cole, eds., *Making Sense of Sentencing.* Toronto: University of Toronto Press, pp. 77–97.

Roberts, J.V., A.N. Doob, and V. Marinos. 2000. *Judicial Attitudes to Conditional Terms of Imprisonment: Results of a National Survey.* Ottawa: Department of Justice.

Roberts, J.V., and T. Gabor. 2004. "Living in the Shadows of Prison: Lessons from the Canadian Experience in Decarceration." *British Journal of Criminology* 44: 92–112.

Roberts, J.V., and P. Healy. 2000. "The Future of Conditional Sentencing." *Criminal Law Quarterly* 44: 309–41.

Rottman, D.B. 1996. "Community Courts: Prospects and Limits." *National Institute of Justice Journal,* August: 46–51.

Sampson, R.J., S.W. Raudenbush, and F. Earles. 1997. "Neighborhoods and Violent Crime: A Multilevel Study of Collective Efficacy." *Science* 277, 1–7.

Sawyer, K. 1985. "Tougher Probation May Help Georgia Clear Crowded Prisons." *Washington Post,* August 16, A1.

Schmidt, A.K. 1998. "Electronic Monitoring: What Does the Literature Tell Us?" *Federal Probation* 62: 10–20.

Sherman, L., P.R. Gartin, and M.E. Buerger. 1995. "Hot Spots of Predatory Crime: Routine Activities and the Criminology of Place." *Criminology* 27: 27–55.

Smith, L.G., and R.L. Akers. 1993. "A Comparison of Recidivism of Florida's Community Control and Prison: A Five-Year Survival Analysis." *Journal of Research in Crime and Delinquency* 30: 267–92.

Taillon, J. 2006. *Offences against the Administration of Justice, 1994/95 to 2003/04.* Ottawa: Canadian Centre for Justice Statistics.

Thompson, D. 1985. *Intensive Probation Supervision in Illinois.* Chicago: Center for Research in Law and Justice.

Tibbetts, J. 2008. "Ottawa to Track Parolees." *National Post*, August 12, A4.

Tonry, M. 1990. "Stated and Latent Functions of ISP." *Crime and Delinquency* 36: 174–91.

Tonry, M., and R. Will. 1990. *Intermediate Sanctions.* Washington, DC: National Institute of Justice.

U.S. General Accounting Office. 1990. *Intermediate Sanctions: Their Impacts on Prison Overcrowding, Costs.* Washington, DC.

Walker, S. 2001. *Sense and Nonsense about Crime and Drugs.* Belmont, CA: Wadsworth.

Wallerstedt, J. 1984. *Returning to Prison.* Washington, DC: National Institute of Justice.

Zion, J.W. 1998. "The Dynamics of Navajo Peacemaking." *Journal of Contemporary Criminal Justice* 14: 58–74.

Court Cases

R. v. Proulx (2000), 30 C.R. (5th) 1 (S.C.C.)

Weblinks

One of the most controversial components of Bill C-41, which was introduced in Parliament in 1996, was conditional sentences. Two of the first cases to reach the Supreme Court of Canada concerning conditional sentences were *R. v. Proulx* and *R. v. Wells* (both 2000). To read the Supreme Court's judgments, go to http://scc.lexum.umontreal.ca/en/index.html and then to the year 2000, Volume 1. *Proulx* was announced on January 31; *Wells* on February 17.

CHAPTER 11

Corrections in Canada: History, Facilities, and Populations

CHAPTER OBJECTIVES

✓ Examine the adult correctional population in Canada today.

✓ Discuss the facilities for women offenders in the federal correctional system.

✓ Discuss the legal rights of inmates.

✓ Understand the effects of being sentenced to prison, including prison violence and suicide.

✓ Outline the main benefits for introducing new-generation correctional facilities.

✓ Discuss the positive and negative aspects of private prisons.

✓ Discuss the different types of legal rights afforded to inmates.

In his book, *Justice Behind The Walls: Human Rights in Canadian Prisons*, UBC law professor Michael Jackson studied two issues relating to the law and Canada's prisons. The first issue was how far recent legislation had gone toward balancing the security of society with the "residual rights of prisoners." The second issue looked at how well Correctional Service of Canada "does at respecting the rule of law while administering the system." Jackson concluded that while the legislation doesn't "do badly at achieving the balance between security and residual rights," Correctional Service of Canada had demonstrated its inability "to respect the rule of law, to adhere to the spirit and letter of its own rules . . . " (Ruby, 2003, 11).

One case that raises issues about the rule of law in the federal correctional system involved Ashley Smith, 19, who died at the Grand Valley Institution in Kitchener, Ontario, on October 19, 2007. Ms. Smith first became involved with the criminal justice system in New Brunswick when, at the age of 14, she was sentenced to one-year of probation in March 2002, for harassing phone calls and shoving strangers on the street. A year later, she was ordered to a youth centre for breach of probation. She then underwent a psychiatric assessment that mentioned she had a possible learning disorder, ADHD, and a borderline personality disorder. In October, 2003, Ms. Smith while at home on probation threw apples at a postal worker and was subsequently returned to the youth centre.

On October 24, 2006, she received a one-year sentence for charges while she was at the youth centre. When she turned 18, Ms. Smith was then transferred to the federal women's correctional centre in Nova Scotia. In less than a year, she was transferred nine times between six different federal correctional facilities. During the time she was in federal custody, Ms. Smith never received a comprehensive psychological assessment. In September 2007, while at the Grand Valley Institution in Kitchener, Ontario, Ms. Smith started to choke herself several times a day. Guards who intervened "were kicked, grabbed, or spat upon" (Ha 2009b, A6). Between August 20 and her death two months later, guards confiscated 50 ligatures from Ms. Smith. Kim Pate, Executive Director of the Elizabeth Fry Society, visited Ms. Smith at the Grand Valley Institution and filed a grievance on her behalf. Ms. Smith indicated to Ms. Pate that she wanted to be taken out of segregation and taken to a hospital. However, the letter Ms. Pate sent to correctional officials went unread until several weeks after her death.

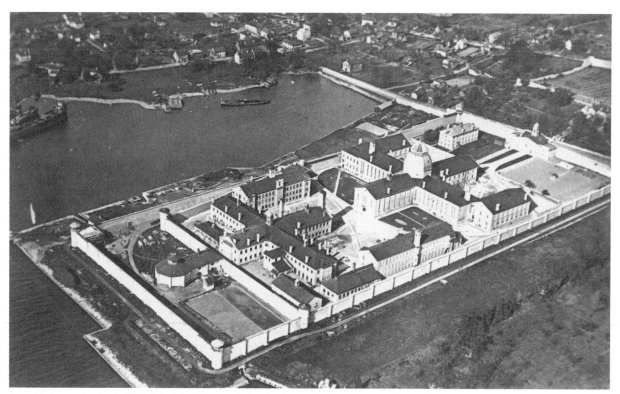

An aerial photograph taken in 1919 of the federal Kingston Penitentiary for Men in Kingston, Ontario. (National Archives of Canada/PA-30472)

On October 15, Ms. Smith was referred to a nearby regional mental health care facility but no beds were available. Four days later, she died in her cell after tying a garrote around her neck. After Ms. Smith's death, Kim Pate stated that Ms. Smith's case "is exceptional but not unique, reflecting the inability of the correctional system in dealing with mentally troubled inmates" (ibid.). During an investigation of Ms. Smith's death by federal corrections investigator, Howard Sapers, it was discovered that managers at the federal correctional institute had repeatedly attempted "to curb the instances where they had to report the use of force" when dealing with Ms. Smith (Ha 2009a, A5). In his report, Mr. Sapers stated that the system had failed to solve an array of problems that had previously been highlighted. He was troubled that Ms. Smith had been moved 17 times within the correctional system, had spent the final year of her life in segregation and had not received the mental health care she required. In his report, Mr. Sapers found that the Correctional Service of Canada "violated the law by keeping Ashley in solitary confinement without review, and continually transferring her without a proper psychiatric assessment" (Ha 2009b, A6). Although the use of solitary confinement is, "by law, subject to automatic review by regional correctional authorities after six weeks, Ms. Smith never received a single such review in nearly a year of solitary" and while federal policy "forbids the transfer of suicidal inmates . . .

Ms. Smith was transferred 17 times" ("Ashley Smith's . . ." 2009, A14). Mr. Sapers made 16 recommendations for improvements in a number of areas, including compliance with the law and policy in correctional operations, governance in women's corrections, and inmate complaint and grievance procedures (Meaney 2008).

After profiling the adult correctional population, this chapter will cover some of the most important issues facing Canadian corrections today. These issues include prison violence, prison suicide, and the challenges of surviving prison life. In addition, the legal rights of inmates will be discussed, including the requirement for the Correctional Service Canada to treat inmates fairly.

Offenders who have been convicted of a criminal offence may be sentenced to a period of confinement in a federal or provincial/territorial correctional institution (see Figure 11.1). Canada's correctional system was established in the early 1800s in Ontario with the opening of Kingston Penitentiary. The correctional system has grown since then in response to the growing number of individuals sentenced to a term of **incarceration**. In 2003, there were 186 correctional facilities across Canada. Seventy of these were under federal jurisdiction and the remaining 116 were under provincial/territorial jurisdiction. Sixteen of the 70 federal institutions were community correctional centres with a capacity of 505 spaces. There were also 54 federal institutions containing with 14,515 spaces.

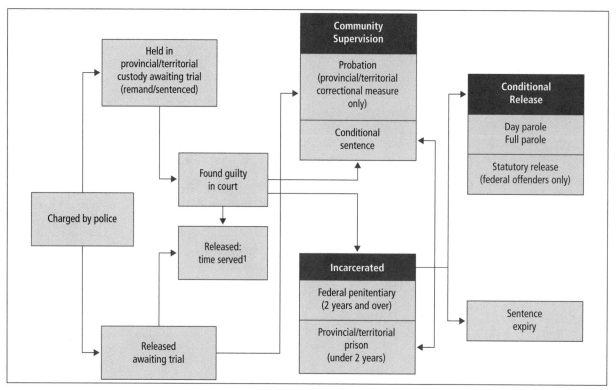

FIGURE 11.1

An Overview of Events in the Adult Correctional System

[1]An individual whose sentence approximates time already held in custody (i.e., while awaiting trial) is generally released by virtue of having already served his sentence.

Source: Juristat, April 1999, p. 3. Statistics Canada catalogue 85-002.

Five of these 54 institutions are regional women's institutions and another is an Aboriginal healing lodge for women. All of the women's institutions (except the Aboriginal healing lodge) are classified as multilevel security. There are also three mental health units across Canada. The remaining 45 federal facilities are for male inmates. According to the Correctional Service of Canada (CSC), most federal inmates are housed in facilities built between 25 and 60 years ago. Twenty-nine of the federal institutions were built between 30 and 65 years ago while another six are more than 65 years old (Robinson et al. 1998).

THE ADULT CORRECTIONAL POPULATION IN CANADA TODAY

In 2005–06, the federal and provincial/territorial adult correctional services processed 232,810 admissions into custody and 109,539 intakes into community supervision.

This represented a 3 percent increase compared to 2004–05. While the total number of individuals admitted into adult corrections in Canada has increased by 1 percent since 1996–97, there has a significant change in the composition of these admissions, most specifically in the provinces and territories. Ten years ago, adults remanded to custody while awaiting their next court appearance and adults those admitted to serve a sentence represented approximately equal percentages of all admissions to provincial and territorial custody. In 2005–06, the total number of remanded admissions into provincial/territorial custody were 22 percent higher than in 1995–96, while admissions to the provincial and territorial custody declined almost 28 percent (Landry and Sinha 2008).

Compared to 2001–02, the total number of remands increased in 12 jurisdictions during 2005–06. In terms of actual number of individuals remanded, the largest increases were found in Ontario (from 56,370 to 60,635, an increase of 7.1 percent) and British Columbia (from 10,687 to 13,580, an increase of 21.4 percent). Quebec was the only province to experience a decline in the same time period (from 27,341 to 26,921, a decrease of 1.5 percent). In terms of sentenced admissions, six jurisdictions experienced an increase between 2001–02 and 2005–06. In terms of actual number of individuals sentenced to custody, the largest increases occurred in Alberta (from 15,164 to 17,249, an increase of 12.1 percent) and in New Brunswick (from 1,555 to 2,285, an increase of 31.9 percent). The largest drop in sentenced admissions was experienced in Quebec (from 14,372 to 8,001, a decrease of 44.4 percent). At the federal level, the total number of sentenced admissions to custody increased by 4 percent (ibid.).

With the exception of conditional sentences, which declined from 18,890 to 18,580 individuals (a decrease of 1.6 percent), admissions increased to all forms of community supervision programs in 2005–06 compared to 2004–05. Admission to probation increased from 79,652 to 81,430 individuals (an increase of 2.2 percent) and provincial parole (from 1,762 to 1,875 individuals, an increase of 6.4 percent). Most (93 percent during 2005–06) admissions to community supervision programs during are under the control of provincial and territorial officials, while admissions to full parole, day parole, and statutory release (which increased by 7 percent during 2005–06) are under the responsibility of the federal authorities. During 2005–06, probation intakes were most common for violent offences (41 percent), followed by property offences (28 percent) and "other" Criminal Code offences (20 percent). The majority of probationers (41 percent) spent 12 months on probation; 17 percent received a probation order of two years or more; 14 percent received six months; and 9 percent received 18 months. Overall, admissions to all types of community supervision increased by 2 percent in 2005–06 compared to the previous year.

In 2003–04, most admissions (97 percent) were at the provincial/territorial level. Compared to 2002–03, all provinces except Newfoundland, British Columbia, and Alberta reported declines in the number of people sentenced to custody. Those three provinces experienced stable rates of sentences to custody. The largest decreases were in Nunavut (−29 percent), Prince Edward Island (−18 per cent), Quebec (−11 percent), and the Northwest Territories (−10 percent). Since 1995, the number of admissions to custody in all provinces and territories has decreased by 32 percent. Admissions to federal custody have decreased by 17 percent over the same time period.

During 2005–06, at least 89 percent of all offenders in each jurisdiction across Canada were sentenced to custody for Criminal Code offences; in Quebec and Alberta, though, this figure was only 69 percent. Sentences to custody for violent crimes were most common in Nunavut (74 percent), the Northwest Territories (63 percent), and Manitoba (60 percent). For property crimes, the highest rates of admissions were found in both Ontario and British Columbia (28 percent) and New Brunswick (25 percent). Admissions to sentenced custody for "other" Criminal Code offences, such as failure to comply with an order, were most common in Saskatchewan (48 percent) and Alberta (39 percent) (ibid.).

Almost 54 percent of admissions to sentenced custody in the provincial/territorial correctional system are for 31 days or less. During 2003–04, 24 percent of admissions to provincial/territorial custody were for between one and three months and 7 percent were for greater than 12 months. At the federal level, the percentage of offenders admitted to custody for sentences of between two and three years was 55 percent in 2003–04, an increase from 42 percent in 1999–2000. The percentage of those serving a sentence of three to four years remained stable, while the percentage of offenders serving a sentence of between four to five years fell from 12 percent to 9 percent. Declines were also evident for sentences of five to ten years (17 percent to 11 percent) and for life sentences (7 percent to 5 percent).

In federal correctional institutions during 2005–06, males accounted for the vast majority of admissions (94 percent); the same year, males accounted for 89 percent of all admissions to provincial/territorial facilities. The highest rates of females sentenced to provincial or territorial custody were found in Saskatchewan and Alberta during 2005–06 (13 percent). Aboriginal people made up 24 percent of all admissions to provincial/territorial facilities; for federal facilities, this figure was 18 percent. This highest rates for Aboriginal people sentenced to custody in a territory were found in Nunavut (99 percent) and the Northwest Territories (89 percent). The highest proportions of sentenced admissions to custody in provincial jurisdictions for Aboriginal people was in Saskatchewan (79 percent), Manitoba (71 percent), and Alberta (38 percent) (ibid.).

Most women remanded or sentenced to a correctional facility in Canada today are placed in provincial/territorial institutions. In 2005–06, women represented 11 percent of all provincial/territorial and 6 percent of all federal admissions to sentenced custody. This proportion of women admitted to provincial/territorial custody has remained stable since 1998–99. The proportion of women admitted to sentenced custody since 1998–99 has also slightly increased, from 4.8 percent of all admissions in 2002–03 to 5.6 percent of all admissions in 2003–04 and to 6.0 percent in 2005–06. The lowest number of women admitted to sentenced custody in a provincial jurisdiction during 2005–06 occurred in Nunavut (2 percent) and Newfoundland and

Labrador (4 percent). Newfoundland and Labrador was the only jurisdiction to report a significant decrease in the proportion of women admitted to sentenced custody over the past ten years (from 7 percent in 1996–97 to 4 percent in 2005–06) (ibid.).

EUROPEAN ANTECEDENTS TO THE MODERN PRISON

The first institutions resembling prisons emerged in Europe during the seventeenth and eighteenth centuries. Three major changes during this century dramatically influenced how most Western societies would run their correctional facilities in the coming centuries. The first was a philosophical shift away from the punishment of the body (such as flogging and torture) toward the punishment of the mind (Cohen 1985). Many people felt that punishments should focus on depriving people of their liberty instead of physically punishing them. According to Foucault (1995, 11), "the punishment-body-relation [was no longer] the same as it was in the torture during public executions. The body now serves as an instrument or intermediary: if one intervenes upon to imprison it, or to make it work, it is in order to deprive the individual of a liberty that is regarded as both a right and as property."

This new approach had its clearest beginnings with the work of the Philadelphia Society for Alleviating the Miseries of Public Prisons, a society operated by the Pennsylvania Quakers. In 1794, Pennsylvania became the first state to permanently abolish the death penalty for all criminal offences except first degree murder. The Quakers were also instrumental in restructuring the first jail in America (originally built in 1776 in Philadelphia) in order to introduce a humanitarian approach to housing inmates and changing their behaviour (Taft 1956).

The second major change involved the passing of laws that made it illegal to imprison anyone who had not been convicted of a crime. This led to the segregation of criminals from the rest of society. Gradually, the courts began to hand out sentences involving terms of imprisonment as opposed to physical punishments. According to historians, these changes emerged slowly in different European countries at different times. Spierenburg (1995) notes that the first criminal prison in Europe was opened in Amsterdam in 1654; he adds, however, that in other parts of the country, people were still being imprisoned for non-criminal offences—a practice that continued for another 100 years or so.

The third and biggest change was the beginning of the Age of Enlightenment. The Enlightenment had a strong impact on the criminal justice systems of Western nations, by influencing the form and content of corrections over the next two centuries. In terms of changes in imprisonment, two figures had the greatest impact: Cesare Beccaria and Jeremy Bentham (see Chapter 3).

Beccaria (1738–1794) was a member of a progressive intellectual group that in the late 1750s began publicly criticizing Italy's criminal justice system. Basing much of their social critique on the work of like-minded thinkers in England and France, they ultimately wrote a book titled *On Crimes and Punishments*. (Beccaria was credited as sole author. The others feared that the authorities would respond harshly to their critique. Beccaria, who belonged to an aristocratic family, would probably be safe.) In this short book, Beccaria outlined a utilitarian approach to punishment. He argued that some punishments could never be justified since they were more "evil" than any potential good they could ever do. Among the punishments that Becarria categorized as "evil" were torture and the use of ex post facto laws (i.e., laws passed after someone had committed a crime; the offender was then punished for actions that had not been illegal at the time). One of his strongest arguments was that punishments should be swift, since that would achieve the greatest amount of deterrence. Also, he argued that punishments should not be overly severe.

Bentham (1748–1832) was a famous British philosopher and jurist. He was a utilitarian—that is, he supported the principle that the goal of public policies (such as imprisonment) should be the greatest good for the greatest number of people. He also believed that people are motivated by pleasure and want to avoid pain and that a proper amount of punishment can deter crime (this is the "hedonistic calculus"). Accordingly, people by nature choose pleasure and avoid pain. Thus:

- Each individual calculates the degree of pleasure or pain from a given course of action.
- Lawmakers can determine the degree of punishment necessary to deter criminal behaviour.
- Such punishment can be effectively and rationally developed into a system of criminal sentencing.

Bentham drew up the plans for the first prison. Known as the "panopticon" (Greek for "all-seeing"), it was designed to put utilitarianism into practice by reforming offenders. A significant feature of the panopticon was its design: the plans called for a circular structure with a glass roof and a window in each cell. This would make it easy for the staff, who were located in a circular room in the centre of the building, to observe (or "surveil") each cell and its occupant. Solid walls separated each cell from the others, ensuring that the offenders, who were housed one to a cell, could not talk to one another. No panopticon was ever built, apparently because Bentham insisted that they be built near large urban centres in order to achieve the maximum amount of deterrence. Local residents, however, opposed the building of these structures and succeeded in defeating Bentham's dream of building progressive places for incarcerating offenders.

A BRIEF HISTORY OF FEDERAL CORRECTIONAL FACILITIES IN CANADA

It is only in recent decades that Canada, like all other Western nations, has increased its use of confinement as the main approach to punishing offenders. Between 1832, when the first federal prison was built in Kingston, and 1950, a total of eight federal prisons were constructed. During the 1950s, three federal institutions were built, followed by eight in the 1960s, five in the 1970s, and six during the 1980s.

The first prisons in North America were built in the United States. Two different types were originally constructed. The **Pennsylvania system** reflected a strong Quaker influence: inmates were isolated not only from the outside, but also from one another. They had one hour a day to exercise by themselves in an outside yard; they were expected to spend the rest of their time in their small cells, reading the Bible provided to them, reflecting on their illegal actions, and "repenting" their crimes (Jackson 1983).

Another style of prison was built in Auburn, New York. Referred to as the **Auburn system,** this institution held inmates in what is known as the "congregate system." This system was based on the belief that the most efficient way for inmates to reform their actions was through hard work. During the day, inmates worked together both inside and outside the walls, although they were not supposed to talk to one another. Prisoners ate together, but also in complete silence. When the inmates were not working or eating, they were locked in their cells. A different prison architectural style characterized the Auburn system. The Pennsylvania prison was built on one floor; the Auburn system had a number of floors of cells built in tiers, as they were called (Rothman 1971). The Auburn system, originally built between 1819 and 1823, quickly became the most copied style of prison and ultimately was considered to be the "international prototype of a maximum-security prison" (Anderson and Newman 1993, 349). The Auburn system was to become the basis for Canadian prisons. The first prisons in Canada were built by provincial

authorities. The first of these was completed in 1835 in Kingston; this was followed by the New Brunswick Penitentiary (1841) and the Nova Scotia Penitentiary (1844). In 1868, the federal government took over all three of these institutions and proceeded to build four new ones over the next 12 years. While the Canadian authorities followed the Auburn model, Pennsylvania system continued to survive in one particular form: solitary confinement. Most correctional institutions today contain within them areas set aside for more severe forms of punishment for inmates who have violated prison rules and regulations or who are considered to be troublemakers.

For the rest of the nineteenth century, the federal government operated its prisons in a very harsh manner. Conditions were harsh, discipline was extreme, and solitary confinement was regularly used (up to 18 months at a time). These approaches, it was argued, clearly demonstrated their "superiority [in terms of] the treatment of incorrigibles and criminal crooks" (Jackson 1983, 38–39).

At the beginning of the twentieth century, significant changes were introduced to the federal correctional system. Parole was introduced, correctional officials began to receive training, and inmate classification systems were developed. Also, inmates began to be housed on the basis of their needs and crimes, which led to the minimum-, medium-, and maximum-security designations (see below). The treatment of inmates was now based on the "policy of normalization," which specified that inmate programs were to be in a controlled environment (i.e., not an oppressive one) in order to better reflect conditions in society. Education programs and vocational training were also introduced at this time. In reality, the living conditions of inmates remained harsh; handcuffs and the ball and chain continued to be used until the early 1930s (Eckstedt and Griffiths 1988).

In 1935, the federal government decided to change its approach toward the treatment of inmates. Clear (1994, 80) notes that this change came about for three reasons. First, the correcting of offenders was now considered a "science," and as a result, highly educated individuals were beginning to take more dominant positions in the correctional administration hierarchy. Second, trained specialists were beginning to enter the institutions as case management workers and psychologists, with the goal of "correcting" offenders. Third, the belief that offenders could be corrected was leading to an infusion of money into the correctional system. Gradually an approach was adopted (referred to as the "medical model of corrections)," which favoured the provision of a variety of programs and therapies for "curing" inmates of their problem behaviour. It advocated medical solutions for problem behaviour, with treatments to be prescribed by "experts" in human nature, such as psychiatrists and psychologists. The impact of this new approach was immense: in 1920, there were approximately 1,200 federal inmates; by 1937, this figure had increased to 4,000. Over the same years, the number of federal correctional facilities increased, from 8 in 1937 to 19 in 1961.

Despite this change to a more rehabilitative ideal, inmates still experienced a harsh environment. Between 1932 and 1937, 16 riots broke out in federal correctional facilities. In 1937, the first of many Royal Commissions began investigating conditions in federal facilities. This commission, known as the Archambault Commission, produced a report that was harshly critical of the existing system. Instead of finding a system that was humane and based on the rehabilitative ideal, the commissioners found many problems. They made 88 recommendations, the general goal of which was to make federal correctional institutions more humane and progressive. But before any of these recommendations could be implemented, the Second World War began, leaving concerns about prison conditions as a low priority.

The end of the war led to a renewed interest in the federal correctional system. Of particular note was the creation, in 1953, of a committee of inquiry to study the operations and activities of the federal correctional system. The resulting report, the Fauteux Report, popularized the term "corrections" in Canada—a word the committee defined as "the total process by which society attempts to correct the anti-social attitudes or behaviour of the individual" (Carrington 1991, 374). This report's recommendations included the provision of aftercare programs and the construction of facilities with different security classifications. It also recommended a liberalizing of the parole process, automatic review of parole, increased use of pre-sentence reports, and the creation of a National Parole Board. However, support for rehabilitation was waning at this time, and by the early 1960s, treatment programs had been reduced in favour of incarceration.

In 1963, the medical model began to decline in importance, to be replaced by the reintegration model. This approach favoured community-based correctional facilities, in particular, the elimination of the coercive aspects of "treatment" and greater use of community resources for correcting offenders. This approach reflects the justice model of corrections (see Chapter 3), which maintains that inmates must be protected from any potential harmful actions of correctional officials through the introduction of legal rights for inmates and the increased use of community sanctions. In the mid-1970s, the Law Reform Commission of Canada committed itself to the reintegrative ideology, calling for a reduction in the use of imprisonment as a sanction. According to the Law Reform Commission of Canada (1975, 25), "restricting our use of imprisonment will allow more people for other types of penalties . . . positive penalties like restitution and community service orders should be increasingly substituted for the negative and uncreative warehousing of prison."

This approach was dominant until the 1990s, when the federal government merged the reintegration model with the psychological-based risk prediction ideology (see Chapter 12). The dominant approach today emphasizes the increased use of community resources; the assessment of offenders' risks and needs on entering the correctional facility; and the creation of individual programs addressing those risks and needs. This approach has since become recognized in other countries as the most effective way to treat inmates.

A BRIEF HISTORY OF FEDERAL CORRECTIONS FOR WOMEN

The earliest prison for women in Canada was located within Kingston Penitentiary. The original design called for separate units for male and female inmates; however, the first two women sentenced there were placed in the infirmary. By 1859, 68 women were serving their sentences in this facility, creating a serious problem for administrators. As Faith (1993) points out, female inmates were viewed as an "inconvenience" by prison administrators. Women continued to be moved to various locations within the penitentiary over the years; basically, they were "confined wherever and in whatever manner best served the administration of the larger male population" (Cooper 1993, 5).

Construction of a separate institution for female inmates was not begun until 1914. This facility, known as the Prison for Women ("P4W"), was actually built within the walls of the male prison in Kingston. Construction of a completely separate facility for women was begun in 1925. When it was completed in 1934, this new facility was designated as a maximum-security facility. No outside windows were built into the walls, all letters were censored, and there were no opportunities for education or vocational training of the type available to male inmates. Reports of sexual abuse and harsh living conditions led many reformers to demand that conditions be improved.

Beginning in 1968, numerous reports, investigations, and commissions investigated the P4W, and the final reports all made the same recommendation—that the facility be closed. They recommended that all inmates be located in their home provinces or in regional correctional facilities, which should be built and operated by the federal government. Many of these reports made basically the same point in support of their demands—that is, that female offenders are different from male offenders and thus should have different programs available to them. Programs were to be woman-centred—that is, all policies should be restructured to reflect the realities experienced by women as distinct from men. This was reflected in the report *Creating Choices: Report of the Task Force on Federally Sentenced Women* (1990), which advocated the empowerment of female inmates. It was recommended that women inmates be offered meaningful choices, respect and dignity, supportive environments, and shared responsibilities (Correctional Service of Canada 1990, 126–35). This reports also recommended that the federal government open regional facilities for women (including a healing lodge for Aboriginal women), increase programming for women, and make those programs more relevant so that when women were released they would be able to reintegrate quickly into society.

Two inquiries into the conditions of federally sentenced women in the P4W made a number of recommendations about how conditions for female inmates could be improved. The first was in 1989, when the federal government appointed the Task Force on Federally Sentenced Women to study the needs of female offenders, as well as their experiences, especially with regard to physical and sexual abuse. One of the goals of the inquiry was to evaluate whether the correctional model used for the male prison population was appropriate for women. The task force's final report, *Creating Choices: Report of the Task Force on Federally Sentenced Women* (Correctional Service of Canada 1990), recommended that the P4W be replaced by five new correctional facilities for women, all of which would feature community-based programs.

Perhaps the most significant event in the history of federal correctional institutions for both women and men in Canada was in 1994, when "a series of events occurred in the Prison for Women in Kingston . . . would go on to define the new 'face' of corrections in Canada" (Erdahl 2001, 43). On the evening of April 22, 1994, an Emergency Response Team made up of male correctional officers from the neighbouring federal facility in Kingston became involved in a "brief but violent physical confrontation with eight female inmates." The officers had been ordered to take them out of their cells in the segregation unit and strip search them. The following day, these women were sent to a psychiatric centre before being returned to the P4W. A second inquiry was held in 1995 to investigate the 1994 incident. The final report of this investigation, *Commission of Inquiry into Certain Events at the Prison for Women in Kingston* (also known as the Arbour Commission) was released in 1996. It made a series of recommendations, the general thrust of which was for fundamental and systematic changes for federally sentenced women. Its findings included these:

1. The CSC was not responding to outside criticism and was not prepared to give an honest and fair account of its actions. Instead, it was choosing to deny any errors in judgment and resist any criticism. Also, it was failing to properly investigate allegations of misconduct.
2. The CSC was part of a prison culture that did not value individual rights.
3. The CSC was failing to promote a "culture of rights" (Jackson 2002).

Between 1995 and 1997, the federal government opened new women's facilities across Canada (Correctional Service of Canada 1997). These regional facilities were located in Truro, Nova Scotia; Joliette, Quebec; Kitchener and Kingston, Ontario; Maple Creek, Saskatchewan; Edmonton, Alberta; and Burnaby, British Columbia. The Burnaby facility was managed under an Exchange of Service Agreement between the CSC and British Columbia Provincial Corrections. In September 2002, the federal government announced that those women serving federal sentences in Burnaby would be moving to a new federal women's facility in Abbotsford. This facility opened in the fall of 2004.

When the new women's correctional facilities first opened, all women, regardless of their security level, were housed together. However, a series of violent incidents at the Edmonton facility in its first few months of operations

The Edmonton Institution for Women was opened in 1995 and can accommodate up to 123 inmates. It is a multi-level facility; medium- and minimum-security inmates are accommodated in living units within a Structured Living Environment. Maximum-security inmates are accommodated in the Secured Unit. (CP PHOTO/Edmonton Sun/Christine Vanzella)

CHAPTER 11 Corrections in Canada: History, Facilities, and Populations in 1996—including two serious assaults on correctional staff, self-injury by a number of women inmates, a homicide, and seven escapes—led to all of the women classified as medium- and maximum-security risks being transferred to Alberta provincial facilities (where they would remain until late August 1996) under Exchange of Service Agreements. Soon after, the CSC decided that for safety reasons, no women classified as maximum security would be placed in the new regional facilities.

Yet another investigation of female inmates' needs was conducted at the time of the incidents in Edmonton. The resulting report, the Rivera Report, concluded that some women offenders required both a secure environment and long-term intervention/treatment for needs that pre-existed their incarceration and that could be exacerbated by certain aspects of their incarceration (Watson 2004, 4). One of the conclusions of this report was that the CSC should create a safe environment for at least three distinct subgroups of federally sentenced women.

It was realized that new resources would have to be built for maximum-security federally sentenced women in the new regional facilities. It was decided to place the maximum-security female offenders in small units in two federal male institutions (Springhill Institution and the Saskatchewan Penitentiary), both of which housed female inmates until 2003. A third facility, the Regional Reception Centre in Quebec, housed women inmates until 2004.

In May 1998, the Structured Living Environment (SLE) approach was implemented at each institution. This approach allowed higher security levels so that federally sentenced women would be able to remain in the regional facilities together with other offenders. Around-the-clock assistance and supervision were to be provided by staff with specialized training. However, concerns were raised about having maximum-security women living so close to lower security offenders. As a result, in 1999, Secure Units were introduced in order, to provide high-level intervention and supervision by specialized staff for women classified as maximum security with the exception of the women's facility at Maple Creek, Saskatchewan, all facilities currently have, or will eventually contain, Secure Units.

A BRIEF HISTORY OF FEDERAL CORRECTIONS FOR ABORIGINAL PEOPLE

Aboriginal peoples make up about 4 percent of Canada's population in 2006, yet they accounted for 18 percent of the federal custodial sentences in 2005–06. In 1991, the Royal Commission on Aboriginal Peoples was established to investigate many issues confronting Aboriginal people in the broader Canadian society, including justice issues. In response to the commission's five-volume final report, the federal government launched the "Gathering Strength" initiative, which amounted to a plan to recast the relationship between the government and Canada's Aboriginal people. The plan was built on the principles of mutual respect, mutual recognition, mutual responsibility, and sharing.

In compliance with the Royal Commission's recommendations and the federal government's initiative, the CSC reviewed its mandate to provide services to Aboriginal offenders as reflected in ss. 79 to 84 of the Corrections and Conditional Release Act. These clauses are intended to allow Aboriginal inmates to benefit from the positive spiritual and holistic aspects of their culture. They also invite Aboriginal communities and Elders to play an active role as service providers and advisers on policy formulation and implementation.

Sections 81(1) and (3) of the act state:

> 81 (1) The Minister, or person authorized by the Minister, may enter in to an agreement with an Aboriginal community for the provision of correctional services to Aboriginal offenders and for payment by the Minister, or by a person authorized by the Minister, in respect to the provision of these services . . .
>
> (3) In accordance with any agreement entered into under subsection (1), the Commission may transfer an Aboriginal offender to the care and custody of an Aboriginal community, with the consent of the Aboriginal offender and of the Aboriginal community.

As part of this initiative, starting in the mid-1990s, the federal government entered into agreements with Aboriginal communities and organizations relating to correctional services, including custody, for Aboriginal offenders. Since this time, at least eight healing lodges for Aboriginal offenders have been established. Healing lodges are designed to offer services and programs reflecting Aboriginal cultural traditions. The needs of Aboriginal offenders are addressed through Aboriginal teachings and ceremonies—with an emphasis on the spiritual values—in order to assist Aboriginal offenders in their successful reintegration. Almost all of these healing lodges are located away from urban centres. The first healing lodge was opened by the federal government in 1995; this was the 30-bed Okimaw Ohci Healing Lodge in Maple Creek, Saskatchewan, for use by

Okimaw Ohci Spiritual Lodge. (Correctional Service Canada. Reproduced with the permission of the Minister of Public Works and Government Services Canada, 2009.)

Aboriginal female offenders. Since that time, seven more healing lodges have been opened for Aboriginal men. These are located near Hobbema, Alberta (the Pe Sakastew Centre); Prince Albert, Saskatchewan (the Grand Council Spiritual Healing Lodge); Edmonton (the Stan Daniels Healing Centre); Chehalis, British Columbia (the Elbow Lake Healing Village); Crane River, Manitoba (the Ochichakkosipi Healing Lodge); Duck Lake, Saskatchewan (the Willow Creek Healing Lodge); Montreal (the Waseskun Healing Centre); and Yellowknife (the Some Ke' Healing Lodge). In addition, in 1999, the federal government opened the first healing lodge within the walls of a federal correctional facility, in Stony Mountain Institution, a medium-security facility north of Winnipeg. In this healing lodge, inmates do not live in the lodge, but do attend the facility for Aboriginal programming, spiritual teachings, and ceremonies.

Section 81 of the Corrections and Conditional Release Act allows Aboriginal communities to provide correctional services. The Okimaw Ohci and Pe Sakastew healing lodges are managed by the CSC; the remaining lodges are managed by Aboriginal agencies and/or communities. There are a number of differences between the lodges operated by the federal government and those run by Aboriginal agencies/communities. The federal lodges focus on traditional Aboriginal cultural traditions and holistic methods and are classified as minimum-security facilities (although Okimaw Ohci also accepts medium-security offenders). Some of the staff of both these facilities were CSC correctional officers before the lodge became a healing lodge. An offender who wants to transfer to one of these healing lodges follows the same process as for a transfer to any other correctional facility within the CSC. Between

1995, when the first healing lodge opened in Canada, and October 2001, 530 offenders resided in a healing lodge. Since 1998, over 100 individuals have been transferred to a healing lodge each year.

Healing lodges managed by Aboriginal communities are privately operated and follow guidelines as outlined in their contracts with the CSC. They do not necessarily follow the structured approach found within CSC-operated facilities. Transferring to a s. 81 healing lodge involves a slightly different process. Only those who are classified as minimum security can apply for a transfer. Once a healing lodge receives an application for a transfer to its facility, a meeting is held between the applicant and members of the healing lodge. Factors such as the applicant's involvement in traditional culture, motivation to change, commitment to the healing plan, and behaviour in the current correctional facility may influence the outcome of the application. Some healing lodges have other stipulations—for example, Waseskun has an agreement with the local community not to accept an applicant who has been convicted of a sexual offence (Trevethan et al. 2002).

Federal healing lodges have spaces for 30 to 40 individuals; the healing lodges under s. 81 offer spaces for anywhere between 10 and 100. Also, Crutcher and Trevethan (2002) report several differences between Aboriginal offenders in healing lodges and those in a minimum-security CSC facility: overall, the "residents of healing lodges appear to have a slightly more extensive criminal history than Aboriginal offenders in a minimum security" (ibid., 52). A larger proportion of healing lodge residents had been previously segregated for disciplinary infractions (25 percent versus 17 percent) and for attempted/successful escapes (34 percent versus 21 percent). Also, they were rated as at higher risk for re-offending (53 percent versus 45 percent) and as having a lower reintegration potential (45 percent versus 33 percent).

THE ROLE OF CORRECTIONAL INSTITUTIONS IN CANADIAN SOCIETY

Correctional facilities are built to make society a safer and better place. What goes on behind their walls is important in the sense that it is here that the goals of punishment (see Chapter 10) take over. The guiding philosophy of a given correctional system is a function of the operating preferences (e.g., deterrence, rehabilitation) of correctional facilities. Since correctional facilities were first introduced, three general models of correctional facilities have emerged to describe the different ways of thinking about them:

- *The custodial model.* This model is based on the idea that prisoners are incarcerated for the purposes of incapacitation and deterrence. All decisions are made in the context of maintaining maximum security and discipline. There is tight control over inmates in all phases of prison life. This model was the first to emerge, and the early prisons built in Canada reflected this style of thinking and operation.
- *The rehabilitation model.* Here, the emphasis is on individualized treatment. Concerns about security and control are secondary to the well-being of inmates. Treatment programs are available for (and often forced on) inmates in order to help them change their criminal and antisocial behaviours. This model came into popularity in the 1950s, but that popularity began to fade in the 1970s with the emergence of critiques of rehabilitation brought about by the work of Robert Martinson and his colleagues (see Chapter 12).
- *The reintegration model.* Here, correctional facilities attempt to prepare inmates for reintegration with the broader society. Facilities that take this approach help inmates work on their specific needs and risks so that they will not engage in criminal behaviour once they are living in the community again. During incarceration and their time on conditional release, responsibility and accountability are stressed. This model is the most influential one in Canada today.

Security Levels

The major objective of correctional institutions is confinement; it follows that the key factor in determining an inmate's classification level is security. On a general level, security has three components: (1) the likelihood that an inmate will escape or attempt to escape; (2) the likelihood that an inmate will place a correctional officer or another inmate in danger; and (3) the likelihood that an inmate will attempt to violate institutional rules (Anderson and Newman 1993). Until 1981–82, the CSC employed a classification system for offenders based on the likelihood that the offender would try to escape from an institution and the potential harm to the community if he or she succeeded. Accordingly, the CSC defined three levels of security as follows:

1. *Maximum security.* The inmate is likely to escape and would cause serious harm in the community.
2. *Medium security.* The inmate is likely to escape but would not cause serious harm in the community.
3. *Minimum security.* The inmate is not likely to escape, and if he or she did, would not cause

harm in the community. (Eckstedt and Griffiths 1988, 191).

The CSC's parole officers assign every inmate a security classification on entry into the institution. In most cases, this is followed by an interview with a placement officer, who assesses the inmate to determine his or her security needs. However, this initial assessment does not necessarily determine to which type of security-level facility the inmate will be sent. An inmate classified as maximum-security may be sent to a medium-security institution, depending on his or her prior record as well as the types of programs offered by the institution.

Maximum-security facilities are usually surrounded by high fences or walls (depending on when they were built), which are typically around 6 metres in height and surrounded by guard towers at strategic points. Intrusion detection systems ensure that the perimeter is not "compromised." Parts of the facility are separated by gates, fences, and walls, and inmates are usually required to have special permission forms when they are moving

A perimeter guard tower located at the Kingston Penitentiary for Men. (Copyright © 2006 HER MAJESTY THE QUEEN IN RIGHT OF CANADA as represented by the Royal Canadian Mounted Police (RCMP). Reproduced with the permission of the RCMP.)

between sections of the institution outside normal times of movement. A number of inmates live in solitary confinement, either owing to behavioural issues or out of concern that they will be attacked by other inmates, usually because of the crimes they are in prison for (e.g., sex offenders are in particular danger in prison). Maximum-security facilities usually have a number of educational and treatment programs, including adult basic education, high-school equivalency courses, and various skills development programs, such as carpentry.

Medium-security institutions are typically enclosed by chain link fences topped with barbed and razor wire. Relative to maximum-security facilities, medium-security institutions allow more freedom of movement for inmates. Many of these facilities have modern surroundings and training centres; a variety of educational and treatment facilities are also available. Minimum-security prisons usually have no fences or walls around them. In fact, any inmate can walk out of the facility, since the surrounding security is much more relaxed. There are no armed guards, no towers, and no barbed wire; nor is there any electronic surveillance equipment to ensure that prisoners stay in the institution. Staff and inmates often mingle and are indistinguishable from one another, since prison clothes are not issued. Inmates are housed in better living arrangements, in private or semiprivate rooms. In addition, inmates may be on work release programs that allow them to hold jobs during the day.

In 2008, the CSC reported that 14.3 percent of all male and female inmates serving a custodial sentence in the federal system were in a maximum-security institution. The remaining offenders were in medium-security, minimum-security, or multilevel institutions (Correctional Service of Canada 2008). A multilevel facility combines features of two or more of the security levels described earlier in this section. Some facilities use the same buildings to accommodate inmates classified at different security levels; others operate separate structures for each level. The majority of female inmates in the federal system are housed in multilevel security institutions, as are a significant number of all male inmates and 35 percent of female inmates serving a custodial sentence in the provincial/territorial correctional systems.

Since 1981–82, the CSC has operated on the basis of seven security levels. Level 1 facilities are community correctional centres; level 2 institutions are minimum-security facilities such as forestry and work camps. Levels 3, 4, and 5 are medium security; level 6 is maximum security. Level 7 is the highest level of security and is reserved for violent offenders. Level 7 units are often referred to as special handling units, or "super-max."

Federal female offenders are classified according to a different scale: the Security Management System,

which was approved for the new women's federal facilities in April 1995. The guidelines developed by this system govern the daily management of each facility as well as the inmates' participation in programs and activities and freedom of movement inside each facility. This system focuses on the majority of the female population in federal institutions, rather than on the few who persistently commit crimes in a violent and aggressive manner. It comprises six management levels, of which five are related to security classification and one is used exclusively for admission status (Finn et al. 1999).

PRISON ARCHITECTURE AND CORRECTIONAL FACILITIES

Correctional facilities must confront many serious issues, including drug use, suicide, violence between inmates, and attacks on correctional officers. Some prison officials began looking at these issues and developing new ways to approach the housing, guarding, and treatment of convicted offenders. They felt that how correctional facilities were operated was just as important as why they were built. As a consequence, some correctional facilities in Canada have been moving away from traditional designs and turning themselves into **new-generation facilities**.

In traditional facilities, known as first-generation facilities, often there is a separate building or cluster of buildings separated from the "outside" by high walls of reinforced concrete topped with barb wire and guard towers. Cell blocks have a linear design—that is, they are located along a long hallway. To supervise inmates when they are in their cells, correctional officers walk up and down these halls; as a result, their ability to see beyond the specific cell they are looking at is extremely limited. This style of supervision is referred to as "intermittent supervision." There is minimal contact between correctional officers and inmates, unless the officers are responding to an incident requiring their assistance. Many inmates misbehave or engage in illicit activities since they are not under the surveillance of correctional authorities.

Second-generation facilities began to emerge in the 1960s. In these designs, correctional officers keep the inmates under constant supervision from secure control booths that overlook all of the hallways and other areas (e.g., weight rooms) where inmates gather in groups. This type of surveillance is generally referred to as "indirect supervision." Cells are clustered around common living areas, where the inmates can watch television or meet. The cells have metal doors with unbreakable windows and usually have enough room for one or two inmates. Rooms have a bed, a desk, a sink, and perhaps

EXHIBIT 11.1 Supervision Models

According to the prison officials, there are six objectives of the direct supervision model:

1. Staff, rather than inmates, control the facility and inmates' behaviour.
2. Inmates are directly and constantly supervised, and correctional officers direct and control the behaviour of all inmates.
3. Rewards and punishments are structured to ensure compliant behaviour.
4. Open communication is maintained between the correctional staff and inmates.
5. Inmates are advised of the expectations and rules of the facility.
6. Inmates are treated in a manner consistent with proper standards of conduct and are treated in a fair and equitable way regardless of their personal traits or crimes they committed.

There are also seven behavioural dimensions necessary for the effective supervision and control of inmates in the pods. Many of these dimensions were developed from the general principles found in effective personnel supervision:

1. Resolving inmate problems and conflicts.
2. Building positive rapport and personal credibility with inmates.
3. Maintaining effective administrative and staff relations.
4. Managing the living unit to ensure a safe and humane living environment.
5. Responding to inmate requests.
6. Handling inmate discipline.
7. Supervising in a clear, well-organized, and attention-getting manner.

Sources: Nelson and O'Toole 1983; Gettinger 1984; Zupan 1991.

---

a toilet. They can be made of concrete or reinforced metal bolted to the wall or floor. Overall, there is little interaction between correctional officers and inmates. Early facilities of this type continued to use reinforced concrete walls topped with barbed wire; many later facilities used fences topped with razor wire.

Because of increasing prison violence starting in the late 1960s and continuing through the 1970s, other efforts were made to change the architecture of prisons. These attempts were based on the idea that inmates' physical surroundings were having an impact on their behaviour. In addition, important changes were made in the management philosophies of correctional facilities, so as to allow for more personal contact between correctional staff and inmates. Prison officials altered the traditional designs of correctional facilities to arrive at what are now known as "new-generation" facilities (sometimes these are referred to as third-generation or direct-supervision facilities). These new facilities are very different from their predecessors. The physical structure is based on a **podular design**—that is, each "pod" contains 12 to 24 one-person cells extending from a common area. These cells are usually situated in a triangle, enabling correctional officers to be in the centre of the triangle and have visual access to all, or nearly all, the living units and common areas. Daily activities, such as eating and recreational activities, take place in this common area. Other types of facilities, such as treatment and interview rooms, are located within the pod; all of this allows correctional officers greater access to and contact with inmates.

Another change in these facilities is the provision of comfortable furniture and rugs, as well as a "communal" room that allows inmates to get together to watch television, listen to a radio, or make a telephone call.

The podular design also differs from the traditional model in that it allows each unit to be directly supervised (see Exhibit 11.1). Throughout the day there are physical contacts among correctional officers (who are stationed within the pod), prison authorities, and inmates. During the day, inmates must stay in common areas and can only be in their cells with permission. This model allows correctional officials to identify problem behaviours quickly; it also allows them to observe the daily activities of all inmates. Prison officials have reported that the new-generation facilities have led to a dramatic reduction in the number of violent incidents as well as escapes (Zupan 1991). Studies have verified the positive effects that new-generation facilities have had on inmate behaviour, including lower rates of destructive behaviour, fewer escapes, and reductions in the number of suicides and violent incidents (Senese 1997). Applegate, and colleagues (1999) concluded that new-generation designs were not increasing recidivism and might lead to reduced post-offence offending.

Female Inmates

In 2004–05, women accounted for 6 percent of all offenders in provincial/territorial custody. There was strong variation among the provinces and territories with regard to the sentenced-custody admissions of women. Fifty-six percent of new female admissions were serving sentences of less than three years, continuing a trend that started in 1996–97. Female offenders usually account for larger proportions of probation and conditional sentences than of custody admissions. During 2005–06, for example, they accounted for 18 percent of all admissions to probation, ranging from a low of 14 percent in Quebec to a high of 23 percent in Saskatchewan. Seventeen percent of all admissions to conditional sentences were female, ranging 10 percent in Yukon to a high of 22 percent in Newfoundland and Labrador.

A small number of women are sentenced to a term in a federal institution each year. Overall, the number of women sentenced to federal custody has remained at approximately 5 to 6 percent since 1998–99. In 2007–08, the CSC reported that 307 women were incarcerated in federal correctional institutions. In 2006, just over one-half (55 percent) of federally sentenced women were serving a sentence for a violent crime while 25 percent were in custody for drug offences. These proportions remained relatively stable between 1997 and 2006. Compared to women in the Canadian population, the average age of women in federal custody was 37.7 years of age in 2006, compared to the average age among females aged 18 years and older in the general population was 48.1. Almost one-half (47 percent) of all federal female inmates were single, while just over 33 percent were married or living in a common-law relationship prior to their being sentenced to federal custody. In comparison, in the general population, women aged 18 years and older are much more likely to be married or living in a common law relationship (62 percent) compared to those who are single (21 percent). Twenty-five percent of all women serving a federal sentence in 2005–06 were Aboriginal, Women who were serving a term period of custody in three provincial systems (Nova Scotia, New Brunswick, and Saskatchewan) in 2006, had an average age was 32 years of age, single (55 percent), and less likely to be married or living in a common-law relationship (30 percent). Three of every ten female offenders admitted to provincial/territorial custody during 2004–05 were Aboriginal.

Female inmates are convicted and placed in a correctional facility for different offences than men, and for fewer offences. Data from four provinces (Newfoundland and Labrador, Nova Scotia, New Brunswick, and Saskatchewan) in 2002–03 indicates that 23 percent of all females released from an adult provincial correctional institution returned to that same jurisdiction's correctional service system within two years

(compared to 32 percent for males). In the federal system in 2006, 85 percent of women serving a term had either no, or only one, previous term of federal incarceration, compared to 70 percent of male inmates (Kong and AuCoin 2008).

Female and male inmates differ in terms of the offences for which they have been convicted. Women sentenced to a federal correctional facility are less likely than male inmates to be incarcerated for a violent crime. Nineteen percent of women were incarcerated for a violent crime, compared to 38 percent of men. The most common violent crime for which women were convicted during 2003–04 was "common assault," while the most common conviction in the category of crimes against property was "theft." Men were also most commonly convicted of these same two offences during 2003–04. Since 1997–98, the number of women admitted to federal jurisdiction increased 32.3 percent, from 232 in 1997–98 to 307 in 2007–08. Overall, the number of women admitted to federal correctional facilities represented 6.1 percent of the total number of admissions to federal jurisdiction. As of April 2008, there were 495 women incarcerated in federal correctional facilities across Canada (Correctional Service of Canada 2008).

Aboriginal Inmates

A major correctional issue is the well-documented fact that Aboriginal people are overrepresented in Canada's correctional facilities . In 2001, Aboriginal people represented 3 percent of the national population, yet they were 21 percent of provincial/territorial inmates, 18 percent of federal inmates, 16 percent of probation intakes, and 19 percent of conditional sentence admissions in 2003–04. The proportion of sentenced admissions to custody represented by Aboriginal people increased from 20 percent in 2001–02 to 21 percent in 2003–04 in the provincial/territorial correctional system and a decrease (from 19 percent to 18 percent) in the federal correctional system (Beattie 2005). The proportion of admissions to sentenced provincial/territorial custody has consistently increased each year, from a low of 15 percent in 1994–95. The largest increases in provincial custody during this time period were in Saskatchewan (72 percent to 78 percent) and Manitoba (from 61 percent to 68 percent). Provinces with the largest numbers of Aboriginal people in the adult population reported a larger representation of Aboriginal offenders in their sentenced admissions. The largest overrepresentation of Aboriginal offenders in sentenced custody compared to their representation in the adult population occurred in all of the western provinces (British Columbia, Alberta, Saskatchewan, and Manitoba) as well as in Ontario (ibid.).

A study comparing Aboriginal versus non-Aboriginal peoples in Nova Scotia, New Brunswick, and Saskatchewan between 2002–03 and 2003–04 revealed that almost 40,000 adults were involved in correctional services. Of this total, almost 11,400 (or 30 percent) were Aboriginal people. Aboriginal men and women represented relatively high proportions of all men and women in the adult correctional services of these three provinces (28 percent and 35 percent respectively). Similar to their representation in the general population, Aboriginal adults in correctional services were younger than non-Aboriginal adults, had attained lower levels of education, and were less likely to have been employed. More specifically, Aboriginal adults were, on average, three years younger than their non-Aboriginal counterparts in the three provinces (30.8 years versus 33.7 years of age). In addition, the majority (42.3 percent) of Aboriginal adult offenders were between 20 and 29, compared to 35.2 percent for non-Aboriginal offenders in this same age bracket. In addition, about three-quarters of all Aboriginal adults involved in correctional services had not completed high school compared to one-third of non-Aboriginal adults. Aboriginal people were also to be less likely to have been employed at the time of their admission to correctional services compared to non-Aboriginal people (35 percent versus 44 percent) (Brzozowski et al. 2006).

Prison Life

Most people believe that prisons can change the lives of inmates. Prisoners are separated from the outside world, experience a life under the constant scrutiny of prison guards and other staff, and are required to follow strict daily regimes or endure strict disciplinary sanctions. Prisons are commonly referred to as **total institutions**. According to Goffman (1961), total institutions have four distinct elements:

1. The inmate lives under the watchful eye of a centralized institutional authority.
2. The inmate shares his or her space with other inmates, who are all treated alike and who are forced to enact the same routines.
3. All of an inmate's time is tightly scheduled by a body of rules and administrative orders imposed by those in charge.
4. The entire system of enforced activities, and time and space control, is organized around the institutional goals of correction and/or treatment.

Goffman was interested in the ways that structural properties of institutions affect and alter the identities of the residents. According to Goffman, prisons are total institutions that force inmates to live regimented and dehumanizing lives. This overwhelming control forces inmates to "fight back" against this authority, leading them to commit more criminal acts. This process of dehumanization starts while the new inmates are being admitted, and it gives them a "clear notion of their plight." They quickly find that the requirements of the institution far outweigh any concerns about individual needs. This transition from the outside world to prison life is referred to as "civil death" by Goffman. At this time, the new inmate enters into a total institution that involves significant psychological and social changes that undermine the sense of self.

But this traditionally accepted view of prisons as total institutions has since been challenged. Farrington (1992) argues that prisons can better be described as "not so total" institutions. Here, he points out that Goffman's view is no longer consistent with the one that underlies most modern prisons. He notes that prisons are never totally isolated from society, as most require a constant supply of goods and services from the broader society. Prison staff work only in the prison, and every day when they leave, they take the prison into the community; they also bring back information from outside the prison and can answer inmates' questions. Furthermore, inmates are able to maintain contacts with many aspects of their former lives. The trend toward relatively shorter sentences and various programs that allow inmates to leave the prison for brief periods of time mean they have consistent contact with their communities. In addition, the correctional system today, through its emphasis on community corrections, emphasizes the reintegration of inmates.

Notwithstanding Farrington's view, prisons remain in many ways total institutions. Residents must dress according to institutional rules, and many human activities are strictly curtailed, including family relations, friendships, heterosexual activities, and a choice in deciding the daily activities in which one wants to participate.

Inmate Society

For decades, experts on prisons and prison life have stated that inmates form their own world—one with a unique set of norms and rules referred to as inmate subculture (Irwin 1980). The basis of inmate subculture, they argue, is a unique social code of unwritten rules and guidelines that tell inmates how to behave, think, and interact with prison staff and other inmates. Clemmer (1958) introduced the idea of inmate social codes when he wrote about life in a maximum-security prison. He identified a unique language used by prisoners, known as argot (Caron 1982), consisting of such words as "jointman" (a prisoner who behaves like a guard) and "yard" ($100). Clemmer also identified what he termed the "prisonization process"—the manner in which an individual assimilates into the inmate subculture by adhering to norms of behaviour, sexual conduct, and language. According to Clemmer, inmates who become the most "prisonized" are the most difficult to reintegrate into mainstream society.

When studying **prisonization**, criminologists have looked at two areas: how inmates adapt their behaviour to life behind bars, and how life in a correctional facility changes as a result of inmate behaviour. Sykes (1958) identified the "pains of imprisonment," that is, five deprivations inflicted on inmates that constitute the defining elements of imprisonment. The five pains of imprisonment identified by Sykes were:

- loss of liberty
- deprivation of goods and services
- loss of heterosexual relationships
- deprivation of autonomy
- deprivation of security

Inmate society compensates for the losses of things generally taken for granted in the outside society by creating an inmate subculture that offers differing degrees of comfort to those who successfully adjust to it. Sykes (ibid.) and Sykes and Messinger (1960) used Clemmer's work to identify the most important aspects of inmate subculture. They discovered what they called a "prison code"—that is, a system of social norms and values established by inmates to regulate their own behaviour while they were serving their time. According to Sykes (1958), these norms and values include the following:

1. Don't interfere with inmates' interests—for example, never betray another inmate to authorities.
2. Don't lose your head, and refrain from emotional displays (e.g., arguing) with other inmates.
3. Don't exploit other inmates.
4. Be tough and don't lose your dignity.
5. Don't be a sucker, don't make a fool of yourself or support guards or prison administrators over the interests of the inmates.

Sykes and Messinger (1960) identified the major theme of the inmate social code as prison or group solidarity. The greater the number of inmates who follow the inmate code, the greater the stability of the prison population and the less prison violence.

Cooley's (1992) research on prison victimization attempted to find out whether the inmate social code existed in Canada. After interviewing 117 inmates, he concluded that the inmate code, as traditionally defined, did not exist in the five institutions he studied. Instead he found a set of informal rules of social control (ibid., 33–34). Following are the most important informal rules of social control:

1. *Do your own time.* These rules define the public and private realms of prison life. They encourage group cohesion by defining proper prison behaviour, which promotes order and minimizes friction. They also discourage prisoners from asking for help from others.
2. *Avoid the prison economy.* These rules warn inmates of the consequences of conducting business in the informal prison economy. High interest rates exist in this economy, and if debts aren't paid off, physical violence may occur. These rules promote social cohesion by warning inmates of the consequences of not paying debts.
3. *Don't trust anyone.* These rules, which caution inmates to be wary of whom they associate with, are a consequence of the existing informant or "rat" system. The fewer people to whom a prisoner divulges personal information, the better. But if you do find some other inmates you can trust, support and help them so that they will respond in kind to you.
4. *Show respect.* This set of rules prescribes how inmates should interact with one another during their daily activities. These rules contribute to social cohesion in the prison by defining appropriate and inappropriate conduct between prisoners. They also determine a prisoner's status within the prison hierarchy. Those who follow the rules are respected. Those who violate the rules may be physically assaulted.

According to Cooley, these rules can bring the inmate population closer together or isolate its members. The resulting environment can best be described as partially unstable, in the sense that the prison is neither in conflict nor in consensus. The informal social control system described by Cooley establishes an inmate's status within the prison. Lifers and serious violent offenders usually maintain a high status, unless an inmate loses that status by engaging in behaviour not accepted by the other inmates. For example, while Donald Marshall was imprisoned at the medium-security federal institution near Springhill, Nova Scotia, he was told that another inmate, a "greenhorn," hadn't delivered some MDA (a powerful hallucinogenic drug) to him. When Marshall confronted the other inmate, it became obvious that the new inmate didn't know about "the code that applied when a greenhorn had a 'beef' with a lifer" (Harris 1986, 279). When the other inmate refused to admit he hadn't delivered the drug, Marshall knocked him unconscious.

An alternative to the **deprivation model** for understanding how inmate society develops is the importation model (Irwin and Cressey 1962). This model posits that inmate society is shaped by external rather than internal factors—that is, by the attributes that inmates bring with them when they enter the prison. An inmate who engaged in criminal offences on the outside and was friends with similarly minded people will bring those norms and values into prison and keep them while incarcerated, resisting any changes to make him or her more law abiding. Conversely, an individual who abided by societal norms on the outside will be open to following those norms while incarcerated, and will be more amenable to taking programs and services while in prison.

This inmate social code has changed over the years. In the earliest studies of inmates, researchers concluded that an unwritten set of rules guided inmate conduct. An inmate's position in a prison was determined by whether he or she followed the prison code: those who failed to do so were ignored and rejected by the prisoners who did follow the code. Some inmates were ignored; most were relatively safe from the violent actions of others unless they "ratted out a con." Starting about two decades ago, however, correctional facilities began to change as the prison code lost some of its power to maintain social relationships among inmates. This was owing to the rising numbers of younger offenders and drug offenders, who were originally viewed by those embedded in the traditional prison code as only "looking out for themselves" and as unwilling to follow the code and pay homage to other inmates. As a result, violence began to increase among inmates. With the increase in prison gangs in Canada and other Western countries, the traditional prison code has largely disappeared, having been replaced by another in which loyalties to the gang are the most important factor. One result has been a rise in inmate-on-inmate violence. In response to the different gangs now developing in the federal system, the CSC has started to send inmates in Quebec who are linked to rival gangs to different facilities. Maximum-security inmates, for example, are typically sent to the Donnacona Institution, where Aisle 119 is reserved for members and associates of the Bandidos Motorcycle Club and Aisle 240 for members of Hells Angels. There is also evidence that gang violence is escalating among other gang members serving time across Canada—a situation that may lead to "tremendous violence" within prisons (Humphries 2002, A3).

A large number of federal inmates have children under the age of 18. Families left behind not only suffer financial hardships but psychological and emotional problems as well. (AP/Ed Wozniak)

According to Dobash, and colleagues (1986), female inmates experience prison and the pains of imprisonment differently from male inmates. This is referred to as the gendered pains of imprisonment, which take into account the unique deprivations associated with women's incarceration and their responses to it. As Ishwaran and Neugbauer (2001, 135) point out, female inmates "cope with the loss of emotional relationships by developing and maintaining significant relationships of 'pseudo families' with other prisoners." Hannah-Moffat (2001, 233) states that "one manifestation of the pains of imprisonment experienced by female inmates is self-injurious behaviour." Self-injurious behaviour (or self-harm as it is also called) is a serious problem among women in the Canadian correctional system. Shaw (1991) reported that 59 percent of all federal female inmates at the time of her federally sponsored study of incarcerated women had engaged in some self-injurious behaviour. Presse and Hart (1996) studied 26 patients in the Intensive Healing Program at the Prairie Regional Psychiatric Centre and found that 19 of them had injured themselves. And the 1990 *Survey of Federally Sentenced Aboriginal Women in the Community* (Sugar and Fox) reported that Aboriginal women continued to slash themselves after being released in order to relieve their tension and anger. Fillmore and Dell (2001, 105) point out that to effectively deal with self-injurious behaviour, it is important to interconnect "the health concerns of self-harm [with] the broader issues of poverty, child care support, housing, education, job training, employment, discrimination, and racism."

Another difference experienced by female inmates relates to the disruption of their family life. At the time of their offence, at least half of incarcerated female offenders are living with at least one of their children. As a result, many must make special child-care arrangements with family or friends. Some lose custody of their children to the authorities. Many provincial governments have some type of limited policy regarding mother-and-child contact, but this was not so for federally sentenced women until recently. Shaw (1991), in her survey of federally sentenced women, reported that separation from children and concerns about child custody were a major source of anxiety for incarcerated women. The federal government's Task Force on Federally Sentenced Women reported that about 70 percent were mothers, many of whom were sole supporters of their children. In addition, most women had a limited education and few marketable skills, and were either on social assistance or working at low-paying jobs when arrested (LeBlanc 1994). When the regional centres for federally sentenced women were opened, the Mother-Child Program was established, which allows children to live with their mothers in the facility (Watson 1995).

PRISON VIOLENCE

Conflict leading to violence is an ever-present reality of prison life. Violence can involve different sets of actors: inmate versus inmate, staff versus inmate, inmate versus staff. According to official data, major assaults on inmates declined yearly between 1983–84 and 1988–89, but started to increase dramatically in 1989–90—a trend that has continued. The CSC produces the equivalent of official police reports (i.e., the Uniform Crime Reports); however, the actual occurrence of incidents that happen within the walls is not known, so the true picture of prison violence is not available. Between 1995–96 and 1997–98, for example, 144 major assaults among inmates were recorded. In addition, there were 10 major assaults by inmates on correctional staff, 9 murders by inmates, 8 hostage takings, and 13 major fights among inmates (Correctional Service of Canada 1998).

Attacks on staff varied between one and ten annually between 1984–85 and 1991–92. On average, there are two to four major assaults on staff each year. Furr (1996) examined the characteristics of sexual assaults on female prison staff in the federal correctional system and studied 11 inmates who had committed (or attempted to commit) at least one sexual assault against female staff. These inmates had committed crimes that had resulted in more physical harm to the victims, including the murder or attempted murder of past victim(s). A large proportion of these inmates suffered from psychoses, severe personality disorders, or mental/behavioural instability. Most had been identified as at high risk to sexually assault a female staff member—in some cases, they themselves had warned the staff about the risk before attacking them. Most of the assaults on the female staff occurred after the inmate had experienced hopelessness—for example, after being rejected for a conditional release program by the National Parole Board.

Violence can also involve all of the inmates in a correctional facility. Culhane (1985) documented nine examples of prison violence in Canada between 1975 and 1985. She described the degradation of inmates by prison officials and the resulting prisoner violence. One such incident occurred at Archambault Prison, north of Montreal, in 1972. Although 50 inmates were identified as having actively participated in the riot, between 75 and 150 were sent to solitary confinement. These inmates were accused of "participating passively" and therefore "had to pay the social price." Complaints about this treatment reached the attention of federal politicians; a federal inquiry failed to materialize because the guards who had allegedly been involved denied that they had participated, and there was a lack of corroborating evidence (Culhane 1985; Ruby 1985).

In 2007, Howard Sapers, the federal correctional investigator, released a report in which he studied the 82 deaths (all homicides, suicides, and accidental deaths) that occurred in federal correctional facilities between 2001 and 2005. It was discovered that more than 60 percent of these deaths were suicides, the majority of which were by hanging. Most homicides were the result of stabbings, while drug overdoses accounted for 80 percent of all accidental deaths. In his report, Mr. Sapers accused the federal correctional system of poor record keeping and communication involving troubled inmates, as well as having poor policies in place to respond to emergencies and failing to routinely check on inmates to ensure that they were safe. According to Mr. Sapers, the Correctional Service "has failed to incorporate lessons learned and implement corrective action over time and across regions, with the same errors and observations being made incident after incident" (Tibbetts 2007, A6). In his report, he did add that it may "possess a bias" since the study did not look at those cases in which the lives of inmates were saved by the actions of prison staff.

Prison Suicide

Suicide is the leading cause of death in Canadian prisons. Burtch and Ericson (1979) reported that between 1959 and 1975, the suicide rate of inmates in

Canada's federal institutions was 95.9 per 100,000 inmates, compared to 14.2 per 100,000 non-prison males in Canada. Between 1996–97 and 2005–06, 111 of the 525 offenders who died while in federal custody had committed suicide (Correctional Service of Canada 2008).

Concern over suicide rates during the early 1990s led the CSC to develop a suicide prevention program. In order to gain as much information as possible about male and female inmates who had committed suicide, Green and colleagues (1992) studied 133 suicides that occurred between 1977 and 1988. They found that most suicides were male (129, or 97 percent) and that 115 (or 80 percent) were White. The study also found that suicide was distributed across all age groups. In terms of marital status, half of those who committed suicide were single, 38 percent were married or living common-law, and 12 percent were divorced. Sixty percent had no children, 14 percent had one child, and the rest had two or more children.

The researchers reported that hanging was the most common suicide method (80 percent) among inmates. Almost all of the suicides occurred inside the inmate's own cell. In terms of offence and sentence characteristics, 51 suicides had committed a non-sexual offence of violence as their most recent offence, 34 had a robbery or weapons offence, 25 had a property offence, and only one individual was a first-time offender. Green and colleagues discovered that a high number of suicides occurred early on in a sentence—25 percent within 90 days of sentencing and 50 percent within a year of sentencing.

In an attempt to rectify this situation, the CSC developed a comprehensive approach that encompassed assessment, prevention, intervention, treatment, support, evaluation, research, and training of staff. Specific actions included these:

1. Providing a safe, secure, and humane environment for those suffering from mental illness and for those coping with the stresses of life in a correctional environment.
2. Increasing the awareness and understanding of both management and staff concerning suicide and self-injury.
3. Developing staff skills to prevent suicide and self-harm, so that suicide risk can be identified, pre-indicators can be monitored, and crisis intervention and support services can be provided.
4. Developing and implementing support services for survivors as well as affected staff and inmates.

These measures may be appropriate for men; but Grossmann (1992) argues that they are not applicable to

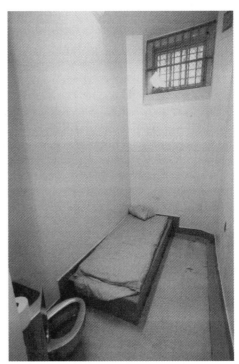

A view into one of the segregation cells at Kingston Penitentiary. (CP PHOTO/Kingston Whig Standard/Michael Lea)

Aboriginal women. She contends that correctional officials should better understand the needs of these women in the context of their socioeconomic position and victimization experiences. Responses to these needs should include a variety of culturally sensitive methods of assistance that focus on their "violent pasts and various forms of personal victimization, as well as opportunities to redress their education and employment deficiencies" (ibid., 412). The Task Force on Federally Sentenced Women (Correctional Service of Canada 1990) recommended assistance to abused women, improved counselling services, more culturally sensitive spiritual supports, and the maintenance of relationships between offenders and their families and communities.

Gangs in Prison

Prison gangs are one of the most significant developments in Canadian prisons in recent years. Their presence is attributed to increased gang activity in general across Canada as well as to criminal justice interventions, such as anti-gang legislation. Boe et al. (2003) studied the prevalence of gangs in Canadian federal correctional facilities and found that the proportion of federal inmates affiliated with a criminal organization had increased from 821 in March 1997 to 1,696 in November 2002. In 2008, there were 55 different gangs identified within the CSC. As of December 30, 2007, there were 1,882 offenders identified as either members or associates of criminal organizations. Of these offenders, 66 percent were in custody, while the other 34 percent were under various types of community supervision. Some of these offenders were associated (5) or affiliated (48) with Aboriginal gangs, with most (86 percent) serving their sentence in Alberta, Saskatchewan, or Manitoba. The number of individuals affiliated with street gangs increased 119 percent between 2000 and 2007, from 213 to 467 members. It is now estimated that the members of street gangs slightly outnumber members of outlaw motorcycle gangs in the federal correctional system (Bentenuto 2008).

Gangs in Canadian correctional facilities tend to vary according to region. Aboriginal gangs are typically concentrated in the Prairie region. Motorcycle gang members are overwhelmingly found in the Quebec region, as are members of traditional organized crime groups. Street gang members are predominantly located in the Prairie and Quebec regions, as are members of Asian gangs. White Supremacist gangs are most commonly found in the Pacific and Prairie regions.

Gang members are being blamed more and more for an increasing number of offences against both staff and other inmates. Leger (2003) reports that the presence of gang members poses various challenges for prison officials—challenges relating to power and control issues, the availability of drugs, gang recruitment, and the intimidation and corruption of staff. These individuals are more likely to be directly involved in assaults on other inmates and staff members than are non-gang members. As a result, some gang members have been placed into Canada's Special Handling Unit (SHU), located at Ste-Anne-des-Plaines in Quebec (see Exhibit 11.2). Howard Sapers, in an investigation into the deaths of inmates between 2001 and 2005, attributed a number of killings and suicides to gang-related activities. He noted that the federal correctional system "lacks anti-gang strategies and trained security intelligence analysts" (Tibbetts, 2007, A6).

Two explanations for the emergence of gangs as powerful forces within Canadian correctional facilities are deprivation and importation. As pointed out in this chapter, the argument underlying the deprivation model is that inmates develop a social system as a way to adapt to the pains of imprisonment. Since inmates are deprived of, for example, their liberty, they develop a culture that allows them to access what imprisonment has taken from them. The importation approach emphasizes that inmates' pre-prison attitudes and values guide their behaviours as well as their responses to the internal conditions of a correctional facility. Groups often bring their illicit activities with them when they enter prison.

PRISONERS' RIGHTS, DUE PROCESS, AND DISCIPLINE

Over the past few decades, prisons have been reformed most often through the intervention of the courts. Before the 1970s, Penitentiary Service Regulations required prison officials to provide inmates with certain basics, such as adequate food and clothing, essential dental and medical services, and sufficient time to exercise (MacKay 1986). These rights represented only the core of the Standard Minimum Rules for the Treatment of Prisoners (1957) adopted by the United Nations, which covered such issues as religion, transfers, and disciplinary procedures. Starting in 1980, inmates began to receive limited rights and access to justice within federal correctional facilities. Yet it remained difficult for them to question prison rules and regulations or the decisions of prison officials. Perhaps the most important reason why inmates lacked legal rights was that provincial and federal courts hesitated to intervene in the administration of prisons unless there were obvious, excessive, and indiscriminate abuses of power by prison officials. This policy, referred to as the **"hands-off" doctrine**, had three planks:

1. Correctional administration was a technical matter best left to experts rather than to courts, which were ill equipped to make appropriate evaluations.
2. Society as a whole was apathetic to what went on in prisons, and most individuals preferred not to associate with or know about offenders.
3. Prisoners' complaints involved privileges rather than rights.

The effect of this doctrine was "to immunize the prison from public scrutiny through the judicial process and to place prison officials in a position of virtual invulnerability and absolute power over the persons committed to their institutions" (Jackson 1983, 82). But as a result of prison disturbances during the 1970s and complaints made by inmates about their treatment during and after these incidents, government officials began inquiring into the conditions faced by those serving sentences in federal correctional facilities. The federal government established a committee to investigate prison conditions in the mid-1970s; its final report (tabled in 1977) emphatically pointed out that the prison system was not rehabilitating offenders and that "imprisonment . . . itself epitomizes injustice" (House of Commons Subcommittee on the Penitentiary System in Canada 1977, 85). To alleviate this situation, the committee recommended that the rule of law (see Chapter 1) and justice be introduced into the prison system.

At the end of the 1960s, prisoners and prison-rights advocates were already challenging the hands-off doctrine in the courts over the specific issue of due process rights within correctional facilities. In the first such case, *R. v. Institutional Head of Beaver Creek Correctional Camps ex parte McCaud* (1969), an inmate challenged the prison's authority to make disciplinary decisions without providing inmates with due process protections, such as the right to a fair hearing and the right to legal counsel. Also challenged were the arbitrary powers found within s. 229 of the Penitentiary Regulations, which outlined a number of activities for which inmates could be disciplined. The Ontario Court of Appeal ruled that while natural justice also applied to inmates, there were situations in which prison officials had the right to place an inmate in segregation without proper due process safeguards and the possibility of a review of the administrative decision in question. However, while the court ruled that administrative decisions are reviewable when they involve questions about the civil rights of inmates, this specific case involved a decision purely administrative in nature and therefore wasn't reviewable by the courts.

The first case to significantly challenge the administrative power of prison officials was *McCann v. The Queen* (1975). Jack McCann had been placed in solitary confinement in the British Columbia Penitentiary for 754 days under the authority of s. 2.30(1)(a) of the Penitentiary Service Regulations, which states: "Where the institutional head is satisfied that for the good maintenance of good order and discipline in the institution . . . it is necessary that the inmate should be kept from associating with other inmates." McCann argued that his period in solitary confinement infringed on his right to freedom from cruel and unusual treatment or punishment under s. 2(b) of the Canadian Bill of Rights (Jackson 1983). The court held that prison administrators had the right to place inmates in solitary confinement with no prior hearing, unless their civil rights were in jeopardy. But it ruled that the use of solitary confinement in this case did, in fact, constitute "cruel and unusual punishment" (ibid., 101–33).

However, the Supreme Court of Canada, in *Martineau v. Matsqui Institution Inmate Disciplinary Board* (1980), formally recognized that "the rule of law must run within penitentiary walls." It also stated that although prison officials make administrative decisions, they are still subject to the duty to act fairly. In this case, two inmates at the Matsqui Institution in British Columbia had been found guilty of being in a cell where they shouldn't have been. They argued that "they were not provided with a summary of evidence against them;

that the evidence of each was taken in the absence of the other; that the conviction was for an offence unknown to law; and that Martineau was never given an opportunity to give evidence with respect to the charge" (ibid., 126–27). As a result of this ruling, all those who make administrative decisions concerning the rights or liberties of inmates now have a duty to act fairly (Pelletier 1990).

The Duty to Act Fairly

What does it mean to "act fairly," especially for inmates in a correctional facility? The duty to act fairly involves two basic rights: (1) the right to be heard, and (2) the right to have an impartial hearing. As Pelletier (1990, 26) notes, the right to be heard means that all citizens have the right "to be informed of the allegations made against them and to respond to those allegations." The right to an impartial hearing means that "a decision must not be rendered against a person for discriminatory or arbitrary reasons."

In Canada, two areas of legal concern are related to the duty to act fairly: (1) administrative segregation (or solitary confinement), and (2) discipline of inmates. What powers do prison officials have to place inmates in administrative segregation? Obviously, some situations, such as prison riots, may require immediate segregation. But what about other situations? In *McCann v. The Queen* (1975), which was the first case to argue the fairness of the decision to segregate, Mr. Justice Heald ruled that the decision to place an inmate in solitary confinement was "purely administrative" and therefore not subject to legal review.

This interpretation was reinforced by the decision in *Kosobook and Aelick v. The Queen and The Solicitor-General of Canada* (1976). In this case, the complainants had been told that they were being placed in solitary confinement after an administrative inquiry into the stabbing of an inmate, but no charges had been laid against them. They argued that their segregation was a denial of natural justice and their right to an unbiased tribunal, the result of a decision made in an arbitrary manner, and an infringement of the Canadian Bill of Rights. They claimed that they had not been provided with due process protections and that as a result they had been held in arbitrary detention. The judge ruled that the prison authorities did not have any judicial or quasi-judicial functions, but rather performed the role of an administrative body. Thus they could not violate the Canadian Bill of Rights.

However, in *Martineau v. Matsqui Institution Inmate Disciplinary Board* (1980) the Supreme Court of Canada ruled that correctional officials have a duty

EXHIBIT 11.2 Special Handling Units: Canada's Super-Maximum Institutions?

In the United States, about 30 states are experimenting with super-maximum prisons. Recently, much attention has been paid to the super-max prison in Tamms, Illinois. Formally known as Tamms Correctional Center, it isolates all inmates for 24 hours a day. In essence, all programs and services come to each inmate either through a television located in each cell or by individual attention from priests or staff who go to a specific cell to talk to an inmate. At the present time, four inmates serving time in Tamms are involved in a class-action suit alleging that the structure of Tamms will lead to sensory deprivation based on the nearly total isolation, which results in "tormenting pain" (Campbell 1999).

The closest any correctional facilities in Canada come to this type of super-max prison are the Special Handling Units (SHUs). The CSC opened two SHUs in 1977 to house male inmates "who could not be managed adequately in a maximum-security institution because of the high level of risk and danger they posed to staff and other inmates" (O'Brien 1992, 11). These units were housed in two sections of existing federal correctional institutions, one in Millhaven, Ontario, the other in the Correctional Development Centre in Quebec. Two institutions built specifically as SHUs were opened in 1989 in Prince Albert, Saskatchewan, and Ste-Anne-des-Plaines, Quebec.

A new policy on the control of dangerous inmates in the federal system was introduced in 1990. SHUs began to offer limited programs, such as anger management and treatment for substance abuse, and only those inmates who were assessed as high-risk to staff and other inmates were sent to these facilities. The objective of SHUs is to safely reintegrate prisoners into a maximum-security prison. This allows other institutions to become safer, thus enabling them to work with larger numbers of offenders in the hope of successfully reintegrating them into society (ibid.).

In 1991–92, 50 to 60 inmates with an average age of 31.5 (ranging from 24 to 52) entered the Prince Albert SHU. The most common offence for those admitted was first degree murder (21.1 percent); the most common sentence was life imprisonment (42.1 percent). At the other SHU, in Quebec, the average age of inmates was 33, with a range of 22 to 55. Their most common offences were second degree murder and robbery (20.6 percent each); 26.5 percent were serving a life sentence. Of those admitted to the Quebec SHU, 32.4 percent were serving their first federal sentence.

In 1998, the SHU in Prince Albert was closed. In September 2003, 72 inmates were being held in the SHU at Ste-Anne-des-Plaines, which has a capacity of 90 inmates. Inmates at Ste-Anne are divided into groups of five or six on each of the floors (also known as "ranges"). This facility is the only one in Canada where correctional offices are allowed to carry firearms and live ammunition during their patrols. Inmates in an SHU are not totally isolated from one another; they are allowed to exercise in small groups and to watch a communal television. Some inmates are locked in their cells for 24 hours a day, but these are the ones who refuse to participate in any programs or to take advantage of the limited work activities available. Most of the inmates were transferred to this facility because they assaulted other inmates (21) or staff (20). The rest were transferred to the SHU after committing acts such as murdering another inmate, attempting to escape, or threatening others. Fifty-four percent of the SHU population had been there for a year or less; 22 percent had been housed there for between one and two years. Twelve percent had been in the SHU for five years or more (Correctional Service of Canada 2004).

Sources: R.L. O'Brien 1992; Campbell 1999; Humphries 2002.

to act fairly when making disciplinary decisions. According to Cole and Manson (1990, 63), this case "opened the modern era of prison law in Canada and exposed internal parole and prison processes to judicial scrutiny." In essence, the Supreme Court concluded that the rule of law must be upheld within correctional facilities. As a result of *Martineau*, the CSC changed its policies to fit more closely with the fairness doctrine. For example, in terms of administrative segregation, inmates now had the right to be heard within the correctional context, and prison authorities were obliged to (1) inform an inmate, in writing, of the reasons for the placement in segregation within 24 hours following this placement; (2) notify an inmate in advance of each review of the placement in segregation, in order to permit the inmate to present his or her case at a hearing in prison; and (3) advise the inmate, in writing, of decisions concerning his or her status.

The impact of the Charter of Rights and Freedoms has not been as great in the area of prisoners' rights as many had first expected. Some thought that it would bring about great changes, but the Supreme Court has often held in its decisions that the state can justify, within reasonable limits, intrusions into fundamental rights and freedoms afforded to Canadians (e.g., the right to freedom from search and seizure). In other words, "the concept of liberty is not an all or nothing proposition" (Jackson 2002, 60). However, the Charter has had an impact in terms of procedural protections for inmates.

The Office of the Correctional Investigator (OCI) was established in 1973 after a Royal Commission examined the events surrounding recent prison riots at Kingston and Millhaven. This report recommended major changes "in the accountability and oversight of the federal correctional system," which has led the OCI to be seen by many as "an important part of safeguarding the rights of offenders" and of ensuring that inmates are treated fairly (Sapers 2006, 31).

The OCI has the power to investigate a broad range of offender issues and problems. While it can only recommend solutions to the problems that inmates bring to its attention, it can often get information that the inmate is requesting and that has not yet been provided by the correctional administration.

In 2003–04, the OCI received 6,892 complaints, a slight decline from the 6,988 it received the year before. The ten most common complaints dealt with by the OCI in 2003–04 related to health care, institutional transfers, visits, cell property, correctional staff issues, administrative segregation, the conditions of confinement, case preparation for decisions, grievance procedures, and file information.

PRIVATE PRISONS

Prisons have always been controversial in our society. A current issue in Canada revolves around the idea of **private prisons**. These prisons would be built and operated by private corporations specializing in corrections and supposedly would save large amounts of money for federal and provincial governments.

In the spring of 1995, New Brunswick signed a contract with a private corporation specializing in the building and management of correctional facilities. In that contract, Wackenhut Corrections Corporation of Florida agreed to build and operate a facility for young offenders. At the same time, New Brunswick announced that it was considering calling for private proposals to build and possibly also operate an 80-bed adult facility. The Nova Scotia government then issued a press release stating that it was looking at the feasibility of involving the private sector in operating its nine provincial correctional centres. Both provincial governments cited cost savings as the rationale for exploring private prisons as an alternative. New Brunswick noted it might save as much as 15 percent of the costs of building and operating a facility, while Nova Scotia stated that it was looking for ways to reduce the provincial debt. The government of New Brunswick later decided to staff the new facility with provincial employees; even so, its contract with Wackenhut raised the issue of private prisons in Canada.

Canada and other countries, including Great Britain, Australia, and France, have experimented with privatizing prisons, but the only country that has actually implemented such prisons is the United States, where an estimated 3 percent of prisons and jails are now privately run. In 1991, Corrections Corporation of America—the largest contractor of private prisons—was operating 14 secure adult facilities and 3 juvenile facilities, totalling about 48,000 beds; Wackenhut was operating eight adult facilities with 3,200 beds. Today, more than 50 private correctional facilities for adult inmates are operating in the United States. Most of these are minimum- or medium-security institutions, and most of them have been built in the three states—California, Florida, and Texas—with the largest inmate populations. Besides operating these facilities, private corporations are designing and building them, and maintain that they can build a facility twice as quickly and 20 percent cheaper than a state government can. The private sector is also involved in the financing of new construction.

In all other countries that are experimenting with private prisons, such as Great Britain and Canada, citizen approval of debt for capital projects is not required. For this reason, private financial support of prisons is "less attractive . . . because the cost of raising capital is higher when the debt instruments are not backed by the full faith and credit of the government" (McDonald 1992, 391). Experiments with private prisons were conducted largely on the basis of claims that private contractors could relieve governments of the costs of running these facilities while maintaining the same level of custody and the same quality of services. State governments, facing large increases in the number of inmates, the high costs of constructing prisons (up to $75,000 per bed), and demands by the public to reduce taxes, turned to private prison contractors in the hope of saving money.

At first, claims by private prison contractors seemed to be borne out (Meddis and Sharp 1994). However, a 1996 study by the U.S. General Accounting Office, the investigative unit of Congress, compared studies of public and private prisons on the basis of two factors: (1) operating costs, and (2) quality of service. The final report concluded that the results were mixed: some private operations were cheaper and yet able to provide quality services, while other private facilities were more expensive to operate and/or offered poorer services. It concluded that these studies provided little guidance for jurisdictions hoping to reduce the costs of their prisons.

Nevertheless, advocates of privatization contend that for several reasons, private prisons have distinct advantages. First, they are more productive because they are not caught in public-sector bureaucracy and red tape. Second, they are more efficient, because private employees are more productive and because private facilities are more willing to experiment with cost-cutting measures. Third, these institutions are able "to buy in larger quantities of discounts and from a wider range of possible suppliers," thereby reducing the costs of supplies (ibid., 399).

Critics of privately operated prisons argue that prisons cannot be operated according to the bottom line. They point out that the labour-intensive nature of prisons does not allow for significant amounts of technological innovations of the sort that would reduce costs. Instead, any cost savings will come at the expense of reliable and well-trained employees. And any advantage that private corporations hold over their public-sector counterparts may be reduced if their employees unionize.

Furthermore, these critics argue, privately run prisons will not be committed to providing quality programs for inmates. Charging that the private sector is more interested in "doing well" than in "doing good," an American Bar Association committee wrote that "conditions of confinement will be kept to the minimum that the law requires" (American Bar Association 1986, 6).

All researchers who have studied both public and private correctional institutions have commented on how hard it is to make direct comparisons. Even advocates of privatization believe that private prisons will not always be cheaper than public-sector facilities; they add, however, that the strength of private facilities lies in their ability to be more innovative and to implement changes more quickly and more efficiently.

The Central North Correctional Centre in Penetanguishene in fall 2001. When it opened in 2001, it was the first private provincial correctional facility in Canada. It is now operated by the Province of Ontario. (© Queen's Printer for Ontario, 2009.)

To date in Canada, private prisons have not been a big issue. More than a decade ago, the federal government ruled out any involvement with the private sector. The provinces, though, have been much more active on this issue. New Brunswick's private youth-training facility was mentioned above. The first adult facility to be built and operated by a private contractor is in Penetanguishene, Ontario. It was built by and is being operated by Management and Training Corporation (MTC), based in Utah. This facility has the capacity for 1,184 maximum-security adults (1,152 men and 32 women). It has six interconnected octagonal pods, with each pod containing six living units (two offenders are housed in each cell). It also has an enclosed exercise area as well as program and visiting areas. MTC was awarded a five-year contract worth $170 million for its bid of just under $80 per inmate per day—a bid $60 lower than the average provincial cost (Patchmar 2001).

Supporters of private prisons argue that private corporations have shown that they perform the same services as government-run facilities at a cost 10 to 15 percent lower. However, Shichor (1995) contends that there is no consensus on the cost savings achieved by private prisons. Supporters of private prisons argue that labour costs are saved by flexible staffing, by electronic surveillance used in lieu of human surveillance, and by substituting fringe benefits with profit-sharing arrangements (Logan 1990). Critics argue that this model may lead to reduced safety within these institutions and to less security for surrounding communities (DiIulio 1991).

THE ISSUE OF CREDIT FOR PRETRIAL CUSTODY

From 1996–97 to 2005–06, the total number of admissions to adult corrections increased only slightly (+1 percent). However, during this time period there was a substantial shift in the composition of the admissions. In 1996–97, the percentage of adults remanded to custody and the percentage of adults admitted to serve a sentence were almost equal. In 2005–06, remanded admissions accounted for 63 percent of admissions to provincial/territorial custody. According to Landry and Sinha (2008), the number of admissions to remand was 22 percent higher in 2005–06 than in 1996–97, while admissions to provincial and territorial sentenced admissions declined almost 28 percent in the same time period. In addition, individuals sentenced to remand are now spending longer periods of time in remand custody. During 1996–97, the number of adults serving one week or less of remand decreased from 62 percent of all those individuals remanded while the number of individuals who spent three of more months in remand increased from 4 to 7 percent.

One of the reasons for the increased use in remand custody has been changes in the Criminal Code. Section 515(10) of the Criminal Code provides the reasons for which custodial remand is justified. It states that the prosecutor must "show cause" in order to justify the detention of the accused in custody. In the case of certain specified offences, e.g., murder, the onus is upon the accused to "show cause" as to why they should not be detained in custody. Traditionally, the detention of accused persons can be justified on the basis of (1) if it is shown that there is a risk they will not appear for their court date; and (2) if they are considered to be a danger to themselves or to others. In 1997, this section of the Criminal Code was expanded to allow the use of remand when "the detention is necessary in order to maintain the confidence of justice having regard to all the circumstances." In 1999, another amendment was added to ensure that the safety concerns of both victims and witnesses are taken into consideration in decisions involving remand. In addition, non-compliance with court orders has increased, police-reported data indicating that there has been an increase of 40 percent in such violations over the past decade (Silver 2007). For example, since 1999–2000, Saskatchewan has experienced an overall increase of 23 percent in admissions to remand for bail violations.

On March 27, 2009, the federal government introduced legislation (Bill C-25) in an attempt to limit judicial discretion in granting credit for pre-sentence custody. The most common credit for pretrial custody at the time of sentencing in Canada is two for one—six months in pretrial custody ends up being 12 months toward the sentence. The proposed legislation, entitled An Act to Amend the Criminal Code (limiting credit for time spent in pre-sentencing custody), if passed, will limit judicial discretion when it comes to sentencing offenders. It is also referred to as the "Truth-in-Sentencing" Act. Truth-in-sentencing laws are used by over 40 states in the U.S. to mandate that violent offenders serve at least some of their sentence in prison (Sobel et al. 2002). While they were first enacted in 1984, most truth-in-sentencing laws came into existence after the U.S. Congress passed the federal Violent Crime Control and Law Enforcement Act (1994). The Act awards grants to states to expand prison space to punish violent offenders, if they can prove that offenders convicted of violent crimes (e.g. murder, manslaughter, sexual assault, robbery) serve at least 85 percent of their sentence.

If the new legislation passes, it will replace s. 719(3) of the Criminal Code, which states:

719.(3) In determining the sentence to be imposed on a person convicted of an offence, a court may take into account any time spent in custody by the person as a result of the offence.

In its place, the federal government proposes to replace s. 719(3) of the Act with the following:

(3) In determining the sentence to be imposed on a person convicted of an offence, a court may take into account any time spent in custody by the person as a result of the offence but the court shall limit any credit for that time to a maximum of one day for each day spent in custody.

(3)(1) Despite subsection (3), if the circumstances justify it, the maximum is one and one-half days for each day spent in custody unless the reason for detaining the person in custody was stated in the record under s. 515(9.1) or the person was detained in custody under s. 524(4) or (8).

(3)(2) The court shall give reasons for any credit granted and shall cause those reasons to be stated in the record.

(3)(3) The court shall cause to be stated in the record and on the warrant of committal the offence, the amount of time spent in custody, the term of imprisonment that would have been imposed before any credit was granted, the amount of time credited, if any, and the sentence imposed.

(3)(4) Failure to comply with s. (3)(2) or (3)(4) does not affect the validity of the sentence imposed by the court.

Why has the two-for-one pretrial credit sentence continued to be a part of the Canadian criminal justice system? One reason given is that pretrial detention facilities across Canada are often overcrowded with sometimes two or three individuals sharing the same cell. Individuals may be locked-down for 18 hours or more each day and there are very few programs or activities available.

Another reason is that pretrial custody does not count toward parole eligibility. For example, if an individual is denied bail and spends six months in pretrial custody before they are found guilty in court and subsequently sentenced to four years with a two-for-one credit, they will be able to apply for parole after having served 18 months. In comparison, an accused who is granted bail and receives the same four-year sentence can apply for parole after serving 16 months in custody. According to one defence lawyer, two-for-one credit "is only fair, given the jail conditions and the fact that the time does not count towards parole" (Kari 2008, A5).

In *R. v. Wust* (2000), the Supreme Court of Canada upheld the lower court decision to grant the defendant a credit of one year for their pre-sentence custody of seven and one-half months of custody, although in this case the credit resulted in a period of incarceration below the mandatory minimum sentence. According to the Supreme Court of Canada, mandatory minimum sentences must be interpreted and administered in a manner consistent with the criminal justice system's overall sentencing approach.

According to recent court decisions in Ontario, two-for-one credit is not a right. The Ontario Court of Appeal in 2006 held that the credit is not automatic, particularly when a judge determines someone remains a danger to society and has very little chance of being granted early parole. In *R. v. Francis* (2006), the Court of Appeal upheld a lower court decision not to apply the two-for-one credit because the offender posed "a serious danger to society and that he would not likely receive parole."

In 2007, the Ontario Court of Appeal once again ruled on the two-for-one credit. In *R. v. Thornton* (2007), it upheld a lower court decision not to grant credit for pretrial custody when it appeared that an offender was taking advantage of this system by intentionally accumulating time in pretrial custody so as to reduce his sentence.

Questions
1. Should pretrial remand custody only be an option for those individuals deemed to be violent?
2. What type of measures could be taken to reduce the amount of individuals in pretrial custody?
3. Do you think that Bill C-25 will be effective in terms of limiting judicial discretion in terms of handing out two-for-one pre-trial credit?
4. Do you think the federal government should introduce a truth-in-sentencing policy for all sentences?

SUMMARY

The ideas underlying our contemporary correctional institutions originated in the United States in the nineteenth century. Two competing systems emerged: the Pennsylvania system and the Auburn system. Both approaches treated their inmates with great discipline and rigidly enforced rules, but it was the Auburn system, which allowed groups of inmates to work together and then isolated them at night, that formed the basis of the Canadian correctional system.

Canada's federal and provincial/territorial correctional populations were increasing slowly until five years ago; since then, they have grown by a phenomenal 31 percent. Besides those serving time in a correctional facility, there are in excess of 120,000 offenders serving their time in the community.

At present, more than 40 federal correctional facilities are operating in Canada. They are classified according to security level. Significant differences exist between them when it comes to their physical appearance and the amount of freedom they offer inmates. Five new regional facilities for federally sentenced women are now operating and are providing new and innovative programs designed specifically for women. Many of the programs are offered in the community.

Until recently, little information was available about prison society. Certain codes or rules exist for inmates to follow, but the prison environment is very unstable since changes are always occurring. There is much violence in Canadian prisons: suicides, murders, and assaults occur regularly, and many inmates try to isolate themselves from other inmates as well as from situations that they feel may lead to violence.

Today, inmates have significant (albeit limited) legal rights. Inmates can take their grievances to various officials and request a hearing. Various courts, including the Supreme Court of Canada, have recognized that inmates possess these rights and have often ruled in their favour.

Discussion Questions

1. Do you think that reintegration is a positive approach to dealing with inmates? Why or why not?

2. Discuss the issue of prisoners' rights and the evolution of law concerning such rights in Canada.

3. Should we build more federal prisons in Canada?

4. Describe the classification of inmates and correctional facilities. Do you think that there is a better way to classify offenders?

5. Discuss the special issues surrounding female offenders.

6. Discuss the needs of Aboriginal offenders. Do you think they can be met by the existing correctional systems? Do you think any changes should be made?

7. Discuss "prisonization." What are the negative aspects of this process? Can we change it?

8. Can prison violence ever be eliminated?

9. What is the best way to solve the issue of gangs in Canadian correctional facilities?

10. Should more provincial/territorial governments allow private prisons to operate their correctional facilities?

11. Can anything be done to better control gangs in prison?

Suggested Readings

Eckstedt, J.W., and C.T. Griffiths. *Corrections in Canada: Policy and Practice,* 2nd ed. Vancouver: Butterworths, 1988.

Faith, K. *Unruly Women: The Politics of Confinement and Resistance.* Vancouver: Press Gang Publishers, 1995.

Jackson, M. *Prisoners of Isolation: Solitary Confinement in Canada.* Toronto: University of Toronto Press, 1983.

McMahon, M.W. *The Persistent Prison? Rethinking Decarceration and Penal Reform.* Toronto: University of Toronto Press, 1992.

References

American Bar Association. 1986. *Report to the House of Delegates.* Chicago: American Bar Association.

Anderson, P.R., and D.J. Newman. 1993. *Introduction to Criminal Justice,* 5th ed. Toronto: McGraw-Hill Ryerson.

Applegate, B., R. Surette, and B.J. McCarthy. 1999. "Detention and Desistance from Crime: Evaluating the Influence of a New Generation Jail on Recidivism." *Journal of Criminal Justice* 27: 539–48.

"Ashley Smith's Inhumane Death." 2009. *The Globe and Mail*, March 10, A14.

Beattie, K. 2005. *Adult Correctional Services in Canada, 2003/04.* Ottawa: Canadian Centre for Justice Statistics.

Bentenuto, L. 2008. "Street Gangs: A Federal Correctional Perspective." *RCMP Gazette,* 70: 20–21.

Boe, R., M. Naketh, B. Vuong, R. Sinclair, and C. Cousineau. 2003. "The Changing Profiles of the Federal Inmate Population: 1997 to 2002." Research Report R-132, Ottawa, Ontario Correctional Service in Canada.

Brzozowski, J., A. Taylor-Butts, and S. Johnson. 2006. *Victimization and Offending among the Aboriginal Population in Canada*. Ottawa: Canadian Centre for Justice Statistics.

Burtch, B.E., and R.V. Ericson. 1979. *The Silent System: An Inquiry into Prisoners Who Suicide/and Annotated Bibliography*. Toronto: Centre for Criminology, University of Toronto.

Campbell, M. 1999. "Buried Alive?" *The Globe and Mail*, December 7, R1, R2.

Caron, R. 1982. *Go-Boy!* Toronto: Hamlyn.

Carrington, D. Owen. 1991. *Crime and Punishment in Canada: A History*. Toronto: McClelland and Stewart.

Clear, T. 1994. *Harm in American Penology: Offenders, Victims and Their Communities*. Albany, NY: SUNY Press.

Clemmer, D. 1958. *The Prison Community*. New York: Holt, Rinehart, and Winston.

Cohen, S. 1985. *Visions of Social Control*. Cambridge: Polity Press.

Cole, D.P., and A. Manson. 1990. *Release from Imprisonment: The Law of Sentencing, Parole and Judicial Review*. Toronto: Carswell.

Cooley, D. 1992. "Prison Rules and the Informal Rules of Social Control." *Forum on Corrections Research* 4: 31–36.

Cooper, S. 1993. "The Evolution of Federal Women's Prisons." In E. Adelberg and C. Currie, eds., *Women in Conflict with the Law: Women and the Criminal Justice System*. Vancouver: Press Gang.

Correctional Service of Canada. 2008. Corrections and Conditional Release Statistical Overview. www.publicsafety.gc.ca. Retrieved April 24, 2009.

———. 2004. *Commissioner's Directive: Special Handling Unit*. Ottawa: Correctional Service of Canada. www.csc-scc.gc.ca. Retrieved April 16, 2006.

———. 1998. *Performance Report for the Period Ending March 31, 1998*. Ottawa: Correctional Service of Canada.

———. 1997. *Corrections in Canada*. Ottawa: Correctional Services Canada.

———. 1990. *Creating Choices: Report of the Task Force on Federally Sentenced Women*. Ottawa: Correctional Service of Canada.

Crutcher, N., and S. Trevethan. 2002. "An Examination of Healing Lodges for Federal Offenders in Canada." *Forum on Corrections Research* 14: 52–54.

Culhane, C. 1985. *Still Barred from Prison: Social Injustice in Canada*. Montreal: Black Rose.

DiIulio, J.J. 1991 "The Duty to Govern: A Critical Perspective on the Private Management of Prisons and Jails." In D.C. McDonald ed., *Private Prisons and the Public Interest*. New Brunswick, N.J. : Rutgers University Press.

Dobash R.P., R.E. Dobash, and S. Gutterridge. 1986. *The Imprisonment of Women*. New York: Basil Blackwell.

Eckstedt, J.W., and C.T. Griffiths. 1988. *Corrections in Canada: Policy and Practice*, 2nd ed. Toronto: Butterworths.

Erdahl, E. 2001. "History of Corrections on Canada." In J.A. Winterdyk, ed., *Corrections in Canada: Social Reactions to Crime*. Toronto: Prentice-Hall, pp. 27–48.

Faith, K. 1993. *Unruly Women: The Politics of Confinement and Resistance.* Vancouver: Press Gang.

Farrington, K. 1992. "The Modern Prison as Total Institution? Public Perception versus Objective Reality." *Crime and Delinquency* 38: 6–26.

Fillmore, C., and C. Dell. 2001. *Prairie Women, Violence and Self-Harm.* Winnipeg: Elizabeth Fry Society of Manitoba.

Finn, A., S. Trevethan, G. Carriere, and M. Kowalski. 1999. *Female Inmates, Aboriginal Inmates, and Inmates Serving Life Sentences: A One-Day Snapshot.* Ottawa: Juristat.

Foucault. M. 1995. *Discipline and Punish: The Birth of the Prison*, trans. Alan Sheridan. New York: Vintage.

Furr, K.D. 1996. "Characteristics of Sexual Assaults on Female Prison Staff." *Forum on Corrections Research* 8: 25–27.

Gettinger, S.H. 1984. *New Generation Jails: An Innovative Approach to an Age-Old Problem.* Washington, DC: National Institute of Corrections.

Goffman, E. 1961. *Asylums.* New York: Doubleday.

Green, C., G. Andre, K. Kendall, T. Looman, and N. Potovi. 1992. "A Study of 133 Suicides among Canadian Federal Prisoners." *Forum on Corrections Research* 4: 20–22.

Grossmann, M. 1992. "Two Perspectives on Aboriginal Female Suicides in Custody." *Canadian Journal of Criminology* 34: 403–16.

Ha, T.T. 2009a. "Officials Tailored Reports Involving Use of Force on Inmate, Transcripts Show." *The Globe and Mail*, March 11, A5.

———. 2009b. "Instructed to Curtail Crushing Red Tape, Guards Watched Girl Die in her Cell." *The Globe and Mail*, March 3, A1, A6.

Hannah-Moffat, K. 2001. "Limiting the State's Right to Punish." In J.A. Winterdyk, ed., *Corrections in Canada: Social Reactions to Crime.* Toronto: Prentice-Hall, pp. 151–69.

Harris, M. 1986. *Justice Denied: The Law versus Donald Marshall.* Toronto: Totem.

House of Commons Subcommittee on the Penitentiary System in Canada. 1977. *Report to Parliament.* Ottawa: Minister of Supply and Services.

Humphries, A. 2002. "Prisoner Tried to Hurt Mom." *National Post*, August 16, A3.

Irwin, J. 1980. *Prisons in Turmoil.* Boston: Little Brown.

Irwin, J., and D. Cressey. 1962. "Thieves, Convicts, and the Inmate Culture." *Social Problems* 10: 142–55.

Ishwaran, S. and R. Neugebauer. 2001. "Prison Life and Daily Experiences." In J.A. Winterdyk, ed., *Corrections in Canada: Social Reactions to Crime.* Toronto: Prentice-Hall, pp. 129–50.

Jackson, M. 2002. *Justice Behind Walls: Human Rights in Canadian Prisons.* Vancouver: Douglas and McIntyre.

———. 1983. *Prisoners of Isolation: Solitary Confinement in Canada.* Toronto: University of Toronto.

Kari, S. 2008. "Pretrial Credit on Trial." *National Post*, August 5, A5.

Kong, R., and K. Aucoin. 2008. *Female Offenders in Canada.* Ottawa: Canadian Centre for Justice Statistics.

Landry, L., and M. Sinha. 2008. *Adult Correctional Services in Canada, 2005/06.* Ottawa: Canadian Centre for Justice Statistics.

Law Reform Commission of Canada. 1975. *Our Criminal Law*. Ottawa: Information Canada.

LeBlanc, T. 1994. "Redesigning Corrections for Federally Sentenced Women in Canada." *Forum on Corrections Research* 6: 11–12.

Leger, S. 2003. *Criminal Organizations: Identification and Management of Gangs and Criminal Organizations in CSC*. Ottawa: Correctional Service of Canada.

Logan, C.H. 1990. *Private Prisons: Cons and Pros*. New York: Oxford University Press.

MacKay, A.W. 1986. "Inmates' Rights: Lost in the Maze of Prison Bureaucracy?" *The Correctional Review* 1: 8–14.

McDonald, D. 1992. "Private Penal Institutions." In M. Tonry, ed., *Crime and Justice: A Review of Research Volume 16*. Chicago: University of Chicago Press, pp. 361–419.

Meaney, K. 2008. "Report Cites Federal Prison Danger." *National Post*, June 25, A8.

Meddis, S.V., and D. Sharp. 1994. "Prison Business in a Blockbuster." *USA Today*, December 13, 10.

Nelson, W.R., and M. O'Toole. 1983. *New Generation Jails*. Boulder, CO: Library Information Specialists, Inc.

O'Brien, R.L. 1992. "Special Handling Units." *Forum on Corrections Research* 4: 11–13.

Patchmar, K. 2001. "Ontario Introduces Private Prison to Canada." *RCMP Gazette*, 63: 30–31.

Pelletier, B. 1990. "The Duty to Act Fairly in Penitentiaries." *Forum on Corrections Research* 2: 25–28.

Presse, L.D., and R.D. Hart. 1996. "Variables Associated with Parasuicidal Behaviour of Female Offenders During a Cognitive Behavioural Treatment Program." *Canadian Psychologist* 40.

Robinson, D., F.J. Porporino, and W.A. Millson. 1998. *A One-Day Snapshot of Inmates in Canada's Adult Correctional Facilities*. Ottawa: Juristat.

Rothman, D.J. 1971. *The Discovery of the Asylum*. Boston: Little, Brown.

Ruby, C.C. 2003. "Do Canadian Prisoners Have Rights?" *Literary Review of Canada*, November, 10–11.

———. 1985. "Violence In and Out of Prison." *The Globe and Mail*, June 29, E6.

Sapers, H. 2006. "The Correctional Investigator." *LawNow* 30: 3031.

Senese, J.D. 1997. "Evaluating Jail Reform: A Comparative Analysis of the Podular/Direct and Linear Jail Inmate Infractions." *Journal of Criminal Justice* 25: 61–73.

Shaw, M. 1991. *Survey of Federally Sentenced Women: Report of the Task Force on Federally Sentenced Women on the Prison Survey*. Ottawa: Corrections Branch, Ministry of the Solicitor General of Canada.

Shichor, D. 1995. *Punishment for Profit: Private Prisons/Public Concerns*. Thousand Oaks, CA: Sage.

Silver, W. 2007. *Crime Statistics in Canada, 2006*. Ottawa: Canadian Centre for Justice Statistics.

Sobel, W.J., K. Rosich, K.M. Kane, D.P. Kirk, and G. Dubin. 2002. *The Influence in Truth-in-Sentencing Reforms on Changes in States' Sentencing Practices and Prison Populations*. Washington, DC: Urban Institute Justice Policy Center.

Spierenburg, P. 1995. "The Body and the State: Early Modern Europe." In N. Morris and D.J. Rothman, eds., *The Oxford History of the Prison*. New York: Oxford University Press.

Sugar, F., and L. Fox. 1990. *Survey of Federally Sentenced Aboriginal Women in the Community*. Ottawa: Native Women's Association of Canada.

Sykes, G. 1958. *The Society of Captives*. Princeton, NJ: Princeton University Press.

Sykes, G., and S. Messinger. 1960. "The Inmate Social Code." In R. Cloward et al., eds., *Theoretical Studies in the Social Organization of the Prison*. New York: Social Science Research Council, pp. 6–9.

Taft, D.R. 1956. *Criminology*, 3rd ed. New York: Macmillan.

Tibbetts, J. 2007. "Prison Staff Blamed for Inmates' Deaths." *National Post,* June 28, A6.

Trevethan, S., N. Crutcher, and C. Rastin. 2002. *An Examination of Healing Lodges for Federal Offenders in Canada*. Ottawa: Research Branch Correctional Service of Canada.

Watson, L. 1995. "In the Best Interest of the Child: The Mother-Child Program." *Forum on Corrections Research* 7, 25–27.

———. 2004. "Managing Maximum Security Women in Federal Corrections 1989–2004. *Forum on Corrections Research* 16: 3–7.

Zupan, L.L. 1991. *Jails: Reform and the New Generation Philosophy*. Cincinnati, OH: Anderson.

Court Cases

Kosobook and Aelick v. The Queen and The Solicitor-General of Canada (1976), 1 F.C. 540

McCann v. The Queen (1975), 29 C.C.C. (2d) 377

Martineau v. Matsqui Institution Disciplinary Board (1980), 1 S.C.R. 602

R. v. Francis (2006), Ontario Court of Appeal ONCA 41

R. v. Institutional Head of Beaver Creek ex parte McCaud (1969), 2 D.L.R. (3d) 545

R. v. Thornton (2007), Ontario Court of Appeal ONCA 366

R. v. Wust (2000), 1 S.C.R. 455

Richardson and McKnight, 117 S. Ct. 2100 (1997)

Weblinks

One of the key debates concerning prisoners' rights in Canada has been over the right of federal inmates to vote. One federal inmate in particular, Richard Sauve, challenged the policy that inmates cannot vote in federal elections. For two decisions by the Supreme Court of Canada, go to http://scc.lexum.umontreal.ca/en/index.html and open the following pages: *Sauve v. Canada (A.G.)*, 1993, Volume 2, May 27; and *Sauve v. Canada (Chief Electoral Officer)*, 2002, Volume 3, October 31.

CHAPTER 12

Community Reintegration

CHAPTER OBJECTIVES

✓ Understand the different community sanction programs that exist today in Canada.

✓ Understand the operation and purpose of the "faint hope" clause.

✓ Examine the rates of recidivism for the community sanction programs.

✓ Look at the relationship between recidivism rates and the race, gender, marital status, and employment status of offenders released on community sanction programs.

Although some people would like to see criminals put away in prison forever, the reality is that over 90 percent of offenders are released back into society. Some offenders are placed on probation as soon as they are sentenced or shortly thereafter, while others—considered good risks not to re-offend—are ultimately released on some type of conditional release program such as **parole**. The beliefs about the role of conditional release programs in the criminal justice system have changed dramatically over the past few decades. As will be discussed below, these programs were once criticized as "not working," while today they are seen by correctional officials as necessary if offenders are to become law-abiding citizens after their sentences are completed.

This chapter begins with a brief discussion of the history of conditional release programs in Canada and how the approaches underlying these programs have changed in recent decades, from those emphasizing rehabilitation (based on medical models) to those which focus on what is known as **reintegration**. It then outlines the reintegration model and how it is practised in today's federal correctional system. A discussion then follows of some of the issues relating to reintegration, such as the importance of risk prediction. The roles played by the National Parole Board and the Corrections and Conditional Release Act (1992) in this area are also reviewed. Finally, the different types of conditional release programs and the recidivism rates of those who participate in them are reviewed.

In the spring of 2003, the Auditor General of Canada tabled a report in the House of Commons that focused upon the reintegration of women offenders. This report reviewed all aspects of the Correctional Service of Canada's (CSC) reintegration programs for women offenders. While the report noted the efforts and advances made by the CSC since 1990 in the area of facilities and programming for women, such as the construction of the Aboriginal healing lodge as well as the new federal facilities and the development of gender-based rehabilitation programs, it also advanced a variety of recommendations on issues that would lead to greater successes of women offenders reintegrating into the community.

Among the recommendations made by the Auditor General was that the CSC implement its gender-specific substance abuse program, prompting the CSC to introduce the Women Offender Substance Abuse Program in all federal facilities. This led to the CSC adjusting some of its programs so that participation was based on an open entry approach. In addition, some other programs were adjusted in order that small group or one-on-one programs became possible. In addition, some programs were

An offender released into the community. Reintegration helps offenders by connecting them with resources that allow them to support themselves in society. (David Cooper/getstock.com)

changed in order that participants could enter them at an earlier date. The Auditor General also noted that in order for women offenders to better prepare for future employment opportunities, the CSC should create and introduce a Women's Employment Strategy. In addition, the Auditor General recommended that the CSC look at and evaluate those factors contributing to the large number of women whose conditional release is revoked although they have not committed a new offence (Squires 2006).

COMMUNITY RELEASE UNDER ATTACK

In the early the 1970s, all forms of community sanctions, and particularly parole, came under attack by an outraged public that felt that any program whose goal was to place offenders into the community as part of their sentence was soft on criminals. These criticisms were followed by a series of policy changes developed by criminal justice practitioners, who argued that all community sanctions were too discretionary and were failing to protect the due process rights of offenders. Critics also asserted that the rehabilitation ideal and its related treatment programs, which had been designed to reintegrate offenders into the community, were misplaced. For many reasons, parole was abolished in a number of American states, beginning with Maine in 1975. By 1984, the number of states without parole had increased to 11, although the following year Colorado reinstated parole after having abolished its parole board in 1979. In 1987, the Canadian Sentencing Commission recommended the elimination of parole in this country, but its proposals were never implemented.

"Nothing Works"

In 1974, Robert Martinson published an article that was to have a tremendous impact on how community sanctions would operate over the following decades. Titled "What Works? Questions and Answers about Prison Reform," this article questioned the very existence of rehabilitation. This essay was drawn from a larger work (Lipton et al. 1975) that assessed 231 studies of treatment programs operating between 1945 and 1967. At the end of his article, Martinson (1974, 25) commented that with "few and isolated exceptions the rehabilitative efforts that have been reported so far have had no appreciable effect on recidivism."

In his last section—"Does Nothing Work?"—he pointed out that the studies he had just reviewed were no doubt flawed in many ways, and that these flaws might explain why he had not been able to find any significant treatment successes. Even so, he concluded (ibid., 49) that it might be impossible for rehabilitation-based programs to overcome or reduce "the powerful tendencies of offenders to continue in criminal behavior."

Most people who read Martinson's article failed to heed his acknowledgment that rehabilitation might work sometimes. Instead, as Walker notes (1984, 168), the phrase "nothing works" became an instant cliché for critics—one that exerted enormous influence on both popular and professional thinking. Five years later, Martinson (1979, 244, 252) clarified his position: "Contrary to my previous position, some treatment programs do have an appreciable effect on recidivism . . . Some programs are indeed beneficial. New evidence from our current study leads me to reject my original conclusion . . . I have hesitated up to now, but the evidence in our surveys is simply too overwhelming to ignore."

Although his original article is one of the most frequently cited in criminology, his second remains virtually ignored (Cullen and Gendreau 1989). By the time his second article appeared, the critique of rehabilitation was too powerful and entrenched. Martinson himself, after reviewing the few research projects on parole, concluded that when parolees and non-parolees were compared, parole had at best only a delaying effect on recidivism (Waller 1974). This doubt cast on the benefits of parole led to questions concerning the grounding of parole in rehabilitation (Canadian Sentencing Commission 1987).

DISCRETION AND DISPARITY

Another issue raised by the critics of community sanctions was that parole boards held immense discretionary power. These critics were concerned not only about the arbitrariness of many parole board decisions but also about the inability of the boards to develop criteria for predicting which offenders were ready to be released into the community. Parole authorities were accused of knowing little about the criminal personality and of making contradictory decisions (Frankel 1972).

In addition, parole boards often shortened the sentences of offenders by releasing them on a conditional release program (e.g., parole). In this way they became, in effect, the main sentencing agent in the criminal justice system. The Canadian Sentencing Commission (1987, 240), after examining statistics on both the original sentences and subsequent parole board decisions across Canada, concluded that "there is a substantial difference between the sentence a judge hands down and the length of time an offender actually serves in prison."

This discretion, critics argued, was leading to disparities in the time served by offenders. Specifically, the Canadian Sentencing Commission (ibid.) noted that "offenders serving longer sentences are more likely to get released on parole than are offenders sentenced to shorter terms." Harman and Hann (1986, 27–29), for example, reported in their study of individuals sentenced for manslaughter between 1975–76 and 1981–82 that the percentage of the prison sentence served before parole release ranged between 51 and 64 percent. They also found that more people convicted of manslaughter were being released on parole than those convicted of break and enter.

CONDITIONAL RELEASE IN CANADA

Many types of conditional release programs are being carried out in Canada today. Some of these programs are relatively new, while others have existed for many years.

However, most are in a state of flux in the sense that citizens' demands for tighter control of offenders in the community have led correctional officials to tighten eligibility for these programs in order to enhance public safety.

The earliest form of conditional release in Canada was known as "remission." Its importance in the correction of offenders was such that it was included in the first Penitentiary Act (1868). This program utilized a point system, allowing offenders to receive an early release at the maximum rate of six days per month for good behaviour. Merit (and demerit) points were awarded for good behaviour and attitude as well as for industrious work. A few years later, this policy was changed to allow inmates to receive up to 10 days' remission on having earned 72 days under the existing scheme (i.e., they had been "model" inmates for one year). This formula—which had the potential to release inmates after they had served three-quarters of their time—remained in practice until 1961.

The first piece of legislation involving the conditional release program of parole was found in the Ticket-of-Leave Act (1899). This act specified that inmates could gain a form of early release (known as "clemency") that was independent of earned remission. Clemency gave Canada's Governor General the power to release an inmate early under certain conditions. In effect, this program introduced a system of administrative discretion of release; it also reduced an inmate's time served to a greater extent than what had been allowed under the policy of remission (Carrington 1991; Ryan 1990). The first parole officer (who worked for the Salvation Army) was appointed in 1905. In 1913, the Remission Service of Canada was established and placed under the control of the federal Department of Justice.

Between the early 1900s and 1958, the ticket-of-leave system evolved until it resembled the modern-day parole system. In 1958, the Parole Act was proclaimed and the authority to grant release and to issue **revocation** orders was transferred to the newly founded National Parole Board. This board operated on the premise that "interviews between Board members and inmates do not serve a sufficiently useful function . . . The Board should not be required to grant inmates an opportunity for a personal interview" (Cole and Manson 1990, 171). All information in support of parole applications was to be collected from a variety of official sources and then submitted in written form. However, the Parole Act provided little guidance regarding the criteria that the members of the National Parole Board were to consider when reviewing applications for early release. A significant change introduced by this new legislation was the principle that there should be a statutory term of parole supervision in the community before the inmate could be said to have completed his or her sentence. At this time, the policy of **temporary absence (TA)** was also introduced; this allowed inmates to be released into the community for relatively short periods of time.

Over the next decades, the federal government commissioned numerous reports concerning parole and other forms of conditional release. Most of these recommended expanding the conditional release system, and as a result, new policies were gradually introduced (such as mandatory supervision and day parole). One of the most significant reports was produced by the Ouimet Committee (1969), which recommended that the parole system be expanded. In the late 1980s, however, the Canadian Sentencing Commission (1987) recommended that the system of **full parole** be abolished (it also recommended that a system of earned remission be retained). This recommendation was not accepted—the following year, the Daubney Committee proposed that the conditional release system be expanded but that the system of earned remission be abolished. Of these two reports, the recommendations made by the Daubney Committee had a greater impact on the system of conditional release.

The Reintegration Approach

The CSC has since expanded the conditional release system so that most, although not all, inmates are released into the community prior to the end of their sentence. This is referred to as "reintegration," and it involves placing offenders in the least restrictive setting possible. Conditional releases and temporary absences are also available. The former, however, can be revoked when it is considered necessary for public safety (Motiuk and Serin 1998). Reintegration is based on two assumptions: first, that only the most serious offenders should be sentenced to a period of incarceration in the federal system, and second, that the use of alternative sanctions (such as conditional sentences) should be maximized. According to Latessa and Allen (1997, 28), reintegration is "a broad correctional ideology stressing the acquisition of legitimate skills and opportunities by criminal offenders, and the creation of supervised opportunities for testing, using, and refining those skills, particularly in community settings."

The reintegration approach takes the position that the key predictors of recidivism are known and that each individual offender must be assessed in terms of these predictors so that programs can be developed that will enhance their reintegration to society. These key predictors of recidivism are as follows: (1) "antisocial/procriminal attitudes, values, beliefs and cognitive-emotional states (that is, personal cognitive supports for crime)";

Lucie McClung, the first woman to be appointed Commissioner of the Correctional Service of Canada, favours reintegrating inmates into the community. (Correctional Service Canada. Reproduced with the permission of the Minister of Public Works and Government Services Canada, 2009.)

(2) "procriminal associates and isolation from anticriminal others (that is, interpersonal supports for crime)"; and (3) antisocial personality orientations such as low self-control, impulsiveness, risk-taking, and egocentrism (Andrews 1995, 37). Recidivism is also predicted by a history of antisocial conduct going back to childhood; by poor childhood training by parents, such as inadequate support and supervision; and by "low levels of personal educational, vocational or financial achievement," including an "unstable employment record" (ibid.). Some of these predictors are "static," but most are "dynamic"—that is, most of them can be changed. These dynamic factors are called "criminogenic needs." To determine what the likelihood is that an offender will recidivate, the individual's risks and needs are assessed on entry into a federal correctional facility. On the basis of this assessment, correctional personnel select the proper response.

This approach has been practised by the CSC for more than a decade. The key piece of legislation guiding that organization, the Correctional and Conditional Release Act, has as one of its main goals the reintegration of offenders into the community (see Exhibit 12.1). The main tool for achieving this goal is the Offender Intake Assessment (or OIA), during which an extensive

One of the purposes of the Corrections and Conditional Release Act is to help rehabilitate offenders and reintegrate them by providing programs in penitentiaries and in the community. Offender reintegration is defined as all activities and programs conducted to prepare an offender to return safely to the community and live as a law-abiding citizen. To understand offender reintegration, one must understand the variables considered in decisions about releasing offenders to the community. For each offender, the Correctional Service of Canada (CSC) does the following:

- Collects all available relevant information about the offender, including items such as the judge's reasons for sentencing and any victim impact statements.
- Assesses the offender's risk level (the likelihood that he or she will re-offend) and criminogenic needs (life functions that lead to criminal behaviour).
- Reduces the offender's risk level by increasing his or her knowledge and skills and by changing the attitudes and behaviours that lead to criminal behaviour.
- Develops and implements programs and individual interventions that effect change in areas that contribute to criminal behaviour.

- In cooperation with the offender, develops a plan to increase the likelihood that the offender will function in the community as a law-abiding citizen.
- Motivates and helps the offender follow the correctional plan and benefit from correctional programs and interventions.
- Monitors and assesses the offender's progress in learning and changing.
- Makes recommendations to the National Parole Board as to the offender's readiness for release and the conditions, if any, under which he and she could be released.
- After release, helps the offender respect the conditions of the release and resolve day-to-day living problems.
- Makes required programs and interventions available in the community.
- Monitors the offender's behaviour to ensure that he or she is respecting the release conditions and not indulging in criminal behaviour.
- If required, suspends the offender's release, carries out specific interventions, and reinstates or recommends revocation of the release as appropriate.

Source: Thurber 1998, 14–18.

amount of information is collected, including the offender's prior criminal record, his or her potential for violence, and the nature of the most recent offence. During the OIA, a criminal risk assessment is developed and the offender's case needs are identified. These serve as the basis for the Correctional Plan Overview, which evaluates the total case record of the offender (typically, it is updated every six months). All of this becomes the basis of the Custody Rating Scale (CRS), which is used to determine the security classification of the offender (see Figure 12.1).

The Offender Risk Assessment is based on the risks and needs of each offender. (The risk of an offender is also evaluated by the National Parole Board if the inmate has applied for early release on a conditional release program—see below.) Risk assessments are intended to identify those individuals most likely to re-offend and the types of needs that correctional officials must address when developing a personalized plan to assist the incarcerated offender. The CSC implemented the Offender Risk Assessment and Management strategy in 1986 and uses it to assess all inmates, except for some who may receive a very early release date (Taylor 1998).

The Theory of Risk Assessment

Underlying the OIA is the theory of risk assessment. This theory focuses on the social psychology of criminal behaviour. It posits that individual and social/situational factors combine to create in offenders values, cognitions, and personality contexts that facilitate criminal behaviour. To a large extent, these ways of thinking, behaving, and reacting are learned and reinforced and ultimately lead to individual differences in criminal actions.

There are three key factors in a risk assessment: risk, need, and responsivity. The first principle, risk, states that the level of supervision and treatment should be commensurate with the offender's level of risk. This means that the most intensive correctional treatment and intervention programs should be reserved for those offenders identified as higher risk (Andrews et al. 1990). However, as Andrews (1989, 14) points out, "the belief persists that treatment services, if effective at all, only work for lower risk cases." Thus, high success rates for low-risk offenders on a conditional release program may be incorrectly interpreted to mean that those offenders benefited from treatment. This may not be so because, being low-risk, they

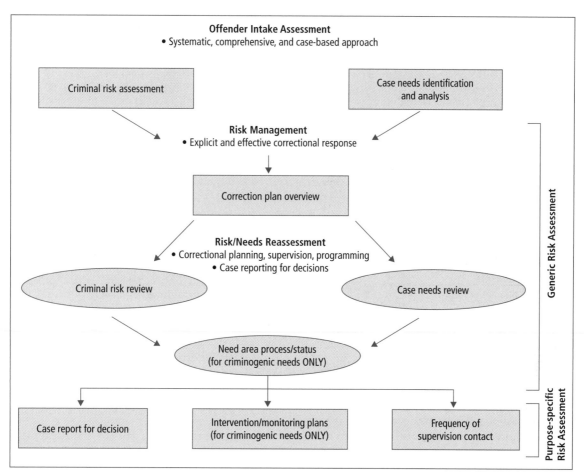

FIGURE 12.1
The Offender Risk Assessment and Management Process
Source: Taylor 1998.

might have had high success rates even without treatment. As Andrews (ibid., 19) points out, "such errors involve confusing the predictive accuracy of pretreatment risk assessments with the issue of who profits from it." If high-risk offenders are improperly assessed as low-risk, they will no doubt have high recidivism rates. In his research on probation supervision programs in Ottawa, Kiessling (1989) found that higher-risk cases in a regular supervision program had a recidivism rate of 58 percent, compared to 31 percent of high-risk cases placed in a high-risk supervision program. So it is essential to make a correct determination of risk in order to match the offender with the type of program from which he or she will benefit. Lipsey (1995), in his meta-analysis of 400 studies of the effectiveness of treatment programs with youth offenders, found greater reductions in re-offending when higher-risk offenders were treated than when lower-risk offenders were treated.

One essential component of risk assessment is the determination of which risks are considered static factors

and which are considered to be dynamic. Static factors include the prior record of the offender as well as his or her prior record (if any) when placed in a conditional release program. Dynamic factors (sometimes these are referred to as "need" factors) involve those characteristics of the offender that can be changed through correctional programming. These include level of education, the level and type of cognitive thinking skills, occupational skills, and interpersonal skills. Dynamic factors differ from static factors in that they can be changed. Some needs may be viewed as criminogenic—that is, if they are not dealt with, there is a significant chance that the offender will re-offend on release.

The second principle, need, asserts that "if correctional treatment services are to reduce criminal recidivism, the criminogenic needs of offenders must be targeted" (Andrews 1989, 15). Research has found that offenders with criminogenic needs are much more likely to fail when they are placed in a conditional release program and that assessments of offender risk and needs are good predictors of outcome on parole (Motiuk and Brown 1993). The combined assessment of risk associated with criminal history and need levels of offenders has been found to increase the predictive power of risk assessments (Taylor 2001). Motiuk and Brown (1993) found that higher-risk/higher-need offenders were four times more likely to fail while they were in conditional release programs that were lower-risk/lower-need offenders.

Research in this area points to the importance of distinguishing between criminogenic and non-criminogenic needs. For example, Dowden (1998) found after analyzing the need principle that non-criminogenic needs were not related to, or were negatively associated with, reductions in recidivism. Criminogenic needs, however, were positively correlated with reduced recidivism. Overall, 75 percent of the individual criminogenic need targets led to significant decreases in recidivism.

Specific needs vary among individuals. That said, Andrews (1989, 15) found that the following needs can be dealt with in a rehabilitative program:

- Change antisocial attitudes.
- Change antisocial feelings.
- Reduce antisocial peer associations.
- Promote formal affection/communication.
- Promote formal monitoring and supervision.
- Promote identification and association with anti-criminal role models.
- Increase self-control, self-management, and problem-solving skills.

Responsivity, the third principle, has to do with selecting appropriate targets for change as well as styles of service. Responsivity factors are individual targets that affect the treatment goals (Bonta 1995, 36). Two types of responsivity are related to success in the treatment of offenders: (1) general responsivity, which involves the styles or types of service (such as behavioural, social learning, and cognitive-behavioural strategies) that work for offenders; and (2) specific responsivity, which matches service with personality and motivation as well as ability with demographics such as age, gender, and ethnicity. In essence, this principle addresses effective correctional supervision and counselling. The assumption underlying the responsivity principle is that not all offenders are the same. Characteristics such as verbal skills, communication style, inadequate problem-solving skills, and poor social skills become important not only in classifying offenders but also in the ways that offenders themselves respond to efforts to change their behaviour, thoughts, and attitudes (ibid.).

Research in this area has found that many risk factors overlap with the types of responses needed to teach offenders prosocial attitudes. An important part of this principle is that offenders need to be matched to parole officers' characteristics. Research indicates that parole officers who scored higher on interpersonal sensitivity and awareness of social rules received higher scores from their clients and were also more likely to display prosocial behaviours and to disapprove of antisocial behaviours (Andrews 1980; Andrews and Kiessling 1980).

According to Taylor (2001, 15), studies related to these three principles for correctional treatment "demonstrate that assessing a variety of static and dynamic risk factors using actuarial methods, providing more intensive levels of treatment to higher-risk offenders, and targeting criminogenic needs in a manner consistent with the characteristics of the offender results in considerably reduced rates of recidivism."

Note that there is another principle, the principle of professional discretion, which states that correctional staff should use the information about offenders attained through the proper application of the risk, need, and responsivity principles in an informed manner. Professional judgment can be used to override objective-based results in exceptional cases, and this can improve the accuracy of assessments (Taylor 2001).

The Case Management Process

Case management is defined as "a systematic process by which identified needs and strengths of offenders are matched with selected services and resources in corrections" (Enos and Southern 1996, 1). The essential objectives of this system are the following:

- Provide for the systematic monitoring of an offender during his confinement.
- Facilitate the graduated release of an offender back into the community.
- Prevent an offender from re-offending after he or she has been released into the community.

This system (1) establishes a program for each inmate that provides for a level of structure so that any needs will be dealt with; (2) balances the protection of the community with the need for offender rehabilitation; (3) prepares an inmate for successful reintegration back into the community; and (4) assists in effective supervision while an offender is serving his or her conditional release program. The case management process is illustrated in Exhibit 12.2.

THE NATIONAL PAROLE BOARD

The National Parole Board (NPB) plays a significant role in the conditional release of inmates into the community. While it once held significant discretionary powers under

EXHIBIT 12.2 The Five Phases of the Case Management Process

I. Initial Assessment and Institutional Placement

- identification of inmate risks/needs
- development of correctional plan

II. Correctional Planning and Institutional Supervision

- correctional plan initiated
- institutional programs (work, treatment, skills upgrading)
- institutional transfers
- institutional releases (temporary absences, work releases)
- ongoing monitoring of inmate progress

III. Preparing Cases for Release Decisions

- institutional progress reports
- community assessments

IV. Parole Board Decision and Release

- temporary absences, day/full parole, statutory release

V. Community Supervision

Source: Griffiths and Cunningham 2000.

---

the Parole Act (see above), it gradually changed its approach as a result of concerns about the lack of due process guarantees and procedural safeguards for inmates during parole hearings. For example, the Report of the Task Force on the Release of Inmates (1973) criticized the criteria for parole release for being vague and unclear, with the effect that "neither inmates nor members of the Board are able to articulate with any certainty what positive and negative factors enter the parole decision" (Task Force on the Release of Inmates 1973, 32). The task force recommended that offenders be allowed to appear before the parole board members, giving them "the opportunity to hear from the decision-makers themselves the reasons for their decision" (ibid., 34). The reasons for any decision were now to be written down and a copy given to the applicant. Also, a parole hearing would now be granted when an inmate requested it. In addition, the National Parole Board (1981) published a list of factors that its members could consider during a hearing. These included the following:

- Any criminal record, the kinds of offences and their pattern, and the length of crime-free periods between convictions.
- The nature of the current offence and its seriousness.
- The understanding the inmate appeared to have gained of the situation that brought him or her to prison, and what that individual had done about it.
- The effort the inmate had made while in prison to take training and to take advantage of educational and employment upgrading activities.
- The institutional behaviour and offences of the inmate.
- Previous parole violations, if any, of the inmate.
- The plans the inmate had for employment or training and how definite those plans were.

An important component of the legislation governing the federal correctional system (the Corrections and Conditional Release Act, which replaced the Parole Act) is what is referred to as "schedule offences." These are offences under the Criminal Code prosecuted by way of indictment. Offences found in Schedule I are violent crimes, such as murder, attempted murder, and sexual offences, as well as offences of criminal negligence in which the result was severe harm or death. Severe harm may be physical or psychological. Schedule II offences are offences under the Narcotic Control Act and the Food and Drugs Act and are prosecuted by way of indictment. Offences included in Schedule II include all drug offences and conspiracy to commit a drug offence (charges for simple possession are excluded). The importance of these schedules lies in their influence on how offenders are classified, the types of programming they are offered, their need for a psychiatric or psychological assessment, and their qualification for a conditional release program (Leonard 1999).

Today, before offenders leave a federal correctional facility on a conditional release program, they agree to a correctional plan developed by the National Parole Board with the assistance of correctional officials (such as institutional parole officers). The correctional plan outlines an individualized risk management strategy for each offender and specifies the interventions and monitoring techniques that will be required to address the risks associated with the offender's re-offending. It typically involves the placing of certain restrictions on their movement and activities. It also specifies certain constructive activities, such as working and attending counselling.

The assumption behind this approach is that people become involved in crime because of problems in their lives, such as substance abuse, lack of skill in anger management, lack of employment opportunities owing to a lack of job training and skills, and so on. The correctional plan is based on information selected from risk assessment evaluations conducted by the CSC as well as the case management group to which the offender belongs while in custody (Correctional Service of Canada 1997).

The release of an offender into the community entails the addressing of three related issues: supervision, programming, and community involvement. Supervision is the direct monitoring of and communication with offenders once they are back in the community. This is usually conducted by parole officers or trained volunteers, depending on the offender involved. Not all offenders are adequately supervised, however, according to the 1999 report by the Federal Auditor General's office. That office conducted a random sample of 150 offenders under community supervision in five major urban centres and reported that 10 to 20 percent "were not contacted with the required frequency" (Bellavance and Alberts 1999, A6). According to the CSC, supervision alone does not help offenders change. Therefore it is combined with "programming," which requires the supervised offender to participate in programs designed to meet his or her needs. These programs are located in the community, with the idea that they will help the offender reintegrate (Correctional Service of Canada 1997).

CONTEMPORARY COMMUNITY SUPERVISION IN CANADA

The law specifies that offenders must receive penalties for their crimes, but it also allows for the mitigation of sentences. Some offenders serve their time in a provincial or federal institution, of course, but the majority remain in the community—at home and at work—under the supervision of probation or parole officers. During 2006–07, more than 367,000 adults were under the jurisdiction of the various federal and provincial correctional agencies in Canada. Of these, almost 107,000 (about 29 percent) were under some type of community supervision.

In most cases, offenders complete their sentence in the community on a conditional release program after serving time in a correctional facility. A key difference between probation (see Chapter 10) and a conditional release program is that probation is imposed by a judge after an individual has been convicted of an offence. By contrast, a conditional release program is not a sentence imposed by the courts but rather a release decision made by correctional authorities or a parole board after an offender has completed part of his or her sentence in a correctional facility.

Conditional release programs were implemented as a result of dissatisfaction with the role of prisons. Prisons are viewed as being too expensive to operate, as having harmful effects and disrupting family relationships, and as having success rates about the same as probation and conditional release programs. As previously mentioned, correctional institutions are expensive to run. Food, medical and dental services, vocational and literacy training, 24-hour security, and escorted leaves are expensive. Community sanctions are much less expensive. Guards are not needed, and capital costs are lower since no expensive security devices are required. The offender is usually working as well as paying taxes and family support (and in some cases restitution to victims).

In addition, community sanctions are thought to mitigate the harmful effects of incarceration on individuals. Life in a correctional facility does not resemble life in society. The violence, controlled environment, and lack of employment programs in prisons have led many to conclude that prisons do more harm than good. Community sanctions allow offenders to maintain connections to society—to work, to be in supportive relationships, and to benefit from community resources. Finally, those who receive community sanctions usually have lower recidivism rates, since they are considered lower risks. So placing these individuals in a correctional facility could be counterproductive, as it would disrupt their lives and their families and make it more difficult for them to reintegrate into society.

RISK OF RECIDIVISM

Even though it had introduced these procedural changes, the NPB came under increasing public criticism for its release decisions, especially after a series of homicides in 1987–88 by individuals on conditional release. At the time, some of the public felt that offenders released into the community were potential high-risk offenders.

However, studies of inmates placed in community release programs found that rates of recidivism were related to the type of conditional release program in which offenders were placed. A profile of readmissions to federal correctional institutions over a six-year period conducted by the CSC found a substantial difference between recidivism rates for those on full parole and those on mandatory supervision. Of the 8,751 offenders released on full parole, 30 percent were readmitted, compared to 58 percent of the 17,769 offenders placed in mandatory supervision.

The majority of offenders returned to a federal institution for violating the terms of their conditional release did so within 12 months of release. Also,

81 percent of all offenders who failed on full parole or mandatory supervision were readmitted within 24 months. After 24 months, however, the incidence of inmates being returned to a federal institution dramatically declined. According to the Correctional Service of Canada (1990, 12), "after the two-year follow-up point, the number of offenders returning to federal institutions dropped to 2 percent and gradually tapered off each subsequent year. At the six-year follow-up point, fewer than 1 percent of offenders were readmitted." This study revealed that for offenders on mandatory supervision, the critical point for readmission to a federal institution arrives within six months of release, whereas for offenders on full parole, the second six-month period is the most critical.

Because of concerns about recidivism rates, the CSC instructed the National Parole Board (NPB) to shift its focus to risk factors as the primary consideration when considering the release of offenders. This change was introduced in November 1986, when the NPB identified its main goal as the protection of society. To achieve this goal, the board made risk assessment of future crimes by offenders after release its major focus (NPB 1987). And in 1988, the NPB released its policy on pre-release detention, which was intended to identify the criteria for parole board decisions.

These policies were based on three key assumptions: first, that risk to society is the fundamental consideration in any conditional release decision; second, that the restrictions on the freedom of the offender in the community must be limited to those that are necessary and reasonable for the protection of society and the safe reintegration of the offender; and third, that supervised release increases the likelihood of reintegration and contributes to the long-term protection of society (Bottomley 1990; Larocque 1998; NPB 1988).

In 1992, the Corrections and Conditional Release Act replaced the Parole Act. The new act identified fundamental principles that were to guide the correctional system in the changing social and legal contexts of Canadian society. The CSC is now guided by a statement of principles that declares, first, that the purpose of the federal correctional system is to maintain "a just, peaceful and safe society" (Haskell 1994, 45). Section 3 of the new Act states that this purpose is to be achieved through the following means:

1. By carrying out sentences imposed by the courts through the safe and humane custody and supervision of offenders.

2. By assisting the rehabilitation of offenders and their reintegration into the community as law-abiding citizens through the provision of programs in penitentiaries and in the community.

Those who drafted the new Act hoped to enhance for all concerned—offenders, correctional staff, and the

A halfway house. These facilities provide a place to live as well as a range of personal and social services for offenders in the process of being reintegrated back into society. (getstock.com)

public—an understanding of and appreciation for the principles and purposes behind correctional decision-making. To this end, it provided improved guidance for the NPB. The hope was that the board would become "more consistent and straightforward in its functioning" (ibid., 46).

To achieve its goals, the Corrections and Conditional Release Act authorizes the disclosure of all relevant information to offenders (subject to certain limited exceptions) when a decision adversely affects their conditional release application. The Act also allows for the disclosure of some information to victims, in the hope that this will "lead to greater awareness of the legitimate reasons behind decisions that may appear arbitrary, inappropriate or even unfair" (ibid.). Furthermore, the Act requires the release of all information to the NPB about the offender's background that could affect the board's conditional release decision. This information includes the nature of the offences as well as police and prosecution files and sentencing information.

Risk Assessment

The Corrections and Conditional Release Act requires the NPB to distinguish between offenders on the basis of risk factors. All board members are required to "specifically assess whether an offender will commit an offence, in particular a violent offence, while on conditional release" (Sutton 1994, 21). To enhance their decision-making ability, board members are now required to take training in risk assessment as well as in the tools and research currently available.

NPB decisions, then, are made on the basis of risk assessment, risk prediction, and risk reduction. They are based on a general knowledge of the social-psychological perspective on criminal conduct, including the assumption that criminal behaviour is usually learned behaviour. When making decisions about conditional release, parole board members make assessments in five areas of an offender's situation (ibid., 22):

- behavioural history
- the immediate situation
- mental and emotional outlook favourable to criminal activity
- pro-criminal social supports
- other personal factors, including level of development, self-regulation, problem-solving skills, impulsivity, and callousness

The Task Force on Reintegration of Offenders, formed by the CSC in 1997, noted in its report that the service has been mandated to use the least restrictive measures consistent with protecting the public. As such, it recommended implementing a risk-related differentiation process that would place offenders in one of three categories on the basis of a risk/needs rating. This categorization would be carried out during the Offender Intake Assessment process. The three levels are (1) release-oriented intervention for low-risk offenders, (2) institutional and community intervention for moderate-risk offenders, and (3) high-intensity intervention for offenders in the high-risk category (Correctional Service of Canada 1997).

To assess the significance of these principles for recidivism rates, Brown and O'Brien (1993) described a study that involved a panel of psychologists and psychiatrists and their assessments of 69 randomly selected federal offenders in the forensic unit of a Canadian hospital. The most common offences were murder (41 percent of offences), a sexual offence (20 percent), and assault or manslaughter (19 percent). The panel used 15 recidivism risk factors—three demographic factors and 12 clinical factors—to complete their assessments. On the basis of risk scores, 26 offenders were identified as "good risks" for release into the community, and all succeeded in completing their terms on parole. Clearly, then, recidivism risks were a factor in the release of these high-risk offenders on parole. However, the success of these offenders on parole was in large part the result of treatment services delivered in the context of risk principles in a community setting.

Conditional Release Programs

Conditional release programs include full parole, day parole, statutory release, and **temporary absences**. Full parole allows offenders to serve a portion of their sentence in the community until that sentence has expired. Most inmates in the federal correctional system can apply to the NPB for full parole after serving one-third of their time or seven years, whichever is shorter. Offenders who face steeper eligibility requirements include those serving life sentences or sentences of preventive detention. Offenders serving a sentence of two years less a day in a provincial institution are eligible to apply for parole after serving one-third of their time. British Columbia, Ontario, and Quebec were the only provinces to operate their own parole boards during 2005–06. The NPB has authority over all provincial inmates in all other provinces (Birkenmayer 1995; Eckstedt and Griffiths 1988). An offender who is released on full parole is placed under the supervision of a parole or probation officer and is required to follow general and specific conditions similar to those granted probationers. As with all types of conditional release, offenders can be reincarcerated if they fail to meet the conditions of their parole or if they break the law.

Day parole differs from full parole in that it is granted only for short periods of time, to a maximum of four months. However, it is renewable for a period of up to one year. Most offenders in federal and provincial correctional facilities become eligible for day parole six months before they are eligible for full parole. The NPB has the authority to grant day parole to offenders in both federal and provincial correctional institutions. Provincial parole boards do not have the power to grant day parole.

Temporary absences (TAs) are granted for four main reasons—medical, compassionate, administrative, and family and community contact. Such absences can last from a few hours up to 15 days. A TA is granted when an offender requires medical treatment not available in a correctional facility. An example of a compassionate TA is when a family member falls seriously ill or dies. Family and community contact TAs are granted to allow offenders to participate in community activities that contribute in their adjustment in the community. An administrative TA is given when an offender needs to make contact with community agencies prior to his or her release (Grant and Belcourt 1992). TAs may be escorted or unescorted. An offender on an **escorted temporary absence** must be accompanied by a representative of the correctional facility. An escorted TA may be granted at any time after sentencing. TAs are the responsibility of the superintendent of the institution, under the authority of the CSC.

Federal offenders not granted parole may, under **statutory release**, be released into the community before the sentence's expiration. Provincial inmates can gain early release for earned remission (good behaviour) and not be supervised in the community; federal offenders released under statutory release are supervised in the community as if they were on parole. However, all inmates leaving a correctional institution on statutory supervision must, before their release, have their cases reviewed by the NPB. The Corrections and Conditional Release Act allows the board to detain an offender on statutory supervision beyond and up to the normal release date. Furthermore, the board has the power to specify that an offender released on statutory supervision will live in a community residential facility if it feels the offender will be a threat to the community or will commit a crime before the termination of his or her sentence.

The NPB does not grant parole to every applicant; in fact, in most years, less than 50 percent of applications succeed. Just over 40 percent of federal and provincial applicants for full parole succeeded in 2007–08. Of the 3,407 male federal inmates who applied for full parole in 2007–08, only 1,398 (30 percent) succeeded. And of the 168 women serving a federal sentence who applied for full parole, 69 (41 percent) succeeded. In comparison, the success rates for those applying for day parole were much higher.

Only 41 of the 302 women (14 percent) who applied for day parole were denied, while the success rate for males was 71 percent (1,592 of the 2,856 males who applied were successful).

It is possible that an inmate will never be released on a conditional release program; in such cases, the inmate is detained until the warrant expiry date. Detainees fall into one of three categories. The first category includes those convicted of offences found in Schedule I of the Corrections and Conditional Release Act. This category is especially likely to contain offenders who are thought likely to commit another offence causing death or serious injury if released into the community through a conditional release program. The second category, too, contains those convicted of offences found in Schedule I—specifically, sexual offences involving children. The third category contains those convicted of Schedule II offences. This category is most likely to contain those believed likely to commit a serious drug offence while on a conditional release program. According to the NPB's own statistics, the number of inmates detained increased from 184 in 1991–92 to a high of 484 in 1995–96; in 2007–08, the number was 266, which was the highest number since 2003–04, when the number of individuals detained totalled 303. According to Leonard (1999), detainees have committed a variety of offences, from violent sexual offences to crimes that did not involve any sexual activity whatsoever.

THE EFFECTIVENESS OF CONDITIONAL RELEASE PROGRAMS

There is much disagreement in Canada today regarding the effectiveness of conditional release programs. Much of this debate has focused on the administration of parole. Roberts (1988), in his study of attitudes toward the NPB, found that two-thirds of Canadians considered the board too lenient. Another study, this one conducted by the Canadian Criminal Justice Association (1987), found that most Canadians felt that the board was releasing too many offenders. Adams (1990, 11) found most Canadians held negative views about parole. Most of the people he interviewed said that offenders "get off too soon, that parole is virtually automatic after one third of the sentence and that the nature of the offender's crime and concurrent risk to society are not given proper consideration." Adams also reported that while parole is actually part of the offender's sentence, it is "not viewed generally by the public as part of the 'punishment' for a crime."

Since offenders commit different types of crimes and have different criminal backgrounds, is it fair to treat all offenders on conditional release programs the same way? Also, offenders have their conditional release orders revoked for different reasons—for example, for a technical violation such as missing a curfew, or for a conviction for an indictable offence while under the supervision of the parole board. The NPB measures the effectiveness of conditional release on the basis of three factors: (1) the rate of success; (2) the number of charges for serious offences committed by offenders while on release in the community, by release type, in eight offence categories that emphasize violent crimes (murder, attempted murder, sexual assault, major assault, hostage taking, unlawful confinement, robbery, and so-called sensational incidents such as arson); and (3) post-warrant-expiry recidivism.

Recidivism Rates

A key factor in assessing the success of an offender on a conditional release program is the **recidivism rate**. In general, recidivism means the readmission, because of a violation, of an offender to an institution. This rate is usually expressed in terms of the number of readmissions within a particular period of time.

The two most common categories applied when measuring recidivism are technical violations and convictions for new offences. A technical violation has occurred when an offender breaks a condition of the release program. This type of violation does not count as a new criminal offence. Nouwens et al. (1993) illustrate the concept of technical violations by discussing a "fraud offender who was told to abstain from alcohol and drugs while on release [and who] decides to celebrate his new-found freedom by getting drunk at a party. The police are called . . . and find out the offender is on parole." Other examples of technical violations include failing to stay within a specified geographical location and failing to maintain a job.

Recidivism rates are considered the most important figures for assessing the success or failure of a conditional release program. In 2007–08, the success rate for male offenders on full parole was 72.2 percent; for female offenders, it was 78.8 percent. Parole was revoked for breach of conditions in 261 cases, for non-violent offences in 106 cases (6.9 percent), and for violent offences in 16 cases (0.9 percent). The rates of successful completion for day parole were higher than those for full parole. The success rate for males on day parole was 83.5 percent, while for women, it was 82.5 percent. Just over 3 percent of day paroles ended with a non-violent offence and 0.4 percent with a violent offence.

Of the three conditional release programs, offenders on statutory release had the highest recidivism rates. The success rate for women on statutory release was 60.3 percent; for men it was 58.6 percent. In 2007–08, 8.7 percent of statutory releases ended with a non-violent offence and 1.9 percent with a violent offence. Most failures on statutory release were for breach of conditions (30.6 percent). (Correctional Service of Canada 2008).

Recidivism rates can also be measured in terms of the different lengths of time that offenders are on a conditional release program. Nouwens and colleagues (1993) compared the short-term and long-term recidivism rates of 1,000 federal offenders. Short-term recidivism was measured by looking at those offenders released over a three-year period (April 1, 1990, to March 31, 1993). The percentage of supervised offenders readmitted to a correctional facility for technical violations was 2.8 percent; for those readmitted for a new offence, it was 2 percent. Long-term recidivists were defined as those offenders released during a ten-year period (April 1, 1975, to March 31, 1985). Over this ten-year period, 15,418 offenders were released on full parole. Of these, 72 percent (11,704) completed their sentence without being returned to custody for any reason. After these individuals had completed their parole, about 10 percent committed a new offence, for which they were returned to the federal correctional system. Over the same period, 27,124 offenders were released on mandatory supervision. Fifty-seven percent completed their sentence successfully; 24 percent had their release revoked for technical violations; and 19 percent were readmitted for a new offence. Thirty-four percent of those offenders who successfully completed their statutory supervision were readmitted to a federal institution after their sentence was finished.

Nouwens et al. (ibid.) also studied readmission rates by type of conditional program release for 1,000 offenders admitted to federal custody for a new offence between April 1, 1988 and March 31, 1989. By June 30, 1993, almost 92 percent of these offenders had been released on some form of conditional release. During this period, the overall readmission rate was 37.1 percent. The highest rate of readmission was for those released on statutory supervision—46.6 percent, which was almost double the rate for those released on full parole (25.1 percent).

But are different types of offenders more successful than others in conditional release programs? Are those who commit a violent crime such as murder bad risks for parole, and do those convicted of a sex offence run a higher risk of recidivism? Edwin (1992) investigated the recidivism rates of 2,900 homicide offenders released between 1975 and 1990 to determine their success rate on full parole. Of these offenders, 658 had been convicted of first or second degree murder. The vast majority (77.5 percent) successfully completed their conditional release program, while 13.3 percent were incarcerated for a technical violation of their full parole and 9.2 percent for the commission of an indictable offence. Of the 69 indictable offences committed by the released offenders, 21 (30.4 percent) were narcotics offences, 12 (17.5 percent) were property offences, 6 (8.7 percent) involved robbery, and 17 (24.6 percent) were for "other" Criminal Code offences (ibid., 7).

Edwin also studied the full parole and supervision success rates of 2,242 offenders convicted of manslaughter between January 1, 1975, and March 31, 1990. Almost all of these offenders (93 percent) were released on a conditional release program. Forty-seven percent were released on full parole and 53 percent on statutory supervision. Twenty-two percent of those released on full parole were reincarcerated: 14.6 percent for a technical violation, 6.5 percent for an indictable offence, and 0.5 percent for a summary conviction offence. Of those released on mandatory supervision, 41 percent had their full parole revoked. Thirty-one percent were revoked for a technical violation of the conditions of their parole order, 10 percent for an indictable offence, and 1 percent for a summary offence.

There is much public concern about the release of "special needs" offenders—such as those diagnosed with mental disorders—on conditional release programs. Porporino and Madoc (1993) compared the recidivism rates of 36 male federal offenders identified as having a mental disorder with those of a matched group of 36 federal offenders without mental disorders. During the four-year study, almost as many offenders *with* mental disorders were released (67 percent) as those without (75 percent). However, offenders with mental disorders were more likely to be released on mandatory supervision (83 percent), while offenders without mental disorders (44 percent) were released more often on parole. In addition, Porporino and Madoc (ibid., 17) reported "a tendency for mentally disordered offenders to serve more time before release and a greater proportion of their sentence."

The same study looked at recidivism at two points during the release period: 6 months after release and 24 months after release. No significant differences were found in the recidivism rates between the two groups during the first six months of conditional release, although more offenders without mental disorders were returned to custody for a new offence or a new violent offence. After 24 months, however, those with mental disorders were more likely to have their conditional release suspended owing to concern about the probability of further violent offences (Madoc and Brown 1994, 11). In contrast, offenders without mental disorders were more likely to have their conditional release revoked for the commission of a new offence.

Post-warrant-expiry recidivism rates are of interest to the NPB, which uses these figures as indicators of long-term effectiveness. However, offences committed after warrant expiry are beyond the control of the NPB. According to Larocque (1998, 22), information concerning the recidivism rates of federal offenders after "warrant expiry on SR [statutory release] indicates that offenders reaching warrant expiry on statutory release are 3 to 4 times more likely to be readmitted to a federal institution than offenders who complete their sentence on full parole." In addition, recidivism rates are higher for all groups of offenders who have been in the community for longer periods, regardless of the type of conditional release program they were in.

Conditional Release and Due Process

Other critics have focused on the lack of explicit criteria used in decisions to grant parole. This lack has led to confusion among those inmates who wish to improve themselves and subsequently improve their chances of being granted parole. Concerns have also been raised about the fairness of parole hearings, in particular "the absence from parole of due process requisites such as the right to a hearing, to know the nature of complaints against one, and to be informed of the reasons for adverse decisions" (Bottomley 1990, 339). These issues have led to what has been called the "pains of parole," a term used to describe the "anxiety, fear, loss of dignity, excessively limited freedom, [and] uncertainty of one's future" (Mandel 1975, 520–26).

In 1977, the Subcommittee on the Penitentiary System in Canada (1977, 151) concluded that inmates are under the impression that the parole board does not, in all circumstances, treat them fairly: "The records contain many examples of inmates whose parole has been revoked because they arrived a few minutes late and who were charged with being unlawfully at large . . . It is, therefore, extremely disconcerting to hear of inmates having their paroles suspended and revoked for essentially trivial questions."

These concerns about the role of the NPB were echoed by the late Chief Justice Bora Laskin, who commented in *Mitchell v. The Queen* (1976), a case involving the matter of parole revocation: "The plain fact is that the Board claims a tyrannical authority that I believe is without precedent among administrative agencies empowered to deal with a person's liberty. It claims an unfettered power to deal with an inmate, almost as if he were a mere puppet on a string."

In 1978, new regulations were enacted under the Parole Act that guaranteed inmates serving a sentence of two years or more a series of due process safeguards—a hearing, disclosure of information, and reasons for the denial of parole. However, these safeguards did not eliminate the perception that the NPB's decisions were unfair. Furthermore, disparities—albeit more subtle ones—continued to exist (Casey 1986).

Confusion about parole board decisions continued among offenders. Eckstedt (1985) found that five years after the new regulations came into effect, offenders who requested parole hearings were still questioning the fairness of board decisions. In an attempt to rectify this situation, reforms were recommended and legal changes were made. Perhaps the most significant statement came from the Canadian Sentencing Commission (1987, 244–45), which recommended that parole in Canada be abolished because it violated the principle of proportionality, introduced uncertainty into sentencing, and transferred the decision-making power of judges. Others, however, are content to apply the Charter of Rights and Freedoms to specific cases as they come forward (Cole and Manson 1990).

Today, the Corrections and Conditional Release Act (s. 147) allows for appeals within 60 days when an inmate's application for parole is denied. Grounds for appeal include the NPB's making a decision that fails to observe a principle of fundamental justice; an error of law; a breach or failure to apply a policy adopted to respect ethnic, cultural, and linguistic differences; a failure to respond to the special needs of women and Aboriginal people; a decision based on incomplete information; and the failure to act with appropriate jurisdiction (Leonard 1999). A judicial review is also possible, at either the federal or the provincial level.

The "Faint Hope" Clause

In July 1976, capital punishment was abolished in Canada with the passage of Bill C-84. This bill established mandatory life sentences, with parole eligibility specified for those convicted of first and second degree murder (25 years and 10 to 25 years, respectively). Bill C-84 also stipulated that offenders convicted of first and second degree murder would be eligible for a judicial review after serving 15 years of their sentence, and, if successful in their application, would be able to participate in a conditional release program. Section 745.6 of the Criminal Code was a component of Bill C-84 and was added to the Criminal Code when it passed.

This section, now commonly referred to as the "faint hope" clause, allowed offenders who had served at least 15 years of their sentence to apply for a reduction in the amount of time they had left to serve before the parole eligibility date specified in their sentence. As Roberts and Cole (1999, 284) point out, s. 745.6 was included in the Criminal Code "out of recognition of the fact that inmates who have served well over a decade in prison may have changed"; they added that "once applications began to be heard by juries, the section becomes possibly the most controversial provision in the Criminal Code."

The faint hope clause states that any offender still serving a sentence after 15 years has the right to apply for a judicial review of parole eligibility. Application is made to the chief justice in the province or territory in which the conviction occurred. The chief justice determines whether the offender is eligible to apply, and, if so, informs the provincial justice minister of the decision. A two-stage process then begins: (1) a preliminary hearing followed by (2) the actual hearing.

The preliminary hearing considers such issues as the evidence to be allowed, as well as matters such as transportation and living facilities. The actual hearing is adversarial in nature, and the applicant is present. A jury determines whether the application has merit and decides on one of three options: (1) no change or reduction in the period before parole eligibility, (2) a reduction in the number of years of imprisonment prior to eligibility for parole, or (3) termination of ineligibility for parole, allowing the applicant immediate eligibility. If the jury selects the third option, it does not mean the offender is released right away, but rather that he or she can apply to the NPB for release prior to the original eligibility date (Brown 1992).

Under the original legislation, juries were not able to consider such issues as "the character of the applicant, his conduct while serving his sentence, the nature of the offence for which he was convicted and such other matters as the judge deems relevant in the circumstances." It was possible that if the jury rejected the application, the Supreme Court of Canada might hear an appeal, although s. 745 made no provision for this. If the Supreme Court were to decide in the applicant's favour, a second hearing would be ordered. In addition, juries did not have to be unanimous in their decision; only two-thirds of the jurors had to agree to allow an applicant to proceed to an NPB hearing.

In December 1996, Parliament revised s. 745(6), by passing Bill C-45. The impetus for this was an application for early release from serial killer Clifford Olson. Olson gained national and international notoriety in the early 1980s when he received $100,000 from provincial authorities in return for revealing where he had buried 11 of his murder victims in British Columbia's Lower Mainland. Public outrage over his application was so great that it became an issue during the 1997 federal election.

As a result, s. 745(6) of the Criminal Code was revised (and the revision was promptly labelled the "Olson Amendment"). No longer can multiple murderers apply for early release. Note, however, that very few cases involving multiple victims are ever processed, and those that are are unlikely ever to be approved by a jury. Superior court judges now have to review all applications and be convinced that they have a reasonable prospect of success (Roberts and Cole 1999). Another change requires the jury to reach a unanimous decision. And when a jury unanimously decides that the number of years to be served is to be reduced, it must decide by a two-thirds majority that a certain number of years must be served before the inmate can apply to the NPB for a possible reduction in the time to be served. If a jury decides that no reduction in time is to be granted, it may set another date of application. If it doesn't set a date, the inmate has to wait for another two years before applying again. These changes are retroactive, to include all individuals who committed their crimes before Bill C-45 was passed. In addition, Bill C-41 (proclaimed in 1995) made it possible for the families of victims to submit victim impact statements as evidence. (Such information was admissible before that year, but only at the discretion of the judge.)

In June 2009, the federal government introduced legislation that proposed to take away the ability of individuals convicted of first and second degree murder to apply for parole after serving 15 years of their life sentence. If the legislation is passed, the new law stipulates that if someone is convicted of first or second degree murder on the day or after the new law is passed, he or she would no longer be able to apply for an early release. Those individuals currently serving a life sentence or awaiting sentencing would only have three months to apply for early release after serving 15 years of their sentence. If they miss the deadline, they would have to wait another five years (as opposed to the current two-year wait) before they could apply again. In addition, a judge would have to rule that there was a "substantial likelihood" that the jury would agree to move up their parole eligibility date (Galloway 2009).

Between the first judicial review and April 2008, there has been a total of 169 court decisions involving a judicial review, and of these, 141 have succeeded in the sense that a jury has reduced the time to be served before possible parole. Of these 141 successful applications, 125 have reached their revised eligibility date. Ninety-five of the successful applicants are being supervised in the community, 15 have been returned to custody, 11 are deceased, 3 have been deported, and 1 is unlawfully at large. Many of the applicants for judicial review had been convicted of a murder: a higher percentage of second degree (86 percent) than first degree (83 percent) murder cases have led to a reduction of the time period required to be served before parole eligibility. Sixty-two of the cases—that is, most of them—involving a reduced time period prior to eligibility have been in Quebec (Correctional Service of Canada 2008).

RISK FACTORS FOR RECIDIVISM

Andrews (1989) reviewed the literature on recidivism and concluded that the findings from past research were consistent in outlining characteristics that indicate an increased risk of crime. These characteristics include the following: having associates who have criminal tendencies or who are antisocial in nature; pro-criminal attitudes, values, and beliefs; generalized difficulties or trouble in relationships with others; and being male. The more risk factors present, the greater the likelihood of re-offending. According to Andrews (ibid., 13), research has established "beyond question, that systematic risk assessment allows the identification of lower and higher risk groups . . . offenders in higher risk groups will be responsible for a majority of the recidivistic offences."

Of course, predictions are not always accurate. Some individuals identified as high risk may never re-offend, while some identified as low risk will. In an attempt to improve the risk classification of offenders, risk assessment criteria have been developed on the basis of behavioural and objective criteria. Behavioural criteria include cognitive-behavioural and social learning factors (Andrews et al. 1990). Objective criteria, which are the ones most commonly used when comparing offenders on conditional release programs, include such measures as race, drug abuse history, and employment status.

Studies by Antonowicz and Ross (1994) and Robinson (1995) have concluded that low-risk offenders have a similar, if not better, response to treatment than high-risk offenders. Andrews (1996) has identified four significant risk factors: antisocial cognitions, antisocial associates, antisocial personality complex, and a history of antisocial behaviour.

Most research on success in conditional release programs compares recidivists with non-recidivists on a number of standard objective criteria, including gender, race, age, marital status, and employment.

Gender

As of April, 2008 there were 495 women offenders incarcerated under federal supervision in Canada. The most commonly cited offences committed by incarcerated women are drug related offences homicide robbery and assaults. Females admitted to federal custody have been found to have different treatment needs than men. Table 12.1 reveals the percentages of women with needs in each of the seven target domains that were identified at intake and post-release. In terms of risk levels assessed at intake, just over half the women were identified as being low risk to re-offend, 35 percent as moderate risk, and 14 percent as high risk. On release, 62 percent of the women were identified as low risk to re-offend, 29 percent as moderate risk, and 9 percent as high risk (Taylor and Flight 2004).

Jones (2004) studied 483 substance-abusing women who were released on a conditional release program between January 1, 1995, and December 31, 2000. The rate of revocation was 48 percent, "considerably higher than that reported in earlier research studies." However, the researchers pointed out that the sample of their study consisted of "only substance abusing women, who are at greater risk for recidivism compared to women who do not have substance abusing problems."

A number of studies have compared male and female offenders on conditional release. These have found some differences in recidivism rates. In general, women seem to have lower recidivism rates than men. Bonta et al. (1992) analyzed 2,985 male and 81 female recidivists released from federal custody during 1983–84 and found that 36 percent of the women committed a new offence within three years of their release compared to 49 percent of the men. Regarding temporary absences, Grant and Belcourt (1992) reported that women (0.01 percent) were less likely to fail on this program than men (1.0 percent). However, Lefebvre (1994), in her analysis of 929 men and 44 women on day parole during 1990–91, found that the overall failure rate for women was 30 percent, compared to 27 percent for male offenders.

Reasons for parole revocation varied between women and men: 5 percent of women had committed a new offence, compared to 10 percent of men. This result supports the conclusion reached by Belcourt et al. (1993), who reported in their analysis of 968 women released from federal custody over a 10-year period that 50 percent had been readmitted for a technical violation, while 21 percent had had their release revoked for a new offence. Blanchette and Dowden (1998) state that federally sentenced women released on either full or day parole have higher success rates on day and full parole than those released on statutory release or on the expiration of their warrant.

Proper programming has a significant influence on reducing recidivism rates among federally sentenced women. Dowden and Blanchette (1998) studied 251

TABLE 12.1 Need Domains

| Need Domains | Percentages of Women with Identified Needs | | | | | | | |
| | At Intake | | | | Post-Release | | | |
	Asset	No	Some	Consid.	Asset	No	Some	Consid.
Family	11	42	31	16	18	42	31	9
Attitude	21	53	17	9	36	49	11	4
Employment	8	39	42	11	14	47	34	5
Substance Abuse	N/A	52	15	33	N/A	62	19	19
Community Functioning	8	56	33	3	15	57	26	2
Associates/Social Interaction	7	39	41	13	18	44	32	6
Personal/Emotional Orientation	N/A	23	45	32	N/A	39	44	17

Note: N/A = Not Applicable, Asset = Asset to community adjustment, No = No need for improvement, Some = Some need for improvement, Consid. = Considerable need for improvement.
Source: FORUM–A profile of federally-sentenced women on conditional release, K. Taylor, J. Flight, Correctional Service of Canada, 2004. Reproduced with the permission of the Minister of Public Works and Government Services Canada, 2009.

federally sentenced women; 143 of them were substance abusers, 108 were non-abusers. All of them had been released on either day or full parole. The researchers found that the substance abusers were at greater risk of being returned to a correctional facility. However, participation in drug treatment programs while in custody was "associated with reduced returns to custody for substance abusers; the rate approximated that of female non-abusers" (ibid., 29).

Race

Most research has found that Aboriginal offenders in conditional release programs have recidivism rates higher than those of White offenders. In their analysis of 282 male Aboriginal inmates, Bonta et al. (1992) reported an overall recidivism rate of 66 percent. They found that 84 percent of these Aboriginal inmates had been incarcerated in the past. Aboriginal offenders placed on mandatory supervision during this three-year study had a much higher recidivism rate (75 percent) than those released on full parole (33 percent).

Belcourt et al. (1993) studied the success of Aboriginal female offenders in all forms of conditional release programs. They reported that Aboriginal women were overrepresented in the group returned to a correctional facility after release. Forty-four percent of Aboriginal women offenders were readmitted, compared to around 19 percent of non-Native female offenders. Dowden and Serin (2000) studied the needs of 113 Aboriginal female offenders placed in conditional release as of May 1, 1999. They found that compared to non-Aboriginal offenders, Aboriginal women were more likely to be assessed as high risk (31.9 percent versus 14.6 percent); non-Aboriginal women were more likely to be placed in the lower risk category (72.1 percent versus 49 percent) or in the medium risk category (13.3 percent vs. 18.6 percent). Also, offenders who were released with significant needs that had yet to be addressed were more likely to recidivate. The authors concluded that when these offenders' needs are not addressed in the community, they are more likely to fail in the community.

Grant and Belcourt (1992) studied temporary absences and found that Aboriginal inmates were underrepresented in all TA programs except for compassionate TAs. However, these differences could be explained in large part by legal variables—namely, the fact that these offenders were more likely to have been convicted of serious violent offences and to have served a greater number of multiple federal prison sentences. Given these facts, they concluded that Aboriginal people "may therefore represent a greater risk to the community and, as with other offenders in these categories, are less likely to be granted TAs."

The reasons for these differences between Aboriginal and non-Aboriginal offenders have been of concern to the CSC, various federal committees studying conditional release programs, and independent researchers. The Daubney Committee (1988, 214), for example, noted that "Native inmates are often not as familiar with release preparation and the conditional release system as other inmates." Zimmerman (1992, 401) reported that Aboriginal offenders "often waive the right for early release." She attributed this in part "to subtle encouragement by case management officers" (ibid., 409). It seems, then, that Aboriginal offenders are the least likely of all groups in the federal correctional system to be released on parole. This is in part due to certain parole criteria being "inherently weighted against aboriginal offenders" (ibid., 408). Johnson (1997) found that Aboriginal offenders have lower rates of application to conditional release programs in part because they mistrust the correctional system. Welsch (2000) found that less than half (48 percent, or 65 of 136 individuals) of Aboriginal offenders who could make their first application for full parole actually did so, compared to 73 percent of non-Aboriginal offenders. In addition, about 59 percent of Aboriginal offenders waived a full parole hearing on their current sentence, compared to 33 percent of non-Aboriginal offenders. In addition, of those offenders who did apply for parole, Aboriginal offenders were more likely to be classified as high risk relative to non-Aboriginal offenders (61.1 percent versus 49.9 percent), while non-Aboriginal applicants were more likely to be classified as low risk (26.4 percent versus 16 percent) or medium risk (29.4 percent versus 20.9 percent).

Aboriginal offenders who are granted parole are more likely to find themselves returned to prison before the expiration of the conditional release program—a fact thought to be the result of the inappropriate conditional release requirements placed on them, more stringent enforcement of release conditions, and inadequate support on their release.

Ellerby (1994, 23) points out that these higher recidivism rates have made the reintegration of Aboriginal inmates into the community on conditional release programs both "difficult" and "challenging." Culturally specific practices have been incorporated into the treatment process in the hope that they will "help aboriginal offenders address their offending and develop the insight and skills necessary to avoid or manage the factors that place them at risk of re-offending" (ibid., 24). Starting in 1987, the Forensic Behavioural Management Clinic in Winnipeg began to include traditional healing practices in its treatment of both Aboriginal and non-Aboriginal participants. These programs involve Elders and present an opportunity for offenders to take part in pipe ceremonies and sweat lodge ceremonies. This program has made treatment more meaningful for the program participants.

Age, Marital Status, and Employment

Sherman and colleagues (1992) have reported that recidivism may be higher among those who are unemployed and unmarried. Citing research from domestic violence studies, they argue that neither race nor a record of prior offences has an impact on reducing recidivism. They have found, rather, that "arrested persons who lacked a stake in conformity were significantly more likely to have a repeat offence than their counterparts who were not arrested" (ibid., 682). This finding suggests that those with a higher stake in conformity are more likely to complete a conditional release program.

Lefebvre (1994) found that the overall failure rate of her sample of day parolees was inversely related to age. For the youngest group (18 to 25 years), it was 41 percent, followed by 25 percent for those 26 to 40 and 14 percent for those over 40. The rate of failure owing to the commission of a new offence was 15 percent for the youngest group, 9 percent for the middle group, and 5 percent for the oldest group. Similar findings were made by Bonta and colleagues (1992), who found that recidivists were, on average, three years younger (26) than non-recidivists at the time of sentencing. In their study of female offenders, Belcourt et al. (1993) found a similar trend. Twenty-nine percent of those between 18 and 25 were readmitted, compared to 22 percent of those 26 to 30, 20 percent of those 31 to 45, 16 percent of those 46 to 60, and 11 percent of those over 60.

Regarding marital status, Lefebvre (1994) found that offenders who were married or involved in common-law relationships at the time of their offence had a lower failure rate (22 percent) than those who were divorced or separated (28 percent) or single (29 percent). Studies by researchers such as Bonta et al. (1992) have consistently found that recidivism rates for single, divorced, or separated offenders are higher than for those who are married.

Lefebvre (1994) studied the impact of employment status and education on recidivism. She found that the overall failure rate for day parolees declined as the offender's level of education increased, from 29 percent for those with a grade 8 education or less to 19 percent for those with a postsecondary education. She also found that those who were employed at the time of the offence were twice as likely to succeed on conditional release programs compared to those who were unemployed (33.9 percent versus 16.8 percent).

HOW INMATES VIEW RECIDIVISM

Most criminological research uses recidivism as an indicator of the success or failure of correctional programs to prepare offenders to live a crime-free existence in the community or as a predictor of future criminal behaviour. However, Zamble and Porporino (1988) argue that both these approaches may be "incomplete because they fail to acknowledge that institutional treatment is not a one-way causal process but rather the outcome of interaction between the correctional system and offenders." Besozzi (1993) interviewed 25 offenders serving their first sentence in a federal institution. Most of the inmates in this study, however, had prior records and had served time in a juvenile or provincial institution. At the beginning of the study, most of them indicated that they hated prison life and, once released, did not want to return. Some even mentioned that their time in prison would deter them from re-offending when they returned to the outside. This attitude quickly changed for most, however, as, on reflection, "the correctional institution became less awful and the determination not to reoffend became less resolute. The deterrent effect of prison seemed to vanish" (ibid., 37).

Besozzi (ibid., 35) also found that inmates "have developed their own theories to explain why 'they always come back.'" One significant theory formulated by inmates is that the very nature of the correctional facility and the parole supervision system are important "causes" of failure. By this, they mean that prison staff are not there to help but rather to ensure that inmates fail when they are released. Programs in the prison are simply viewed "as a way to get out sooner, not as a way to improve the odds of success on the outside" (ibid., 37). This view arises from the inmates' conception of prison as a place in which to be punished, not as a place in which to be rehabilitated or to solve the problems that will likely make them re-offend on release.

Some of these feelings derive from the fact that prison is a negative environment. Most inmates interviewed were unsure of how much they had changed, if at all, while in prison. As one inmate said when contemplating the reality of leaving prison, "I think I will be more aggressive than before, when I get out. Oh yes, that's for sure, because you experience a lot of unfairness here" (ibid.). Another reason given for the negativity associated with prisons is that, although inmates want to change, prisons lack the resources to help them, in terms of both quality and quantity. This was especially true for offenders at the beginning of their sentence (Zamble and Porporino 1988). "The strongest criticisms of the correctional system came from inmates who knew they needed to change, went to prison hoping for some qualified help and think they didn't receive it" (Besozzi 1993, 37).

Some offenders did indicate that they had changed, but added that the change was brought about through their *own* efforts, not as a result of any efforts by the staff. Most of these offenders isolated themselves from the other inmates and thought about how they would live on the outside so as not to re-offend. According to one inmate, his time in prison was a "positive experience" and gave him the "opportunity to think a lot . . . to question values and attitudes" (ibid., 37).

Overall, most inmates had vague and ambiguous feelings about their chances of survival on the outside. According to Besozzi, this uncertainty arose from the fact that they had not developed a well-defined identity, in the sense that they alternately saw themselves as law-abiding citizens and as criminals. The second reason for their uncertainty was a lack of clarity regarding the aims of the correctional system.

CORRECTIONS: THE OLDER INMATE

In 2007–08, 37 percent of all offenders admitted to a federal correctional facility were between the ages of 20 and 29 while 28 percent were between 30 and 39. The median age of the offender population has been increasing, from 30 in 1994–95 to 33 in 2007–08. A trend in the federal correctional system is the increasing proportion of older inmates. The number of offenders between 40 and 49 when they entered the federal correctional system increased between 1994–95 and 2007–08, from 694 (15 percent) to 1,062 (21.1 percent). In comparison, the number of offenders between the ages of 30 and 34 fell from 827 (17.8 percent) in 1998–99 to 718 (14.3 percent) in 2007–08 (CSC 2008).

When we refer to older offenders, we are referring to offenders who are aged 50 or over. In 1996, older offenders serving a federal sentence in Canada ranged in age from 50 to 90. The largest group of older offenders is between 50 and 59, where 368 offenders (353 men and 15 women) were serving a sentence in a federal correctional facility. In 2007–08, 489 men and 20 women over 50 were serving a sentence in a federal correctional facility.

Three types of older offenders have been identified. The first group includes those who were incarcerated while young and who have remained in prison since. In 1996, 155 (or 10 percent) of all older offenders fell into this category. The second category includes chronic offenders who have been incarcerated many times before their latest term of imprisonment. Of all older offenders, 17 percent (261) fall into this group. Most of them are serving time for property crimes. The third category includes those offenders who are serving their first term of imprisonment late in life. They were law-abiding for most of their life and became involved in crime only later (Aday 1994). Most of the older inmates in Canada's prisons in 1996 (1,111 or 73 percent) fall into this category.

Older offenders pose special problems for the correctional system, since they have a reduced ability to cope in prison and to have their needs met there. As a consequence of growing old in prison while serving a long sentence, older offenders have special needs and problems that set them apart from the rest of the adult offender population (Cowles 1990; Walsh 1989). Among other things, these needs relate to accommodation, programming, adjustment to imprisonment, the prison environment, peer relationships while in prison, family relationships, and parole issues (Uzoaba 1998). A study of older inmates in California found that 80 percent had a chronic health condition, 38 percent had hypertension, 28 percent had a heart disease, and 16 percent had cataracts (Zimbardo 1994).

All of this has led to a new program, the Reintegration Effort for Long-term Infirm and Elderly, Federal Offender (RELIEF) program, launched in January 1999 (Stewart 2000). It is located at the Sumas Centre in Abbotsford, British Columbia. This program's goals and objectives are as follows:

- To provide a safe reintegration option for elderly/infirm offenders by addressing the needs and concerns of an aging population in a community setting.
- To provide safe, secure, humane care for offenders at a dependent stage of their life by fostering hope and dignity.
- To provide a caregiving program, in a correctional setting, that will follow the same high standards of care and practice as established by the community hospice movement.
- To train selected offenders, on work release or day parole, to assist in the provision of care to elderly and infirm offenders in the Sumas Centre and in other Pacific region community-based residential facilities.
- To establish and maintain responsible care teams to ensure that offender clients' needs are met and that the wellness of the caregivers is maintained.
- To annually conduct three caregiver training programs of two months' duration at the Sumas Centre.

Despite the high costs of incarceration, some (e.g., Goetting 1983; Walsh 1992) argue that it is inconsistent to argue that older inmates ought to be excused from serving time in a federal institution simply because costs are high. They contend that the needs of older inmates will not create a heavy financial burden on the correctional system. But they also point out that it must be recognized that older inmates require programs that meet their needs.

Specialized care is a general concern in prisons. To date, prisons have operated with young offenders in mind. But some observers (e.g., Vito and Wilson 1985; Wilson and Vito 1988) speculate that prisons will soon become geriatric centres and that staff will have to be specially trained to look after these inmates. Morton (1993, 44) recommends that these staff be trained to identify physical disabilities in older inmates, to develop policies on managing the special needs of older inmates, to be sensitive to the physical and emotional difficulties experienced by older inmates, and to begin developing solutions that apply to specific institutions.

Adjustment to prison life by older prisoners is a contentious issue. Some argue that older inmates experience more psychological and emotional problems—a concern that Vito and Wilson (1985) believe is not being addressed by correctional systems. Others (e.g., Teller and Howell 1981) argue that older offenders are better adjusted, less impulsive, and less hostile than those who are younger. Sabath and Cowles (1988) found that older offenders who maintain family contacts are better adjusted than those who don't, and there is general agreement that first-time older offenders are better adjusted in prison than those who have served at least one previous term of incarceration (Aday and Webster 1979; Teller and Howell 1981).

Other issues facing older inmates arise when they leave a correctional facility. They are by then used to prison life and have established social networks. How will they survive in the outside world? Many of their friends have died or forgotten about them, so questions involving care and a place to stay become paramount. As Hassine (1996, 97) points out, the elderly inmate represents "a growing underclass of dependents in a world of change."

A special category of older offenders is "lifers"— that is, inmates who have spent many years in prison. In 1997–98, 2,433 Canadians were serving a life sentence— 18 percent of the total federal inmate population. The median age of lifers was 39 in 1997–98, compared to 33 for non-lifers. Lifers were more likely than non-lifers to be non-Aboriginal, single, less educated, and unemployed when they committed the offence that led to their incarceration (Finn et al. 1999). These individuals will in all probability spend some of their older years in a federal institution; thus they pose particular issues for federal correctional authorities.

CRITICAL ISSUES IN CANADIAN CRIMINAL JUSTICE

CORRECTIONAL TREATMENT: "WHAT WORKS" AND GENDER-RESPONSIVE APPROACHES

In the years since Robert Martinson' article *Nothing Works* was published, there has been considerable debate over the issue of whether or not rehabilitation is effective. Various researchers (e.g., Wilson and Davis 2006) believe that some treatment programs using the most recent approach to treatment, cognitive-behavioural therapy, have failed to show that treatment has a positive impact on individuals who are released back into the community. Others argue that the continuing belief that "nothing works" is not always true. As early as 1979, Gendreau and Ross were arguing that many correctional treatment programs were, in fact, successful. According to Ross and Gendreau (1980, viii) these successful programs were "convincing evidence that some treatment programs, when they are applied with integrity by competent practitioners in appropriate target populations, can be effective in preventing crime or reducing recidivism." More recently, Lipsey and Cullen (2007) reviewed studies of correctional rehabilitation programs and discovered consistent positive effects in terms of programs reducing recidivism. They also reported that there was considerable variation in the effects of correctional treatment programs depending on the type of treatment, the implementation, and the type of offenders to which the program was applied.

Evaluations of treatment programs within correctional facilities as well as the community have found the following elements to be the most successful in terms of reducing recidivism:

- Cognitive-behavioural therapy.
- Interpersonal skills training.
- Individual counselling.
- Behaviour modification techniques.
- Integration of community programs with those found within correctional facilities to assist re-entry into society (Wilson et al., 2005).

In recent years, questions have been raised as to whether this approach is applicable to all individuals. Since the research on these programs has been conducted almost exclusively upon white males, there have been questions raised about its applicability to women as well as racial and cultural groups. While the cognitive-behavioural approach does not totally ignore the issue of gender, it is considered to be of secondary importance. According to Andrews and Bonta (2006), gender is a specific responsivity factor, that is, gender should be considered in terms of how a treatment program is delivered. However, this approach rejects the idea of gender-specific assessment and treatment interventions. Andrews and Bonta (ibid., 467) state that they have "not found any evidence that the antisocial evidence of demographically defined groups is insensitive to personality, attitudes, associates, or behavioural history. Nor have we found that the impact of RNR (risk-needs-responsivity) adherence and breadth on future offending varies with age, race, or gender."

A number of researchers have examined the considerable differences that exist between the cognitive-behavioural and gender-responsive approaches. Some (e.g., Krisberg 2005) have discovered that most of the research conducted from the cognitive-behavioural perspective has not included females. Others (e.g., Belknap 2001) point out that a gender-responsive approach has an entirely different theoretical base; that is, instead of the psychological approach favoured by the cognitive-behavioural approach, the gender-responsive approach uses a macro-level explanation that attributes the criminal activity of women to social issues such as class and race, both of which are marginalizing forces, creating an environment in which they are able to potentially engage in destructive behaviours.

Another difference between the approaches centres upon the issue of "risk." According to the cognitive-behavioural approach, the level of risk refers to the likelihood of an individual's recidivism. This is based upon the research evidence pointing out that high-risk offenders need intensive levels of services to reduce recidivism and that medium-risk offenders need moderate levels of services (Andrews et al. 1990). Supporters of the gender-responsive approach believe that women, although they may have significant "needs," they are not high "risk."

Criminogenic needs are also thought to differ. The cognitive-behavioural approach makes a distinction between "general" and "criminogenic" needs. General needs refer to those areas that are not considered as strong correlates of criminal behaviour on the basis of research reports. In comparison, criminogenic needs are dynamic factors that have proven to be correlates of criminal behaviour. As such, it is necessary to target the identified criminogenic needs in order to reduce the possibility of recidivism. Supporters

of the gender-responsive approach point out that the source of crime is to be found within societal factors, not within individuals. They also point out that by looking at only a select number of criminogenic needs fails to lead to an understanding of the problems that are the source of women's criminal behaviour as well as the social realities in which women live (Bloom 2003).

Differences are also founding terms of program delivery. According to the cognitive-behavioural approach, it is important to recognize that cognitive restructuring is needed in order that beliefs, values and attitudes become prosocial. In addition, cognitive skills training is required, particularly those that focus upon improving critical thinking and problem-solving skills. Those who support a gender-responsive approach believe it is more important to look at the ways in which the programs are delivered. They favour programs that are trauma-informed (i.e., aware of the history of past abuse in order to create better and more effective programs) and that are relational (i.e., the development of positive interpersonal relationships).

While the cognitive-behavioural and gender-responsive approaches may appear to be incompatible, Law (2007) notes that some recent research efforts have identified substantial overlap between them. On the basis of this research, she recommends an approach that recognizes that variability may be greater in small groups such as women offenders. Furthermore, it is necessary to look for and study gender-informed constructs as well as situational variables. Finally, it is important to have "full consultation with the women being served in the correctional system" (ibid., 35).

Questions
1. Do you think that one treatment approach can "work" for all offenders, regardless of their gender or race?
2. Do you think rehabilitation programs are more cost effective than approaches based on deterrence?
3. Do you think offenders have the right to forgo treatment if there are programs available that can assist them in terms of reducing the risk of recidivism?
4. Do you think that aftercare programs in the community are necessary to ensure that offenders are successfully reintegrated into the community? If so, should it be mandated that all offenders be placed in the community prior to the end of their sentence?

SUMMARY

Conditional release programs can be traced back to 1868, when a formal system of parole was first implemented. Today conditional release programs consist of various parole programs, including full parole, day parole, and temporary absences. But in terms of the number of offenders taking part, probation is the largest conditional release program currently practised today in Canada. Over the past 20 years, largely as a result of increased legal rights for prisoners, a number of programs have been developed to allow better access to both probation and various conditional release programs.

In recent years, prison authorities have begun to emphasize risk factors as the most significant consideration when deciding which offenders to place in these programs. Offenders who are placed in these programs must follow certain rules and conditions. If they violate any of them, their release may be revoked, in which case they are returned to a correctional facility. The Canadian courts have extended legal rights to all those who have applied for or who are in these programs. An individual who is not allowed to participate in a program must be told why. In addition, an individual whose conditional release has been revoked has the right to a full hearing on the issue as well as the right to legal counsel.

Discussion Questions

1. Discuss the use of conditional release in Canada. Should more people be placed in these programs?
2. What is the current role of the parole board? How has it changed over time?
3. Discuss the factors that influence the decision to grant parole.
4. What is the purpose of probation?
5. What are some of the problems associated with probation orders?
6. What type of offenders are most likely to re-offend?
7. Discuss the risk factors used in the decision to grant parole.
8. Should we continue our statutory supervision policy? What purposes does this policy serve?

Suggested Readings

Andrews, D., and J. Bonta. *The Psychology of Criminal Conduct,* 2nd ed. Cincinnati, OH: Anderson, 1998.

Cole, D.P., and A. Manson. *Release from Imprisonment: The Law of Sentencing, Parole, and Judicial Review.* Toronto: Carswell, 1990.

Culhane, C. *Still Barred from Prison.* Montreal: Black Rose, 1985.

Faith, K. *Unruly Women: The Politics of Confinement and Resistance.* Vancouver: Press Gang, 1993.

Gottfredson, D.M., and M. Tonry, eds. *Prediction and Classification: Criminal Justice Decision Making.* Chicago: University of Chicago Press, 1987.

References

Adams, M. 1990. "Canadian Attitudes toward Crime and Justice." *Forum on Corrections Research* 2: 10–13.

Aday, R.H. 1994. "Aging in Prison: A Case Study of New Elderly Offenders." *International Journal of Offender Therapy and Comparative Criminology* 38: 79–91.

Aday, R.H., and E.L. Webster. 1979. "Aging in Prison: The Development of a Preliminary Model." *Offender Rehabilitation* 3: 271–82.

Andrews, D.A. 1996. "Criminal Recidivism Is Predictable and Can Be Influenced: An Update." *Forum on Corrections* Research 8: 42–45.

———. 1995. "The Psychology of Criminal Conduct and Effective Treatment." In J.M. McGuire, ed., *What Works: Reducing Offending.* West Sussex: John Wiley, pp. 35–62.

———. 1989. "Recidivism Is Predictable and Can Be Influenced: Using Risk Assessments to Reduce Recidivism." *Forum on Corrections Research* 1: 11–17.

———. 1980. "Some Experimental Investigations of the Principles of Differential Association through Deliberate Manipulations of the Structure of Service Systems." *American Sociological Review* 45: 448–62.

Andrews, D.A., and J. Bonta. 2006. *The Psychology of Criminal Conduct,* 4th ed. Cincinnati, OH: Anderson.

Andrews, D.A., J. Bonta, and R.D. Hoge. 1990. "Classification for Effective Rehabilitation: Rediscovering Psychology." *Criminal Justice and Behavior* 17: 19–52.

Andrews, D.A., and J.J. Kiessling. 1980. "Program Structure and Effective Correctional Practices: A Summary of the CaVic Research." In R.R. Ross and P. Gendreau, eds., *Effective Correctional Treatment.* Toronto: Effective Correctional Treatment.

Andrews, D.A., I. Zinger, R.D. Hoge, J. Bonta, P. Gendreau, and F.T. Cullen. 1990. "Does Correctional Treatment Work? A Clinically Relevant and Psychologically Informed Meta-Analysis." *Justice Quarterly* 8: 369–404.

Antonowicz, D., and R.R. Ross. 1994. "Essential Components of Successful Rehabilitation Programs for Offenders." *International Journal of Offender Therapy and Comparative Criminology* 38: 97–104.

Belcourt, R., T. Nouwens, and L. Lefebvre. 1993. "Examining the Unexamined: Recidivism among Female Offenders." *Forum on Corrections Research* 5: 10–14.

Belknap, J. 2001. The Invisible Woman: Gender, Crime, and Justice. Belmont, CA: Wadsworth. .

Bellavance, J.D., and S. Alberts. 1999. "20% of Criminals on Parole Lack Supervision." *National Post.* April 21, A6.

Besozzi, C. 1993. "Recidivism: How Inmates See It." *Forum on Corrections Research* 5: 35–38.

Birkenmayer, A. 1995. *The Use of Community Corrections in Canada: 1993–1994.* Ottawa: Canadian Centre for Justice Statistics.

Blanchette, K., and C. Dowden. 1998. "A Profile of Federally Sentenced Women in the Community: Addressing Needs for Successful Reintegration." *Forum on Corrections Research* 10: 40–43.

Bloom, B.E. 2003. *Gendered Justice: Addressing female offenders.* Durham, NC: Carolina Academic Press.

Bonta, J. 1995. "The Responsivity Principle and Offender Rehabilitation." *Forum on Corrections Research* 7: 34–37.

Bonta, J., S. Lipinski, and M. Martin. 1992. "The Characteristics of Aboriginal Recidivists." *Canadian Journal of Criminology* 34: 517–22.

Bottomley, A.K. 1990. "Parole in Transition: A Comparative Study of Origins, Developments, and Prospects for the 1990s." *Crime and Justice: A Review of Research*, vol. 12. Chicago: University of Chicago Press.

Brown, G. 1992. "Judicial Review: How Does It Work and How Does It Affect Federal Corrections?" *Forum on Corrections Research* 4: 14–16.

Brown, R.J., and K.P. O'Brien. 1993. "How Do Experts Make Parole Recommendations and Are They Accurate?" *Forum on Corrections Research* 5: 3–4.

Canadian Criminal Justice Association. 1987. *Attitudes toward Parole.* Ottawa: Canadian Criminal Justice Association.

Canadian Sentencing Commission. 1987. *Sentencing Reform: A Canadian Approach.* Ottawa: Minister of Supply and Services.

Carrington, D.O. 1991. *Crime and Punishment in Canada: A History.* Toronto: McClelland and Stewart.

Casey, M. 1986. "Parole: A Purely Personal View." *Correctional Review* 1: 19–20.

Cole, D.P., and A. Manson. 1990. *Release from Imprisonment: The Law of Sentencing, Parole, and Judicial Review.* Toronto: Carswell.

Correctional Service of Canada. 2008. *Corrections and Conditional Release Statistical Overview.* Public Safety Canada. www.publicsafety.gc.ca. Retrieved April 24, 2009.

———. 1997. *Basic Facts about Corrections in Canada.* Ottawa: Solicitor General of Canada.

———. 1990. "A Profile of Federal Community Corrections." *Forum on Corrections Research* 2: 8–13.

Cowles, E.L. 1990. "Programming for Long-Term Inmates." Executive Summary. *Long-Term Confinement and the Aging Inmate Population: A Record and Proceeding.* Washington, DC: Federal Bureau of Prisons.

Cullen, F.T., and P. Gendreau. 1989. "The Effectiveness of Correctional Rehabilitation: Reconsidering the 'Nothing Works' Debate." In L. Goodstein and D. MacKenzie, eds., *American Prisons: Issues in Research and Policy.* New York: Plenum, pp. 23–44.

Daubney Committee. 1988. *Taking Responsibility: Report of the Standing Committee on Justice and Solicitor-General on Its Review of Sentencing, Conditional Release and Related Aspects of Corrections.* D. Daubney, chair. Ottawa: Queen's Printer.

Dowden, C. 1998. "A Meta-Analytic Examination for Risk, Need and Responsivity Principles and Their Importance within the Rehabilitation Debate." Unpublished MA thesis. Ottawa: Department of Psychology, Carleton University.

Dowden, C., and K. Blanchette. 1998. "Success Rates for Female Offenders on Discretionary versus Statutory Release: Substance Abusers and Non-Abusers." *Forum on Corrections Research* 10: 27–29.

Dowden, C., and R. Serin. 2000. "Assessing the Needs of Aboriginal Women Offenders on Conditional Release." *Forum on Corrections Research* 12: 57–60.

Eckstedt, J.W. 1985. *Justice in Sentencing: Offenders' Perceptions.* Ottawa: Canadian Sentencing Commission.

Eckstedt, J.W., and C.T. Griffiths. 1988. *Corrections in Canada: Policy and Practice,* 2nd ed. Toronto: Butterworths.

Edwin, G. 1992. "Recidivism among Homicide Offenders." *Forum on Corrections Research* 4: 7–9.

Ellerby, L. 1994. "Community-Based Treatment of Aboriginal Offenders: Facing Realities and Exploring Realities." *Forum on Corrections Research* 6: 23–25.

Enos, R., and S. Southern. 1996. *Correctional Case Management.* Cincinnati, OH: Anderson.

Finn, A., S. Trevethan, G. Carriere, and M. Kowalski. 1999. *Female Inmates, Aboriginal Inmates, and Inmates Serving Life Sentences: A One-Day Snapshot.* Ottawa: Canadian Centre for Justice Statistics.

Frankel, M.F. 1972. *Criminal Sentences: Law without Order.* New York: Hill and Wang.

Galloway, G. 2009. "Tories Look to Deny Murderers 'Faint Hope' for Early Parole." *The Globe and Mail,* June 6, A7.

Gendreau, P., and R. Ross. 1979. "Effective Correctional Treatment: Bibliotherapy for Cynics." *Crime and Delinquency* 27: 463–89.

Goetting, A. 1983. "The Elderly in Prison: Issues and Perspectives." *Journal of Research in Crime and Delinquency* 20: 291–309.

Grant, B.A., and R.L. Belcourt. 1992. *An Analysis of Temporary Absences and the People Who Receive Them.* Ottawa: Correctional Service of Canada.

Griffiths, C.T., and A. Cunningham. 2000. *Canadian Corrections*. Scarborough, ON: Nelson Thompson.

Harman, W.G., and R.G. Hann. 1986. *Release Risk Assessment: An Historical Descriptive Analysis*. Ottawa: Solicitor General of Canada.

Haskell, C. 1994. "The Impact of the Corrections and Conditional Release Act on Community Corrections." *Forum on Corrections Research* 6: 45–46.

Hassine, V. 1996. *Life without Parole*. Los Angeles: Roxbury.

Johnson, J.C. 1997. *Aboriginal Offender Survey: Case Files and Interview Sample*. Research Report R-61. Ottawa: Correctional Service of Canada.

Jones, D. 2004. "The Revocation of Conditionally-Released Women: A Research Summary." *Forum on Corrections Research* 16: 31–33.

Kiessling, J. 1989. Cited in D.A. Andrews, "Recidivism Is Predictable and Can Be Influenced: Using Risk Assessments to Reduce Recidivism." *Forum on Corrections Research* 1: 11–17.

Krisberg, B. 2005. *Juvenile Justice: Redeeming our Children*. Thousand Oaks, CA: Sage.

Larocque, B. 1998. "Federal Trends and Outcomes in Conditional Release." *Forum on Corrections Research* 10, 2 (May): 18–22.

Latessa, E.J., and H.E. Allen. 1997. *Corrections in the Community*. Cincinnati, OH: Anderson.

Law, M.A. 2007. "Federally Sentenced Women in the Community: Dynamic Risk Factors." *Forum on Conditional Research* 18: 18–20.

Lefebvre, L. 1994. "The Demographic Characteristics of Offenders on Day Parole." *Forum on Corrections Research* 6: 11–13.

Leonard, S.G. 1999. "Conditional Release from Imprisonment." In J.V. Roberts and D.P. Cole, eds., *Making Sense of Sentencing*. Toronto: University of Toronto Press, pp. 259–76.

Lipsey, M.W. 1995. "What Do We Learn from Research Studies on the Effectiveness of Treatment with Juvenile Delinquents?" In J. McQuire, ed., *What Works: Reducing Reoffending*. New York: John Wiley, pp. 63–78.

Lipsey, M.W., and F.T. Cullen. 2007. "The Effectiveness of Correctional Rehabilitation: A Review of Systematic Reviews." *Annual Review of Law and Social Science* 3: 297–320.

Lipton, D., R. Martinson, and J. Wilks. 1975. *The Effectiveness of Correctional Treatment*. New York: Praeger.

Madoc, L.L., and S.L. Brown. 1994. "Sex Offenders and Their Survival Time on Conditional Release." *Forum on Corrections Research* 6: 14–17.

Mandel, M. 1975. "Rethinking Parole." *Osgoode Hall Law Journal* 13: 501–46.

Martinson, R. 1979. "Symposium on Sentencing: Part II." *Hofstra Law Review* 7: 243–58.

———. 1974. "What Works? Questions and Answers about Prison Reform." *Public Interest* 35: 22–54.

Morton, J.B. 1993. "In South Carolina: Training Staff to Work with Elderly and Disabled Inmates." *Corrections Today:* 42–47.

Motiuk, L.L., and S.L. Brown. 1993. *The Validity of Offender Needs Identification and Analysis in Community Corrections*. Research Report R-34. Ottawa: Correctional Service of Canada.

Motiuk, L.L., and R. Serin. 1998. "Situating Risk Assessment in the Reintegration Potential Framework." *Forum on Corrections Research* 10: 19–22.

National Parole Board. 1988. *National Parole Board Pre-Release Decision Policies.* Ottawa: Ministry of Supply and Services.

———. 1987. *Briefing Book for Members of the Standing Committee on Justice and Solicitor General.* Ottawa: National Parole Board.

———. 1981. *A Guide to Conditional Release for Penitentiary Inmates.* Ottawa: National Parole Board.

Nouwens, T., L. Madoc, and R. Be. 1993. "So You Want to Know the Recidivism Rate." *Forum on Corrections Research* 5: 22–26.

Ouimet, R. 1969. *Report of the Committee on Corrections: Toward Unity: Criminal Justice and Corrections.* Ottawa: Information Canada.

Porporino, F.J., and L.L. Madoc. 1993. "Conditional Release and Offenders with Mental Disorders." *Forum on Corrections Research* 5: 17–19.

Roberts, J.V. 1988. "Early Release from Prison: What Do the Canadian Public Really Think?" *Canadian Journal of Criminology* 30: 231–49.

Roberts, J.V., and D.P. Cole. 1999. "Sentencing and Early Release Arrangements for Offenders Convicted of Murder." In J.V. Roberts and D.P. Cole, eds., *Making Sense of Sentencing.* Toronto: University of Toronto Press, pp. 277–94.

Robinson, D. 1995. "Federal Offender Family Violence: Estimates from a National File Review Study." *Forum on Corrections Research* 7: 15–18.

Ross, R., and P. Gendreau. 1980. *Effective Correctional Treatment.* Toronto: Butterworth.

Ryan, H.R.S. 1990. "Foreword." In D.P. Cole and A. Manson, *Release from Imprisonment: The Law of Sentencing, Parole, and Judicial Review.* Toronto: Carswell, pp. v–x.

Sabath, J., and E.L. Cowles. 1988. "Factors Affecting the Adjustment of Elderly Offenders in Prison." In B. McCarthy and R. Langworthy, eds., *Older Offenders: Perspectives in Criminology and Criminal Justice.* New York: Praeger.

Sherman, L.W., D.A. Smith, J.D. Schmidt, and D.P. Rogan. 1992. "Crime, Punishment, and Stake in Conformity: Legal and Informal Control of Domestic Violence." *American Sociological Review* 57: 680–90.

Squires, K. 2006. "The Reintegration of Federally Sentenced Women: A Commentary." *Forum on Corrections Research* 18: 7–8.

Stewart, J. 2000. "The Reintegration Effort for Long-term Infirm and Elderly Federal Offenders (RELIEF) Program." *Forum on Corrections Research* 12: 35–38.

Subcommittee on the Penitentiary System in Canada. 1977. Report. Ottawa: Supply and Services Canada.

Sutton, J. 1994. "Learning to Better Predict the Future: National Parole Board Risk-Assessment Training." *Forum on Corrections Research* 6: 20–22.

Task Force on the Release of Inmates. 1973. Report. Ottawa: Information Canada.

Taylor, G. 2001. "The Importance of Developing Correctional Plans for Offenders." *Forum on Corrections Research* 13: 14–17.

———. 1998. "Preparing Reports for Parole Decisions: Making the Best Use of Our Information—and Time." Forum on Corrections Research 10: 30–34.

Taylor, K., and J. Flight. 2004. "A Profile of Federally-Sentenced Women on Conditional Release." *Forum on Corrections Research* 16: 24–27.

Teller, F.E., and R.J. Howell. 1981. "The Older Prisoner: Criminal and Psychological Characteristics." *Criminology* 18: 549–55.

Thurber, A. 1998. "Understanding Offender Reintegration." *Forum on Corrections Research* 10: 14–18.

Uzoaba, J.H.E. 1998. *Managing Older Offenders: Where Do We Stand?* Ottawa: Correctional Service of Canada, Research Division.

———. 1985. "Forgotten People: Elderly Inmates." *Federal Probation* 49: 18–24.

Walker, S. 1984. *Sense and Nonsense about Crime.* Belmont, CA: Wadsworth.

Waller, I. 1974. *Men Released from Prison.* Toronto: University of Toronto Press.

Walsh, C.E. 1992. "Ageing Inmate Offenders: Another Perspective. In C.A. Hartjen and E.E. Rhine, eds., *Correctional Theory and Practice.* Chicago: Nelson-Hall.

———. 1989. "The Older and Long-Term Inmate Growing Old in the New Jersey Prison System." *Journal of Offender Counselling Services and Rehabilitation* 13: 215–48.

Welsch, A. 2000. "Aboriginal Offenders and Full Parole." *Forum on Corrections Research* 12: 61–64.

Wilson, D., and G. Vito. 1988. "Long-Term Inmates: Special Need and Management Considerations." *Federal Probation* 52: 21–26.

Wilson, J., and R. Davis. 2006. "Good Intentions Meet Hard Realities: An Evaluation of the Project Greenlight Reentry Program." *Criminology and Public Policy* 5: 303–38.

Wilson, R., A. Bouffard, and D.L. Mackenzie. 2005. "Quantitative Review of Structured, Group-oriented, Cognitive-Behavioral Programs for Offenders." *Criminal Justice and Behavior* 32: 1872–204.

Zamble, E., and F. Porporino. 1988. *Coping, Behavior and Adaptation in Prison Inmates.* New York: Springer-Verlag.

Zimbardo, P.G. 1994. *Transforming California's Prisons into Expensive Old Age Homes for Felons.* San Francisco: Center on Juvenile and Criminal Justice.

Zimmerman, S. 1992. "'The Revolving Door of Despair': Aboriginal Involvement in the Criminal Justice System." *University of British Columbia Law Review:* 367–426.

Court Cases

Mitchell v. The Queen (1976), 2 S.C.R. 577

Weblinks

In early 2000, the Supreme Court of Canada made six decisions regarding conditional sentences. You have read two of them (see Chapter 10). Read the other four cases (*R. v. L.F.W., R. v. R.N.S., R. v. R.A.R.,* and *R. v. Bunn*) that were released on January 31, 2001. To read these decisions and the issues for the use of conditional sentences, go to http://lexum.umontreal.ca/en/index.html and click on Volume 1.

Absolute jurisdiction indictable offence. Offences for which the accused has to be tried by a provincial court judge unless the judge determines that the case must be tried another way. These offences are found in s. 553 of the Criminal Code.

Actus reus. The illegal act. It involves either the commission of an act, such as an assault, or the failure to act, such as failing to take proper safety measures.

Adjudication. The determination of guilt or innocence of the accused by a judge.

Administrative regulations. The laws created by administrative agencies (in the form of rules, regulations, orders, and decisions) in order that they can carry out their responsibilities and duties.

Adversarial system. The procedure used to determine truth in a criminal court system. According to this system, the burden is on the state to prove the charges against the accused beyond a reasonable doubt.

Aggravating circumstances. Any circumstances accompanying the commission of a crime that may justify a harsher sentence.

Appeal Court. A review of lower court decisions or proceedings by a higher court.

Appearance notice. Issued to the accused requiring him or her to appear in court on a specific date and time. The accused is issued an appearance notice instead of being arrested.

Arraignment. The process whereby the accused hears the formal charges being laid and pleads either guilty or innocent.

Arrest. The taking into custody of a person thought to have committed a crime. The legal requirement for an arrest is "reasonable and probable grounds."

Assembly line justice. The idea that the criminal justice process is similar to a production line, in that it handles most cases in as routine a manner as possible.

Auburn system. The prison system developed in New York in the nineteenth century that favoured a tier-based prison facility and congregate working conditions for inmates.

Beyond a reasonable doubt. The standard used to determine the guilt or innocence of an accused.

Boot camp. A short-term militaristic-style correctional facility in which youths and young adults are exposed to intensive physical conditioning and discipline.

Broken window model. Refers to the idea that community disorder leads to criminal behaviour.

Case law. The judicial application and interpretation of laws as they apply in any particular case.

Charge a jury. When the judge informs a jury of the relevant evidence of a case and the types of decisions the jury can reach about the accused.

Charge bargaining. A prosecutor's decision to reduce the number of charges against the accused in return for a plea of guilty and/or for information.

Common law. Early English law, developed by judges, based on local customs and feudal rules and practices. Common law formed the basis of the standardized criminal law system in England.

Community policing. A police strategy that emphasizes the reduction of fear, community involvement, decentralization of the police force, neighbourhood police stations, and order maintenance as an alternative approach to fighting crime.

Concurrence. Forms the legal relationship between the guilty mind and the illegal act.

Corpus delicti. The body of circumstances that must exist for a criminal act to have occurred.

Courtroom work group. The informal social organization of the courtroom, comprising the prosecutor, defence attorney, judge, and other court workers. The informal relationships among the members of this group have far-reaching implications for the treatment of the accused in our criminal justice system.

Custodial interrogation. The questioning of a suspect after that person has been taken into custody. Before any interrogation begins, the individual must be read his or her rights.

Custody. The forceful detention of an individual.

Cybercrime. A crime that occurs online, in the virtual community of the Internet, as opposed to the physical world.

Cyberstalking. The crime of stalking, committed in cyberspace.

Deadly force. Force applied by a police officer that is likely or intended to cause death.

Deprivation model. The theory that states that inmate aggression is the result of the frustration inmates experience at being deprived of freedom, consumer goods, and the like that are common outside prison.

Determinate sentence. A period of incarceration fixed by legislature that cannot be reduced by a judge or correctional officials.

Deterrence. The prevention of crime before it occurs by threatening individuals with criminal sanctions.

Deterrence, general. A crime control policy that aims to stop potential law violators from engaging in illegal behaviour. It favours certain policies—such as long prison sentences—that underscore the fact that the pain associated with crime outweighs the gain.

Deterrence model. One of the four main models of criminal justice. It envisions a criminal justice system with no discretion, more police, and longer prison terms. It is related to the crime control model and the classical school of criminology.

Deterrence, specific. A crime-control policy that advocates punishment severe enough to convince convicted offenders never again to engage in criminal behaviour.

Directed patrol. A police patrol strategy. Police officers are told to spend much of their patrol time in certain areas, to use certain tactics, and to watch for certain types of offences.

Discretion. The use of individual decision-making and choice to influence the operations of the criminal justice system. All the major institutions of the criminal justice system—police, courts, corrections—make decisions that influence the outcome of cases.

Disparity. The lack of uniformity in sentencing, which leads to concern about discrimination against particular groups in society. Disparity involves arbitrary differences between sentences against offenders convicted of the same crime.

Drug treatment courts. Courts whose jurisdiction is limited to drug offences. Offenders selected receive treatment as an alternative to incarceration.

Election indictable offence. An offence for which the accused (or the accused's lawyer) may decide on which type of criminal court to be tried in.

Electronic monitoring (EM). A system designed to ensure an offender completes the terms of a court order. EM is the regulatory aspect of home confinement.

Employment equity. The federal policy that emphasizes that members of minority groups should be represented in the workforce.

Fact bargaining. A type of plea bargaining in which the prosecutor decides not to introduce certain facts about the offence or offender into the court record.

Fine. One of the most common sentences in Canada. Failure to pay a fine is one of the most common reasons for the incarceration of offenders.

First degree murder. Planned and deliberate murder—though it does not have to be planned or deliberate when the victim is a police officer, a prison guard, an individual working in a prison, or a similar individual acting in the course of duty.

Foot patrol. A type of police patrol linked to community policing. It takes police officers out of cars and places them on a beat, which allows them to strengthen ties with community residents.

Full parole. The early release of an inmate from prison subject to conditions established by a parole board. Full parole can be granted to inmates after they serve one-third of their sentence, unless the sentence specifies otherwise.

Habeas corpus. A judicial order requesting that a state representative (e.g., a police officer) detaining another give reasons for the capture and detention. It is a legal device used to request a judicial review of the reasons for an individual's detention and the conditions of detention.

"Hands-off" doctrine. The unwritten policy favouring non-interference by the courts in the administration of correctional facilities.

Home confinement. A type of intermediate punishment that allows offenders to live at home while serving their sentence.

"Hot spots." Concentrated areas of high criminal activity that draw the interest of the police.

Hybrid offence. An offence that may proceed either as an indictable or summary conviction offence. The decision on how to proceed is usually made by the Crown prosecutor.

Identity theft. The theft of identity information, such as a name, driver's licence, social insurance number, or similar. This information is typically used to access the victim's financial resources.

Incarceration. Occurs when an offender receives a sentence that stipulates that he or she spend time in a provincial or federal correctional institution.

Indictable offence. An offence for which the accused must, or has the right to, choose between a trial by judge and a trial by jury, with the exception of a few minor offences.

Infanticide. One of the four types of murder. It was introduced in 1948, and only a woman can be charged. The Criminal Code defines an infant as a child under one year of age.

Information, to lay an. One lays an information when one presents to a judge a sworn written allegation alleging the individual named in the document has committed an offence. Informations are also used to obtain search warrants.

Intermediate sanctions. Sanctions that are more restrictive than probation and less restrictive than imprisonment.

Judicare. A type of legal aid practised in Canada that combines elements of the public defender and judicare models.

Judicial interim release hearing. The condition(s) of pretrial release, typically set by a justice of the peace, in order that an accused may live in the community prior to his or her trial. Also referred to as "bail."

Jury. A group of individuals whose function is to determine the guilt or innocence of the accused. A jury comprises 12 citizens.

Justice model. A model of criminal justice that emphasizes legal rights, justice, and fairness. A main feature of this model is that any punishment should be proportional to the seriousness of the crime.

Legal aid. A government-supported system that allows individuals who are earning below a certain amount to receive free legal services.

Legalistic. An approach that emphasizes the type of crime committed as opposed to any extraneous factors such as the race or social class of the offender.

Lower court. A general term used to describe those courts that have jurisdiction over summary conviction offences. Most pleas are made in these courts.

Management of demand. A police organizational strategy that categorizes requests for service and analyzes them as to their priority, resulting in differential police responses.

Manslaughter. Unintentional homicide requiring either criminal negligence or an unlawful act.

Mens rea. A prerequisite of criminal conduct is the "guilty mind." *Mens rea* is based on the belief that people can control their behaviour and choose between right and wrong. It commonly is used to refer to the intent to commit a crime.

Mitigating circumstances. Any circumstances accompanying the commission of a crime that may justify a lighter sentence.

New-generation facility. A type of correctional facility distinguished architecturally from its predecessors by a design that encourages interaction between inmates and correctional officers.

Parens patriae. A doctrine that holds that the state has a responsibility to look after the well-being of children and to assume the role of a parent, if necessary.

Parole. The conditional release of an inmate from an unfinished sentence of incarceration into the community. The decision to parole an individual is made by a parole board, which determines the conditions of the release.

Pennsylvania system. A prison system developed in the nineteenth century that emphasized solitary confinement for all inmates so they could reflect on individual penitence.

Podular design. The architectural style of the new-generation jail. "Pods" usually contain between 12 and 24 one-person cells, as well as a communal room that allows for social interaction.

Preliminary inquiry. An inquiry made by a provincial court judge in a case involving an indictable offence in order to determine whether there is enough evidence to order the accused to stand trial.

Pre-sentence report. An investigation, usually conducted by a probation officer, before the sentencing of a convicted offender. The report typically contains information about the offender's personal background, education, previous employment, and family as well as interviews with family members, neighbours, and employer.

Prisonization. The socialization process through which a new inmate learns the accepted norms and values of the prison population.

Private prisons. Correctional facilities operated by private corporations.

Probation. A sentence that allows a convicted offender to serve his or her sentence in the community, subject to certain conditions for a designated time period.

Problem-oriented policing. A style of policing that emphasizes focusing on a specific crime problem. It features a proactive rather than a reactive approach to fighting crime.

Procedural criminal law. The rules that define the operations of criminal proceedings. It specifies the methods that are to be followed in obtaining warrants, conducting trials, sentencing convicted offenders, and reviewing cases in the appeal courts. Its main purpose is to describe how substantive offences are to be enforced.

Public defender. A type of legal aid. Legal aid lawyers are employed by a provincial government to help with the legal defence of an accused.

Recidivism rate. The repetition of criminal behaviour. It is measured by criminal acts committed by individuals under correctional supervision or technical violations of individuals on probation or parole.

Rehabilitation. A correctional philosophy that emphasizes the treatment of conditional offenders and their reintegration into the community.

Rehabilitation model. One of the four criminal justice models. It differs from the other models in its support of discretion in the system and the treatment of the offender.

Reintegration. The goal of corrections that focuses on preparing the offender for a return to the community.

Revised UCR system. Reports that record incident-based criminal events. Each crime incident is analyzed for a number of individual characteristics (e.g., the relationship between offender and victim). (*See also* Uniform Crime Reporting System.)

Revocation. The withdrawal of probation or parole orders due to the commission of a new offence or the violation of any condition set out in a parole or probation order.

Search warrant. An authorization, granted to police officers by a judge, that authorizes officers to search a specific place.

Second degree murder. Any murder that is not first degree is second degree. The maximum punishment for second degree murder is life imprisonment.

Selective incapacitation. The incarceration for long periods of time of a select group of "chronic" offenders who commit numerous violent offences.

Selective incapacitation model. One of the four criminal justice models. It emphasizes long prison sentences for the small number of individuals who chronically commit violent crimes. It rejects any type of favourable discretionary actions for those offenders.

Sentence bargaining. A form of plea bargaining that involves the reduction of a sentence in return for a plea of guilty or information.

Sexual assault. Classified as a violent crime. Legislation introduced in 1983 created three levels of sexual assault, which emphasize that these offences involve physical violence directed against an individual.

Social service. A view held by some police officers that their prime function is to assist the public in as many ways as possible. A purely legalistic approach is rejected except in extreme cases.

Specialty courts. Those courts having jurisdiction over one specific area of criminal activity, such as domestic violence or illegal drugs.

Stare decisis. A common law doctrine under which judges are to follow those precedents established by prior decisions.

Statute. Laws created by legislatures in a response to changing social conditions and public opinion.

Statutory release. A program designed to release most incarcerated offenders who have not been able to obtain full parole and who have served two-thirds of their sentence.

Substantive criminal law. These describe our rights and duties as members of Canadian society. The substantive part of the criminal law prohibits various forms of conduct from which society and its members have a right to be protected

Summary conviction offences. Minor offences tried on the basis of the information without other pretrial formalities.

Summons. An order by the court requiring the appearance of the accused or a witness before it.

Superior court. The court where most indictable offences are tried, either by judge or by judge and jury.

Supreme Court exclusive indictable offence. Involves those individuals who are charged with first or second degree murder. The case is tried by a federally appointed judge and jury.

Suspended sentence. A prison term that is delayed by a judge's order while the convicted offender is involved in community treatment. If this treatment is successful, the individual is allowed to remain in the community.

Temporary absence (TA). Permits the release of offenders from federal institutions so that they can access programs and various services within the community.

Temporary absence, escorted. An offender's permitted temporary absence, for a brief period, from a correctional facility, on the basis of having an escort.

Temporary absence, unescorted. An offender's permitted temporary absence, for a relatively long period of time, from a correctional facility, in order to integrate that individual into the outside community.

Total institutions. Institutions that eliminate all daily and normal inmate contact with the outside world.

Uniform Crime Reporting (UCR) system. National crime statistics maintained by the RCMP in Ottawa. Offences are grouped into three categories: crimes against the person, crimes against property, and "other" crimes. (*See also* Revised UCR system.)

Victim impact statement. The option given to the victim of a crime to complete a form and detail what has happened to that victim as a result of the crime. If the victim decides to fill out the form, it is placed in the case file and may have an impact on the case, particularly at the sentencing stage.

Victimless crime. Crimes for which there are no complainants or victims. It refers to consensual social exchanges punished by criminal law (e.g., drug use and selling sex).

Warrant. An authorization that grants an individual, usually a police officer, to do what is specified in the warrant (e.g., to arrest someone).

Warrantless search. Those conditions which allow an individual, usually a police officer, to search a place without a warrant (e.g., doctrine of plain view).

Watchman. A style of policing that emphasizes a reactive style of policing rather than a proactive or preventative style.

INDEX

Electronic surveillance, 228-30
    closed-circuit television (CCTV), 134-35
Employment equity
    and women police officers, 190
Entrapment, 55
Equality rights, 42
Escorted temporary absence, 385
Evidence, admissibility
    Charter and "reasonable-person" test, 45
Evidence, trial, 267
Excuse (legal) defences, 52-53
Eyewitness error, 296

F

Fact bargaining, 258
Faint Hope clause, 388-89
    Olson Amendment, 385
    parole eligibility review, 388
False confessions, 212. *See also* Custodial interrogations
Family temporary absence, 385
Family violence, restorative justice and, 93-94
Female (women) inmates, 354-55
Fines, 284, 325-26
Firearms legislation, 294-96
    mandatory minimum sentences, 295
First degree murder, 56
First Nations Policing Policy (FNPP), 157, 158
Fitness hearings, 16
    special jury, 16
Foot patrol, 144-45
Forcible confinement, 120
Forensic errors, 296-97
Forensics, 147
Forward-looking infra-red camera (FLIR)
    searches and privacy, 234-25
Full answer and defence, right to make, 46

G

Gang peace bonds, 3
Gender
    conflicts/women police officers, 191
    recidivism and, 390-91
Gender-responsive treatment, 394-95
General deterrence, 75
General intent, 48
Global Positioning System (GPS), receivers, 312, 323
Guilt beyond a reasonable doubt, 267
Gun crime
    and criminal justice system, 1-4
    mandatory minimum penalties (MMPs), 294-96

H

Habeas corpus, 43
Hands-off doctrine, 361
Harm, 35, 36, 51

Healing lodges, 351
Heat emissions (FLIR), 234-36
Hedonistic calculus, 346
High-speed pursuits
    police discretion and, 174-75
HIV disclosure, criminality and, 61-63
Home confinement, 322-25
Home invasions, 121
Homicide, 116-18
Homicide rate, 106
Hotspot patrol, 144
Hybrid offence, 36, 56

I

Identity theft, 124-25
Imprisonment, 284
    Charter rights, 41
Incarceration, 18-19, 343
Indictable offences, 55-56
Indictment, 17
    and preliminary inquiry, 17
Individual discrimination, 11
Infanticide, 57
Information, 17, 208-10
Inmates, *see also* Prison
    Aboriginal, 355-56
    older, 393-94
    recidivism views of, 392-83
    women, 354-55
Inmate society, 356-59
    deprivation vs. importation models, 358
    female inmates, 358-59
Innocence, presumption of, 44
Insanity defence, 46-47
Institutionalized discrimination, 10
Intelligence-led policing, 154, 155, 156
    COMPSTAT, 156
Intensive supervision probation (ISP), 321-22
Intent
    vs. motive, 48
    types of criminal, 48, 50
Interim release, 217-19
Intermediate sanctions, 320-22
    success of, 326-28
Intermittent sentence, 284
Internet luring, 128-29
Investigation hearings, 26-28
Investigative detention, 207-208

J

Jailhouse interrogation, 214-16
Judges, 252
Judicial interim release hearing, *see* Bail
Judicially administered sanctions,
    see Intermediate sanctions
Judicial recognizance orders, *see* Peace bonds